THE ROEBLING LEGACY

CLIFFORD W. ZINK

PRINCETON LANDMARK PUBLICATIONS
PRINCETON, NEW JERSEY

THE ROEBLING LEGACY

ISBN: 978-0-615-42805-5

Library of Congress Control Number: 2011920730

First Edition, First Printing

Printed by
Friesens in Altona, Manitoba, Canada

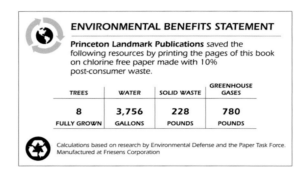

ENVIRONMENTAL BENEFITS STATEMENT

Princeton Landmark Publications saved the following resources by printing the pages of this book on chlorine free paper made with 10% post-consumer waste.

TREES	WATER	SOLID WASTE	GREENHOUSE GASES
8 FULLY GROWN	3,756 GALLONS	228 POUNDS	780 POUNDS

Calculations based on research by Environmental Defense and the Paper Task Force. Manufactured at Friesens Corporation

Also by the author:

Spanning the Industrial Age: The John A. Roebling's Sons Company, 1848-1974
by Clifford W. Zink & Dorothy White Hartman
Trenton Roebling Community Development Corporation - 1992

The Hackensack Water Works, by Clifford W. Zink
The Water Works Conservancy - 2003

Mercer Magic: The Mercer Automobile Company, Founded 1909, by Clifford W. Zink
Roebling Museum - 2009

The Monmouth County Park System: The First Fifty Years, by Clifford W. Zink
Friends of the Monmouth County Parks - 2010

PRINCETON LANDMARK PUBLICATIONS LLC

PRINCETON, NEW JERSEY 08540

princetonlandmarkpublications.com

DEDICATION

To my wife
Emily Davis Croll
My own guiding star

ACKNOWLEDGMENTS

Many people have contributed to my research into Roebling history over the years and deserve much credit for generously sharing their knowledge and enthusiasm.

Darcy White Hartman undertook much of the initial research for our book, *Spanning the Industrial Age: The John A. Roebling's Sons Company, Trenton, N.J., 1848-1974*, which was supported by grants from the New Jersey Historical Commission and published by the Trenton Roebling Community Development Corporation in 1992.

Tami Gobert and Amy Rupert at Rensselaer Polytechnic Institute's Folsom Library have always been exceptionally helpful in providing access to the remarkable legacy of Roebling drawings, family photographs and personal documents in the Institute Archives and Special Collections.

Fernanda Perrone, Al King, Ron Becker and Bonita Grant have likewise provided gracious access to Roebling Family and Company documents in Alexander Library's Special Collections and University Archives at Rutgers University.

Illustrations and excerpts from personal accounts and correspondence from these two institutions significantly enrich the Roebling story herein.

At the Trenton Public Library, Wendy Nardi has always enthusiastically provided access to Roebling materials in the Trentoniana Collection. At Ellarslie, Trenton's City Museum, Brian Hill has consistently provided kind access to Roebling objects and documents on display and in storage.

At the Smithsonian Institution, the late David Shayt graciously provided access to Roebling documents and artifacts largely collected by Robert Vogel, the former curator of civil engineering whose studies of the Brooklyn Bridge and Roebling aqueducts have long been inspirational for me.

Over the last two decades, Donald Sayenga, an historian and former general manager of Bethlehem Steel's wire rope division, has shared numerous documents and images and has provided much insight from his extensive knowledge on the history of wire rope and of John and Washington Roebling.

Dr. Andreas Kahlow, at the University of Applied Sciences in Potsdam and Dr. Nele Guntheroth at the Berlin City Museum Foundation, shared materials from their research on John A. Roebling for a 2006 exhibit at the Mühlhausen Museum. Thomas Müller, the Museum's Project Director, kindly adapted exhibit panels, with English translations by Norma Schadt, that Seth Goldman of the Neversink Valley Museum in Cuddebackville, N.Y., generously shared. Steffi Maass at the Mühlhausen Museum assisted with images.

At the U.S. Environmental Protection Agency, Tami Rossi, the Roebling Steel Site Manager, and Bobbi Dease, Construction Manager, have kindly provided access to the former Roebling Plant on numerous occasions and have also provided images and information on EPA's remediation work.

Many people in Roebling, N.J., have been exceptionally kind over many years in sharing their knowledge and love of the town's history. Donna McElrea, a Roebling native, the President of the Roebling Historical Society and a founding board member of the Roebling Museum, and her husband, Andy, have always been most accommodating and enthusiastic. George Lengel, a Roebling native and retired Roebling School teacher, and his wife Kathie, both founding board members of the Roebling Museum, have been boundless in sharing their knowledge and historical resources. Lou Borbi, a Roebling native, retired Roebling School teacher and the founding president of the Roebling Historical Society, and his wife Carol have also generously shared their knowledge and documentation, including an image of Lou's painting of the Roebling Steel Mill.

Other founding board members of the Roebling Museum have also been most generous with their personal knowledge, documents and enthusiasm. The late Ferguson Reeves, who worked in the Roebling personnel office, happily shared information from his Company experience and his personal collection. Don Jones has shared his enthusiasm of his family's three generations in Roebling, his update of the Roebling Family Tree, and an image of his painting of the Kinkora Works from the Main Gate. Paul Varga, a Roebling native and former plant railroad engineer, provided much information about the Kinkora Works and shared several images. Mark Dimon has continued the generous sharing of enthusiasm about Roebling history always provided by his father, the late "country lawyer" and State Senator John Dimon, who helped found the Roebling Historical Society. Don Cammus and Dennis O'Hara have also shared their enthusiasm and recollections of Roebling, N.J.

Mark Magyar, the founding Executive Director of the Roebling Museum, shared his knowledge of labor history and presciently initiated an oral history project in 2007 that recorded the recollections of 25 former Roebling employees and residents: Alice Mae Agostinelli, Lonnie Brown, Lou Boldizar, Helen Bordash, Lou Borbi, Charles Detterer, Joe Horvath, Ken Ibach, Lulu Jenkins, Bill Lovelett, Al McDowell, Donna McElrea, Ted Mitre, Mary Montalto, Paul Nyquist, Leonard Olschewski, Leroy Paterson, Ferguson Reeves, Joe Sabol, George Sampson, Bill Spenser, George Swanberg, Paul Tymosh, Paul Varga and Mary Yurcision.

In 1993, the late Dennis Starr, a Trenton labor historian, and the author recorded the oral histories of 13 former employees from the main Roebling plant in Trenton: Blair Birdsall, Charles Brenner, Joe Cichocki, Ruth Egan, Calvin Jeffers, Irene Lipson, Tom Malloy, Pat Migliacchio, Jack Nixon, Joseph Olafson, John Smith, Lou Szakacs, and Stephen Toth. These 38 oral histories provide rich personal experiences and insights about the Roebling story, and they were timely as many of the 1993 interviewees and several of the 2007-2008 interviewees have passed on.

Excerpts from the 1993 interviews highlight the film, *Now You're Set For Life*, that Andy Fredericks of Telequest, Inc., produced in 1993 for the Trenton Roebling Community Development Corporation, and excerpts from the 2007-2008 interviews highlight *Roebling Stories*, the Roebling Museum's orientation film written and directed by the author. The N.J. Council for the Humanities provided support for the production of both of these films.

Pat Millen, the Roebling Museum's Executive Director, and Peg Manser, a Roebling resident, Museum Board Member and archivist, have graciously helped with access to documents in the Ferdinand W. Roebling III Archive.

Several Roebling descendants have enthusiastically shared information and resources. Bill Roebling, a descendant of Ferdinand W. Roebling and a founding Museum board member, and his wife Maeryn generously supported my planning and curatorial work at the Museum and my work on *Roebling Stories*. Bill and his sister, Mary Roebling Foster, a current Museum board member, also kindly lent documents collected by their father, Ferdinand W. Roebling III, and Mary sponsored the Museum's Ferdinand W. Roebling III Archive in his honor.

Karl Darby, a descendant of Ferdinand W. Roebling and a founding Museum board member, shared his considerable knowledge and resources on the Mercer Automobile Company. Linda McDonald, a descendant of Laura Roebling Methfessel, the founding Museum president and current board member, shared copies of Roebling letters in the collection of her aunt, Antonia Malone. Martha Moore, a descendant of Ferdinand W. Roebling, a founding Museum board member and the current president, shared her extensive knowledge of the family and research from her 1982 study of Roebling, N.J.

In San Francisco, Ted Schildge, a descendant of Laura Roebling Methfessel, graciously arranged a visit to the Golden Gate Bridge, where Bridge Manager Kary Witt and Public Relations Manager Mary Currie provided a special tour and copies of Roebling Company documents.

Rip Roebling, a descendant of Ferdinand W. Roebling and a founding Museum board member, has graciously provided images and information on numerous occasions about family members, including his parents' donation of Modena Plantation to the State of Georgia to establish the Skidaway Institute of Oceanography. Mike Sullivan and Anna Boyette at SKIO kindly provided information and images.

Tim Kuser shared his considerable knowledge as well as several illustrations and documents on the Mercer Automobile Company, which his grandfather, John L. Kuser, co-founded. George Ott also shared Mercer images and documents from his collection.

Sandra Simpson graciously arranged access to a number of people and historic buildings in Saxonburg, and has answered numerous questions about the town's history. Sandra also shared several of her images of Saxonburg, and Howard Mortimer shared one as well.

Many individuals have provided or assisted with obtaining images of Roebling buildings or specific aspects of Roebling history. George Lengel and Norman Reeves, Ferguson Reeves' son, kindly scanned and shared numerous images. Alice Mae Agostinelli and Ken Ibach provided photographs of themselves from earlier years.

Eleanor Sollenberger graciously shared documents and images collected by her husband, Norman Sollenberger, a former Roebling engineer and Princeton University professor.

John Hatch, a principal architect at Clarke Caton Hintz in Trenton, provided several photographs of his firm's rehabilitations of Roebling buildings. Philip S. Collins, architect of the New Jersey Pavilion at the 1964 New York World's Fair, arranged for access to images of the Pavilion at HDR-CHU2A, where Josh Krayger kindly provided copies.

Dave Frieder provided a George Washington Bridge photo from his remarkable bridge images at davefrieder.com. Frank Jacobs provided a photograph of Art All Night in Trenton from his many fine images at frankjacobsphoto.com.

Andrea Sussman provided a photograph of her company's Roebling Metro Complex from nexusproperties.com. Hillary Swank and Debbie Upp at the Archbold Biological Station near Lake Placid, Florida, provided photographs of the Red Hill Estate, which John A. Roebling II donated to the Station in 1941. Dr. Harm tho Seeth at the Graf von Westphalen Archive assisted with image access. Jeff Macechek assisted with images at the Burlington County Historical Society.

Ruth Markoe of Theater To Go and Mark Violi provided images of Mark's play, *Roebling: The Story of the Builders of the Brooklyn Bridge*, which Ruth produced in 2010 at the Roebling Auditorium in collaboration with the Roebling Museum.

Jordan Antebi, a student and fine young historian at Timberlane School in Hopewell, N.J., provided illustrations and information from his insightful research into Roebling history. Michael Floyd arranged for access to photograph the former Roebling Testing House at the N.J. Housing Mortgage Finance Agency. Michael Farewell of Farewell Mills & Gatsch in Princeton, Ingrid Webbuer, Ron Rice, and Ron Berman all helped with requests for photographs.

Matthew Hirsch assisted with proofreading the text. Gail Hunton assisted with the cover design and printing details.

My wife, Emily Davis Croll, has facilitated my efforts on various Roebling projects in countless ways over the last two decades, and our children, Alexander and Julie, have been consistently supportive as well.

To all of these people and to others who have assisted along the way, I am profoundly grateful.

- Clifford W. Zink, January, 2011

INTRODUCTION

The story of the Roeblings and their family enterprise is a classic American saga spanning two centuries and encompassing immigration, innovation, entrepreneurship, monumental accomplishments, the rise of national capitalism and labor unions, the impact of wars and their aftermath, and ultimately, obsolescence, industrial decline and cleanup, and the adaptation of people and communities.

The epic story of the Brooklyn Bridge has fascinated people since the brilliant engineer John A. Roebling designed a colossal bridge in 1867 to unite New York and Brooklyn. "The great towers will serve as landmarks to the adjoining cities," he wrote, "and they will be entitled to be ranked as national monuments." The bold proposal captured the public's attention and started a 16-year epic drama of tragedy, danger, sacrifice, heroism, perseverance, and ultimate triumph.

After John died tragically from an injury while surveying for the Brooklyn tower, his oldest son, Washington A. Roebling, assumed his father's position. "Here I was at the age of 32," he later recalled, "suddenly put in charge of the most stupendous engineering structure of the age! At first I thought I would succumb but I had a strong tower to lean on, my wife - a woman of infinite tact and wisest council." When Washington faltered from his own construction injuries, Emily Warren Roebling helped him carry on the work, keep his position as Chief Engineer, and complete the daunting task.

The Brooklyn Bridge became, as *The New York Times* noted in 1956 on the 150th anniversary of John's birth, "a universally known symbol of the spirit of New York," but the story of the Roeblings did not end with its completion. In the age-old tradition of passing along a livelihood to one's children, John left his sons a thriving wire rope manufacturing business that he had started on his farm in western Pennsylvania and had developed in Trenton, N.J., into a highly profitable concern.

John instructed his sons to call their business the John A. Roebling's Sons Company, and over the next five decades Washington and his brothers Ferdinand and Charles expanded it beyond anything their father could have imagined. They produced "unthinkable millions of feet" of wire rope and specialty wire for numerous innovations that shaped modern life – long-span suspension bridges, telegraphs and telephones, elevators and high rise construction, tramways, cable cars, electrification, deep mines, oil drilling, and airplanes.

Inspired innovation, bold entrepreneurship, continuous reinvestment, superior quality, and company-employee loyalty characterized the Roebling enterprise.

When competition from new steel conglomerates threatened their business at the beginning of the 20th Century, the Roebling brothers built their own steel mill ten miles south of Trenton. Faced with inadequate housing for their workers, they built a model company town which soon became known as Roebling, New Jersey. "We are building as well as we know how," Charles Roebling told a reporter in 1906, and the quality remains evident today, as David McCullough attested in his fine book, *The Great Bridge*, when he called Roebling: "One of the best planned industrial towns ever built in America - a model in every respect."

Through four generations of Roebling family ownership, the John A. Roebling's Sons Company continued to innovate, most notably in building cables for a series of landmark suspension bridges. In their crowning achievements, Roebling engineers took "another bold leap forward" during the Great Depression with the construction of the massive cables of the George Washington Bridge, which doubled the record span, and the Golden Gate Bridge, which increased it another 20 percent. After the Colorado Fuel and Iron Corporation (CF&I) bought the Roebling business in 1952, Roebling engineers kept innovating with prestressed concrete and suspended roofs.

The Roebling Company was one of New Jersey's largest manufacturers for many decades, employing some 8,000 people at its peak. Thousands of European immigrants and their descendants earned their livelihoods at "Roebling's" while assimilating into the American way of life in Trenton's Chambersburg and South Trenton neighborhoods and in the town of Roebling. "Now you're set for life," John Smith's mother told him when he got a job at Roebling's Trenton Plant in 1939. "She believed it, and I believed it too," he recalled in 1993. But as former bridge draftsman Leroy Patterson recalled in 2007, "It just ended sooner than anybody wanted it to, but that's life." Oral histories conducted in 1993 and 2007-2009 of 38 townspeople and former Roebling employees enrich the Roebling story with personal recollections of work, origins, family life, and community.

After a corporate takeover led to CF&I's closing of its former Roebling plants in the 1970s, the neighborhoods struggled like many other communities in America to adapt to a postindustrial economy. Perseverance, an abiding pride of local history, and new investment have gradually reinvigorated the Roebling communities.

Today, numerous buildings in Trenton and the town of Roebling symbolize America's industrial era and the quality and durability of Roebling design and construction. Thousands of people walk from their neighborhoods or commute to their jobs or to patronize businesses in renovated Roebling buildings in Trenton, while adjacent Roebling mills and shops await rehabilitation for new uses. Residents in the town of Roebling continue to identify with the Roebling Company 36 years after the steel and wire mill closed there. "I am who I am today," Roebling native George Lengel wrote in 2010, "because of the village, the mill, and my family's connection with the John A. Roebling's Sons Company."

Thanks to the U.S. Environmental Protection Agency, Florence Township, the dedication of many local people, and the generosity of Roebling family members and many other donors, the Roebling Museum opened in 2009 and has attracted thousands of visitors, including many students and interns eager to learn about the Roebling story.

The remarkable collections of Roebling documents in several institutions contribute immeasurably to the Roebling Legacy. Recognizing the significance of their work, John and Washington Roebling carefully preserved their drawings, correspondence, notes, reports, and business records.

John A. Roebling II, Washington's son, donated most of the engineering and Brooklyn Bridge documents to Rensselaer Polytechnic Institute, where Washington and Charles Roebling graduated with engineering degrees, and he and other family members donated personal and business records to Rutgers University. Thanks to Robert Vogel, former Curator of Civil Engineering at the Smithsonian Institution, Roebling Chief Bridge Engineer Blair Birdsall donated documents from his 30 years in the Bridge Division to the Smithsonian Archives.

Roebling family members have donated personal objects and paintings to Ellarslie Museum and to the State Museum in Trenton, and other people have donated Roebling items to the Trenton Public Library's Trentoniana Collection and to the Roebling Museum. Thanks to the generosity of a Roebling family member, the Roebling Museum has established the Ferdinand W. Roebling III as a local archive of the family, Company and town.

Objects and documents in all these collections richly chronicle the Roebling story from its roots in Germany through the closing of the Roebling plants, and they will continue to fascinate students and researchers for many years.

Excerpts and illustrations from the rich assortment of Roebling documents significantly enliven the story herein.

Chapter 1 describes John A. Roebling's origins in Germany, his excellent education, his early works, and the influences, including the famous philosopher Georg Hegel, that led him to emigrate to America in 1831. Excerpts from his emigration diary express the universal aspirations of immigrants.

Chapter 2 draws upon his diary and letters home to convey his deliberations on where to settle in America, his thoughts on slavery, and the hopes and realities of starting the village of Saxonburg north of Pittsburgh with his fellow German settlers. Other documents highlight his early engineering projects and his ingenious development of wire rope in 1841.

Chapter 3 chronicles John's move of his family and business to Trenton in 1849, the growth of his engineering practice and reputation as a bridge builder, and ultimately his death in 1869 while preparing to build the Brooklyn Bridge. Excerpts from Washington Roebling's biography of his father, which thanks to Donald Sayenga was published for the first time in 2009, provide a lively filial view of John and his era in Chapters 1-3.

Chapter 4 relates Washington's completion of the Brooklyn Bridge in 1883 with the crucial assistance of his wife, Emily, and the remarkable growth of the John A. Roebling's Sons Company as the Roebling brothers continuously expanded to meet the ever-increasing demand for wire rope and wire.

Chapter 5 describes Charles Roebling's efforts to build a steel mill to survive amidst the increased competition from the new conglomerates U.S. Steel and Bethlehem Steel, his building of the model town of Roebling to house its workers, the growth of labor unrest amidst the economic boom of World War I, and Washington's stoic assumption of the Roebling Company presidency at the age of 84 after the deaths of his brothers and nephew. Excerpts from Washington's memoirs in Chapters 4 and 5 convey his unique view of his brothers and the challenges of running the family business.

Chapter 6 relates the transition of the business to a modern corporation after Washington's death in 1926, the innovations of Roebling engineers in pioneering the massive cables for the George Washington Bridge in 1931 and the Golden Gate Bridges in 1937, the impact of the Great Depression on the business and employees, the struggle to unionize the workers

> *the stuff of dreams...*
> *and an enduring symbol*
> *of America's greatness*

as production climbed for World War II, the impact of the war, the Company's sale of houses and stores in Roebling after the war, cold war tensions, and ultimately the Roebling family's sale of their business to the Colorado Fuel and iron Corporation in 1952.

Chapter 7 highlights the golden age of 1950s prosperity, the gradual decline of American steel production due largely to foreign competition, and the impact of corporate raiders that led to CF&I's shuttering of the old Roebling plants.

The Epilogue chronicles the long-term efforts to clean up and reuse the Roebling plants in order to revitalize the industrial communities around them, the growing recognition of the contributions that the Roeblings and their Company made to the modern age and to their communities, and the establishment of the Roebling Museum.

The greatest Roebling contributions are of course the many suspension bridges and cables around the country that stand as monuments to Roebling ingenuity and accomplishment, and the greatest among them have become icons of their cities: the John A. Roebling Bridge in Cincinnati, the Brooklyn Bridge and the George Washington Bridge in New York, and the Golden Gate Bridge in San Francisco.

At New York City's 125th Anniversary celebration of the Brooklyn Bridge in May, 2008, Mayor Michael Bloomberg told the crowd of tens of thousands: "The Brooklyn Bridge really has been the stuff of dreams, a New York City icon and an enduring symbol of America's greatness."

Even more people will no doubt celebrate the 75th Anniversary of the Golden Gate Bridge in 2012.

The Roebling Legacy continues to captivate and inspire in multiple places and in multiple ways.

ILLUSTRATIONS

Sources of illustrations with initials in the captions:

ABS	Archbold Biological Station	MH	Mortimer Howard
BC	*Blue Center* (J.A.R.'s Sons Co.)	NFPL	Niagara Falls Public Library
BCHS	Burlington County Historical Society	NJSL	New Jersey State Library
BHS	Bessemer Historical Society	NJSM	New Jersey State Museum
BM	Brooklyn Museum	NP	Nexus Properties
Bm	Bridgemeister	NPS	National Park Service
CCH	Clarke Caton Hintz	NYHS	New York Historical Society
CL	Carnegie Library	NYPL	New York Public Library
CT	Cincinnati Transit	TS	Ted Schildge
CRT	Charles Roebling Tyson	PANYNJ	Port Authority of New York & New Jersey
CUH2A	HDR CUH2A	PPL	Philadelphia Public Library
CWZ	C. W. Zink	PSHS	Pullman State Historic Site
DF	Dave Frieder	PU	Princeton University
DJ	Donald Jones	PV	Paul Varga
DM	Donna McElrea	RC	*Roebling Cables* (J.A.R.'s Sons Co.)
DS	Donald Sayenga	RG	Ralph Goldinger,
EM	Ellarslie Museum, Trenton, N.J.		*Historic Saxonburg and its Neighbors*
EPA	U.S. Environmental Protection Agency	RM	Roebling Museum, Roebling, N.J.,
FJP	Frank Jacobs Photography		Ferdinand W. Roebling III Archive
FL	Flickr	RMg	*Roebling Magazine* (J.A.R.'s Sons Co.)
GL	George Lengel	RPI	Rensselaer Polytechnic Institute,
GO	George Ott		Institute Archives and Special Collections
GVW	Graf von Westphalen	RR	*The Roebling Record* (J.A.R.'s Sons Co.)
HAER	Historic American Engineering Record,	RWW	*Roebling War Worker* (J.A.R.'s Sons Co.)
	Library of Congress	RU	Rutgers University,
HB	Historic Bridges		Special Collections and University Archives
HS	Hamilton Schuyler, *The Roeblings*	SI	Smithsonian Institution
HM&L	Hagley Museum & Library	SKIO	Skidaway Oceanographic Institute
KD	Karl Darby	SS	Sandra Simpson
KI	Ken Ibach	SW	Sara Wermiel
KR	Kriss Roebling	TPL	Trenton Public Library
LB	Lou Borbi	TTG	Theatre To Go
LH	Lehigh University	USGS	U.S. Geological Survey
LOC	Library of Congress	UCB	University of California - Berkeley
MANY	Municipal Archives of New York	WIK	Wikipedia
MM	Mühlhausen Museum	WSR	William S. Roebling

With a few exceptions, illustrations without initials in the captions are the author's.

Cover background:
John A. Roebling, "Elevation of Brooklyn Tower, East River Bridge, 1867." Rensselaer Polytechnic Institute
Front Cover:
Center: John A. Roebling Statue, Cadwalader Park, Trenton, N.J. CWZ
Clockwise from top: Brooklyn Bridge 150th Anniversary, 2008. CWZ; Emily Warren Roebling, 1896. BM;
John A. Roebling Bridge, Cincinnati, Ohio, 2008. CWZ; Roebling Works, Trenton, N.J., 2010. BING;
Delaware Aqueduct, Lackawaxen, Pennsylvania, c1990. NPS; Washington A. Roebling, 1880. BM
Rear Cover:
Center: Art All Night at Roebling Machine Shop, Trenton, N.J., 2009. FJP
Clockwise from upper left: George Washington Bridge, 1997. DF; Golden Gate Bridge & Cable Section
by John A. Roebling's Sons Company, 2009. CWZ; Saxonburg, Pennsylvania, 2009. MH;
Mercer Centennial Reunion, Roebling Museum, Roebling, N.J., 2009. CWZ; Roebling, N.J., 2008. EPA;
Art All Night at the Roebling Market and Millyard Park, Trenton, N.J., 2009. CWZ.
Title Page:
Brooklyn Bridge, 2008. CWZ

THE ROEBLING LEGACY

CONTENTS

Figure 1.1: Mühlhausen in Thuringia, Prussia, c1825, MM
The town had about 10,000 residents when Johann August Röbling was born there in 1806.
Four months after his birth, Napoleon conquered Prussia and stimulated many reforms.

Figure 1.2: Prussia, c1815.
Mühlhausen, highlighted in yellow on the lower left, is about 215 miles southwest of Berlin, upper right.
Johann A. Röbling attended Dr. Soloman Ungar's mathemetics institute in Erfurt, about 36 miles
southeast of Mühlhausen for two years, and attended the Royal Building Academy in Berlin for one year.

Chapter 1: *Johann August Röbling*

Figure 1.3: John Augustus Roebling, c1867. TS

Born in June 1806 in Mülhausen, Thüringen,
an old walled town founded in the year 800;
the youngest of four children, three boys and a daughter.

With these words, Washington Augustus Roebling began his "Biography of J.A. Roebling" in 1893 sitting at his desk in his "museum" of minerals in his mansion at 191 West State Street in Trenton, New Jersey. Washington was 56 years and had visited Mühlhausen (Figs 1.1-2) 26 years earlier in 1867, just two years before his father, John Augustus Roebling (Fig.1.3), died while preparing for the construction of the East River Bridge – the monumental suspension bridge that he designed to connect New York and Brooklyn and that would be the culmination of his brilliant career.

Washington succeeded his father as Chief Engineer of the Brooklyn Bridge, and it took him 14 years to complete it. With various distractions, it would take Washington 14 years to complete his biography of his father.[1]

One of the oldest towns in Thuringia, Mühlhausen lies in the upper Unstrut River Valley in an area of rolling hills in the middle of Germany, with the Harz Mountains on the north and the Thuringian Forest on the southwest. With half-timbered and stone houses, medieval churches and a city wall, Mühlhausen was a small town of about 10,000 people in the early 19th century.

"Our ancestors were men of the people – artisans, mechanics, farmers," Washington wrote. Family researchers traced their lineage to Nicholas Rebeling, who was born in 1560 in the nearby town of Tennstedt, about twenty miles east of Mühlhausen, where he was a "wool-weaver, market-master, public weigher and builder of the City Council." The German word "rebe" translates to "vine" in English, and Washington noted: "This shows that the ancestor who first took this surname was a worker in the vineyard."[2]

Nicholas' son Jacobus Rebeling was the treasurer of Tennstedt, and Jacobus' son, Hans Jacobus Röbling, moved to Mühlhausen in 1670. His son, Jacobus Philip Röbling, was the father of Hermann Christian Röbling, born in 1721, who served for many years as a town councilor and bought a large house built in 1587 that came to be known as the Röbling Ancestral Home (Fig. 1.4). Hermann had three sons: Heinrich Wilhelm Röbling, the "rich uncle" who was a wealthy merchant and a philanthropist with a fine town house and a large country house, Ernst Adolph Röbling, who was a master of the Clothmakers' and Sergemakers' Guild of Mühlhausen and a senator, and Christoph Polycarpus Röbling, who became a tobacco "fabricant" or processor and merchant.

"Polycarp," as Washington called him, married Friederike Dorothea Mueller in 1798. Polycarp and Dorothea were both born in 1770 and had four children: Hermann Christian Röbling, born in 1800, Friedericke Amalia Röbling, born in 1802, Karl Friederich Röbling, born in 1803, and Johann August Röbling, born on June 12, 1806. Washington noted that: "Johann and August were common family names."[3]

Figure 1.4: Roebling Ancestral Home, c1900. RU
Built in 1587 on Erfurterstrasse in Mühlhausen, Thuringia.

**Figure 1.5: Mühlhausen Gymnasium, c1800. MM
Johann benefited from Real School reforms instituted at the
Gymnasium after Napoleon's conquest of Prussia in 1806.**

In October of 1806 Napoleon conquered Prussia in decisive victories at Jena and Auerstadt, about 75 miles to the east of Mühlhausen, and life in the old walled town changed dramatically. As Johann and his siblings grew up, Washington noted, "the country of Thuringen and the neighborhood of Mühlhausen were harassed and plundered by the French armies under Napoleon."

Napoleon imposed a "kontinental speere" on Prussia to ban trade with Britain, and smuggling soon became an "honorable" resistance to French rule. Taxes burdened the local populace, but the wartime movement of troops though towns like Mühlhausen generated business for merchants and artisans like Heinrich, Ernst and Polycarp Röbling.[4]

When Washington visited Mühlhausen in 1867, he heard stories about his grandparents and later wrote:

> *Polycarp was gifted with a vivid imagination - every evening he would spin the most delightful yarns about his travels in Brazil, Africa and India, whereas in reality he had never left Mühlhausen. He was a man of most methodical habits, about rising, eating, business, walking and his evening beer in the 'Golden Angel' (tavern)....*
> *My father's mother had the opposite characteristics from her husband, and my father inherited many of her traits; she was of a very positive temperament, had much executive capacity, made everybody work, managed her household, family, the business, and her quarter of the town besides.*[5]

The Röbling brothers - Hermann, Karl and Johann - attended the Mühlhausen Gymnasium, a public school founded in the 16th century during the Reformation (Figs. 1.5-6),

that included elementary, middle and upper levels, with students attending up to the level they desired or merited. Hermann and Karl planned to enter their father's tobacco business, but it couldn't support all three brothers and Johann needed to find another occupation. He was quite fortunate to be born with exceptional talents, and to grow up in a period of educational reform that provided him with excellent learning opportunities of which he took full advantage.

While traditional Gymnasium education focused on the classics and humanities, Rector Schollmeyer, the principal of the Mühlhausen Gymnasium, instituted "Realschule" (Real School) reforms emphasizing practical learning to reflect the growth of commerce and manufacturing brought on by the Napoleonic Wars. The curriculum included religion, mathematics, natural sciences, geography, world history, German, French, Latin, penmanship, drawing, and singing.

Schollmeyer also "reduced the number of Latin classes in the lower grades and introduced a collection of teaching materials for mathematics and physics. He added an institute for draftsmanship to the Gymnasium, in which students of the higher 'Beurgerklasse' (citizens' class) drew models for carpenters and those of the intellectual classes (gelehrten Klassen) drew landscapes and portraits. He also introduced the drawing of architectural layouts and buildings in 1817." Johann was thus 11 when he first studied design and construction.[6]

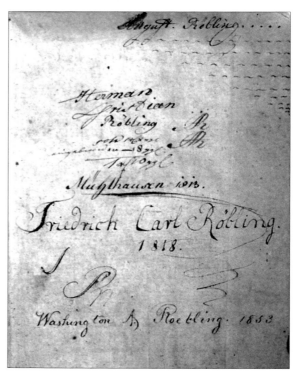

**Figure 1.6: French-German, German-French Dictionary, 1811. RPI
The three Röbling brothers used this dictionary at the
Mühlhausen Gymnasium. Washington signed it
when he visited Mühlhausen with his wife in 1867.**

Johann developed strong skills in mathematics, languages, writing, penmanship and drawing that would serve him well throughout his life. He learned to read and write French fluently, and to play the piano and violin, which he did often until he suffered a hand injury many years later. In 1921, at the age of 15, he made "a decisive step in the direction of his future career as an engineer." He left the Gymnasium before completing the curriculum there to study mathematics and geometry with Dr. Ephraim Solomon Unger in Erfurt, (Fig. 1.7) about 36 miles southeast of Mühlhausen. Dr. Unger ran a small boarding school in his home, teaching theoretical and practical mathematics for students interested in engineering, architecture, mining and similar occupations.

Washington wrote that "Dr. Unger was the foremost mathematician of Thüringen at the time. He was a prolific author of works on arithmetic and its branches, all of which are on the shelves of my library," and were brought to America by Johann. The Unger family had been "one of the first Jewish families to receive the rights of citizenship in Erfurt, and Unger had been a professor at the University of Erfurt until its dissolution in 1816." Dr. Unger started his school in Erfurt in 1920 and within a few years it earned "such a good reputation even outside of Prussia that students came to him from far and wide."[7]

Figure 1.8: Johann August Röbling, 1821. WSR
Johann also developed his artistic skills while studying at Unger's institute, and he signed his work "August Röbling," the name he used in Germany. Washington later wrote across the bottom, "Painted by John A. Roebling at the age of 15 while a scholar at Jena, Thuringia."

Dr. Unger supported the Realschule movement and taught "pure mathematics, practical geometry and geometrical drawing" in the first year of his two-year course of study, and "higher and applied mathematics, particularly for the art of construction and all its subfields, including mechanics and physics," in the second year. Living with Dr. Unger provided the students opportunities to discuss other subjects with him, including philosophy, which became a life-long interest of Johann's. While he was in Erfurt, he apparently acquired his first book by Georg Hegel, the famous philosopher at the University of Berlin, and later brought it with him to America.[8]

According to Washington, Dr. Unger "was very proud of his pupil, John A. Roebling, whose tastes were in the same direction, and the success my father had at Berlin was largely due to the thorough knowledge of algebra and geometry imparted by Dr. Unger....At Unger's school he (also) became a proficient freehand draughtsman. I possess a number of excellent drawings he made at that time" (Fig 1.8).[9]

At Dr. Unger's school, Johann made friends with August Soller, who would become a prominent architect and building official in Berlin, and Edward Thierry, who would later emigrate to America with hopes of establishing a school of architecture and would help Johann obtain some of his first engineering jobs in Pennsylvania. Dr. Unger taught surveying as a practical application of mathematics, and after completing his studies in the Spring of 1923, Johann took his first professional exam in Erfurt and qualified as a surveyor.[10]

Figure 1.7: Dr. Ephraim Solomon Unger, c1820. MM
Röbling studied advanced mathematics for two years starting at the age of 15 at the institute that Unger conducted in his home. Washington called him "the foremost mathematician in Thiringia."

That spring, 17-year-old Johann returned to Mühlhausen, where the family called him August, and a letter he wrote to his brother Karl shows his serious nature and writing skill:

> *Observe all the remarkable things and sites on your trip that opportunity affords. Brother Christel will probably have to join the militia the end of May, then father will need you. I shall also come here the first of May, and shall stay here for half a year, when we can live together, to which I am looking forward. Try to get as much recreation and pleasure on your journey as you possibly can, you will come to beautiful regions....In any case you must get out of military service, which we will try to manage when you are here....*
>
> *When you take your trip, then look around if you can see machines etc. about the tobacco business, and observe them carefully, that can be useful to you. You will undoubtedly have an opportunity to drink a good wine and cheese.*
>
> *Keep a thorough diary, which I also did on my trip to Dresden, and which you will read through here.*
>
> *In the hope that we can soon embrace each other I shall close this letter,*
>
> *Your affectionate brother, August Röbling.*[11]

Washington credited his grandmother, Friedericke, for providing the support Johann needed for his full education:

> *It was her ambition that her youngest son should become a great man, so she schemed and managed and saved to get enough money to send him to the Royal Building Academy in Berlin after he had been at Dr. Unger's pedagogium in Erfurt.*[12]

Johann decided to become a Baumeister – a master builder – and he enrolled at the Königliche Bauakademie (Royal Building Academy) in the spring of 1924. In response to "Germany's quickly expanding industrial development," the Prussian state had established the Bauakademie in 1799 to provide instruction in "all branches in the art of building in their proper inter-relationship, and where theory and praxis go hand in hand in educating the prospective master builder." In a repetition of Johann's good fortune at the Mühlhausen Gymnasium and at Dr. Unger's school, the director of the Bauakademie, Johann Albert Eytelwein, had recently reorganized the curriculum to update and strengthen technical courses. Eytelwein also directed the Prussian Building Administration, and he wanted to increase its effectiveness "by means of a stringent technical education of capable surveyors and of provincial state employees."[13]

The one-year Bauakademie program provided a complete curriculum in two five-month terms. In the summer term,

Figure 1.9: Johann August Röbling, c1824. RU Johann's studies at the Royal Building Academy in Berlin included classical drawing.

from April to September in 1824, Johann studied Physics, Chemistry and Mineralogy and their role in the Field of Construction, plus Architectural Drawing and Drawing and Ornamentation. He attended lectures on General Architecture and Building Construction given by Professor Friedrich Rabe, the Royal architect. According to Washington:[14]

> *Prof. Rabe taught the rules of construction as applied to buildings of stone or wood....*
>
> *Architecture and engineering, which today are separated, then went hand in hand; architecture was predominant and every engineer had to be his own architect. Roebling's correct taste is apparent in his many designs for engineering works. Thoroughly self-reliant, he never employed an architect but always made his own drawings....*
>
> *Under different circumstances he might have become an architect, but Prussia is a land of stone and Berlin a city of stucco. The early object lessons were therefore not intense enough.*[15]

In the winter term, from October 1824 through March 1825, Johann studied Urban Architecture with Professor Rabe, Analysis and Higher Geometry, and most importantly, two courses with the noted Professor J.F.W. Dietlein: Statics and Hydraulics, and Construction of Roads, Bridges, Locks and Canals. According to Washington:

> *Dietlein occupied the chair of bridge engineering. The topics chiefly comprised the theory of stone arches, wooden arch and truss bridges, and chain bridges; also foundations, pumping and the different appliances used in bridge building. Dietlein was an excellent professor, but in practice his students were not backward in criticizing him.*

**Figure 1.10: Johann August Röbling, 1824. RU
While studying at the Royal Building Academy, Johann
developed three-dimensional shading techniques that
he also used in some of his engineering drawings.**

Washington noted the importance of Dietlein's instruction in hydraulics:[16]

Water wheels were the principal source of power. This brought with it the supply of water by damming rivers. Next came canals as the principle means of communication – the pumping of water, drainage, marine hydraulics, etc. For a number of years, my father was considered an authority on hydraulics. He wrote a number of articles on the subject, acted as expert in courts of law, and in his own profession was thoroughly familiar with its principles and applications."[17]

Professor Dietlein's lectures on bridge construction were even more influential on Johann, particularly his lectures on Claude Navier's theory of suspension bridges. Navier, who taught at the Ecole des Ponts et Chaussees (the School of Bridges and Roads in Paris), had studied five iron-chain suspension bridges recently constructed in England. His "Memoire sur les Ponts Suspendus" (Report on Suspension Bridges), which he published in 1823, was the first practical treatise on the theory of suspension bridges.

In 1825, Dietlein published a German summary of Navier's Memoire, and Johann acquired both of these publications and later brought them with him when he immigrated to America. An important part of Dietlein's instruction on suspension bridges focused on "the hazards of inadequate design….as two

of the English bridges had been blown down by the wind." The lessons of these failures impressed Johann strongly and helped ensure his success as a bridge engineer.[18]

Johann's facility with French aided his study of Navier's Memoire and other French publications on bridges and construction. He had picked up some French as a child growing up in Napoleonic Prussia, and he had studied French at the Mühlhausen Gymnasium. In Berlin, he paid for private lessons in French Conversation during both of his terms at the Bauakademie. As Washington noted, "My father spoke French fluently."[19]

During his first term Johann also paid for Drawing Lessons in Architecture and Perspective at the Royal Academy of Art (Figs. 1.9 & 1.10), and during his second term he paid to attend lectures in Geography at the University of Berlin. All of these expenses he carefully listed in the journal of his studies that he began in 1824.

His master passion

In one intriguing entry in his student journal, Johann wrote: "Attended Professor Hegel's lectures on Logic and Metaphysics, costing a Louisdor (a gold piece), and being held five times per week." Georg Wilhelm Friedrich Hegel had taught philosophy at the University of Berlin since 1818, and though his appearance and voice were modest, the famous philosopher had an immense influence on his students. Washington noted Hegel's influence on his father:[20]

The profound ardor with which my father in his leisure hours pursued the study of metaphysics and the higher branches of mental philosophy I have attributed to his relationship with Hegel….(who) occupied at that time the chair of philosophy at the Royal University.
He was the deepest thinker of the day, and while giving his own system preference he yet imparted to his eager listeners a full knowledge of the principles of Kant, Schelling, Fichte, Shoppenhauer, Oken and others. The love for the abstract thus early implanted in my father, grew with age and finally became his master passion, I might say his religion.[21]

Hegel's philosophy appealed to Johann's sense of order and his ambition to become an engineer. Hegel identified Reason as the underlying characteristic of the universe that mankind needed to understand:

Reason governs the world. The movement of the solar system takes place according to unchangeable laws. These laws are Reason, implicit in the phenomena in question…
Reason is the substance and the Infinite Energy of the Universe.

Nature is an embodiment of Reason

Hegel believed that Reason leads to Freedom as the essential characteristic of life, just as "The essence of Matter is Gravity,….the essence of Spirit is Freedom." He viewed social arrangements like slavery as savage, brutal, and contrary to human nature. Slavery limited the freedom of masters as well as slaves, which intelligent people now recognized: "The Greek and Roman world (knew) only that some are free, whilst we know that all men absolutely are free." Hegel's disdain for slavery resonated with Johann's middle class German upbringing and would stick with him throughout his life. In a state of Freedom, according to Hegel, ambitious men can pursue their passions and fulfill their promise:[22]

> *The first glance at History convinces us that the actions of men proceed from their needs, their passions, their characters and talents; and….such needs, passions and interests are the sole springs of action - the efficient agents in this scene of activity.*
>
> *The motive power that puts (ideas) in operation, and gives them determinate existence, is the need, instinct, inclination, and passion of man. That some conception of mine should be developed into act and existence, is my earnest desire: I wish to assert my personality in connection with it: I wish to be satisfied by its execution….*
>
> *Inasmuch as the whole individual, to the neglect of all other actual or possible interests and claims, is devoted to an object with every fibre of volition, concentrating all its desires and powers upon it - we may affirm absolutely that nothing great in the World has been accomplished without passion.*

Within each epoch, Hegel noted, "World Historical Men" envision and accomplish great deeds:

> *What is the material in which the Ideal of Reason is wrought out (on earth)? The primary answer would be - Personality itself - human desires. In human knowledge and volition….Reason attains positive existence.*
>
> *Such are all great historical men - whose own particular aims involve those large issues which are the will of the World-Spirit.*
>
> *They may be called Heroes, inasmuch as they have derived their purposes and their vocation, not from the calm, regular course of things, sanctioned by the existing order; but from a concealed fount - one which has not attained to present existence - from that inner Spirit, still hidden beneath the surface, which, impinging on the outer world as on a shell, bursts it in pieces….*
>
> *They are men, therefore, who appear to draw the impulse of their life from themselves; and whose deeds have produced a condition of things and a complex of historical relations which appear to be only their interest, and their work.*

> *Such individuals had no consciousness of the general Idea they were unfolding, while prosecuting those aims of theirs; on the contrary, they were practical, political men. But at the same time they were thinking men, who had an insight into the requirements of the time - what was ripe for development.*
>
> *This was the very Truth for their age, for their world; the species next in order, so to speak, and which was already formed in the womb of time. It was theirs to know this nascent principle; the necessary, directly sequent step in progress, which their world was to take; to make this their aim, and to expend their energy in promoting it.*
>
> *World-historical men - the Heroes of an epoch - must, therefore, be recognized as its clear-sighted ones; their deeds, their words are the best of that time.*
>
> *It is in the light of those common elements which constitute the interest and therefore the passions of individuals, that these historical men are to be regarded. They are great men, because they willed and accomplished something great.*

Hegel utilized the example of building to illustrate how great men fashion ideas and materials into 'the edifice of human society:'

> *The building of a house is, in the first instance, a subjective aim and design. On the other hand we have, as means, the several substances required for the work - Iron, Wood, Stones. The elements are made use of in working up this material: fire to melt the iron, wind to blow the fire, water to set wheels in motion, in order to cut the wood, etc.*
>
> *The result is, that the wind, which has helped to build the house, is shut out by the house; so also are the violence of rains and floods, and the destructive powers of fire, so far as the house is made fire-proof. The stones and beams obey the law of gravity, press downwards, and so high walls are carried up. Thus the elements are made use of in accordance with their nature, and yet to co-operate for a product, by which their operation is limited.*
>
> *Thus the passions of men are gratified; they develop themselves and their aims in accordance with their natural tendencies, and build up the edifice of human society; thus fortifying a position for Right and Order.*

Hegel idea's provided a rationale and vision for a life directed towards great deeds, and it's easy to see the appeal of Hegel's philosophy to a brilliant and ambitious young man studying engineering and architecture with some of the best teachers of the age.

> *We may affirm absolutely that nothing great in the world has been accomplished without passion.*
> *- Georg Wilhelm Friedrich Hegel*

The land of desire

Hegel's view of governments and the opportunity of citizens under them inspired many young Germans like Johann to seek their fortunes in America:

> A State is well constituted and internally powerful, when the private interest of its citizens is one with the common interest of the State; when the one finds its gratification and realization in the other....
>
> Europe has sent its surplus population to America....Many Englishmen have settled there, where burdens and imposts do not exist, and where the combination of European appliances and European ingenuity has availed to realize some produce from the extensive and still virgin soil. Indeed the emigration in question offers many advantages.
>
> The emigrants have got rid of much that might be obstructive to their interests at home, while they take with them the advantages of European independence of spirit, and acquired skill; for those who are willing to work vigorously, but who have not found in Europe opportunities for doing so, a sphere of action is certainly presented in America. In North America we witness a prosperous state of affairs: an increase of industry and population, civil order and firm freedom.... America is the land of the future. It is the land of desire¸ for all those who are weary of the historical armory of old Europe.[23]

A life of hard work

Johann experienced two intensive terms at the Bauakademie, as recorded in his student journals and as Washington recognized in his own education decades later:

> Of Roebling's University life at Berlin....it seems to have been a life of hard work, of constant intense application. The lecture system was in vogue at that time. Notes were taken of the lecturer's remarks and then written out at night. These notes were bound in book form, afterwords, and number at least ten volumes; they are copiously illustrated with hand and ink sketches.
>
> To one who has not been through such a course, the amount of laborious application seems incredible, and simply shows how much can be accomplished by steady work from early morn till midnight. Thirty years later I went through the same task myself at Troy and I know what it means.[24]

Johann completed his studies in March of 1825 and qualified as a Baukondukteur or building supervisor. He was "one of only six of the 125 students who, due to their diligence and good progress, were nominated for a book award." In his journal, he noted that "within one year a law would be introduced, that everyone wanting to do their second exam (to qualify as Baumeister, or master builder) would have to engage

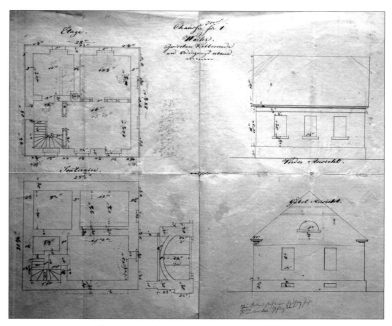

Figure 1.11: Johann August Röbling, Toll Collector's House, Eslohe, Westphalia, 1827. RU Johann designed this house while working for the Prussian government as a 'Baukondukteur,' or master builder.

in practical construction for at least a year with an architect already in royal service." When a candidate completes his obligatory service, as Washington noted:[25]

> He then presents his final thesis, receives his full degree and his membership as government engineer. In Prussia the engineering profession is not open to all comers. The number is limited, they have to be graduates of Berlin, are under government control subject to a chief engineer, with assignment of duty in various districts, regular promotion and fixed salary. The district to which my father was assigned for two years was that of Arnsberg in Westphalia; the duty comprised the laying out and construction of public chaussees (roads). The experience here gained proved of great value to him later on in western Pennsylvania, although rather ahead of the times.

In this first job as a Prussian Baukondukteur, Johann worked out of the local office in Eslohe as a "site manager on a section of the primary road from Meschede to the Rhine," in the Sauerland area of Westphalia. In addition to laying out roads and designing culverts and small bridges, he also designed a collector's house for the toll road (Fig. 1.11).[26]

We wish to convey to him our encouragement

While working in Westphalia, Johann pursued his interest in suspension bridges that he had developed from Professor Dietlein's lectures and Navier's Theory of Suspension Bridges. He corresponded with Dietlein in Berlin, "supplied

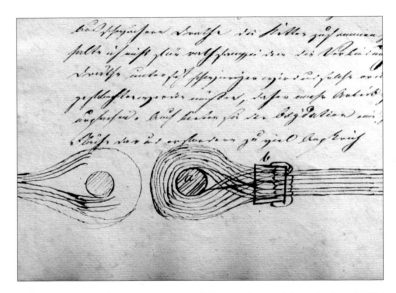

Figure 1.12: Johann August Röbling, Wire Cables, 1828. GVW Johann proposed building a 130 ft. span suspension bridge over the Ruhr River at Freienohl in Westphalia with cables made of bundled wires instead of the iron chains typically used.

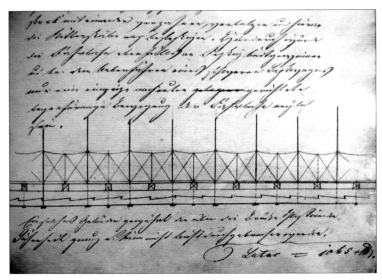

Figure 1.12: Johann August Röbling, Deck Truss, 1828. GVW For his Freienohl Bridge proposal, Johann drew a deck with a stiffening truss to provide the rigidity that he recognized as essential for suspension bridge decks.

himself with the latest publications on suspension bridges to complement the extensive library he had taken along with him to Westphalia (and) very soon he began to think about designing a suspension bridge as an exam project for his (Baumeister) degree."[27]

On a trip along the Ruhr and Rhine Rivers in 1828, Johann became acquainted with Friedrich Harcort, an industrialist who wanted to build a 450 foot bridge across the Ruhr River, a Rhine tributary, near his factory in Wetter, about 40 miles northwest of Eslohe, and Johann proposed a suspension bridge. Nearly 40 years later, he wrote to Washington, who was visiting Prussia: "I stopped three weeks at Wetter an der Ruhr…. I made a survey on the Ruhr, for location of the Suspension Br. which I had to plan as my Thesis for my 2nd Examen."[28]

We wish to convey to him our encouragement

Nothing appears to have come from Johann's first proposal for a suspension bridge, but in the spring of 1828 he developed plans for suspension bridges to be built at two sites that he probably learned about during his winter trip: one over the Lenne River (a tributary of the Ruhr) near Finnentrop, about ten miles west of Eslohe, and the other over the Ruhr at Freienohl, about eight miles north of Eslohe. Johann submitted his plans for the Finnentrop bridge to the regional government office in Arnsberg on June 1, a few days before his 22nd birthday, and he submitted his proposal for the Freienohl bridge that July.

In his description of the Freienhohl bridge, found in the Graf von Westphalen's archive in 1998, he proposed main cables built of "either linked iron rods or sheafs of parallel wire" (Fig. 1.12). He also proposed a rigid deck stiffened by a trussed railing (Fig. 1.13), and saddles with roller bearings on top of towers that could slide back and forth to balance the tension from moving loads. The Superior Board of Construction in Berlin reviewed both proposals.

When Johann's road work in Westphalia came to an end in the fall of 1828, he returned to Mühlhausen and registered with the government building department in Erfurt, the regional administrative center. The official entry in the government ledger described him as a "surveyor, who was employed until autumn for the construction of roads in the county of Arnsberg for the exam in construction and is very willing to improve his mastery of this discipline."

Later that year he received the Interior Ministry's response to his Finnentrop bridge proposal:[29]

The project for this suspension bridge must be rejected, because the chains and especially the rings that connect the chain elements, as well as the wire cables and the anchoring of the chains in the earth are surely too weak.

As well, the non-perpendicular form of the suspenders, the manner in which the roadway is suspended on two independent chains, the iron saddles, the intention of using railings to assist in the suspension, the wooden blocks on the columns under the chains etc. do not have our full approval.

Nevertheless, the industriousness with which the engineer Röbling has completed his suspension bridge project deserves our full recognition, and we wish to convey to him our encouragement.

Figure 1.14: Johann A. Röbling, Journal, c1827. RU
Johann sketched the famous Hammersmith Bridge in London, a chain suspension bridge, from illustrations in his library.

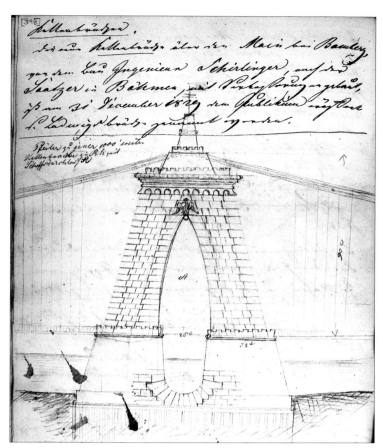

Figure 1.15: Johann A. Röbling, Journal, c1830. RU
Johann sketched a proposal for a 1,000 ft. long suspension bridge over the Rhine River, probably near Rheinhausen.

The Superior Board of Construction also rejected his proposal for the Freienohl bridge. These rejections reflected official concerns about suspension bridges following the collapse in 1825 of an inclined-stay bridge near Nienberg, about 40 miles northwest of Leipzig, that caused several deaths. They also reflected Johann's lowly status as a Baukondukteur within the hierarchical Prussian building bureaucracy.

While his proposals failed, Johann's plans for the Finnentrop and Freienohl bridges show that he was already developing features that would become hallmarks of his later work, including rigid decks stiffened with trusses, saddles with roller bearings on top of the towers, and diagonal stays.

Johann continued collecting publications on suspension bridges and he studied two iron chain bridges built in 1827: the Malapane Bridge in Silesia and the Hammersmith Bridge in London. He sketched the latter in his journal from illustrations in books in his library (Fig. 1.14). Around 1828, Johann outlined a proposal to build a 1,000 ft. long suspension bridge over the Rhine River, probably at Rheinhausen near Freiburg (Fig. 1.15). His design specified a tower in the middle of the river with an opening for ships to pass through.

With great delight

In 1829, an engineer named Johann Adolphus Etzler returned after eight years in America to Mühlhausen, where he was born in 1791, to promote his plan for establishing a community of German emigrants in America. Etzler was 15 years older than Johann Röbling and his reports of the freedom and boundless opportunities in America strongly appealed to his young friend. Fearing that Etzler would convince too many young people to emigrate, the local authorities jailed him for a time, but upon his release he resumed proselytizing about a better life in America.

Washington recalled hearing "my father speak of Etzler, who seemed to exercise considerable control over him. He was a universal genius, conversant with English….and (later) wrote a remarkable book called the new 'Paradise.'" By the spring of 1830, Johann was studying English with Etzler.[30]

In May of 1830, Johann traveled by mail coach to Nürnberg in Bavaria, about 175 miles south of Mühlhausen, and his remarkable dairy of this 20 day trip highlights his curiosity and his skills of observation and analysis. Along the route, he noted the changing landscapes, with their 'ancient' castles, abbeys, 'majestic' ruins, 'manicured' gardens, farms, villages and taverns, and he summarized the history of many of these places. He commented on industrial features like granite works, marble quarries, and copper and iron works, and often cited the number of men who worked in them.

In the towns, he described government buildings and churches in Greek, old German, old Italian, and Gothic styles, and noted their distinctive decorations and artworks. He described hospitals in detail, including their layouts, staffing, treatments, hygiene and meals. He sketched floor plans, elevations and details of several churches and hospitals.

Major errors were made in constructing this bridge

The highlight of his trip and probably the main reason for taking it was the Bamberg Chain Bridge that had opened at the end of 1829. Washington noted:

> *I have always heard my father speak of this trip with great delight because it was at Bamberg that he saw a suspension bridge for the first time. It was a chain bridge over the Regnitz. Of course he sketched it, examined it and made it the subject of a thesis. It was the memory of this structure which turned his attention later on in that direction.*[31]

The 'thesis' Washington referred to was his father's detailed analysis of the Bamberg Chain Bridge in his travel diary. He spent several days studying every part of the bridge, discussed it with the Bamberg building inspector, and sketched many of its details and its overall appearance (Figs. 1.16-17). His assessment included mathematical calculations of its loading and capacity, the quality of its materials and construction, and its aesthetic appeal. His criticism of several aspects of the bridge and his praise of others presaged his future design and construction of suspension bridges that would make him famous.

Johann began his analysis by concluding that the chains of the Bamberg Bridge were undersized. Using Navier's formulas that he learned at the Bauakademie, he calculated that if the bridge were fully loaded with people, there would be too much tension on the chains: "This tension of 27,000 pounds per sq.in. is assumed to be somewhat too large and the chains therefore should be slightly heavier because they are made of iron, not steel."[32]

In several pages describing the costs and details of the iron work, the foundations, and the pillars that supported the chains, he noted flaws in the design of the cast iron saddles at the top of each pillar, a feature that he would pay close attention to in his future work:

Figure 1.16: Johann A. Röbling, Bamberg Chain Bridge, 1830. KR
Johann traveled to Bamberg in Bavaria to study the construction of its well known suspension bridge, which he sketched in his travel diary.

> *The friction in between the chains and the saddles is extremely high. During this year's spring, due to changes in temperature, the chains expanded and all four pillars were slightly bent out of the proper direction. Several cracks have been noted on the outer side of the pillars.*
> *One can see from this how necessary it is to guide the chains over the saddles using rollers which would allow the expansion or contraction of the chains without putting any pressure on the pillars.*
> *On the Bamberg chain bridge, the lever-type motions (at the saddles) will never cease, but will always occur at every temperature change. Because of this fault and other factors it is clear that major errors were made in constructing this bridge.*[33]

His criticism of roadway and ironwork details, which he documented in several sketches, showed the importance he placed on construction practices and aesthetics:

> *According to the design, the roadway was supposed to rise slightly toward the middle. However, in the end, the roadway was laid horizontally. Since the roadway was built in winter when it was very cold, and because it was then laid horizontally, in summer, when considerable heat occurred, the roadway sagged slightly below the horizontal in the middle due to the stretching of the chains, proof of how important the influence of the temperature is.*
> *The ironwork has three coats of black paint. Due to the black coating the chains heat up even more. The entire appearance of the bridge is quite dark and it would've been much nicer if they would have painted it white….*
> *The construction of the ironwork in general is not exact and clean. The hanging rods aren't suspended exactly vertically and are not an equal distance from each other.*

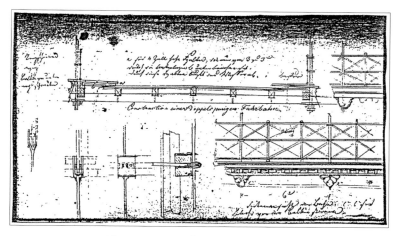

Figure 1.17: Johann A. Röbling,
Bamberg Chain Bridge, 1830. KR
Johann met with the bridge manager, sketched many of the bridge's details, and wrote a critical analysis of its design and construction and how they could have been improved.

When the chains were hung it happened that some were too long and therefore many links were bent and twisted in different directions….All the chain bolts are too long and protruded at least two inches in some spots, which is quite objectionable.

In general, the connections of the chain lengths and the individual blades are not exact and too much clearance has been allowed….

In general, the thickness of the iron components of the entire bridge aren't even.[34]

In reviewing bridge details with the Bamberg building inspector, Johann identified design flaws that affected both appearance and performance:

From the side the bridge roadway doesn't look very good and the appearance would improve, if the suggested wood covers were installed. The handrail rods are not firmly mounted and sometimes clatter against the hanging rods. The entire handrail arrangement is too open and not firmly mounted, with the result that children could fall into the river.[35]

His comments on the importance of the pillars to the overall appearance of the bridge presaged the symbolic emphasis he would place on the pillars and towers of his suspension bridges:

The pillars and all the masonry are very solidly constructed and look quite elegant. If you stand on the bridge or near the pillars, they look strong and secure. A connection between these pillars was unnecessary. The entire appearance of the bridge is enhanced by the pillars and the spaces between them give the structure a special 'look,' almost as if guards were stationed on it.[36]

In recognizing the critical role that a stable deck plays in the performance of a suspension bridge, Johann highlighted one of the keys to his future success as a bridge engineer:

The reason why the heaviest loads don't cause any perceptible bending in the roadway is because the roadbed itself is powerfully and sturdily built. As the chains are stretched by the hanging rods at certain points, they are lifted at others. This stretching doesn't happen often on account of the weight of the roadbed.

Because of the weight of the roadbed, all the hanging rods are under tension, and this explains why even the heaviest load of carriages doesn't cause any perceptible chain movement when they travel over the bridge.

The foregoing observation should apply to the construction of larger bridges.[37]

But, of course, the slaves suffer greatly

After returning to Mühlhausen, Johann wrote a section of his diary in German under a heading, "Notes on America, especially the Union of North America: Information from magazines, newspapers and books," which suggests that he had already developed the ability to read English. He noted many facts about American population, Indians and their resettlement, crops and farming methods, and specific regional conditions and activities.[38]

His notes detailed farming practices and crop prices in several states, especially for sugar cane and cotton in Florida and Louisiana. He cited reports of planting mulberry trees in Baltimore and Delaware for silk worms, growing cotton in Georgia, Virginia, Alabama and Charleston, raising sheep in New England for wool, and growing grapes in Ohio, Illinois and Mexico for wine. He also included many details about Texas geography, farming, and settlements.

In his writing he expressed his concern about slavery, which would influence his choice of where to settle in America. After a lengthy description of highly profitable sugar cane farming in Louisiana, he noted: "But, of course, the slaves suffer greatly. When the sugar simmering starts, it must be watched day and night, and the slaves have to work at all hours."

In discussing Missouri, he wrote that it was "admitted only two years ago to the Union and even then with great political difficulties and after a long debate because Congress didn't grant Missouri the right to come into the Union as a 'slave' state." Since the famous Missouri Compromise of 1820 permitted slavery in Missouri, Johann and many other Germans who were appalled by slavery had no interest in settling there if they had the opportunity to emigrate to America.[39]

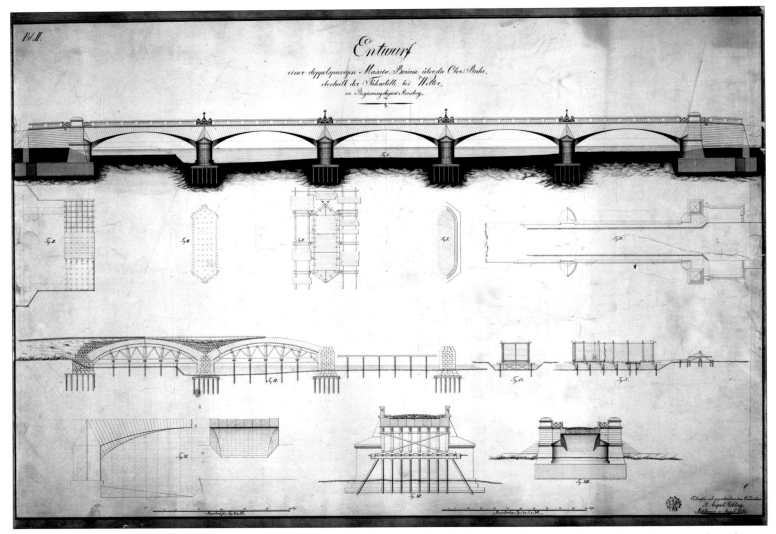

Figure 1.18: Johann August Roebling, "Design of a double lane Massive Bridge over the upper Ruhr above the Ferryplace by Wetter in Arnsberg Administrative Area, Designed and Drawn by Conductor J. August Röbling, Mühlhausen in August 1830." RPI Washington characterized his father's submission to qualify for the Baumeister exam as "a magnificent design for a massive stone arch bridge with full details of construction. This beautiful drawing is still in my possession, as fresh and as clear as it was seventy years ago." In the lower right corner, an official in the Royal Building Department in Berlin stamped its red seal of approval.

This beautiful drawing

During the summer of 1830, Johann continued working on a thesis project that would qualify him to take the Prussian Baumeister exam to become a certified engineer. In spite of his keen interest in suspension bridges, he must have been wary of the official distrust of suspension bridges in Berlin, and for his thesis project he chose to design an arch bridge over the Ruhr River in Wetter (Fig. 1.18).[40]

As Johann was working on his thesis, reform efforts shook up the established order in several European countries and threatened others. The "July Revolution" in Paris deposed the Bourbon regime that had been restored after Napoleon and replaced it with a constitutional monarchy, and an August revolt in Brussels liberated the Belgians from Dutch rule. Encouraged by these changes, German students and intellectuals pressed their own monarchs for constitutional reforms, and they won some concessions on parliamentary rights and press control. Economic progress in Prussia, however, had strengthened the monarchy, and Kaiser Frederick Wilhelm III resisted further reforms and tightened restrictions on students and the press. Prussians hoping for more freedom became increasingly disillusioned.

In addition to this disappointment, Johann carried the burden of his experience with the Prussian building administration, which had rejected his suspension bridge proposals and offered few opportunities for his advancement. Washington described his dilemma:

> *The question of his future life confronted him. Should he remain in the fatherland, tied down to the strict rules of semi-official life, a perpetual subordinate with no opportunity to gratify a laudable ambition, or to follow the bent of his own genius?*
>
> *My father often told me when referring to the Pittsburgh Suspension Aqueduct that he would never have been allowed to build such a structure in Prussia. The dignity and pride of the supervising engineer would have frowned down the ambitious attempt of the young engineer and even proposing such a structure which had no precedent.*
>
> *Or should he in the prime of his youth, seek his fortune in new fields, untrammeled by official supervision. America was the goal which all young men aimed to reach then as well as now. A family council was held at Mühlhausen, his meager patrimony was scraped together and paid him in advance. He now began to think seriously of emigrating to the New World.*[41]

To acquire more happiness for themselves and their loved ones

Johann continued recording facts about America in his diary into the Fall of 1830, though none of his notes pertained to engineering opportunities there. He and Etzler organized an emigration society and in December they published an emigration guide anonymously to avoid censure. They wrote the guide - *General View of the United States of North America, together with a Community Plan for Settlement* - for those who "had enough power and drive to acquire more happiness for themselves and for their loved ones by working independently, yet at the same time have little or no perspective for achieving this in their own country."[42]

For a second edition printed in early 1831, they added an introduction and subscribed their names along with those of two other leaders of their emigration society. While no copies of their emigration guide have been found, it no doubt included Etzler's portrayal of all the resources awaiting ingenious settlers in America, plus his ideas for harnessing natural forces to create an unprecedented era of prosperity (see box).

The Paradise Within Reach of All Men, Without Labour by Powers of Nature and Machinery, - Johann Adolphus Etzler, 1833

I promise to show the means for creating a paradise within 10 years, where everything desirable for human life may be had for every man in superabundance, without labor, without pay; where the whole face of nature is changed into the most beautiful form of which is capable; where man may live in the most magnificent palaces, and all imaginable refinements of luxury, in the most delightful gardens....

The basis of my proposals is, that there are powers in nature at the disposal of man, a million times greater than all men on earth could affect, with their united exertions, by their nerves and sinews....If we have the requisite power for mechanical purposes, it is then but a matter of human contrivance to invent adapted tools or machines for application....

The powers are chiefly to be derived, 1, from wind; 2, from the tide, or the rise and fall of the ocean caused by the gravity between the moon and the ocean; and 3, from the sunshine, or the heat of the sun, by which water may be transformed into steam, whose expansive power is to operate upon machineries....The waves of the ocean are also powers to be applied....Each of these powers requires no consumption of materials....but the materials for the construction of the machineries....

No country in the world is evidently better situated and constituted for the application of the means in contemplation....than the United States. Free from the blast of arbitrary despotism, with an uncultivated territory,

sufficient for the reception of more than 100 millions of men, which might revel here in superabundance of all necessities, comforts and luxuries of life, the United States might easily accelerate their march towards their supreme power and influence over the whole world, by inducing immigrants from Europe to settle in our extensive wildernesses in the West, with the application of the proposed means....(for) the extensive improvements for the benefit of the nation, such as railroads, canals, draining of swamps, dams along rivers against noxious inundations, establishments for new settlers and travelers, vehicles for transporting men, and things of any bulk and weight, over land and water, to the immense benefit of the community at large, which the new means afford....

The fundamental truths are....that the wind, the periodical rise and fall, and the motions of the ocean, and the transformation of water into steam, for ten thousand times more power than the whole human race may ever want for all imaginable purposes; that these powers can be rendered operative uninterruptedly; backed by reflectors the heat of the sun can be concentrated, and any desired heat produced; that by this heat steam can be generated; and sand, clay, and other vitresible substances can be vitrified; that the finest cultivation of soil, and all works in the ground, can be affected by one simple contrivance; and that very large vehicles can be moved by such great powers; and that pliable stuff can be composed and formed into any desired form.

Etzler saw his proposals being accomplished in dedicated communities: "The most profitable, the shortest, and easiest way to put them into operation is to form associations…so as to enable the rich and the poor to participate fully in all the possible greatest benefits of these discoveries." He foresaw that the success of these enterprises required the cooperative efforts of a group of special men: "The execution of the proposals is only qualified for a large body of intelligent men, who associate themselves."[44]

Etzler and Johann's pamphlet was apparently well distributed and quite convincing, as hundreds of people from several German towns - some more than 100 miles from Mühlhausen - committed to join their emigration party. Karl Röbling decided to join his brother in emigrating, and they received a letter from their good friend, Frederick Baehr:

Now dear friends, a last farewell! You have done well. Your names will be glorified by your children's children. You should be highly praised and honored for your brave hearts and the spirit of friendship you possess. I await with longing the hour which will bring us together again.[45]

Washington described the circumstances surrounding his father's departure….

In the spring of 1831 all preparations were made.

Several hundred colonists composed the emigrating party, more than half came from Hesse-Darmstadt, many from electoral Hesse, and the balance from Mühlhausen and its neighborhood. Such companies at the start generally aim to settle at some common point in America, but long before the end of the journey dissensions arose, friends became estranged and they scattered in different directions.

The party was too large for one vessel, so the first and larger half, numbering 230 souls, sailed from Bremen in the ship Henry Barclay. The remainder, with my father and his brother Karl, numbering 90 persons sailed on the American bark August Edward.

He left Mühlhausen on the 11th of May, 1831, never to see it again. The ship sailed on the 20th of May from Bremerhaven, arriving in Philadelphia on the sixth of August after a stormy and wearisome voyage of 78 days. During the voyage my father kept a journal, which was subsequently printed in German at Eschwege, by his cousin E.W. Röbling.[46]

Farewell, my Fatherland

On the first day of his journey, May 11, Johann began writing the emigration journal that he later sent to his cousin, who published it in German in 1832 as the *Dairy of My Journey from Mühlhausen in Thuringia via Bremen to the United States in North America in the year 1831*. In his first entry he wrote:

Today we journeyed from Mühlhausen, took leave from our friends, relatives and acquaintances, and said farewell to our native land, in the hope of establishing a new home, a new Fatherland, which will treat us indeed as a father, in the western continent, beyond the Atlantic Ocean.

Our undertaking has been begun with precaution and circumspection, and it shall be carried out in the same manner. Here nothing has been inconsiderately done. Firm conviction and settled views have led us. We are not going with exaggerated views or extravagant hopes. To what extent America corresponds with our moderate expectations and affords us what we seek, the future must teach. Trustworthy reports will inform you later.

We would tempt no one to emigrate, and up to now we have persuaded none. The decision to settle in America must arise from the personal energy and power of will of each individual; otherwise it is useless for him to go to America.

At the Lengefelde Tower we took farewell of the friends who had accompanied us thus far. Once more we express our thanks for your company and for your sincere sympathy, which has stirred me deeply more than once.

God keep you! We shall never forget you! Farewell, tough native land, which has fostered our childhood, and in which we have enjoyed so many happy moments. Thou too shalt remain unforgettable to us.

It is not contempt for our Fatherland that causes us to leave it, but an inclination and an ardent desire that our circumstance may be bettered and that they may have a decidedly humane aspect. May fate soon grant Germany that which her educated populace can lay claim with most well-founded right, and which has been son long unjustly withheld from her. You know what I mean.

Farewell, my Fatherland.[47]

When his brother, Karl, and other emigrants from Mühlhausen joined him in Bremen six days later, he wrote in his journal that, "All are well-prepared for the journey. The children are well and more cheerful than when they left Mühlhausen." Of the 93 passengers who boarded the 100 ft. long by 27 ft. wide bark, *August Edward*, 44 were members of the Röbling emigration party. To fill up the ship, the captain also took on 49 passengers who were strangers to the Roebling group, but "apparently decent folk," as Johann noted.[48]

The Röbling brothers and five other passengers booked bedsteads in the captain's cabin, while the other 86 passengers, including all the children, slept four and five abreast in steerage. Johann wrote in great detail about "matters of daily occurrence at sea," Washington noted, including: "the trip down the (Wesser) river, entrance into the North Sea, remarks on the first steamship he had seen, seasickness, food, description of the rigging and vessel, navigation, whales, winds and storms, ocean currents, calms, a death on board, American clippers, anxiety to reach land, ending with a description of the Delaware and Philadelphia."[49]

Of the start of their 37 mile sail down the Wesser River to the North Sea at Bremerhaven, Johann wrote:

> As the wind filled the sails from the side, the ship lay quite on her side during this river voyage, and we land-lubbers had hard work to keep our footing on deck without leaning against the rails or the masts….
>
> The afternoon and evening, when we lay calmly at anchor, were very pleasant….Our whole ship's company had been put into a happy mood, which expressed itself in merry choral singing accompanied by a violin and flute. Nevertheless, we noticed soon enough and very clearly that we were not on land amidst society of our own choice and free from constraint, but in the far from pleasant constraint of a ship.[50]

As Johann adjusted to the conditions of living on the ship along with his fellow passengers, he observed much of the world around him and thought often of his destination:

> The sight of the clouds on the western horizon afforded me a pleasant diversion one evening, when the sun was setting beautifully and the calm sea permitted my gaze to follow its last rays.
>
> After these had disappeared, the glorious coloring of the still-illuminated clouds became more and more lovely, and from their fantastic forms the lively imagination created all the pictures, which only the sight of a beautiful shoreline can ever supply.
>
> Thus I dreamed myself back amongst my native fields in Europe, and the scenes of the last farewell again stood vividly before me. With them also were the friends who took part in them and who, perhaps at that very moment, were thinking just as vividly of us as we of them.
>
> But soon the lively imagination also dreamed on and already seemed to see in the remarkable forms and nuances of color, which the light elusively painted before us, the shores of the new, Western World, to which our gaze is ardently directed….
>
> I believe we can reasonably allow ourselves the hope of arriving in America in good time to celebrate the anniversary of the Declaration of Independence with the free citizens of the United States.
>
> This day must be of the greatest interest to every free-minded man, a day in which fourteen million free citizens of the state can thank for their present condition of freedom and well-being, and on which their brave ancestors, with the splendid and high-minded Washington at the head, cast off the servile fetters of the proud and overbearing motherland.
>
> We are all desirous of arriving in time to join in the celebration.[51]

Everything moves more freely now

After a short time, Johann overcame his initial seasickness, but Karl didn't, and his weaker constitution presaged future problems. The lack of wind greatly slowed the progress of the *August Edward*, but Johann used the extended time studying English, reading, playing music, thinking thoughts shared universally by immigrants, and writing in his diary:

> I for my part am now feeling very well and am enjoying all foods with great relish. Brother Karl is more disposed to nausea and does not yet feel so well. I am now entirely reconciled to sea life and so familiar with the sea that, if it goes high, the play of the water and the howl of the wind, which had previously occasioned me nausea, now provide entertainment for me.
>
> One easily becomes accustomed to the sight of the wild waves, which, like great wild animals, often seem to dance upon the deck, in order to devour the ship, but remain satisfied, however, in giving it such a cuff in the ribs that its wooden frame groans at every joint….
>
> Besides the study of the English language and the conversation, the library of Herr Stieweg affords us a pleasant opportunity of passing the time.
>
> In the evening, if the air is mild and the sea is calm, a pair of flutes will be heard on deck, accompanying a chorus of strong, male voices, from which a few can be distinguished.
>
> Thus the most monotonous of living does not lack in entertaining seasoning, and often only the will is lacking to enjoy the present. As much as I wish the end of our voyage to come, I have yet felt no impatience up to now.
>
> The lonely, isolated stay on the ship during a long sea voyage from one part of the world to another has in a certain respect an entirely well-founded utility.
>
> Thus, we see the last of the shores of Europe vanish from our site, we separate ourselves at a single stroke from the Old World that is known to us, and to which by our birth, by our education, by the entire youth that we have lived there, by the nation to which we belong, by its history and our own, by our relatives, and by many other circumstances, which have a bearing on our life, we are bound and continue to be bound, at least in memory, as long as we draw breath.
>
> The influence, which Europe has had on us up to now will, however, be marked. Everything moves more freely now and the sight of the open, wide sea serves altogether to arouse the feeling of personal freedom and natural independence in every breast. The restless activity and chicanery of the little and the great gods of earth and their vassals now seem petty and small. Yet it was necessary and still is necessary to lighten the darkness as time goes on and create more influence and more privileges for reason.[52]

During the long journey, where nothing presents itself, which can gradually lighten in the imagination a passage from one part of the world to another, one has time and leisure enough to make good this lack and prepare one's self mentally for the New World.

All impressions, which America will make upon us, will in reality be new, no matter how familiar we may already have made ourselves with the new continent through reading and hearsay.

A nature divergent from the German, other human beings, a foreign language and customs, an entirely foreign type of national character, new political institutions, which phenomena, in so far as they are derived from men themselves, all bear in themselves the free stamp of the resurrection from the ruins of the institutions of the old world - all these will indicate to us that we are foreigners.

Much that is good, honorable, and humanly great and reasonable, will interest us still more than we already are, in the land, which we have chosen for our new home. However, much also, which does not agree with our former conceptions, will appear offensive to us, and there will be much, which concerns the people, its disposition, and its character, which we cannot approve.

However, the opinions, which are leading us, and which have led us up to now, are mainly based on the natural conditions and national advantages of the country; in general, they are also based on the political order, which does not chain up human activity in any sorts of fetters.

The citizenship is left to itself and affords appropriate protection to the particular individual without occasioning many expenses.

The future will teach us to what degree the picture we have sketched of the United States agrees with the reality. Much may be exaggerated and set forth in too bright a light; yet everything is also very simple and natural, and hence also well-founded.

The greatest art will indeed consist in shaking off the old European prejudices and fitting oneself to the New World; every people demands of a foreigner, who wants to settle permanently among it, that he will assimilate to his environment as soon as possible.

I have undertaken to observe with all possible impartiality, and truth shall ever guide me in my reports to my countrymen.

After being surrounded by water for over two months, Johann and his fellow passengers welcomed the first hint of land in the wind as they approached the American coast:

On the evening of the day before yesterday we had the opportunity to convince ourselves of the truth of the assertion of the seamen that one can smell land at a great distance. On that evening we had a pretty strong, westerly and warm wind, which bore a very noticeable aromatic odor of herbs to us from the vicinity of the American coast.

The odor was strikingly distinct and my earlier doubts regarding this oft-asserted fact vanished. This wide-spread odor would also indicate that the entire American mainland is covered with an almost uninterrupted forest and a great abundance of plants, whereby the atmosphere is saturated with aromatic particles, which the winds blowing away from land carry away to a great distance. This land odor produced a beneficial effect upon all the passengers.[53]

As the *August Henry* sailed into Delaware Bay, the passengers caught sight of Cape Henlopen in Delaware and then the lighthouse at Cape May, New Jersey:

The coast is sandy and flat, and hardly seems to stand out of the water; but in the background thick, compact woods appear, which cut off the further view, and on which our eyes rest with pleasure.

How long have we not been without the sight of land and vegetation! Already it has been over ten weeks since we have seen nothing but sky and water. Everyone is rejoicing and longs to tread the solid earth, which will be a good mother to us also in this new part of the world....How am I to find expression, which would be adequate, to communicate my feelings and my surprise to others, which I myself have experienced, since we came up the Delaware Bay....

The shores are becoming more and more interesting. Although low, yet they present a beautiful appearance on account of the handsome groves of trees and stretches of forest, with which the bank is still ornamented, the remnants of the ancient, venerable primeval of this new part of the world.

Three hundred years must have passed since the sheltered loneliness of these wild surroundings was interrupted by the all-disturbing European. Then a few Indian tribes were living quietly on the property inherited from their ancestors. What changes have come about since that time![54]

The Fouth of July, as the day of the fifty-fith anniversary of the Declaration of Independence, was hailed by us with sympathy and celebrated in our thoughts. In vain had we cherished the hope of celebrating this holiday in company with the free-minded citizens of the Union.
- Johann August Röbling, aboard the *August Henry*, July 8th, 1831

Chapter 2: *The Village of Saxonburg*

At noon we arrived before Philadelphia….the world-famous City of Brotherly Love of the New World, founded by the Quaker, William PENN. For three nights we still remained on board the ship, whereafter all the passengers moved to lodgings in the city….The streets, all of which intersect at right angles, are entirely straight, very roomy and in part planted with rows of trees.[1]

Johann August Röbling compared what he saw in Philadelphia with cities back home in Germany:

Regarding the inner elegance of the residences, and indeed not individual ones, but all together, Berlin, for example, offers no comparison and seems to be a city of poor, oppressed people. What is lavished there upon a few public buildings, is here lavished by every plain citizen upon his home. Elegance and cleanliness in this respect are observed to the highest degree.

Notwithstanding there is no lack of fine public edifices. The building of the Bank of the United States is built in Doric style of Pennsylvania marble, and beside it, there are many other banks, both State and private. Further notable buildings are the Peale Museum, several academies, and a multitude of neatly built churches.

Philadelphia's renowned 'water-works' also caught his attention:

An excellent convenience is provided by the water-mains, which are laid under all streets and squares, and provide every house with water, which serves for drinking and household use and has a clean taste. The water comes from the Schuylkill and is stored by the famous water-works outside the city in wide, elevated reservoirs, from which the pipes lead. These water-works, which we saw on Sunday, are very fine and artistically constructed. The water mains make it possible quickly to extinguish every fire that breaks out, which is the more important, as fires are said to be very frequent here.

Above all else, Johann was impressed by the people in this new land:

The impression, which the populace has made on me, has turned out more favorable that I had expected….

The outward demeanor of the people, of the townsfolk, and their public conduct is more modest here and at the same time more free and unconstrained than I have noticed in any city in Germany….Philadelphia is to be distinguished above other cities on account of its politeness

towards foreigners….I have spoken to no one yet, even when he seemed to be in a hurry, who did not fully reply to my question. Every American, even when he is poor and must serve others, feels his innate rights as a man. What a contrast to the oppressed German population!….

The Negroes here are all free and constitute the domestic class. They go cleanly and decently clad.

The removal of the hat and the frequent greetings, which are so burdensome in Germany, do not exist here.

In Johann's assessment, freedom had enabled the Americans to accomplish a great deal in a relatively short amount of time:

In all institutions and customs, which concern public life, the American proves himself to be long-headed, and in this particular he stands higher than the German. The numerous hindrances, restrictions, and obstacles, which are set up by timid governments and countless posts of functionaries against every endeavor in Germany, are not to be found here. The foreigner must be astounded at what the public spirit of these Republicans has accomplished up to now and what it still accomplishes every day.

All undertakings take place through the association of private persons. In these the principal aim is naturally the making of money; nevertheless a noble and beneficent public spirit also exhibits itself in the public institutions, which have a purely scientific or charitable design. The hospital on the Delaware, the poor-houses, the Peale Museum, the excellent penitentiary, the fire-houses, the temperance societies, churches, schools, and the multitude of endowed academies, all do honor to the citizens.

Someone now may ask how trade and communication are provided for. Whence has the multitude of splendid steamboats, mail-boats, highways, railways, steam-cars, canals, and stages sprung up in so short a time, where previously only wildernesses and wild Indians were to be found? In part, of course, this is the result of the natural and fortunate situation of the land and its manifold resources; but it is principally a result of unrestricted intercourse in a concerted action of an enlightened, self-governing people….

Let one inquire about the gigantic construction of the New York Canal, the Ohio Canal, the multitude of smaller canals, roads, and railways, and the German wonders how all this could have been accomplished without first having had an army of governmental counselors, ministers, and other functionaries deliberate about it for ten years, make numerous expensive journeys by post coach, and write so many reports about it, that for the amount expended for all that, reckoning compound interest for ten years, the work could have been completed.

Johann noted that the portion of his emigration party that had departed from Bremen on an earlier ship, which had included Etzler, had arrived in Baltimore after only 40 days at sea, and after waiting 14 days for the *August Henry* to arrive, they had set sail for South Carolina to stay temporarily on a plantation owned by a German immigrant. With no word from them, Johann and his group pursued their own direction for settling:

Since our arrival we have made the acquaintance of several men of experience and have made numerous inquiries....We have altered our previous opinion regarding the Southern States and in general regarding the slave States, where slavery is still permitted. In consequence of this we have made our decision to settle in a free State. Here one is universally prejudiced against slaveholding States and that with right....

In general it is more difficult to discover a healthful locality in the South than in the North, for in the South most of the river valleys are said to be exposed to floods....

In the northern states there are more localities, on the contrary, which are free from floods and yet full of rivers, which afford good communication. Against the cultivation of cotton the objection is made that the cleaning of the cotton ball in the cotton-gins is a very unhealthful business, on account of the pulverizing of the fibers, whereby the lungs of the workmen are attacked and their lives thus shortened. A Negro, who is much engaged in cleaning cotton wool, is said seldom to become over 40 years of age. This objection to the cultivation of cotton seems well-founded to us.

But in general we have been frightened away from the South by the universally prevailing system of slavery which has too great an influence on all human relationships and militates against civilization and industry with an ever-hindering effect. Earlier we believed that this circumstance would not injure us, in that we would tolerate no slavery.

But now we see already, after a few experiences, how hard it would be to accomplish anything with free German workers in a place where all the work is done by a despised race of men, namely the blacks. In time we should see ourselves compelled to hold slaves, and this would have highly injurious effect upon ourselves and upon the prosperity of the colony.

According to news from New Orleans, a conspiracy and combination of the blacks has recently been discovered there. They had already secretly collected 10,000 weapons, munitions, and the like, had made a plan to massacre the whites, and thus attain their freedom by force in the 'unhealthful' time of the year, namely in the summer, when there is no business and activity there, and when a great portion of the population has gone away. The example of

the Negroes of Santo Domingo, their present independent condition, is too great a provocation of the slaves.

Such scenes and horrors will and must occur as long as slavery continues to exist and as long as the white sons of the gods will not listen to reason. In such situations, however a German character can never feel at ease.

I for my part wish the blacks all good fortune in their endeavors to be free. Again, in some Southern States, the strictest orders have been issued to give the slaves no education, in order not to make them more dangerous still through cultivation than they are already as the result of their condition. Thus the white masters must ever live in fear and anxiety of their slaves.

The Northern States criticize the Southern ones very much, and it is neither lying nor dissembling, and in this all reasonable Americans agree, to say that slavery is the greatest cancerous affliction, of which the United States are suffering. Slavery contrasts too greatly with the rest of their political and civic institutions. The republic is branded by it and the entire folk, with its <u>idealistic</u> and altogether purely <u>reasonable</u> Constitution, stands branded with it before the eyes of the civilized world!

Grounds enough for us not to go into any slave-holding State, even if Nature had created a Paradise there! It is hoped that, little by little, slavery will be entirely abolished; there's been talk about it recently in Maryland.

On the other hand just as little do we wish to go into the far distant western lands, whose boundaries in Missouri and Arkansas have just recently been disturbed by attacks of bands of wild Indians, and where one is cut off from all intercourse and all civilization.

It is now our intention, after we have carefully examined all considerations:

1- To settle in a <u>slave free</u> State in a locality, which has, where possible, good communication with the Eastern coast, with the principal centers of the American civilization, and at the same time communication with the principal markets of the West.

2- In a locality, where culture, civilization and trade have already attained significance, and where a German population is to be found.

> **The German wonders how all this could have been accomplished without first having had an army of governmental counselors, ministers, and other functionaries deliberate about it for ten years, make numerous expensive journeys by post coach, and write so many reports about it, that for the amount expended for all that, reckoning compound interest for ten years, the work could have been completed.**
> **- Johann August Röbling, 1831**

3 - Where the soil affords every advantage to all for agriculture and keeping cattle, namely keeping sheep, and at the same time yet gives an opportunity for other undertakings in the future, such as factories, canneries, mills, and the like. The latter purposes demand a locality, where there are plenty of oak trees, waterfalls, coal beds, minerals, and the like.

4 - In a locality, where we find the opportunity to purchase for our own beginning small farms, already under cultivation, with buildings and all, and where there are still sufficient uncleared lands for the rest of our friends and our posterity later on, and forest lands, which can be cleared when opportunity offers.

By consultation with men of experience we have come to perceive the difficulties, which are involved in pioneering and in settling in an entirely remote and wild locality, and hence we have become convinced that we should be better off from a pecuniary point of view in purchasing little farms, already cultivated, for our beginning than to clear the land ourselves....

We further believe that more is to be made by keeping cattle, and especially sheep, than by agriculture alone. The latter is in more hands, demands more work, and earns less money. Sheep grazing has been taken up very little up to now and wool commands very good prices here, as formerly it could only be obtained from abroad....

According to the prospects communicated to us, the two States of Pennsylvania and Ohio appear to us to be the most suitable for the execution of our project. To be sure there may be localities in the States lying further West, where one can purchase great tracts of land for a very cheap price, which are also well-fitted for sheep raising; but, as already noted above, we have now a strong antipathy to settling in those far-off territories, removed from all communication and all civilization. There only poor Americans wander, accustomed to a wild forest life; these must first clear the path more for the Germans....

If we could still find good and cheap land this side of the mountains in Pennsylvania, we should prefer these localities to all others, on account of their nearness to the Eastern coast; but the high price of the land frightens us away from it....

We are going to take Indiana County mainly into consideration on our journey. Some letters of recommendation for Pittsburgh will be of use to us likewise for the State of Ohio. According to all inquiries, the State of Ohio appears to us the best for our purpose and especially the locality at the upper Ohio, from Pittsburgh on....This locality in the State of Ohio has been especially recommended to us, because it is the hilly and healthful part, has fruitful soil in general, and would be especially adapted to sheep-raising. In that place one has communications with Cincinnati, Pittsburgh and with New York....

Our plan is now as follows:

We shall journey at the end of this week in a canal boat up from here past Reading, Harrisburg, and Huntington, to Pittsburgh. On the way we shall gather information about the land in Indiana County in Pennsylvania.

If we do not settle in Indiana County, we shall travel on to Pittsburgh, from whence we shall seek a place in the State of Ohio. It is very likely that we shall settle in the State of Ohio.

We begin our journey with the conviction that our friends in South Carolina will follow us, as well as that our friends in Germany will approve our plan.

- J.A. Röbling

In the neighborhood of Pittsburgh

Once Johann and his brother Carl had rejected settling in the South, as Washington noted:

They finally concluded to go either to Ohio or Western Pennsylvania, not into an uncleared wilderness, but to buy small farms already cleared, and then to start mills and enterprises of various kinds, and especially raise sheep on a large scale.

Throughout western Pennsylvania, numerous small farms were for sale, most of them had been started by men from the East, who became tired of their location after a few years and obeying the national impulse of moving further West were ready to sell out for a song. There were many such in the neighborhood of Pittsburgh, and this was one inducement which determined my father to move in that direction.

On August 22, 1831, the party left Philadelphia for Pittsburgh by the canal. It consisted of himself, his brother Carl, three friends from Mülhausen and a German family. What a falling off from the 150 who had left Bremen together! It shows that the Germans do not hang together and are inclined to be quarrelsome.

The incidents of this canal trip, the subsequent sojourn in Pittsburgh and the events which finally led to the settlement of what was later on called Saxonburg, in Butler County, Pennsylvania, have been preserved in quite a remarkable and unexpected manner.

It appears that on his arrival in Pittsburgh my father wrote a series of long letters, or properly speaking a voluminous report to his old friend Frederick Baer, in Mülhausen, the whole forming a quarto volume of 101 pages.

It was written in accordance with a promise given on his departure, and was the means of inducing other colonists to come out, among them Herr Baer himself...

He looks at everything with the eye of a man who is going to be a farmer. You would never dream that he had been educated as an engineer....

The journey took nearly a month, as they arrived in Pittsburgh September 19, 1831....The canal was then finished to Huntington, Pa., thence (they traveled) by wagons to Hollidaysburg, where the Portage Railroad took them across the mountains to Johnstown, thence again by canal down the Kiskiminitas and Allegheny to Pittsburgh.[2]

Our future in America is assured

Johann didn't record his first impressions of the portage railroad, which would change his career ten years later, but he wrote enthusiastically to Baer from Pittsburgh on November 2 that: "My brother Carl and I....have advanced so far in our undertaking, that we can say: our future in America is assured."

They had found land to purchase and Johann was convinced that they had made the right choice to forgo their original intention to settle in the South:

No educated man can feel well there where he is surrounded by slaves; slave states will never make progress in culture and in human education, never will factories and manufacture blossom there, they will always remain barbarian states.

In Philadelphia we got the news and I myself read it in the newspapers that a great association among the blacks in New Orleans had been discovered in time to stop the plan of the slaves to murder all the whites during the feverish time of the year.

This was the first news that dampened my prejudice for the South. Soon after all the newspapers were full of news about the conspiracy of the slaves, almost in all Southern states....

The whites are superior to the blacks, but the latter will revolt just as long as they are contrary to nature being suppressed and robbed of their human rights. I wish them all luck.[3]

In a foreshadowing of future problems, Johann reported to Baehr:

My brother Carl during the last week of our trip also became feverishly ill and so weak that I could transport him only in a hammock, which was strung up in a freight wagon. My brother, who up to now had to keep to his room constantly, is now fairly well restored, although still quite weak.

As far as my health is concerned it has constantly been the best and I have always felt well and strong.

After observing what he called "pale suffering faces" in Philadelphia and along the canal route, Johann was pleased to be in Pittsburgh, where he found "the most undeceptive proof of healthy water is the blossoming *appearance* of the people. In part the American way of life contributes to the unhealthy appearance, especially of the feminine persons, who have less exercise."

Johann saw great promise in Pittsburgh:

Twenty years ago Pittsburgh was only an insignificant place of several hundred inhabitants and now contains 25,000 inhabitants, it is the first manufacturing city in America, the main place of work between East and West and the key to the great Western River region of the Mississippi. By virtue of its situation on the Ohio....Pittsburgh holds the first rank as interior place of storage and of trade.

As a place for factories Pittsburgh has endless advantages, because nature here has done everything which is necessary for the existence of factories.

The vicinity of Pittsburgh is rich in bituminous coal beds, which are inexhaustible....Pennsylvania is rich in iron ore is, which all go to Pittsburgh.

The time is not distant when this place will have developed into a city of 100,000 inhabitants.

He would have made an excellent land promoter

Washington noted that:

Considering that my father was only 27 years old then, he understood the situation very well. The special advantages of Pittsburgh, to which it owes its prosperity today, he sets forth well. Expeditions were made into the neighboring counties to look at farms and lands....

Finally he hears of the lands in Butler County belonging to the Widow Collins in Pittsburgh - a lady land rich, not land poor, owning 20,000 acres which she was anxious to sell. Mrs. Collins was a native of Trenton, New Jersey, remarkably....

The two brothers bought 1600 acres together at $1.75 per acre ($2,800 total – about $118,000 in 2009)....with the right to buy 2000 acres more at the same price and 3000 acres more at one dollar per acre. These lands were purchased afterwards and sold to the colonists from Mülhausen and neighborhood....

The descriptions he gives of the country are wonderfully true to nature and of the rosiest character. He would have made an excellent land promoter at the present day.

Of course everything was new to him, forests entirely different from those of Germany, sky brighter, air bracing, meadows finer, the lay of the land more inviting, he was young and enthusiastic and anxious to go to farming.

Some land was also bought for his oldest brother Christel, who was to come over - he even tried his best to induce his parents to come.[4]

22

Nach der Natur gezeichnet von T. Gosewisch im Juli 1835.   Steindruck von E. W. Röbling in Mühlhausen.

Sachsenburg,
Colonie von Thüringern und Sachsen bei Pittsburg.
(Von der Südseite.)

12 Herting,   10. Muder.   9 Tolle,   8 Bernigau   7 Stübgent Schmidt Mül Dunkelhaut Eckman Lamp 3 Leineder   2 Bär.   1 Geb. r. Röbling
Schneider.   11 Unbekant Raffassen aus   Fischler.   Seh.   Wohfingt Herd Fasermann   aus Sachsen.   Kung aus Sachsen.
                                Leizig.

Figure 2.1: Saxonburg, Pennsylvania, 1835. HS
**Johann Röbling designed many of the buildings in the village he and his fellow immigrants founded in western Pennsylvania,
about 35 miles northeast of Pittsburgh. He and his brother Carl built house No. 1 on the right for themselves.**

Where nature is beautiful

In his November letter to Baehr about Saxonburg (Fig. 2.1), Johann wrote:

>   These lands offer everything for farming: a good, partly best soil, extended meadow lands, such as I have seen nowhere else, the most beautiful water supply; a great number of pure springs and several rich mineral springs....
>   When this region is cultivated and especially when the low meadow lands have been cleared this can become a paradise. Extensive cultivated fields, gently sloping, will then alternate with beautiful valleys with meadows, and on the higher spots the spared forests will form a beautiful interruption.
>   Everywhere there are living springs which never go dry and near which there are suitable places for dwellings. My description is not an exaggeration; and that which I until now have seen in America, and if this region is cultivated by industrious people and worked by them, I would compare it to none in Germany.
>   On the western boundary, a small brook runs through, which has enough water and fall to drive machines....
>   In the middle lies a level area of about 300 acres of farmland at the boundary of which springs are situated and which run in all directions and form meadow valleys. This middle level is best suited for building a house and the center of barns. From that point one can overlook almost

>   everything. We intend to begin with cultivation there and in the future to build a house there. This place everywhere affords an open view into the distance....
>   I would not have obtained these lands so reasonably if the people in Butler had not been eager to attract newcomers and especially German farmers to their county and thus to raise the value of their own lands.[5]

In December, Johann wrote to Baehr from the small farmhouse that came with the land:

>   We are now entirely well and we are happy in our present circumstances and are satisfied with the fate that we have chosen of our own free will. We now live as free men in a land whose reasonable and humane Constitution assures every inhabitant his natural rights; where no unnatural compulsory rule robs a person of that which he acquired by his own efforts; where no laws exist that hinder human endeavor; but where everyone can go his free and unchecked way as long as he keeps peace with his fellow men.
>   Further we live in a section of the country where nature is beautiful and where every diligent person can easily earn a livelihood; and also, we are in one of the most advantageous sections of America, in the vicinity of a good market, which is improving from year to year, where we can dispose of all products for cash, with little trouble - what more do we want just now?

23

Nothing more than some honest, cultured German countrymen, who are capable of forming a happy, free, and sociable community circle; we mean by this yourself and your friends, and, if possible, during the coming year - then we will live a contented, undisturbed life, in German manner, and will never long to be back in our unfortunate Fatherland in the realm of compulsory rule and slavery....

As Johann wrote about the land, he also expressed a longing for his family and friends back in Germany:

This country is adaptable for any kind of farming, for cattle raising and sheep raising and especially horse breeding. Further, it is also suitable for any manufacturing enterprise.

The nearest town along the Pennsylvania Canal, namely Freeport, is about five or 6 miles distant....Several places here would be suitable for laying out a small town, where farming and industry could be combined....

The beginning is hard, and in the first year there are many expenses; after the first difficulties have been overcome however, and if one then has some capital, it is possible to do a good business. If this region is built up by industrious Germans then it can become an earthly Paradise....

The keeping of silkworms is very profitable here and is carried on with much success; this is an occupation for the women and children. Further, we can look forward to doing a good business and manufacturing vegetable oil. We can, jointly, build the gristmill and oil mill....

Brother Christel seems to have the earnest intention of coming over with you. Please tell him we will welcome him and his family with open arms, but even more happy would we be if our parents would also come. As it is a sad thought for us to see our parents forsaken by their children, so far away.

If we can all live together, and if more good Germans came over, than our parents could live a comfortable, carefree and tax-free life, in a beautiful scenic spot; and in the circle of their family they could peacefully spend the rest of their days and enjoy everything that beautiful nature and the companionship of friends offer.[6]

Johann wanted Baehr, their brother, Christel, and their parents to join their settlement for family reasons, but they also wanted them to bring money to help pay for it. Facing two annual payments on their 1,600 acres, Johann wrote:

We have, to be sure, more expenses than our present funds permit. But we will never regret the purchase we made....Ten years from now, when this section is more settled, every acre will be worth ten dollars. I would very unwillingly give up this land.

Figure 2.2: Johann A. Röbling, Saxonburg Church, c1834. RG Röbling designed a "suitable building to honor the highest being" for Saxonburg, but with their limited resources, he and his fellow villagers built a much simpler "German Evangelical Christian Church" in 1837.

When Brother Christel comes over at some future date, then each of us brothers will have land enough to support our family. For now, whether we keep this land depends on whether my father will aid us with five hundred dollars. If we should be forced to give up some of the land, then we can sell at a profit a few years hence, as our purchase price is so low.

Please talk with my father and brother about this matter. The money will be safe here and well invested....

My friend Baehr, if you come, either with or without my parents, and you accept our propositions, then in the spring we must build a house, for which, however, we lack capital. I intend building a spacious house and making it habitable, for from five to six hundred dollars, which would suffice for both you and us.

It is necessary to have your advice about this as soon as possible, and we must be assured of the money....

Come as early next year as possible; bring all your machines, tools, and household utensils, whatever you can move; bring a supply of locks, chains, carpenters axes, key bits, shovels, hoes, pick axes, scythes, sickles, linen cloth, durable gray trousers, and beaver jackets for the winter. Provide yourself with everything possible for the next ten years, for everything is so expensive here.

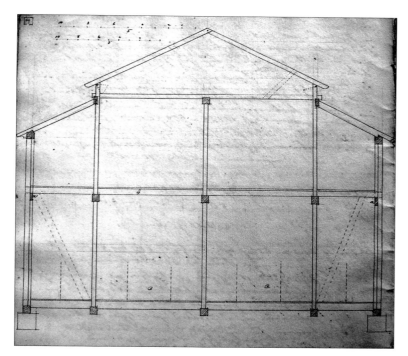

Figure 2.3: Johann A. Röbling, Barn Framing, c1835. RU Röbling designed houses and barns for himself and other villagers and carefully detailed the required materials and costs in notebooks.

The hardships that are connected with emigration

When Johann wrote again to Baehr in January, 1832, he started to acknowledge the limitations of rural Pennsylvania:

> *From the time we left Mühlhausen up until the time we settled here we were restless, but now we live quiet and contented lives, not disturbed by anyone; our thoughts are often with our friends, and we cherish the hope but they may soon follow and enjoy with us the quiet peace of an independent country life....It would give us great joy if a little German town would flourish here like a plant whose growth was forced by diligent industry and farming....*
>
> *The American farmer lives a very happy life indeed, enviable in comparison with the German farmer; he raises all his necessities himself, makes his own clothing, and has a surplus of the necessities of life. Contented people can in truth lead a happy, free, and unconstrained life here.*
>
> *The American farmer does not work half so much as the German farmer and lives like a prince as far as his necessities are concerned but he must deny himself luxuries, as he cannot afford them....*
>
> *We doubt, now, whether we can maintain the big bulk of land, as we do not believe that father is inclined to make an additional allowance and we could not expect him to make further sacrifice. We regret that we have already asked him for such; also, we now prefer to own less land and keep more funds on hand to invest in cattle raising.*

> *If we had enough money to maintain the land, without debt, and some funds to spare, then we would not part with a single acre, but as it is now our means are too small....it costs a good deal for our family to live through the winter....*
>
> *What I here communicate to you and our friends has not, before God, the purpose of persuading any man to come over to America and eventually to our place.*
>
> *The booklet published by Etzler and me was in many respects persuasive, and for that reason I wish it had never been printed; the hardships that are connected with emigration, especially for the one who is taking the first step, are not given enough prominence therein.*
>
> *I blame Etzler's carelessness and bold, unfounded assertions for this....*
>
> *I would not, for any price, persuade any person to come here, even if we should have to be here alone for the rest of our lives - we would not want to deceive anybody, as much as we desire to have our countrymen with us.*
>
> *I assure you that I do not feel disappointed, and in the main part I have found all that I sought: a free, reasonable, democratic government and reasonable, natural relationship of the people toward each other; freedom and equality; a peaceful, generous, beautiful country the blessings of which are not forcefully and deceitfully taken away from the land toiler by tyrants.[7]*

Johann again reiterated his contempt for slavery and predicted trouble for the South:

> *It was our good faith that kept us from going to the Southern states, as we had at first planned.*
>
> *There, freedom and equality are in bitter contradiction on account of the detestable slavery of the black race which is still permitted.*
>
> *These unfortunate Negroes will use their natural rights and will revolt anew each year - will murder their oppressors, guilty or innocent - to secure a final freedom for themselves; the slave owners will then continually become more tyrannical, and despair will force the Africans to risk all and commit horror and crime.*
>
> *No white man works in the South, because labor is only performed by a despised race, and the wages of the white man there are much lower than here.*
>
> *How would we small planters be scorned there if we tilled our land ourselves!....*
>
> *How could an educated German feel happy under such conditions in the South if he must regard every Negro as a natural enemy, where even the law strictly forbids him to treat the Negro humanely, to educate him, to draw closer to him with kindness, or even to set him free?*
>
> *If you free a slave, the law puts the strange responsibility on your shoulders of giving security for his future behavior.*

Figure 2.4: John Augustus Roebling. RM

Figure 2.5: Johanna Herting Roebling. RM

Washington noted that his father had found the freedom he wanted in America, but he remained restless:

> I presume my father was happy for a short time. That freedom from social and political tyranny for which all Germans sigh he had at last attained. But having it, it was no longer appreciated. To be in a country where no one cares a rap for you and where you can do as you please, becomes rather monotonous, a person must have ties....
>
> He proposes to found the village of "Germania" and fill it with German artisans, mechanics and practical working people who would supply the wants of the surrounding agricultural population, and this scheme was practically carried out. To amuse the people he proposes to build a theater, dance hall, concert hall, school and even a church, all of which was done on a small scale. The name "Germania" was changed to Saxonburg because most of the settlers came from the Prussian province of Saxony....
>
> Colonists arrived by degrees, lands were sold to them, and they settled either as farmers or mechanics. My mother's family did not arrive for three or four years....
>
> The surveying of land and laying out of roads, and plotting of the village of Saxonburg was a task which came along the following year. The village had one street, perfectly straight and running east and west, called Main Street. Parallel to it, on lower ground was Water Street, so-called because the ground was wet....The church stood at the head of Main Street on the highest ground....Main Street was laid off in lots, from 100 to 200 and 300 feet wide and running back to Water Street, most of the people having barns, stables and other houses on their places....Main Street was less than a mile in length. It formed the ridge of a watershed - on

> one side the water ran towards the Allegheny, and on the other towards Thorn Creek, a branch of the Conequenessing and Beaver River....the extension of Main Street west, led towards Bauer's dam and gristmill, where all the boys went fishing for sunfish, and learned to swim....
>
> The country was by no means a wilderness as there were a few old settlers gathered around who had moved in from Susquehanna County, Pennsylvania, some five or six years previous.[8]

In 1836, Johann married Johanna Herting, who Washington described as "a handsome young woman of 18 or 19, of an amiable and gentle disposition." She was the daughter of Ernest Herting, who Washington described as "a well-to-do tailor" in Mühlhausen. Washington spent a lot of time at his grandparent's house, which he called "my favorite abode."

Washington related that, "My father's desire to become independent led him into many schemes." He tried sheep farming, growing sunflowers and rape seed for oil, raising canaries, growing mulberry trees and raising silkworms for silk, and fabric dying. For crops, Washington noted, "In reality the soil was heavy, cold and clayey, subject to early frosts." With little to show for his farming efforts, Johann turned his attention elsewhere:

> I know that my father had a hard time learning to farm, and realized before long he was not fitted for that kind of work, but he gave it a faithful trial. His brother Carl married, built himself a house a mile to the south of ours. He had two children and then suddenly died. This was also an inducement to give up farming.

Figure 2.6: John A. Roebling House, Saxonburg, c 1930. HS Johann and his brother Karl built this house in 1834. Washington A. Roebling was born here in 1837.

In the mean time my father gathered experience and learned the language and customs and ways of the people, for whom he really had very great respect….

Selling lands in small parcels, giving deeds, mortgages, making agreements, contracts, etc. made my father very familiar with legal papers and with the common law of the country, which was of great use in later life. He had great respect for the true common sense of the American lawyer as contrasted with the antiquated legal forms of the old country.

Owing to the fixed purpose of making Saxonburg a German settlement only, Americans had no object coming there, and the English tongue was seldom heard.

I myself did not learn to speak English until I was along towards ten or eleven years of age, and most of the older settlers never learnt it. My father, however, made the most determined efforts to speak nothing but English.

I think it was in 1833-4 that the house in which I was born was built (Fig. 2.6). It stands at the head of the main road near the church. The Saxon style of building was in vogue, that is, an open framework of hewn scantling, filled in with smaller sticks and then plastered up with mud and clay, cool in summer, warm in winter….The raising of the framework of a new house or barn was always made the occasion of a frolic, the neighbors lending their aid gratuitously. They wound up with a bountiful feast, which I usually attended.

The great drawbacks of Saxonburg were felt early on. They were the difficulties of communication and the distance from markets; this was the main reason why he left in 1848.[9]

I shall embrace the first opportunity

Washington noted that his father's interest in engineering returned as he lost interest in farming:

After the excitement of laying out Saxonburg was over, after the settlers had been located, houses built for them and their affairs started in the right way, my father was occasionally reminded of the circumstance that he had been raised for the engineering profession.

His frequent trips to Pittsburgh and country kept him in rapport with what was going on in that line. How the first opportunity came about I do not know, but in 1833 and 1834 we find him employed as assistant engineer on the slack water navigation of the Beaver River, about 40 miles from Saxonburg.

His special duty was the construction of dams, a delicate and difficult task, requiring the utmost care and caution to arrive at permanent success - many of these dams still stand. They were of course not massive stone dams but usually timber cribs filled with stone and puddle. Every dam had its backwater, which at times of high water flooded the lands of the farmers for miles back. This led to lawsuits, which my father had to settle, because he was the only engineer with sufficient knowledge of hydraulics to understand such problems. The study of Eytelwein at Berlin thus came into direct light. His reputation as hydraulic engineer rose high, he began to write on the subject in the journals (Franklin Institute and others) and was even summoned as an expert in a celebrated case on the Croton River Aqueduct….

We next find him on the Sandy and Beaver Canal, a work intended to connect the waters of the Ohio with Lake Erie, but not carried out to a full completion. On such works he was constantly in contact with other assistants, mostly engineers, and by no means did he stand last, usually first….

The last employment in canal work was the location of a feeder for the Pennsylvania Canal along the Allegheny River, extending from the neighborhood of Kittanning to Freeport….Associated with him on this was a young engineer named Leslie,….an accomplished English scholar, a thorough grammarian and fluent speaker. He undertook to train my father in the English language and in his literary style. I have often heard him speak of Leslie in terms of gratitude and admiration. The forceful English my father could use both in speaking and writing was largely due to Leslie….

My father's connection with hydraulic works brought him to the notice of American engineers such as Solomon Roberts, Milnor Roberts (both engineers on the Allegheny Portage Railroad), John Jervis, who had just completed the Croton aqueduct, and others. He maintained friendly relationships with these gentlemen throughout his life. Mr. Jervis was chief engineer of the Delaware and Hudson Canal, where my father had much to do with him….

During the winter, while work was suspended, he returned to Saxonburg, attended his affairs and made plans for a great variety of projects. Good engineers were scarce then; we had no engineering schools; young men who aspired to excellence in that line had to study in Europe.

Engineering was very uncertain employment and in times of enforced idleness he could always go back home and extract a living from his farm, at least enough to keep from starving. When I say he did the farming I ought to qualify it by saying that my mother did most of it. Her patient foresight kept things moving at their proper time....

As it became possible to live off the farm it enabled my father to save his engineering salaries, and thus by degrees accumulate a little capital for other enterprise. Capital acquired by saving is always carefully looked after.[10]

The promise of Johann's early engineering work on canals was temporarily thwarted by economic hard times. The success of canals and the first railroads had lead to excessive speculation in real estate, and a financial panic began in May of 1837 that depressed investment and employment for several years. Johann wrote to several prospective employers but none had work for him.

In a June letter to E.H. Gill, the engineer for whom he had worked on the Sandy and Beaver Canal, Johann noted that "the gloom of the times" was forcing employers "to reduce their engineering corps instead of increasing them." He nevertheless remained optimistic for the country and confident of his own abilities and he started to develop some ambitious inventions and proposals:

As the general impetus of business and public improvements, the circulating capital, is at present almost reduced to its lowest state, the prevailing calamity in consequence will soon have reached the point of culmination and this induces me to believe that the dawn of better days may surely be expected after a while.

Although in possession of a fine library and my time being principally occupied by interesting studies, I cannot reconcile myself to be altogether destitute of practical occupation and I shall embrace the first opportunity, which offers itself to me to enter service again....

During the time of my present leisure I have improved the idea of some new plans and constructions regarding engineering....The first improvement is a new plan altogether for dams and locks to improve the navigation of large Rivers as the Ohio, Monongahela, and Allegheny, by Slackwater. These dams and locks will render the shallowest water navigable during the dry season, without being an obstruction to rafting, without accumulating the sediment into River Channel and without swelling the water much in time of a flood above the former River. I am confident that these dams can be built in a very solid and permanent manner, with an expense but little increased of what common dams would cost.

Another plan of mine has reference to the improvement of the channel of the mouth of the Mississippi R. below N.O.

for which purpose large sums of money have been already expended since a number of years without having obtained any permanent beneficial results from the operations executed.

The channels of this noble River are filled up every year more and more and the City of N.O. after some time will cease to be the port of entrance for the large kind of sea vessels, unless they adopt a better and more effective plan, suitable to the nature of that river to keep its channel open and deep. The plan I suggest to that effect, is extremely simple and cheap, and I am perfectly satisfied would fully answer the purpose if executed.

Another improvement of mine regards a simple contrivance in the construction of railroads to make switches and movable rails in turn outs and passings altogether dispensable. This plan will not increase the costs and recommends itself for its simplicity. I have also computed a number of tables, being useful in tracing Rail Road curves in the field. Any Engineer, familiar with the use of these Tables will find them preferable to any other tables, calculated for that purpose and which I know of.[11]

His fertile mind

The range of projects and the efforts that Johann devoted to them at this time illustrate his remarkable inventiveness and discipline. He spent countless hours devising improvements to existing machinery and to inventing new machinery (Fig. 2.7). Working in his house with his characteristic precision, he filled large notebooks with detailed drawings and technical descriptions covering dozens and dozens of pages. Washington recalled his father's meticulous efforts:

His fertile mind perfected many useful inventions. I find complete drawings of a patent steam plow, dating back to the thirties: also drawings for multi-tubular steam boilers specially adapted for ocean propellers and men of war. (Fig 2.7) Steam propellers engaged his attention, locomotives, agricultural machinery, etc....

The notebooks which my father kept were marvels of neatness and concise perfection. His figures were beautiful - the large round old handwriting was the result of learning to write Latin at school. In arithmetic he never made a mistake. These books, all of which I have, are freely illustrated with pen and ink drawings. He made it the rule of his professional life to write up his notebooks full and complete every night, even if it took him until one o'clock. In this matter procrastination and dependence on memory are always fatal.

In the Mechanics' Magazine of June 15, 1840, we find the following editorial note: "The communications of Mr. Roebling have one unusual character, which has always rendered them doubly welcome - they are written in the plainest possible hand, and the extraordinary neatness of

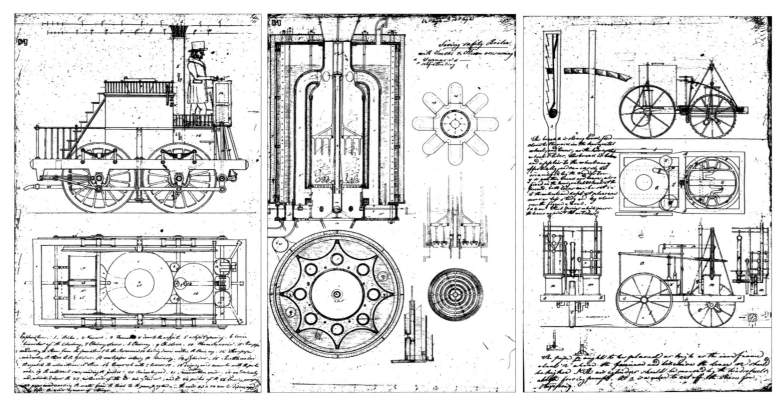

Figure 2.7: John A. Roebling, Saxonburg Notebooks, late 1830s. RU
After becoming an American citizen and anglicizing his name, John hoped to earn money from his inventions,
including a steam locomotive, left, a steam boiler, center, and a steam tractor, right.
In 1838, he wrote to the Patent Office in Washington seeking a "caveat," a recognition of the intent to file a patent application,
for "a new and improved way of constructing steamboilers and rendering them safe from bursting."
He built and submitted a model of his steamboiler and one for his steam plow.

*his diagrams and formula, have saved us much trouble, and
himself much mortification in correcting errors.*"[12]

The year 1837 brought other major changes to John's life
that propelled his focus onto his work. His brother Karl, who
had been weak ever since their journey from Mühlhausen to
Saxonburg, died suddenly that year, leaving a young wife and
two children whom Johann had to help raise. The Röbling
brothers had shared their vision of migrating to America to
found a German settlement, and Karl's untimely death further
diminished Johann's enthusiasm for the effort.

Washington was born in the spring of 1837, and as he noted
decades later:

In 1837 my father had in his (work) *party a young fellow
from Richmond, Virginia, named Washington Gill (E.H.
Gill's younger brother), who acted as a leveler. Being
a Virginian he was very proud of his surname, and I have
always understood that my father named me Washington
for him, and not directly for the father of his country. I
appeared in this world May 26, 1837. My middle name is
Augustus, same as my father's middle name.*[13]

With the responsibility for his brother's family and for his
own, Johann needed to earn more money. To further establish
himself here, he applied for citizenship and became an
American in 1837. He adopted the Anglicized name of John
A. Roebling, replacing the German umlaut 'ö' in Röbling with
'oe' to reflect English spelling of the pronunciation.

John's training and experience in surveying in Germany
and his growing reputation helped him obtain more work
on canals. In 1838, he worked for the Pennsylvania Canal
in surveying routes for a canal extension and a feeder near
Kittanning on the Allegheny River. His work on the feeder
project for Chief Engineer Charles Schlatter led to his next job,
in 1939, when Schlatter hired him to help survey a railroad
route across the Allegheny Mountains:

*My father's work on the Allegheny feeder of the
Pennsylvania Canal, naturally brought him in personal
contact with state officials. Hence, when the State
commenced its surveys across the Allegheny Mountain
system for three alternate lines of railroad, he had no great
difficulty in getting a position as assistant engineer in charge
of one of the surveying parties....*

The chief engineer in charge of the whole survey was Mr. Charles Schlatter, next came Mr. Benjamin Aycrigg....I have always heard my father speak of both with the highest respect, especially Mr. Schlatter. This was not a common thing for him to do, as he could be a sharp critic.

What he admired about these men was the eminent practical common sense with which everything was done, no red tape or bureaucracy. So utterly different from the German ways of doing things. These surveys were matters of the greatest importance to the State at large, as well as to individual counties and communities. Wherever the main line would be located, there it would probably remain forever, to the great benefit of its own neighborhood and detriment of remoter sections....

Much of my father's time was spent in Harrisburg, the headquarters of the Survey, especially in the winter; the surveys were plotted there, maps made, profiles laid out, notes written up and reports made. His notebooks were models for everyone – correct and reliable and written up every night so that errors were almost impossible. He gained the respect and esteem of his superiors whom he later on surpassed....This work brought my father in personal contact with the prominent men of the State, brought him reputation and valuable acquaintances, who were useful to him. At a railroad convention in 1840 in Pittsburgh he was a delegate.[14]

My favorite occupation

In early 1840 John read an article by Charles Ellet, Jr., in the *American Railroad Journal* about wire suspension bridges. Ellet had studied at the School of Bridges and Roads in Paris and was the chief engineer on the James and Kanawha canal in Virginia. He described wire suspension bridges in France and detailed his plan to build one across the Schuylkill River in Philadelphia to replace the Colossus, a wooden arch bridge that had burned in 1838. Recalling his own studies in Europe of wire suspension bridges, John wrote to Ellet:

The following communication, I fear, will appear to you inopportune and add an uncalled for obtrusion upon your time, however, I flatter myself that an appeal to the great interest which I have felt for the subject of suspension bridges for a number of years and am still feeling, you will be disposed to accept my apology.

The study of suspension bridges, formed for the last few years of my residence in Europe, my favorite occupation; as this matter however appeared to be little cared for by Engineers in this country, I had no occasion whatever to bestow any further attention on it, while engaged in professional pursuits here.

Some publications of yours, which appeared in the R.R. Journal on the subject of Suspension bridges, revived in me the old favorite ideas, and I was very agreeably apprised by the report of your being now actually engaged in making preparations for constructing a wire cable bridge over the Schuylkill at Philadelphia and another one over the Mississippi at St. Louis, which latter indeed would form the greatest construction of the kind in existence.

I have been informed that a like great undertaking is now in progress in Europe, the construction of the cable suspension bridge across the river Danube at Perth, which River resembles the Mississippi in nature and extent.

I cannot refrain from congratulating you upon the spirit with which you appear to enter upon this important undertaking, and which together with your familiar knowledge of the subject will no doubt ensure your complete success. Let but a single bridge of the kind be put up in Philadelphia exhibiting all the beautiful forms of the system to the best advantage, and it needs no prophecy to foretell the effect, which the novel and useful features will produce upon the intelligent minds of the Americans.

You will certainly occupy a very enviable position, in being the first Engineer, who, aided by nothing but the resources of his own mind and a close investigation, succeeds to introduce a new mode of construction, which here will find more useful application than in any other country.

Let me request the favor of some data respecting your plans over the Schuylkill and the Mississippi. Perhaps I should be able to suggest to you an improvement in the construction of the saddles, applied by Mr. Telford on the Minai bridge, in supporting the chains on top of the towers, calculated to facilitate the motion of the chains in the saddles in consequence of the contraction and expansion of the chains or cables.

I am at present engaged as principal assistant on the Harrisburg and Pittsburgh R.R. under Mr. Ch. L. Schlatter. Should you at some future period be desirous of engaging an assistant for the construction of suspension bridges, who is competent for the task, and at the same time would execute with pleasure all the necessary drawings, please bear me in mind.

Let me request you to look upon this communication as a professional homage due to you, and to accept of the high regard, with which I remain your most obedient servant.[15]

Ellet replied graciously but uncommittedly:

It has given me much pleasure to learn that you have not neglected the subject of suspension bridges, in pursuing your professional studies abroad, and that you consequently appreciate the merits of that system of construction. It is my intention to endeavor to introduce this improvement to the United States; and shall accordingly pursue those means which appear to be most suitable to convey information to the public, and extend a knowledge of their powers and the principles of their equilibrium.

I have already had one adopted at Philadelphia, and am now engaged in a report for another, and a much more important one, for the Mississippi at St. Louis. You correctly estimate the character of the American people, in supposing that they will not fail to recognize the merit of these structures, when furnished with one respectable specimen.

Should the system prevail, as I have reason to believe it will, I hope to have the pleasure of engaging the services of one who is familiar with the subject, and whose aid cannot but be invaluable.[16]

Given their strong personalities and firm ideas, it was unlikely that John and Ellet could work together and they soon became rivals. With his interest in suspension bridges rekindled, John wrote an article for the *American Railroad Journal* in 1841, demonstrating his knowledge of the subject and the preferability of wire cables over chains (Fig. 2.8).

John aligned himself with a Philadelphia engineer named Andrew Young who initially won the contract to build the suspension bridge over the Schuylkill River, but Ellet soon convinced some city officials to rescind the contract and award it to him. Ellet built his 358 ft. span "Fairmount Bridge" in the French method by making ten small cables on land, pulling them out over the river and then hoisting them onto the bridge towers, placing five on each side of the bridge. As John had predicted, the success of this first major suspension bridge in America brought Ellet much notoriety.

But here he saw a chance

In his surveying for railroad routes, John had the opportunity to study a major problem on the Allegheny Portage Railway, and his solution would launch both his wire rope enterprise and his bridge building career. As Washington related:

These surveys caused my father to make journeys over the Allegheny Mountains across the Portage railroad, which extended from Hollidaysburg to Johnstown, forming a series of 20 or more inclined planes. Every canal boat was built in three or four sections. In order to cross the mountains these boats were dismembered, each section placed on a car and hauled over to Johnstown, or vice versa, and then put together again in the water. Each plane had a double engine and the rope used was a heavy hemp rope, nearly 3 inches in diameter, mostly made in Pittsburgh from Kentucky hemp.

He paid much attention to the machinery, and noticing the wear and tear of these ropes and their high price, conceived the idea that they could be replaced to advantage by a lighter and stronger rope made of iron wire. He had heard of wire ropes being made in Germany at the Harz and in Freiberg, but I doubt if he had ever seen one. He spent his leisure time devising plans how to make wire rope.[17]

AMERICAN RAILROAD JOURNAL, AND MECHANICS' MAGAZINE.

No. 6, Vol. VI. New Series.]   MARCH 15, 1841.   [Whole No. 378. Vol. XII.

We take great pleasure in presenting the following paper of Mr. *Roebling*, on the subject of Suspension Bridges. The labors of Mr. *Ellet*, have contributed to bring this matter into general notice, and we are glad to find that other Engineers are turning their attention in that direction. No time can be more suitable for the discussion of Suspension Bridges, and we hope soon to see this class of structure coming into general favor.

SOME REMARKS ON SUSPENSION BRIDGES, AND ON THE COMPARATIVE MERITS OF CABLE AND CHAIN BRIDGES.—*By J. A. Roebling, Civil Engineer. No. 1.*

The subject of suspension bridges is beginning to engage the attention of the profession. To cause public opinion to incline in favor of this species of structure, can only be accomplished by the successful erection of some good specimens. The ocular demonstration they will offer, will advance this cause more than all treatises. Among the profession, however, this matter cannot be too much discussed, provided the discussion is carried on by men who are familiar with the features of the system.

Figure 2.8: John A. Roebling, 1841. RU
John wrote "Some Remarks on Suspension Bridges and on The Comparative Merits of Cable and Chain Bridges" to promote suspension bridges and to show his command of the subject.

John thought that wire rope could be a product that would supplement his engineering income, as Washington related:

My father had realized quite often that professional engineering was an intermittent precarious occupation. Working very hard all summer, when winter came the parties were generally laid off and you spent all the money you might have saved in the summer. Then in the spring you had the pleasure of commencing over again on nothing.

He, therefore, never lost sight for one moment of the desirability of engaging in some kind of manufacturing business, which might go on without much special attention, leave him some time for engineering and yet bring in enough money to tide over a rainy day and gradually lay out a small competency. The small efforts he made heretofore had amounted to nothing. But here he saw a chance.

He also felt that while he might succeed after a while in making a pretty fair rope, the main thing was to get the opportunity to have one put on a portage incline for trial, and also to get the necessary permission to alter the machinery for adaptation to the use of wire rope. To bring all this about he found that his acquaintances among political people, engineers and business people would be of the greatest advantage. The hemp rope interest was bitterly opposed to him and had money to fight him. Fortunately he made friends with the Superintendent of the planes who gave him a chance to make one rope, some 1100 feet long on trial.[18]

Figure 2.9: Inclined Plane No. 6, Cresson, Pennsylvania, c1850. In 1841, John saw an opportunity to replace the problematic hemp ropes, which plane operators used to haul canal boats over the Allegheny Mountains, with ropes made of wire.

In a section in his memoir titled "Rope Making," Washington recalled his father's efforts to develop a wire rope for the Portage Railway (Fig. 2.9):

After all the (railroad) surveys were finished, reports made, maps and profiles filed, the year 1841 had arrived. My father had not lost sight of the wire rope project on the portage, but in view of his complete ignorance of the art of rope making, want of machinery and appliances and small capital, prudence suggested that he first make a small rope by way of experiment and learn something about it. At Johnstown there was a small subsidiary plane some 400 feet in length. He induced the proprietor to let him make a rope for him of that length and about ¾" thick. It was made on the meadow at Saxonburg (see box).[19]

An English inventor named Andrew Smith and a Harrisburg inventor named Isaac McCord had received English and American patents in 1839 for their respective methods of twisting iron wires into a rope on typical hemp ropewalks. John's initial idea was to make a cable by laying wires parallel to each other in sufficient numbers to pull the canal boats up the incline. To keep the wires together, he devised a wrapping

machine to "serve" or wind a wire tightly around the parallel wires. When he filed a patent for his wrapping machine in the Spring of 1841 (Figs. 2.10-11), his patent agent, Thomas Jones, who had also assisted McCord, warned him that the "wrapping would be very liable to brake, uncoil, and produce trouble." When John sought Ellet's advice on his parallel wire design, Ellet cautioned that it was "wholly impracticable…to answer your purpose."[20]

John's second son, Ferdinand W. Roebling, was born in 1841, and despite Jones' and Ellet's cautions, he installed his parallel wire cable on the Johnstown plane, as Washington noted:

It proved a complete failure, because it was not even a twisted rope, but was made of parallel wires served (or wrapped) with annealed wire by means of an ordinary serving mallet. Of course as soon as the serving broke the whole rope went to pieces. However, nothing daunted, he bravely went to work again and studied the whole subject thoroughly. The experience gained by one failure is often of the greatest value in pointing the way to the right path.
He knew that wire rope had been made in Europe some years before, first at Clausthal in the Harz by Herr Albert, the superintendent of the mines in 1832….and later on, in 1836 at Frieburg, Saxony, for use in the Royal mines. These were not made on machines, but on rope walks, and were all seven-wires-to-the-Strand ropes.[21]

John decided to make a wire rope composed of six 19 wire strands "laid" or twisted around a 19 wire core strand. He wrote to the Pennsylvania Canal Board proposing to install this rope "entirely at my own expense" on an inclined plane. If the rope "answered" its purpose, the Board would pay him 75 cents per foot.

After the Board gave its approval in March of 1842, John set to work making the strands by "laying" 18 wires in three succeeding circles around a core wire to create a 19 wire strand. The process is called "laying" from the task of laying out the wires horizontally on a long rope walk. A major challenge

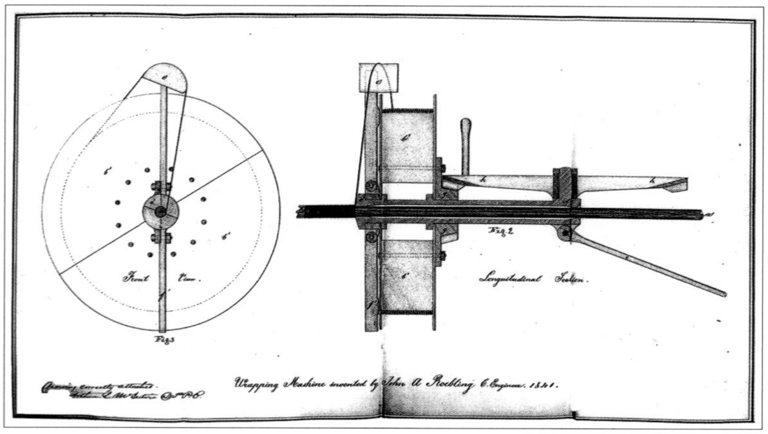

**Figure 2.10 (left):
John A. Roebling,
Cable Wrapping Patent Drawing
1841. RPI**

**Figure 2.11 (right):
John A. Roebling,
Cable Wrapping Patent Model,
1841, at the Smithsonian.**

Rope Making, "Biography of J.A. Roebling" - Washington A. Roebling, 1893

About the particular method of manufacture (in Europe) my father knew nothing. He had everything to learn, everything to evolve from his own brain. He knew that hemp ropes were laid up with a wooden top, hence the first thing was to devise an iron top with proper grooves. Behind this top the wires laid themselves up into a strand. I think it very remarkable that the first top he designed was arranged for 19 wires to the strand. In fact he never made a rope with seven wires to the strand until he moved to Trenton. In Europe the reverse practice obtained. They commenced with seven wires to the strand and stuck to it for twenty years until they learned from him how to make a 19-wire strand, and even then they did not make it in one operation, but first made seven wires and then overspun it with 12.

He had no tracks, no carriages to hold the tops, nothing but the rough meadow to work on. The strand top was carried on a crossbar by 2 strong men who walked along, regulating their speed and the lay of the wire in the strand entirely by their eye...At the end of the meadow was a simple twisting machine, spurwheel, pinion and crank by which 2 men turned the twist into the strand. They had to make so many turns per minute, taking a rest every 15 minutes, and then the top men stopped also when they saw that no twist was coming forward.

At the other end were appliances for letting the twist out of the wires by means of small brass swivels; to these were attached small hemp ropes, leading over a pulley with the weight attached so as to keep a uniformed equal strain on all the wires....As the strands were finished they were cut off in each end and a loop made, through which pegs were driven into the ground to keep the ends from twisting....

According to the length of the proposed rope, the end twister was moved back and forth. To keep the individual wires from tangling up they were laid out 2 inches apart in small grooves on what were called gauge boards, horizontal boards on edge, attached to an upright stuck in the ground. The wires were hauled out by a man dragging them on the ground, and then laid in their proper places. After that they were oiled with linseed oil and a sheepskin, arranged in an oiling box. To make a thousand feet of strand always took a day or more, sometimes two days. Rain and snow often interfered....

The first ropes, in fact all Saxonburg ropes, were made with one size of wire....Strand is composed of 3 circles; a center wire, then the inner circle of 6 wires, next the middle or second circle of 6 wires, and then the outer circle of 6 wires. The wires of the outer circle must necessarily project as the mathematical arrangement of circles compels it. Later on, 3 sizes of wire we used in a strand to avoid these projection....

Alongside the strand walk was the rope walk, where the seven strands were laid up into the rope....At the end was a twisting machine, with a pinion and gear wheel which was operated by a vertical capstan attached to the pinion shaft operated by four men.

At the shop end was the counter twist machine, a sort of juggernaut on rough wooden wheels which ran on the ground. This machine untwisted the separate strands as fast as the twist was put in at the other end. It had a master wheel and seven pinions attached to the end of each strand. This master wheel was also turned by a vertical capstan operated by six and eight men, twice as many as at the other end.

This machine was held back by a long double wire rope fall to a frame in which hung a heavyweight which gradually raised as the machine advanced in obedience to the shortening of the strands due to the twisting of the rope....The operation of turning in the twist and taking it out of the strands were all conducted by the watch. Warneck usually did the counting, he would count about 20 in one minute and then the men would take 20 yanks at the capstan. It was hard work, compelling a rest every 6 or 8 minutes. At the other end they did the same thing; the resting spells were indicated by signal flags.

The top where the rope was laid up was carried by 4 men. As the twist which forged the top ahead was very powerful, the men had to exercise great care not to get long lays in the rope; to avoid too sudden jerks a rough log was tied to the top by the rope, and yanked along, acting as a sort of a break. The log was called the alligator, from a fancied resemblance. It used to be my delight to sit on it and he knocked off by the sudden jerk.... The length of lay was tolerably uniform by these means and the ropes lasted a long time.

When a rope was finished the ends were cut off and it was wound up on a horizontal real with a capstan bar worked by a man, and it was put on a heavy wagon by a winch attached to a tall gallows frame. The loaded wagon with four horses was next driven to Freeport, 10 miles, where the rope was loaded into a canal boat and usually sent east....This rope hauling was wretched business in muddy weather....

For strand making there was a permanent gang, but for laying up rope men were collected from around the neighborhood. My mother fed them; they commenced work in summer at 5 a.m., came to breakfast at 6:30; at 10 a.m. I carried down a basketful of rye bread and whiskey, at 12 I blew the horn and they came to dinner, at 4 p.m. I carried down a basketful of rye bread with butter and more whiskey, and at 7 p.m. they came up for supper. This is the way the Germans work in Germany....

An ordinary rope was usually laid up in a day, but a long one took a day and a half. After the first year or two rope making did not require my father's constant presence, but when things went wrong he could make everyone stand around lively. It was very plain that this way of making rope was very expensive, with many drawbacks to overcome.[22]

was figuring out how to take the twist out of the wires that occurred as the men laid or twisted them around the core.

While John had been disappointed that more educated Germans had not immigrated to Saxonburg, many of the ones who did had the right skills and temperament for helping him in making wire rope. Washington had fond memories of the German farmers and craftsman who learned how to make wire rope along with his father:

> *The people my father had hoped would come there, came not. In their place came men of a humble walk of life – mechanics, people with a trade, small farmers, all hard workers and much better adapted for life there than more educated people....*
>
> *One cause which led to my intimate relation with many of the people arose from a simple circumstance. In the process of rope making, seven strands are first manufactured, by a regular force working daily. But when the strands were laid up into the large rope, a force of twenty men was required for one or two days; this force had to be summoned from all the neighborhood and I was a little messenger who did the running. As the men were only too glad to get an occasional job with cash pay and plenty to eat, the little harbinger was very welcome. In that way I became intimate with every family and knew every path and byway for miles around.*[23]

Washington wrote of pleasant German farmers named Sommer, Muder, Gertsner, and Schleitz who helped make rope whenever they were needed. A shoemaker named Bauer also helped and he and Sommer later helped John build an aqueduct. A weaver named Kunze made rope for eight years and followed John to Trenton and worked there for a year as a boss in the rope shop there. Washington noted that a locksmith and blacksmith named Stuebgen "did a variety of work for may father in rope machinery." A storekeeper named Schwietering hauled rope for John in his wagon. In fondly recalling these and other men, Washington wrote: "Now they are but dreams of a happy past to me."

The foundation of his fortune

After more than a year of service on Plane No. 3 near Ben's Creek, the Canal Board reported that John's wire rope "realized all expectations." Washington noted his father's efforts to ensure its success:

> *The first rope made for the Portage railroad was about 1100 feet long, 1¼" thick, of good charcoal iron and lasted longer than any of the subsequent ropes. The plane hands took the best of care of it and were proud of it. The business of introducing wire rope on the portage was not confined merely to rope making. It required special rope drums*

and double engines with counterweights below to keep up the tension. They were designed by John A. Roebling and put in under his superintendence, requiring perhaps more engineering than the making of the rope.

> *By degrees all the planes were altered, supplied with new engines and adapted for wire rope. I have often heard him speak of the difficulties he had to overcome, the reluctance with which the powers that were came over to his views, the bitter hostility of the hemp rope interests. But he carried through with undaunted energy and thus laid the foundation of his fortune.*[24]

As word spread of his success, John received inquiries about how his wire rope worked and how much it cost. The secretary of the Beaver Meadow Railroad and Coal Company wrote:

> *I have been informed that you made an iron wire rope for an inclined plane on the State Road at Hollidaysburg. We have it in contemplation to try the use of one on our road. Will you please inform us how the wire rope at Hollidaysburg answers the purpose? How long it has been in use? Does it show any signs of failing in anyplace? Is it affected much by rust?....What would be your price for making one suitable for the length and height of our plane and the weight we pass over it? What size of wire would you propose using? How many wires would you use? Would they be twisted or not? Would you serve or wrap the wires the whole length or only bind them together in places?*[25]

In his reply, John wrote:

> *I will give you with pleasure all the information you want on the subject of Wire Ropes. I will in the first instance remark that I am the only person in the U.S. who has made essential improvements in the construction of Wire Ropes and Wire Rigging. My claims are secured by patent and do not interfere with those of Smith in London, the Patentee for Wire Ropes in England, nor are my ropes in imitation of those which have been since three years in use in the mines of Germany.*
>
> *The main feature of my improvements consists in the Spiral laying of the wires around an axis <u>without twisting</u> them, and while they are exposed to a uniform and considerable strain, for the purpose of making the ropes pliable and giving all the wires a uniformed tension, which object has never been obtained before. I likewise hold a patent for wrapped Ropes, but I do not recommend a rapping for running ropes, only for stationary cables, as in Suspension bridges.*[26]

To explain his wire ropes to other prospective users, John wrote an article for the *American Railroad Journal* (Fig. 2.12), stating that wire rope was preferable to hemp rope "in all

AMERICAN
RAILROAD JOURNAL,
AND
MECHANICS' MAGAZINE.

Published Monthly at 23 Chambers-st. New York, at $2 a-year, in advance, or 3 copies for $5. | By GEO. C. SCHAEFFER, and D. K. MINOR, Editors.

No. 11, Vol. I. Third Series. | NOVEMBER, 1843. | Whole No. 430. Vol. XVI.

For the American Railroad Journal and Mechanics' Magazine.
AMERICAN MANUFACTURE OF WIRE ROPES FOR INCLINED PLANES, STANDING RIGGING, MINES, TILLERS, ETC. BY JOHN A. ROEBLING, CIVIL ENGINEER.

The art of manufacturing ropes of *wire* is comparatively new. Numerous attempts have been made in Europe and here, and most of them have proved failures. A collection of parallel wires, bound together by wrappings in the manner of a suspension cable, is no rope and not fit for running, it can only be used for a stationary purpose. The first rigging made in England, was of this description. The difficulty in the formation of wire rope arises from the unyielding nature of the material; iron fibres cannot be twisted like hemp, cotton or woollen; their texture would be injured by the attempt. To remove this obstacle, some manufacturers have resorted to *annealing*, and thereby destroyed the most valuable properties of iron wire, viz. its great strength and elasticity.

**Figure 2.12: John. A. Roebling, 1843. RU
"American Manufacture of Wire Rope for Inclined Planes, Standing Rigging, Mines, Tillers, Etc."**

exposed situations, and where great strength and durability is required." He noted that his "process of manufacture" ensured the flexibility needed for "running rigging" such as in tillers on ships, and he recommended wire ropes for "standing rigging" on ships. As with his article on suspension bridges in 1841, this wire rope article demonstrated his thorough knowledge of the subject and simultaneously proffered his services.

You are lost in your present seclusion

While John was promoting his wire ropes, his friend and former superior, Charles Schlatter, who had become Harbor Superintendent in Chicago, cautioned him about the limits of his location: "My opinion is that you are lost in your present seclusion, and that it would only be necessary for you to be long enough at Washington to become known to the proper persons, and your success will be certain, whilst your reputation and fame will spread as I know it deserves to spread." Schlatter was enthusiastically promoting John's wire ropes in Chicago, and in the Fall of 1843 he wrote: "Dear Roebling,....I do assure you that we all have the wire rope fever, and we are planning many ways to introduce tillers and rigging upon the Likes." A few months later Schlatter wrote: "Your indomitable courage and perseverance will render sure....that you will be before long at the head of the list of those benefactors to mankind, who employ science to useful purpose."[27]

With his limited capabilities in Saxonburg, John thought of licensing his wire rope patents to an established manufacturer. At the end of 1843, D.K., Minor, the editor of the *American Railroad Journal*, wrote to him:

I communicated your wishes to a gentleman in the city engaged in the manufacture of wire on a limited scale, Peter Cooper, Esq., a very candid man – and asked him if he could point me to anyone who would be likely to engage in the business. He said he did not know anyone – though he thought the time <u>would</u> come when it would become an important branch of manufacture....I asked Mr. Cooper if he would bear in mind your enquiry and let me know if any opportunity should offer to aid you in carrying out your views, and if he would also like to hear from you on the subject – to which he assured me he would give me any information in his power and would gladly receive any communication you might feel disposed to make.[28]

Peter Cooper's advice would soon influence John in one of his most important decisions. Washington noted how his father's success and the locations of his customers convinced him that he needed to find a place to build a wire rope factory in the east where he could ship his wire rope easily to his customers:

The reputation he gained on the portage led to numerous inquiries from the East and he made several journeys to the Lackawanna Valley. His friend, the engineer Archibald, who had charge of the planes and collieries of the Delaware and Hudson Canal, was enthusiastic in favor of wire rope and at once adopted it for the planes on their gravity road between Carbondale and Honesdale, which are running to this day (1897).

He took stock in pay for many of the ropes and this proved a profitable investment. A little later an offshoot of the Delaware and Hudson came into existence, called the Pennsylvania Coal Co., which built the gravity road between Carbondale and Hawley on the Lackawaxen, sending their coal from there to New York by the Delaware and Hudson Canal....They had as many planes as the Delaware and Hudson, and used as much rope. For this also my father took stock, which again proved a very profitable investment. These two companies were his best customers for many years....

The most important customer, however, that he captured in those days was the Morris Canal which runs from Easton to New York. They had no less than 22 planes operated at that time by chains, which constantly broke. Mr. Talcott, the engineer, concluded to adapt the machinery for wire rope and one complete set of ropes was made in Saxonburg. For these and later ropes he took part stock, which also proved a profitable investment. These ropes were no less than 2 1/4" in diameter, and up to 2300 feet in length. Their construction taxed the Saxonburg rope walk to its utmost capacity. The wire was large and stiff and so hard to handle, and many more men were required to lay up the big rope.

But the greatest trouble was the handling and the

transportation of the heavy reels, hauling them 10 miles through mud to Freeport and loading them in canal boats.

These drawbacks made my father think he was located in the wrong place, but labor was cheap in Saxonburg, an important item for a beginner with small capital. Fortunately his three main customers were so located that ropes could be delivered by canal directly to their planes.

Most of the prominent merchants, businessmen and capitalists of New York and Philadelphia were invested in the Delaware and Hudson Canal, the Pennsylvania Coal Company and the Morris Canal, so that his circle of acquaintances with prominent men was greatly enlarged, and much to his pecuniary benefit, which he was not slow to take advantage of.

With the completion of the Pennsylvania Railroad he foresaw that the portage railroad would be doomed, and that Saxonburg was then the last place to make rope, his main customers being all in the East. So during every visit East he kept on the lookout for a place with long level ground suitable for a rope walk with good transportation facilities both by Canal and Railroad. It was not until 1848 that he found such a place and the move was not completed until 1849. That move was the death knell of Saxonburg!

Having practically no competition, he could charge a fair price for ropes, and accumulate some capital, besides defraying the expenses of a growing family. He weathered the panic of 1837, mainly because he had but little money to lose, but he gained financial experience which enabled him to weather the next panic, 20 years later, without losses of any account. It was also fortunate for him that his chief rope customers were perfectly sound, so that he received no financial slap at the beginning, and lastly he operated with saved capital, not burrowed capital, the secret of most success....

By the years 1842-3-4 the mechanical problems of rope making had been sufficiently solved for the time being, the business was on a sound financial basis and was gradually increasing, it no longer demanded his whole time and his engineering ambition became roused again into activity.[29]

In March of 1844, John wrote to his father and brother in Germany about his family and about his progress in his new wire rope business:

My family now consists of Washington, a six-year-old, well-built, sturdy, quiet boy, Laura four years old, who has been suffering a great deal for two years from a protracted illness, Ferdinand, two years old, who is a promising lad with good prospects, and Frederick Baer's favorite....

My present business, wire cable manufacture, is going pretty well, but is only in its early stages. Another year must pass in order to put its duration and suitability beyond any doubt, then I hope to make out fine. My slender means have limited me very much up to now. So far as the work itself is concerned, it may be regarded as completely successful in every respect. My wire cables are the best ones to be had.[30]

Everything was new, everything required an invention

John was buying wire for his ropes from Robert Townsend of Pittsburgh, and in May of 1844 Townsend wrote to him: "We send by mail this day a paper with a proposal from the Aqueduct Committee offering a premium of $100 for the best plan for a wooden or suspension aqueduct. Now is the time for you to strike, the aqueduct is at present impassable." The Pennsylvania Canal's aqueduct over the Allegheny was nearly 16 years old and ice storms had damaged it beyond repair. John immersed himself in designing a suspension aqueduct, calculating the loads, drawing elevations, sections and construction details (Figs. 2.13-14), and building a model in his meadow. He prepared a 28 page proposal for a "Wire Suspension Cable Aqueduct over the Allegheny River" and submitted it in July. Washington related his father's determined efforts to build his first suspension bridge:[31]

The construction of the Pittsburgh aqueduct was in many respects the greatest feat of his life, and in my opinion even surpassing the Niagara Bridge, mainly because it had to be accomplished in the short space of nine months, during a severe winter with snow and ice in the river. It was likewise an untried problem, without a precedent and undertaken in the face of violent opposition, raised by the press, by rival contractors, engineers, canal men, merchants, etc.

This opposition had to first be overcome by personal effort, by constant argument, by writing in the papers and scientific journals and by marshaling his many personal friends in his behalf.

The board of Canal Commissioners had to be brought over to his views. The City Council of Pittsburgh was won over with difficulty. He conquered everything with that wonderful personal force, a power which only fed on opposition and knew no defeat. I consider the effort of merely getting started fully as great as that of actually executing the work.

In addition to the undertaking was the circumstance that he was obliged to take the work in contract and be his own engineer at the same time, without an assistant. Everyone who expected to furnish supplies of course helped him. The Townsends who were to furnish the wire; the firm of Lyon and Shorb who made the blooms for the wire; the foundrymen, lumber men, stone men, iron men all helped and endorsed the new departure, so different from the wooden arches that stood there before and had rotted in less than twenty years. Without his wire experience in Saxonburg, he could never have built the seven inch cables of the aqueduct.

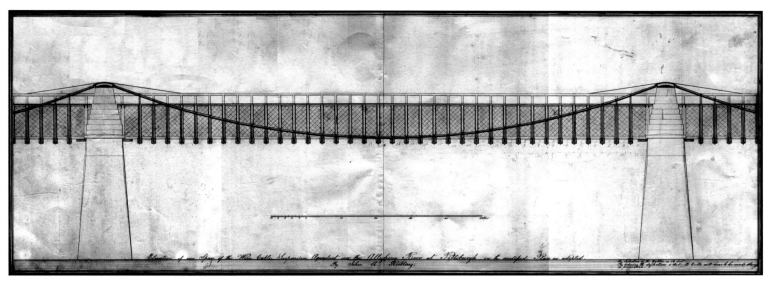

Figure 2.13: John A. Roebling, 1844. RPI
"Elevation of the Span of the Wire Cable Suspension Aqueduct over the Allegheny River at Pittsburgh on the modfied Plan as adopted."
John drew an elegant presentation drawing for his first suspension bridge in America.

The Pittsburgh Aqueduct consisted of seven spans of 162 feet each, with a wooden trunk wide enough for the passage of one boat. The trunk was supported by two continuous wire cables, one on each side, and seven inches in diameter, made of No. 10 wire, charcoal stock. At each end were the stone anchorages with the anchor bars, arranged in a quarter circle and embedded in the masonry.[32]

In constructing the Pittsburgh Aqueduct, John developed a number of techniques that improved on previous wire suspension bridges and became standard procedures for subsequent suspension bridges.

This aqueduct was in many a respects a typical construction (for my father). For instance the cable was made of strands, which were afterwards compressed together and wrapped into one solid cable. Each strand was practically one endless wire, the wires passing around a cast iron shoe at the ends into which they were laid....

In those days...wire was apt to be wavy and kinky, hence my father found it necessary to make the strands under tension, so as to get the wires to bear alike and lie parallel....

In the old French system of cable making the strands were made on shore, with little or no tension, and were then hauled over and suspended separately, side by side. The location here was such that it was impossible to make the strands on shore in line with the bridge, hence they had to be made in place. Their consolidation into one compact cable was a great step forward....

Wrapping the cable was another great step. The wrapping machines were original inventions and remarkable in their way. They have never been improved upon...They consist of a cast iron barrel in two halves which slides on the cable; around it turns a loose reel, which is filled with wire by hand. In operating, the wire passes from this reel, over a flyer, around the cable behind the machine which is thus wormed forward; it is turned by hand and used to wrap 35 to 50 ft. per day.

The method of strand making and getting the wires across is also an original patented invention derived from Saxonburg experience. The same principle has been followed

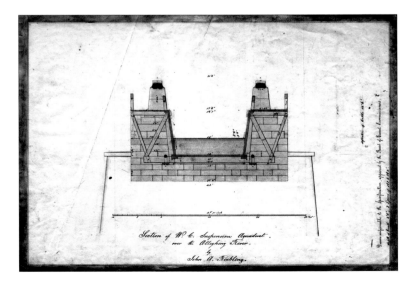

Figure 2.14: John A. Roebling, 1844. RPI
"Section of W. C. (Wire Cable) Suspension Aqueduct over the Allegheny River."
The original idea upon which the plan has been perfected, was to form a wooden trunk, strong enough to support its own weight, and stiff enough for an aqueduct, or bridge, and to combine this structure with wire cables, of a sufficient strength to bear safely the great weight of water.
- J. A. Roebling[33]

in laying up all the subsequent cables. The wires are first spliced, then wound on large drums, passing through a straightening heddle at the same time. The wires are taken over by an endless rope, propelled by a horizontal wheel, and moving alternatively back and forth. To the rope is attached a light revolving grooved wheel, by means of a gooseneck and retaining bridle. The wheels are always moving in opposite directions. The bight of the wire is passed over the wheel, hence the lower wire is laid down stationary and the upper one travels twice as fast. Each wheel goes back empty. The running wire runs on rollers on the towers and cradles. When the wheel has reached the other side the wire is taken off and thrown over so that the dead wire lies on one side of the strand and the moving wire on the other.[34]

John brought several of his Saxonburg wire rope makers to Pittsburgh to help build the aqueduct, and Washington attributed the timely completion of the bridge cables to their combined experience:

Without the Saxonburg wire experience and the skilled man, John A. Roebling could not have made these cables in time. Everything was new, everything required an invention. There was no time for failures.[35]

A German-American carpenter working on the aqueduct caught John's attention for his skills and detail work, and this began a long-term relationship that would benefit both men tremendously. Washington noted:

Among the young carpenters was a bright eyed, black haired, red cheeked chap named Charles Swan, who distinguished himself by his daring, his handiness, adaptability to all kinds of work, and that good natured honesty which characterizes the German. A native of Breslau, Silesia, and only son and support of a widowed mother, he at once attracted my father's attention who saw in him a man of capacity and of future usefulness.

When the rope business was moved to Trenton, he selected Swan to take full charge of it, both mechanically and commercially, an arrangement made necessary by his own prolonged absence on important engineering works. The mutual respect and esteem and the implicit confidence and trust which my father reposed in him grew with age and only ended with his life.[36]

In reporting on the completed aqueduct, he described his method of anchoring cables under an enormous load of masonry:

The extremities of the cables on the aqueduct do not extend below ground, but connect with anchor chains, which in a curved line pass through large masses of masonry, the last links occupying a vertical position....The extreme links are anchored to heavy cast-iron plates of 6 feet square, which are held down by the foundation, upon which the weight of 700 perch of masonry rests. The stability of this part of the structure is fully insured, as the resistance of the anchorage is twice as great as the greatest strain to which the chains can ever be subjected.

The plan of anchorage adopted on the aqueduct varies materially from those methods usually applied to suspension bridges....The chains below ground are embedded and completely surrounded by cement. In the construction of the masonry this material and common lime-mortar have been abundantly applied. The bars are painted with red lead: their preservation is rendered certain by the known quality of calcareous cements to prevent oxidation.

If moisture should find its way to the chains, it will be saturated with lime, and add another calcareous coating to the iron. This portion of the work has been executed with scrupulous care, so as to render it unnecessary, on the part of those who exercise a surveillance over the structure, to examine it.[37]

One great success leads to others

Convinced that his cable making process and anchorage design held great promise, John filed patent applications for both of them (Figs. 2.15-16). Washington credited his father's success in designing and building the Allegheny Aqueduct as rapidly launching his bridge building career.

I myself saw the aqueduct for the first time in May, 1845, just before the opening having been brought down from Saxonburg to go to school in Pittsburgh. Although I was only eight years of age, I remember it's appearance very well....

The aqueduct was opened triumphantly by a procession of boats. John A. Roebling had become a great engineer, his fame spread throughout the land, other engineers acknowledged it, all but Charles Ellet Jr., his great rival....

One great success leads to others. John A. Roebling in place of seeking work, was now sought after. The Wheeling Suspension Bridge took shape and its incorporators opened negotiations with him.

The great fire of Pittsburgh in April, 1845, just before the aqueduct was completed, had destroyed the wooden Smithfield Street bridge across the Monongahela. The rebuilding of that structure came to him almost without an effort, most of the directors being his personal friends.[38]

While Washington described the traffic on the old Smithfield Street Bridge as "very heavy, an endless procession of wagons laden with pig iron and bar iron and coal," the load was less than the weight of the water on the Allegheny

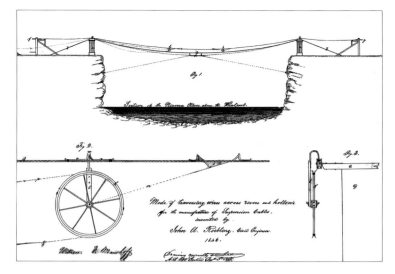

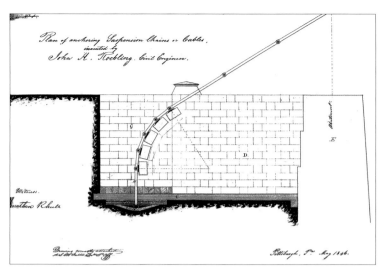

Figure 2.15: John A. Roebling, Cable Making Patent. RPI
"Mode of traversing wires across rivers and hollows
for the manufacture of Suspension Cables,
invented by John A. Roebling, Civil Engineer, 1846."

Figure 2.16: John A. Roebling, Cable Anchoring Patent. RPI
"Plan of Anchoring Suspension Chains or Cables,
invented by John A. Roebling, Civil Engineer,
Pittsburgh, May, 1846."

John's invention of a traveling wheel, or traveler, to lay wires individually for suspension cables and anchoring the cables
with an iron plate under a massive weight of masonry have guided the builders of traditional suspension bridges ever since.

Aqueduct. John designed smaller cables for the new bridge over the Monongahela River and employed the French method of making them in sections on shore, hauling them out onto the river on boats, lifting them into place, and securing them with pendulum connectors on top of the towers. Washington described his father's construction of the cables and the difficulties he had to overcome:

The Monongahela Bridge was commenced in 1845, consisted of eight spans, each 188 feet in length, with two abutments, a double roadway and too narrow sidewalks…. The cables were not continuous, but were made in short lengths from tower to tower where they were attached to pendulums swinging from a cast-iron seat above….

The cables, 4½ inches in diameter and made of No. 10 charcoal wire were made on land in the usual style, stretched between posts under tension and wrapped there. The attempt to move them, however, came near proving disastrous, and it could only be accomplished by putting each one in a long close wooden box, then skating that down to the flatboat on which two were placed and floated over in the span where they were hoisted in place by tackle worked by a capstan….

The pendulums would swing a little to counterbalance inequalities in the loads of adjacent spans, sufficiently so as not to overthrow the towers. They were in fact so sensitive that a load on one would be felt at the other, each set of pendulums swinging a little less and less….The pendulums were a new idea and worked admirably.[39]

While completing the Monongahela Bridge in 1846, John explained his design in the *American Railroad Journal*:

The peculiar construction of the Monongahela Bridge was planned with the view of obtaining a high degree of stiffness, which is a great desideratum in all suspension bridges; this object has been fully attained.

The wind has no effect on this structure, and the vibrations produced by two heavy coal teams, weighing seven tons each, and closely following each other, are no greater than is generally observed on wooden arch and truss bridges of the same span.

This bridge is principally used for heavy hauling; a large portion of the coal consumed in the City of Pittsburgh passes over it in four and six horse teams. As a heavy load passes over a span, the adjoining pendulums, when closely observed, can be noticed to move correspondingly - the extent of this motion not exceeding one half inch.

By this accommodation of the pendulums, all jarring of the cast iron towers is effectively avoided.

Two of the piers of the old structure had once given way in consequence of the shaking and pressure of the arch timbers, when subjected to heavy loads. Such an accident can never take place on the new structure, as the piers are only subjected to the quiet and vertical pressure of the towers.

I do not recommend the application of pendulums in all cases; but in this, it appeared to me the best plan which could be adopted.[40]

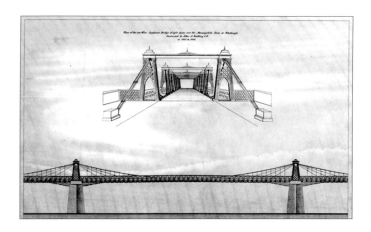

Figure 2.17 (left): "View of the new Wire Suspension Bridge of eight spans over the Monongahela River at Pittsburgh Constructed by John A. Roebling in 1845 to 1846." RPI
Figure 2.18 (right): Smithfield Street Bridge, c1890, CL Roebling built his first suspension bridge for vehicles and pedestrians with cables of wire ropes he made on land and hauled into position for each of the 188-ft. spans.

D.K. Minor, the editor of the *American Railroad Journal* wrote in the same issue: "The Monongahela Bridge (Figs. 2.17-18) is a credit to Pittsburgh and to the ingenious constructor. As the traffic is a very heavy one, the test to which this beautiful structure has been subjected well, we think, convince those who have heretofore doubted, that the suspension type may be adopted, not only with the entire safety, but also with great economy, on railroads." When the Monongahela Bridge opened, the editor of the *Pittsburgh Morning Post* wrote: "It is in every way a most wonderful work." Many years later, the distinguished bridge engineer David B. Steinman wrote about this bridge: "The accomplishment was notable as the first suspension bridge scientifically designed and constructed to provide against all the forces with which a bridge must battle."[41]

While John was completing the Monongahela Bridge, several opportunities arose to build much larger suspension bridges. Major Charles B. Stuart, a retired officer and the first New York State Engineer, proposed a railway suspension bridge as the long-sought solution to crossing the Niagara Gorge, and he invited comments from leading bridge engineers. When John, Ellet, and two others responded positively, Stuart pushed for a charter to build the bridge.

John was keenly interested because he believed that railroads would open up the country for development, as he told members of the Pittsburgh Board of Trade (Fig. 2.19). Stuart favored Ellet but John persevered to try to win the Niagara contract.

A clear and concise style

Meanwhile, a group of businessmen in Pittsburgh who wanted to link manufacturing, residential and coal areas around the city asked John to design a three-part bridge at the convergence of the Monongahela and Allegheny Rivers. John drew up plans for a 900 foot span over the Allegheny and a 750 foot span over the Monongahela, which would have been quite a marvel, but steamboat opponents blocked it because they feared it would impede river traffic.

The success of John's work in Pittsburgh brought another bridge project to him in 1846 that would take more than 20 years to complete, but he characteristically never lost faith that he would build it. As Washington related:

While the Monongahela Bridge was in progress, my father received an invitation from some leading men of Cincinnati to visit that city and make a report on a proposed suspension bridge over the Ohio. A visit in May resulted in a report and plans on the following September, 1846….
The design (a noble plan, never executed) calls for a central tower in the middle of the river with the anchorages located well back from the water so as not to interfere with water way or wharf rights. Each land span was nearly 800 feet long….Diameter of cables 11.28 inches (Fig. 2.20).[42]

The newly-formed Cincinnati & Covington Bridge Company hired John to design the bridge across the Ohio that year, but the opposition of steamboat operators to its central tower and disagreements about where to place the bridge would delay its construction for years. Reflecting on these delays and his father's report to the bridge company, Washington wrote:

A civil engineer must be endowed with broad views, he must look to the future and must-have force of character to override the shortsighted views of his board of directors, who are usually influenced by property and real estate interests and are afraid to place themselves in opposition to local interests which might be temporarily injured. An engineer must be a Haussman (Baron Georges-Eugene Haussman, who rebuilt Paris in the 1850s).

In this report the characteristic features of the Roebling type of suspension bridges are clearly set forth, and to this type he adhered all his life....

This report is the first of the many model reports, in the writing of which my father excelled. Every part of the project is treated in a clear and concise style with short telling sentences. The language is plain and forcible, and everyone can understand what is meant. There is nothing ambiguous and no essentials are left unsaid.[43]

While the proposed suspension bridges in Pittsburgh and Cincinnati soon stalled, the directors of the Delaware & Hudson Canal Company were eager to improve their coal transportation from Carbondale, Pennsylvania, to the Hudson at Kingston, New York. To alleviate delays that occurred when their canal boats crossed the Delaware River, they decided to build two aqueducts at Lackawaxen, Pennsylvania – one across the Lackawaxen River and another across the Delaware (Figs. 2.21-24).

The company had been buying wire rope from John for several years for its gravity railroad between Honesdale and Carbondale, and after inspecting his Pittsburgh bridges, the directors contracted with him in early 1847 to design and build the cables and the superstructures of the two aqueducts for $60,400 (about $2.4 million in 2009). That year he lost two big bridge projects to his rival, as Washington related:

While the Monongahela Bridge was underway, the Wheeling bridge matter had taken shape. My father had made his plans, estimates, and given his figures at which he would take the work in contract.

Read and Circulate.

AMERICAN
RAILROAD JOURNAL,
Extra.

THE GREAT CENTRAL RAILROAD,
FROM
PHILADELPHIA TO ST. LOUIS.

BY JOHN A. ROEBLING, C. E.

Read before the Pittsburg "Board of Trade."

Railways appear to be destined to supersede all other means of intercommunication. Among the great mass of modern inventions and improvements, none perhaps are of greater importance, and will contribute more to the great and *common* interests of mankind, than RAILROADS and TELEGRAPHS. It is not improbable, that in a country like Russia, whose Autocrat has ordered the construction of *railways* upon a gigantic scale, this system of iron bands may first prove another powerful mode of enslaving more thoroughly the masses of the people, but it will surely aid in their eventual emancipation. Railroads and Telegraphs may be hailed as the latest offspring of the spirit of the present age; they have imparted a new and most powerful impulse to the social movement, from which will yet flow a vast train of beneficial results.

One of the best proofs of the advancement of mankind in *true* civilization is, that the industrial efforts of nations are no longer squandered upon the creation of vast monuments of pride and of war. The partial attempts at improvements during the middle age, have been followed by a generous rivalry among nations, states, and communities, in the construction of public works of general utility and vast extent, particularly highways, canals and railroads. So far has this system been successfully developed, that we may project works with unerring certainty in advance of population and traffic. In place of railroads growing out of commerce and wealth, the former are now creating the latter: Like a *magic wand*, they open the slumbering resources and long-hidden treasures of the earth; convert stone and iron into gold; draw into bonds of union and amity isolated individuals, as well as communities and nations; unchain long-cherished prejudices and selfishness, and cause to be made more simultaneous, exertions in all that is useful and good. The nobler feelings and sentiments of man are likewise partaking of the benefit of this general move; they will be roused to greater activity by the enlarged scope rendered accessible by the increased facilities of communication.

While *canals* and *turnpikes* (ever since their general introduction) have experienced but little improvement, because they are not susceptible of it—railroads, on the other hand, have undergone a constant change towards the better. Since their nature admitted the application of mechanical power, they have largely partaken of the benefits, which have resulted from the late astonishing developments of mechanical science. To the successful application of the mighty agency of steam, the vast extension of the great usefulness of railroads is mainly to be attributed; time itself and space have almost been annihilated. But, I may well ask, where is the country on earth, as much to be benefitted by these modern improvements, as our own? We abound in the elements of wealth, but want the means of moving, working and distributing them! Inexhaustible supplies of coal and iron invite us to use and apply them for the construction of these and other useful works of art.

The geographical features of the Mississippi valley, it is said, afford the best guarantee for the stability of this Union. But I think, that with greater

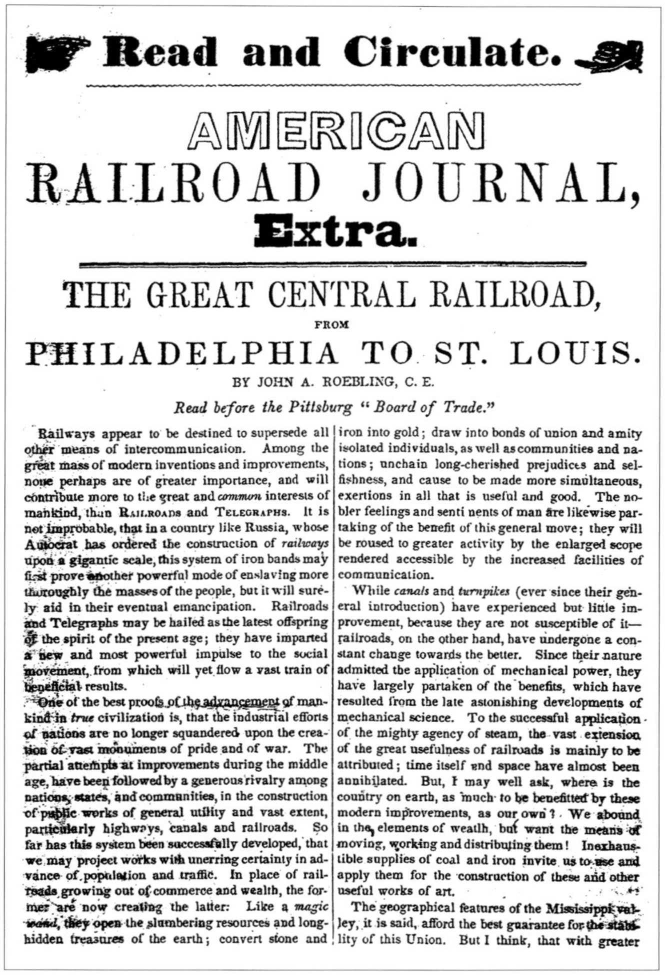

Figure 2.19:
"The Great Central Railroad from Philadelphia to St. Louis," John A. Roebling, 1847. RU

Railways appear to be destined to supercede all other means of intercommunication. **- J.A. Roebling**

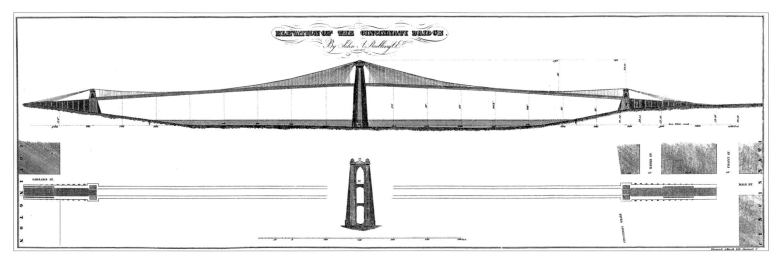

Figure 2.20: "Elevation Of The Cincinnati Bridge, by John A. Roebling," 1846 RPI Two 800 ft. spans with a central tower.

This bridge, when constructed, will possess great claims as a national monument. As a splendid work of art and as a remarkable specimen of modern engineering and construction, it will stand unrivaled upon the continent. Its gigantic features will speak loudly in favor of the energy and enterprise of the community which will boast of its possession. **- John A. Roebling**

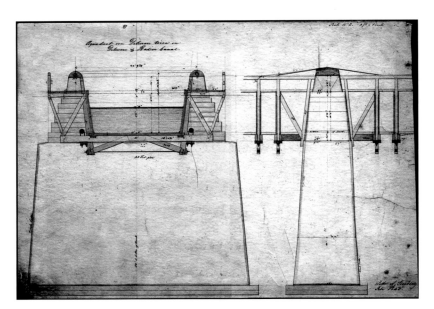

Figure 2.21: John A. Roebling, "Aqueduct over the Delaware River on the Delaware & Hudson Canal, Feb. 1847." RPI

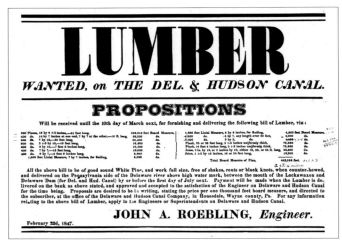

Figure 2.22: "Lumber Wanted, on the Del. & Hudson Canal, John A. Roebling, Civil Engineer, 1847." RPI Roebling built four aqueducts for the Delaware & Hudson Canal Company between 1848 and 1850, but railroads soon supplanted canals, as he had predicted.

This was a more ambitious work, the span being no less than 1010 feet with a height above water of 80 or 90 feet....

When my father arrived there, he found a lion in his path; Charles Ellet, Jr., engineer of the Fairmount Suspension Bridge over the Schuylkill River at Phila. and an engineer of reputation otherwise....

I have heard my father say that if Ellet had been in the country during the aqueduct time he never would have let him build them; he would certainly have maneuvered him out of the job.

Ellet at once laid his plans to capture the Wheeling bridge. While perhaps less virulent in his arguments, he was more plausible, more politic in his actions, more polished and put on immense airs of superiority. Being a Virginian himself, State pride came in, as Wheeling was then located in Virginia. In short, he succeeded in convincing the bridge

company that they would make a great mistake in taking Roebling in place of himself; so he was made the engineer and their troubles commenced.

In architecture Ellet had taste; as a constructing engineer of common sense he was a failure, due largely to a French education. The towers are handsome pieces of masonry of fine design....But when it came to practical details Ellet was a failure. In cable making he adhered to the old French type of a lot of small cables hung up side by side, each one as limber as a whip and possessing no inherent stiffness. They were made on land and hauled over....

His pride probably prevented him from imitating the Roebling type of solid compact cable....In floor and truss construction his ideas were still cruder. His mind had not risen to the level of the stiffening truss to check undulations.

Given the above conditions and circumstances, only one

Figure 2.23: Delaware Aqueduct, c1900. NPS
After the canal ceased operations in 1904,
a local businessman operated it as a toll bridge.

Figure 2.24: Delaware Aqueduct, c1995. NPS Restored by the National Park Service in the 1980s for vehicular traffic, it is the now oldest suspension bridge in America.

result was possible. He swamped the company financially, through incompetent management, and the first little gale that came along destroyed the bridge....

Most engineers would have considered such an experience as rather damaging to their reputation, but Ellet's self-esteem easily survived it and actually extracted enough credit from it to demand and obtain the position of chief engineer of the Niagara bridge.[44]

Can a suspension bridge be made stiff enough

When Charles Stuart, the Commissioner of the Niagara Bridge Company, solicited proposals in 1847, John submitted a handsome elevation and a report with calculations and details for the towers and cables (Figs. 2.25-26), noting in it:

I have bestowed some time on this subject, and have matured plans and working details. Although the question of applying the principle of suspension to railroad bridges has been disposed of in the negative by Mr. Robert Stephenson - I am bold enough to say that this celebrated engineer has not at all succeeded in the solution of this problem....

It cannot be questioned that wire cables, when well-made, offer the safest and most economical means for the support of heavy weights. Any span within 1500 feet can be made perfectly safe for the support of railroad trains as well as common travel.

The greater the weight to be supported, the stronger the cables must be, and as this is a matter of unerring calculation, there need be no difficulty on the score of strength. The only question which presents itself is: Can a suspension bridge be made stiff enough, as not to yield and bend under the weight of a railroad train when unequally distributed over it; and can the great vibrations which result from the rapid motion of such trains and which prove so destructive to common bridges, be avoided and counteracted?

I answer this question in the affirmative, and maintain that wire-cable bridges, properly constructed, would be found hereafter the most durable and economical railroad bridges for spans over 100 feet....

The locality of the Niagara Bridge offers the very best opportunity for the application of a system of stays, which will insure all the stiffness requisite for the passage of railroad trains at a rapid rate.

The plan I have devised for the structure will convince you that the rigidity will be ample.[45]

John confidently offered "to construct the bridge with two tracks for common travel, two footwalks, and one railroad track, within fifteen months, for $180,000 (about $7 million in 2009), subscribe $20,000 to the capital stock, and give security for the complete success of the work in all its parts." His design specified four 10 1/2-in. cables with a main span of 800 ft. but he lost the contract to Ellet in late 1847, largely because Stuart favored Ellet.

Around that time, the Delaware & Hudson Canal Company contracted with John to build two more aqueducts in New York over the Rondout Creek at High Falls and the Neversink River at Cuddebackville. John spent much of his time in 1848 to 1850 designing and building the four Delaware & Hudson aqueducts at their remote locations.[46]

His business will no doubt be a large one

With his Saxonburg rope works stretched to its limits and his high shipping costs, John "wrote to Peter Cooper on December 23, 1847, that he wished to establish a wire rope manufactory near Trenton, and would like to know if five or ten acres of dry level ground could be obtained near the railway and the canal." Cooper was famous for building the Tom Thumb locomotive for the Baltimore & Ohio Railroad, but had also become well

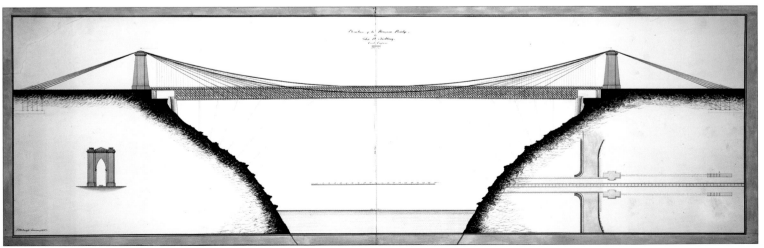

Figure 2.25: John A. Roebling, "Elevation of the Niagara Bridge, by John A. Roebling, Civil Engineer," 1847. RPI
John offered to "give security" for constructing his proposed 800 ft. span bridge, but he lost the contract to his rival, Charles Ellet.

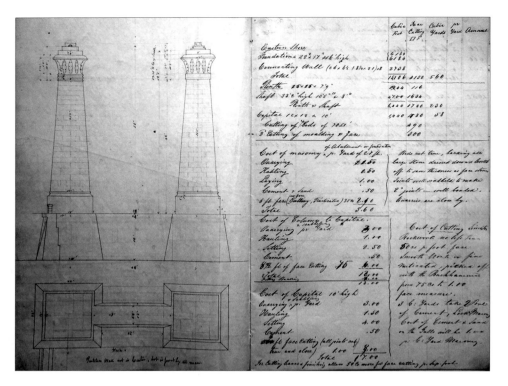

known and wealthy for manufacturing glue and iron. After operating iron works in Baltimore and New York, he had established the South Trenton Iron Company in 1845 at sites on the Delaware River and the Delaware and Raritan Canal.[47]

With easy access to coal and pig iron in the Delaware Valley, iron makers established forges in Trenton by the early 1730s and Benjamin Yard began making steel there by 1745. Canal and railroad construction in the 1830s provided inexpensive access to raw materials and connected Trenton to New York and Philadelphia, two of the biggest markets in the country, which attracted investors like Cooper.

By the end of 1846, Cooper's employed 500 men in Trenton making rods, bars, and wire and rolling rails. Cooper saw John's wire rope business as a customer for his wire, and John needed a ready supply to meet rope orders he already had on hand. Washington related his father's attraction to Trenton:

The years 1848-9 were perhaps busier years for my father and more fraught with successful results than any two previous years. He had fully determined to move his family and his business to the East....when his engineering engagements demanded it and the product of his rope making was also consumed in the East. Financially the latter was more important than engineering.

In the choice of a location he followed the advice of Peter Cooper, who had recommended Trenton, New Jersey, a place where he himself had recently established extensive iron works. The place possessed many advantages. As he still intended to make rope on a walk, it was necessary to find a

level piece of ground at least 3500 feet long; combined with this must be convenient shipping facilities. Both of these he found at Trenton....

As he intended to put up a small wire mill and draw his own wire, Mr. Cooper's mill was very convenient for rolling Swedish bars into rods, or he could buy common wire from them or from the Stewart mill at Easton, only forty-five miles away by canal.

Trenton was about halfway between the two largest cities of the continent, New York and Philadelphia; the canal connected with the Pennsylvania system of canals which led to the coal regions through the valleys of the Lehigh, the Schuylkill and the Susquehanna. The Morris Canal was easily reached and also the Delaware and Hudson by way of the Hudson River. The canals were as yet paramount and railroads still in their infancy....

From Captain Hunt of the U.S. Navy he bought a narrow strip of the above length, area about 25 acres, at $100 per acre. The western end abutted on the Delaware and Raritan Canal and the Bordentown branch of the Camden and Amboy Railroad, this giving him all the necessary shipping facilities in all directions.[48]

In August, 1848, the *Trenton State Gazette* reported John A. Roebling's purchase of Captain Hunt's property:

The establishment of his factory will create a new source of wealth in the city and be of special advantage to (Cooper's) new rolling mill which is already adapted to the making of wire....The wire rope made by Mr. Roebling enjoys a high reputation and his business will no doubt be a large one.[49]

Chapter 3: *First class facilities*

Trenton in 1848 was a thriving little Quaker town of 11,000 people. A few years previous it had been awakened from its lethargy of half a century or more by the completion of the Delaware and Raritan ship Canal and the Camden and Amboy Railroad, finished in 1835. These gave the place first-class facilities for cheap and speedy communication with the rest of the world. But there were not many commodities to ship, until the enterprising Peter Cooper brought about construction of the Trenton Water Power canal (which) attracted the attention of manufacturers from New England and Middle States, who established mills and factories from 1843 to 1845. The machine shop and foundry facilities were especially good, an important factor in my father's business.[1]

As Washington related, Trenton was a logical place for his father to build a wire rope factory. With the Delaware and Hudson aqueducts keeping him in New York State, John delegated the construction of the factory and a house for his family to a young man in whom he saw much promise:

My father had always kept track of Charles Swan, the young carpenter of the (Allegheny) aqueduct, so when the land purchase from Capt. Hunt was completed (Fig. 3.1), he arranged with Swan to move to Trenton with his family and commence the erection of buildings, but before going, Swan spent ten days at Saxonburg to learn the practical art of rope making from Kuntz.

The manufacture of ropes at Saxonburg as a matter of course had to continue until everything was ready in Trenton….So my father had to divide his time between three places – Trenton, Saxonburg and the Delaware and Hudson aqueducts.[2]

John completed the Delaware and Lackawaxen Aqueducts at the end of 1848 and started working on the High Falls Aqueduct in the spring of 1849 and on the Neversink Aqueduct that summer. With Swan erecting the first buildings and laying out the rope walk in Trenton, John's family was preparing their move from Saxonburg, as Washington recalled:

The summer of 1849 was spent getting ready to move. The children were glad, but my mother wept and the old folks went under compulsion. We had an auction of goods and chattels that were not needed in Trenton….The party that moved comprised my grandfather and grandmother, aunt Mary, my mother, myself, Ferdinand, Laura, Elvira and Josephine….I was 12 ½ years old and Josephine, the youngest, perhaps three. As I was the only one who knew English well I served as an interpreter. The two Kuntzes went along to help with rope making.

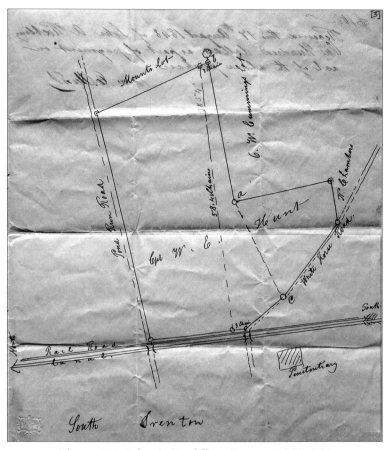

Figure 3.1: John A. Roebling, Survey, 1848. RU
For his new wire rope factory, John bought 25 acres of farmland for $3,000 from Captain C. W. Hunt USN in Chambersburg, at that time an independent borough southeast of Trenton. The land had excellent transportation access with frontage on the Delaware and Raritan Canal, the Trenton-Bordentown branch of the Camden and Amboy Railroad, and South Broad Street.

My father did not accompany the party, being busy on the aqueducts. The auction brought in just about enough money to see this little party through to Trenton.

We left on a Sunday afternoon, the middle of September for Freeport in four wagons. The whole village turned out to see us off; many cried, all looked sad, because our departure was the death knell to the prosperity of the place. We left the friends and companions of 20 years, most of whom were never to see each other again. I think my mother grieved more than anyone, the change in her life was to be so great….

The journey took about a week, as we arrived in Trenton the following Saturday….Sunday evening we occupied the hotel in Freeport, sleeping on sofas, and even the floor, it was so full; at 3 a.m. we were all routed to get on a Philadelphia packet, a canal boat drawn by four mules and averaging four miles an hour. This boat was not over crowded and the party soon got accustomed to the narrow quarters. The

weather was fine, we sat on deck, laid down flat every time we passed a bridge, read books, threw stones at things on shore, and admired the scenery....

Late Tuesday we arrived at Johnstown, the western terminus of the Portage Railroad. Here I saw the first locomotive! As our boat was not a section boat it could not cross the mountains....

Friday morning early we reached Lewistown on the Juniata, in Midland County, the western terminus of the Pennsylvania Railroad. We were transferred to the cars and managed to reach Philadelphia that same night about nine o'clock....

The next morning after the baggage had been collected and counted we started for Trenton via Camden. In crossing the Delaware I saw a ship for the first time, quite an event in a boy's life.

Trenton was finally reached at 11 a.m. Saturday, on the seventh day of the journey....The weary party trudged down the muddy towpath, and finally entered their new home where Mrs. Swan was cooking dinner. How she opened her eyes when she saw that hungry army invade her premises.

A shade of disappointment passed over the faces of most of us, at the first impress of the new home, yet we were all so glad to be under one roof tree once more, and have regular meals and regular times for sleeping that there was no audible grumbling. The house was small for so many. Before everything was regulated, there were many bickerings and divisions of opinion.

My father was not there, he did not arrive for a month, being busy on the aqueduct. The work at Trenton he directed by correspondence. Swan had a small force of carpenters and laborers putting up buildings and machinery.[3]

With urgent rope orders backing up, John wrote to Swan: "I wish you to hurry on with our works <u>as fast as it can be done</u>." He instructed Swan to hire mostly Germans and told him how much to pay them, he itemized materials that he had ordered,

sketched machinery details, sent bank drafts, and often pressed Swan to get more done. John would be away from Trenton building bridges for much of the next two decades, and he relied on Swan to run the factory. While Swan kept books in Trenton, John kept his own journals, meticulously detailing his purchases, the hours worked by Swan's men, the results of wire tests, and wire rope orders.[5]

In November of 1849, just a year after acquiring the Chambersburg property, John noted the completion of his first wire rope there. It consisted of three 2,330 ft. long sections, each 1-9/16 in. in circumference, for splicing into a continuous "driving rope" nearly 7,000 ft. long to run his complicated rope walk (Figs. 3.3-4). In December, his men made a 3,030 ft. long, 4-1/8 in. circumference wire rope for the South Carolina Railroad Company in Charleston. After completing the superstructures on the High Falls and Neversink Aqueducts, John returned to Trenton, and Washington later recalled some important events:

On the 12th of December, 1849, Mr. Roebling's third son, Charles, was born....This boy as he grew up was more like his father than any of the others; he resembled him more in features, stature, walk, manner and mental peculiarities, exhibiting much of the same intensity and force of action, but while he had a kinder heart after it was once found, he lacked a certain breath of mind, polish of manner and that comprehensive intellect which stamped Mr. Roebling senior a great man among his fellows.

Of course there was a great difference between their respective early environments and circumstances, yet my observation tells me that nine-tenths of all mental characteristics are inborn and both parents influence it....

Shortly before Christmas a very serious accident happened to my father by which he nearly lost his life and was permanently injured. The rope making machinery had just been successfully started, and while watching its operation he stood near the weight box of the counter twist

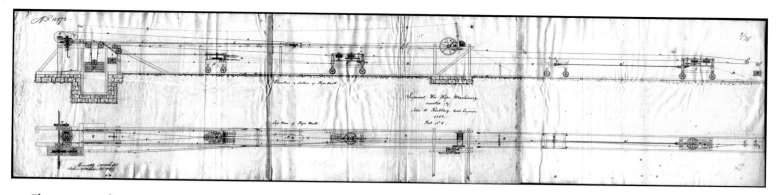

Figure 3.3: John A. Roebling, "Improved Wire Rope Machinery, 1851." RPI John's patent drawing for his Trenton rope walk illustrates his machinery for laying strands and ropes up to 3,030 ft. long, double the length possible on his Saxonburg rope walk.

The rope walks were on the same general type as at Saxonburg, (but) here the top carriages were pulled by endless wire ropes, so that the lay was uniform throughout the rope, a great desideratum." - Washington A. Roebling
This machinery is so perfect that every strand of the wire rope will bear its due proportion of the strain to which the whole shall be subjected. - Trenton State Gazette[6]

machines; unconsciously seizing hold of the wire rope which pulls it up, his left hand was drawn in, into the groove of the rope sheave. His cry of agony was fortunately heard by Swan who happened to stand near the engine; he instantly reversed the machine, and the mangled arm was slowly liberated, and he fell backward into the pit apparently lifeless.

After a time he rallied. Dr. Coleman attended to the crushed wound which had lacerated the end fingers. The fingers remained stiff for life, while the movement of the hand and wrist was much impaired....

After a month he walked about again in the house and in February was able to travel. I went along to help dress him and act as a sort of young nurse, a part I played for two or three years. The mental shock of such an accident was very great, as so much depended at that time on his personal health, and he could not know how his wound would heal....

All flute playing and piano playing (except with his right hand) came to an end, while drawing was more difficult and many actions were seriously impaired; and yet it was after he had been handicapped in this way that he accomplished his greatest engineering works.[7]

Another important event for John took place that December. Charles Ellet had built a footbridge across the Niagara Gorge as the first step in building his suspension bridge. As Washington noted, "By the time this footbridge was completed Ellet was in trouble with his directors….He took possession of the footbridge, allowed no one to cross except on paying tolls to him, fortified both ends, planted cannon, armed his men and defied the militias of both sides, including the sheriff. It took a regiment to dislodge him, but that ended him."

Ellet had been keeping the tolls for himself, even though the footbridge belonged to the International Niagara Bridge Companies that paid for it. By the end of December, the directors of the two companies were fed up and they terminated

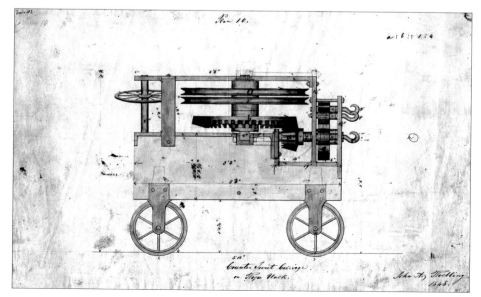

Figure 3.4: John A. Roebling, "Counter Twist Carriage on Rope Walk," 1848. RPI

The driving of the counter-twist machinery for the large rope by an endless rope drive was a remarkably ingenious invention on the part of my father; it has always challenged my admiration…. I think of all the men on the place only my father and Swan understood the operation of the whole system; certainly no outsider ever got it through his head.

- Washington A. Roebling[8]

their contract with Ellet. As David Steinman noted much later, "Now the officials of the Niagara Bridge companies were sorry that they had not dealt with Roebling in the first instance."[9]

With his last two aqueducts nearly completed and recovering from his injury, John mostly stayed in Trenton, as Washington noted: "During 1850 and 1851 my father laid public works to one side, partly because his private business took up his whole time, but mainly because his arm would not permit him to do much work. But this was getting better and he employed every day at drawing, designing and planning various schemes. He always kept his mind on the Cincinnati Bridge, keeping it alive by frequent correspondents with the prominent men." John also began corresponding with the directors of the Niagara Bridge Company.[10]

While recuperating in Trenton, John read a proposal by John Wilkins in the January, 1850, *Journal of Commerce* "to sink a strong wire upon the bottom of the ocean" for a trans-Atlantic telegraph. Samuel Morse had invented and patented an electric telegraph at the Speedwell Iron Works in Morristown, N.J., and he demonstrated it in 1838. Morse and several partners established the first commercial telegraph in 1846 and by 1850 dozens of companies operated telegraphs.

These companies strung their wires between cities along railroad right-of-ways. For long distances such as across rivers, they used wire rope made by John and a few other suppliers. John endorsed Wilkins' concept and he developed a plan for the trans-Atlantic telegraph based on his "experience in the construction of wire cable suspension bridges and aqueducts, and in the manufacture of wire ropes" (Fig. 3.5). He estimated the cost to be $1.3 million (about $54.7 million in 2009) and called upon Congress to support a survey "to obtain a correct profile of the bottom of the Atlantic....in consideration of the great national importance of the project." John apparently did not pursue his proposal, but when Cyrus Field laid the first successful transatlantic cable in 1858, it contained seven parallel wires wrapped like John had suggested.

Intense activity and self reliance

John spent much time studying and testing wires and experimenting to find the best ways to draw them into smaller diameters. As Washington related: "Wire drawing was not such a simple art as it seemed to be. The wire had to be annealed, pickled in acid to remove scale, and coated with rye flour or lime to make it fit for drawing. In none of these processes had my father any experience. They were the results of the English practices of a century or more, resulting more from rule of thumb than from scientific deductions." John also tested his wire ropes against hemp ropes and iron bars to show their superiority and he listed the results for his customers (Fig. 3.6).[11]

When John recovered sufficiently to travel to Neversink and High Falls in New York State to inspect some final work on his aqueducts, he took Washington with him:

Figure 3.5: John A. Roebling, "Transatlantic Telegraph," *New York Journal*, **April 20, 1850. RU**

Who will think of writing a letter?

The application of electricity for transmitting intelligence through the medium of metallic wires, on an extensive scale, is a most beautiful illustration, how matter can be rendered subservient to mind....
My plan proposes to lay down a Sub-Marine Telegraphic Wire Rope....composed of twenty strands of No. 13 or 14 wire, perfectly separated from each other and isolated, so that they will form twenty different and distinct transmitting wires, by which twenty machines can be operated at each end, and twenty messages dispatched at one time.... The revenue of the line will be in proportion to the number of messages, which can be transmitted, and these will be immense. Who will think of writing a letter, and waiting from four to five weeks for an answer, when he can receive the same intelligence in so many minutes? Would this not be worth paying for?.... It is not proposed to twist the wires, but to lay them parallel to each other, similar to the mode of practice in the construction of wire suspension cables.

New York Journal

SATURDAY MORNING, APRIL 20, 1850.

JOURNAL OF COMMERCE.

TRANSATLANTIC TELEGRAPH
JOHN A. ROEBLING, Civil Engineer.
Trenton, N. J., March 1st, 1850.

The application of electricity for transmitting intelligence through the medium of metallic wires, on an extensive scale, is a most beautiful illustration, how matter can be rendered subservient to mind. Electricity appears to be the all pervading and great regulating agency of the universe, actuating all physical as well as all organic and mental operations. As a propelling agent, this subtle fluid causes the rapid transmission of thoughts from the brain through the extensive ramifications of the nervous system; and while animal life and sensation appears to be

PATENT WIRE ROPE of JOHN A. ROEBLING,
Civil Engineer, Trenton, N. J.

MEMORANDUM:

When substituting Wire Rope for Hemp Rope, it is good economy to allow for the former the same weight, which experience has approved of for the latter, per foot run or per yard.

As a general rule, Wire Ropes will last from two to three times as long as Hemp Ropes.

To guard against rust, stationary ropes should be oiled with Linseed Oil, or painted with Red Lead, Spanish Brown, or any other durable paint, or they should be tarred from time to time. Running Rope, when in use, requires no protection. Wire Ropes will run on the same sized sheaves as Hemp Ropes of equal strength, but the greater the diameter the less the wear.

The adhesion of Wire Ropes is the same as that of Hemp Ropes. When giving orders, the diameter of sheaves, kind of machinery, and duty to perform, should be described. The size of wire and rate of twist will be determined accordingly. Wire Ropes should not be coiled or uncoiled like Hemp Ropes, but should be reeled, so as not to affect the twist. The manufactured rope is reeled upon a drum, which, when mounted upon a wooden spindle, between two supports, and made to revolve, will pay off the rope in the same manner in which it received it.

Wire Ropes are substituted for Hemp Ropes and Chains, on Inclined Planes, for Standing Rigging on board of Sailing Vessels and Steamers, Ferry Ropes, in Mines, for all kinds of heavy hoisting, with or without blocks and tackles, in Foundries, for stays on derricks, Cranes and Shears, for staying Chimneys and Masts, for Tillers, Towlines, Lightning Conductors, for Suspension and other Bridges, Crossing Rivers for Telegraph uses, &c, &c.

TERMS CASH.

Figure 3.6: "Patent Wire Rope of John A. Roebling, Civil Engineer, Trenton, N.J.," 1852. RU John favorably compared his wire ropes to hemp ropes and listed a variety of uses.

As a general rule, Wire Ropes will last two to three times as long as Hemp Ropes....on Inclined Planes, for Standing Rigging on board of Sailing Vessels and Steamers, Ferry Ropes, in Mines, for all kinds of heavy hoisting, in Foundries,....for Tillers, Towlines, Lightning Conductors, for Suspension and other Bridges, Crossing Rivers for Telegraph uses, &c, &c.

The shock of his accident had been so great that for a time he could not write with his right hand even, so that I served as a very poor amanuensis, writing from dictation. I was only 12 1/2 years old, with an undeveloped handwriting of my own, the cause of much parental complaint. There were no stenographers in those days. The journey was commenced in very cold weather. I went along to help him....

Having no overcoat or underclothes, I nearly perished from the cold - shall never forget that ride.[12]

Washington also accompanied his father on short trips to Philadelphia, New York and Harrisburg, and once on an inspection of the Morris Canal, which used Roebling wire ropes on all but one of its 22 inclined planes. These trips provided Washington the opportunity to see bridge construction sites, wire rope in use, and his father at work:

The leading feature of my father's character was his intense activity and self reliance. I cannot recall the moment when I saw him idle. He commenced work right after a morning meal, drawing, planning, scheming, always devising something or perfecting an old idea. I am not out of the way when I say that for every bridge that he actually built he made about fifty plans that were never executed. All the drawings he made with his own hands; he could not tolerate a so-called assistant.[13]

Power and influence and dividends

In spite of the injury to his left hand, John's output was remarkable. In 1850 and 1851 he drew plans for several suspension bridges: three over the Schuylkill River in Philadelphia - at Gerard Avenue, at Market Street, and a 500 foot span at Chestnut Street; a span over the Susquehanna River at Clarks Ferry near Harrisburg; another over the Allegheny River at Bayardstown near Pittsburgh; a 500 foot span over the Cumberland River in Nashville; and a 400 foot span railway bridge over the St. Lawrence River near Montreal.

He continued developing plans for the Niagara Bridge and in early 1852 he contracted with the Niagara Bridge Companies to build his bridge for a fixed fee for engineering and supervision. He no longer had to bid on the construction as in his earlier proposals; the bridge company would now pay for all materials and labor. He also invested his money in the project, as Washington noted: "My father was one of the largest stockholders. He made that a rule in all his bridges because it gave him power and influence and dividends."[14]

John began building the Niagara Bridge in the Fall of 1852. As he was securing the stays for the lower deck in May of 1954, news came that a heavy gale had torn apart Charles Ellet's Wheeling Bridge, which he had completed in 1849, plunging the deck and half the cables into the Ohio River. Ellet had beaten John in competitions for the Niagara and Wheeling Bridges in 1847, and now with the Wheeling collapse, John emerged as the country's supreme suspension bridge engineer.

In 1854, John sent Washington, who was then 17 years old, to study engineering at Rensselear Polytechnic Institute in Troy, New York, "at that time the best engineering school in the United States." His second son, Ferdinand, who was 12 years old, attended the Trenton Academy on Academy Street, where Washington had studied since 1851. Concerned about Ferdinand's progress, John wrote to Samuel Backus, the vice principle at the Academy: "I am desirous that my son Ferdinand, who is progressing but very slowly, should receive private instructions. Please let me know what you are willing to devote one hour to each day to teach him privately, and in such branches, as you think most necessary for him."[15]

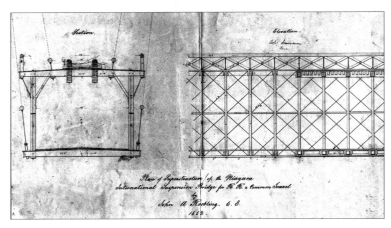

Figure 3.7: John A. Roebling, "Plan of Superstructure of the Niagara International for R.R. and Common Travel, 1852." RPI

The Roebling plan provided for a double decked bridge, 20 feet wide, double track for teams, with a railroad track and sidewalks on the upper floor; the whole supported by four cables at different elevations. The lower bridge and cables would be built first so as to establish a regular highway bridge for at least a year in advance of the railroad track. When the upper bridge was finished it would be connected with an efficient stiffening truss with the lower work.

- Washington A. Roebling [16]

The passage of trains is a great site

Pleased with the progress on the Niagara Bridge, John wrote to Swan: "My Bridge is the admiration of everybody; the directors are delighted. The woodwork goes together in the best manner (Fig. 3.7). The Suspenders require scarcely any adjustment at all." Many skeptics, however, continued to doubt that John's bridge could carry the weight of a locomotive and freight cars, as Washington recalled:[17]

A railroad suspension bridge was looked upon as a novelty at that time and pronounced an impossibility by most foreign engineers. An attempt had been made in England to run a locomotive over an unstiffened chain bridge, resulting of course in lamentable failure. His own bridge directors had implicit faith in the success of the project and never wavered when others derided it....

Sir Robert Stephenson, England's greatest engineer, and builder of the Menai tube (bridge) came to Canada in connection with the Victoria Bridge at Montreal. He paid a visit to Niagara when the work was half done, shook his head and threw cold water on the project. The directors only laughed at him, and in less than two years the laugh was entirely on their side....

The weight of the locomotive of that day was 25 tons, decidedly light when compared with the 90 ton locomotive of the present day. A whole train weighed 300 tons. When the bridge opened many tests were made, confirming the accuracy of the calculations. This was a proud day for my father.[18]

Figure 3.8: Currier & Ives, "The Rail Road Suspension Bridge Near Niagara Falls," 1870. LOC

Whenever necessity calls for new works of art, new expedients will be discovered and adapted to the occasion. It will no longer suit the spirit of the present age to pronounce an undertaking impracticable. Nothing is impracticable which is within the scope of natural laws.

- John A. Roebling, *Niagara Bridge Report*, 1852.

In March of 1855 John wrote to Swan:

Last Sunday I opened the Bridge for the regular passage of trains. The first one was the heaviest freight train that will ever pass, and was made up on purpose to test the bridge. With an Engine of 28 tons we pushed over from Canada to New York twenty double loaded freight cars, making a gross weight of 368 tons; this train very nearly covered the whole length of the floor between the towers....

No vibrations whatever. Less noise and movement than in a common truss bridge....yesterday the first Passenger train from the East with three cars, crowded inside and on top, went over in fine style.

Altogether we passed about twenty trains across within the last 24 hours. No one is afraid to cross. The passage of trains is a great site, worth seeing it.[19]

Weight, girders, trusses and stays

The Niagara Suspension Bridge opened to great acclaim and represented two milestones (Figs. 3.8-9). It was the first bridge to support the enormous weight of railroad trains on suspended wire cables. As John noted in 1862 in his *Report to the Directors of the International Niagara Falls and Suspension Bridge Companies*:

One single observation of the passage of a train over the Niagara Bridge will convince the most skeptical that the practicality of Suspended Railway Bridges, so much doubted heretofore, has been successfully demonstrated.

Figure 3.9: Niagara Suspension Bridge, c1870. NFPL
Carriages and pedestrians entered the lower deck
beneath the upper deck railway at the towers.

Figure 3.10: Niagara Suspension Bridge, Lower Deck. NFPL

The Niagara Bridge was also the first suspension bridge built with a stiffened truss (Figs. 3.7 & 3.10) to resist the uplifting force of high winds, which had destroyed Ellet's Wheeling Bridge and several earlier suspension bridges:

The destruction of the Wheeling bridge was clearly owing to want of stability, and not to want of strength....

There was no provision in the whole structure which could have had an effect in checking vibrations....

What means have been used in the Niagara Bridge, to make it answer for railway traffic? The means employed are Weight, Girders, Trusses and Stays. With these any degree of stiffness can be insured, to resist either the action of trains, or the violence of storms, or even hurricanes. And I will here observe that no Suspension Bridge is safe without some of these appliances.

The catalog of disastrous failures is now large enough to warn against light fabrics, suspended in the defiance of the elements only to be blown down. A number of such fairy creations are still hovering about the country, only waiting for a rough blow to be demolished.[20]

The Niagara Bridge made John famous (see box), and he predicted the building of suspension bridges of great length:

The appearance of the cables is not only pleasing, but their massive proportions are also well calculated to inspire confidence in their strength. The reflecting man, however, will naturally inquire: Is this mass of wire put together so that the different strands bear all alike? Does each individual wire perform its duty, so that when exposed to a great strain, they will resist with united strength to the last? I can answer this question in the affirmative, and can assure you that the tension of these 3640 wires, composing each cable, is so nearly uniform that I feel justified in using the term perfect....

You drive over to suspension bridge and divide your misery between the chances of smashing down two hundred feet in to the river below, and the chances of having a railway-train overhead smashing down onto you. Either possibility is discomforting taken by itself, but, mixed together, they amount in the aggregate to positive unhappiness.

- Samuel Clemens, Niagara Falls, 1871.[21]

What I consider of most importance to the durability of the cables, is the fact that their strength is nearly six times as great as their ordinary working tension, and equally important is the fact that their strength will never be impaired by vibration....

Bridges of half a mile span, for common or Railway travel, may be built, using iron for the cables, with entire safety. But by substituting the best quality of steel wire, we may double the span and afford the same degree of security.[22]

Niagara Falls, September 17, 1860
Mr. John A. Roebling

Sir - I have the honor, on behalf of the Prince of Wales to acknowledge the address which was presented to him this afternoon by yourself and other Directors of the Inter-national Niagara Falls Suspension Bridge Company, and to express to you all his Royal Highness' thanks for so obligingly meeting with Him and accompanying Him across the beautiful work of Engineering skill erected under your superintendence.

The Prince was greatly interested in this grand and useful structure. It's graceful design and remarkable solidity do honor to the ability of the Eminent Man who conceived and completed the work - but it is still more interesting as forming an additional bond of mutual interest and another commercial link between the two great Countries which are connected by its span.

*- Henry Pelham-Clinton, Duke of Newcastle
Secretary of State for the Colonies*

The family mansion is a very spacious three-story brick building covered with stucco work and surrounded with greensward and thick shrubbery. It is unpretentious in style, and was evidently built for use and comfort and not for show....The dimensions are about 35 feet each way and in the rear is a long extension....It contains about 27 rooms, many of which are much larger than the whole of the ground floor of many modern houses. In front is a very handsome iron portico, which harmonizes very admirably with the general appearance of the mansion. Choice engravings, rare and costly paintings, and groups of statuary adorn different rooms, and silently proclaim that the most refined taste had been exercised in their selection. In several of the rooms are engravings of some of Mr. Roebling's great engineering triumphs, such as a fine engraving of the Niagara Falls Suspension Bridge. - Brooklyn Eagle, 1869[23]

As Washington recalled about this period:

John A. Roebling found himself now endowed with a worldwide reputation as a suspension bridge engineer. The fruits therefore came rapidly. Even before the Niagara Bridge was finished he made a contract with the Kentucky Central Railroad to build a railroad suspension bridge over the gorge of the Kentucky River near Nicholasville in central Kentucky.[24]

John designed this bridge with 9 ½ in. diameter cables and a 1,200 ft. span, 50 percent longer than the Niagara Bridge span, and he designed a similar bridge for crossing the Ohio River at Steubenville. He also started working on the design of the Cincinnati Bridge again, but problems in the credit markets worried him, as he wrote to Swan:

You are aware that the prospects of the money market are not brightening, and there is little prospect of Public works being prosecuted with vigor. I cannot calculate on the Kentucky bridge going on....The general derangement in the money market and deficient harvests will stop more works and stop extensive building in the cities....[25]
The Niagara Bridge company has paid me $17,000 (about $600,000 in 2009) already on Wire, Rope & Salary, all this has gone into the Trenton business....My balance sheet of the Trenton business next New Year will be no brag, but very little if any over minus. It would show a loss perhaps without the Bridge orders, which have greatly helped and which have been promptly paid.[26]

Figure 3.12: John A. Roebling,
"Vertical Section Through Furnace Room," c1854. RPI
In John's "very explicit plans, six rooms of 18 feet square each heated pleasantly at one time," he designed a central heating system that drew fresh air into the basement, humidified it, and then distributed it to rooms on the three stories above.

While barely making a profit, John went out of his way to help loyal employees, as he instructed Swan: "Fritz Buttendorf wrote to me and inquires if I would not advance him $100 or guarantee the purchase of $100 of furniture to furnish his home. He wants to marry now and has got no money to do it with. I think it will be safe to trust him. I therefore request you to offer him either the cash in advance or my credit." Three generations of John's heirs followed his practice of assisting loyal employees.[27]

John invested some his Niagara earnings in an Italianate mansion for his family (Figs. 3.11-12), which now included six children, and instructed Swan to build it expeditiously, noting, "I do not wish to make a long job of it, but to get all of it under roof this season." This was the first of many mansions that Roeblings would build in New Jersey and elsewhere.[28]

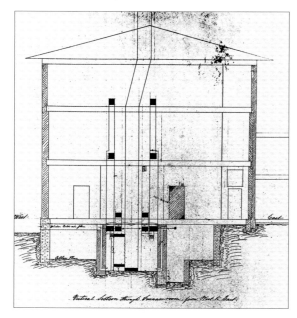

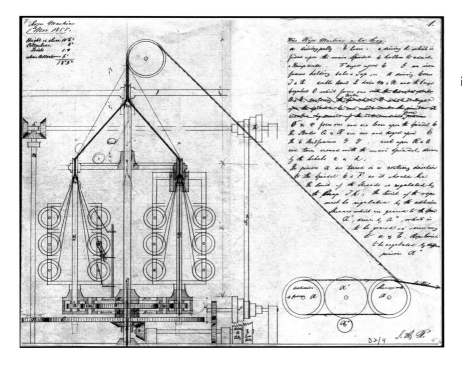

Figure 3.13: John A. Roebling, "Wire Rope Machine, Nov. 1855." RPI
John's design for this 7 x 19 vertical wire rope machine illustrates his mechanical engineering ingenuity, combining six 19 wire stranding operations with one rope laying operation to make "fine rope." He mounted six stranding frames on an iron base called a spider, and each frame held 18 reels that played out wires to a closing head that wound or "laid" them around them around a core, or 19th wire, as the strand was pulled out. The six strands were laid around a core strand, which came up through the central spindle, by another closing head to form a rope. Belts, pulleys, gears, and cogwheels on the 10 1/2-ft. tall steam-powered machine could all be adjusted for different size ropes. The finished rope was rolled around "register" sheaves, or wheels, to measure its length before being rolled onto wooden reels for shipping. Some of John's machines remained in production into the 20th century, and his sons continued developing vertical machines for several decades.

To take the twist out of the wires

While living in his new mansion in 1855, John devoted much time to improving his wire rope production. His complicated outdoor rope walk was difficult to operate, couldn't be used in bad weather, and could only make ropes about 3,000 feet in length. In 1847, a Trenton inventor named Edward S. Townsend had patented a small vertical machine for twisting wires or strands from four bobbins positioned around a spindle into cords or ropes. By soldering the ends of wires together, Townsend could make extra long cords or ropes for telegraph companies and other businesses that needed long lengths. John needed to produce longer ropes to stay ahead of his competition, and in one of his notebooks he cited "machinery at Camden for making Telegraph Cords & Ropes capable of making 6 miles of 3, 4, or 7 ply cord per day. Each spool of Wire revolves in its frame so as to avoid twist."[29]

John expanded upon this vertical concept for twisting or "laying" wires around a core wire to make strand, or laying strands around a core strand to make ropes. He designed an elaborate vertical Rope Machine (Fig. 3.13) that combined

strand and rope making to produce 7 x 19 ropes consisting of six 19 wire strands laid around a 19 wire core strand core. John designed all the components of this machine in detailed drawings, and over the next several years he designed many additional vertical machines to make various types of strands and ropes. To associate his wire rope with his reputation as the leading suspension bridge engineer, John put out a circular prominently featuring the Niagara Suspension Bridge (Fig. 3.14).

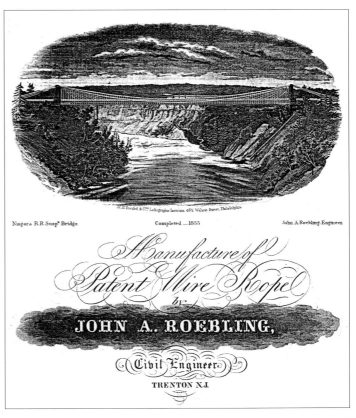

Figure 3.14: *Manufacture of Patent Wire Rope by John A. Roebling, Civil Engineer, Trenton N.J.* **RPI**
An astute businessman, Roebling marketed his wire rope with circulars prominently displaying the Niagara Suspension Bridge. In a letter to Swan, he wrote:
Whenever you address a new man, always send him one or two circulars - if living in a large industrious place like Rochester and New York send him three or four copies, this is the cheapest and best mode of advertising and making our rope known through the country."[30]

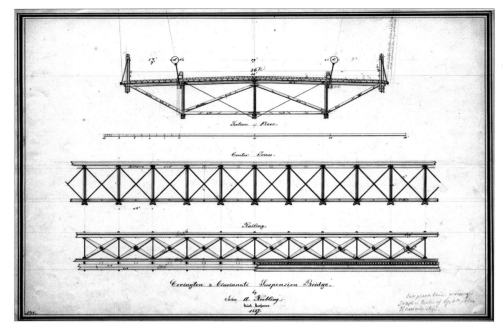

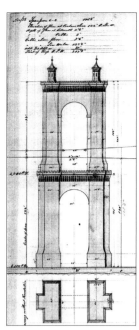

Figure 3.15 (left): John A. Roebling, "Cincinnati & Covington Suspension Bridge," 1856. RPI John's early design for the deck showed a central carriageway with wide pedestrian walkways outside the suspender ropes.

Figure 3.16 (right): John A. Roebling, Cincinnati-Covington Bridge, 1856. RPI John intitally designed the towers with crenellations like a castle.

Railroad construction boomed, as Washington recalled:

The great era of railroad building was in full swing. My father took the greatest interest in their development. He was a member of the national convention held in Philadelphia for building the Pacific Railroad....

His work at planning and designing went on all day long. He never took a rest or vacation. Among other works he made plans and estimates for a high-level (railroad) suspension bridge across the Hudson at Albany. This was never built, more on account of cost than feasibility. Truss bridges on piers were already driving out all short span suspension bridges.[31]

In Cincinnati, business and political leaders resolved to start the long-awaited suspension bridge over the Ohio River, and the State legislature approved a new charter for the bridge with a span of 1,057 feet. John developed the designs and specifications for the deck and the towers and workers began building the towers in 1856 (Figs. 3.15-17).

As a work of engineering the bridge will be without a rival

In 1856, New York businessmen approached John about a bridge over the East River across Blackwell's island to link Manhattan and Queens. John sketched a plan for them showing a narrow 22 ft. wide wagon and pedestrian bridge with 800 ft. spans over each of the East River channels and a 500 ft. cantilevered middle section over the island.

In early 1857, he decided that a bridge further downriver linking Manhattan and Brooklyn would be more financially feasible, and he developed alternate designs for 322 ft. high

towers for this "Brooklyn Bridge" (Figs. 3.18-19). John wrote a letter to his friend Abram Hewitt, Peter Cooper's son-in-law and a partner in their Trenton Iron Company, stating the feasibility of building a bridge that would "bring the City of New York within a five minute ride of the City Hall of Brooklyn." As he noted to Hewitt:

The importance of a permanent connection between Brooklyn and New York appears to be strongly felt just now. This feeling will continue to ebb and flow, as the necessity of the case becomes more or less urgent....

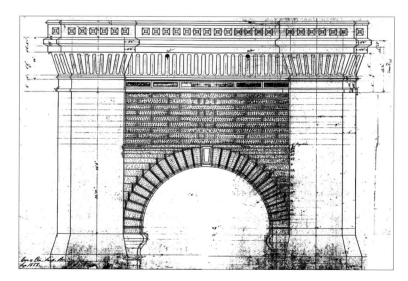

Figure 3.17: John A. Roebling, *Cincinnati & Covington Suspension Bridge*, September, 1858. RPI John later designed the towers as triumphal arches. Masons built the towers to the height of the roadway, about 80 ft. above the river level, but had to stop when the Bridge Company directors couldn't raise any more money.

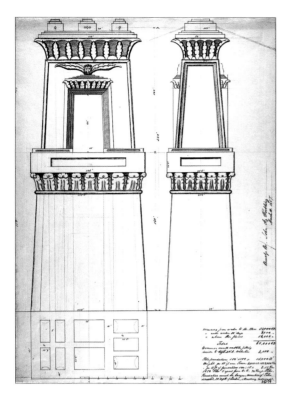

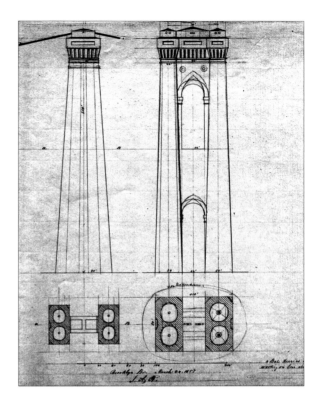

Figure 3.18 (left): John A. Roebling, "Brooklyn Br., March 10, 1957." RPI John first designed 322 ft. tall bridge towers in an Egyptian Revival Style, which he had also used in an early drawing of the towers for the Cincinnati-Covington Bridge. These massive portals would have associated his bridge with the great monuments of ancient Egypt.

Figure 3. 19 (right): John A. Roebling, "Brooklyn Br., March 24, 1857." RPI John subsequently designed towers with semi-circular and Gothic variations for the arches.

That in the course of time such a structure will be wanted and erected, irrespective of cost, on a magnificent scale, there can be no doubt. Such a work is not only perfectly practicable, but will also become absolutely necessary. Its erection is only a question of time.[32]

Hewitt wrote back, "I cannot see why it is not a perfectly feasible plan," and sent John's letter to the *Journal of Commerce*, which published it on January 22, 1857, with the comment:

The following communication, on the subject of a bridge from New York to Brooklyn is from a gentleman well known as the greatest living authority on the subject of Suspension Bridges, and as he never expresses an opinion or makes statements without due deliberation, reliance can be placed on the estimate of costs, as well as upon the feasibility of the project.

Two months later, John wrote to the editor of the *New York Herald Tribune* about his proposed "Bridge Over the East River Between New York and Brooklyn:"

The plan in its general features proposes a wire suspension bridge crossing the East River by one single span at such an elevation as will not impede the navigation....As a work of engineering the bridge will be without a rival. It will form one of the grandest and most attractive features of the two sister cities. The tops of the towers, elevated over 300 feet, would afford the best opportunity for putting up Government lights, observatories, lookouts, &c.[33]

As the Panic of 1857 strained some banks, John directed Swan to keep their men employed with funds from specific banks that remained solvent:

To make good use of Philadelphia money in Jersey, you should go to Philadelphia one day and purchase with Philadelphia money a lot of provisions, say $2-$300 worth, say 10 barrels to 20 barrels of flour, some bacon, ham, coffee, sugar, molasses, rice etc. for our own use, and your household and all the hands in our employment.

Let all the hands understand, that they will have to take one half of their wages in provisions and groceries and coal, which will be weighed off and sold, once a week with a small profit, enough to cover all expenses and loss by waste....

Say to Mrs. Roebling that she must not buy any more provisions and groceries in Trenton – all must come from Philadelphia at wholesale prices, bought for bills of the Philadelphia bank.

This will not only be a Saving all around, but also a great Service to our hands. We may be able by this means, to employ our old good hands all winter and make rope ahead, and also wire.[34]

While John worried to Swan that: "There will be a wholesome reduction of Credit throughout the Country," he also had his eye on new business: "I wish you would prepare a handsome set of samples for the Navy Department, set into a mahogany frame." The Navy Department would eventually purchase large amounts of Roebling rigging and hoisting ropes for its ships.[35]

Figure 3.20: Washington A. Roebling, age 19, at Rensselear Polytechnic Institute, Troy, N.Y., 1856. RPI

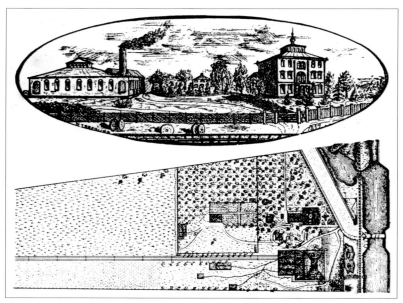

Figure 3.21: Washington A. Roebling, John A. Roebling house and factory in Trenton, 1857. HS

On each side of the rope walk was some arable land which was carefully cultivated and crops of all kinds were raised.... There was a large garden, a fine orchard, barn, outhouses, icehouse, &c. Ferdinand even raised flowers for sale. It was this small flower business that also interested Charles, and led to his subsequent expansion into an orchid fancier.... All disappeared in course of time as the irresistible desire for expansion filled up acre after acre with buildings.

– Washington A. Roebling[37]

In the spring of 1857, Washington completed his thesis project – "Design for a Suspension Aqueduct" – and was graduated from Rensselear Polytechnic Institute (Fig. 3.20). He returned home to Trenton, sketched the family house and garden and the adjacent wire rope factory on the canal (Fig. 3.21), and went to work in the factory for Sawn:

> *As I was not especially engaged in anything, I learned the mysteries of rope making under Swan....*
>
> *The skies were bright and prospects lovely. Then came the unexpected, which always happens. The great bank panic of 1857 set in, when all banks but one suspended specie payments. Work on the Cincinnati bridge stopped for an indefinite period, most people thought forever....none of the stockholders could pay their assessments, even the city of Covington could not do so and quit.*[36]

Fortunately for John, Pittsburgh officials arranged financing for a new Allegheny Bridge, thanks to the reliable income from tolls on the old wooden bridge. As Washington recalled:

> *My father was very much pleased to receive the position of Engineer of the Allegheny Bridge at Pittsburgh. This was the oldest bridge in the that part of the West, having been built in 1804 to 7, with a provision in its charter that it should be made free at the end of fifty years, provided, that at the end of that time it should not be deemed to build a new bridge in its place. Of course it was so deemed. It was a highway bridge, double roadway and two sidewalks, the old bridge being built with wooden arches and covered.*

> *My father's reputation in Pittsburgh was great as a bridge builder. He had lived there much of his life and kept his acquaintance among the best citizens of the town. He had a faculty of forming valuable connections and strong friendships with the important people, which all helped him in a business way. It was therefore natural that he should be put in charge of this work.*
>
> *He always said, though, that he considered this structure a small affair alongside of the Niagara or the Cincinnati.*[38]

In the spring of 1858, John put Washington to work on the Allegheny Bridge as his assistant engineer and soon wrote to Swan: "Washington is doing very well here." With iron production improvements, John was able to design much of the Allegheny Bridge in iron (Figs. 3.22-25) in contrast to the stone towers and wooden trusses at Niagara. That summer he corresponded frequently with Swan about iron and steel:

> *Respecting the great improvements in the manufacture of Wire in England, by which the Strength is doubled....this Wire is made of good iron in the usual way, and converted into Steel Wire afterwards - it is Steel Wire, hence its great strength. I have no longer doubt, that this improvement will <u>revolutionize</u> the whole Wire Rope business and if our*

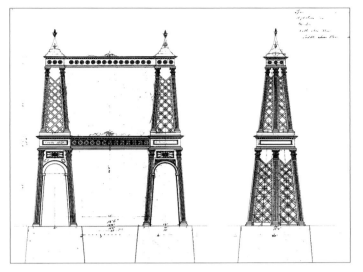

Figure 3.22: John A. Roebling, early study for the Allegheny Suspension Bridge towers, 1857. RPI

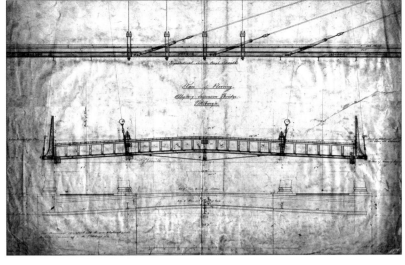

Figure 3.23: John A. Roebling, "Plan of Flooring, Allegheny Suspension Bridge, Pittsburgh, 1858." RPI

This is the first of Mr. Roebling's bridges in which iron beams were used, both for floor beams and trusses. The towers were made of cast iron columns, of large size, difficult to cast and to erect on the narrow piers. - Washington A. Roebling [41]

businesses is to continue successfully we will have this fall to work at once to experiment and if possible manufacture the same kind of wire.[39]

Mindful of the hot conditions at the factory that summer, John wrote to Swan: "I have no doubt about the temperature in that Sweating Box where the new machine is. I advise you to get it plastered with a good rough coat, this will make a great difference….and perhaps another window or openings at both sides….I think it advisable to give our hands a long 4th July to enjoy themselves during the dog days."[40]

In the Fall of 1858, John sent 16-year old Ferdinand to Columbian College in Washington, DC, which in 1904 became George Washington University. Ferdinand wrote to Washington: "I am studying Algebra, Trigonometry, Geometry, and Chemistry. We are going to commence Surveying pretty soon." He also wrote about collecting minerals for Washington, playing chess, and flowers that he was growing. Unsatisfied with "this one horse college," he switched in 1860 to the Polytechnic College of Philadelphia, where he wrote to John about studying mechanics, mineralogy and trigonometry.[42]

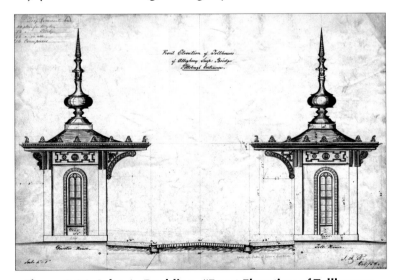

Figure 3.24: John A. Roebling, "Front Elevation of Tollhouses, Allegheny Suspension Bridge, Pittsburgh Entrance, 1859." RPI

Figure 3.25: Allegheny Suspension Bridge c1880. RPI Roebling designed the tollhouses and towers to stand out.

When entirely completed this Bridge will make a splendid appearance; Gilded domes on the Towers & well shaped spire on the Tollhouses, with Cornishes projecting 10' 6" so as to cover sidewalks….We are now finishing Tollhouses and the ornamental parts of the Work, which is a slow business. The bridge will be beautiful. - John A. Roebling[43]

In his second year of college, Ferdinand lived at home and took the train to Philadelphia. In a letter to John he wrote:

Having no lecture to write out tonight I will do the next best thing; that is write to you….

I am getting along pretty well now in my studies; I pay more attention to chemistry than to the other studies. I stay down 2 days every week, and work in the laboratory….

I also have a number of things here, which Washington left, so that I can work out many of the tests at home….

I pruned all of the new grapes back to one eye. I made slips of the cuttings which I planted. I guess most of them will take root. Everything about the place looks fine and is in good order.[44]

Ferdinand, Washington and Charles all developed an interest in horticulture by helping the gardener their father employed to take care of the gardens and orchard behind his house. Ferdinand completed his studies at the Polytechnic College of Philadelphia with a specialty in chemistry. While he lived at home during his college studies, he helped Swan at the mill and learned the wire rope business. Washington learned bridge construction details with his father, the master builder, on the Allegheny Bridge, as he recalled:

Outside the masonry no work was done by contract. We did it ourselves; a blacksmith shop was built, machine shop and carpenter shop. All the erection was done by day's work. Nowadays an engineer lets out the work either as a whole or in part to others, who can do it much better than he can. To do it all yourself requires a hundredfold the labor.

Mr. Roebling made all contracts for materials, hired men, paid them and was there all day long. Being a director in the company he took part in the larger financing. Having

absolute control of everything, he was saved all the friction which results from divided authority. This is a position he endeavored to establish in all his works….

On this bridge I first saw actual cable-making and learned something about it under David Rhule….A temporary footbridge was built to accommodate travel and was used in cable-making.

The middle cables (10 inches diameter) were made first, the main floor suspended and foot travel started; then the outer small cables were constructed, which supported the outer ends of the floor beams….

The bridge opened to light travel in 1859….

Much of his time was taken up in corresponding about new projects, all of which he attended to himself. After a bridge was finished, time was lost waiting for another one and he found it the better plan to have the new one started before the old one was finished….He lost no opportunity to promote the resumption of work on the Kentucky Bridge and the Cincinnati….

The winter of 1859 found us both at home. The troublesome political condition which preceded the rebellion excited him very much, as he had but little sympathy with the South. Occasionally he had little pamphlets of his own printed on the situation for private or semi-public distribution.

The month of January was always devoted to financial matters. He now devoted much needed time to the rope business, by designing rope machinery which would do away with the long rope walk.[45]

With his success in substituting iron for wood in bridge trusses, John developed designs for building rail road cars of iron instead of wood (Figs. 3.26-27). When he and Washington returned to Pittsburgh in early 1860 to "finish Tollhouses

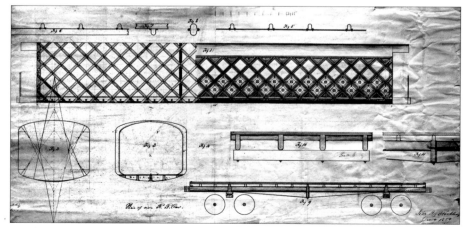 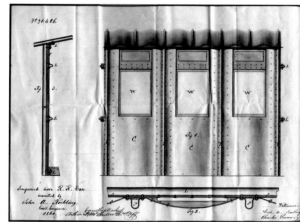

Figure 3.26: John A. Roebling, "Plan of new R.R. Car, 1859." RPI John designed and patented a durable railroad car made of iron.

Figure 3.27: John A. Roebling, "Improved Iron R.R. Car, 1860." RPI

My father invented and patented a system of iron pressed cars, now called steel pressed cars, working out all the details, but they were ahead of the times; iron at that time could not compete with wood, and he sold his patents without engaging in the manufactory to any extent. - Washington A. Roebling[46]

**Figure 3.28: John A. Roebling,
"Susp. Br. across the Channel between Dover
& Calais 19 miles, Jan 25, 1861." RU**
In response to a French engineer's proposal in 1857
to build a tunnel under the English Channel,
John sketched out a plan for building a
suspension bridge across the Channel.

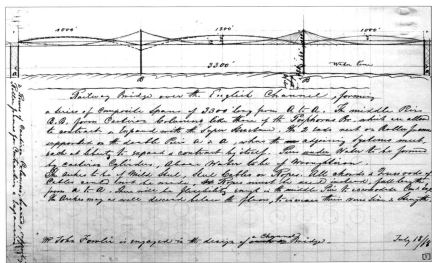

**Figure 3.29: John A. Roebling,
"Railway Bridge over the English Channel, July 18, 1868." RU**
After a second French engineer proposed a channel tunnel in 1865,
John returned to his original concept and sketched a suspension bridge
across the channel, with "a series of composite spans of 3,300 feet long"
supported by stone piers and iron columns in between the piers.
His design combined suspension cables with parabolic arches,
a construction method that he continued to study.

> *The project of a Tunnel is entertained by the French but deserves no support. The cost of such a work can scarcely be estimated, and when done, who will go through a tunnel 19 miles long, if he can avoid it? A suspension bridge on the other hand is perfectly practicable and can be put up at such a cost, as will prove a good investment. Make Spans about one half mile long, use Steel wire for the Cables.*
>
> - John A. Roebling

and the ornamental parts of the work" on the Allegheny Bridge, John again wrote to Swan about producing steel wire from scrap steel, a requirement that his sons would have to face some four decades later to remain competitive:[47]

*We will have to prepare for working Steel in the future....
On leaving Trenton I met Mr. Abbot (of Peter Cooper's Trenton Iron Company) on the Cars and he told me that they are making a Superior Cast Steel by remelting Scrap steel, which they buy at 2 ½ to 3 cents per pound. The Converting and remanufacture cost them 2 cents per pound for a total of 4 ½ to 5 cents, and they sell it for 14 cents per pound - pretty good profit.*

Their melter is an Englishman, imported by Charles Hewitt, who understands his business, and by thoroughly selecting & mixing & slow converting will invariably produce a better quality than the Scrap. Their scraps are principally old files and Tools. Abbot says they can get enough of it.

Now this would certainly be the easiest and cheapest way of getting steel for wire. All the investment would be a few melting pots, a hammer & a freshly imported John Bull or maybe a German melter, if one could be had. We must keep this in mind, but first we must try to get at the proper working of Steel, after the Steel is made.[48]

At home in the winter of 1860-61, John studied a proposal that a French engineer had presented to Napoleon III in 1857 to build a rail road tunnel under the English Channel. John dismissed the tunnel as unsupportable and outlined a plan to build a suspension bridge, which he considered "perfectly practicable" (Fig. 3.28).

Seven years later, when other proposals came forth to cross the channel, he again studied the feasibility of a suspension bridge, this time incorporating parabolic arches in conjunction with suspension cables (Fig. 3.29).

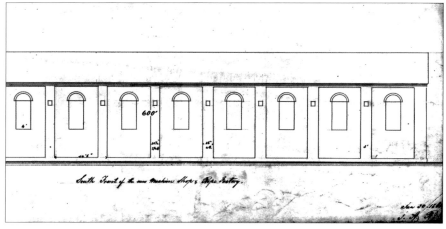

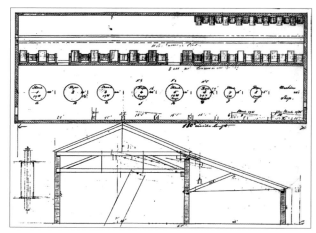

Figure 3.30: John A. Roebling,
"South Front of the new Machine Shop & Rope Factory, 1860." RPI

Figure 3.31: John A. Roebling,
Plan of Machine Shop and Rope Factory, c. 1861. RPI.

John designed his new 180 ft. by 66 ft. rope factory for four vertical and two horizontal stranding machines, and four vertical rope machines in the main section, and a "Rope House" in the rear for winding strand and rope onto reels.

Many stirring events

As the economy recovered, John designed a new Machine Shop and Rope Factory to finally replace his 1849 rope walk (Figs. 3.30-31). He also designed all the complicated machines for it (Figs. 3.32-33).

As the election of Abraham Lincoln and other events leading up to the Civil War unfolded, John, Washington and Ferdinand were all working at the wire rope works in Trenton. As Washington recalled:

In 1860 to 1861 public affairs engrossed the attention of everyone....As the excitement in public affairs increased my father's excitement at home increased. He constantly lamented that his health and age would prevent him from taking an active part in the conflict.

Had he been a little younger he would have entered the army he said and become its commander-in-chief in a year!

One day, about Fort Sumter time, we were eating dinner when my father suddenly remarked to me, 'Washington, you have kicked your legs under my table long enough, now you clear out this minute!'

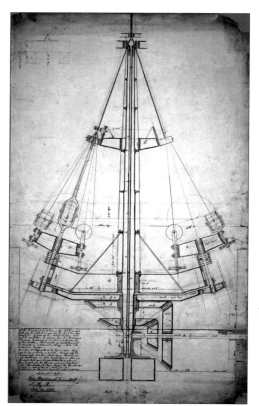

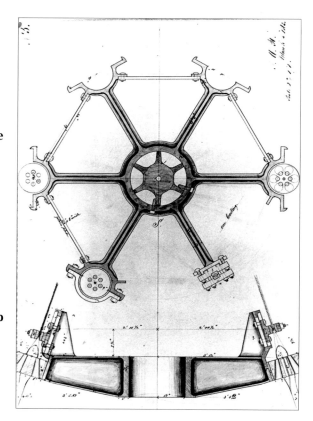

Figure 3.32 (left):
John A. Roebling, "Rope Machine No. 5 7 x 7, Feb. 14, 1863." RPI. John's meticulous drawing shows his mechanical engineering and drafting skills. The machine drew wire from seven spools mounted on the outer edge of the lower armature, known as a spider, to the closing heads on the outer edge of the upper spider to form six strands. The machine then closed the six strands around a central strand that came up through the hollow spindle to form a 7 x 7 wire rope at the closing head at the top.

Figure 3.33 (right):
John A. Roebling, Spider for No. 5 Rope Machine, Mar. 5, 1863. RPI. This upper spider, 2/3 of the way up the spindle (left), held six closing heads for laying six wires around central wires to form six strands, which were then layed around the central strand to form the 7 x 7 wire rope at the top (left).

A potato that I was guiding to my mouth fell on the plate, I got up, put on my hat and walked out. Then I went over to Mr. Swan, our superintendent, borrowed a few dollars from him, I being penniless, then took the next train to New York. On the way I picked up a paper and saw that the 9th New York State Regiment needed a few more men before leaving for the war. I started for their armory, was sworn in that evening, slept on the floor and had something to eat, including a potato.

Two weeks later we went to the war to Washington, and curiously enough passed down the Bordentown branch (of the railroad), close by my home (no longer so) which looked silent and deserted. Many stirring events passed before I saw it again.[49]

John was eager for his eldest son to join the war effort to help fight the south to abolish slavery. When Fort Sumter fell on April 13, President Lincoln called for a states' militia force of 75,000, and Washington joined the New Jersey State Militia to protect Trenton on April 16. After two months of guard duty, he joined the 9th New York Regiment. He served with an artillery brigade in Maryland and Virginia, where he witnessed the battle of the Monitor and the Merrimack.

In Trenton, John sketched plans of a "Shotproof War Steamer and Ram," and sent them to the U.S. Navy (Fig. 3.34). To support the Union cause, he bought $100,000 in U.S. bonds (about $3.7 million in 2009) and solicited others to so as well.

In 1862, Laura Roebling, John's second child and oldest daughter, married Anton Gottlieb Methfessel, a German immigrant and teacher who founded the Methfessel Institute on Staten Island. John sent his third son, 12-year-old Charles, to live with the Methfessels and to study at the institute, and he soon wrote to his father: "I am now studying geometry and I need a compass box to draw angles and other figures....Mr. Methfessel made a plan for money, he said that I should get $1 fore perfect 80 cts fore good, 60 cts fore putty good 40 cts for middle 20 cts for bad, and 0 cts for failure, that is if you are willing to do it. I got good for this week." Methfessel later merged his institute with the Staten Island Academy and Latin School, which is now the Staten Island Academy.[50]

Washington was promoted to Lieutenant in 1862, and that spring, as he recalled:

After the Merrimack first came out, the army in Washington was terribly frightened; they saw the capital already bombarded by her. So the first idea was to barricade the Potomac some distance below.

Two plans were proposed – one, to load a number of canal boats with stone and sink them in the channel. Another, to support a lot of chain or big wire ropes on buoyant logs and

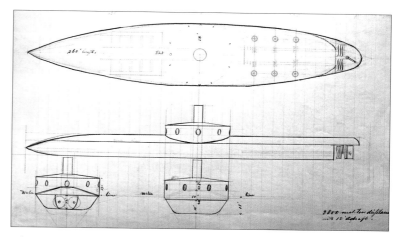

Figure 3.34: John A. Roebling, Shotproof War Steamer and Ram, 1861. RU John sent his drawings for a steam ram to the U.S. Navy headquarters in Washington.

anchor them to each shore. Large chains would have taken too long to make, so General Montgomery Meigs (the Army Quartermaster) telegraphed to Trenton for John A. Roebling to come down and make the necessary arrangements to blockade with wire ropes. He came and got the order....

While he was consulting with General Meigs, the General stated that light military suspension bridges would be a good thing for the army to have. My father thought so too, mentioning at the same time that he had a son in the army with sufficient technical experience to put them up....

Arriving in Washington, I was ordered to write a book on military suspension bridges, which I did in three weeks.[51]

Lt. Roebling wrote home about this book, *Construction of Military Suspension Bridges*:

The written instructions are being printed very nicely. The drawings are being engraved in Philadelphia. I have received several proof sheets already for correction. The engraving is very well done - 500 copies are to be struck off. I wish they were done; it would save me a heap of trouble and explaining to folks.[52]

General Meigs assigned Lt. Roebling to build a suspension bridge near Fredericksburg, Virginia, in replace of a bridge the Confederates had destroyed. With little in the way of materials or skilled labor, Washington erected a 1,000 ft. long bridge on fourteen piers from the old bridge, using wire ropes supplied by his father. As he later recalled:

It was in use over a month. When the place was evacuated General Burnside blew up the Anchorage, precipitating the bridge and cables into the river. The rebels later fished them out and used them as ferry ropes down south....

One never knows at what moment military exigencies may compel the abandonment of such structures.[53]

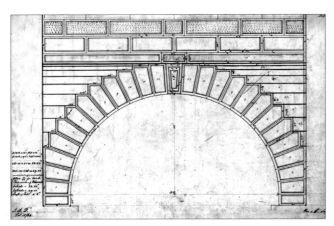

John A. Roebling, Cincinnati-Covington Bridge, 1864. RPI Figure 3.35 (left): Tower Arch; Figure 3.36 (right): Deck Railing.

In early 1863, as Washington recalled, "I was turned over to General G. K. Warren, Chief Topographical Engineer of the Army, with whom I contracted a lasting friendship and with whom I served during the remainder of the war." Swan wrote to Washington that his father had "gone to Cincinnati on bridge business" (Figs. 3.35-36). As Washington explained:[54]

The Cincinnati suspension bridge had been commenced in 1856 and 1857 and then held up for the time being. In the spring of 1863, seven years later, the artificial prosperity induced by the war had struck in at Cincinnati.

This city was the gateway to the Southwestern army operations through Kentucky, Tennessee and states south of it. The army traffic through it was exceedingly large. There was no permanent bridge of any kind over the Ohio, but two pontoon bridges had been laid over the river, and even these, supplemented by two steam ferries, were inadequate to handle the traffic.

So people thought, why not finish the great suspension bridge commenced so auspiciously seven years before?

Public meetings were held, new enthusiasm created; the bridge company was reorganized, a preferred stock created, the old stock practically wiped out, new capitalists with heavy real estate holdings in Covington, Ky., interested them selves in it; presently word was sent to Trenton for Mr. Roebling to come on at once to resume work, which he did....

That summer's work was a heavy burden on my father's shoulders because everything had to be created anew....An engineer had to design and execute everything himself, which made engineering so much harder in those days. Inclined planes were built from the water's edge to deliver stone at the anchorages....new derricks were built for the towers, with horizontal booms on which ran heavy weights to balance the stone....The work made good progress in 1863 and 1964.... The members of the bridge company were well satisfied.[55]

After Lt. Roebling (Fig. 3.37) helped General Warren secure Little Round Top at Gettysburg, the General wrote:

Lieut. W.A. Roebling's services to me are invaluable and by his ability and exertions he has won the promotion....

Lt. Roebling built the wire suspension bridge over the Shenandoah, and has just repaired serious damage done to it by our troops on evacuating Harpers Ferry, a delicate operation which no one but an expert in this kind of bridge could have safely performed.[56]

Washington recalled that: "The Shenandoah suspension bridge consisted of three spans, at 250 or 275 ft. each....The bridge was double tracked with three wire rope cables and wire rope suspenders." In early 1864, Washington organized the 2nd Army Corps' officers ball for General Warren and wrote on February 28 to his sister, Elvira, about this big event:[57]

We had the grand 2nd Corps Ball, the most successful ball ever given by any army or by anybody....At least 150 ladies graced the assemblage, from all quarters of the Union and at least 300 Gentleman from General Meade down to myself. I received numerous congratulations on the success of everything....

The most prominent ladies of Washington were present, from Miss Hamlin, Kate Chase and the Misses Hale down, last but not least Miss Emily Warren (Fig. 3.38), sister of the General, who came especially from West Point to attend the ball; it was the first time I ever saw her and am very much of the opinion that she has captured your brother Washy's heart at last. It was a real attack in force, it came without any warning or any previous realization on my part of such an occurrence taking place, and it was therefore all the more successful and I assure you that it gives me the greatest pleasure to say that I have succumbed.

On March 5, he wrote to Elvira:

I don't suppose you can imagine the splendid opportunities we have for courting each other; the General went away to Baltimore leaving her in my entire charge and care and I assure you I perform the duties to our mutual satisfaction.

Figure 3.37 (left):
Washington A. Roebling, c1864. RPI
Washington was commissioned
a Major and Aide-de-Camp to
Major General Gouverneur K. Warren
on May 26, 1864, his 27th birthday.

Figure 3.38 (right):
Emily Warren Roebling, c1865. RPI
Born in 1843 in Cold Springs, New York,
the eleventh of twelve children,
Emily attended the Georgetown Visitation
Preparatory School in Washington, D.C.

Washington and Emily met in February,
1864, in Culpeper, Virginia at the 2nd Army
Corps Ball, which Lt. Washington organized
for General Warren, Emily's older brother.
They became engaged in March, 1864,
and they married on January 18, 1865.

You are my guiding star

Lt. Washington A. Roebling
Sunday evening, March 27, 1864
To Miss Emily Warren, Cold Spring, New York,

Think about me dear Emmie when you go to sleep tonight; I have before my mind's eye a vivid picture of a certain young lady as she stood in the parlor with a sort of half disconsolate air, watching a young man putting on his gloves and being watched by a certain married lady who thereby spoiled the proper demonstration of affection due to the occasion.

Lt. Washington A. Roebling, March 30, 1864
To Miss Emily Warren,

Oh how I wish I had just one of those sweet kisses that you can give; my lips have fully recovered from your attacks and are in excellent fighting trim to receive you.

Lt. Washington A. Roebling, April 1, 1864
To Miss Emily Warren,

I notice now that the oftener I write the more I want to write and then your dear letters only add fuel to the flames. I have often wondered how two lovers can be true to each other if they don't know how to write, they must believe in each other with a very blind faith....

You know, darling, that your presence always made me feel so good, a kind of contented feeling pervaded me if you were only near me, it was not necessary to say anything, perfect silence was as much companionship as the liveliest chatter; and that state of mind only exists when there is a perfect accordance between two souls; such I feel is the case with us, isn't it with you dear Emmie?

It is needless to put the interrogation because I would bet my life you will say yes....

My happiest hour in the day is in the morning when I first awake; I turn over then on my face and just lie for about an hour half dozing half dreaming and vainly trying all the while to cheat myself into the belief that you are near me, oh my! If you only were, it makes me sad to find nothing but a great big pillow....

One thing is certain however that I now only look upon other girls with an eye of comparison to see wherein you excel them; not one possesses that amiability, those mouth, them tooths, that eyes, in fine no one loves me as you do, that's the real secret is it not dear fun aside?

Lt. Washington A. Roebling
Saturday night, April 2, 1864
To Miss Emily Warren,

Don't it strike you that we are remarkably alike in our sentiments - if you write anything I am sure to have written the same thing that same evening - don't you think so?

Pray don't fail me, darling....I put my faith in you; you are my guiding star....

Goodnight sweet guardian angel of my existence - six years ago I dreamt three nights in succession of a veiled lady, who the spirit of my dreams told me would be my helpmate during life; the face I did not see, but months passed away before the impression wore off. Need I say that I feel more and more convinced that you are the one thus foreshadowed....

Kiss me good night before I go to bed and give me one embrace, darling - Your Wash.

On March 30, 1864, John wrote to Washington from Cincinnati where he was working on the big bridge:

My Dear Washington,

Your communication of the 25th came to hand last night, and I hasten to reply. The news of your engagement has not taken me by surprise, because I had previously received a hint from Elvira in that direction. I take it for granted, that love is the motive, which actuates you, because a matrimonial union without love is no better than suicide. I also take it for granted, that the lady of your choice is deserving of your attachment. These two points being settled, there stands nothing more in your way except the rebellion and the chances of war.

These contingencies having all passed away, you and your young bride, as you know beforehand, will be welcome at the paternal house in Trenton. Our house will always be open to you and yours, and if there's not enough room, a new one can be built on adjoining ground, or one can be rented.

As to your future support, you are fully aware, that the business at Trenton is now suffering for want of superintendence, and that no increase or enlargement can be thought of without additional help. Of course I do not want to engage strangers, and it is you therefore, who is expected to step in and help forwarding the interests of the family as well as yourself individually.

For your services you will be either entitled to a sufficient salary or per centage or both, as may be agreed on between us. You and Ferdy know, the whole business will be one day your own, including your younger brothers.

If on the other hand the Bridge here should proceed satisfactorily I shall like to have your assistance during the construction of the Cables and Superstructure, provided you can be spared from Trenton. Perhaps it can be so arranged, that you spend some time here and some in Trenton, as may be most needful and convenient.

Should you be in want of money at any time, let me know. I conclude with the request, that you will assure your young bride of my most affectionate regards beforehand, and before I shall have the pleasure of making her personal acquaintance.

Your affectionate father, John A. Roebling.

Amidst the family's joy in Washington's engagement, Johanna Roebling's health had been declining. On April 25, 1864, John wrote to Swan from Covington about her condition: "I fear....that her protracted weakness and illness is only the approach to her final dissolution. This thought is gloomy and depressing. I am anxious to see her health restored and her life spared for awhile."

John asked Swan to have her doctor send him a diagnosis in writing so that he could consult with three distinguished physicians he knew in Cincinnati. That summer, Washington wrote to Emily from Virginia that his mother, who was born in Germany, had not had the advantage of a good education and had only learned to speak English comfortably within the last fifteen years. On the other hand, he wrote:

My father has enjoyed the best education that could be given in his days - wherever he is he always moves in the first society of the place and although he acquired the English language after coming to this country, he is as seldom taken for a foreigner as I am.[58]

In October, Washington came home to Trenton on leave and found his mother in poor condition: "She is almost too weak to move and suffers a great deal." When he returned to camp, he reported to Emily:

Father arrived about three hours before I left and of course had not expected to find me at home. He wants to know for certain whether I can leave the service the latter part of December so that he can make his arrangements to have me appointed assistant engineer in time to go out with him next spring.

Everything has progressed finally this year in Cincinnati, the work is much farther advanced than I had any idea of, and father is proud of his work which he says will be the finest bridge in the world.[59]

During his stay in Trenton, John went to New York, and later reported to Washington:

I met Miss Emily and she accompanied me to Trenton, where she remained two days. I like her very much and have not the least bit doubt that your union with her will be a happy one.[60]

Johanna Herting Roebling passed away at the age of 48 in November, 1864, and John later wrote in the family bible:

Of those angels in human form, who are blessing this Earth in their unselfish love and devotion, this dear departed wife was one.

She never thought of herself, she only thought of others. No trace of ill will toward any person ever entered her unselfish bosom.

And O! What a treasure of love she was towards her own children! No faults were ever discovered - she only knew forbearance, patience and kindness.

My only regret is that such pure unselfishness was not sufficiently appreciated by myself.

In a higher Sphere of Life I hope I meet you again my Dear Johanna! I also hope that my own love and devotion will then be more deserving of yours.[61]

In December, 1864, the Army commissioned Washington a lieutenant colonel for his valiant service. In early January of 1865 he resigned after serving more than three and half years, during which he participated in the battles of Second Bull Run, South Mountain, Antietam, Chancellorsville, Gettysburg, the Wilderness, Spotsylvania and Petersburg. Washington wrote extensively of his experiences in the war with the attention to detail that characterized all his writing and his work. After the Civil War, nearly everyone referred to him as Colonel Washington A. Roebling or simply Colonel Roebling. On January 18, Washington and Emily were married in her hometown of Cold Spring, New York.[62]

After President Abraham Lincoln died on April 15, 1865, John wrote in a letter to Swan from Cincinnati:

The sad bereavement of the Nation by the foul assassination of President Lincoln has produced a strong and deep feeling of bitterness against the Rebels about here. The rebels have lost their best friend, and the North has to mourn over the fall of a great and good man.[63]

It far surpasses my expectations

Washington joined his father as assistant engineer on the Cincinnati Bridge in May, 1865. John was pleased to have his new assistant and within a week he wrote to Swan:

Ms. Elvira informs me, that our grounds look beautiful, and that the new dining room will be the most cheerful and pleasant room in the house. I shall not be able to enjoy it much before this Bridge is completed. After that I expect that I shall take all the comfort I can get at home and leave Bridge building to younger folks.[64]

A week after he arrived in Cincinnati, Washington wrote to Emily: "Our bridge here is an immense thing, it far surpasses my expectations, and any idea I had formed of it previously." In a letter home to Trenton he wrote: "The towers are so high a person's neck arches looking up at them. It will take me a week to get used to the dimensions of everything around here." As he later recalled:

The long interruption in the progress of the Cincinnati Bridge had in the meantime been attended by many advances in the science of bridge building, especially in the matter of material to be used. Where formerly plans were made in wood, now iron beams were used. Thus my father was compelled in 1865 to redraw the first designs of the superstructure, which were of wood and replace the parts in iron, all of which involved many changes, also increase of weight, and hence of cable power....

During 1865 the towers were finished. Saddles and

saddle plates were hoisted in position, always difficult and dangerous work. We were all glad when the bulk of the masonry work was behind us....

On this bridge we did all the work ourselves; shops were built on the anchorage for cable making, a machine shop was built, also a blacksmith shop and carpenter shop and a planing mill. Nowadays such things are let in contract and the engineer can go fishing....

Middle of December, 1865, we went home for Christmas, where my dear sister Elvira was keeping house. I returned to the bridge the following month. This winter period was always a season of great activity for my father. He had to attend to his financial affairs, and having been away nearly a year it took some time to resume the threads of his manufacturing business, managed by our Superintendent Swan, an honest, trustworthy, faithful man. My uncle Riedel who had been working with Swan was finally sent back to Saxonburg, my brother Ferdinand taking his place....

Making rope on a rope walk had been given up. More machines were built to make ropes in a shop. The first elevators were being built about this time. I think it was this year that the first elevator rope was made; it was 5/8 of an inch in diameter, made of fine wire, took a long time to make. In fact it was such a nuisance that Swan wished he would never have to make another one. And yet, today, 40 years later, we are making millions upon millions of feet per annum, and their manufacture comprises nearly one half of our business. All beginnings are difficult, but don't give up.[65]

John and Swan made their first elevator wire rope for Charles and Norton Otis, the sons of Elijah Otis, who developed the elevator safety brake and installed his first elevator using hemp rope in the 1850s. After Elijah died in 1861, his sons founded Otis Brothers and Company, which eventually became the Otis Elevator Company. John and his heirs would have a highly profitable relationship with Otis Elevator for many decades.[66]

As Washington recalled about returning to Ohio:

1866 was the era of cable making at Cincinnati (Fig. 3.39). The cables were to be 12 1/2 inches in diameter, a great step in advance of the 10 inch cables at Niagara....

Preliminary to cable making a light foot bridge was built, 2 1/2 feet wide, only hanging from two wire ropes; 28 feet above it were suspended two cradle cables, same size, to support a cradle platform where the wire regulators stand during cable making....

The maintenance of a long narrow foot bridge in the winter gales was a matter of difficulty. It tore apart several times; to fix it was my job, always at the risk of my life. On one occasion I could only return by walking on the main cable back to the top of the tower. Before reaching it my strength gave out, below me was sure death.

**Figure 3.39: Cincinnati-Covington Bridge, 1866. RPI
Of cable making, Washington wrote,
"Few men have the nerve to do it."**

How I managed to cover the last 100 feet is still a hideous nightmare to me....

To break in a lot of new hands at cable making is always an ugly job, particularly in such a windy situation. Few men have the nerve to do it. It was expected that six months would suffice to make cables, but it took nine, owing to the winds....

The stay ropes were made in Trenton and I had to put them up, a hard, steady grind; in cold weather from 7 A.M. to 6 P.M., bossing gangs of men. After the men went home and ate and slept I had to prepare the work for the next day....

Every day meant hard work on the bridge. The regulating of the floor, trying to make stays and suspenders harmonize (an impossible thing), made much unsatisfactory work.

The screwing up of the truss rods was another impossible problem. You might screw and unscrew all your life and not get any equilibrium....

The towers themselves were notable pieces of architecture, properly designed and more than strong enough, having been intended for a longer span. My father had studied architecture in Berlin to some purpose. He could design a stone bridge tower in proper proportions, without indulging in useless ornamentations....

While the Cincinnati Bridge was not a railroad bridge, still my father considered it a greater bridge than the Niagara Bridge. He had made the first plans in 1846, long before the Niagara episode. Hence for many years it was the favorite child of his anticipations. He was proud of its final completion, never losing his faith that it would be finished after its various vicissitudes.

This work furnished a striking example of what can be accomplished by one man in overcoming great difficulties. Few people that I ever met possessed such an amount of vital energy, coupled the same time with an amazing perseverance which never rested, weekday or Sunday, from early morning to dewy eve and later. His mind was incessantly at work.

We all know that mere thought without expression or action is useless. His every thought was at once put down in the shape of the drawing, a plan, or in writing. Of these I have hundreds and thousands packed away in boxes, all antiquated by this time, mere memorials of past activities surpassed by the combined progress of innumerable other minds, each of which is, however, an essential unit, without which the whole cannot exist....

My four years of service in the Civil War left me with broken down nerves. The incessant excitement, risk of life and hardships leave their mark.

The building of a large suspension bridge is nearly as bad. There is the constant risk from high winds, the dangerous work aloft, requiring the steadiest nerves to keep from being dashed to pieces below. In recognition of these conditions it was planned that I should make a short trip to Europe with my wife (my first voyage).[67]

When John asked Washington to study caissons in Europe, he responded: "Your kind offer of having me go to Europe next summer I accept with pleasure; Emily is especially delighted, to her the idea of going to Europe is something exceedingly grand." In the spring of 1867, John married Lucia Cooper and Ferdinand married Margaret Allison, the daughter of the New Jersey Secretary of State. John also completed his Cincinnati Bridge report (see box), writing in it:[68]

Man is a social being, and the interests of society can only be advanced and maintained by rapid and easy means of transit. Indeed the advance of the nation may justly be measured by its facilities of intercommunication; there is no better scale....

Bridging our western rivers is one of the great means of facilitating intercourse, commercially, as well as socially and politically. Commercial, social and political contact and friction is essential to American life. And our bridge is well calculated to forward this benign process.[69]

John's and Washington's completion of the Cincinnati and Covington Bridge (Fig. 3.40) convinced some visionary New

Public works should educate public taste

In the earlier periods of the art of bridge building, large spans could not be attempted. So long as the builder was confined to stone and timber, no great watercourse could be crossed without intermediate supports. But by the application of iron the construction of larger spans became practicable....

Iron and steel are the materials which preeminently stand foremost as elements of civilization. That nation which attains to the highest perfection in its skillful production and application to the various arts of life, will rank also highest in the scale of social advancement and political power.

If the government of a nation refuses to protect those branches of industry, which more than any others are calculated to give it power and wealth, and to make it independent, such nation will find itself rapidly outstripped by other people who have better comprehended this fact. The material forms the basis of the mental and the spiritual; without it the mind may conceive, but cannot execute.

It was left to modern engineering, by the application of the principle of suspension, and by the use of wrought iron, to solve the problem of spanning large rivers without intermediate supports....

Where strength is to be combined with lightness and elegance, nature never wastes heavy, cumbrous masses. Architects of the middle ages fully illustrated this fact by their beautiful buttresses and flying arches, combinations of great strength and stability, executed with the least amount of material....

It is a difficult task to produce any proper architectural effect when designing towers for a suspension bridge of large dimensions. Highly ornamented masonry may be built, but it looks out of place, and the general impression should be that of simplicity, massiveness and strength.

Figure 3.40: Cincinnati-Covington Bridge, c1870. CT
The bridge has a pleasing effect. - John A. Roebling

On the other hand, a public work which forms a conspicuous landmark across the great river, which separates two large cities, both abounding in highly ornamental façades, should also serve as a model of appropriate architectural proportions.

Public works should educate public taste; at any rate, should not violate it. In the erection of public edifices, therefore, some expense may and ought to be encouraged in order to satisfy the artistic goal aspirations of the young and growing community....

As it is, the bridge has a pleasing effect, and at the same time presents strong and reassuring proportions, which inspire confidence in the stability of the work.[70]

Report of John A. Roebling, Civil Engineer,
to the Covington and Cincinnati Bridge Company,
Trenton, New Jersey, April 1, 1867

Yorkers that the time had finally come to build the bridge between Manhattan and Brooklyn that John had proposed in 1857. William C. Kinsley, a wealthy Brooklyn Contractor, and State Senator Henry Murphy, a former Mayor of Brooklyn, led the group. With Kinsley promising to subscribe to a substantial amount of the capital stock, Senator Murphy convinced the New York State Legislature to approve a charter to incorporate the New York Bridge Company on April 16, 1867.

On May 23, the Bridge Company trustees appointed John A. Roebling as Chief Engineer at a salary of $10,000 (about $220,000 in 2009). John sent Washington to Europe to study caissons for building the tower foundations for the bridge, as Washington recalled:

We sailed July 1, 1867. Circumstances lengthened my stay abroad to nine months, much of the time being spent at Mühlhausen, my father's native place. Here my son was born and baptized in the same church as his grandfather.

For me it was really an engineering trip, which took me through many countries and brought me in contact with many eminent people. I was then comparatively young and strong and enjoyed everything.

My special investigations, however, were directed towards deep foundations, more particularly to the use of compressed air in caissons, all of which had a bearing on a possible Brooklyn Bridge of the future.

The Cincinnati Bridge had only been a steppingstone to this greater ambition of John A. Roebling.[71]

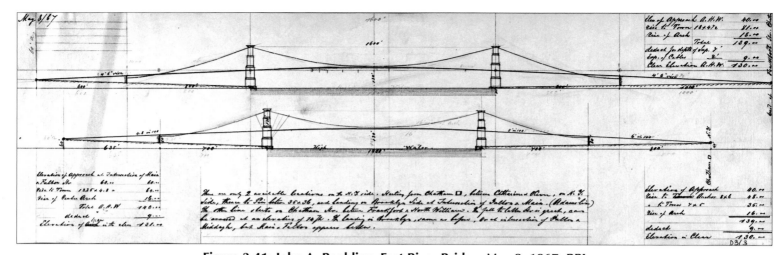

Figure 3.41: John A. Roebling, East River Bridge, May 8, 1867. RPI
John sketched a 1,600 ft. span elevation, top, for a bridge from Fulton Street in Brooklyn to Frankfurt Street in Manhattan, where the bridge was built, and an alternate 1,400 ft. span elevation for a bridge from Fulton Street to Catherine Street in Manhattan.

The bridge will form a great avenue between the two cities

Working at home in Trenton, John immersed himself in his East River Bridge proposal, producing drawings, (Figs. 3.41-43) descriptions of the towers, foundations, anchorages, deck, and the overall strength of the structure. In his report to the Bridge Company directors (see box), he predicted:

> *The city of New York will become the great commercial emporium, not of this continent only, but of the world. In another half century, Liverpool and London, as commercial centers, will rank second to New York. This is no futile speculation, but the natural and legitimate result of natural causes....*
> *The Bridge will be certain of an overwhelming patronage, in consequence of its superior access and facilities, at all seasons and at all hours of day and night....*
> *Of the same width as Broadway, the Bridge will form a great avenue between the two cities.*[72]

John estimated the construction cost at $6,600,000 (about $146 million in 2009), and calculated that toll revenues would return a ten percent profit to the investors. He also projected that property values in Manhattan and Brooklyn would rise by two percent per annum, which "would pay for the whole cost of the work in less than three years."[73]

That fall, John sent 18-year-old Charles to Rensselear Polytechnic Institute in Troy, where Washington had studied engineering and graduated ten years earlier. In a letter to his father on the day he arrived, Charles wrote: "I feel very lonesome and I wish you and mother had come up with me, and I hope you will come soon. I don't like Troy at all, and I wish I was back in Trenton again. Tomorrow I will be examined, and see whether I can enter the Institute."[74]

On their European trip, Washington and Emily visited England, France and Germany. Washington toured steel works and suspension bridges, and met with prominent engineers. He wrote some 50 letters to John describing wire production, steel making and caissons. He wrote to John and Ferdinand suggesting that they license a patented engine that burned coal gas. John declined, but Ferdinand proposed that he and Washington raise $200,000 (about $4.4 million in 2009) to license the patent for $150,000 and split $50,000 for themselves. They could sell the license or raise more money to produce the engines. Nothing came of this, but it illustrated Ferdinand's business acumen, which he would put to great use.

While Washington traveled around Germany, Emily stayed in Mühlhausen with Roebling cousins, who Washington wrote, "are so kind and attentive and take the best care of us." On November 21, Emily gave birth to a boy and wrote to John:

> *As our boy is your first grandson and born in your native place I have claimed for him the honor of bearing your name. He was christened yesterday in the Unter Markts Kirche (where John was christened in 1806) and according to the German custom you were named as his godfather.*
> *The name of John A. Roebling must ever be identified with you and your works but with a mother's pride and fond hopes for her firstborn I trust my boy may not prove unworthy of the name though I cannot hope that he will ever make it famous as you have done.*
> *The boy is very big and strong....He has a very broad full chest....I hope soon to be once more with you with my boy to show you what a fine little fellow he is.*[75]

Three weeks before giving birth to John A. Roebling II, Emily fell down a flight of stairs in Mühlhausen and had to spend many weeks recuperating. John II was their only child.

The completed work,
when constructed in accordance
with my designs,
will not only be
the greatest bridge in existence,
but it will be
the greatest engineering work
of the continent,
and of the age.

It's most conspicuous features,
the great towers,
will serve as landmarks
to the adjoining cities,
and they will be entitled
to be ranked
as national monuments.

As a great work of art,
and as a successful specimen
of advanced bridge engineering,
this structure will forever testify
to the energy, enterprise
and the wealth of that community
which shall secure its erection.

- Report of John A. Roebling,
Civil Engineer
to the President and Directors
of the New York Bridge Company
on the Proposed East River Bridge,
September 1, 1867.

As a whole, no work of the same
character, yet executed,
approaches this in magnitude.
It will undoubtedly be
the crowning work of Roebling's life
and we may, not unreasonably,
conclude that it will hand his name
down to posterity as one of the
greatest engineers of modern times.

- Engineering, London, July, 1867.

Figure 3.42:
John A. Roebling, 1867. RPI
"Front Elevation of Tower
of
East River Bridge
1400 ft. Span
by
John A. Roebling, C.E."

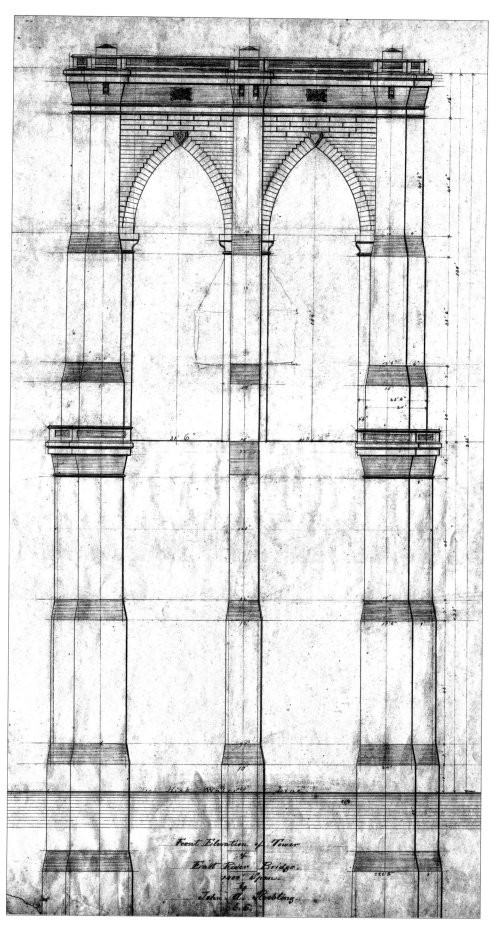

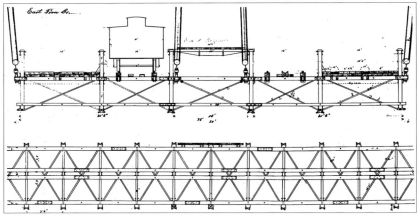

It is beyond doubt entirely practicable

After nearly eight months abroad, as Washington later recalled, "I returned from Europe in March, 1868, and found to my surprise a large amount of preliminary work done on the Brooklyn Bridge. My father had engaged two young engineers, Hildenbrand and Greiffenberg, to help him. Hildenbrand was a valuable man and afterwards was of great service to me." William Hildenbrand would periodically work with Washington and his brothers over the next four decades.[77]

While waiting for the East River Bridge approvals, John worked on various projects like an elevated railway to relieve traffic on Broadway in New York (Fig. 3.44). He designed bridges for crossing the Delaware River at Market Street in Philadelphia, the Ohio River in Kentucky, and the Mississippi River in St. Louis, and he worked on drawings and text for a book on railroad bridges. John asked Wilhelm Hildenbrand to do a rendering of the East River Bridge for the New York Bridge Company trustees, and Hildenbrand produced a superb drawing depicting the completed bridge (Fig. 3.45).

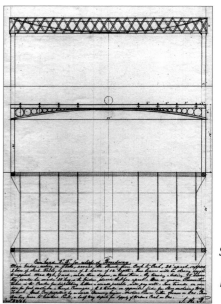

Figure 3.44: J.A. Roebling, "Overhead R.R. for relief of Broadway, 1868" RU.

One or more pneumatic tubes in the center for dispatching letters and small parcels, will pay well. Two tracks on one side for fast motion and through Passengers; and two tracks on the opposite side for slow motion and Way Travel. Each car propelled by a small Dummy Engine. Motion Power from either Steam or Gas. From Bowling Green to Central Park, a half way depot for supply of Water & Coal or Gas.

The Bridge Company trustees appointed Washington as Assistant Engineer at a salary of $6,000 (about $134,000 in 2009), which he later called "entirely too small." He designed the tower foundations with digging devices and airlocks, which he had studied in Europe. As he later recalled, "I moved my family from Trenton to Brooklyn, renting a small brick house on Hicks Street near Orange, little thinking that it would be 16 years before I would leave Brooklyn for good."[78]

Ferryboat owners, shipping interests and political opponents raised objections to the East River Bridge, citing among other issues its cost and the proposed New York subsidy, which most everyone thought Tammany Hall politicians would largely divert to themselves. *The New York Times* reported that: "There is great danger that the East River Bridge project, of which we have lately heard so much, will, for the present, at least, end in smoke."

William Kingsley wrote to John: "Another argument is made against your plan that no other eminent or distinguished Engineer endorses it, and this idea with some well meaning people is rather embarrassing." As Washington recalled:[79]

Every possible accusation was made. The Bridge would fall down, the wind would blow it down, it would never pay, nobody would ever use it, it damaged shipping interests, it was too long to walk over, it never would compete with the ferries, the cost would be so great that the cities would be ruined, etc.…

Public works are always encompassed by false accusations. Certain papers take the opposition side, disseminate false statements continually, distort facts to help their side, do not hesitate downright lies and make charges that are absolutely false. There are two ways to meet these conditions. One is to maintain dignified silence, the other is to hire a paper and fight every accusation as fast as it comes, and above all be polite to reporters. The fighting plan is the best. When you keep silent, the public takes it for granted that you are guilty and have nothing to say for yourself.[80]

Figure 3.45: Wilhelm Hildenbrand, East River Bridge, 1868. RPI When John asked his 23-year old assistant for a rendering, Hildenbrand drew the bridge soaring over the East River towards Brooklyn with late afternoon sun light on the New York tower.

At Kingsley's suggestion, John in 1869 assembled a Board of Consulting Engineers to examine his plans: Horatio Allen, an engineer on the Croton Aqueduct; Julius Adams, a veteran Army engineer who had also designed a bridge across the East River; William McAlpine, the engineer for the Brooklyn Navy Yard and President of the American Society of Civil Engineers; Benjamin Henry Latrobe, engineer for the Baltimore & Ohio Railroad and a bridge builder; John Serrell, a suspension bridge builder; J. Dutton Steel, Chief Engineer for the Reading Railroad;

and James Kirkwood, builder of the 1,040 ft. long Starrucca Viaduct, the world's longest stone-arched railroad bridge, in Wayne County, Pa. The Board of Consulting Engineers met twice a week, beginning in March, 1869, with Washington serving as secretary. As he recalled, "It required courage and resolution on the part of Mr. Roebling to defend his thesis, as it were, against all comers." After visiting his Niagara Falls and Cincinnati-Covington Bridges (Fig. 3.46), the engineers endorsed John's plan as "beyond doubt entirely practicable."[81]

Figure 3.46: Charles Bierstadt, Falls View Suspension Bridge, Niagara Falls, New York, 1869. RPI
John took members of the East River Bridge Board of Consulting Engineers and New York and Brooklyn officials on a tour to see his Niagara Suspension Bridge and his Cincinnati-Covington Bridge.
Bierstadt photographed them on a narrow pedestrian and carriage bridge completed in early 1869 that provided a broad view of his bridge nearby.
John is on the bottom right in the light coat.
Washington is on the bottom left with the top hat.[82]

It is beyond doubt entirely practicable to erect a steel wire suspension bridge of 1600 feet span across the East River in accordance with the plans of Mr. Roebling, and that such structure will have all the strength and durability that should attend a permanent connection of a bridge by the cities of New York and Brooklyn.
- Report of East River Bridge
Board of Consulting Engineers, May, 1869

John's satisfaction from the endorsement of his fellow engineers suddenly evaporated, as Washington recalled:

We were getting impatient to begin active work of which owing to financial reasons there was no immediate promise.

Instead of work came the crowning catastrophe of all in the death of John A. Roebling as a result of an accident received on the 28th of June, 1869. We had gone down after lunch to inspect the site of the Brooklyn Tower in the spare ferry slip. In order to see better we climbed on a heap of cordwood, and from that on top of the ferry rack of piles.

Seeing a boat coming, and fearing that a heavy blow would knock him off, I cried to him to get down. In place of getting down all the way he stepped from the fender rack down on the string piece of the permanent outside row of piles. The blow from the boat was severe, sending the fender rack so far in that its string piece overlapped the other one, at the same time catching the toe of his boot on the right foot and crushing the end of the toes. When he uttered a cry I did not realize at first what had happened....

As quickly as possible I got him into a carriage and....took him to my house. With great difficulty we got him upstairs, where I undressed him and laid him on the bed, which he never left....He did not rally from the first shock until the next day. Then when Dr. Barber came he told him that he would take command of his own case himself and would take not orders or treatment from him....A tinsmith was ordered; he fixed up a big tin dish, supplied with a hose of running water. Into this dish Mr. Roebling put his foot, the stream of water playing on it all the time.

When Dr. Barber saw that he exclaimed 'You are inviting sure death for yourself. Nature in endeavoring to cure such a severe wound must have recourse to pain, fever, in order to supply the increased vitality necessary to the healing process. If the pain is too severe take a temporary anodyne.'

All this was a challenge to Mr. Roebling. He ordered Barber out of the room, in a violent manner, and resumed his own treatment....After three or four days I noticed an inability to eat or speak in the patient. Barber ventured up and at once pronounced it lockjaw, incurable at that....

Now came ten terrible days. As the jaws set, eating and swallowing became impossible. With feverish haste he started to write all kinds of directions about his treatment, about the bridge and his financial affairs. As his powers waned the writing became more and more illegible, nothing but scrawls in the end.

As there was no trained nurse, I assumed that function, with an occasional friend to sit up nights....Daily and hourly I was a miserable witness of the most horrible tetanic convulsions, when the body is drawn into a half circle, the back of the head meeting the heels, with a face

Figure 3.47: *John A. Roebling,* **HS**
An engraving of a photograph taken c1868.
The most common of only five known images of John.

drawn into hideous distortions, each attack sapping the rapidly waning vital forces.

Hardened as I was by the scenes of carnage on many a bloody battlefield, these horrors often overcame me. When he finally died one morning at sunrise, I was nearly dead myself from exhaustion.

We all have to die. It is useless to tax one's self as to whether life could've been prolonged or death hastened by this or that treatment.

Tetanus will set in under the best care and in the most skillful hands. I will say that when he died the wound had almost healed....

After a week I had become sufficiently composed to take a sober look at my own situation. Here I was at the age of 32, suddenly put in charge of the most stupendous engineering structure of the age!

The prop on which I had hitherto leaned had fallen; henceforth I must rely on myself. How much better when this happens in early life, before one realizes what it all implies.

In addition to the bridge I had to pay some attention to the business at home. As the principal executor of

Figure 3.48: *John A. Roebling, Presented to W.A. Roebling, Esq., Fr. Greiffenberg, W. Hildenbrand, 1869.* **RPI**
John had hired Greiffenberg and Hildenbrand as assistants on the East River Bridge in 1867, and the young engineers drew a tribute to their deceased mentor depicting his Cincinnati, Niagara, and Allegheny Bridges, his proposed East River Bridge, and the "Roebling Residence" and "the Roebling Wire Mill" in Trenton.

my father's will much responsibility was placed on me in dividing his considerable estate. I was also guardian of my youngest brother.

Fortunately these things do not come on you all at once. You presently realize that they are spread over weeks and months, and therefore do not overwhelm you.

At first I thought I would succumb, but I had a strong tower to lean upon, my wife, a woman of infinite tact and wisest counsel.[83]

With these words, Washington concluded his 280 page biography of his father (Fig. 3.47). Everyone involved in the East River Bridge was stunned and moved by John's untimely death, and two of his assistant engineers drew a tribute to him and his accomplishments (Fig.3.48).

On the day of his funeral in Trenton, *The Brooklyn Eagle* reported on the large number of people who came to pay their last respects to John's body as it lay in his study at his home on South Broad Street, where Washington and other members of the family met them:

There were at least two thousand persons assembled in and around the mansion. The majority of course belonged to the working classes, and it was a very sad and affecting sight to see tears in the eyes of many of the powerfully built mechanics as they passed out of the room in which the body of their deceased master was lying.[84]

The great advantages occurring to navigation

Besides the East River Bridge, John left behind another unrealized dream, as Washington recalled decades later:

In the summer of 1868, Mr. Roebling commenced work on a long projected scheme of his, namely the writing of a book on long and short span railway bridges. The book was not quite finished at the time of his death, but near enough for me to finish it.

Assuming that long span bridges were destined to be the bridge of the future, he sets forth their merits by citing the great advantages occurring to navigation by having a clear water way in the river, giving the steamboats, the great tows of coal fleets on our Western rivers, a free passage at all times. The saving of numerous piers in deep water was another important item. This he proposes to accomplish by suspension cables stiffened by parabolic trusses. Taking the situation of St. Louis as a model, he makes a number of alternative designs, of great beauty and utility (Fig. 3.49). The cables were to be made of an aggregation of steel ropes....

No bridge of this type has ever been executed....The constantly increasing weight of locomotives and cars as well as speed of passage has forced a weight of structure far beyond what Mr. Roebling had in mind....

This book of Mr. Roebling's is handsomely printed, with many steel engravings of beautiful bridge designs, surpassing anything he had done in that line before. It attracted much attention at the time. With his forcible personality he undoubtedly would before long have found the place where this new type of structure would have become a reality under his guiding hand.[85]

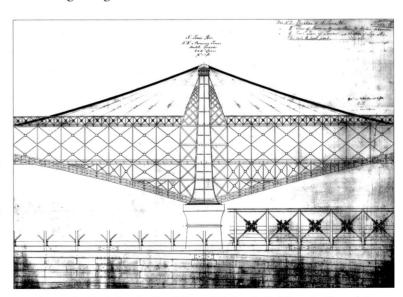

Figure 3.49: John A. Roebling, "St Louis Bridge, Railroad & Common Travel, double Track, 600 ft. span," c1868. RPI
In his design for a railway bridge over the Mississippi River, John combined suspended cables with parabolic arches.

The general theory of bridge construction

In an introduction to his father's book on *Long and Short Span Railway Bridges* (Fig 3.50), Washington wrote:

> *This book was still in press at the time of Mr. Roebling's death. It was the intention of the author to have followed this volume by several more on the same subject. They would have comprised the general theory of bridge construction, and also complete plans and detailed descriptions of some of the larger works erected by him.*
>
> *The only accounts we have of these bridges we find in his original reports. These give very full descriptions of the works as they stand after their completion; but they allude in a very brief manner to the peculiar modes of construction employed, to the methods of making the cables, or to the intricate overhead work. It was especially in the actual construction of works, that the fertility of Mr. Roebling's mind and resources was so preeminent. The question with him was never how to do a thing, but which method to select of the number that occurred to him.*
>
> *A large suspension bridge embraces a vast variety of detail in construction as well as execution, dependent upon its location and the nature of the traffic it is to accommodate. In view of this we can partly explain why all his bridges are so essentially different from each other, both in general arrangement and minor details. But it also seems to show that the originality of his mind was such as to forbid it from imitating even itself.*
>
> *In temperament Mr. Roebling was hopeful and sanguine, even to the degree of enthusiasm. When we read one of his preliminary reports on a bridge enterprise, we are struck with that feature. But when we read the concluding report of the same structure, be it 3, 5 or 10 years subsequent, we find that all his predictions have been more than fulfilled....*
>
> *While engaged in laying out the towers for the East River Bridge, Mr. Roebling received the accidental injury which ultimately resulted in his death.*
>
> *He at no time expected to see the great work upon which he was engaged finished, but did desire to live long enough to see it fairly launched upon its way toward completion.*
>
> *He looked upon the task before him with that calm confidence that knows its own power. Numerous difficulties were expected to rise, novel in their character, difficult to overcome. Yet similar difficulties had been overcome before successfully, and would be again provided there was left to him the time and health necessary to accomplish it.*
>
> *In view of that, the injury he received was as much a mental as a physical shock. He felt that at his age he could ill afford to lose any time - this circumstance, combined with the prospect of being crippled to some extent, had a most depressing influence on his spirits.*[86]

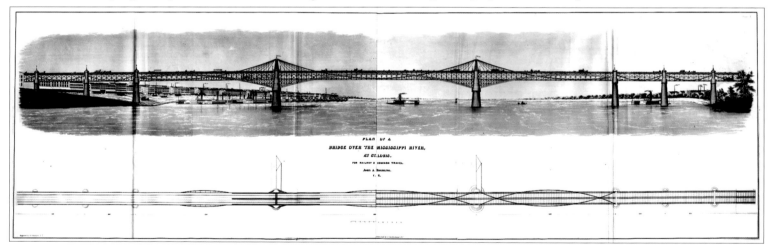

Figure 3.50: John A. Roebling, *Long and Short Span Railway Bridges*, 1869. LU

No continent can boast of a more magnificent system of water courses than ours, and on no other continent will there be a greater development of internal commerce, by land as well as by water. The construction of long span railway-bridges over our large navigable rivers, such as will not materially interfere with their free and easy navigation, becomes therefore a question of national importance....

Economy in construction will be the test of the future. Sooner or later those plans and systems alone will survive in practice which are the most economical; those alone will be adopted by the competent engineer which will afford the greatest amount of strength for the least amount of cost....

The principle of suspension will of necessity become the main feature in our future long span Railway Bridges.

Theoretically considered, the principle of the arch, in an upright as well as a suspended form, is the most economical. It will hold equally good in practice, if properly applied.

To obtain the largest degree of economy however, the two positions of the arch, the upright as well as the inverted or suspended, must be combined into one united system....

The principle of the Parabolic Truss forms the main feature of the designs herewith presented. As time and health shall permit, others plans will be prepared, to follow this number, designed for long span as well as short. - John A. Roebling, Trenton

Chapter 4: *John A. Roebling's Sons*

Figure 4.1: John A. Roebling's Sons, along the Delaware & Raritan Canal, c1874. The core of John's original factory (see Fig. 3.2) is behind the hipped roof wire mill on the left, his 1861 Rope Shop (see Figs. 3.30-31) is in the center, and his house, orchard and garden are on the right. Charles Swan and Charles Roebling built the rolling mill on the upper left in 1872.

I bequeath unto my four sons, Washington A. Roebling, Ferdinand W. Roebling, Charles Roebling and Edmund Roebling, to hold as equal tenants in common, All the Factory Buildings erected for and in use in the business of manufacturing wire rope, situated in the Township of Hamilton, together with the Land occupied by said buildings and the Land fenced off for said business....Together also with all the Fixtures, Buildings and Machinery necessary and used for carrying on the business of manufacturing wire rope....

It is my wish and I hereby request of my sons that they continue the manufacturing business after my decease, under the name of "John A. Roebling's Sons," and also that they associate with them as a partner in said business, my present manager, Charles Swan.[1]

In his will of June, 1868, John A. Roebling also left $20,000 (about $445,000 in 2009) to Charles Swan, and $5,000 (about $111,000) to the widows of his brother Karl and his friend Julius Riedel in Saxonburg, and his friend Frederic Overman in Camden. He gave $30,000 (about $668,000) each to the Widows and Single Women's Home and the Union Industrial Home Association for destitute children, both of Trenton, and $10,000 (about $223,000) each to the Pittsburgh Infirmary, the Orphans Farm School located at Zelionople, Butler County, Pennsylvania," and "The Wartburg Farm School, Mount Vernon, Westchester County, New York."

He gave the remainder of his personal estate in eight equal shares to his seven children from his first wife and to his second wife, "Provided However, that from the share thus given to each shall be deducted the amount advanced by me, in my lifetime, to each of them respectively....as the same appears in the entry of my private ledger, and from the share of each of my sons shall be deducted the value of the share of each in the manufactory, land buildings and fixtures."

John valued his factory (Fig. 4.1) at $150,000 (about $3.3 million in 2009). Two months after his death the appraisers of his estate valued his personal property at $5,777 (about $134,000), with a piano listed as the most valuable item at $800 (about $18,500). They valued his stocks, bonds and cash holdings at $1,088,468 (about $25.2 million), listing his largest holding as $165,700 (about $3.8 million) in the Pennsylvania Rail Road. He had $149,070 in bonds and shares of the Covington & Cincinnati Bridge Company and City of Covington bonds, and substantial investments in other clients and projects: the Niagara Bridge Company, Allegheny Bridge Company, Delaware & Hudson Canal Company and Fayette County, Kentucky. He also had investments in several other railroads, in iron and coal companies, in state bonds, in banks, and in the Morris Canal Company, one of his major customers. He had $89,000 (about $2 million) in bank deposits, receivable notes, cash and silver.

His appraisers valued his inventories of coal, wire, rods, billets, wire rope, boards, etc., at $98,593 (about $2.3 million). With his factory, personal property, investments, cash, inventories and land, John had accumulated an estate that the appraisers valued at $1,370,000 (about $32 million). In 1874, the executors valued his house and 8-1/2 acres in Trenton at $13,000 (about $336,000), and 2,750 acres of land he owned in Iowa at $19,250 (about $497,000).

John had invested more than three quarters of his wealth in securities, about a fifth in his factory, and less than half of one percent in personal belongings. His limited factory investment reflected his focus on bridge building, and as Washington noted, John believed the factory was large enough for the wire rope business. Besides his engineering accomplishments, John achieved the traditional goal of setting up his sons with livelihoods and he left them money to operate and expand.

Each of the three brothers assumed part of what John had done on his own. Washington succeeded him as bridge engineer and builder. Ferdinand had gradually assumed the financial management of the business since he started working there in 1859. After her was graduated from Rensselaer Polytechnic Institute in 1871, Charles joined Ferdinand and Swan at the factory and gradually took over production. The three brothers would build the family business far beyond their father's greatest expectations. Edmund, the fourth brother, would work for the business briefly when he came of age. The brothers bought the family house and land from his estate for $29,000 (about $723,000 in 2009), and turned the house into their office. Within a few years they would erect factory buildings where they had grown up playing and working in the garden, orchard, and field.

Factory workers at that time earned about $1-$2 a day, or $300 to $600 a year (about $7-14,000). The 1870 Census reported that John A. Roebling's Sons employed 75 males over the age of 16 plus ten children (Fig. 4.2), who together earned a total of $52,000 (about $1.2 million). The Census listed the firm's capital at $250,0000 (about $6 million), its steam engines generated 250 horsepower, and its workers produced 700 tons of wire rope worth $250,000. Output had nearly doubled since 1860 but the value had increased more than three times.

Figure 4.2: Roebling Mill, 1871. BC
John A. Roebling's Sons employees in front of John's original half-timbered factory (see Fig. 3.2). About three quarters of the men had German names and the remainder had English-Scotch-Irish names. Three German boys sat in the front.

Figure 4.3: Charles Swan, c1870. HS
John had first hired Swan as a promising young carpenter on the Allegheny Aqueduct in 1845, and in 1848 he sent Swan to Trenton to build his factory and house. Over the next two decades, Swan significantly expanded the factory and house and ran the business while John was away building bridges. An ever loyal employee and friend, Swan also helped Mrs. Roebling and the children a great deal.

Charles Swan (Fig. 4.3) had devoted his life to John Roebling and the wire rope factory and had even built his house adjacent to his employer's. Although John had requested in his will that his sons make Swan a partner, they were reluctant to share profits or control. Washington offered him a $6,000 salary (about $139,000) plus incentives of $2 for every 1,000 lbs. of wire rope produced and $500-$1,000 for each rope machine he "put up." He showed Swan that he would make more from his salary and bonuses than from his share of profits as a partner, which he suggested would not increase since the price of wire rope was declining.

Washington noted to Swan that: "By taking a salary you avoid all risk, and it makes our own business relations much simpler than they otherwise would be and fewer conflicting interests would arise." The brothers contracted with Swan to stay on as "Superintendent and Manager of the Wire rope Works" at the proposed salary "until Charly comes of age, then it has to be renewed."[2]

And no one else was

John had designed the overall layout of the East River Bridge and the elevation of the New York tower, and he had drawn construction details, including a caisson for the tower foundations. Washington (Fig. 4.4) dutifully stepped into the huge void left by his father's untimely death and assumed the task of building the world's greatest bridge, as he recalled:

After my father's death and burial, I remained home in Trenton for some time settling up his estate....

When I returned to Brooklyn I was appointed Chief Engineer without any question - for three cogent reasons -

1st - I was the only living man who had the practical experience to build those great cables, far exceeding in size anything previously attempted, and make every wire bear its share;

2nd - Two years previous I had spent a year in Europe studying pneumatic foundations and the sinking of caissons under compressed air. When the borings of the New York Tower site developed the appalling depth of 106 ft. below the water level, all other engineers shrank back and I had to face this enormous dangerous task, spending nearly 2 years in compressed air, more or less, and nearly losing my life;

3rd - I had assisted my father in the preparation of the first designs, he of course being the mastermind, and I was therefore familiar with his ideas and with the whole project and no one else was.[3]

Figure 4.4: Washington A. Roebling, c1869. RU

Here I was at the age of 32, suddenly put in charge of the most stupendous engineering structure of the age!
- Washington A. Roebling

Washington had to design numerous details, prepare the specifications for the contractors, and supervise all of the work. A skilled draftsman like his father, Washington drew the construction drawings for the caissons - larger than any previously built - based on his father's sketch and on his study of caissons in Europe three years earlier (Fig. 4.5).

Carpenters built the Brooklyn caisson and tugboats eased it into place in May, 1870, and as workers excavated the riverbed inside and masons piled stone on top, it gradually sank. When a fire broke out in the caisson that December, Washington supervised the efforts to put it out and after many hours in the caisson, he became so ill that he had to be helped out. As the work proceeded, many workers became ill and some died, and Washington suffered along with them.

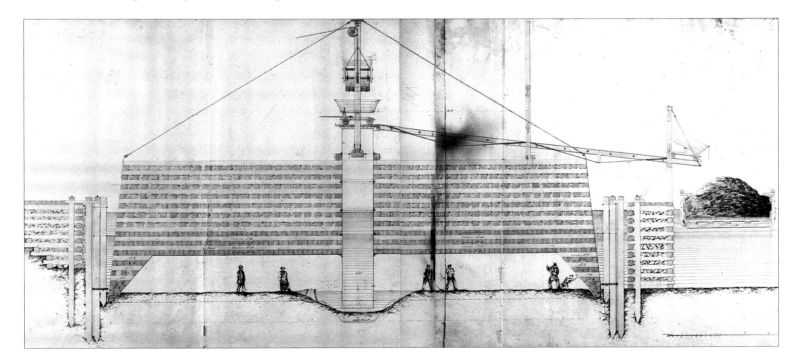

Figure 4.5: Washington A. Roebling, Caisson in Position, Brooklyn Side, September 28, 1869. MANY
After steamboats eased the 168 ft. by 102 ft. Brooklyn caisson into place, masons began erecting granite blocks on top to sink it. When the caisson reached the riverbed, workmen pumped air into the hollow bottom, while others used a clamshell to remove dirt and rocks through an airlocked shaft. For every two feet that the caisson descended, the pressure increased one pound. After climbing out of the caisson, many workers suffered from "caisson disease," later called "the bends," a painful condition but unknown at that time wherein dissolved gases form bubbles in the blood when depressurization occurs too quickly.

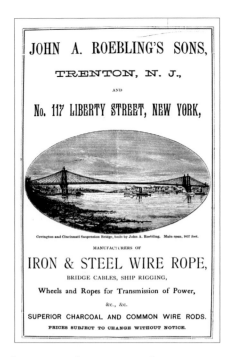

JOHN A. ROEBLING'S SONS,

TRENTON, N. J.,

AND

No. 117 LIBERTY STREET, NEW YORK,

MANUFACTURERS OF

IRON & STEEL WIRE ROPE,

BRIDGE CABLES, SHIP RIGGING,

Wheels and Ropes for Transmission of Power,

&c., &c.

SUPERIOR CHARCOAL AND COMMON WIRE RODS.

PRICES SUBJECT TO CHANGE WITHOUT NOTICE.

Figure 4.6 (left):
*John A. Roebling's Sons,
Trenton, N.J., Manufacturers of
Iron & Steel Wire Rope, 1875.* **RU**
**The Roebling brothers followed
their father's example and used
prominent Roebling suspension
bridges to promote their wire
rope products. Their 1875
catalogue proudly featured the
Cincinnati-Covington Bridge.**

Figure 4.7 (right):
**Charles G. Roebling, 1871. RPI
After he was graduated from
Rensselear Polytechnic Institute
in Troy, N.Y., at the age of 21,
Charles immediately joined
his brothers at J.A.R.'s Sons.**

Manufacturers of Iron & Steel Wire Rope

He was his father over again

Washington's work as Chief Engineer for the Brooklyn Bridge occupied nearly all of his time. Ferdinand managed sales and correspondence with the knowledge he gained working under his father and Swan over more than a decade. John had recognized Ferdinand's business skills early on and had refused to let him join the army during the Civil War. Now that he was in charge of the business at the age of 28, Ferdinand expanded sales by opening an office in New York in 1871, and he promoted Roebling products on stationary, catalogues, and trade cards displaying John A. Roebling's landmark suspension bridges (Fig. 4.6). Like his father had done, Ferdinand invested most of their profits in securities to maintain a ready source of capital for expansion.

While business expanded westward in the 1870s through the growth of railroads, manufacturing, and communications, the Roeblings manufactured most of the wire rope produced in the United States but wire makers like Washburn and Moen in Worcester, Massachusetts, and the Trenton Iron Company also manufactured wire products. As innovations like telephones and electrical transmission created new markets for wire and wire rope, producing the new products required financing and mastering new production techniques, such as wire insulating.

When new opportunities arose, the Roebling brothers adapted or expanded their production and sales efforts to seize a big share of the market ahead of their competition. In this era of cheap labor and few taxes, the business generated ample surplus to expand, and like their father, the brothers never resorted to borrowing money.

In the spring of 1871, when 21-year-old Charles (Fig. 4.7) joined Ferdinand and Swan at the factory, he focused on improving production and soon began a building campaign that he basically continued for the rest of his life. Like his father, he attended to all the planning, construction and operation of everything from machines to buildings to the entire new factory and town that he and his brothers would eventually build south of Trenton. As Washington noted, "he was his father over again, to a far greater degree than any of the other children, (with) the concentrated energy which drives one to work and be doing something all the time."[4]

One of his first jobs was to modernize rod rolling to produce more wire. The brothers bought land along South Clinton Avenue north of their original parcel, and Charles and Swan built an innovative rolling mill there with automated returns to send rods repeatedly through a train of rollers (Fig. 4.8 & see Fig. 4.1). Within a couple of years Charles demolished his father's 1849 wire mill and rope shop (see Figs. 3.2 & 4.1) and erected a new wire mill there (Fig. 4.9).

As Charles took charge of production and with Ferdinand handling sales, they gradually pushed Swan to the side. Washington later noted: "Swan had grown up with John A. and not with these younger men. It was not long before a little friction developed and it grew and grew. It was not exactly jealousy, but they could not look upon Swan as an equal.... After three years of it Swan left suddenly, he couldn't stand it any longer." Washington and Ferdinand persuaded Swan to return, but he left for good in a short time. The brothers had no time to for sentimentality, as Washington recalled:

Figure 4.8: John A. Roebling's Sons, Rolling Mill, 1889. SI
In 1872, Charles and Swan built an innovative rolling mill with an iron floor and an auomated drive train for rolling rods into wire.

Figure 4.9: John A. Roebling's Sons, c1889. RPI Charles next built a two and three-story wire mill adjacent to the one-story rope factory that John built in 1861 (see Fig. 3.30).

The telegraphs of the country were assuming enormous proportions, expanding daily. Thousands and thousands of lines were demanded to cover the United States. Our output grew until it exceeded that of the famous Washburn mills in Worcester. Ferdinand was especially active in expanding this part of the business and was very successful.[6]

Charles spent much time and money learning how to heat, clean and galvanize wire for telegraphs and other uses. "There were at least fifty difficulties to be solved satisfactorily," wrote Washington, "else the business would not pay. This was the sort of schooling Charles had to go through, day after day from year to year." On his father's old field he built a galvanizing shop that "held six or seven trains, working day and night and Sunday, and it was still unequal to the demand." Steel wire posed another challenge for Charles, as Washington recalled:[7]

The era of Bessemer steel had arrived in the early 1870s and was gradually taking the place of the costly Swedish iron and American charcoal iron. The treatment of this material cost Charles many an anxious hour and years of experimenting. One of his most striking characteristics was that he wanted to do everything and find out everything himself. That disposition has great merits with a few demerits, because sometimes it is much cheaper to buy what you want them to waste thousands in experimenting.

This tendency of self-reliance was one of Charles's chief points. It strengthened his capacity for successful work and enabled him in later years, when he was in his prime, to undertake great projects where he had no precedents and was forced to rely upon himself alone.

This period in a busy man's life lasts only a few years. The time inevitably arrives when it is necessary to train someone to take your place. With him that time never came, simply because he could not tolerate the idea of rising up an equal. On the other hand, it is a great thing to have a man at the manufacturing head in whose infallibility every subordinate had the most profound confidence.[8]

It requires courage to face a band of infuriated men

The changes created some tension among the employees, and Washington described their "first serious strike:"

As the employer of labor it was Charles' duty to fix wages and settle strikes when they came, a most difficult task, because it is necessary to be just to both sides.

For many years we had nothing but Germans in our employ, a peaceful and tractable race. The number of operatives was comparatively small so that most everyone was known by sight or name. This could not last. Wire drawing, a special trade, was gradually monopolized by Englishmen.

About 1875 our Worcester competitors established a saving in the costly wiredrawing plates, by substituting a cheap cast-iron die which could be reamed to gauge by a few men, the mere drawing of the wire and taking it off the block could then be done by ordinary labor. The high wages of wire drawers had been due to the skill needed in setting up the holes, hammering the conical hole into shape and tempering the plate.

When this went into effect every Englishman, about 50 in number struck and refused to use chilled dies. They sat around on the fence for a couple of days, and then left. This was the first serious strike.

Charles was a good fighter. When he felt he was right he would not give in. This was the forerunner of many a subsequent strike, especially when he began to employ many different nationalities – Italians, Poles, Russians, Hungarians, Scandinavians, Croats, Romanians, Greeks.

The hardest test comes when it is imperative to reduce wages in hard times. It requires courage then to face a band of infuriated men. Charles possessed that courage to the highest degree.[9]

Figure 4.10:
John A. Roebling's Sons Company blotter with Allegheny Bridge, c1876. RPI
The Roebling brothers incorporated their wire rope business in 1876 with Washington as president, Ferdinand as secretary-treasurer and Charles as vice president.

Workers protesting wage cuts or working conditions had little power since they were unorganized and other men would readily take their jobs. Like most other employers, the Roeblings refused to negotiate with their employees. As Washington noted: "It is low wages that count the most in profits," but the Roeblings tried to keep their men employed in slow times by distributing work among them, including maintenance. They believed that they treated their employees well and expected their loyalty. When workers protested or went on strike, the brothers felt that they were ungrateful.

Washington's work on the difficult foundations of the Brooklyn Bridge left him exhausted much of the time from "exposure, overwork and anxiety," as he later recalled. In the winter of 1872, after spending far too much time in the New York caisson, he collapsed from the effects of the bends with such pain that he had to be carried out and almost died in the

Brooklyn house where his father had died four years earlier. He recovered enough to work part time but his poor health forced him to request a leave of absence in the spring of 1873, and he and Emily and John II spent that summer in Wiesbaden in Germany so he could recuperate. When they returned he tried to resume work but his doctors recommended further rest and in early 1874 he moved to Trenton with his family and stayed there for three years.[10]

From 1870 to 1875, J. A. Roebling's Sons (Figs. 4.10-11) annual revenues increased $250,000 to $763,000 (about $20 million in 2009) and profits averaged $165,000 (about $4.2 million). The Roeblings were manufacturing three quarters of the wire rope made in the United States and the value of their Company grew from $350,000 (about $8.4 million) to $894,000 (about $23 million). In 1876, the brothers incorporated John A. Roebling's Sons Company with $500,000 in capital (about

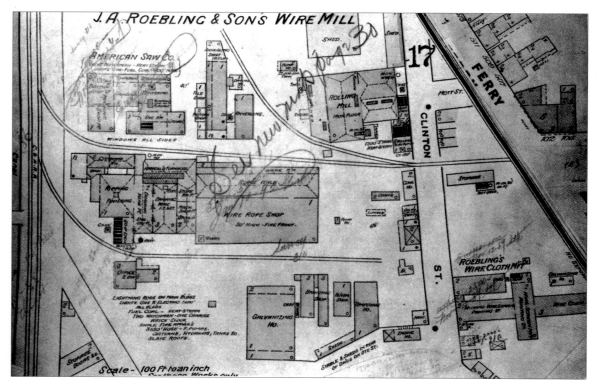

Figure 4.11:
Sanborn Insurance Company Map, 1876. NJSL
"J. A. Roebling & Sons Wire Mill"
The map depicts the Company Office in John's 1855 house, lower left; the wire mills and rope shop, left center; the 1872 Rolling Mill, and boiler houses, upper center; galvanizing and tempering shops, lower center; and Roebling's N.J. Wire Cloth Company, lower right.
The Roebling brothers soon took over the American Saw Company site on the upper left.

$13.5 million) and "real assets in the mill of nearly $400,000." They issued 1,000 shares of stock: 300 each to Washington, who became President (see Fig. 4.10), Charles, Vice President, Ferdinand, Secretary & Treasurer, and 100 shares to Edward, First Assistant Bookkeeper. The brothers also retained Charles Swan as General Superintendent for a short time.[11]

The Roeblings anticipated that J.A.R.'s Sons Co., as they called it, would get the contract to furnish the wire for the Brooklyn Bridge cables, and they mounted an impressive exhibit at the 1876 Centennial Exposition in Philadelphia with full-size cable sections (Fig. 4.12). When some New York Bridge Company trustees suggested that J.A.R.'s Sons Co.

shouldn't bid on the wire contract while Washington served as Chief Engineer, he resigned his position as President of the Company and sold his 300 shares to his brothers. Charles became President and held the post for more than 40 years until his death. Ferdinand reluctantly submitted a bid to supply the bridge wire, but some Bridge directors underhandedly arranged to award the wire contract to a Brooklyn firm.

When the Bridge Company trustees learned that the Brooklyn wire firm was supplying defective wire, they cancelled the contract and awarded a new wire contract to J.A.R.'s Sons Co. Washington later bought back his Company shares and became Vice President.

Figure 4.12: John A. Roebling's Sons Company Exhibit in Machinery Hall at the Centennial Exhibition in Philadelphia, 1876. SI

The exhibit itself is most artistically arranged, in Machinery Hall, a large space has been set aside for the company, and every inch of room has been utilized for display. At the Southside, a large framework of the breath of their space has been erected, and every size of their wire rope, from the minute as to the largest, is arranged upon it in circular rayed forms, and is very attractive to visitors. The platform is surrounded with a unique railing made of a monstrous wire rope 3 1/2 inches thick, and inside of this are displayed pieces of the ropes used in the various suspension bridges. Prominent among these is a piece of the cable which is to be used in the East River bridge....At the west end of their space is a large pencil drawing, made by William Hildenbrand, assistant engineer, representing the New York and Brooklyn Bridge as it will be on its completion (see Fig. 3.45)....The exhibit of this company will not suffer in comparison with any other.

- Brooklyn Daily Eagle, August 11, 1876[12]

"How the Wire is Made - A Visit to the Factory in Trenton," *Brooklyn Daily Eagle*, August 11, 1876

Mr. F. W. Roebling courteously showed me through their works and explained their operation. Their grounds cover fourteen acres, and within the walls are five wire rolling mills, ten steam engines, eight annealing furnaces, and all the buildings needed for their 350 workmen and office purposes. They use the best billets of Swedish as well as American blooms, and the various grades of foreign and domestic steel. Their products amount to three fourths of all the wire rope made in this country.

It was a rare sight to watch these busy workmen taking blocks of red-hot steel and their tongs from white-hot furnaces, passing them through rolling mills which stretched them until they lay upon the iron floor like interlacing snakes in bizarre shapes, ready to be carried by other hands to annealing furnaces, and thence through other draw plates until the wire was prepared to bind together either the delicate handiwork of the jeweler or the two cities of New York and Brooklyn with their million of inhabitants.

In a store room devoted to galvanized steel wire was Col. Paine, of the New York and Brooklyn Bridge, carefully testing every ring of water to be used in the cables and the temporary bridge in Brooklyn, and taking great pains that not a single piece should fall short of the severe standard required.

They are now making of the No. 7 wire 60 miles per day, and the average of all sizes, down to the hair breadth, is 440 miles daily. Some idea may thus be formed of the extent of this industry.

Nor is it strange that so much wire is needed, when we think on the uses to which it is applicable - for ship rigging, hoisting, bridges, fences, clothes wire, tiller ropes, telegraphs, etc.

It was well worth my visit to watch the attention given to the details of their widely extended business. In accounting houses there was no flurry; at the furnaces the workmen were warmed up to their work, and did it mechanically; around the annealing furnaces, rolling mills and acid baths, everything seemed to move along rapidly and pleasantly, notwithstanding the thermometer stood at 102.

Once J.A.R.'s Sons Co, had the contract to produce the bridge wire, everyone felt assured of its quality (see box), but Washington's absence from the bridge site remained an issue for some. He continued as Chief Engineer but his fragile condition forced him to work from his house in Brooklyn Heights (Figs. 4.13-14). His wife, Emily (Fig. 4.15), became his chief assistant, transmitting communications between him and his assistant engineers at the bridge site.

As construction continued, few people got to see the Chief Engineer and newspapers printed rumors of his demise. In September, 1882, Brooklyn Mayor Seth Low tried to replace Washington, alleging that his health problems had delayed construction. Incensed that Washington was considered unfit to finish the bridge after all he had sacrificed, Emily assured the Bridge Company trustees of her husband's "perfect sanity and ability as an engineer," and they voted to retain him.

Figure 4.13: Brooklyn Bridge Construction, May 29, 1877. SI Three days after Washington's 40th birthday, bridge directors gathered on the footbridge to mark the first passage of the traveling wheel (upper left), invented by John A. Roebling, that carried individual wires across the spans to build up the cables.

Figure 4.14: Washington A. Roebling, 1880. BM After he became ill from the bends, Washington supervised the construction of the bridge from his house in Brooklyn Heights.

Figure 4.15 (left): Emily Warren Roebling, c1885. RU
Figure 4.16 (right): Col. & Mrs. Washington A. Roebling's invitation to a reception at their home in Brooklyn Heights following the ceremonies opening the Brooklyn Bridge. RU

Figure 4.17: *Bird's Eye View of the Great New York and Brooklyn Bridge*, **Opening Day, May 14, 1883. BM**

The Eighth Wonder of the World

The bridge cost $15,000,000 (about $421 million in 2009), more than twice John's 1867 estimate, and it took nearly three times as long to build as he had predicted. When Bridge Company Trustee Abram Hewitt, a partner in the Trenton Iron Company and a future mayor of New York, cited the bridge as an example of progress, Washington wrote:

It took more than twenty years for Cheops to build his pyramid, but if he had had a lot of Trustees, contractors, and newspaper reporters to worry him, he might not have finished it by that time. The advantages of modern engineering are in many ways overbalanced by the disadvantages of modern civilization.[13]

On May 24th, 1883, a "glorious spring day" just two days before Washington's 46th birthday, the City opened the bridge with a huge celebration of parades, speeches, receptions and fireworks (Figs. 4.16-17 and box). Emily made a ceremonial first crossing in a carriage with a rooster, a symbol of prosperity, on her lap, as Washington watched from his study in Brooklyn Heights. *The Brooklyn Eagle* called it "the Eighth Wonder of the World - eighth in point of time but not in significance." Brooklyn Mayor Seth Low said, "No one shall see it and not feel prouder to be a man." In his speech, Bridge Company Trustee William Kingsley, one of the early proponents of the bridge, said: "With one name, this Bridge will always be associated - that of Roebling." Abram Hewitt paid homage to:[14]

> *The wonder and the triumph of this work of our day is in the weaving of the aerial span that carries such a burden of usefulness, by human thought and skill, from delicate threads of wire that a child could almost sever.*
> -"Brooklyn Bridge," *Harper's New Monthly*, May, 1883
>
> *When we turn to the graceful structure at whose portal we stand, and when the airy outline of its curves of beauty, pendant between massive towers suggestive of art alone, is contrasted with the over-reaching vault of heaven and the ever moving flood of waters beneath the work of omnipotent power, we are irresistibly moved to exclaim, "What has man wrought!"*
> - Abram Hewitt, Opening Address, May 24, 1883
>
> *"It so happens that the work which is likely to be our most durable monument, and to convey some knowledge of us to remote posterity, is a work of bare utility; not a shrine, not a fortress, not a palace, but a bridge."*
> - Montgomery Schuyler, *Harper's Weekly*, May 24, 1883

John A. Roebling, who conceived the project and formulated the plan of the Bridge; Washington A. Roebling, who, inheriting his father's genius, and more than his father's knowledge and skill, directed this great work from its inception to completion, in the springtime of youth, with friends and fortune at his command, braved death and sacrificed his health to the duties which had devolved upon him, as the inheritor of his father's fame, and the executor of his father's plans....

With this bridge will ever be coupled the thought of one, through the subtle alembic of whose brain and by whose facile fingers, communication was maintained between the directing power of its construction and the obedient agencies of its execution. It is thus an everlasting monument to the self-sacrificing devotion of woman, and of her capacity for that higher education from which she has been too long debarred. The name of Mrs. Emily Warren Roebling will thus be inseparably associated with all that is admirable in human nature, and with all this is wonderful in the constructive world of art.[15]

83

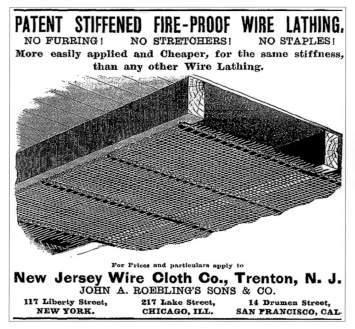

Figure 4.18: New Jersey Wire Cloth Co. ad., *American Architect & Building News,* **March 6, 1886. SW The new Roebling subsidiary targeted the emerging wire cloth market.**

Figure 4.19 (left): J.A.R.'s Sons Co. catalogs featured new electric wire and wire cloth products, c1892. RU; Figure 4.20 (right): A Spanish version targeted new business in Latin America, 1891. RU

To consume the extra output

New power looms made wire cloth affordable in the 1870s, and the Roeblings chartered the New Jersey Wire Cloth Company in 1878 to manufacture it. Charles hired William Orr, Jr., a foreman with the Clinton Wire Cloth Company in Massachusetts, to run the business and erected a building for it east of South Clinton Avenue where John had built his rope walk. When New York and other cities adopted fire codes in the mid-1880s, Orr patented woven wire plaster lath for fire proofing floors (Fig. 4.18), and the subsidiary generated good profits until competitors caught up. As Washington noted,[16]

Every new branch of business was always a pet for several years, until the novelty wore off, and the initial profits, which were large, had become reduced by competition and the unfortunate fact that jobbers really controlled the profits. As time went on we consoled ourselves with the delusion that the wire cloth business must be continued in order to consume the extra output of the wire mills.[17]

By 1880, J.A.R.'s Sons Co. revenues increased sevenfold to $1,769,000 (about $53 million in 2009), and the payroll expanded to nearly 500. The "Mongrel Tariff" of 1883 increased duties on the import of English wire products and encouraged other American firms to enter the wire and wire rope business. The Roebling's share of the market gradually declined but new uses for wire rope generated increasing demand for several decades, pushing Company sales and revenues steadily upward.

Going mad about electricity

With the rise of telephones and electrical power, the Roebling brothers created the Insulated Wire Department in 1883 to supply the emerging markets. Charles learned how to manufacture various types of "annunciator" and electrical wire (see box), and Ferdinand issued new catalogs (Figs. 4.19-4.20), including Spanish and French versions for customers in Latin America and Quebec. As Washington recalled:

The electrical age had begun; everything was done electrically - lighting, communication, power lines and the hundreds of other appliances connected with it. All this meant copper wire, large and small, in untold quantities, not only bare but also insulated. We had never drawn or rolled copper wire: it was a new problem which Charles of course, had to solve, and as usual he succeeded after some failures.

Our rolling mill passes had to be adapted; we had to learn how to heat copper properly, then came annealing and quenching in water. The drawing of the wire was easy in large sizes, but had to be done through jewels in the fine sizes....

The methods of insulation where many. First came ordinary braiding with copper yarns; later paper insulation was largely used....

The whole manufacturing world was going mad about electricity. From an early period Ferdinand was fascinated by the magnet-wire business, affording an outlet for very fine copper wire covered with green and other shades of high priced silk thread - it was a delicate, nice, clean business - a successful venture, much to the credit of F. W., who deserves it.[18]

Figure 4.21: John A. Roebling's Sons Company Exhibit, World's Columbian Exposition, Chicago, 1893. RU
The Roebling exhibit proudly displayed the Brooklyn Bridge along with electrical wire and "traction" ropes for cable cars.

Our own exhibit to my surprise is one of the finest and most imposing in the place. It possesses three great features which impel the passer-by to stop, hence it is crowded all day. Location and light are excellent. **- Washington A. Roebling**[19]

The electrical entrepreneurs George Westinghouse and Nikola Tesla illuminated the fairgrounds and exhibits at the World's Columbian Exposition in Chicago in 1893 (Fig. 4.21), and thereby introduced most of the 26 million visitors to electrical lighting for the first time. Washington and Emily were much impressed with the fairgrounds when they visited, as he wrote to his 17-year-old son, John II, on September 22:

Figure 4.22: John A. Roebling Son's Co. Catalog, c1890. RU
Ferdinand's marketing of Roebling products prominently featured the Brooklyn Bridge for many years.

I think to Mr. Frederick Law Olmsted belongs the greatest honor. While many eminent architects have distinguished themselves in the construction of separate buildings, to him belongs the credit of conceiving the Court of Honor around which the various buildings are grouped in one harmonious whole....The vista is so magnificent that the heart threatens to burst its confines in its exultant joy.

Washington and Emily moved to Troy in 1884 and enrolled John II in engineering at Rensselear Polytechnic Institute, where Washington and Charles had graduated. At their annual convention in New York in 1885, members of the American Society of Civil Engineers elected Washington as President for a one year term. J.A.R's Sons Co. continued to capitalized on the Roebling association with the Brooklyn Bridge (Fig. 4.22).

"History of the Insulated Wire Department," Frank S. Newberry Sr., *Blue Center*, December, 1925

Electric lighting had not yet started, and the only use for insulated wire was to connect up electrical bells and annunciators, and this type of wire took the name of annunciator wire and consisted of soft copper covered with two wraps of cotton, saturated in paraffin....

The telegraph companies used, in wiring their offices, copper covered with two or three braids of cotton, the outer braid of which was a peculiar pattern of red and white threads. This was known as office wire.

When the electric light companies were started there was a demand for house wires, which were called "Underwriters" and since that time "Slow Burning." This soft copper wire was covered with three braids, saturated with white paint, and when properly made it will not burn.

Outside the demand was for weatherproof wire, consisting of three braids of cotton, saturated with an asphalt compound and then run through wax and polished.

There was a demand from the companies making electrical apparatus, such as dynamos and motors, for wires to use on these machines, and this wire became known as magnet wire. All these wires were made in the Insulated Wire Department between 1883 and 1890.

After 1890, the Bell Telephone Company in Philadelphia had us make up for them 55-pair telephone cables insulated with dry paper and covered with a cotton braid. These cables were 1 ¾ in. in diameter....

With the increase of electric lighting there came a demand for rubber covered wires for house wiring, and in order to meet this demand a rubber mill was started in 1895.

The growth of the Insulated Wire Department has been made possible by the demands of the various kinds of wire used in the electrical industry, and as this demand called for a certain kind of wire, the Department would add that particular kind of wire to its output.

Figure 4.23:
Clinton Avenue Rolling Mill, 1886. BC
In this timber-framed mill with wood siding, 2-1/2 ft. wide leather belts drove a train of rollers that reduced red-hot billets to rods.
The smokestack under construction vented four 150 horsepower steam boilers that sat between the mill and houses facing Mott Street (see Fig. 4.11).
The Company's stable is visible in the left background on Hudson Street with a pasture for mules and horses in front.

With his usual zeal

By the 1880s, innovations in steel hardening and rolling machinery enabled competitors to produce three to four times as many rods for the same cost as the Roeblings in their 1872 Rolling Mill (see Fig. 4.8) Washington noted that "Charles tackled the problem with his usual zeal," and he erected a new rolling mill in 1886 east of Clinton Street with a rail extension to supply it (Figs. 4.23-24).

When engineers at the Washburn & Moen wire mill in Worcester, Massachusetts, improved their wire drawing capacity, Charles (Fig. 4.25) refused to be outdone and he built a new wire mill to stay competitive. With row houses crowding the Roebling plant on its north, east and south sides, Charles had no choice but to build up, as Washington recalled:

Our wire drawing capacity having proved too small, Charles became ambitious and planned a large five-story mill on Elmer Street, to be equipped on Worcester lines and superintended by a Worcester man.

Wilhelm Hildenbrand, my former Brooklyn Bridge assistant, helped to draw the plans. Property had to be bought and part of Clark was vacated. This mill was a wonder and a success (Fig. 4.26-27).[20]

The Roebling brothers had acquired land along the Canal north of Elmer Street to build another rope shop, and Charles erected the Elmer Street Rope Shop there right behind row houses on the west side of Clark Street, leaving room for additional buildings between the new rope shop and the Canal. Charles remained typically unfazed by the need to fill the building with numerous machines, as Washington recalled:

Figure 4.24:
Clinton Avenue Rolling Mill Employees, c1890. BC
Of the 28 men identified in *Blue Center*, 18 had English-Irish-Scottish names, and 2 had German names, which was far fewer Germans than 20 years earlier (see Fig. 4.2).
The large flywheel behind the men kept the rolling train runing at a steady speed despite the the impact of the billets as they first came in contact of the rollers.

**Figure 4.25: Charles G. Roebling, c1875. HS
Charles kept expanding the plant whenever
a need arose to remain competitive.**

*The demand for small-sized elevator rope had become
so great that we could no longer devote the slow and
cumbersome machines in the old rope shop to do this
work profitably. Charles proceeded to erect a long three-
story building, nearly 600 feet long for elevator cables and
galvanized strand.*

*Many small-sized upright 19 wire strand machines were
put in; also a number of horizontal machines for 19 wire
strands, together with a number of rope laying machines,
and very small fast running machines for Tiller rope strand.
All of this machinery was built on the place and had to be
designed and properly proportioned in Charles's office.*[21]

In 1888, Washington traveled to Niagara Falls to assist
his fellow RPI alumnus, Leffert L. Buck, in renovating John

A. Roebling's famous suspension bridge over the gorge. To
carry larger locomotives and freight cars, Buck reinforced
John's cables, replaced his stone towers with steel towers and
replaced the wooden deck trusses with steel trusses.

Washington immersed himself in this work, but noted in
a letter to John II, that "putting in about twenty hours out of
the twenty four makes it a little wearing." His frustration with
his physical limitations from his experience of building the
Brooklyn Bridge over so many years was also apparent:[22]

*I do not know if my last letter to you was pitched in a
more doleful key than is usual with me or whether my
plaintive mood has become fixed upon me and I can no
longer be as cheery as of old however hard I may try.*

**Figure 4.26 (above):
Elmer Street Wire Mill, c1890. RPI
With no room to expand horizontally,
Charles erected this first of several multi-story
buildings at the Roebling works, but they were fire
hazards and inefficient because of the extra expense
of moving men, materials and power vertically.
On the south side of the four-story mill,
the Company photographed a huge reel
of street car cable being picked up by
the Pennsylvania Railroad.**

**Figure 4.27 (left):
Elmer Street Wire Mill Employees, 1894. BC
Of the 44 men identified in *Blue Center*,
27 had English-Irish-Scottish names,
and 17 had Germanic names.**

There is something mysterious in the sight of these flying reels of steel....whizzing round and round like indefatigable moths around a big steel candle, or a dervish around his own spinal column on a spot of ground the size of a dinner plate, and the rope, hard, shining, round, packed around its core of hemp or steel, noislessly gathering all this strength and energy unto itself for use in the days of need. When you see it on the spool at the side, shining with its coat of lubricant, ready for work and able to do it, it is a little hard to associate so respectable and dignified a fabric with the rusty heap of iron that lay in the Kinkora yard.

- John Kimberly Mumford,
Outspinning the Spider, 1921.[24]

A prosperous period for rope making

Cable car railways emerged as another large market for wire rope in the 1880s. Andrew Hallidie, an Englishman whose father held a patent on wire rope in England, moved to California in 1852 and manufactured wire rope and built some small suspension bridges. In 1873, he built the first cable car line on Clay Street in San Francisco. By the 1880s, cable car companies were building rail lines in many cities, creating a big demand for long wire ropes. As Washington recalled:

A prosperous period for rope-making had now arrived, namely, making long ropes for cable roads. This surpassed all expectations, so much so that Charles had to start another wire rope shop alongside the old one, and build especially another big rope machine which could lay up 30,000 feet of 1 1/2 inch diameter common lay and lang lay rope, all of which he designed and executed in 1893, and none too soon.

For awhile we had all the cable road business to ourselves, but could scarcely handle it, which brought on competition....

Constant additions of machinery and strand machines were being made to the new rope shop. In designing these machines Charles did his own work, making all the drawings himself, besides attending to all the work and the shops. His industry was indefatigable.[23]

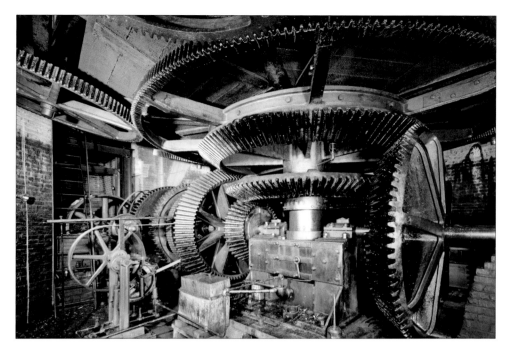

Figure 4.30: 1893 80-Ton Rope Machine, 1987. Jet Lowe, HAER
Charles designed the 60 ft. tall machine with six revolving reels
and a core reel to produce 1-1/2 in. ropes more than 30,000
foot long and weighing up to 80 tons for cable car systems.

Figure 4.31: 1893 80-Ton Rope Machine, 1987. Jet Lowe, HAER
Enormous bevel and pinion gears below the floor drove the
multiple components of the machine to counter twist
the six strands as they were laid around the core strand.

Charles modernized the Company's capacity for making large wire ropes with new buildings and a new generation of rope machines (Figs. 4.28 & 4.30-31). To produce the long wire ropes that cable car and mining companies needed (Fig. 4.32), he built vertical "rope layers" similar to his father's vertical machines (see Figs. 3.32 & 3.33). Charles' 30-Ton and 80-Ton Rope Machines were so big that they required special rope rooms 2-1/2 stories tall with basements, and these rooms have survived several generations of alterations.

The vertical rope layers had three movements: as the spindle and platform rotated, the cradles holding the reels turned in the opposite direction to counter twist the strands to prevent kinks as the strands played off the reels to the closing head at the top. Their operation mesmerized observers for generations, and the 80-Ton Rope Machine survives in place partially intact. It took Charles more than eight years to modernize the rope shops, but the investment enabled the Company to meet the demand for extra long wire ropes for the next three decades.

Figure 4.32: Roebling Rope Shops,
***Blue Center*, February, 1927.**
The 1893 Rope Room housing the 80-Ton Rope Machine is visible on the left.
In 1927 rope shop employees paused to show off their latest product made on the 80-Ton Rope Machine: an 8,025 ft. long, 3 in. diameter wire rope that weighed 62 tons and had to be shipped on three reels.
The Company made the rope with a breaking strength of approximately 375 tons for the Spanish-American Iron Company in Cuba, for hauling ore cars up an incline with a grade of 25%.

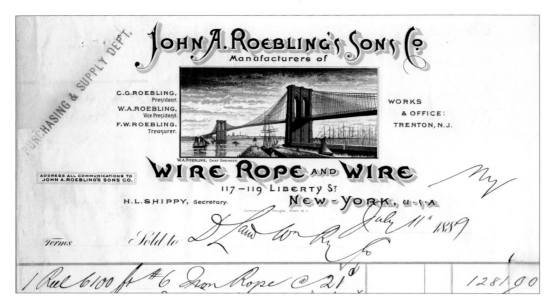

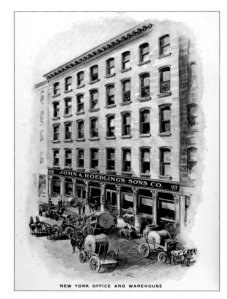

J.A.R.'s Sons Company - Figure 4.33 (left): N.Y. Office Invoice, 1889; Figure 4.34 (right): N.Y. Office & Warehouse, c1900. RU

Expansion was the order of the day

With significant growth in the sales of wire cloth, insulated wire, elevator and mining ropes and cable car cables, J.A.R.'s Sons Co. revenues rose more than two and a half times from $1,769,000 (about $53 million in 2009) in 1880 to $4,553,000 (about $137 million) in 1890, and profits more than tripled from $250,000 (about $7.5 million) to $879,000 (about $26 million). With the additional production capacity and Ferdinand's aggressive marketing, sales continued to grow dramatically in the early 1890s. Washington recalled:

We had our stores in San Francisco, in New York and Chicago and elsewhere; agents all over (Figs. 4.33-36). Our salesman Shippey (head of the New York office) had become

a globetrotter. Cable ropes in quantity went to Australia and elsewhere. Expansion was the order of the day. Every branch of the business was run at top notch.[25]

William Orr, Jr., the Superintendent of the New Jersey Wire Cloth Company subsidiary, devised new ways for fire-proofing floors and partitions, as Washington remembered:

This was the new era of fireproof buildings. Mr. Orr proposed concrete floors stiffened by reinforcing with round rods, all in panels put together in the shop.[26]

With favorable tests and aggressive marketing, the Wire Cloth Company sold many tons of fire-proofing products (Figs. 4.37-39) to a growing list of builders and architects (Fig 4.40).

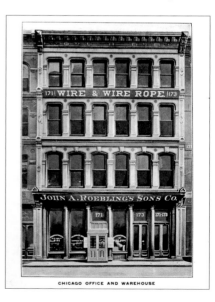

J.A.R.'s Son Co. - Figure 4.35 (left): San Franscisco Office Invoice, 1992; Figure 4.36 (right): Chicago Office & Warehouse, c1900. RU.

Figure 4.37: *A New Method of Fire-Proofing Buildings*, New Jersey Wire Cloth Company, 1892. RU
The J.A.R.'s Sons Co. subsidiary developed its fire-proofing to protect floors and partitions with wire lath covered in concrete.

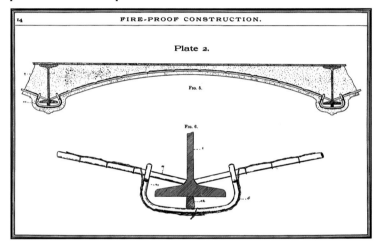

Figure 4.38: *A New Method of Fire-Proofing Buildings*. RU
The system used prefabricated rods and clips to support Roebling Patent Wire Stiffened Lath to hold the concrete in place.

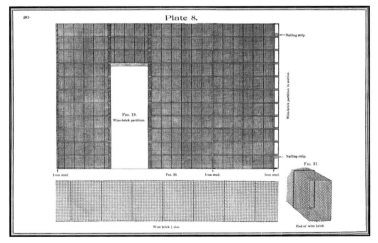

Figure 4.39: *A New Method of Fire-Proofing Buildings*. RU
Plate 8 - The system used "wire bricks" assembled into wall panels between iron studs, all covered in concrete. Wooden inserts provided nailing places for door frames and trim.

A New Method of Fire-Proofing Buildings

The importance of erecting fire-proof buildings is becoming each year more apparent. Not only in large cities but in the larger towns, blocks of buildings are crowded closely together, a fire in one of which endangers the whole, so that, too often, a whole block or square and, in many instances, a large portion of the business parts of our best cities has been reduced to crumbling walls and ashes in a few hours....

We illustrate our method of fire-proofing buildings by the union of concrete or mortar with iron wire and rods, supported by the beams and studding, whereby we not only thoroughly protect the iron beams but construct ceilings and floors impervious alike to fire and water....

We feel assured that all who carefully study the system wll be convinced of its supriority over the old and the present methods of fire-proofing....

We will be pleased to furnish samples of any of our products, or to answer any inquiries, either in regard to lathing, or to our light fire-proof construction, or to give estimates of the cost of our material, either furnished, or furnished and applied.

- Yours respectfully, NEW JERSEY WIRE CLOTH CO.

Amidst all the sales, however, the Roebling brothers worried about getting the best steel and iron, as Washington noted:

Bessemer stell was being replaced by open-hearth steel. Most of our fine steel rods for wire rope were imported from Sheffield (England). Iron rods for telegraph wire came from Sweden and steel billets had to be bought in this country, and even abroad, wherever we could get them. We were beginning to feel that we were laboring under a great handicap because we could not produce our own steel.[27]

Figure 4.40: Broad Street National Bank Brochure, 1900. BOA
Architect William Poland used the Roebling System for Trenton's "New Fire-Proof Bank and Office Building."

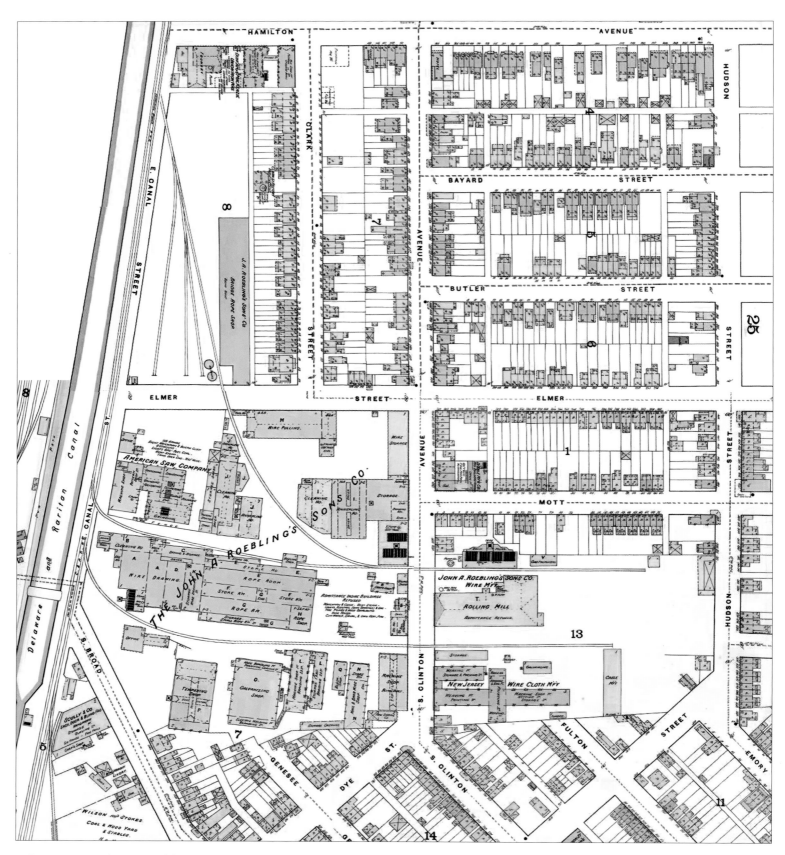

Figure 4.41: John A. Roebling's Sons Co., Trenton, Sanborn Map Compamy, 1890. Brick buildings, pink, wood buildings, yellow. With the new Rope Rooms, the Elmer Street Wire Mill, Tempering and Galvanizing Shops and the Machine Shop on the main block, the Rolling Mill east of South Clinton Avenue, and the Rope Shop north of Elmer Street, Charles had more than doubled the factory since the 1876 Sanborn recording (see Fig. 4.10). Rowhouses now crowded the factory on three sides.

Figure 4.42: 1890 Machine Shop, 1987. Jet Lowe, HAER
Charles employed the Basilica nave and aisle form for a large shop to make and repair the Company's machines. It is now the oldest intact Roebling building.

Figure 4.43: 1890 Machine Shop, 1987. Jet Lowe, HAER
Used as a lumber warehouse in 1987, the Roebling machinists had operated lathes and milling machines in the nave and aisles and pattern makers had worked on the second floor galleries.

When John Roebling set up his Trenton wire rope factory in 1849, he included a workshop in it to build and maintain his rope walk. In 1861, he included a "Machine Shop" section in his new Rope Factory to make all the new strand and rope machines he designed. With the 1870s and 1880s expansions for existing and new products, Charles had to build a freestanding Machine Shop to produce all the machines and parts needed in the various mills and shops (Figs. 4.41-4.44).

Charles established apprenticeships for machinists and for masons, carpenters and electricians to train men for life-time employment. John Cichoki started working in the Machine Shop in 1941, became a tool and die maker and worked there 33 years. In a 1993 interview in the Machine Shop, he recalled:

When I got up in the morning I just couldn't wait to park my car out here and and get in the shop. It was so nice. If anything broke all through the mill, they would say, we need this, and you went ahead and made it....

There were eight tool and die makers in there at that time....It was real interesting to make dies. You're working on a lathe, or on a milling machine or a shaper or a drill press....It was always more or less different work and I loved it....When I would make a die I would shine it; it was so beautiful....I just loved Roebling's work.[28]

Charles also established sports teams to keep his men occupied while they weren't working, and Company sports activities became quite popular over the years (Fig. 4.45).

Figure 4.44: Machine Shop Employees, 1894. BC
Machinists and apprentices gathered outside the arched entrance, which was later enlarged for trucks (see Fig. 4.42). The Company ran apprenticeship programs in several trades.

Figure 4.45: Roebling Baseball Team of 1891-1892. BC
The Company sponsored sports teams to provide wholesome leisure activities for employees. Champions of the Trades Baseball League, this team lost only one game in two years.

Figure 4.46 (left):
Washington & Emily Roebling House West State Street side, c1895. RU
A prominent porte cochere sheltered visitors at the front entrance, and the Brooklyn Bridge stained glass window provided a popular view for passers-by, especially when it was lit from inside at night.

Figure 4.48 (right):
Washington & Emily Roebling House Stairhall, c1895. RU
A large fireplace and the Tiffany stained glass window of the Brooklyn Bridge dominated the grand stair hall, where Emily posed on the staircase.

The finest house in Trenton

When their son, John II, was graduated from Rensselear Polytechnic Institute in 1888, Washington and Emily moved back to Trenton and bought a property at 191 West State Street with a fine view of the Delaware River flowing southward. They commissioned George E. Harney, a prominent architect from Cold Spring, New York, Emily's home town, to design a suitable house. Emily knew Harney from his design in 1869 of the Episcopal Church of St. Mary in the Highlands in Cold Spring, which she attended and where he served on the vestry. In 1885, Harney had completed a 27 room mansion, now part of the Newark Museum, for John H. Ballantine, the eldest son of the famous Newark Brewer, Peter Ballantine, and he had also designed several prominent buildings in New York City.[29]

For Emily and Washington's home, Harney designed "a commodious mansion after the Tudor style of architecture, surrounded by ample grounds" (Figs. 4.46-47). Emily oversaw many aspects of the design and decoration and after they

Figure 4.47 (left):
Washington & Emily Roebling House South Side, c1895. RU
The rear of the house and property commanded a fine view of Stacy Park, the Delaware and Raritan Canal and the Delaware River.

Figure 4.49 (right):
Washington & Emily Roebling House "Museum," c1895. RU
Washington's study contained more than 16,000 mineral specimens.

The Geological Congress has been holding sessions at Princeton University, and yesterday six of their mineralogists swooped down on me and for five long hours I was busy showing them 'the best collection in the world.' That is what they said.

- Washington A. Roebling, 1914[31]

the back stairs and through a butler's pantry into the huge dining room. In 1931, Hamilton Schuyler, the Roebling family historian, simply characterized 191 West State Street as "the finest house in Trenton."[32]

Washington and Emily had purchased the property in her name and she left it to her grandson Siegfried with a life estate for Washington. When he died, *The New York Times* reported: "Colonel Roebling's will provides that Siegfried receive $100,000 (about $1.3 million in 2009) to invest, the income to be used to carry the property. An additional bequest gives $25,000 a year for three years for the upkeep of the place." In 1927, Siegfried offered to sell the property to the State for a Governor's residence, but with concerns about the upkeep, Governor Arthur Moore chose to remain in his Jersey City home. The State later acquired the property, demolished the house and built the State Library on the site.[33]

moved in, she commissioned a series of photographs on glass plate negatives to document the house. She entertained guests frequently at the house and participated in many social activities there. With its imposing façade and lavishly decorated interior, the Roebling Mansion embodied the stature and wealth of Trenton's most prominent couple.[30]

Harney's design included a grand hall with a Tiffany stained-glass window of the Brooklyn Bridge, (Fig. 4.48) a "Museum" for Washington's mineral collection (Fig. 4.49), a lavish parlor (Fig. 4.50) and six second-floor bedrooms, three of which Emily decorated in "Colonial," "Dutch" and "Empire" styles. The house had a Conservatory for Washington's orchid collection, nine fireplaces, and several bedrooms on the third floor. From the basement kitchen, servants carried meals up

Figure 4.50 (above): Washington & Emily Roebling House Parlor, c1895. RU Emily oversaw all the decorations, including the elaborate "Renaissance Style" parlor, which she embellished with European furniture and polar bear and tiger skins.

The cabinets and cases containing these treasures extend all the way about the walls of his study, which is a room as large as the entire first floor of a dwelling of moderate size. It is asserted by expert mineralogists that this collection contains all but 12 of the minerals ever discovered in the world and the missing ones are not now attainable at any price. When Colonel Roebling exhibits his collection to a visitor for the first time, he usually asks, 'Is there any precious stone or mineral of any kind that you have never seen and that you would like to see?'
- Hamilton Schuyler, *The Roeblings*, 1931[34]

Figure 4.51: Ferdinand W. Roebling Residence, c1918. HS
Ferdinand's Italianate townhouse at 222 West State Street was the
most modest of the Roebling houses on Trenton's best street.

Figure 4.52: Ferdinand W. Roebling, Jr., Residence, c1948. TPL
Ferdinand, Jr., renovated his father's house to resemble the
architecture of his grandfather's home town in Germany.

Ferdinand bought a town house at 222 West State Street (Figs. 4.51-52) just northwest of Washington and Emily's mansion. The most outgoing of the Roebling brothers, Ferdinand had the largest family (Figs. 4.53-54) and participated in many civic activities. He served as the first president of the Trenton Free Public Library and oversaw the construction of its Academy Street building in 1902. He chaired the Building Commission for Trenton City Hall, built on East State Street in 1910 with murals in the Council Chamber celebrating Trenton's pottery and steel industries.

Figure 4.53: Ferdinand W. Roebling,
c1905. Pach Brothers, NYHS
Ferdinand had the largest family
of the three Roebling brothers.
For the relationships of his
family in Fig. 4.54, see the
Roebling Family Tree, page 283.

Figure 4.54: Ferdinand W. Roebling Family at 222 West State Street, c1913. KD
Back row standing: Anne Allison Perrine, Ferdinand W. Roebling, Jr., Margaret Perrine,
Karl G. Roebling, Augusta Henrietta Roebling White, William T. White.
Middle row seated: Blanche E. Roebling, Margaret Allison Roebling,
Ferdinand W. Roebling, Margaret Roebling Perrine, Ruth Metcalf Roebling.
Children seated middles row: Caroline Roebling, Ferdinand W. Roebling III,
Joseph M. Roebling, John Augustus Roebling Perrine.
Children seated front: Ferdinand Roebling White, Margaret Roebling White.

Figure 4.55: Roebling Row, c1900. TPL
In 1885 Ferdinand commissioned
the noted Trenton architect
William A. Poland
to design a row of
seven townshouses from
198-210 West State Street.
The N.J. League of Women Voters
has occupied 204 for many years.

He also served as a director of corporations in which J.A.R.'s Sons Co. invested, including Otis Elevator, Public Service Corporation, Mercer Automobile Company, Equitable Life Assurance Society, and several banks and railroads.

In 1885, Ferdinand built seven elegant row houses on West State Street as an investment project (Fig. 4.55). He and his wife, Ruth Metcalf Roebling, bought a farm in Ewing Township northwest of Trenton for a country estate. They had four children, including Karl and Ferdy, the only third generation Roeblings who spent their careers in the family business.

Charles bought a large elegant house at 333 West State (Fig. 4.56), a block west of Washington's house, and expanded it until it was nearly as big as his brother's (see Fig. 4.46). With his

fondness for gardening, which he acquired in his youth while helping his father's gardener on South Broad Street, Charles had studied botany at RPI and had become quite interested in orchids. He built a conservatory on his property where he grew rare specimens, including some he hybridized.

Charles served one term in the State Legislature but declined to run for re-election. Beyond his endless duties as Company president, he mostly cherished his privacy and home life. He and his wife, Sarah Mahon Ormsby Roebling, of Pittsburgh, had five children, but one boy died in infancy and another at the age of five. Sarah died after only ten years of marriage at the age of 32. Emily Warren Roebling's sister, Mrs. Cornelius Hook, moved into Charles' house to help raise the three surviving children. Charles never remarried.

Figure 4.56: Charles G. Roebling Residence,
333 West State Street. c1900. HS
Charles bought and expanded this large
Queen Anne Style house,
which included wrap-around porches
facing the street and the Delaware River.
He grew prized orchids in his conservatory,
which had a larger footprint than the house,
on the west side of the lot.
The house was torn down in the 1960s
to make way for the
Carteret Arms Apartments.

Washington reported to John II in early 1893 that the big rope machines "now run day and night," and at the wire cloth division, "They work day and night and Sunday and have sold 1 ½ million more square feet than can possibly be made." In the Insulated Wire Division, "Galvanized strand for electric roads (trolleys) and railroads has increased enormously in product; the suburban extension of electrical roads is unprecedented. They are extending to all small towns and villages contiguous to large towns and will thus check the unhealthy engorgement of our American towns! We have no village life here as it exists in Europe. This will become possible now." The Roeblings would soon be creating some village life not far from Trenton.[35]

While orders kept coming in, the low quality of the steel available to make wire was causing ropes to fail sooner than expected. As Washington complained:

Our ropes have done so poorly on an average that we have had to replace many more than formerly, which makes double work….Much of the trouble has arisen in trying to use American steel in place of foreign. In itself this is very proper, but the open hearth people in this country have not succeeded as yet in making a good uniform wire steel. The Washburns (in Worcester) *make their own open hearth steel, with fair success….Our competitors are very active.*[36]

By making their own steel, competitors could better control the prices as well as the quality of their products, as Washington noted:

In all manufacturing business you are at the mercy of your competitors to fix selling prices for you. To exist at all you must buy the raw material always at the bottom price. That requires a long-headed merchant who feels instinctively when markets have touched bottom and is not deceived by temporary fluctuations.[37]

In the copper market, Washington noted that Anaconda Copper and other producers had invested large amounts of capital to increase production:

Their output is steadily increasing and the tendency of prices is downward….This is one of the wonderful anomalies of these times, namely, that an enormous demand has reduced prices….due I think to the great increase of capital in this country.
Capital is always the savings of money earned, but we used to waste it in high transportation charges, in paying fancy wages, in throwing away waste materials, in unstable currency and in political uncertainties which have ceased since the war.
We used to live on the virgin products of the soil, the forests and mines. These have been skimmed off and the next step

Figure 4.57: 1897 Mott Street Generating Station, 1987. Jet Lowe, HAER Charles built the Company's first electric generating station in 1897 with steam-driven dynamos for 350 arc lamps and 5,000 incandescent lamps throughout the plant. The proportions of the one-and-a-half story building recall the classical forms of ancient Greek temples.

is aggregation of large capital and an enormous production. England led the way and we followed and are beating them.[38]

While investment in iron, steel and copper production was growing significantly, over speculation in railroads and in silver started a financial panic in mid-1893 that ruined many businesses and banks and pushed unemployment above 20 percent. As demand for wire rope and wire slackened, Charles reduced wages and had to settle a strike at the South Clinton Avenue Rolling Mill. As Washington recalled:

I was present when he addressed the rolling-mill men and certainly did not envy him the task. When there is much of this a man's temper becomes hardened; there is no help for it, you have to face the music. As usual he was the only man to do it.[39]

With the slowdown, Washington recalled: "All kinds of juggling were resorted to keep the place a-going and supplied with work. Then it is the time one suffers from over expansion. But it is also the time when everything is cheap and therefore the time for laying the foundation for future expansion." Charles took this opportunity to expand the Company's electrical capabilities. He bought rowhouses along Mott Street and erected a one-and-a-half story generating station on the corner of Mott and South Clinton Avenue to power electric lights around the plant (Fig. 4.57). The boiler house for the South Clinton Avenue Rolling Mill (see Fig. 4.41) provided the steam for the station's twin engines and dynamos.[40]

With growing demand for both residential and commercial wiring, Charles bought land on the same block facing Hudson

Figure 4.58: Insulated Wire Department, 1925. BC
Charles expanded the Company's IWD along Hudson Street
in the 1890s with, left to right, a five-story Rubber Mill, one-
story Lead Covering Shop, and a two-story Braiding Shop.

Figure 4.59: 1897 Lead Covering Shop, 1987. Jet Lowe, HAER
The south end of the shop on Hudson Street is the only
extant section of the Insulated Wire Department
at the Roebling Works in Trenton.

Street and erected three buildings for the Insulated Wire Department, including a five-story shop that was the largest building at the works. The new IWD buildings included a Rubber Mill, a Rubber Covering Shop, a Braiding Shop, and a Lead Covering Shop (Figs. 4.58-59). IWD workers (Figs. 4.60-61) produced Weatherproof, Rubber, Magnet, German Silver, and Office Wire, and Power, Telephone, Telegraph, Aerial, and Submarine Cables.

Roebling sales dipped in 1896, but rebounded with the election of President William McKinley, who Republicans promoted as "the advance agent of prosperity" because he promised to promote banking and to support a high tariff to protect American industry. The outbreak of the Spanish American War in early 1898 further stimulated industrial production and J.A.R.'s Sons Co. revenues jumped in 1899 to $10,874,000 (about $322 million in 2009).

WIRE
IN
Electrical Construction
JOHN A. ROEBLING'S SONS CO.
TRENTON, N. J.
1897.

*Charles educated his own foreman, very few men
came from outside. By this method we had men
attached to the place and faithful to the management.
A carpenter soon became a millwright,
a plain wire drawer could become a foreman,
office men were often put in charge of stores.*
– Washington A. Roebling

Figure 4.60: Clerical Staff, Insulated Wire Department, 1905. BC
The group includes one office boy, third from left.

Figure 4.61: Foremen, Insulated Wire Department, 1905. BC.
The foremen appear to be in the 1897 Lead Covering Shop.

Figure 4.62: H.B. Longacre, *Works of John A. Roebling's Sons Company, Trenton, New Jersey,* **1898. NJSM**
The Roebling brothers commissioned Philadelphia artist H. B. Longacre to illustrate their works (see Fig. 4.41) at the 50th anniversary of John A. Roebling's founding of his wire rope factory in Trenton. The bird's eye view depicts the Elmer Street Rope Shop (far left) and the four-story Elmer Street Wire Mill (see Fig. 4.26) adjacent to it, the General Office (bottom center) in John A. Roebling's 1855 house (see Fig. 3.11), the Wire Mill (see Fig. 4.9) and Rope Shops (see Figs. 4.29 & 4.32) behind it, the Rolling Mill (see Fig. 4.8) (center), the Tempering and Galvanizing Shops (bottom right), and the Machine Shop (see Figs. 4.42-43) and N.J. Wire Cloth Company (upper right). The view shows canal boats, trains and horse drawn wagons (bottom left), and electric trolleys on South Clinton Avenue (center right). The black smoke is from boilers, and the white puffs are releases of steam.

The largest single industry in Trenton is the works of the John A. Roeblings Sons' Company, an industry famous not only in this country but all over the world for its production of wire rope, cables and wire of all varieties and for all purposes. For Trenton the significance of the establishment of the enterprise many years ago was more momentous than could then be realized.
- Daily True American, June 25, 1897

Among the great industrial establishments of America

In 1898, J.A.R.'s Sons Company marked its 50th anniversary in Trenton (Fig. 4.62). Local newspapers prominently featured Roebling accomplishments (see box), with *The Daily State Gazette* calling the Brooklyn Bridge:

> *The greatest piece of engineering ever attempted in any country in this world. No grander monument has ever been left by any man of modern times than this structure; no work has proven of more lasting commercial value to the people of this country.*[41]

Charles turned 50 in 1899, having been born in Trenton just a few months after his family had moved from Saxonburg. Ferdinand was 57 and Washington was 62, ages when most men were retired or ready to retire. In the 30 years since they had inherited the business with its 100 employees, the Roebling brothers had developed it into a large corporation shipping many tons of wire and wire rope products around the globe and employing some 2,000 people at it works (Figs. 4.63-64).

Figure 4.63: *Wire: Its Manufacture and Uses,* **1900. RU**
J.A.R.'s Sons Company won a Grand Prize for its wire and wire rope at the Paris Exposition in 1900.

100

"John A. Roebling's Sons Company, Cast Steel, Iron, Copper, Plough Steel Wires and Wire Rope," - *Daily State Gazette*, Trenton, N.J., July 31, 1897

The achievements of this corporation have been instrumental in no small way in giving the State her prominent position in the industrial world....

Each year since its inception improvements and additions have been made until today the entire plant....covers twenty-two acres

This company produces eighty per cent of the large cables in use by the street railways in the United States, shipments being made frequently to the various cities throughout the country, as many as five of these cables, representing half 1,000,000 pounds, have been shipped in a day.

This company manufactures electric, telegraph, telephone, trolley, coppered, galvanized, tin, market, spring, fence, insulated and feeder wires; wire rope for street railways, hoisting, haulage, rigging, transmission, tramways, flats, suspension bridge hawsers, and tillers; plus Jersey poultry netting, window screen cloth and Roebling wire lathing, all of these various lines being made of the best material and the finest of workmanship.

The company furnishes the large telegraph and telephone companies of this country with galvanized wire, hundreds of thousands of miles of their wire being in use by these companies throughout the United States.

Nearly fifty per cent of the entire amount of wire rope used in this country is made at the works of the John A. Roebling's Sons Company, they also produce the largest part of the copper wire used for electrical purposes and much of the wire cloth, wire lathing and wire netting manufactured on this side of the Atlantic.

An idea of the extent of the business can be obtained from the statement that the average amount of material handled annually reaches a total of 150,000 tons, while $4,000 (about $125,000 in 2009) worth of oil is used in oiling the machinery annually, 14,000,000 pounds of water are used daily, and 6,000 horse-power are required for running machinery.

The reputation of the company is not confined to this country, as their productions are to be found in all countries, the export trade growing steadily....

It reflects no small credit upon the genius of its founder, as well as the ability of his successors to be able, in the face of the inventions and improvements of the age, to still occupy the leading and commanding position which they have maintained from the inception of the plant until the present day.

In a city like Trenton....the importance of having such an immense plant such as that of the John A. Roebling's Sons Company cannot be overestimated. Employing, as they do, from 2,000 to 2,500 hands, among whom are 200 females, the weekly payroll averaging $20,000 (about $625,000)....

It should be a pride to every citizen of our community for the name Roebling has made its mark among the great industrial establishments of America.

Outside of the mechanical force, there is an office force at the works numbering fifty, while in the various cities where branch offices are maintained, such as New York, Chicago, Cleveland and San Francisco, there are 300 employees who are on the payroll of the company....

Under its careful and conservative management the affairs of the company are in a flourishing condition, and it has succeeded in furthering the interests of the company in a most efficient and capable manner, giving Trenton an air of progressiveness and enterprise that no other concern located here is capable of giving our city.

The Company's 50th anniversary in Trenton also marked a crucial turning point for the Roeblings. Washington's prediction in 1893 of an "aggregation of large capital and an enormous production" had come true in just five years. Buoyed by President McKinley's expansionist policies and favorable view of consolidation, capitalists were viewing the steel industry as the next great opportunity since railroad investment had peaked. John W. Gates, who had made his first fortune selling barbed wire in Texas, had gotten control of the American Wire Company in Cleveland and the Illinois Steel Company in Chicago. People called him "Bet a Million Gates" because of his penchant for gambling.[42]

Gates now saw the potential in consolidating steel and wire companies in one conglomerate that would own ore mines, blast furnaces, rolling mills, and nail and wire mills. Gates collaborated with Wall Street financier John Pierpont Morgan to lead a syndicate of investors in a "Wire Trust." As *The New York Times* reported: "The plan of the consolidation is to buy up all the wire plants in the country and incidentally secure a number of furnaces and steel mills....The capacity of the plants which it is expected eventually to include in the new company is about 50,000 tons a week of rods, wire and wire nails." With this amount of capacity, the Wire Trust could produce about 2.6 million tons of steel products annually.[43]

J.A.R.'s Sons Co. had grown along with competitors like Washburn and Moen in Worcester that were close in size or smaller. The proposed Wire Trust would have more than 17 times the annual capacity of J.A.R.'s Sons Co.'s 150,000 tons, and it would produce its own raw materials. *The Times* noted that: "The object of the new corporation is primarily to lessen the cost of production. Most of the concerns joining own their own iron and coal mines, and the corporation will not have to go outside of its own members for any material they will use in the manufacture of their products."[44]

Gates approached all the wire and nail manufactures in the country and convinced 14 of them to join the Wire Trust. J.A.R.'s Sons Co. and Washburn & Moen were among "five concerns that had been invited to join," *The Times* noted, "but had placed their figures so high that it was impossible to even consider them....Before they can be admitted their estimate of the value of their plants will have to be considerably reduced."

Gates incorporated the Wire Trust as the American Steel and Wire Company in Chicago in April, 1898, with himself as chairman and with J.P. Morgan's syndicate controlling three quarters of the $24 million in capital (about $750 million in 2009). The new corporation's general manager told a reporter: "The move to create the combine is made in order to drive out competition....The combine will control 75 percent of the output of the country." Three weeks later, the general manager started reducing wages between 9 and 33 percent. In August, 2,100 men, a third of the new corporation's work force, went on strike.[45]

By January, 1899, Gates had taken over Washburn & Moen and eleven other wire producers to create, as *The New York Times* described, "a practical monopoly of the wire business of the country." He had increased American Steel and Wire's capital to $90 million (about $2.7 billion), and he was talking with J.P. Morgan about merging American Steel and Wire into a much bigger iron and steel combine. In a February, 1899, letter, Washington described the Roebling brothers' negotiations with Gates:

> *Our negotiating with the American Steel and Wire Company culminated in their making an offer of $8,000,000. This we refused. They then put their expert accountants on the books to ascertain the actual value of the property and before the report was made they raised their offer to $10,000,000 cash (about $308 million)....This was satisfactory to me. Our profits for the year 1898 were $1,500,000 (about $46 million)....*
>
> *For the Washburn concern they paid $8,000,000 million on a basis of $800,000 profits. This was a very high price, but it was essential for them to control the Waukegan (iron ore) portion of the Washburn business, which was a direct competitor of theirs - for the Worcester end they did not care as much....The Washburn plant in Worcester is twice the size of ours, but does not begin to make the money (we do), having been managed by people on salaries who owned very little stock....*
>
> *Their accountants....cut down our profits to below $1,250,000....When the matter came to be decided on February 9, Ferdinand and Charles came to the Waldorf and announced that they had reconsidered their offer and would now take no less than $12,000,000 cash (about $370 million)....Mr. Gates laid this before his people and they declined to accept, but reduced to their offer to $9,000,000 (about $277 million). So the sale is off.*
>
> *The reasons for refusing the price are about as follows: copper had suddenly advanced 3 to 4 cents a pound and as we had already contracted for one year's supply at a low figure, a profit of nearly a million is assured from this source alone.*
>
> *Another reason and a powerful one is that in all the negotiations Mr. Gates insisted on retaining Charles as Superintendent of the mechanical department and the manufactory. But on no account would he consent to retain Ferdinand in any capacity. It hurt Ferdinand's pride and made him mad....*
>
> *Another most potent factor lay in the almost irresistible pressure brought to bear by our numerous employees, clerks,*

store managers, foreman, traveling salesman, agents etc., every one of whom expected to be discharged under the new regime....

Ferdinand says I was too anxious to sell. In the mean time things will go on as before....Ferdinand promised positively to divide half the surplus.

Charles did not want to sell anyhow. He says he has been bossing his own place so long that he could not stand to boss it for someone else....Ferdinand's feelings were mixed - his untrammeled judgment told him he ought to sell. Yet he insisted on a price which was bound to forsake it.[46]

Washington wanted to sell because he had little say in how the Company operated and he was unsatisfied with the dividends that Ferdinand had recently been issuing - on average only five percent of profits in the 1890s, versus the average 30 percent he had issued in the 1880s. Ferdinand had been investing most of their profits into the plant or into securities, and Washington thought that he could make more money investing the value of his 30 percent share of the Company himself. Because he was not involved in managing the Company like his brothers, he had fewer relationships with employees who would be affected by selling it.

Ferdinand wanted to keep the business and keep investing in it partly for his two sons, 25-year-old Karl, who had started working there since he was graduated from Princeton University in 1894, and 20-year-old Ferdy, who was studying mechanical engineering at Lehigh University in Bethlehem, Pennsylvania. Washington and Charles each had one son but neither of them was interested in working for the Company.

Like his father had done, Ferdinand often bought customers' stock, like the Otis Brothers Elevator Company, or accepted stock as payment from them, which helped ensure future business. In 1899 the J.A.R.'s Sons Co. listed $975,000 (about $30 million) in investments, about eight percent of its total assets, which helped the Company survive cyclical downturns in the wire and wire rope business. Also like their father, the Roebling brothers refused to borrow money, as Washington recalled in 1919: "Enlargements and increases made entirely out of our own profits, no outside capital ever being required." This financial independence enabled the Roebling brothers to run J.A.R. Sons' Co. without interference from outside financial interests.

Washington claimed in 1898 that Ferdinand's management would "ultimately lead to bankruptcy," but it substantially increased the wealth of all three brothers over the next two decades. Sales and profits both grew substantially in 1899, and to mollify Washington, Ferdinand distributed $500,000 (about $15.4 million) in dividends, a 20-fold increase over the average annual dividends of the rest of the 1890s.

Washington's recollections of Roebling family and Company history were usually accurate, but he was not beyond altering facts to polish his own legacy. While he wrote in 1898 about Gates' offer, "Charles did not want to sell....Ferdinand's feeling were mixed," and he himself wanted "a sale even at a sacrifice," some 20 years later after Charles and Ferdinand had died, he wrote about the offer: "Ferdinand insisted on taking it; even Charles favored it. But I am free to say that I violently opposed it, and the deal did not go through."[47]

The girls were anxious to work

The New Jersey Wire Cloth Company employed many women to operate the looms used to make wire screens, just as women operated most of the looms in textile mills in the New England states and in other states. In May, 1899, the *Sunday Times Advertiser* reported "trouble at Roebling's mills," as "another committee of girls" complained to Trenton's Deputy Factory Inspector about being unfairly discharged:[48]

The girls objected only to the hours of work. Ten hours is said to constitute a regular day's work, and the girls allege that they worked three hours extra for four months. The girls were anxious to work, but said they could not stand the strain.

They had no fault to find with the rate of wages, but having been discharged for refusing to work overtime, they are now invoking against the Roeblings the law limiting the hours of labor in factories....

The mill's side of the case is that it was pushed with work and could not dispense with the overtime in the evening. Other girls, it was claimed, would take the places of those who didn't like the situation. The girls, however, claimed that they were physically unable to keep up under the strain, which had been going on for five months.

The girls are....claiming that it is illegal to work employees over ten hours per day, except in cases of emergency. Others are hoping that a settlement of the difficulty may be had, as the girls are in many cases the chief supporters of their homes.

The Inspector told a reporter: "I hope that this trouble will be settled amicably," and he recommended that the girls appeal to their employer. A week later the *Advertizer* reported:

The 20 girls who struck against overtime at Roebling's wire cloth department were notified by Charles G. Roebling yesterday that he could not interfere in their behalf....

Mr. Roebling told them that under the system in the Roebling mills, each foreman was held responsible for his department and in such matters would be the final arbiter. In as much as the girls had discharged themselves (by refusing overtime), he could do nothing for them.[49]

One of the strongest floor systems in use

As skyscraper construction proliferated in the 1890s, many cities adopted codes requiring fire-proofing in high-rise buildings. In 1896, New York City fire officials tested and approved the Roebling System of Fire-Proofing. To capture more of the fire-proofing business, Ferdinand incorporated the Roebling Construction Company in 1899 to contract for the installation of Roebling fire-proofing materials. *The New York Times* reported that, "The new concern will engage in the manufacture of iron (products) for fireproof buildings in all parts of the world," but Washington had reservations:[50]

The superintendent of the New Jersey Wire Cloth Company was anxious to retrieve the low price of cloth and chicken netting, and had introduced the use of stiffened wire lathing for fire-proof partitions and walls - a very good thing. This was the new era of fireproof buildings. He then proposed concrete floors stiffened by reinforcing with round rods, all in panels put together in the shop ready for use. This was all very well in a small way and brought in some business for several years.

Then the idea was broached why not take the contract for the entire building and get the profit of the middlemen? Now this was an entirely different proposition; it was the tail wagging the dog; it meant taking risky contracts of $500,000 to $1,000,000 (about $30 million in 2009) for the sake of a few thousands of profit to the New Jersey Wire Cloth Company....

My point was that such a large and intricate business would require the constant attention, every day, of both F.W. and C.G. to make any kind of a success; that the buildings were scattered all over the country and the work had to be entirely left to subordinates....

No business can flourish unless it is to a large extent under one's personal supervision, and there is a limit even to that.[51]

In his *Architect and Builder's Pocketbook* of 1906, Frank Kidder noted that the Roebling system of fire proof construction (Fig. 4.65) "is now so widely known that it requires but a brief description. It has been used in many of the best buildings in the eastern states and has proved one of the strongest floor systems in use."[52]

When the great earthquake and fires struck San Francisco in 1906, 18 buildings with Roebling Fire-Proof Floors survived better than most others. The Roeblings produced a book illustrating the success of their fire-proofing in contrast to buildings that had collapsed. The Roebling Construction Company installed its fire-proofing system into a number of impressive buildings (Fig. 4.66), but as other companies entered the business, profits became more elusive.

> ### *The Roebling System of Fire Proof Construction*[53]
> *The permanent character of fire-proof buildings, their superior sanitary conditions, the immunity they offer the owner from loss by fire, the security of life and property to the tenant, as well as the greatly reduced rate of insurance, are advantages which fully warrant the additional expense.*

Figure 4.65: *The Roebling System of Fire Proof Construction,* Roebling Construction Company advertisement, c. 1905. RPI After New York officials approved it in 1896, the Roebling System became the "STANDARD OF FIRE-PROOF CONSTRUCTION."

Figure 4.66: Roebling Construction Company advertisement, *Architectural Record*, c. 1905. The 1904 St. Regis Hotel in New York City is one of many prominent buildings erected with Roebling Fire-Proofing.

Figure 4.67 (left):
Charles G. Roebling and William Hildenbrand, c1900. PU
Charles worked on the cable plans with Hildenbrand, who had assisted both John and Washington on the Brooklyn Bridge.

Figure 4.68 (right):
Williamsburg Bridge Cable Construction, 1902. NYPL
For the footbridges, Charles produced twelve wire ropes, "each three thousand feet long, as thick as a man's wrist," on the 80-Ton Rope Machine.

Charles' ambition was fired

Having resisted selling out to Gates, the Roebling brothers had to expand to compete with his Wire Trust, and in a fitting coincidence with the Company's 50th anniversary in Trenton and Charles' 50th birthday, a big suspension bridge stimulated the expansion. Charles was eager to build the cables (Fig. 4.67), in part to show that he could do it better than his brother and he got his chance in December, 1899, as Washington recalled:

The contract for the four cables of the Williamsburg Suspension Bridge (Figs. 4.68-69) was let to J.A.R.'s Sons Co. of New York for $1,389,000 (about $43 million) to be finished in 10 months. Mr. Leffert Buck was engineer of the bridge and had prepared the specifications. All the work on this bridge was done by contract, nothing by days work - just the reverse of the old Brooklyn Bridge. Charles' ambition was fired; he was determined to build the cables. They were more than twice the size of the Brooklyn Bridge cables; consequently the honor would be twice as great.

Charles had a double task; to build the cables and make the wire - a big job in itself....Charles had not built large cables before; as an assistant he had William Hildenbrand, who had been my assistant on the cables of the Brooklyn Bridge, and was familiar with the vital points....

Charles attacked every problem with his usual energy. On the Brooklyn Bridge the footbridge cables had been taken over on small carrier cables, so as not to interfere with navigation, ferry boats being very thick there. But here vessels were much fewer and Charles adopted the plan of

placing all four cable reels at once on one barge, towing it across and letting all the ropes payoff into the water at once, and then raising them to their place afterwards....

Since the Roeblings made the wire it became possible to splice the wire together in long lengths and wind it up on wooden wheels at Trenton, which were sent to the anchorages and returned empty, thus reducing the splicing of wire on site to a minimum. The next great improvement consisted in transporting wires across double; he invented a double wheel, that is, the traveling wheel carried wires both in going over and in coming back, thereby reducing the time of cable-making over a third....

Cable making itself did not take seven months....The engineer, perhaps because the Brooklyn Bridge cables were made of galvanized wire, had ordered the wire to be merely oiled. This was a great mistake. Similarly he deprecated the beautiful wrapping which makes the cables look like solid cylinders. Sheet steel covers were put on instead, but afterwards they were taken off and the cables wrapped between the suspenders.

The wire was made in Trenton and oiled in a building on the corner of Elmer and Clinton streets.[54]

Figure 4.69: Williamsburg Bridge, c1910
Leffert L. Buck, Chief Engineer of the "New East River Bridge," had studied at RPI along with Washington in the 1860s, and he designed it 4 ½ feet longer than the Brooklyn Bridge to be the world's longest suspension bridge. With advances in steel fabrication, he designed the towers in steel instead of stone, and he specified larger cables to support subway trains.

Figure 4.70: Clinton Avenue Wire Mill, 1925. BC
Charles erected the five-story wire mill on S. Clinton Avenue in 1899 to supplement his 1880s Elmer Street Wire Mill, upper left.

Figure 4.71: Clinton Avenue Wire Mill, 1987. Jet Lowe, HAER
The first two stories of Charles' huge wire mill remained intact after the upper floors were removed in the 1950s.

The greatest danger

To make the Williamsburg Bridge wire, Charles erected the Clinton Avenue Wire Mill at the corner of Elmer Street in 1899 (Figs. 4.70-71 & see box). Washington ironically recalled Charles' limited interest in fire-proofing:

> *Hildenbrand assisted in getting out the plan of the building, which was provided with two elevators. In a five-story mill the capacity of the elevators measures the capacity of the mill....The greatest danger in these tall buildings is that of*

fire. If one starts there is no hope...Charles always turned up his nose at any suggestion about protection against fire, but our two large fires gave him a jolt which he did not forget until his dying day....

> *The most difficult part was the transmission of power by means of belts to the various floors. The stories being of average height, these vertical belts had to be short and worked under great tension to do their work, and this is not economical. This was not fully recognized and led to an entirely different plan at Kinkora when those great mills were designed, and where there was ample room to put everything on one floor.* [55]

"Roebling Plant Still Reaching Out: The New Buildings Going Up,"
- *Trenton Sunday Times Advertizer*, May 20, 1900

The new five-story wire drawing mill....is the largest single wire mill in the country and when it is in full operation the Roebling plant will be the largest of its kind in the world....The towers are a little over 100 feet tall. It will have a capacity of 100 tons of wire a day, and between three and four hundred workmen will be employed. The ground floor is rigged up for drawing rods of wire of the heavier sizes, having 98 wire-drawing blocks....The second floor will be used for making finer wire and there will there be 400 blocks.

A monster engine....capable of 2,000 horsepower has been placed in position together with twelve new boilers. This engine drives with three big four-foot wide belts, two of which lead down into the cellar from the second floor, transmitting the necessary power to the floors above. There is all together a mile of shafting....

There are over two million bricks in the structure. The new mill is equipped to draw copper and steel wire at the finest grades. Nearly 5,000 tons of wire will be manufactured for the new East River Bridge in New York....

Recently the Roeblings....made the finest steel wire ever

drawn. This wire is one-thousandth part of an inch in diameter or about half the thickness of an average human hair....One quarter of an ounce of this fine wire will measure a mile, there being 64 miles to a pound. A billet weighing 100 pounds and measuring 4 inches wide and 2 feet long will make 2,100 miles of this fine wire which is used in resistance coils in electrical work. It is valued at $50 a pound, and is therefore worth $100,000 a ton (about $3 million in 2009). The original cost of the material was probably not over $70 a ton, so that the difference means that a vast amount was paid out for labor in its manufacture. Extreme care was required in the manufacture of this wire....

All of the engineering work and designing of machinery connected within the Roebling plant is done under the personal supervision of Charles G. Roebling. In the construction of the building just completed and those under way, the workers are of the regular force and almost all the machinery used in the plant is manufactured in the mills.

Very few such plants are able to manufacture their own machinery and construct their own buildings.

Figure 4.72: "Lower Works of John A. Roebling's Sons Co., Trenton, N.J.," Roebling Catalog, c1910. RU Also known as the 'Buckthorn Plant.'

With demand growing for fireproofing and electrical products, Charles needed to expand the N.J. Wire Cloth Company and the Insulated Wire Division, but there was no space available at their works. The Roeblings bought the Buckthorn Fence factory along the railroad and the canal about a mile south of their works and erected several two and four-story buildings there for the two operations (Figs. 4.72-73). They called this new site the "Buckthorn Plant" or "Lower Works" to distinguish it from their original plant, which they now called the "Upper Works" (Figs. 4.74-75).

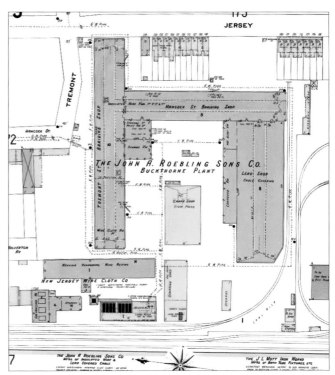

Figure 4.73: John A. Roebling's Sons Co., Buckthorn Plant, 1908. Sanborn Map Company
In 1902, Charles expanded the Insulated Wire Division and the N.J. Wire Cloth Company at the former Buckthorn Fence plant between Jersey Avenue and the canal.

Figure 4.74 (above): J.A.R.'s Sons Co. "Upper Works," c1910.
This east panarama of the original Roebling factory shows the three-story Elmer Street Rope Shop, left center, the five-story Elmer Street Wire Mill, center background, and the one-story Elmer Street Galvanizing Shop, right center. Materials are stockpiled along the canal and the adjacent Bordentown Branch of the Pennsylvania Railroad.

Figure 4.75 (right): J.A.R.'s Sons Co. "Upper Works," c1912. TPL This southeast view was taken from the roof of a Trenton Iron Company building on the west side of the Delaware & Raritan Canal.

Figure 4.76: J.A.R.'s Sons Company General Office, c1903. RU
Charles' Neo-Classical expansion of his father's 1855 Italianate mansion had a grand cornice and balustrade, columned porticos, a cast-iron fence along South Broad Street, and a two-story entrance on the south side, where his father formerly had a garden.

The addition to the office is directly in front of the old office and is to be about the same size, except that it will be four stories in height.... It is being built somewhat on the plan of the old building and will have a rough cast finish... A fourth story will be placed on the old office building and the dining room will then occupy the entire top floor except what is reserved for the kitchen and sleeping apartments of the servants.

- Trenton Sunday Times Advertizer, May 20, 1900[57]

It was just like a family atmosphere

By 1900, John A. Roebling's 1855 Italianate mansion (Figs. 3.11 & 4.62) was no longer adequate for the Company's General Office, and Charles began a series of office expansions that would continue for three decades. In a large Neo-Classical expansion that completely subsumed the house he grew up in, Charles added a fourth story on top of the old building and built a new four-story addition on the front, more than doubling the original size (Fig. 4.76).

Ferdinand organized the General Office into departments for finance, employment, sales, purchasing and disbursements, and adopted modern bookkeeping. Within a few years,

Charles erected another addition on the south side of the building with a new sales office and a large dining room for the office employees (Figs. 4.77-79).

Ruth Egan joined the office staff in 1944 right out of high school and worked there for 30 years, retiring as secretary to the plant engineer. As she recalled in a 1993 interview:[56]

You got good training in industry. It was busy all the time because of the war, and if that phone rang twice, somebody was looking at you....how come you weren't picking it up?
Everything that happened, everybody knew it. If somebody got engaged, they came down and congratulated you from all over the place. It was just like a family atmosphere. We

Figure 4.77: J.A.R.'s Sons Company General Office, c1910. RU
To provide space for the staff of the Company's office departments, Charles had to erect more additions to the General Office within only a few years of his first expansion. He built a four-story addition on the southeast corner and a one-story addition on the southwest corner. Striped window awnings provided relief from the sun's heat in this era before air conditioning.

**Figure 4.78:
J.A.R.'s Sons Company
Sales Office,
c1908. RPI**
**Ferdinand furnished the
Company's spacious sales office
with roll top desks,
oriental rugs, and
lighting fixtures that
operated with either
gas or electricity.
Large windows also
provided ample daylight.**

cared for each other. When somebody got sick everybody sent cards, everybody sent flowers. Whatever happened to anybody, happened to us too. It was really unique.

Half of the fourth floor was the kitchen and dining room. When you were hired they assigned you a number and a seat, and you had that seat forever. We had cooks, most of them were women, that came in every day. You could smell the cooking during the morning. We went up and waited, and we all went in at once, first seating or second seating.

They served full-course meals family-style. They did all their own baking and it was a different meal every day. They had the best cherry pie in the world.

It was wonderful. It was a social place in a family atmosphere. We worked hard but we really had fun, too.

They had to get a Roebling

While Washington often grumbled about Ferdinand's tight financial control of the Company, he also credited him for it's remarkable growth. Other family members also took pride in Ferdinand's accomplishments, especially when business leaders recognized his financial acumen by electing him to their boards. As John II noted in a letter to his father, Washington:

> *I think the whole family feels very proud over F.W.'s appointment as a Director of the Equitable Life Insurance Company. It shows that when they got into real peril....and had to have someone whom the people could trust – they had to get a Roebling.*[58]

**Figure 4.79:
J.A.R.'s Sons Company Dining Room
c1908. RPI**

The dining room is a feature of the Roebling office and is provided by the firm for their office employees. As many as 30 have been seated at luncheon in this dining room at one time and it has proven a great convenience beside a saver of valuable time.
- Trenton Sunday Times Advertizer, May 20, 1900[59]

Figure 4.80: Emily Warren Roebling at the coronation of Czar Nicholas in 1896. BM

When we were wandering all over the Kremlin Palace looking at and admiring all the furniture, royalties and jewels, it made me think of the way Trentonians stray around in my second story when I have a reception. - E.W. Roebling, June 6, 1896

Still acting as a monitor and guide

In 1896, Emily Warren Roebling attended the coronation of Czar Nicholas in Moscow (Fig. 4.80). In 1899, she completed the Women's Law Class at New York University and won a $50 prize (about $1,500 in 2009) for her essay, "A Wife's Disabilities," about laws that limited a married woman's ability to manage and inherit money and property.

Three years later her health started to decline, possibly from a muscular ailment, and she died in February, 1903, at the age of 60. In 1893, Washington had written that when his father died suddenly in 1869, and the burden of building the Brooklyn Bridge had fallen on him,

At first I thought I would succumb, but I had a strong tower to lean upon, my wife, a woman of infinite tact and wisest council.

On the first anniversary of her death, Washington wrote:

One year ago today my dear wife Emily died.
A dreary landscape marks the anniversary, emblematic of a year of sorrow, trouble, turmoil, personal misery and unhappiness.
May I be more content and resigned the coming year.

On his birthday three months later, May 26, he wrote in German:

Washington A. Roebling is 67 years old today. He feels more contented than he did a year ago. The contentment of old age is stealing over him and he is becoming resigned to the inevitable. The image of his wife floats before him as the fading image of the past – still acting as a monitor and guide – a spiritual vision which may again become a reality to me in the distant future. - W.A.R.[62]

The way out of it is to buy a place

In 1901, J.P. Morgan and his investment partners merged Carnegie Steel, Federal Steel, National Steel, American Steel & Wire, American Bridge and six other companies to create the United States Steel Corporation. Morgan had organized the American Bridge Company the previous year by merging 24 structural steel and iron companies, including Abram Hewitt's New Jersey Steel & Iron Company on the Delaware River in Trenton, and he had made Hewitt a director of U.S. Steel.

With a capitalization of $1.4 billion (about $41 billion in 2009), U.S. Steel was the largest corporation in the world and in its first full year of operation it produced two-thirds of the steel made in America. Charles Schwab, who had started at Carnegie Steel as a stake driver and became its president in 1897 at the age of 35, became the president of U.S. Steel, but after a fallout with J.P. Morgan in 1903, he left to run Bethlehem Steel in Bethlehem, Pennsylvania, and built it into the country's second largest steel producer.

U.S. Steel, which was about 120 times larger than J.A.R.'s Sons Company, and Bethlehem Steel controlled most of the steel production in the United States, and they had the ability to squeeze the Roeblings out of business by providing steel cheaply to their own wire subsidiaries. As Washington described the situation to John II:

We need another rolling mill and some open furnaces to make our own steel. The only man to do it is Charles and he is getting old and does not want to work so hard anymore. The way out of it is to buy a place, provided we can find one nearby.[60]

Hewitt, who had also founded the Trenton Iron Company in 1847 on the Delaware & Raritan Canal with his father-in-law, Peter Cooper, died in 1903 and Washington wrote to John II:

The U.S. Steel is negotiating for the Trenton Iron Co.'s plant across the canal and will buy it very cheap. We do not know whether to be sorry or pleased. Now that it is gone we feel that we should have bought it.[61]

Chapter 5: *We are building as well as we know how*

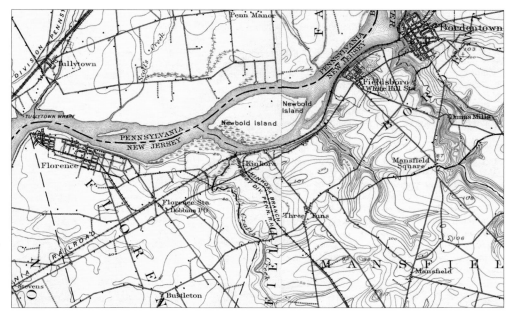

Figure 5.1: U.S.G.S., 1906. The hamlet of Kinkora between Florence and Bordentown in Burlington County grew around the junction of the Pennsylvania Railroad's Amboy Division with its Kinkora Branch. For their steel and wire mill, the Roebling brothers purchased three farms to the west of Kinkora between the Amboy Division and the Delaware River.

For some years it had become apparent that if we did not make our own open-hearth steel we would soon be left behind in the race. Buying rods abroad was unsatisfactory. It took too long, delivery was slow and uncertain. The tariff made the price high. Rods could not be bought in the United States. Neither could we buy billets of the proper quality. Even telegraph wire was made now of very low carbon open-hearth steel, all of which we had to buy. After examinations of the propositions it was found to be of great magnitude and would cost from five to ten millions (about $277 million in 2009).[1]

As Washington related, the Roebling brothers' expansion into steel making was an enormous endeavor:

There were many considerations. The proper site should be not too far from Trenton, with proper railroad facilities, supplemented by water transportation.

The first effort was made to acquire the Lalor tract just below Trenton. We had bought a part of it years before. This fell through because the old lady refused to sell at any price! She preferred peace and comfort to money and worry.

Charles then made a systematic search between Trenton and Burlington, finally selecting a site 1 mile south of the little station of Kinkora on the old Camden & Amboy R.R. (Figs. 5.1-2 and box below). Here he bought a farm having a front on the water of over a mile (afterwards increased to two miles), costing $200 per acre (about $5,500 in 2009). An extended riparian line promised to give ample room for dumping slag and ashes, a very important consideration.

The farm being a little hilly, an even level plane was created by dredging and filling in. The Pennsylvania Railroad people were delighted with the prospect of a real big business in place of peaches and potatoes.

Figure 5.2: Kinkora Works, 1905. BC
To level the site, Charles moved over one million cubic feet of soil and had to excavate down forty feet in some places.

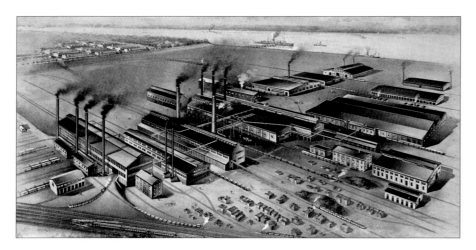

Figure 5.3:
"Kinkora Works of John A. Roebling Sons Co.,
Roebling N.J.," Roebling Catalog, c1910. RU

One of the defects of the old Trenton works
was they had simply grown up without any plan
- there was no room to make a plan.
The consequence was that transportation
of material between the various shops cost
two to three times more than it ought to.
All this was obviated at Kinkora. Everything
proceeded in a quiet, orderly manner....
All railroad tracks were conveniently arranged
for delivery of material where wanted.

– Washington A. Roebling[3]

The location between the railroad and river would facilitate transporting scrap steel and other materials and shipping the finished products (Figs. 5.3-5.4). As Washington related:

A number of things had to be planned....
A line of open-hearth steel furnaces, making large ingots;
a billet mill to roll the ingots into billets; a new huge rod
mill to consume the billets; two new wire mills, all on one floor, for heavy and finer wire; an annealing house; a large tampering shop; a galvanizing shop; a large pump house with engine; an electric light station; machine shops; cleaning houses; offices; laboratories; storerooms; storage yards for pig iron, scrap, limestone, coal and general supplies, and above all for billets.

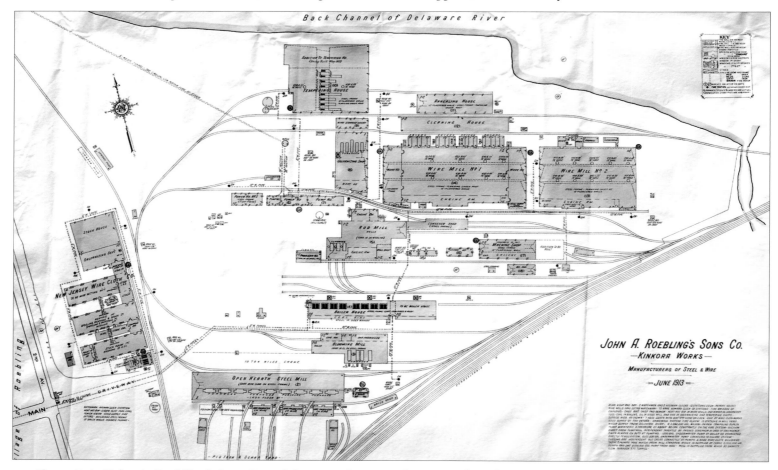

Figure 5.4: "John A. Roebling's Sons Co., Kinkora Works, Manufacturers of Steel & Wire," Fire Insurance Map, June, 1913.
By 1913, Charles had moved the N.J. Wire Cloth Co. to the site, erected a second wire mill, and still had room to expand.
Railmen transported scrap steel from the scrap yard (bottom) to the Steel Mill, ingots from there to the Blooming Mill to make billets, billets to the Rod Mill, rods to the Wire Mills, wire coils to the Galvanizing and Tempering Shops, and finished wire to the N.J. Wire Cloth shops (left) and onto rail cars or trucks for shipping to customers or to the "Upper Works" to make wire rope.

Figure 5.5: Steel Mill and Blooming Mill Employees, 1907. BC
Seven of these nine men had Swedish names.

*To build steel furnaces was a new departure for Charles.
He procured the services of a so-called expert from Worcester,
a Swede, who brought with him some Swedish workmen.*
- **Washington A. Roebling.**[5]

*All those buildings had to be properly located to
best advantage and afterwards connected by suitable
communicating lines operated by our own locomotives.*

As Washington noted, Charles had to learn how to make steel:

*To make good steel is not easy. You have to learn how to
make both acid and basic steel and prepare your bottoms
(the charge) accordingly....It took months to learn how to
make steel with different degrees of hardness....What kind
of pig iron to buy and what quality of scrap. A good testing
laboratory was necessary from the beginning....*

*Charles found it necessary to become an expert
metallurgist. He knew all about the physical properties of
steel and its chemical constitution; he kept pace with the
progress and microscopic examination of steel.*[4]

*After all, vitality supported by good judgment is the best asset.
Charles did so much work every year, no matter if the times
were good or bad, and in most cases it was found that he had
not built enough. Whenever common sense dictated that a
certain work should be done, he did not dream about it or
postpone it but went right ahead, almost before his brothers
knew it. Ferdinand always said that Charles had the building
fever bad; no one could stop him, always building and
building. He had to have an outlet for his boundless energy.*
- **Washington A. Roebling**[6]

Figure 5.6: Steel Mill Charging Floor, 1926. BC
On the "charging" side of the nine open hearth furnaces,
workers loaded scrap steel along with some pig iron, lime, and
other materials according to the "recipe" of the steel required.

Figure 5.7: Steel Mill Pit Side, 1926. BC
Workers emptied the molten steel into ladles lowered into
pits, and skimmed off the slag of impurities at the top.

Figure 5.8: Steel Mill Pit Side, 1926. BC
Workers emptied the molten steel into ingot molds in pits.

Washington also noted that Charles improved rod rolling and wire drawing operations at the new Kinkora mills:

> *With the possible exception of the Williamsburg Bridge cables I think the large rod mill at Roebling (Fig. 5.9) is the proudest achievement of Charles's career….It has been admired by many mechanical engineers of the country….*
>
> *The great wire mills (Figs. 5.10-11) differed radically from those in Trenton, by being arranged all on one floor, giving an oversight at once of everything, doing away with elevators and also with the ever present danger of fire.*[7]

Joe Sabol recalled drawing wire in a 2008 interview:

> *You made a point on your wire and you'd place it in your die. Your point would be sticking out and the puller would grab it and you'd pull it out. Each motor was synchronized to go at a certain speed and you would draw the wire around the block and put another point on it and pull it down to the next die, and then around another block and you just progressively drew the wire down to the size you needed.*
>
> *You worked your eight hours and as long as that machine was running, you were making money. You only had 15 minutes for lunch. You're splicing wire together, you grab a sandwich, back and forth, grab a cup of coffee, you didn't have a chance to get fat. Believe it or not you felt good.*
>
> *I enjoyed working down there. I didn't feel like I was going to work….You made money doing it but you always kidded around and you got the chance to work with the older people….It was hard but it was enjoyable working with those old timers….*
>
> *I started at 22; I just come out of the service.*
>
> *You go in there and first thing you hear, 'Hey Joe. Who's the president of the United States? - John A. Roebling.' 'Hey Joe. Who's the vice president? Mrs. Roebling.'*
>
> *It was fun….you really enjoyed yourself.*[8]

Figure 5.10: Will Mill, Kinkora Works, c1915. BC
Drawing fine wire on continuous wiredrawing machines - a grand sight to see when they are all in operation.
- **Washington A. Roebling**[10]

Figure 5.11: Will Mill, Kinkora Works, c1915. BC
After passing through the last die, the wire coiled around "swifts." Wire workers stripped the coils from the swifts and bundled them onto carts for moving around the mill.

A so-called model town

The Roeblings initially invested around $4 million (about $110 million in 2009) in the Kinkora Works, and a similar amount for housing its workers. Washington wrote that Kinkora was "a Scotch Irish name not Indian," and recalled:

> *Perhaps the most troublesome feature of Kinkora - so named at first - was the utter lack of houses where the working man could live. This could only be overcome by building an entire town, a so-called "model town."*
>
> *Once having the town meant that it had be taken care of. It required a large general store where everything a man needed could be bought and was sold to him at a moderate price. It meant a bakery, a drugstore, a good hotel. It demanded a water system with pure water, gas, electricity, sewers, drainage, a sewage disposal system, good streets, watchmen, policemen and a jail, a doctor.*
>
> *As more houses were built they were made less pretentious, more suitable for the poor man. Then came a public school, of which our share was $80,000. With it came taxation problems. The man who owns a town often wishes he had never been born.*[11]

In building workers' housing, the Roeblings followed the examples of prominent industrialists. The most famous in Europe was Alfred Krupp, founder of the Krupp Works in Essen, Germany, who starting in the 1870s had sought, as he later told employees, "to improve the workers' lot by building housing for them - 20,000 people have already found accommodation - to establish schools for them, and to set up facilities to allow them to purchase necessities at affordable prices."[12]

In Chicago, the sleeper car magnate George Pullman famously built a town for his workers. When he built a new factory for his Pullman Palace Car Company in 1880 on open land about eight miles south of his main plant, he resolved to break the cycle of absenteeism, low productivity and unrest in his shops that he attributed to the sanitation, drinking and crime problems in the neighborhoods where his workers lived.

Pullman was inspired by the "model tenement movement" promoted by Alfred White, who believed that: "A public-spirited man could erect well-designed and decently constructed buildings which offered clean, light, and ventilated rooms while still receiving a seven percent return on his investment." White wrote in 1879 that: "Fair return for fair rents, simple justice and not which is falsely called charity, is what the industrious laboring classes ask, and what they are entitled to." Pullman exemplified the enlightened businessman who wanted to improve the lives of his employees for their sake but also to avoid strikes and increase profits. Four years after starting his community on 500 acres he wrote:[13]

> *The object in building Pullman was the establishment of a great manufacturing business on the most substantial basis possible, recognizing….that working people are the most important element which enters into the successful operation of any manufacturing enterprise. We decided to build, in close proximity to the shops, homes for working men of such character and surrounding as would prove so attractive as to cause the best class mechanics to seek that place for employment in preference to others.*
>
> *We also desired to establish the place on such a basis as would exclude all baneful influences, believing that such a policy would result in the greatest measure of success….from a commercial point of view.*[14]

As Pullman told a reporter, "The Pullman scheme….is simplicity itself – we are landlords and businessmen. That is all there is to it….I have faith in the educational and refining influences of beauty, and beautiful and harmonious surroundings, and I hesitate at no necessary expenditure to secure them." Pullman hired Solon Beman, a 27-year-old New York architect who had remodeled his Chicago mansion, to design his car shops and the adjacent town, and he specified brick construction for all the buildings for fireproofing, aesthetic appeal, and long-term value. He hired Nathan Barrett, the 35-year-old landscape designer for "Fairlawn," his summer house on the Jersey Shore in Long Branch, to landscape the town.[15]

The beautiful manufacturing city bearing his name

Pullman named his town after himself and in the center he built an elegant 50 room hotel, which he named the Hotel Florence after his favorite daughter. Next to the hotel, he built a block-long, 90 foot tall arcade building with a 1,000 seat theatre with a balcony and 30 shops, and a five room library and meeting rooms on the second floor. He leased the Arcade shops to merchants that he selected and ran the theatre to keep out productions he deemed improper for a family audience. He built a Market Hall with stalls for local farmers and a meeting room on the second floor for 600 people. He established the Pullman Savings and Loan Bank with offices in the arcade to handle the financial needs of residents.

Beman laid out the town on a grid pattern with wide streets and narrow alleys in the middle of the residential blocks. For skilled craftsman and their families, he designed single family homes that made up about one-third of the housing units, and for unskilled workers and their families he designed tenements with multiple apartments. Barrett planted elm, maple and linden trees along the streets, and lawns with flowerbeds at intersections. He built a park next to the arcade and along Lake Calumet with a recreation area with baseball, cricket and football fields, tennis courts and a grandstand.

Pullman built a three-story school with 13 "light and cheerful" classrooms, a play room in the basement and a playground outside. He built a non-denominational stone church for religious groups, but few could afford the fees he charged and it remained unused much of the time. He started the Pullman Athletic Association with $10,000 (about $300,000 in 2009) to maintain fields and to sponsor sporting events.

Since many of the car shop workers were single, and men outnumbered women in the town by nearly two to one, Pullman made an effort to employ women. He established a Women's Union to help newcomers settle into the community and to work with the library and the school. To control drinking, Pullman made sure that his hotel had the only bar in town, but he provided ample diversions, as he told a reporter:

> *We allow no liquor in the city; now take strong drink away from men who have been accustomed to it, and not furnish something to fill the gap is all wrong - there is a want felt, a vacuum created and it must be filled; to do this we provide a theater, reading room, billiard room, and outdoor sports, and by these means our people soon forget all about drink, they find they are better off without it, and we have an assurance of our work being done with greater accuracy and skill.*[16]

Imagine a perfectly equipped town of 12,000

Pullman initially invested $5 million (about $137 million in 2009) in his town. In 1883, *Appleton's Railway Guide* noted his "worldwide reputation" for his sleeping cars, but added: "His greatest work, however, as will be better realized here after, is embodied in the beautiful manufacturing city bearing his name." By 1893, the town had 1,740 housing units. Leases allowed the Pullman Company or the tenant to terminate on ten-days' notice. While evictions were rare, turnover in the units averaged about 4-1/2 years because of the turnover in the car shops. With the town's high operating expenses, his return averaged four percent instead of his projected six percent.[17]

**Figure 5.12: Pullman, Chicago, c1883. PSHS
George Pullman established his 'model town' in 1882 with attractive housing for his workers plus a Market Hall, right.**

That year, many of the 26 million visitors to the World's Columbian Exposition in Chicago arrived on overnight trips in Pullman cars, including Emily and Washington Roebling. They visited for two weeks and admired the fairgrounds and the J.A.R.'s Son Co. exhibit (see 4.21). They no doubt also visited Pullman's popular exhibits on his Palace Car Company and his town, and read in one of Pullman's brochures:[18]

> *Imagine a perfectly equipped town of 12,000 inhabitants, bordered with bright beds of flowers and green velvety stretches of lawn....A town where the homes, even to the most modest, are bright and wholesome and filled with pure air and light, a town, in a word, where all that is ugly, and discordant, and demoralizing, is eliminated, and all that inspires to self respect, to thrift and to cleanliness of person and of thought is generously provided.*
> *Imagine all this....and you will then have some idea of the splendid work, and its physical aspect at least, which the far-reaching plan of Mr. Pullman has wrought.*[19]

When Pullman's business dropped off after the fair, he had to cut wages and payroll. He took car orders at a loss to keep men working but refused to negotiate wages or rent, and many of his workers joined Eugene Debs' new American Railway Union. By May of 1894, 35 percent of Pullman's workers were union members and 3,000 of them went out on strike. When Debs called a national boycott of Pullman cars, vandals shut down some rail lines and President Grover Cleveland had to send Federal troops to Chicago and Pullman to protect railcars and shops. The sight of the Illinois First Regiment encamped on the lawn of the Hotel Florence dealt a major blow to Pullman's vision of a model town housing contented workers.

After the strike ended, a presidential commission concluded that Pullman's wage reductions and failure to reduce rent had caused the strike, noting that the town's "aesthetic features are admired by visitors, but have little money value to employees, especially when they lacked bread." Pullman's friend, Charles Perkins, President of the Chicago, Burlington & Quincy R.R., later said: "He thought he was doing a great deal for his employees and would never have strikes; the fact is, the more you do for your men the more they want." A resident later said about the town, "Pullman was never the same after the strike."[20]

Despite the strike and his tarnished reputation, Pullman considered his model town a success that made the lives of his workers "about 40 per cent better." He was particularly pleased when the International Hygienic and Pharmaceutical Exposition in Prague in 1896 recognized Pullman as "The World's Most Perfect Town." When he died in 1897, he left $1.2 million (about $36 million) of his $8 million estate (about $243 million) to support the Pullman Free School of Manual Training for Pullman residents and employees.[21]

The longest service and best mill record

As the Roebling brothers thought about building their own town, they embraced Pullman's idea that a good living environment would attract the best workers and keep them as loyal employees. They also recognized that it would not prevent strikes and they determined to exercise less control over their tenants' lives to avoid resentments that had arisen in Pullman. By keeping the town small in comparison to the factory's payroll, they ensured a steady waiting list for housing that enabled them to reward loyal workers with "the longest service and best mill record."

By hiring multiple family members and promoting from within the plant, the Roeblings sought to achieve more stability and longevity in employment and residency than Pullman had achieved. The Roeblings emphasized the practical business

"The New Roebling Works," *The Iron Age*, April 26, 1906
All the plans for the new plant, as well as for the town, have been worked out by the company's engineers, and while contracts for grading, erection of structural buildings, for much of the equipment, &c., have been let to other concerns, a large portion has been done in its own works and under the direct supervision of the officers of the company, and particularly under that of its president, Charles G. Roebling. While the plant and model town are both known as being located at Kinkora, it is thought highly probable that it will ultimately be known as 'Roebling's,' after the name of the company building the town.

sense of their investment and projected a realistic four percent return instead of Pullman's planned six percent. The Kinkora town plan spanned the existing Knickerbocker Way with three parallel and ten perpendicular streets (Fig. 5.13).

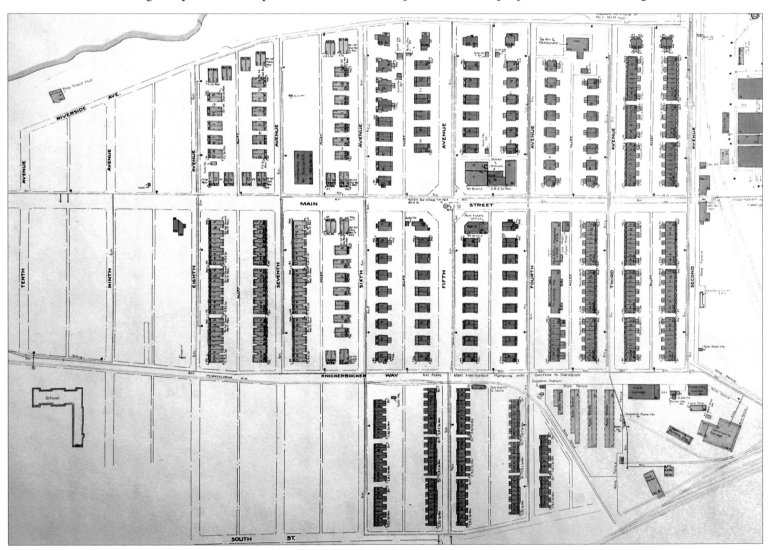

Figure 5.13: "Tenements, John A. Roebling's Sons Company, Roebling, N.J., October 26, 1944."
Charles sited the town on the bluff overlooking the Kinkora Works on the east and the Delaware River on the north.
Each house has access to an alley where merchants originally sold meat, bread and vegetables from wagons.
"Private Property" monuments enabled the Company to chain off the streets once a year to preserve their private status.

"Kinkora: America's Latest Model City Not Built Upon Ideals," *New York Herald*, April 22, 1906

John Roebling's sons - do not profess to be idealists. On the contrary, they protest that they are spending $4,000,000 (about $110 million in 2009) and providing almost ideal homes for their employees only because business forces them to do so.

It is not to avoid labor troubles - they have had none of more than trifling importance in the 60 years since the first little wire plant was built in Trenton. They do not anticipate better work from their men merely because of bettered home surroundings, they say, materialistically professing that it is steady work at living wages, not libraries and coddling, that workmen seek.

And yet, without conscious ideals of the new Utopia in which master and man shall cooperate for mutual betterment, the Roeblings are building a real 'model city.' Not only is every possible material want of their employees being provided for, but the aesthetic side of the proposition is being worked out to the satisfaction of an extreme idealist.

The workmen will not only have homes in which all creature comforts are provided for, but they will have a carefully laid out park at their doorstep. The streets will be macadamized, but instead of being only 40 or 50 feet wide, they will have a width of 100 feet, with a parkway running through the center and bordered with shade trees. The houses are set 15 feet back from the street and the lawns in front will be cared for by the company, besides having the best of plumbing.

Water will be free and it will be filtered by the most improved process. A single man can live for $2.50 a week in one of the company's hotels, with the room 8 x 12, lighted by electricity and heated by steam. A man with a family need pay not more than $8-$14 a month for a separate house for which he would have to pay twice that rent in Trenton.

Colonel Washington A. Roebling is frankly skeptical as to the results of which will be attained and Charles G. Roebling, under whose direction the project was planned and is being carried to completion, regards it as a purely business proposition.

'We are doing only what we are driven to do by force of circumstances,' they say, they do not expect any substantial returns in the form of improvements in the quality or quantity of their product....

The time and expense involved in compelling the employees to travel between Trenton and the new mills below Kinkora put that out of the question as a place for the men to live in. Something radically different had to be done, and it is as a solution to this purely business problem that the new city was evolved.

'Having determined upon Kinkora as the site for the expansion of our mills we were forced to build houses for the men who will be employed there,' is the simple explanation of the Roeblings. 'Inasmuch as we had to build houses anyway, we are building as well as we know how and incidentally we are providing some other things for the benefit of our employees. The rentals presumably will pay the interest on the investment. We do not ask or expect any other returns and we certainly are not posing as idealists or reformers.'

In a long talk the other day, Charles G. Roebling did not give utterance to a single expression of hope that his employees would be uplifted by their surroundings, but deliberately, dispassionately, he has planned so well that it is doubtful whether an advanced idealist would add greatly to what is already finished or in course of completion. Certainly nothing would be subtracted from what the Roebling's have provided....

Disavowing all that is altruistic, the Roeblings are planting fruit trees in the backyards and choosing the varieties with as great care as if they were providing for their own homes. Flowering shrubs will be set out where ever good taste calls for them and will be nurtured by the municipal gardener....

Being in absolute possession and ownership of the houses and hotels, the Roeblings will be in a position to dispense with the company of any man who abuses his privileges. By declining to rent him a house or to house him in one of the hotels it would be made so difficult for him to reach his work as to virtually drive him elsewhere, or by discharging him they would remove any reason for his desiring to remain in the city....

The company will do its own street cleaning and public lighting, will maintain the grounds and dispose of the refuse, conduct its own hotel and bar and store, and limit privileges to those who conform to reasonable roles of conduct. But at the same time every possible effort will be made to get as far as possible away from paternalism.

'The only requisite is for a man to do his work well and to behave himself as a householder and a citizen,' is the dictum of the Roeblings. 'Otherwise we wish him to feel as free as if he were living in his own house on his own land. As far as possible we shall not interfere with his absolute freedom and nothing will be more thoroughly impressed upon him than this fact. We are not giving anything away and the men will be getting only what they pay for. They will be under no obligation nor we to them as far as life in the city is concerned.

'We shall charge enough in rents to provide a fair interest on our investments in houses and their surroundings. While the store, for instance, will not be conducted for the purpose of making a profit, there is no thought of running it in a loss, and the same principal holds throughout the project. It is pure business with us, though we would not go into it if we did not consider it good business, and if the men find it as good business for them we shall be satisfied....

'In fact we propose to keep our hands off everything except where we take the place of the usual city officials, such as commissioners of lighting, street cleaning, parks and the like.

'Workingmen don't want to be coddled and patronized. They would rather have steady work the year-round and decent wages than all the libraries in the world. Fortunately, we have been able to provide the work, and the best of the men are making as much as $50 a week, whilst few are getting as little as $10.

'For reasons over which we have no control we are also providing them with places to live, and in doing so we have built comfortable and substantial houses but more than that we have not attempted and shall not attempt to.'

Whatever else the project may be, it does not include the attempted placating of labor unions, for there are none in the Roebling works, which has the distinction not only of being the largest plant of its kind outside the United States Steel Corporation, but is generally recognized as one of the main strongholds of the open shop principle.

Now and then there have been momentary differences between employer and employees, but in the 60 years since the business was established there has been nothing approaching a general strike.

'Our men themselves do not care to join the unions,' said Mr. Roebling. 'Sometimes they pay trifling dues to save trouble, I suppose, but there is no real organization among them, and apparently no prospect that there will be any. Constant but vain efforts are being made by organizers to gain men over to their way of thinking, but there is no encouragement for them. The men know that they are well off, and while they have steady employment they are not likely to jump to the fire by making impossible demands.'

One of the secrets of the freedom of the Roeblings from labor troubles has been the close association between them and their employees. The three sons of John A. Roebling grew up in the business, and it was not so long ago that they could call every workman by his first name and knew his family history.

There are even yet, in spite of the great growth of the business, men in the employ of the Roeblings whose fathers and grandfathers worked in the mills before them and whose sons are now being trained to take their fathers' places. For many years it has been the custom of the men to go direct to headquarters with any grievances they had, real or imaginary, and to talk as freely with their employers as among themselves.

Colonel Roebling retired from active work several years ago, but his brothers, Charles and Ferdinand, have maintained the family's traditional policies, with the result that the mills are as near family affairs as seems possible with 6,500 men concerned.

'So you see,' the president of the company explained, after reciting the history of the company with regard to its policies, 'we are not building at Kinkora with any thought that improved conditions of living will lessen the danger of strikes. We do not believe that what we are doing would effect that situation one way or the other. The attempts to carry out

ideals in the National Cash Register works, in Pullman and elsewhere, have surely not been encouraging to employers, and we are going ahead without any illusions in this regard.

'The explanation of our project is, in fact, of the simplest. Every available foot of room at our works in Trenton is in use, and we are still crowded up to the limit of efficiency. It became imperative for us to expand, but when we tried to buy adjoining property in Trenton we've found that prices were prohibitive....

'Near Kinkora we found the site available for our mills, but there were no accommodations for the men we would have to employ there. Consequently we had to build houses for them to live in, and in doing so built for permanence and incidentally for the control of our men. That's all there is to it, and to make the project out as altruistic in any respect is a charge to which we do not plead guilty.

'We are providing for the extension of our business....At Kinkora we have many advantages, such as plenty of free water, which is an item that alone will reduce the cost of production by $.25 a ton. Under our feet there is a large supply of silicate, which is an important item in the making of steel. By means of the Delaware River we shall have water carriage to our doors for the receiving of raw material and shipping of the finished product....

'As rapidly as it may be necessary to extend our business the plant in Kinkora will be increased. So far we have planned for two rod mills there and one steel making plant. We expect to be running within a few weeks, when at the start we shall employ about fifteen hundred men. Within two years this number will certainly be doubled and what will occur after that remains to be seen'....

One of the remarkable features of the building and planning of Kinkora is the fact that all of the designing and engineering has been done entirely by the office force of the Roeblings. Not a single plan has gone outside, and the carrying out of the work has likewise been solely in the hands of the Roeblings and their employees. Charles G. Roebling, president of the company, has devoted a great part of his energies for the last year to the carrying out of the project.

The new 'model city' is without a settled name. The Pennsylvania Railroad has unofficially dubbed it 'Roeblings,' while the men who are carrying the project through speak of the site as Kinkora. But a mile up the river there is a Kinkora which has borne the name for many years and could not be expected to relinquish it with good grace. It has its own railroad station, while the new city will have another of its own, and one far more pretentious than its neighbor if the hopes of the 'model city's' founders are realized.

'Roeblings' it will probably be known, despite the evident desire of its founders to use another name, and, ideal without ideals, it promises to endure as a monument to their name far beyond the lifetime of Trenton's great industry.[22]

The Pennsylvania Railroad's Amboy Division ran north, as seen from Knickerbocker Avenue, later named Hornberger Avenue, towards Trenton, and south towards Burlington and Camden. The Roeblings called their village Kinkora after the nearby hamlet to the north (see Fig. 5.1), but the railroad already had a stop there and it named this stop Roebling. Within a short time everyone called the village Roebling.

Pleasantly situated

With the new Roebling Station providing access (Fig. 5.14), workers broke ground on the village in 1905, and *The Iron Age* soon reported on "The only private town in New Jersey:"

> *The Roeblings will provide paved streets, a water system of filtered water, a sewer system, gas and electric lights, schools, churches, a library, fire department, police and street cleaning departments, and all other adjuncts of a modern city. The site of the town is pleasantly situated on the high banks of the Delaware River, possessing natural advantages of health and beauty. The streets are exceptionally wide and will be planted with trees. A park will be maintained on the river slope. Each home will have ample ground for the cultivation of flowers and vegetables, and this will be encouraged by the company, which will do everything possible to promote the welfare of the employees.[23]*

Like Pullman, the Roeblings built for the long-term with brick walls and slate roofs, which reduced maintenance and continued the Roebling tradition of substantial construction. Company engineers employed Italianate, Queen Anne and Colonial Revival details on the buildings.

I know damned well you'd get drunk yourself

The Company erected the Roebling Inn with a bar as the first structure in town to lodge construction workers (Fig. 5.15), and *The New York Herald* reported:

> *It the hopes of the Roeblings are fulfilled theirs will be the only bar within more than a mile of their city. Semi official assurances have been given that no other licenses will be issued in the neighborhood, leaving a clear field to the club bar to work out its own salvation.[24]*

Despite the assurances, entrepreneurs set up saloons and other businesses on non-Roebling land south of the railroad tracks, and "The Row," as villagers called it, became a popular destination for a variety of activities, some operating beyond the law. The Roeblings tolerated it, as Charles told a reporter:

> *Haven't they a right to get drunk out of hours if they want to? That's their business, not mine. If you had to work nine or ten hours before an open hearth furnace I know damned well you'd get drunk yourself (see box).[25]*

Charles built some commercial buildings in the middle of town and developed four kinds of housing for employees, with the size, design and location of each type reflecting the employment hierarchy within the works (Fig. 5.16).

Figure 5.15: Roebling Inn, Roebling, N.J., c1970. BC
The Roebling Inn, beautifully situated, overlooking the river, where the only licensed bar in the village, a billiard room and bowling alleys are run for the benefit of the working man and where transients may be comfortably accommodated.
The Iron Age, August 6, 1908.[27]

> *There is no use in trying to make a mollycoddle out of a mill man. When he wants a drink he is going to get it, especially the foreign-born. We don't propose to pick his drinks for him. If he wants whiskey, it's a good sight better for us that he should be able to get it here like a human being than to travel into Trenton and take a chance with the stuff that goes over the bars where a working man drinks. The whiskey here isn't gilt-edged but it's decent and worth what it costs.*
> *- Charles G. Roebling[26]*

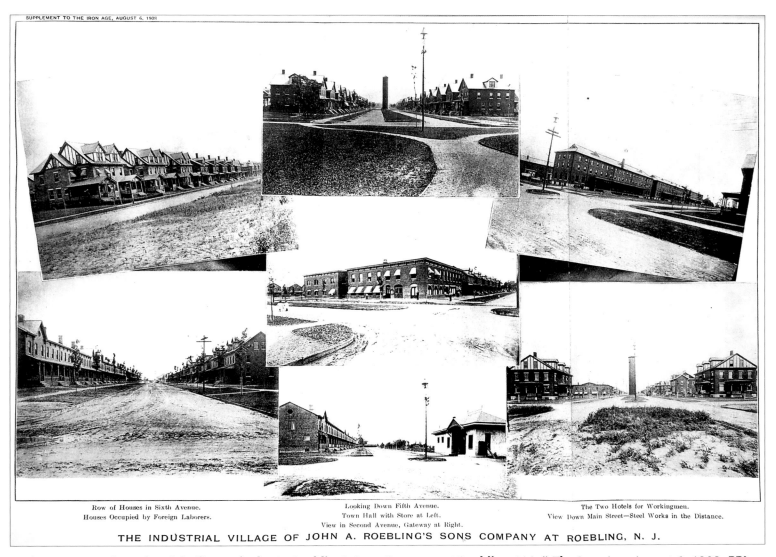

Row of Houses in Sixth Avenue.
Houses Occupied by Foreign Laborers.

Looking Down Fifth Avenue.
Town Hall with Store at Left.
View in Second Avenue, Gateway at Right.

The Two Hotels for Workingmen.
View Down Main Street—Steel Works in the Distance.

THE INDUSTRIAL VILLAGE OF JOHN A. ROEBLING'S SONS COMPANY AT ROEBLING, N. J.

**Figure 5.16: "The Industrial Village of John A. Roebling's Sons Company at Roebling, N.J.," *The Iron Age*, August 6, 1908. PPL
Although the streets remained unpaved, the Company had completed much of the village in just three years,
including planting trees in front of the houses and erecting the "Gateway," bottom center, to the Kinkora Works.**

"The Industrial Village at Roebling," *The Iron Age*, August 6, 1908

One of the marked tendencies in connection with industrial progress at the present day is found in the provisions made by large manufacturing concerns for the comfortable housing of their employees and those dependent upon them.

It goes without saying that laborers whose home surroundings are attractive and pleasant and who can enjoy to probably the fullest extent the comforts of life compatible with the circumstances of wage earners, are likely to prove more efficient than those who are otherwise domiciled.

There is the incentive on the part of the men to become more and more proficient in the department of work in which they are engaged, so that their terms of service may be lengthened and they and their families continue to enjoy the privileges and comforts which come from a residence in the model village provided for them....Many projects for the betterment of the

working man's conditions have been started in this and other countries, and with results in many instances which have strikingly demonstrated the wisdom of the undertaking....

A model industrial village for working men which has been attended with market success is that which the John A. Roebling's Sons Company has built at Roebling, N.J., 10 miles below the city of Trenton, on the south bank of the Delaware River. When it was decided some three years ago to erect a steel plant at this place it was obvious that dwelling houses for the workmen would be required, as there were no housing accommodations in the vicinity.

As a result....a village was laid out immediately adjacent.... the idea being to make it a model in its way and to provide comforts which would render the place attractive to the workmen as a home to themselves and their families.

Figure 5.17: Second Avenue and Main Street, c1906. BCHS
The Company erected rowhouses for common workers across
from the plant and put up a gate at the foot of Main Street.

For unskilled and semiskilled laborers and their families, the Company built rowhouses in blocks of ten and twelve on the streets near the works (Fig. 5.17), south of the railroad, and near the athletic fields on the west. The Company built two three-story Workingmen's Hotels, also known as Boarding Houses No. 1 & No 2, on Fourth Avenue between the center of town and the works (Fig. 5.18 & see box below). In No. 1, the Company set up a post office, a doctor's office and a small hospital with two wards, and in No. 2 it opened a school for grades 3-6. Younger children attended school in a nearby row house.

For steelworkers, wire drawers and other skilled employees, the Company built semi-detached houses on the streets closest to the center of town and near the river (Figs. 5.19-20). On Riverside Avenue facing the park, the Company erected six free standing houses in the Colonial Revival Style for supervisors and department heads (see box opposite).

Figure 5.18: Workingman's Hotel No. 1 & No. 2, c1910. RM
Besides renting rooms to single men in these boarding houses,
the Company provided meals there plus a lounge, a doctor's
office with a sick ward, and classrooms for schoolchildren.

The Roeblings calculated the rents for the modest return of four percent on their investment. As *The Iron Age* reported:

The rents for the various types of houses are based on the costs of each and are so proportioned that the interest on the original investment is but a small amount after deducting the cost of operation. The entire idea is to afford to the employees of the company a maximum of convenience and comfort in the way of living accommodations for the amount of capital invested and to meet all the reasonable requirements.[28]

The initial rents ranged from $2.50 per week at the boarding houses to $25 per month for a supervisor's detached house, about half the cost of similar accommodations in Trenton, although wages were the same at both plants. The Pullman Company deducted rent from employees' pay, but J.A.R.'s Son Co. collected rent when it was due. While Pullman's leases provided for termination by landlord or tenant on ten day's notice, the Roeblings' leases more strictly specified that "tenancy may be terminated at any time upon one week's notice by John A. Roebling's Sons Company."[29]

Both Pullman and the Roebling brothers avoided evicting tenants except for extraordinary circumstances, but both also tried to influence the politics of their employees. One Roebling worker from Eastern Europe related that the plant manager took him aside the day after he became a citizen and instructed him to register as a Republican. Company crews painted and wallpapered the houses every three years, allowing the tenants to choose standard paint colors and wallpaper or to pay an additional cost for fancier options. Leases required the tenants to report any maintenance problems within five hours of discovery, and Company workers promptly made the necessary repairs.[30]

The two hotels for single men - where good board and a single room may be had for the modest sum of five dollars per week - are finished in a thoroughly first-class manner, are light and airy and equipped throughout with the modern conveniences. On the main floor is a sitting or reading room, a large dining room and a well lighted and equipped kitchen, and at the counter are periodicals, cigars and other equipment, such as to be found in the usual hotel lobby. On the second and third floors are 63 single sleeping rooms and two large double rooms. Smaller rooms are each furnished with a single bed, two chairs, chiffonier, and table, with a rug of sufficient size to nearly cover the entire floor area.... On the second floor is also a sitting or lounging room. In the basement (in No. 1) is a lunch or "grill" room.... where the wants of the transient visitor may be supplied.
- *The Iron Age*, August 6, 1908

Figure 5.19: 5th Avenue, Roebling, N.J., c1910. RM

Figure 5.20: 6th Avenue below Main Street, c1910. RM

The Company rented semi-detached houses on Fifth Avenue and the streets to the west to skilled workers and managers.

Company workers maintained the streets, sidewalks, medians and front lawns, while leases required tenants to maintain their backyards. When some residents started piling up garbage in their , R.H. Thompson, the town manager, began offering cash prizes for the best looking yards, and many residents created attractive gardens of vegetables and flowers to try and win the prizes. The Company maintained this incentive for many years, and gardening became a tradition in town that continues today through individual efforts and through the Roebling Garden Club.

"The Industrial Village at Roebling," *The Iron Age,* August 6, 1908 - *Types of Houses*

In the village at present are 10 types of houses all constructed of brick with slate roofs in most substantial manner, and fitted with modern conveniences.

Type No. 1 is a two-story four room and attic dwelling with a shed extension in the rear containing a toilet. It has yellow pine trim finished natural, and is built in blocks or rows of 10. These houses are occupied by the foreign laborers, and rental is $8.50 per month. The foreign laborers are principally Hungarians and Slavs, and their houses are inspected regularly to prevent overcrowding, no one house being allowed to shelter more than six adults.

Type N. 2 is a semi-detached two-story and attic dwelling, a "twin" or "double" house, containing seven rooms, including a shed kitchen. It has yellow pine trim, finished natural, and rents for $9.50 per month.

Type No. 3 is also semi-detached, two stories and attic in height, and contains eight rooms with attic. It is steam heated, has cypress trim, finished natural, and rents for $15 per month.

Type No. 4 contains six rooms, with den and shed extension, is steam heated, and is of a semi-detached style; renting for $12 per month.

Coming to the better class of dwelling and designed for employees receiving a larger income:

Type No. 4 is semi-detached and two stories and addic in height. It has nine rooms, with baths, reception hall, butler's pantry and shed extension. The interior trim is of cypress, finished natural. It is heated by steam and is lighted by

electricity. It has a laundry located in the cellar.

Type No. 6 is three stories in height and contains 10 rooms and attic, thus adapting it to still larger family requirements. It is 20 feet wide, has yellow pine trim, finished natural, laundry in the cellar, is steam heated and lighted by electricity. This type is built eight houses to the street block.

Type No. 7 is two stories and attic in height, has eight rooms and bath, butler's pantry, reception hall and vestibule, has cypress trim, finished natural, steam heat, electric lights and laundry in the cellar.

Type No. 8 is semi-detached, two stories and attic in height, contains eight rooms and bath, with reception hall and vestibule, and has cypress trim, natural finish. It is heated by steam, lighted by electricity and has a laundry in the cellar.

Type No. 9 is two stories and attic in height, contains eight rooms and attic, has cypress trim, natural finish, steam heat and electric lights.

Types Nos. 5, 6, 7 and 8 rent for $20 per month while type No. 9 brings $18 per month. The exterior treatment of these houses is varied to produce attractive street architecture, the resultant effects being such as to reflect great credit upon the designer of them.

Type No. 10 is a handsome detached cottage two stories and attic in height, which contains 11 rooms and bath, with modern plumbing, butler's pantry and reception hall. It is trimmed in cypress, finished natural, is heated by hot water and lighted by electricity. It has every convenience of a thoroughly up-to-date residence. It rents for $25 per month.

Main Street, Roebling, N. J.

Figure 5.21: Main Street, Roebling, N.J.; c1915. RM
The standpipe in the center of town equalized water pressure
to all the buildings, including the General Store, left.

4th Avenue and Main Street, Roebling, N. J.

Figure 22: Roebling Town Hall, c1915. RM
The first floor contained a drug store, barber shop and bakery,
and the second floor held the town's Executive Office, a library
and an Assembly Hall for meetings and entertainments.

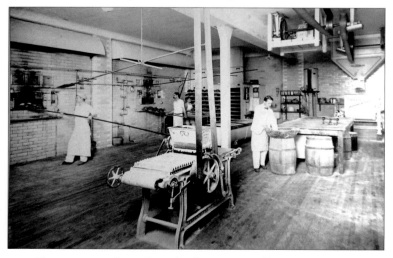

Figure 5.23: The Bakery in the Town Hall, c1915. BCHS
The bakers specialized in "the Hungarian loaf of rye," and
delivered their products to village residents on a bread wagon.

The store is conducted on a cash basis, or if preferred, accounts may be settled weekly, depending upon the credit of the customer. No script is issued by the company to its men and no money is deducted from the pay envelope for store purchases. It is left optional with the men whether they trade at the store or will secure their supplies elsewhere, as nothing is done to restrict the free exercise of their wishes as to the place they may purchase their goods. There is strong competition by reason of the stores in Trenton....and by the fact that peddlers are permitted to sell their goods through the streets of the village....Twenty-two clerks and four teams are kept busy supplying the wants of a population of 1,400 souls. As Manager Samuel Major puts it, the establishment is a cross between a 'general store' and a department store.
- The Iron Age, August 6, 1908

The Roeblings' built their model town about one-third the size of Pullman. Instead of Pullman's large arcade with shops he rented to hand-picked merchants, the Roeblings built a two-story General Store in the center of town (Fig. 5.21), and operated it themselves. They opened the store with two clerks in 1906 when just nine families had moved into town.

Next to the General Store on Main Street the Company erected a Town Hall with a drug store, a "sanitary" barber shop, and a bakery on the first floor (Figs. 22-23). The second floor contained an Assembly Hall, the town's Executive Offices, and a library with "4,300 well-selected volumes." While Pullman built a church and charged religious groups for its use, the Roeblings were more liberal with their Assembly Hall, as *The Iron Age* noted:

The Assembly Room or hall has a seating capacity of 250, where meetings, entertainments, or dances, fairs, etc. are held....The use of this hall is given free of charge for the

The bread baked here is two ounces heavier than the regulation loaf....The bake room on the ground floor is lighted by four large windows, thus enabling passersby to watch from the outside the operations which are going on within. The bake room is lined with white enamel brick or tile, and the ovens are fired from the rear, so that there is no dust or ashes in the bake room.... Much of the bread that is baked is the Hungarian loaf of rye, which is exclusively used by the foreign employees of the company.... The arrangement of the equipment and the general conduct of this bakery has won for it the commendation of the State Inspector, who pronounced it 'the finest in the State.'
- The Iron Age, August 6, 1908

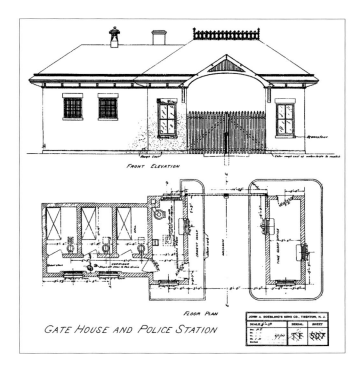

FRONT ELEVATION

FLOOR PLAN

GATE HOUSE AND POLICE STATION

JOHN A. ROEBLING'S SONS CO., TRENTON, N. J.

Figure 5.24 (left): J.A.R.'s Sons Co., Gate House & Police Station, 1907. RM Figure 5.25 (above): Gate House and Mills, 1910. BCHS

For the temporary detention of malefactors a small prison containing three cells is provided at the left in the building constituting the gateway to the steelworks and which is located at the foot of the Main Street of the village. On the right of the gateway is the timekeeper's office, the time of each employee being taken as he passes to work and again when he returns to the village.
- The Iron Age, August 6, 1908

meetings of the various religious denominations…At the present time no one denomination is sufficiently strong to maintain a church of its own, and therefore the services are held in this hall until such time as the natural growth of the village warrants the erection of church edifices or chapels.[31]

The Assembly Hall contained a large stage with dressing rooms on each side. Pullman had personally selected or approved the offerings in his hall to ensure wholesome entertainment for his men and their families, but the Roeblings chose to let their employees pick their own entertainments. As Charles told a *New York Herald* reporter:

This will work itself out naturally. When enough persons are living here it will be profitable for vaudeville shows to include in their programs, and without doubt the men will get up entertainments of their own. But we have no desire or intention to take part in the village life to that extent.[32]

At the entrance to the factory from the town, the Company erected a Gate House and Police Station with a covered

---

Roebling, New Jersey
One of the best-planned industrial towns ever built in America, a model in every respect. In the view of many old admirers of the family, it was a fitting extension of ideas that had spurred John Roebling on at Saxonburg many years earlier.
- David McCullough, *The Great Bridge*

---

entrance, a Time Clock Room, a Watchman's Room, and three jail cells (Figs. 24-25). The Company organized a volunteer fire department of 50 members. As *The Iron Age* noted:

In a large measure, the department is a social organization as well as a firefighter, and the men take great interest in it. They expect at no very distant day to have independent quarters of their own, which will be more in the nature of the social club.[33]

No expense is being spared

For recreation, village residents naturally focused on the Delaware River, as *The Iron Age* reported:

Many of the villagers are owners of motor, rowing or other pleasure boats, for the use of which the Delaware affords excellent opportunity. For the convenience of these boat owners, the company is building a dock of sufficient size to allow even the landing of river excursion steamers.
Several hundred yards above the dock are bathing houses for the free use of the villagers, and no expense is being spared to provide everything within reason for the comfort and health of those within the community.[34]

In addition to the tennis courts at the southern end of the park, the Company the built a recreation center on Knickerbocker Avenue at Sixth Avenue with billiard tables, a bowling alley, and a lunch room. On the southern end of town the Company built athletic fields, including a baseball diamond with a 1,500 seat grandstand and a football field, and a Boy Scout lodge on the river bank to foster American values.

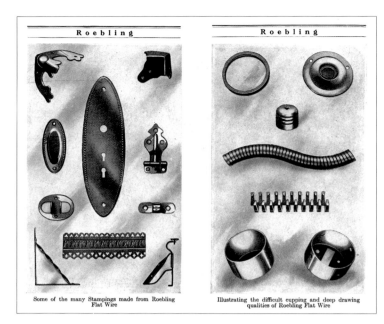

Some of the many Stampings made from Roebling Flat Wire

Illustrating the difficult cupping and deep drawing qualities of Roebling Flat Wire

Figure 5.26: Roebling Flat Wire, 1931.

Low carbon flat wire is used for many purposes, among them grill work, hardware, metal hose and tubing, metal buttons, buckles, toys, shoe hooks and eyelets, electrical novelties, and metal specialties and stampings.... High carbon flat wire may be depended upon to give particularly good service when used in the manufacture of clock springs, trusses, door checks, snap springs, lock springs, brushes, etc. The wire can be furnished untempered, oil tempered, and in bright, black, polished or colored finishes. Articles made from flat wire by stamping or drawing, are steadily replacing small castings and forgings produced in automatic machine work. The smooth surface readily lends itself to plating and superior finish.
- Roebling Wire Rope and Wire, 1931.

Back in Trenton, Charles expanded the capacity for cold rolling steel rods into the various types of flat wire that other companies bought to make a variety of products (Fig. 5.26). He bought a row of houses along Mott and Hudson Streets in 1905 and replaced them with the Mott Street Annealing House and the Mott Street Flat Rolling Shop (Figs. 5.27-28).

Great strength and toughness

Two big public construction projects soon demonstrated the wisdom of building the Kinkora Works. In 1906, Congress approved the Panama Canal as a lock canal, which would cost a lot less than building it at sea level. Ferdinand sent a Company representative to Panama to see what kinds of wire rope and wire were needed, and he ultimately secured more than 50 contracts to supply the Canal construction (Fig. 5.29). For dredging the Canal, the Company produced a 3-1/4 in. diameter wire rope and soon advertised its special qualities:

Where wire rope is subjected to extra heavy tugs and pulls, to scraping and grinding that tend to its rapid destruction, Roebling Improved Plow Steel Wire Rope, because of its great strength and toughness, should be chosen above all others.[35]

Figure 5.27: Mott Street Annealing Shop, 1987. J. Lowe, HAER

Wire drawing hardens most materials so much that it is necessary to anneal the wire at various stages, and thereby restore its ductility, so that it may be able to withstand further drawing. By successive annealings and drawings it may be made so fine that it weighs less than one fourth of an ounce to the mile....In the annealing houses there are many rows of large pots, arranged beneath the floor for convenience in charging. Coils of wire are put into the pots, which are then hermetically sealed. Heat is applied to the outside until the temperature is raised to the right point, and then the pots are allowed to cool. In this manner wire is annealed.

- Price List, John A. Roebling's Sons Company, 1903.

Figure 5.28: Mott Street Flat Rolling Shop, 1987. J. Lowe, HAER
Charles erected the shop in 1905 and rebuilt it in 1911 after the second of four great fires destroyed the roof. Star beam anchors from the rebuilding punctuate the walls.

Figure 5.29: Panama Canal, Gatun or Miraflores Lock, c1913, - *The Wire Rope at Panama*, c1915. RPI

An important part of the mechanical equipment for digging the canal, one which impressed itself on every observer, was the number and size of the wire ropes in use.

The Wire Rope at Panama, John A. Roebling's Sons Company, c1915

When the digging of the canal began the Roebling Company sent one of its wire rope experts to Panama to study conditions and obtain information which would assist in supplying wire ropes for different parts of the work. The wisdom of this move was fully justified by subsequent events, for over fifty contracts for wire rope, wire strand and wire were placed with the firm by the Isthmian Canal Commission. The wire rope and strand called for by these contracts, if placed in a single line, would reach from Colon along the entire length of the canal to Panama and thence twenty miles outward on the Pacific....

Roebling rope was used on cable ways for controlling the movements of buckets and for cables along which the buckets ran in the transportation of the materials across wide spans. It was used also on unloader ploughs dragging them through flat

cars piled high with earth and rock, sloughs clearing the cars as the ropes pulled them along. Great steam shovels and dipper dredges which cleared the way for the canal were also equipped with Roebling wire rope. The rope used for the dipper dredges was in some instances over 3 inches in diameter, this being the largest wire rope every used for a like purpose....

It is interesting to note that in the Roebling Mills, where the steel wire for the ropes was made, there was also drawn a large quantity of bronze wire to make the screens for protecting windows and porches against flies and mosquitoes.

The screens were made by the New Jersey Wire Cloth Company, an allied Roebling concern, and the protection afforded by them aided materially in preserving the health of those employed on the canal work.[36]

In early 1907, Ferdinand secured a contract for the cables of the Manhattan Bridge to be erected across the East River between the Brooklyn and Williamsburg Bridges. By April, Washington reported to John II: "The Kinkora mill is pushed to get the bridge wire in time and is taxed beyond capacity." Charles developed a traveler with two sheaves to speed the cable making, and set up a construction company to do the work (Fig. 5.30). Washington noted in 1908:[37]

The Manhattan bridge cables are progressing with remarkable rapidity and may be finished this year. Not only are wires hauled back and forth from both sides but the large size of the cables permitted their being divided in two parts lengthways so that strands can be made on two sides of the same cable at once. Motors are used for each of the driving ropes. The wire is so heavy that the wind does not affect it.

By the end of October we will have all the wire made.[38]

Figure 5.30: Manhattan Bridge, March 1909. WIK J.A.R.'s Sons Co. created a subsidiary company to build the cables and to install the suspender ropes for hanging the deck.

The work of several years swept away in a few hours

The success of the Manhattan Bridge cables was soon eclipsed by the first of four great fires at the Roebling Works in Trenton within seven years. The fire destroyed the Clark Street Rope Shop, idling 750 men (Fig. 5.31), as Washington recalled:

The demand for small sized elevator rope had become so great that we could no longer devote the slow and cumbrous machines in the old shop to do this work profitably. Charles proceeded to erect a long two-story building, nearly 600 feet long with a short extension on the canal side for cable work and galvanized strand. Many 19 wire strand machines were put in together with a number of rope-laying machines and very small fast-running machines for Tiller rope strand.

All of this machinery was built on the place and had to be designed and properly proportioned in Charles' office. A carpenter shop was built on the same lot and a coal yard established. The boiler house was provided with automatic stokers - first on the place. After running most successfully for less than ten years the building with all its valuable contents was totally destroyed by fire one bitter cold night, zero weather and heavy snow. It started as usual between shifts when no one was there. No one knew how it originated. This was in February 1908.

This was the first great fire we had on the place and was a great blow to us all, especially Charles. He saw the work of several years swept away in a few hours; he realized the heavy monetary loss, and more than that the prospective loss of business. Added to this came the thought of all the work ahead to put up a new building and replace all the machinery....Fortunately, there was much rope machinery available within the Insulated Wire Department and Buckthorn plants. Working day and night and Sundays in all shops helped wonderfully.[39]

While the original Clark Street Rope Shop had wood floors and roof trusses, Charles rebuilt it with steel beams and trusses that would soon be tested for fire resistance.

Pretty girls keep men home

Charles decided to relocate the New Jersey Wire Cloth Co. to the Kinkora Works in 1908, as *The New York Times* reported under the headline "Pretty Girls Keep Men Home:"

A representative of the Roeblings said that the chief reason for the move of the New Jersey Wire Cloth Company is to give the employment to the women in Roebling and thereby keep the man there from wanting to come to Trenton.

The concern found that there were women in the industrial village who wanted employment, and also that the men sought the brighter lights of Trenton every night, so they decided to move the wire cloth plant, where women are mostly employed, and bring girls from Trenton to the industrial village.

There are many pretty girls employed in the Roebling wire cloth plant, and the theory of the management is that when they are located in Roebling the men will make fewer trips to Trenton.[43]

How these things come about is a mystery

In the Spring of 1908, Washington married Mrs. Cornelia Farrow in Pittsfield, Massachusetts. Cornelia, aged 40, was living in Charleston, South Carolina, with her teenage son when Washington met her. As Washington wrote to John II:

A second marriage late in life cannot be judged by the standard of the first because its motives are usually quite different, and if it should not prove happy, death soon remedies all troubles....

How these things come about is always a mystery, and I feel somewhat guilty inflicting myself upon Cornelia....I am not strong and feel like breaking down without some support. I have no one to help me and must do everything myself.[41]

On June 30, 1908, Washington and his bride joined his brothers and their spouses, other family members, nine bands,

Figure 5.32: John A. Roebling Statue, Cadwalader Park, Trenton, c1915. William Couper, the sculptor, modeled Roebling holding plans for the Brooklyn Bridge on his lap.

*Brooklyn Bridge is a thing of art, beautiful in itself...
All the latent poetry of the mathematician - and in its
highest reaches mathematics becomes divinest poetry;
all the estheticism of the architect; all the musician's
sensitiveness to harmony; all the mysticism of an idealist
philosophy; whatever of faith, feeling, reverence John
Roebling cherished in his heart, was here voiced like a
ringing cry. As if conscious of his pending doom his genius
stands embodied in this final form - an inscription invisible
- a soul's bid for immortality!....As if his nature had been
subdued to what it worked in, the Ironmaster of Trenton
was a man of iron. Iron was in his blood and sometimes
entered his very soul - a man of iron, with the virtues of
iron and the peccancies of iron to his account, and John
A. Roebling, as he was, as you knew him, head bared to
the blows of fortune, or the storms of heaven, eyes fixed
unwaveringly on whatever object he had in hand,
poised, confident, unyielding, imperious and proud
- John Roebling is there - seated forever on yonder pedestal.*

- Henry Estabrook, Keynote Address
John A. Roebling Statue Unveiling, June 30, 1908

and 6,000 Roebling employees – 5,000 from Trenton and 1,000 from Roebling - in a parade from the Roebling Works to Cadwalader Park to unveil a bronze statue of John A. Roebling by the sculptor William Couper of Montclair, N.J. (Fig. 5.32). Emily Roebling, Charles' eldest daughter, unveiled the statue, and Henry Estabrook, general counsel of the Western Union Telegraph Company and the father-in-law of Karl G. Roebling, delivered a "notable oration" (see box above).

Washington chose the Niagara Suspension Bridge for a bronze relief on the left side of the granite pedestal and the Brooklyn Bridge for the right side. Several years later he noted: "The features of the statue resemble me to a certain extent for the reason that I sat for it several times. The photographs of my father were not satisfactory to Mr. Couper and he had never seen the original. I also composed the inscription" (below).[42]

*To John A. Roebling, civil engineer, designer
and builder of many suspension bridges, founder of
Trenton's greatest industry, and energetic worker,
inventor and man of affairs, devoted to his adopted
country and in whose progress he had unswerving faith,
a patron of arts and sciences and benefactor of
mankind, this monument was erected by
the citizens of Trenton and his sons in 1907.*

John A. Roebling Statue, Cadwalader Park, Trenton

Spits flames of fire in all directions

In the first decade of the 20th Century, automobiles captured the attention of Americans, and especially of people like the Roeblings who could afford the marvelous new machines. Washington wrote to John II in 1903 that "Automobiling is all the rage here," and both Ferdinand and Charles bought automobiles for motoring through the countryside.[44]

In 1904, Washington wrote to John II:

C.G.R.'s new automobile is still astonishing the natives - a Columbia - body of aluminum - 50 mph." In 1908, he reported, "My nephew's 120 H.P. machine is finished - it is called the Roebling-Planche – Planche designed it. It goes like hell - spits flames of fire in all directions.[45]

Washington's nephew and namesake, Washington A. Roebling II, was Charles' third child and only surviving son, born in 1881. The family called him "Washy" to distinguish him from his uncle. Washy shared his father's fascination with automobiles at an early age, and after working for J.A.R.'s Sons Co. for a few years, he went to work for the Walter Automobile Company on Whitehead Road in Hamilton, a suburb of Trenton. Washy collaborated with Etienne Planche, a French designer at the Walters plant, to build their Roebling-Planche racer. As the *Trenton Evening Times* reported, "It is probably one of the costliest cars in this country....Mr. Roebling and the Frenchman gathered the parts and it was constructed in one of the Roebling mills."[46]

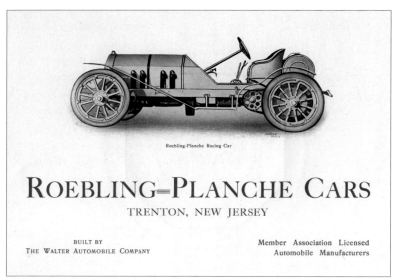

Roebling-Planche Racing Car

ROEBLING=PLANCHE CARS

TRENTON, NEW JERSEY

BUILT BY
THE WALTER AUTOMOBILE COMPANY

Member Association Licensed
Automobile Manufacturers

Figure 5.33: Roebling Planche Cars Catalogue, 1909. GO From their race car, Washington A. Roebling, 2nd, and Etienne Planche developed street cars "for a select class of American gentlemen who appreciate thoroughly the artistic lines."

Proud of their work

The Walter Automobile Company started manufacturing Washy and Etienne's car in 1909 (Fig. 5.33), offering "a powerful 50 horse power for grand touring and a moderate power four cylinder 20 horse power for city use:"

Both cars are designed along modern lines, combining elegance and strength, comfort and speed, simplicity of mechanism and perfection in all details.

The name of the car is the Roebling-Planche, a strong alloy of the mechanical strength of the greatest bridge builders in the world with new automobile blood which has the vigor of the youth, a strong factor in securing success....

Mr. E. Planche and Mr. Washington A. Roebling, 2nd, who present these cars to the public, feel proud of their work. They do not intend to build many of these types, but they build them with the best material obtainable, at great expense, from abroad; they build them for a select class of American gentlemen who appreciate thoroughly the artistic lines and the taste which presided over the elaboration and the building of the best car ever made.[47]

Walter Automobile produced a few Roebling-Planche cars and Ferdinand bought one of them, but the company went into receivership in June, 1909. Ferdinand and Charles raised $244,000 (about $5.9 million in 2009) with Anthony Kuser, president of the South Jersey Gas & Lighting Company, and his brother John Kuser, both of Hamilton, and bought the Walter factory on Whitehead Road at auction. They incorporated the Mercer Automobile Company, named after Mercer County, to manufacture cars that "a private individual may take out on the

road and safely and consistently drive at a speed between 70 and 80 mph." The directors appointed Ferdinand as president, Charles as vice president, John L. Kuser as secretary, and Etienne Planche as chief designer. Planche soon got to work developing a "sports car."[48]

When Rensselear Polytechnic Institute graduated its largest class to date that spring, Washington commented to John II:

A graduating Class of 90 is something I never expected to see. The speeches made by the various orators are wise and prophetic – all point to a special technical education. The days of the old fashioned college which only produced fools are over. Our own condition at J.A.R.'s Sons Co. has become one requiring the utmost technical skill to survive the competition of abler and more up to date concerns.[49]

With sales of wire and wire rope steadily increasing, Charles built additions onto the steel and blooming mills and the tempering shop at the Kinkora Works in 1909, and he erected a second wire mill there in 1910. Washington noted one of the special orders that were coming in:

Today we finished a rope on the grand old cable rope machine, weighing 60 tons, heaviest we ever made – 3 in. in diameter about two miles long for the Juragua iron mines, 40 miles N.E. of Santiago, Cuba. It had to be coiled on two cars – the reel was too heavy to be handled.[50]

As the Company hired more men at the Kinkora Works, the population of Florence Township increased 2.4 times in the first decade of the 20th century to 4,731, compared with an increase of just 33 people during the 1890s. Most of the residents in Roebling had emigrated from Eastern Europe and the Company leased houses to these "foreigners" on Second to Fourth Avenues north and south of Main Street and on Fourth to Sixth Avenues south of Knickerbocker Way.

With many Romanians living on the streets south of Knickerbocker and some of them wearing ethnic clothing, the area became know as Gypsytown. The Company leased houses on Railroad and Amboy Avenues to some Eastern Europeans and to African Americans. When the "original nine Swedes" (see Fig. 5.5) had came to town from Worchester, Massachusetts, to oversee the steel making at the Kinkora Works, the Company had placed them away from the plant in semi-detached houses west of Fifth Avenue, along with other "Americans" of English, German, and Irish descent.

For most of the Eastern European immigrants, the freedom and opportunity they found in Roebling fulfilled and in many cases surpassed their hopes in coming to America (see box).

For the African Americans living in Roebling, the steady work at the plant and the quality of the housing provided more than most blacks had elsewhere. Although the Company had a fair amount of control over their lives, most of the workers in Roebling considered themselves fortunate to live and work there and were typically more loyal than the Company's Trenton workforce.

When an immigrant got a job at the mill, he usually tried to get relatives jobs as well. When an immigrant became a foreman, the plant superintendent often assigned immigrants who spoke the same language to that foreman's department, and portions of the mills and shops gradually became associated with specific ethnic groups. The increasing numbers of immigrants in the plants gradually isolated managers from their workforce because of language and cultural differences.

In Trenton, immigrants from southern and eastern Europe gradually replaced many of the German, English and Irish employees from earlier waves of immigration, and they also settled into ethnic neighborhoods. Italian immigrants gradually dominated the Chambersburg area north and east of the factory, and Romanians, Poles, Czechs, Hungarians and Slovaks settled predominantly in the area south of the plant.

Like earlier immigrants, the new ethnic groups built their own churches to preserve their heritage, such as St. Stanislaus Polish Catholic Church, the Hungarian Magyar

Reformed Church, Sts. Peter & Paul Roman Catholic Slavic Church, and St. Basil Romanian Catholic Church. Most of the congregations built convents and schools next to the churches to provide religious education consistent with their heritage.[52]

Serious trouble is feared here

By 1910, workers in many cities were becoming more militant in their demands. In March, the Amalgamated Association of Street and Railway Operatives of America encouraged the trolley workers of the Trenton Street Railway Company to go on strike for 23 cents an hour and ten-hour work days. The Roeblings were major stockholders in the Inter State Railways Company, which controlled the Trenton Street Railway Company, and Ferdinand served as a director. When the directors dismissed three workers who were helping the union, some strikers began damaging trolley cars, but Mayor Walter Madden refused to send the police out in force. A committee of Trenton businessmen backed the strikers because the public needed the trolleys, and the directors conceded to the union's demands and rehired the dismissed employees.

In April, several thousand workers went on strike at the Roebling Works in Trenton "after their demands for an increase in wages were refused." Charles had offered a modest pay increase and he shut down the plant to show that the Roeblings weren't going to capitulate like the Trenton Street Railway directors had done. The Kinkora Works employees kept working. *The New York Times* reported that for the first time "National labor leaders from Washington" were trying to organize Roebling workers in a union:

> *It has been the boast of the Roebling Company for many years that labor troubles were unknown at the plant, and they have never before had a union to contend with. Serious trouble is feared here when the Company is obliged by trade conditions to reopen the works. At the present time there is sufficient stock on hand to meet orders for several weeks....*
> *Charles G. Roebling told the men that they could have an increase from $1.35 to $1.42 a day to begin at once, and that the amount would be increased to $1.50 a day as soon as trade conditions warrant. The men at first were for accepting this offer and returning to work, but the labor union organizers got in their work and the men stayed out.*[53]

Charles told the Trenton strikers that he would never settle with then and within two weeks they gave up and went back to work, except for a couple hundred workers "whom the Roeblings considered instigators of the strike. Charles' firm hand had apparently decided the issue of the striking workers at the Roeblings' Trenton plant, but the city was experiencing an increased wave of labor unrest, and the Roeblings expected that things would get worse."[54]

> *When my mother came over from Hungary she said she cried because their row house on Second Avenue was so wonderful because it had running water and indoor plumbing. A lot of people didn't have that so my parents were grateful to the Roebling Company for providing them with such good housing besides giving them a job so that they could make a living.*
> **- Paul Varga, Kinkora Works Railroad Engineer, 2007**[51]

Figure 5.34 (left):
Karl G. Roebling, c1918. HS
The oldest son of Ferdinand W. Roebling, his parents named him Charles Gustavus Roebling II after his uncle, but he changed his name to Karl to avoid confusion. Karl served as Company President from 1918 until his premature death in 1921.

Figure 5.35(right):
Ferdinand W. Roebling, Jr., c1926. RU
The youngest child of Ferdinand W. Roebling, "Ferdy" served as Company president from 1926 until his death im 1935.

A source of deep satisfaction

Shortly after this strike, Washington wrote to John II: "Karl & Ferdy have landed the contract for furnishing the Torpedo netting & crane outfit for two 27,000 ton Argentine battleships....It will take about one year to make 58,000 sq.ft. of netting by hand." Karl G. Roebling (Fig 5.34) and Ferdinand W. Roebling, Jr. (Fig. 5.35), who most everyone called Ferdy, were the only third generation Roeblings in the business, and for Ferdinand:[55]

> It was a source of deep satisfaction that his two sons, both well qualified by their training and natural endowments, should have fulfilled his desires for them and have each taken his appropriate place in the Roebling Company.[56]

Since graduating from Princeton University in 1894 and starting with the Company as a common millhand, Karl had worked in the machine shop and in several other departments and was now working in the sales office. Ferdy was graduated from Lehigh University with a degree in mechanical engineering in 1901, and had gone to work in the Company's engineering department for his uncle Charles and had assisted him on the Manhattan Bridge cables. After a visit from his nephew, Washington wrote to John II:

> Young Ferdy Jr. spent the evening here. He has a sound mind, good judgment and looks at matters from a sound standpoint.[57]

Thanks to Karl and Ferdy's efforts and to events in Europe, submarine netting would soon become a major Company focus.

The most talked about car in America

In 1910, Finley Porter became the chief designer at Mercer Automobile. He had worked at the Worthington Pump Company in Stroudsburg, Pennsylvania, and he developed the Mercer Raceabout, a 36 horsepower two-seater guaranteed to run a mile in 51 seconds. Porter shared Washy's enthusiasm for racing, believing it "improved the breed because it brought weaknesses to the surface quickly." Washy placed second in a race in Savannah in November 1910 (Fig. 5.36) and Mercer drivers won five major races in 1911. The Mercer Raceabout soon became "the most talked about car in America."[58]

Figure 5.36: Mercer Automobile Co., *American Motorist,* 1910. GO
The automobile company prominently featured the second place finish by Washington A. Roebling, II, "an amateur" racer.

The party who makes nothing but rope is ruined

In December, 1911, the J.A.R.'s Sons Co.'s second great fire nearly destroyed the Mott Street Flat Rolling Shop and ruined $50,000 (about $1.1 million in 2009) in machinery and many thousands of dollars' worth of wire. As Charles rebuilt the shop (see Fig. 5.28), he and his brothers were again considering selling the Company. However, in January, 1912, Washington reported to John II: "The sale of our business was given up for the time. I voted against it. F.W. had become indifferent on account of our good balance sheet and C.G. wanted more money for it....We are buying Otis Elevator Stock." Ferdinand also wanted to keep the Company for his two sons.[59]

In February, the original four stockholders, Washington, Ferdinand, Charles and Edward, increased J.A.R.'s Sons Co. capital stock from the $500,000 set in 1875 (about $13.5 million) to $15 million (about $343 million), a 30-fold increase. The Company issued new stock certificates, including shares for Karl and Ferdy, and for Frank Briggs, Ferdinand's brother-in-law and head of the New Jersey Wire Cloth Company, and all three became Directors. Within a short time Washington wrote about a drop in orders - "our business is rather slow"- and attributed this decline to unfair competition from the giant "steel trusts:"

My brother Charles wants to have the U.S. Steel Corp. dissolved - they are ruining us with their cheap prices and want to ruin all competitors. Last year our mill profits were about 5% on the money actually invested in the concern. This is not enough because a manufacturing business must make 10% in order to survive the many contingencies that constantly threaten it and tend to destroy it.

This was largely caused by the U.S. Steel Corp. They can easily for example put wire rope below cost for a couple of years and scarcely feel it, because their rope profits are only about 2% of their total profits – whereas the party who makes nothing but rope is ruined and must sell out to them – and they do not conceal their intentions in that respect.[60]

"Two Young Men's Heroism,"
- *The New York Times*, April 20, 1912

Mr. Roebling and Mr. Case bustled our party.... into the boat in less time than it takes to tell it. They were both working hard to help the women and children. The boat was fairly crowded when we were pushed into it and a few men jumped in at the last moment. But Mr. Roebling and Mr. Case stood at the rail and made no attempt to get into the boat. They shouted good-bye to us. Mr. Roebling stood there.... I can see him now. I am sure that he knew that the ship would go to the bottom. – Mrs. William T. Graham.

Figure 5.37: Washington A. Roebling II, c1910. RU Only son of Charles G. Roebling to survive into adulthood, and a key proponent of the Mercer Automobile Company, "Washy" perished on the Titanic on April 15, 1912, at the age of 31.

Smiling as he waved farewell

In early 1912, Washy (Fig. 5.37) and his friend, Stephen Blackwell of Trenton, the son of former U.S. Senator Jonathan Blackwell, traveled to Europe to "motor" with Washy's chauffeur, Frank Stanley. Blackwells and Roeblings had been friends and associates for many years, and Jonathan and Ferdinand served together on the committee that erected Trenton City Hall in 1910-1911. Washy and Stephen boarded the *Titanic* in Southampton, England, on April 10 to return home.

When news reached Trenton of the *Titanic* sinking on April 15, Karl, Ferdy, and Jonathan Blackwell rushed to New York to meet the *Carpathia* in hope of finding Washy and Stephen aboard. Instead, they met Caroline Bonnell, of Youngstown, Ohio, who told them that Washy bid her a cheerful farewell as he helped her into a lifeboat, saying: "You will be back with us on the ship again soon." She reported her last sight of Washy, "smiling as he waved farewell to her and her party."[61] (see box)

Karl traveled to Halifax, Nova Scotia, to meet a ship carrying Titanic victims, but the bodies of Washy and Blackwell were not among them. Many people sent condolences to Cornelia Roebling at 191 West State Street, thinking that Washington Roebling himself had gone down with the Titanic. Charles and Jonathan Blackwell received letters that Washy and Stephen had mailed in England, "telling of the pleasant trip they had and of their hope to soon be with loved ones at home." The death of Charles' only surviving son was a "terrible grief to him, and it was feared ay one time would result in terrible consequences to his health." He and Ferdinand gradually lost interest in the Mercer Automobile Company.[62]

Figure 5.38: N.J. Wire Cloth Company, Kinkora Works, 1928. BC Charles erected "unrivaled" buildings for the new "screen shop" near the village so that women working there wouldn't have far to walk from the Main Gate, up the drive on the left.

Figure 5.39: N.J. Wire Cloth Company, Kinkora Works, 1928. BC As it had in Trenton, the "screen shop" provided the only opportunity in the Roebling mills and shops for women, who operated looms making insect screen and hardware cloth.

On the usual grand and complete scale

Despite his grief, Charles completed new shops "expressly designed" for the New Jersey Wire Cloth Company at the Kinkora Works in 1912 (Figs. 5.38-39). As Washington noted, "This was accomplished on the usual grand and complete scale....A large loom shop of three stories adjoins the village; next comes a wire lathing room, storerooms, a galvanizing department and more storerooms for chicken netting, an establishment sufficient for years to come." The Wire Cloth Company continued employing many women, as it had done at the Roebling Works in Trenton, to run looms for making insect screens and hardware cloth.[63]

That year, the Kinkora Works employed about 1440 people, and 1,200 of them - 86 per cent - were reportedly Hungarians, 100 were Russians and 100 were Lithuanian. By then the Company had erected 312 homes in Roebling. Large families were common at the time, and several in the village had ten or more children. In early 1914, *The New York Times* reported:

> *The model town established here by the John A. Roebling's Sons Company glowed with just pride a few years ago when it gained a national reputation by its record birthrate, but today it knows it must pay the price of many children, for the Roebling company has announced its intention no longer to pay the expense of the town school.*
>
> *Time was when the company was willing to educate all the children of Roebling, but there are so many now that this has become a vast responsibility – too vast....Plans have been drawn for a $75,000 school building, large enough to accommodate rapidly increasing classes (Fig. 5.40).[64]*

By this time the Roebling System of Fire Proofing had been surpassed by newer construction methods and Ferdinand lost interest in it, as Washington reported to John II:

> *My brothers are getting old especially F.W. - he is <u>wisely</u> going to do what should have been done years ago – wind up the 'Roebling Construction Company.' It has never been a source of profit. On the contrary it has tied up a large Capital, and met with heavy losses and at all times severe competition. When we began it, we manufactured much of the constructive parts used, but the fashions change and that fell away. I was opposed to it at its inception because the owners had not the time to give it the close attention that such an intricate business demands. Everything had to be left to assistants.[65]*

Washington claimed that the subsidiary lost a total of $1.5 million (about $32 million in 2009). The experience reinforced his belief that they should stick to wire rope, as he later wrote: "I have always thought that our legitimate business, which is thoroughly understood, afforded every avenue of expansion that the future might offer, and I still think so."[66]

Figure 5.40: Roebling School, c1930. BC Florence Township built the school on Knickerbocker Avenue with classrooms for Grades 1-8 in 1914, and Washington later recalled: "Our share was $80,000" (about $1.8 million).

They are marching daily around the mill

Militant workers in the Trenton rope shops struck for higher wages in March, 1913, as Washington reported to John II:

> *Strike as bad as ever. Men are desperate - but determined – nothing to eat, no coal. Thermometer 14°. They are marching daily around the mill - it looks like a small army. The demand for rope is something fierce. All elevators in N.Y. will stop - what then - it is becoming a national affair.*
>
> *We could make lots of rope at the Buckthorn works and in the rubber shop. We have the machinery but the men say they will all go out if we do. You see it is a fight for life on our part.... The men individually want to come back. It is false pride which prevents them and the supreme satisfaction of being able to injure the employers. Curious enough the rest of the mill is very busy. Of course we are making too much rope wire but that is not to be regretted. We are arranging to import rope from England. But the English rope is not adapted to our elevators. We are one of the few plants not unionized in this cursed town.*
>
> *We are both sick (himself and Cornelia) – my mouth & her asthma & colitis. We are talking of taking a house at Spring Lake (New Jersey) for the summer.*[67]

The Trenton strikers returned to work when the Company started importing wire rope but they continued to agitate. "The whole of Trenton is a hotbed of unions and strikes," Washington noted, "The disease has not taken hold of Roebling as yet, manly because we own all the houses and control the saloon." While Charles had said in 1906 that: "We are not building at Kinkora with any thought that improved conditions of living will lessen the danger of strikes," the Company's control there clearly had that effect, as *Town Development* noted (see box).[68]

"Profitable Philanthropy…as a Producer of Wealth and Happiness to Labor and Capital," *Town Development*, 1914

This town of Roebling has passed safely in the precarious stage of immaturity that has proved fatal to so many similar projects. It has grown and flourished, and has provided its founders with labor that is competent to produce the highest grade of work, and has secured for these workers the highest comfort, health and happiness at the least expense.

In theory the project was fantastic; in fact it has proved highly practicable and profitable from its inception. The policy that dominates and controls Roebling is autocratic, patriarchal. The Company owns all land, houses, stores, industries, even the fire and police departments. The Company supplies work, shelters the worker; and should that worker prove unworthy he is summarily discharged and deprived not only of his wages but of his habitation as well. Out he must go, bag and baggage beyond the village limits. Stern and drastic indeed is the authority of the officials; and not infrequently the innocent must suffer with the guilty.

To Raymond H. Thompson, the manager, is entrusted the prosperity of the Company and the welfare of the worker. Health, sanitation, education, police and fire regulation, housing, water supply, every phase of commercial and social life are under the manager's supervision.... The result is a town of over 3,000 people living a sane and comfortable life in the open country; a town of broad scrupulously clean streets, green grass and trees; a town where disease seldom cripples the worker, so injuring his work; a town where every man may be sure of just and sympathetic judgment upon all his demands; and finally with all this apparent vigor of supervision, a town where every individual has the utmost liberty.

The only rules that are applied with Draconian severity are the rules governing industry, decency and cleanliness. Not more than five adults are allowed to live in one house, and if children multiply too fast, the parents are obliged to move to roomier quarters. Cleanliness is preserved by constant watchfulness as is necessary to regulate so cosmopolitan a community - composed of Hungarians, Swedes, Romanians, Poles, Irish, Germans and Russians. Only with the specific provision that inspection may be made any hour of the day are houses rented….

On the lower lands are situated the shops, great brickpiles with towering chimneys, from which the flare of the furnaces and the smoke of the fire pour day and night. Encompassed by the railroad yards and the omnipresent piles of scrap, this portion of the town suggests nothing so strongly as the suburbs of Pittsburgh. But up above the shops, where row after row of low brick buildings range themselves in parallel files, we find the homes of the Roebling workers….

The children of Roebling are the most striking earnest of the success of this communal development. Streets, lawns, open grass plots, the broad fields are literally alive with scampering little tots and their older brothers and sisters. Every known variety of game, and many to an American unknown, is being played everywhere. There are no petty "keep off the grass" restrictions, no irksome street or traffic regulations, and indeed there need not be for the only danger to be avoided is the lumbering march of the coal wagon. A school and thoroughly equipped playgrounds are supplied by the town management for the education and further amusement of the juvenile population. There are no sickly, puny children in Roebling; red cheeks and well filled little paunches are the universal fashion....

'And to what end is all this trouble taken?,' asks the hard headed and perhaps hard hearted businessman.... The Roeblings saw that the proper treatment of the laboring man is the most sensible and efficacious solution of labor troubles, which are the intangible but malignant destroyers of industry. The vision was true, and as Roebling, New Jersey, completes the ninth year of its existence, the officials of the Company point proudly to a record clean of strikes, lockouts, or the kindred curses of labor.

Washington noted the relative calm at the Kinkora Works:

Compared to Trenton, the works in Roebling seem to be quiet as the grave, yet the efficiency is double. There is an absence of street noise, with teams handling the freight, the railroad trains are farther off, buildings are larger and further apart. There is an absence of the busy street crowds surrounding the main office, or of the gangs of yard men seen in Trenton - matters move on a more majestic scale.[69]

The Mercer automobile became world famous in February, 1914, when Eddie Pullen "a Trenton man driving a Trenton-made car, won what was considered to be the automobile championship of the world, the Grand Prix in Santa Monica, California." Pullen set a world record of 77 miles per hour in the 400 mile race, finishing with a 40 minute lead. "There was a giant victory parade in Trenton. A general half-day holiday allowed 25,000 people to line the streets and watch a 250 vehicle parade led by Eddie Pullen in his Mercer."

We are not very prosperous at present

That June, the International Association of Machinists demanded a standardized wage scale at 24 industrial plants in the Trenton region, and 11 plant owners agreed to 33-44 cents per hour and a nine-hour day. The directors of Mercer Automobile Co., J.A.R.'s Sons Co., DeLaval Turbine, and several other companies refused and the machinists walked out. The directors organized the Trenton Machinist Employers Association, hired scabs, and refused to negotiate.

Meanwhile, political tensions in Europe slowed orders for wire products. On August 1, the day Germany declared war on Russia, Washington wrote to John II: "I was up at Trenton yesterday. It looks like a funeral, working four days a week. We have discharged a number of men again – no work for them in the Insulated Wire Department….We are not very prosperous at present and the future is not bright."[70]

When 400 striking machinists attacked scabs at Mercer Automobile, Karl, Ferdy, and other Employers Association members appealed to Governor James F. Fielder for help. The Governor criticized city officials for not trying "to stop the trouble," and threatened to call out the militia, stating: "If the trouble-makers are allowed to proceed without hindrance it is a sure thing that they are going to further excesses." Union leaders believed the Governor and called off the strike on September 1. The Roeblings and other owners blacklisted some of the machinists, which generated much resentment.[71]

As European nations mobilized, business picked up in the U.S., and in November, Washington noted a British order for one million wire rope traces for harnessing horses to cannons: "It will take 250 men 5 months working day & night & Sunday to do this job." Ten days later he reported, "Preparations for making the English Trace chains are progressing with feverish haste – C.G. solves all difficulties."[72]

With business improving, the Roebling brothers squabbled over dividends at their Annual Meeting in January 1915. "We made a dividend of 4 per cent," Washington reported to John II, "F.W. wanted only 2 per cent and C.G. 6 per cent. There was quite a fight but I compromised. F.W. senior can always carry the vote with his two sons….The British harness contract has consumed 2-1/2 million feet of small rope! We received another order - quite a godsend."[73]

The biggest fire that ever occurred in this city

Disaster struck just a few days later at the Company's 12-year-old Buckthorn Plant (see Figs. 4.72-73), as the *Trenton State Gazette* reported: "The biggest fire that ever occurred in this city last night destroyed the insulated wire department of the John A. Roebling's Sons Co….gutted 15 houses in that neighborhood and badly damaged many more" (Fig. 5.41). Washington suspected that machinists angry about the 1914 strike had set this third big fire, as he recalled:

Figure 5.41: Trenton's biggest fire to date destroyed the Roebling Company's Buckthorn Plant on Jersey Avenue in 1915. BC

On January 18, 1915, the great calamity came. The entire Buckthorn works were destroyed by fire, absolutely - not a vestige left, and undoubtedly set on fire by an incendiary. The fire occurred between six and seven in the evening when the man were away. The fire alarm was systematically cut so that fifteen minutes were lost waiting for fire engines.

It started in a room where no work was being done, but there were quantities of cotton, jute, etc., stored there, all inflammable, and lastly a man was seen running away from the room. The fire burned all night; there was so much to burn that the flames went sky high; the intense heat scorched the adjacent buildings; by morning nothing was left....

The loss has been estimated at 1-1/2 to 2 million (about $43 million in 2009). The great stocks of copper were burnt and oxidized. The lead and tin melted and formed a solid floor of metal in the cellars. The machinery was all scrapped....This was the era of advancing prices due to the war; hence the metal salvage was great. Before deciding the question of rebuilding, the ruins had to be cleared off. That was a job, taking months. As usual the rebuilding came on Charles' shoulders, but he finally built on a reduced scale, putting up only two stories in place of three, which proved more than ample because we lost very much business.[74]

Charles didn't want to rebuild the Insulated Wire Division plant, as Washington noted shortly after the fire:

Charles is still violently opposed to rebuilding the Buckthorn works on the ground that it does not pay and that the annual loss has to be carried by the Rope business which has to carry everything. If F.W., myself and the two boys (Karl and Ferdy) vote for it he will go ahead and do it - not otherwise. F.W. thinks it is a wrong policy to give up an established business. My own inclination is to have them rebuilt - even if it is not backed by hard sound common sense. There are always other considerations.

Charles is getting to feel his years and this may be the last big job he undertakes....Is there ever a time in life when you can sit down in peace and contentment?[75]

One month later, with the rebuilding of Buckthorn underway (Fig. 5.42), Washington reported,

The rope business is on the boom – working day and night, even Saturday night – cause, foreign orders – Pacific Coast orders, nine flat ropes at once, Strand orders for riveting Mississippi River banks. The Argentine has waked up and sends large orders for oil drilling lines which would have gone to Germany.

Flat shop runs day and night – ditto tin shop – mostly fine stuff meaning much labor and more machinery. We expect more British Navy orders....Even the Trenton Iron Co. runs day and night on war orders....

Our U.S. Navy is talking torpedo nets – must be double to counteract the double headed torpedo – But the days of the Dreadnoughts are passed. The future Navy will consist of fast cruisers and submarines – until someone finds a way to knock the submarines.

I understand the English Channel is zigzagged by huge nets to entangle submarines. We could have made them but had no way to transport them in large sections, several hundred feet square.[76]

With several shops and mills operating overtime, Charles decided to build an Amusement Hall on Main Street at Seventh Avenue in Roebling to promote Company pride and loyalty among the employees and residents (Fig 5.43). With removable seating for 800 people, a balcony with seating for 100 and a paneled meeting room on the second floor, the Hall had one of the area's first air conditioning systems, using ice to chill air circulated in ducts. On the stage, Charles installed a wide curtain painted with a scene of the Brooklyn Bridge.

Figure 5.42: Buckthorn Plant, 1930. HM&L
After the 1915 fire, Charles rebuilt the Buckthorn Plant, which housed the Company's Insulated Wire Division, with two and three-story concrete-frame buildings with steel-frame windows.

Figure 5.43: Roebling Amusement Hall, 1927. BC
The Company built an air-conditioned auditorium in Roebling in 1915 so that employees and their families could enjoy movies and live entertainments and hold meetings.

Ousted from their homes

Despite amenities like the Amusement Hall, wartime tensions continued to affect production at the Roebling plants. As *The New York World* reported: "Many of the workmen are Hungarian and there is some agitation among them because the firm is understood to be working on orders for the Allies."

In the summer of 1915, the Roeblings reduced the pay of soft wire drawers at the Kinkora Works from $.87 to $.37 per 100 pounds of drawn wire, due to a "scarcity of orders and because the price of tempered steel had dropped." When ten men demanded the old rate, the superintendent dismissed them and more than a hundred of their co-workers walked out. Charles evicted the dismissed men from their homes in Roebling, and *The Newark Eagle* reported:[77]

An exodus of former employees, ousted from their homes by the Roebling company, after they had gone on strike, has begun. Many families are quitting the town for Trenton or other nearby cities....

Some of the strikers, who were notified to vacate their houses yesterday, are still in possession, and agents of the company.... have threatened to put them into the streets.

As Charles intended, the evictions were: "an extraordinarily powerful warning for the rest of the workers as to the consequences of striking." Few serious labor problems arose again at the Kinkora Works until the Second World War. As orders poured in, Washington wrote to John II, [78]

A commander in the Italian Navy is here inspecting some work for their Navy. He brings an order for half a million feet of rope (and more to come) which they formerly bought from the Germans and English.....

The mill has seldom been so busy. Russia put $40,000 (about $860,000 in 2009) to our credit in N.Y. yesterday for which we send hundreds of drilling lines to Baku, cables for a Suspension Bridge in the Urals, besides Rope wire, Telegraph wire and barbed fence....The automobile tire wire orders are immense – they come in 100 million feet at once - This year's product will be 550 million feet – we are buying machines outside to make it, and are now short of wire!

Panama ordered 6,000 feet of No. 2 rope. We are now supplying Brazil and Argentina with rope – they used to go to England and Germany for it. The Swedish government sent a large order with a guarantee that it will be consumed at home (in which case the English will not seize it). We hope to retain some of our war customers after the war is over.

Our flat shop production is rapidly increasing and almost equal to the two rope shops. We refuse many orders because we can not get the wide sizes which are made at Western mills....The only lame duck is the wire cloth department....

Of all our production only about 10% is export – the rest goes into home consumption....If all the inquiries became realities we would be swamped. When all the mills run full the overhead charges are reduced to a minimum percentage which means profit.[79]

We live in a reign of terror.

While the evictions had quieted the Kinkora Works, the Roeblings had far less control over their Trenton employees. While expanding production, the Roeblings suffered another huge setback (see box opposite), as Washington recalled:

Charles determined to build another rope shop opposite the Buckthorn building as quickly as possible. Scarcely was it finished when the second great calamity of 1915 came to pass. At 2 a.m. Nov. 11 our new Rope shop (at the Trenton works) was destroyed by fire – absolutely and completely – none of the machinery can be saved. The fire started in the second floor – nothing happened to make a fire or to start one incidentally, so the supposition is that it was set on fire....

This country depended on us for elevator ropes, mining ropes, every variety of hoisting rope – all gone. It is a national calamity....The old shop is running as usual, but is already overtaxed in making heavy rope, and can help but little.[80]

This fourth great fire consumed the Elmer Street Rope Shop (Fig. 5.44), which Charles built in 1908 to replace the previous shop that burned that year (see Fig. 5.31). As Washington noted,

The fire started in the Clark Street Annex, second story, where the large stocks of hemp centers were stored and tarred. As usual, the fire alarm wires were cut or out of order, causing the fatal delay. No foreman being about, there was only disorder. Owing to the long strike of the previous year we had many disaffected foreigners working in the shop, especially Austrians. The probability is that it was incendiary. The fire spread and spread. The imaginary fireproof construction of the iron beams and brick arches was worse than useless. As the beams became red hot the whole construction collapsed. Soon the entire building was in flames and all the valuable machinery was doomed. About 160 machines were ruined, large and small.

The war demand for ropes, especially foreign, was so great that we were fairly overwhelmed with orders at high prices. A million dollars in prospective profits was gone. This was another great shock to Charles, not so much the loss of nearly 2 millions, but the prospect of rebuilding that had to be done. But he went at it with surprising energy.

Our other rope shops, including the Insulated Wire Department, did what they could, working night and day and Sundays. Wire was rushed to several other factories. At Clinton, Mass., Charles bought a whole rope factory

Figure 5.44: "Ruins of New Rope Shop fire on Elmer Street Nov. 11, 1915, Loss nearly 2,000,000, Trenton, N.J." RU
Photographs of the ruins depict indescribable masses of tangled beams, machinery, columns, wire and wire rope.
- Washington A. Roebling

and another small one at Plainfield, N.J. He bought strand machines in Providence and Easton. Our own machine shop was rushed to death. One machine after the other was added; a full year elapsed before we reached equilibrium.[81]

Arsonists soon tried again, as Washington reported:

This attempt consisted of an elaborate incendiary pyre.... built in an unfrequented corner of the cellar of the rubber mill – first a small amount of waste soaked in oil and that was covered by a massive sea grass and scraps – all it needed was a match to set it off, which would have happened that night, and destroyed that important building. We have traced the material – the sea grass came as packing from a box containing magnesium asbestos steam pipe covering in our yard. This shows that the incendiary was familiar with the place and is probably a workman.

We live in a reign of terror. Everyone expects the whole mill to go in which case we will be ruined. Further testimony about the fire confirms the incendiary plot – a ball of fire was seen coming through the ceiling under the jute pile directly after the fire started.[82]

We are making submarine netting for the Philadelphia Navy Yard, to be lowered into the Delaware River. The first section is 1,000 ft. long by 36 ft. deep with meshes 12 ft. square made of heavy wire and strand soldered at the intersections. When rolled up it is about 7 or 8 ft. in diameter and can be loaded on a long flat car. To test it you get into a submarine, run into the net and if you do not come up it's a __success__.
- Washington A. Roebling, December 29, 1915[84]

The big rope shop of the John A. Roebling's Sons Co, nearly 700 ft. long and 90 ft. wide, was destroyed and several other buildings on Clark Street were damaged by fire which threatened to wipe out a section of houses in that neighborhood.

The burning building was only a few years old and all its machinery and equipment were entirely new...When the windows were burned out and the heavy north wind forced a draft there was no stop to the fire. Flames shot in all directions and licked up everything that would burn.

As the fire ate its way towards Hamilton Ave. it cleaned out the interior of the long shop and the thick walls then began to topple and fall...Many firemen narrowly escaped serious injury and death when section after section of high and thick walls crashed onto Clark and Elmer streets. The flames were so hot that firemen had to bathe their faces while they stood in the street and faced the danger.

As each wall fell the fire appeared to be renewed and great sparks shot up and ignited other nearby buildings. For a time the six-story wire mill at South Clinton Avenue and Elmer Street (see Fig. 4.70) was threatened. The top of it caught fire several times and streams had to be turned from the main blaze.
- Trenton State Gazette,
November 11, 1915.

The 1915 fires cost the Roeblings about $3.5 million in buildings, machinery and inventory, and $1 million in lost business (about $96.8 million total). The heartache of seeing years of planning and hard work destroyed by arsonists was incalculable. In the midst of all the rebuilding, Charles had to meet all the wartime orders for wire rope and special products like torpedo and submarine nets (Fig. 5.45 and box below). Admiring his work, Washington wrote to a friend: "My brother Charles ranks as high as any engineer in the country."[83]

Figure 5.45: Roebling Workers with torpedo netting, c1915. J.A.R.'s Sons Co. made great quantities of this during the war.

Figure 5.46: J.A.R.'s Sons Co., Roebling Works, Trenton, 1987. Jet Lowe, HAER
1916 Boiler House, right, and 1917 Engine House, left. The Boiler House produced steam for heating and operating the older shops, and for powering turbine generators in the Engine House that produced 4,000 kw of electrical power. The railroad tracks were built in the 1930s after the Delaware & Raritan Canal was filled in. In 1993, the State built N.J. Route 129 along the canal right-of-way.

It takes a man with a stiff upper lip

In early 1916, Washington wrote:

> *All the rope factories in the US cannot relieve the rope famine – neither can we supply them with wire. We are overwhelmed with copper mine rope orders. The Otis people are scared. Labor is getting scarce. We raised wages this week.*

A month later, torpedo net makers and boiler stokers went on strike, and Washington complained,[85]

> *I have been living in a fool's paradise. When I went to the mill this morning expecting to be diverted by the perpetual performance of epicycloidal motion I was met by an ominous silence. Knots of men standing around – entire mill closed and every sign of a strike. Overnight the Socialists took possession and we are in for a long fight. The demands are 8 hours and double pay. We are going to fight it out to the bitter end and it may take two months.*
>
> *Wire rope will sell for its weight in silver. We have raised wages right along, but the fight had to come. One month's complete stoppage means a year's profit….It takes a man with a stiff upper lip to stand a situation like this.*[86]

The Mercer County Central Labor Union, a local associated with the American Federation of Labor, announced plans ten days later, "to organize all the workers in the employ of the John A. Roebling's Sons Company." Anthony Spair, an AF of L organizer, told a reporter:

> *I cannot believe that the owners of the Roebling concern are acquainted with the actual working conditions which exist in the plant controlled by them.*
>
> *I realize that modern industry has separated the interests of the workers and investors. Too much is left to be done and said by their dependents, the shop bosses.*
>
> *The workmen of the Roebling company are left without friends, and they have become nothing but automatic working machines. They are worked to death, and their wages are the lowest paid in this country for similar work.*
>
> *In the case of the 'stokers' the weekly wages paid for such work elsewhere is $17.80 for eight hours per day, whereas in the Roebling plant…in order to make a decent wage they are*

> *compelled to toil in the 'earthly hell' for 12 hours at a stretch, and they received only $15.84.*
>
> *I venture to say that there have been more strikes in the Roebling plants than in any other similar plants in the country and these strikes have taken place without any outside influence whatsoever, thereby showing that the working conditions are vile, and nothing is being done to right them. My persistency in fighting the battles of the workers of that plant to some may seem personal, and in a way it is. Workman like myself who receive decent treatment at the hands of their employers cannot afford to stand idly by and see their fellow workers badly treated.*
>
> *We are going to organize the workers in that plant, if it takes years to do it. The local labor movement is going to center its forces to bring this about. The form of organization will be industrial – that means, all of them will be taken into one big organization, which will be a close and secret one, and will be in charge of those who want their fellow men treated like men instead of slaves.*[87]

In May, rope shop employees went on strike, and with rope orders backed up for six months, the Roeblings had to raise the men's wages, as Washington reported to John II:

> *The long expected strike of the rope makers eventuated on Friday last. We had to give in as we were helpless – it amounts to 5 to 7% of a raise. We hope it will not extend to the entire mill which would be disastrous.*
>
> *We took the occasion to standardize the various classes of rope making. The big rope machine men get now $2.50 a day – next size 2.40 – big strand machines 2.35 – small 2.30 – spoolers 2.25 and so on. We have been raising wages here and there during the spring. Many men also leave to better themselves and then straggle back one by one.*
>
> *A raise of 10% all around means $550,000 (about $11.7 million in 2009) a year – disastrous. The men also insisted on stopping work Saturday afternoon and on Sunday night.*[88]

Figure 5.47: J.A.R.'s Sons Co., Roebling Works, Trenton, 1987. Jet Lowe, HAER

To meet wartime demand for small ropes, Charles erected the Elmer Street Rope Shop, center, and the Clark Street Rope Shop, right. in 1917 to replace the shops destroyed in the 1915 fire (see Fig. 5.44). The great fires lead Charles to adopt the concrete frame and floor construction that had become common for fireproof factories, and the development of steel sash windows permitted huge openings for maximum daylight. Charles used brick on the exteriors to relate these "modern" factories to the traditional Roebling shops and mills. The Elmer Street Rope Shop was demolished in 1999 to provide for parking for a nearby arena.

At the Kinkora Works, many men left for better paying jobs in munitions plants or to join the service, as Washington noted:

I went to Roebling yesterday. Was shocked to see the plant only half working – nearly half the wire drawers have run away. Our trouble at Roebling is that none of the owners live there and seldom appear. That has a depressing effect on the bosses who need moral support.[89]

Charles was preoccupied rebuilding the block between Clark Street and the canal, where the fire the previous November had destroyed everything. He started by completing a new Boiler House and an Engine House (Fig. 5.46) along the canal to provide electrical power instead of the steam that had powered the previous rope shops, and then built new rope shops with fireproof concrete construction (Fig. 5.47). He was also busy erecting a 775 ft. span suspension bridge over the Ohio River between Belpre, Ohio, and Parkersburg, West Virginia. In February of 1917, the United States severed diplomatic relations with Germany over its unrestricted submarine attacks. As the War Department installed harbor defenses and began preparing for war, Washington reported to John:[90]

We are swamped with orders especially by the Government. Every harbor is being mined – the mines are anchored with durable rope spun over with tarred hemp marline. We are making 800,000 feet and more coming. Also 1,000,000 feet of phosphor bronze rope for salt water work, endless quantities of antennae wire and aviation wire (Fig. 5.48).[91]

**Figure 5.48:
Roebling Aircraft Products,
Aerial Ace Weekly, 1919.**

The manufacture of fine rope for airplanes, guys and stays was conducted on a stupendous scale; an incredible quantity was manufactured - hundreds of millions of feet. The new rope shop at the Buckthorn plant was taxed to its utmost capacity night and day. With this aircraft strand came the various fastenings that went with it, 50,000 pieces a week or more; all had to be thought out and contrived.

- Washington A. Roebling, 1919[92]

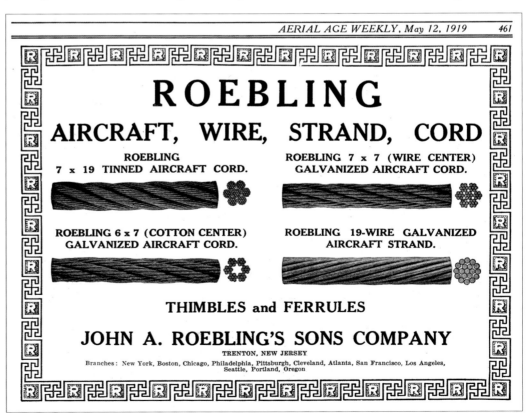

141

*In commercial matters F.W. was _supreme_*

The strikes, fires and wartime production demands all took their toll on Charles and Ferdinand. In early March, 1917, Washington wrote to his son John II: "My brother Ferdinand has been critically ill, dangerously so – A trifle better today – after effect of grip. He is old you know – 75 last week – was unable to attend his own birthday celebration."[93]

After a month of illness, Ferdinand (Fig. 5.49) died on March 16 at his home at 222 West State Street in Trenton. Washington wrote to his son: "F.W. had many underlying _wonderful_ business qualifications….In commercial matters F.W. was _supreme_. His disposition caused him to fight all competitors tooth and nail and win out in the end." While he and Ferdinand often disagreed about the Company's finances and some personal matters, Washington wrote an admiring tribute to his brother that he presented at the next Directors meeting (see box).[94]

The great necessity

At Ferdinand's death, Ferdinand, Jr., (see Fig. 5.35) age 39, assumed his father's position of Secretary and Treasurer, and Karl (see Fig. 5.34), age 44, became second Vice President. Karl and Ferdy had to deal with their father's estate, which was eventually valued at $10.5 million (about $207 million in 2009), but the wartime production requirements were far more pressing and created a lot of stress on them. Just six days after Ferdinand died, Washington reported:

Our Navy contract for 275 nets is done and shipped far ahead of time. The Gov. is so pleased that another contract has been signed now for half as much more….We have Gov. orders for heavy gun slings – also for 2000 miles copper field telegraph along the Coast and the Rio Grande. Every day something new comes in on top of what there is already.[95]

When Congress declared war on Germany on April 6, the need for wire and wire rope became more urgent than ever:

To meet the emergency, the American Iron and Steel Institute at the request of the government formed a committee to manage the production and distribution of wire rope and Karl G. Roebling was appointed chairman, and the Roebling works in Trenton were designated as the official headquarters. Here the committee held its constant meetings and determined ways and means of increasing production and the apportionments to be assigned to the various wire manufacturing plants of the country. There was no possible question of rivalry as to the amount to be allocated to each. It was rather a question of how much each plant could produce under the pressure of the great necessity.

All the orders for wire rope emanating from the several government departments, Army and Navy, with their various bureaus, were centered at the Roeblings' offices in Trenton. A host of government inspectors and experts were drawn thither, with a corresponding number of military and naval officers, all pressing the respective needs and urgent necessities of their respective requirements….
The part taken by the Roeblings in the manufacture and supply was a predominating one among several concerns furnishing wire and wire rope for war purposes. The long and varied experience of this company in manufacturing a high grade of wire specialties stood it in good stead when the call came. Especially in the production of aircraft wire and strand and cord for all the parts involved was their efficiency to be noted. Having from the very inception of aviation paid particular attention to the requirements of this service the Roeblings were spared the necessity of hurried experimenting in this difficult field, for they had learned it all before.[96]

The government instituted a draft and wartime security measures that soon started to discourage workingmen from striking, as Washington reported to John II:

The rope shop strike suddenly ended in a curious way. One third of the men are subject to conscription – but if they are on government work like making mats or telephone cables or netting etc. they are exempt. As soon as they found this out they rushed back in a body and we had 100 more men than we could use – but 10 days of valuable time are lost. At 'Roebling' the situation is still serious. Common laborers who had $3 dollars a day demand $4 – clearing house and annealers - they stop the whole mill.[97]

Just one week later, he wrote,

Today there is no strike anywheres. All foreigners are being registered. It is surprising how few real Germans we have, not more than 50 among 6000.
Not being officially at war with Austria-Hungary the Hungarians and Slavs do not count.[98]

When the government issued an appeal for people to buy war bonds, the Roeblings and their employees responded patriotically, as Washington reported:

I took another lot of $50,000 (about $987,000) of Liberty Bonds yesterday….the Trust Company is crowded with people making small subscriptions at the last moment. The company took $200,000 (about $3.95 million) at the last moment. C.G.R. are also took a large block. The men in the mill took $200,000 – it was rather impressive to see an ordinary wire drawer pull 4 or 500 dollars out of his pocket, ready to pay for it.[99]

Written in loving memory by his brother – Washington A. Roebling, **April 15, 1917**

It is our sad duty to record the first death in the small circle of officers of the John A. Roebling's Sons Co. Ferdinand W. Roebling has passed away. We miss him from his usual seat at his desk and at table. Accustomed as we all have been to look to him for decision in important matters, we realize the great loss we have suffered....

At an early date Mr. John A. Roebling recognized the business ability of his son. He often told me that he was the only one of his four sons who had the true genius of the merchant. When Civil War broke out Ferdinand's services were so valuable that his father refused to let him go...

His talents came into special play, in getting orders, making contracts, cultivating friendly relations with the many new companies constantly springing up, and sometimes taking stock in payment....

Enlargements and increases became the order of the day, paid entirely out of our own profits, no outside capital being ever required....

Ferdinand's mind rose to every occasion, and no opportunity for advancing the business was neglected, processes were perfected, new ones were quickly adopted and the old ones scrapped....

As business grew and prospered his mind broadened and looked farther into the future. To swim with the current is easy, but to weather the periodic reverses which always come, only aroused in him a dogged resolution to fight it out.

When sunshine appeared again after reverses he was one of the first to recognize it and take advantage of the new conditions.

At home he was the most genial host. When you had crossed his threshold all antipathies were forgotten. While just and fair to his office force, he had the faculty of making them understand their position and their duties....

The secret of success in many a business consists in the ability of weathering hard times, of keeping your organization intact, in keeping your workingmen employed even at a small loss. That he always looked out for. In later life his enthusiasm was tempered by considerable caution....

He had the pleasure of seeing branches of the business, which commenced with the humblest beginning, branch out into the most important departments....

**Figure 5.49:
Ferdinand William Roebling
1842-1917 KD**

When the great addition of our plant was begun at "Roebling" (the creation and chef-d'oeuvre of Charles Roebling) it also became necessary to enlarge end systematize the office force, also the Selling Department, and to establish new stores, and new agencies and connections – in fact, to do a worldwide business; all of which Ferdinand attended to with the skill and judgment born of long experience and an intuitive knowledge of the character of men....

I am a great believer in heredity. Fully nine-tenths of our qualities are the consequence of direct inheritance; the other tenth comes from experience, from contact with the daily business surroundings, usually forced upon you by circumstances and also by chance.

Chance plays a large part in our progress through life. In my brother's mental attributes I could see the combination of a father's terrific energy, tempered by the calm and good sense of a devoted mother.

To get ahead of a competitor by even one year he considered good policy. He knew that conciliation and cooperation produced better results than an open fight to the death.

From one great trouble which besets most corporations he was happily freed from. I mean the matter of funds. Owing to his own conservatism, coupled with that of his brothers, there were always ample means at hand for enlargements, improvements, and for experimenting, the latter being an important item....

Went the disastrous fires had visited our plant, I was struck by the philosophic calm with which Ferdinand received the news. I could not quite understand it. It must be that with advancing age the mind realizes that you cannot control everything and must bow to the inevitable.

There is one other point in which I am sincerely grateful to him: during the years that I was incapacitated by illness, he carefully and honorably preserved my interests in the business, which meant a great deal to me and mine.

As time goes by, our memories retain only the good. The other things fade away. What death really means I do not understand, and do not want to. We enter life without knowing it, and leave it unconscious. Cut off thus at either end, all we can do is to obey the dictates of the infallible conscience with which we are endowed by nature.

But who succeeds in doing that?

By November, 1917, the Company was working on its biggest project for the war, as Washington noted:

> *The mill is overwhelmed with an order for untold millions of feet of rope, 50 to 100, for netting and mining purposes – destination a secret – it may be for closing the North End of the North See.*
>
> *If you hear, don't tell me – I am not supposed to know. Other mill business poor, no copper or common wire – Wire Rope prices have been fixed by the U.S. We have been treated fairly well.*[100]

The Allies used 78 million feet of galvanized wire rope to deploy 70,000 mines in the 230 mile long, 25 mile wide "North Sea Mine Barrage" (Fig. 5.50 and box). J.A.R.'s Sons produced about one-third of this wire rope despite having lost about half of its rope production capacity in the great fires, and it produced 4.4 million feet of wire rope for the Adriatic Sea Mine Barrage, plus three million feet for protecting harbors and fleets at home. In March, 1919, Captain Reginald Belknap, Commander of the U.S. Mine-Laying Squadron, reported in *Scientific American*:

> *The latest report is that the Germans admit twenty-three submarines lost and other authorities ascribe the fleet's surrender and the final armistice largely to the defeat of the submarine campaign which the Northern Mine Barrage forced the enemy to accept.*[101]

Figure 5.50:
Wire Roping the German Submarine: The Barrage that Stopped the U-Boat, John A. Roebling's Sons Company, Trenton, c1920.

Every industry owes it to itself to record for the benefit of posterity the part it played in the greatest struggle that ever tested the moral fibre of mankind.

Everybody wants it

With all the war demand for wire and wire rope, Charles built a series of additions onto the mills and shops that nearly doubled the size of the Kinkora Works. When crucial supplies became scarce, he experimented with new methods of production to keep the mills operating, as Washington noted in the spring of 1918:

A Reminiscence of the World War - Washington A. Roebling, c1920

Toward the end of the war with Germany, the German submarines had become such a frightful menace that it became necessary to abate it at any cost. Access to the open sea was obtained by them by way of the North Sea….

At the narrowest point, the North Sea was still 200 miles wide, which seemed to forbid the laying of the net. Encouraged, however, by the success the Roebling firm had achieved in protecting most of the harbors on our Atlantic Coast by the use of their nets, the problem was reconsidered and resulted in a contract being entered into with our firm to construct a net 200 miles long by 400 feet deep at the deepest point.

Time being an important element, a force of 300 men was immediately organized, working night and day with feverish haste under bonds of secrecy. The net had to be built in sections, heavy and strong, to withstand the impact of the enemy submarines. All crossings of strands were soldered. To bury up the net and keep it in a vertical position, novel appliances were introduced. Throughout its length copper hooks were attached on which to hang submarine bombs.

Rapid progress was made, due largely to the unfailing energy of our former president, Charles G. Roebling, aided by the skill of such experts as Mr. C. C. Sunderland, Mr. Wm. Craig, Mr. Wm. Riedel.

When finished the many sections were shipped to the Eastern Coast of Scotland, were then joined together and sunk in place by the united efforts of special detachments from the United States Navy and the British Navy.

I was informed at the time that during the first week, no less than seventeen submarines became entangled – their crews all perished – meeting the same fate which they had so ruthlessly meted out to other nations.

The German plan to continue submarine operations and receive more favorable terms in case of peace received a crushing blow. A few more boats were captured, then came an unexpected peace, in the consummation of which the Roebling firm played an important part and deserves the fullest praise.

The people of Trenton have never fully realized the great activities of the Roebling Company during this war. Besides the above feat, the manufacture of 10,000 units of Artillery harness seems a trifle, but it was not. Of rigging out aeroplanes, the number was almost incredible. On other kinds of war supplies every department was worked to its full capacity. Suddenly the end came.

Figure 5.51:
Charles Roebling (left) and Washington Roebling (center) at a flag raising ceremony in June, 1918, marking the completion of a new 138 ft. tall flagpole that the Company installed at the Kinkora Works Main Gate to inspire patriotism during the First World War. RWW Charles died four months later at the age of 69.

We have only a week's supply of low phosphorous pig on hand and don't seem able to get any – due to Government bossing, to delayed transportation & overwhelming demand from everybody. C.G is making an experiment to mix charges from an acid furnace with those of a basic furnace, half & half, to see if that will help – the product has not been tested yet. We have the reputation of making the best high carbon steel wire in the country and everybody wants it.[102]

In May, rope makers at the Trenton plant saw the huge demand for wire rope as an opportunity to demand more money, and they went out on strike, but Charles had little patience for them. As *The New York Times* reported:

Three hundred employees of the rope making department of the John A. Roebling's Sons Company, after being on strike for several days for increased pay, have been discharged.

Other men have taken their places. The strikers insisted on a 10 per cent increase. The firm met the demand by offering to change the work from day to piece work, which would have meant an increase over what the men had been getting. This proposal was rejected.[103]

There is no one to take his place

By the summer of 1918, all the work and stress caught up with Charles (Fig. 5.51) and he became ill in August. As his condition worsened, Washington wrote to his son, John II:

My brother's sickness is a matter of supreme consequence to me, on account of the position he has occupied in our business. He was the directing head, the man who looked ahead, planned and worked and designed and executed with tireless energy year in year out, and usually successfully.

*He never copied, was always original even when at times it might have been wiser to attain these results in some other way, but it all helps to strengthen one for future efforts….
Now to fill the place of Charles is a serious problem.*

Of course he is still alive and will probably recover from his present acute attack – but a man with high blood pressure, hardened arteries, impaired kidneys and tired heart is handicapped beyond relief.

Never having been seriously ill before he takes the darkest view of his condition, not realizing that he can be an invalid for a long time by resting, which he cannot do. Consequently in his characteristic impulsive fashion he at once goes to extremes. He works with his lawyer every day and has absolutely determined to sell his mill stock of 45,000 shares.

Even goes so far as to offer his house and place for sale, and expects to leave Trenton forever. With that I cannot concern myself, but the mill stock is a matter of great importance. Primarily he desires to save the huge inheritance tax of 33 1/3%, amounting to $3 million in cash, which his daughters would have difficulty in paying….

I have often felt it desirable that some outsiders were in it – but who will buy his stock? That is the question. A man like Schwab (Charles Schwab, President of Bethlehem Steel) who tries to rival the Steel Trust (U.S. Steel) might do it – but he would want control! Two years ago, the Lewisohns….made us an offer for all our stock but we declined. There is only one way to keep it in the family and that is to bond the concern for $9,000,000 (about $151 million in 2009) at 7% making an annual encumbrance of $630,000 (about $10 million). With the money thus raised we could manage it - I mean myself, Karl and Ferdie.[104]

Five weeks later, on October 5, 1918, Washington wrote to his son:

My brother Charles passed away this morning at 9:15 – the family including myself were at his bedside. It was a very peaceful death after much suffering. A few final gasps, then the eyelids fell and it was all over. His face bears that same indomitable look, so characteristic of him. He therefore looks natural; and a day or so as the skin turns white he again will look like a boy.

The effect on our mill prospects will be serious. There is no one to take his place – no one with real engineering ability, his industry, his energy to overcome obstacles, and above all he was a fighter and could keep the men in order, which is one of the most unpleasant but essential tasks in a large business. Our many foremen and assistants all realize that the <u>head</u> *upon which everyone relied is gone.*[105]

To Mrs. Stockton, Dear Madame,

Your kind and sympathetic note touches my heart. By the death of Charles, I not only lose a friend and brother, but Trenton loses its greatest citizen and the country at large its foremost mechanical engineer. He was a paragon of industry. We all relied on him. With his wise counsel, his instant decision and effective action we all felt we had a strong tower to lean upon. We already miss him and look around in vain for someone to take his place....

Time, which usually heals all things, cannot replace him. Coming so soon after the death of F.W. it seems like a double stroke of fate. He was never aware of his condition until it was too late. In the face of growing weariness he kept on planning and working until sheer exhaustion forced him to his bed, from which he could never rise. Most men would have taken alarm in time but that was not his way - He preferred to die in harness.

One winter evening, on December 9, 1849, I was sitting next to a room where a woman was in labor; presently I heard a faint cry of a newborn child. Last Saturday I heard the last sigh of that same child. When I think back on the great work, the vast accomplishments and undertakings achieved between these two sighs, it surpasses my understanding. May he rest in that piece of which he saw so little during his lifetime.

- Washington A. Roebling, October, 1918

"C.G. Roebling is Called by Death at 69," *Trenton Evening Times*, October 6, 1918

Mr. Roebling's extraordinary genius as an engineer was destined to make the Roebling name famous throughout the world, adding to the fame that came to this family through his father and through Colonel Washington A. Roebling and Ferdinand W. Roebling, his brothers.

Mr. Roebling was recognized in the engineering world as one of the most brilliant engineering minds of all times....

Mr. Roebling's greatest accomplishment as an engineer is the town of Roebling, New Jersey, which was his own idea. He drew plans for the layout of the village, planned the great iron mills and the machinery with which they are equipped and planned the dwelling of the workmen. To carry out the company town program up to this time has cost the Roebling company approximately $15 million (about $252 million in 2009) and the end of development has not been reached. This model city was very dear to Mr. Roebling's career, and much of his time was devoted to its development and expansion.

Mr. Roebling was the engineering genius of the Roebling Company, as his brother, Ferdinand W. Roebling, was the financial genius. Ferdinand developed the business fields of the company and took care of the gigantic financial problems, while Charles provided equipment, buildings and machinery with which to carry on the business cultivated by the brother. The business and engineering policies of these two men are inseparably interwoven in the success of the Roebling enterprise and will always remain the inspiration and basis of the company.

A tribute to the ability of Charles G. Roebling as an engineer and builder of industry is contained in the mere statement that when John A. Roebling died the business was worth $150,000 (about $3.5 million), as shown by his will on file in the Mercer County surrogates office, and gave employment to 150 men. Today the book value of the property of this company is approximately $50 million (about $840 million) and employment is given to about 8,000 men.

The Roebling plant when Charles entered the business in 1871 was a healthy industrial infant, consisting of a single mill. Today there are scores of mills, embraced in three general groups, the upper or main Trenton plant, the Buckthorn plant and the plant at Roebling, N.J. All of the buildings and the machinery in them as now constituted were designed and erected by Charles, to care for the business demand created by Ferdinand's business ability, which made him an acknowledged captain of industry of the world in his day....

It was probably through the genius and foresight of Charles Roebling that the Roebling Company has kept pace with competition in the iron and steel industry and survived. The masterstroke of Mr. Roebling in providing for conditions to meet competition was the creation of the great mills at Roebling, N.J. If it had not been for the steel furnaces that he planned and built there, this company would likely have been lost in the race....

Throughout his life Mr. Roebling was awake to the future needs of the business of which he was for so many years its head. It was he who designed all the intricate, special and costly machinery that was needed by the company's pass from one to another of the wonderful developments in the steel and rope business....Fire several times all but wiped out the company's physical property, but each time Charles Roebling rebuilt and equipped on a far greater scale than before.

When New York wanted to bring Cleopatra's Needle from Egypt, Mr. Roebling was called upon to design the machinery to do this, and he performed the task in such a way that this wonderful obelisk was taken from its original place along the Nile, brought overseas and erected in Central Park without being even chipped.

Mr. Roebling was a man of few hobbies, but in his busy life he found leisure to become the owner of the greatest private collection of orchids in the world. He made a specialty of hybridizing and his efforts were attended with wonderful and amazing results that won for his orchid collection each year many blue ribbons in orchid shows in New York, Boston and Philadelphia. His conservatories on West State Street, adjoining his home, are duplications of tropical conditions where wonderful flowers are always in bloom.

At rare intervals, once in a century, a man appears that towers so high above his fellows that his activities and accomplishments surpass a hundred, yes, a thousand-fold those of the average man. Such a man was Charles G. Roebling.

I'm a strong believer in heredity. He was his father over again, to a far greater degree than any of the other children. He inherited his temperament, his constitution, that concentrated energy which drives one to work and be doing something all the time....

Charles' older sister, Laura, had married a German schoolteacher from Mühlhausen named Methfessel, who established a boarding school and pedagogium in Stapleton, Staten Island. Thither the boy was sent when he was 12 or 14; he thrived under his sister's motherly care and followed the usual academic course for three or four years. He developed great ability as a piano player, and became a brilliant performer, by far the best in Trenton. (His father before him had been a virtuoso on the flute and piano until his left hand was mangled.)....

When he was 18 he was sent to the Rensselaer Polytechnic at Troy, where I had graduated in 1857....When Charles graduated in 1871, he came at once to Trenton where everything was prepared for him to make his entrance into business life an easy one. His father was dead, he was his own master; his guardian, Charles Swan, my father's old superintendent, turned over to him $300,000 (about $7.5 million in 2009) in good securities.

He took his place as an equal partner in the partnership of the two older brothers, Washington and Ferdinand, established by the father's will. Being an engineer he naturally took to the manufacturing end of the business. He did not have to go through the grinding apprenticeship that most young men have to undergo. The history of Charles G. Roebling is practically the history of the Roebling company from then on....

Charles was born with a "high blood pressure" constitution. Persons thus endowed have their destiny marked out for them. It forces them to work hard to the end of their lives; there is no rest for them. Thus we find him down at the mill every day of the year, early and late. That was his pleasure and delight. He shared it with his brother Ferdinand. An occasional business trip gave him all the relaxation he needed....

When brothers are in business together the proper amenities are frequently neglected. Not to speak to each other for six months was by no means uncommon, and still the business went on; each one performed his part with grim determination.

Charles had one very strong point - he never copied. He tried to solve every problem according to the best of his ability. Every task was an education to him....

Everyone who came in contact with him in a business way was impressed by his ability and power, but in arguing with him you had to be sure of your ground, else it would be met with a snort of disdain. Charles did not like to write.

Figure 5.52:
Charles Gustavus Roebling
1849-1918 CRT

I never received a letter from him. A few scraps and memoranda were enough for him; he trusted much to his memory - even about such important subjects as the cables of the Williamsburg Bridge he never wrote a line. He might at least have written a short monograph so as to get credit.

He loved his work; it was his life, his happiness....

His death made a gap in our forces at the mill which will be felt for many a long day.[106]

"Famous Orchids Sold," The New York Times, June 12, 1919
A remarkable collection of orchids, mostly grown by the late Charles G. Roebling, President of the company which built the Brooklyn Bridge, has been sold by the Roebling estate to Mrs. Frederick E. Dixon of Elkins Park, Penn. for $28,000 (about $400,000). Roebling sent expeditions into the mountains of South America to search for rare varieties, and his collection is estimated to have cost several hundred thousand dollars. It consisted of several hundred species and varieties and several thousands of Trenton-grown seedlings.

The executors of Charles' estate settled it in 1921 with a value of $15,335,000 (about $165 million). Thanks largely to the efforts of Ferdinand and Charles, the value of the family business was about 240 times greater than it had been when they inherited it from their father, John A. Roebling, in 1869.

Washington's work with his father building bridges, his Civil War duties, and his poor health had kept him from taking an active role in managing the Company, but the death of his two brothers soon forced him to become more involved in the Company's operations than ever before.

Unthinkable millions of feet

Upon Charles' death, his 45-year-old nephew Karl became President of J.A.R.'S Sons Co. (see Fig. 5.34). When the Allies signed the Armistice with Germany on November 11, 1918, the Company's production had increased 75 percent from the start of the war. As Hamilton Schuyler noted in 1929: "Perhaps no one knows exactly how much wire and wire rope were produced during those feverish years, but the estimated quantity runs into unthinkable millions of feet." The war's end brought new concerns about keeping the men employed and about profits. Ferdinand, Jr., 40, suffered a stroke at a hotel in Philadelphia, and Washington worried about the stress on Ferdinand, Jr., and Karl in an ominous letter to John II:[107]

> *F.W. Jr. is at White Sulphur Springs trying to find health. This leaves Karl to carry the whole business on his shoulders and he will soon break down, too. In the town of Roebling is where a head is needed the most. There can only be one end to this condition of affairs.*[108]

In the midst of grieving over his brothers' deaths and worrying about the future of the Company, Washington's middle grandson, Paul Roebling, died suddenly in December, 1918, at the age of 25. Faced with some complicated financial issues relating to Paul's estate, Washington wrote to his son, Paul's father: "All this trouble comes on me in old age, when I should be relieved from my anxieties." Washington had lost his two brothers and partners within 19 months and felt weary at the age of 81, but he was remarkably vigorous mentally. In the remaining years of his life he would assume responsibilities and make decisions that would affect the J.A.R. Sons Co. for decades and the Roebling family for generations.[109]

By March, 1919, Washington reported to John II: "The mill is getting by on a 50% basis - no orders - but high wages continue - also high costs and taxes." As Karl struggled to manage the Company's adjustment to peacetime production, Washington soon reported, "My responsibilities are growing daily - I wonder if my poor old shoulders can stand it."[110]

That year, to keep up with the wartime expansion of the Kinkora Works, the Company expanded the Main Gate to provide employment offices and other facilities (Fig. 5.53).

A broken down octogenarian

By the summer of 1920, the strain on Karl was obvious. Washington wrote to John II in August, "To conduct our business is a terrible burden and Karl shows it." Just a few weeks later he wrote:

> *Karl had a severe attack of angina pectoris, which laid him up and alarmed him very much. The doctors have ordered a rest cure. Who is to take his place I do not know - no business can run without a head....*
>
> *The commercial end of our business is the easy end. The manufacturing, with a little engineering, but most of all handling of man is the hard part and tests his capacity to the utmost. The circumstances under which all work is done nowadays is of the most trying character.*
>
> *Last Monday twenty three wire drawers walked off without a word of warning - and got jobs at the Trenton Iron Company.*
>
> *I wish you could see your way towards taking an interest in our business. Scammell thinks our outlook is dubious – nobody to run it – which I knew long ago.*[111]

MAIN GATE TO WORKS, ROEBLING, N.J.

Figure 5.53:
Main Gate to Works,
Roebling, N.J., 1927. BC
Before his death, Charles planned a large expansion to the village entrance to the Kinkora Works. Completed in 1919, the design incorporated the 1907 Main Gate (see Figs 5.24-25), which includes the first door and the bay window left of the entrance arch. Employees entered through the three narrow doors to the right of the entrance arch to pass through chutes to pick up and punch their time cards. The double doors on the far left led to an ambulance garage. Charles & Washington dedicated the 120 ft. tall flag pole in 1918. (see Fig. 5.51)

The Roeblings had originally hired Scott Scammell, a Trenton lawyer and an acquaintance of Karl's, to do some legal work related to taxes and their interests in Trenton trolleys. When Ferdinand died, Karl and Ferdinand., Jr., appointed Herbert Nobel, a law partner of Karl's father-in-law, as attorney for Ferdinand's estate. Charles hired Noble to write his will and appointed him as a co-executor of his estate along with his two daughters, Emily and Helen.

After Charles died, Noble had given himself one share of stock, called an enabling share, from the estate so he could serve as a Director to represent the estate's interests on the Board. Around this time, Nobel and Scammell formed a law partnership in Trenton. When Ferdinand, Jr., had his stoke, Scammell assumed temporary control of his financial affairs. As Washington later recalled:

It was shortly after CG Roebling's death that Noble and Scammell conceived the conspiracy of acquiring control of the Roebling business for their own ulterior aggrandizement. F.W. Jr. had had a stroke, and was near death and probably would never recover to do anything worthwhile.

I was looked upon as a broken down octogenarian who knew nothing about the business with only a year or two to live. There was then really only one person to deal with, namely Karl. To their secret delight they heard from doctors, after Karl's election to the presidency, that Karl had a mortal disease.[112]

With Nobel controlling Charles' estate and serving as a Company Director, and with Scammell managing Ferdinand, Jr.'s, affairs, the two lawyers had full access to the Company's books and to much of the family's financial and legal matters.

Washington assumed more responsibility in Ferdinand, Jr.,'s absence, and when Karl took a long vacation trip to Panama in 1920, he proudly reported to John II, "I am running the 'mill' very satisfactorily." The prospects of building suspension bridge cables intrigued him, and presaged the Company's return to large cable projects. Washington worked with Karl and Charles C. Sunderland, a highly capable engineer who had started with the Company in 1899, on a bid to build the cables for a bridge across the Delaware River linking Camden and Philadelphia. By the end of March, 1921, Washington reported to John II:

Karl is becoming a great engineer - he has prepared estimates for the Camden Bridge Cables, including Saddles, Cable bands, Suspenders - fastenings and temporary working bridges. Cable wire amounts to 7500 to 8000 Tons - we need that work badly. Our figures were presented to the three Bridge Commissioners yesterday while they were here inspecting our works, which impressed them very much.[113]

Concerns about Karl's health soon changed Washington's mind, as wrote to John II: "The Camden Bridge is to be a Suspension Bridge - Cables 29" in diam. I am opposed to taking the cables in contract. We would only lose on it as we did in N.Y. (the Manhattan Bridge). There is no one to look after it & it is hard and risky work. Karl thinks so too." Five weeks later, on May 29, 1921, Karl collapsed while playing golf at the Spring Lake Country Club in Spring Lake, N.J., and died at the age of 48. Washington called a special meeting of the Directors in the "Mill office" on June 7 (see box), and expressed "deepest sorrow and regret" over Karl's death in a board resolution:[114]

At the moment it seems impossible to replace him. His knowledge of our whole business: his grasp of our troublesome affairs: his genial relations and affable intercourse with all our staff, as well as workmen, cannot be reproduced in any one person. That the great responsibility must have been beyond his powers is evidenced by his untimely demise. Although always cheerful, hopeful, and filled with an inexhaustible desire for work, this sense of human limitation must have been ever present.[115]

On the death of Karl G. Roebling

To all J.A.R.'s Sons Co. employees,

To attempt to state the loss this company has sustained in the death of our late beloved President would be almost impossible. He was a worthy successor to his great father and distinguished uncle.

Under his care, the company took its part and did its full duty in the World War, and the organization has grown and has been perfected under his management. His genial personality, his tact, and firm and wise decisions are fully known to you and serve to mark more clearly our great loss.

The directors have asked me to accept the Presidency and I have agreed to do so. They have also asked Ferdinand W. Roebling Jr. to accept the vice presidency and he has done so.

The Management desires to express most fully to you its appreciation of your loyal cooperation in meeting the problems of the past, and I'm writing this letter to you to further say that you will be expected to maintain your organization at its highest pitch; to use your ability in securing new business, in extending the company's activities, and in maintaining the character of its product.

We know your loyalty to us, and you know the support that we will give you.

There will be no marking of time. We will proceed to make the Company greater and to increase its business and prestige, so that its name will not only remain an honor to its founders, but that it will furnish an opportunity for usefulness to our sons and their sons.

Keep at your work and report in the usual manner.

- Washington A. Roebling, June 3, 1921[116]

As Washington later recalled:

Karl's death implied the election of a new President. Not withstanding my age I was still in possession of all my faculties, although impaired in bodily health. I was the first President of the Co. in the early seventies. My duties as engineer of the Brooklyn Bridge became so onerous that I felt obliged to turn over the Presidency to my brother Charles, retaining the title of Vice President....Throughout this I managed to keep in active touch with the business.

During the past 30 years I have lived in Trenton and have visited the works almost daily. There is no branch of our extensive business with which I am not thoroughly familiar (see box). During these 51 years I've never drawn one dollar in salary - my motive being to allay the natural jealousies that are unavoidable among brothers.

"Keeping Young on the Job at 84 years: Col. Roebling, Factory Head, Tells How," - Marguerite Moore Marshall, *New York Evening World*, June 8, 1921

A little old soldier of 84, Col. Washington A. Roebling, the man who built Brooklyn Bridge and the son of the man who planned it, is fighting today his last fight; is fighting to GET HIS WORK DONE in spite of all his enemies - illness, debility, pain, loneliness, bereavement, that terrible depression of the man who has outlived his generation. This is the quietly dramatic situation behind the terse announcement that Colonel Roebling, at four years past fourscore, has been elected president of the John A. Roebling's Sons Company, cable and wire manufacturers, to succeed his nephew, Karl G. Roebling, who died suddenly, in the prime of life, about ten days ago.

'How do you keep young and on the job at 84?,' I asked Colonel Roebling, when I saw him in his office, a slight, wiry man, whose iron gray hair is still plentiful, whose shoulders are only a trifle bent, whose blue eyes are keen, who appears not a day over seventy. But when he began to speak, I learned that the remarkable thing about Colonel Roebling is not his spurious juvenility; it is that he does his work despite all the infirmities and unhappiness of age.

'I haven't kept young and fit,' he told me sadly. 'I can't hear out of this ear' - touching the right one – 'I can't see out of this eye,' - laying a finger beside the left eye – 'my teeth aren't right, my chest hurts me when I talk; it takes me ten minutes to go up and down stairs. If I could only feel well I could stand anything else. But I don't even for a few minutes at a time.'

'Yet you are on the job,' I persisted, 'and you've just been elected to this most important position. How do you do it?'

'Because it's all in my head,' he answered quickly. 'Sixty years I've known it all, and it's all there yet. It's my job to carry the responsibility. And you can't desert your job; you can't slink out of life or out of the work life lays on you. I haven't any new business plans, but I've lived through hard times before and I can do it again....

'After breakfast I begin my work. I have a lot of my own interests to which I must attend, outside the factory here. For instance, I have to take care of all my correspondence. I don't have a secretary, but answer all my letters in longhand....

'I go down to the office when I get ready, taking the trolley in front of my home on W. State St. I've never ridden in a motor car. You can go back and say you've seen a man who never put his foot inside a motor car! My health won't permit it.

Years ago I strained the muscles of my chest and can't stand the jilting up and down of a motor car or carriage. Even talking for too long gives me a pain across my chest, although my heart and lungs are sound as a bell....

'I like to lunch at the office; we have a special kitchen and dining room for our office force of over 130, and we give them better meals than they can get outside. The chicken today was delicious. My appetite is pretty good; I still eat plenty of pie....

'I manage to keep busy the regular business day, from 9 to 5. When I'm not working, I have my home, my wife, my dog. He's an Airedale, and his name is Billy Sunday. Then, I read a good deal, especially novels. They're a mild form of mental intoxication, but they rest me and help me to forget - all this.'

He glanced rather wearily around the big, comfortably furnished office. 'But why don't you give it up, and enjoy yourself with your friends?,' I queried.

'How can you give up what's part of you?' he asked slowly. 'In Germany, men retire at 50; you never see that in America. I guess it's a good thing; as long as you keep on with your work you have an object in life. As for my friends,' - the thin old voice hesitated, then went on – 'my friends are all dead. My nephew died, and he shouldn't have gone. I don't know why I've lived so long. I've buried eighty doctors. There were ten years of my life, the time I was 40 till about 50, that I never stirred out of one room. There was a time when I thought I'd be blind.'

'But how did you overcome all these troubles and how would you advise others to live as long?,' I asked.

'I wouldn't advise them to do it!,' stubbornly insisted Colonel Roebling. 'I know that I'd be glad to go anytime, but you've got to take the days that are sent you.

'There's just one rule for keeping well as long as you do live, and that's commons sense. There's a monitor here,' – he tapped his wrinkled forehead – 'that tells you how to use it. But people don't obey. I didn't; lack of common sense is responsible for everything that ever ailed me. We should have common sense in eating, drinking, working, playing, and choosing a wife. A good wife is a great help in living many years.'

'And I wish you many more of them,' I told Colonel Roebling, as I rose to go, for I knew he was too tired to talk any longer.

'I'm not worrying about that,' he answered simply. 'I never borrow trouble today about what may happen tomorrow.'

I was therefore the logical candidate and was elected.[117]

At the 1921 Annual Meeting, Noble got Scammell elected as a Director to fill a vacancy. As Washington recalled:

I proposed that Mr. William Anderson, our general superintendent, be elected to fill the other vacancy. He had been with us for over 35 years, filling the most important positions in our works, having full charge of all steelmaking at the Roebling Mills, the big Rod mills, our six big wire mills and their many accessories both in Trenton and at Roebling, an indispensable man, a relative (Ferdinand, Jr.'s, first cousin) and devoted to the Roebling interests.[118]

Noble and Scammell blocked Anderson's election and got Scammell appointed to the Executive Committee. Over the next six months they directed much of the Company's legal work to their law firm and tried to gain control of Edmund Roebling's affairs. Scammell resisted Washington's efforts to increase the role of the Company's Operating Committee, made of "highly trained, efficient and loyal" men, and, Washington noted, Scammell "worked with feverish activity to get a smattering of our manufacturing process, matters which it has taken us 50 to 70 years to learn – he wants to absorb it in a few weeks for his own purposes."[119]

Washington complained that: "One club that Nobel & Scammell hold over us is that they have been our tax lawyers for four or five years, both for the business itself and for individual stockholders." The Roeblings' complicated tax affairs included "questions of depreciation, the valuation of inventory, and the amount of excessive profits tax," which the federal government had imposed during the war. How the lawyers negotiated these matters with the IRS could have a big impact on the stockholders. As an example, Washington noted that Nobel and Scammell had obtained a stay on the IRS's efforts to collect $366,000 (about $4.4 million in 2009) in back taxes it claimed he owed, and he noted that Scammell is "abundantly able to drop the thing out of revenge and subject me to a great loss."[120]

Washington believed that Scammell wanted to become president of J.A.R.'s Sons Co. after he was gone, at a high salary. For decades, Ferdinand and Charles' annual salaries had been $10,000, and the family had increased this to $15,000 (about $180,000) during the World War. When Karl became President his initial salary was $15,000. Noble and Scammell soon suggested that since manufacturers the size of the Roebling Company paid their Presidents a salary of $100,000 (about $1.2 million), Karl was entitled to at least half that. Washington had reluctantly agreed to this, and he now believed that Scammell had his eye on making $100,000 a year as President. Washington also believed that Scammell planned to remove all Roebling family members from the board.

As Washington lamented "the present situation of affairs:"

Just think of it! In three or four years four important men have suddenly died, a fifth is incapacitated by illness and a sixth, myself, suffers from the handicap of old age and its attendant ailments. Such a sequence of events might not happen again in hundreds of years!

The temptation was irresistible for Noble & Scammell. They see in it the control of a vast business - handling of an invested capital of 50,000,000 of dollars - an opportunity for huge salaries - an unchallenged right to exact great legal fees for legal services, many of which should be gratuitous directors' services - fees which are already staggering our ledgers with their amounts. My imagination fails to grasp all the possibilities in store for them. But enough of this.

Now what is the remedy. It must have legal scrutiny. It lies in the hands of the stockholders whose annual meeting will take place next January.…It is imperative to have an outside disinterested lawyer present at the meeting, familiar with such occasions.[121]

Washington enlisted the help of three third generation Roebling women who owned large blocks of stock - Emily and Helen Roebling, Charles' daughters, and Blanche Roebling, Karl's widow. Blanche recommended that Washington hire George Wharton Pepper, a prominent Philadelphia lawyer and U.S. Senate candidate, to assist the family. At the Annual Meeting, the stockholders elected Blanche and two trusted managers - William Anderson and William Gummere, the Superintendent of the Steel Mill - to replace Noble, Scammell, and Edmund Roebling, who never came to meetings. Washington triumphantly reported to John II: "After Herculean efforts on my part I have succeeded in ousting Noble and Scammell from our board of directors. For this I deserve a little credit." Nobel and Scammell, however, were not yet ready to give up.[122]

The good days are over

Washington had preserved his family's control of the Company but privately he foresaw limited prospects for the future. At the end of a long narrative on the Noble and Scammell affair, he wrote: "The prevailing idea that the John A. Roebling's Sons Co. is a concern of boundless wealth is fallacious - it has seen its best days." The buildup of war production had created more competition than ever before, as he had noted earlier: "The good days are over. There are 17 rope factories and another one being built by the Wrights at Worcester. During the war there was work for all - today for only 1/3 and they are slaughtering prices just to keep agoing. We ourselves have one rope shop too many. No one anticipated the war slump." As Washington described some of the slowdown to his son:[123]

I have no good news to impart – it is all bad. For the first three months of 1921 the business profits were only $44,000 (about $474,000 in 2009) in place of one million. Two weeks ago we lowered our prices, but orders fell off instead of increasing. In the copper line we are down and out - 15 years ago we handled 25,000 tons of copper - last year 5000.

We are forced to reduce our wage scale - and that is hard on men who work only three days a week. In that respect the men in Roebling are better off than those in Trenton because we sell them from our store all their food, clothing, shoes and other requirements at fifty percent less than they can buy them from the profiteers in Trenton, and yet most men don't want to give us credit for that.[124]

By the 1920s, family-owned and operated manufacturing concerns were becoming increasingly rare. The World War had accelerated the decline of "civic capitalism" – in which business owners live where their companies are located, interact regularly with their employees, participate in local social and philanthropic activities, and consider the welfare of their employees and fellow residents in making business decisions.

Companies like U.S. Steel and Bethlehem Steel epitomized the growing trend of national capitalism – in which huge corporations are owned by large numbers of stockholders who typically have no involvement in the business, and remote executives have limited interest in the cities and towns where their plants are located. In national capitalism, and even more in today's global economy, corporate executives invest resources where they will generate the best returns, with little regard for the local impacts of their decisions.

Many local manufacturers concluded that they couldn't compete against national conglomerates with multiple plants and integrated production, and sold out to them. Despite his infirmities (see box), Washington convinced the family stockholders to invest in modernizing production so they could compete with "the gigantic establishments out west."[125]

We are proposing a lot of improvements and changes for more economical operation, as our present plant is too costly to run. The total cost will be $750,000 (about $9 million in 2009)....

Everything possible is being electrified....

The rolling mill in Trenton must be transferred to Roebling to avoid duplicate handling of material. More labor saving devices must be introduced to hold our men....Labor and overhead expenses are still so high, that the more mere operating of the plant will show little if any profit this year.

Basic steel is now made 1 1/2 cents per pound cheaper than acid steel which we principally use - its quality is almost as good, hence most customers are buying it and leaving us. Price beats quality every time.[126]

Figure 5.54: Lalor Street Plant, 1928. BC
To meet the demand for Roebling Electro Galvanized Wire, the Company opened a new Electro Galvanizing Shop in 1922 to galvanize wire for special products like telephone and telegraph wire and aircraft cord.

As part of Washington's modernization program, the Company bought land "with ample trackage and yard room" on Lalor Street on the Trenton-Hamilton Township border, a mile from its Trenton Works, and moved its galvanizing operations there in 1922 (Fig. 5.54). The Lalor Street Plant was the Company's third plant in Trenton and fourth overall.

In March, Washington reported to John II: "The Camden Bridge engineers came to see me yesterday. They want me to bid on the cables and I do not see very well how to get out of it. There will be some competition. I do not want it unless there is a chance for profit." John II replied: "You need every ounce of help you possess in order to keep the mill going. You cannot afford to take on the heavy responsibility of the cable making contract." Washington immediately responded: "We need work for the mill and rope shop."[127]

I love the work, the excitement and responsibilities

In early 1922, Herbert Noble telegraphed Washington repeatedly that "someone wanted to buy us out," but he refused to consider it. In May, Washington reported that George Pepper, who was now a U.S. Senator, came to see him about "the banking firm of Seligman & Co., N.Y., who offered to buy our whole business out right (no merger) – part cash, part bonds, with the condition however that Nobel and Scammell should be lawyers of the new company. That condition betrayed to me the origin of the scheme...Pepper is in favor of a sale - he claims it will solve all difficulties and complications. But it is up to me to say Yes or No - the two fatal words - without my assent nothing can be done." Pepper subsequently wrote to Washington:[128]

The Bankers are not only desirous of retaining the name of the Company as at present but are desirous that you should retain official relation to the organization in an important executive capacity and that Mr. F.W. Roebling, Jr. should also retain some official relationship to it in a capacity subordinate to yours….If members of the family desire to retain some of their stock the bankers will be satisfied with the purchase of a majority of shares instead of all. This…. indicates pretty strongly that what the purchasers have in mind is continued independent operation and not a merger with other concerns….The bankers, if encouraged, will make a substantial offer for the purchase of all or some of the stock of the Company (at) *a price appreciably above $200 a share.*[129]

Washington expressed his suspicions to John II:

The Seligmans have someone behind them - they would not buy for themselves. I have a suspicion that the Otis Co. may be behind it. Their capital and resources are about the same as ours - taxes about the same. Scammell has made great efforts to be a director there. Their president is very efficient and has a talent for financial operation….

You know in case of a sale there is a heavy tax by the government…My health is very bad, but it is not aggravated by my attention to business - just the reverse.[130]

As Washington outlined the offer: "The investment account would be retained by the old stockholders - it is $10,000,000 and over (about $120 million)….The basis of the sale is our book value - call it $46,000,000 - and secondly goodwill, which has a considerable value, at least $1,000,000, because, at even prices, we always have a preference." The total value of $47 million (about $565 million) less the $10 million in investments would net $37 million (about $445 million),

which worked out to $246 (about $2,966) per share. Washington conveyed his dilemma to his son:[131]

This is a very serious proposition, with two points of view. The chief one is my advanced age and increasing difficulty as to control and management. My obvious successor should be Anderson, as he has all the necessary experience and much force of character. He has been in our employ many years. The Nobel-Scammell influence would be opposed to him.

On the other hand, at present our business is doing much better….All prices seem to be advancing now, this naturally induces increased demand for our products, as is shown by a large increase in orders recently - people are no longer afraid to stock up….Labor is becoming so scarce that we can scarcely fill what orders we have.

I stick to this business because it has been my lifelong occupation - I do not know any better. The idea of selling out is therefore repugnant to me. I love the work, the excitement and responsibilities, which are largely imaginary.[132]

I hold on as a matter of pride

A few days later Washington wrote to his daughter-in-law:

Our business affairs seem to be subject to occasional Tornadoes of excitement. This is the fourth offer I have had this year to sell. The present offer is very favorable. All contingencies are based on my tenure of life. After me comes the deluge. I can attend to the business easy enough, but too much of my time is taken up by outside matters. Noble & Scammell want to sell….I do not. I hold on as a matter of pride. Our business has improved wonderfully - we have more work than we can do and cannot get workmen to do it. I claim a small part of this is the result of my management.[133]

Raymond Arnot, Esq., Rochester, N.Y., August 31, 1922
Dear Sir,

For me to write an autobiography when I am approaching 86 and can scarcely find time to attend to my own affairs is out of the question….I doubt if any man's true and inner life was ever portrayed in a biography. I suffer from the usual ills that accompany old age - have gone blind with one eye and can scarcely see with the other. Am also deaf. Today I am in bed with bronchitis (a relapse), not to mention a number of other ailments which only get worse, none better. In face of all this, I am expected to smile and look happy….

Through the recent death of my two younger brothers, I have once more become the head of a great Steel and Wire Cable business employing over 6000 men. Having been familiar with it all my life, the feeling of responsibility is somewhat mitigated.

In all business, someone must say the potent words, yes or no! And in order to say them right, he must keep in intimate touch with all details. He must be able to gauge the future - be

a judge of human nature, on which all depends, and act at once. When competition kills some department, his inventive faculty must create a new departure. One has to be a financier, a tax expert, a lawyer and a technical expert.

With an endless string of untoward happenings cropping up almost daily, a man must have stability enough to take them at their face value, and not lose his balance.

My long civil war experience was to me of great interest. Through chance as much as merit, I was thrown into positions where campaigns and battles were planned and as often reduced to naught by an enemy who always had to be reckoned with….

You must excuse me from writing about the Brooklyn Bridge, which took up twelve years of my active life. But I assure you that the periodic outbursts about its downfall are all fakes, inspired by other would-be bridge builders at new locations, who think that by decrying the old structure they can promote the prospects of their enterprises.[116]

- Yours sincerely, Washington A. Roebling

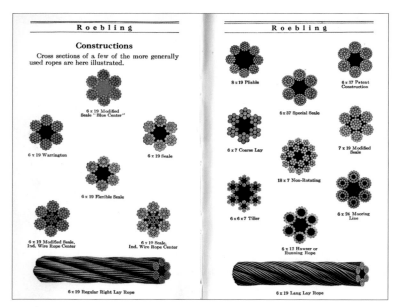

Figure 5.55: *Roebling Wire Rope and Wire*, 1923. "Roebling Wire Rope is fabricated in many constructions to any individual operating requirements," including "Blue Center Steel Wire Rope - from a superior grade of steel made in our own furnaces."

This necessitates the training of new men

Senator Pepper visited Washington later that summer, this time about bidding on the Camden Bridge cables. In a long letter that he showed to Pepper, Washington wrote:

> *The opportunity to build large cables occurs only at long intervals. Between the Cincinnati cables and the old Brooklyn bridge cables 11 years elapsed. Between the Brooklyn Bridge and the Williamsburg Bridge, 25 years. From the latter to the Manhattan Bridge, 11 years. The interval between the latter and the Camden Bridge will be about 12 years.*
>
> *One of the results of this condition is that many actors in these dramas have died in the meantime; others have disappeared or sought other employment or become too old to amount to much, like myself. This necessitates the training of new men, which means time and money, and, above all, someone who can do the training and transpose mere knowledge into concrete facts.*
>
> *This is the rub in this instance....The modern engineer only makes plans - very seldom does he execute them himself. He looks around for an abler contractor to execute them for him. Formerly this was not the case....*
>
> *I regret to say that owing to death, to old age and other disabilities, the firm of J.A.R.'s Sons no longer has anyone at its disposal who could take entire charge of such a work....*
>
> *A Three Million Dollar contract, with a time limit, with heavy responsibilities and the hardest kind of work, is a burden that an old broken down old man of 85 should seek to be relieved from, especially as the prospects of any profit are remote. Competition is inevitable.*[134]

Despite his age and infirmities, Washington oversaw efforts to modernize management and production. The Directors increased the capital stock from $15 million to $34.5 million (about $408 million in 2009) and declared a stock dividend of 1.3 shares to raise the total shares from 150,000 to 345,000. To retain and attract good employees, the Directors allocated some "surplus and undivided profits" to offer benefits similar to their competitors: an Employees Pension Plan" of $2 million (about $25 million), and "Group Insurance of Employees" with life insurance and a $500,000 (about $6 million) "compensation insurance fund" for injured employees.[135]

While the Company proceeded with its "extensions and improvements for increased economy in production," it also started marketing its best wire rope made of 'Blue Center' Steel, which a new catalogue noted: "Combines the highest strength with maximum fatigue and wearing qualities" (Fig. 5.55).[136]

The Bridge pot is boiling

John A. Roebling had built his High Falls Aqueduct over the Rondout Creek near Kingston, N.Y., for the Delaware & Hudson Canal Company in 1850, and in 1921 the Company completed the cables for a Route 9W bridge downstream between Kingston and Port Ewan (Fig. 5.56).

In early 1923, J.A.R.'s Sons Co. won the contract to build the cables for a much bigger bridge over the Hudson River between Peekskill, New York, and Bear Mountain. It would be the first vehicular bridge crossing the river south of Albany. Howard C. Baird, consulting engineer for the Bear Mountain Hudson River Bridge Company, designed the bridge with a 1,632 ft. main span, just 32 ft. longer than the main span of the Williamsburg Bridge, so that it would be the longest span in the world.

Figure 5.56: Kingston-Port Ewen Suspension Bridge, 2010. Bm J.A.R.'s Sons Co. completed the 9-in. cables for the 705-ft. main span bridge, also known as the Rondout Creek Bridge, in 1921.

Construction of Parallel Wire Cables for Suspension Bridges, John A. Roebling's Sons Co., Trenton, New Jersey, 1924.

Figure 5.57 (left): Bear Mountain Bridge Cable Making, 1923. The arrow points to a traveling wheel, which John A. Roebling patented in 1846 (see Fig. 2.15), laying a wire for the cable.

Figure 5.58 (right): The Company heralded its return to cable making with a summary of its suspension bridge history and striking photographs of its cable-making innovations on the Bear Mountain Bridge.

With input from Washington's, Charles Sunderland, the Company's chief engineer, developed several innovations for making the Bear Mountain Bridge cables (Figs. 5.57-59):

The construction of the cables for the Bear Mountain Bridge....may be said to have been the turning point in the history of parallel wire-cable fabrication, as several new theories, put to a rigid test during construction, proved very successful and opened the field to cables of practically any diameter and number of wires.[137]

With this bridge and bid preparations for the Camden Bridge, Washington reported: "We are terribly busy at the mill – 2 bridges on hand at once." After a visit from Gustav

Lindenthal, the Swiss-born engineer who designed a bridge to span the Hudson River at 57th Street in Manhattan, and another visit from the Camden Bridge engineers, Washington exclaimed to John II: "The Bridge pot is boiling." After much agonizing that summer, however, he wrote:[138]

We have formally concluded not to bid on the cable making of the Camden Bridge. There is no one to do the work, which is not easy, everything being thrown on the contractor with heavy penalties. The contractor also has to assume the mistakes of the Engineering Staff. But we propose to bid on the wire and the rope. If we get it, which is very doubtful.... it would come on top of the Bear Mountain Contract, on which we have made a beginning....The two bridges coming together makes the wire question a tremendous job and a heavy burthen to carry. We have to build a new wire mill because we cannot afford to lose our regular routine business. The amount wanted in a short time is too great.[139]

When U.S. Steel won the contract to build the entire Camden Bridge, Washington confided to Senator Clarence Case: "I regret very much that so much time and thought has been wasted by us on this work in the last two years, all to no purpose. We have knowledge and practical processes to make such cable wire exactly right, which no one else knows. The cables can only suffer in consequences." Washington soon wrote to John II: "Footbridge cables going up at Camden - one slipped, breaking a man's leg. One of the cables was two feet too short - causing trouble and delay. These ropes are all in three pieces. They did not have machines big enough to make a rope in one piece from anchorage to anchorage." Charles Sunderland would soon address this problem on a much bigger bridge.[140]

Figure 5.59: Bear Mountain Bridge, 2010. WK With Charles Sunderland's innovations, J.A.R.'s Sons Co. completed the 18-in. cables for the 1,632-ft. main span bridge in record time.

The labor situation

As Washington turned 86 in mid-1923 (see box below), the Company completed the biggest of its modernization projects, the No. 2 Rod Mill at the Kinkora Works for rolling 4 in. steel and copper billets into rods and flat strips. As *The Iron Age* reported: "The construction of the entire mill, including the erection of the fabricated steel, which was purchased, was carried out by the company's own organization, and most of the mill equipment was built in the company's shops."[141]

Among "several causes" for building the new rod mill in Roebling instead of in Trenton, *The Iron Age* noted: "Not the least of these is the labor situation, which is much easier to control in an industrial community, such as that at Roebling, than it is in the larger center." *The Iron Age* followed up with a feature on the "Industrial Village" (see box & Figs. 5.60-61).[142]

William Anderson soon introduced a plan for investing $1.2 million (about $14.8 million in 2009) for a bigger round of modernization projects, including $400,000 (about $5 million) for a new "Main office" at the Trenton plant and $10,000 (about $125,000) for "village sundries" in Roebling.

By this time, the Company had erected 767 houses in the village and about 1,400 workers lived there, most of them with families. Of the 4,000 total residents, about 70 per cent were "foreigners" – primarily Hungarian and Romanian immigrants, but also Slovaks, Poles and Russians – living in "ethnic neighborhoods." Overall the village provided housing for about 40 percent of the Kinkora Works employees.[143]

"Col. W.A. Roebling is 86,"
The New York Times, May 27, 1923

Colonel Washington A. Roebling,
builder of the Brooklyn Bridge and head of
the John A. Roebling's Sons Company here,
today celebrated his 86th birthday anniversary.
Despite his attainment of years when the average
captain of industry turns from active pursuit
of business to the golf links or similar diversion....
he is to be found at his offices in the plant almost daily.
At present Colonel Roebling is interested in the erection
of the new rolling mill at Roebling, New Jersey,
and the change in the operative power
of the local plant from steam to electricity.
A factor in the joy of the birthday celebration
was "Billy Sunday," Colonel Roebling's Airedale dog
and constant company. The dog is one of the few
in the city privileged to ride on the trolleys and
is often seen curled beneath the seat of his master
on route to work at the Roebling plant.

"Industrial Village on Sound Basis,"
The Iron Age, June 3, 1924
Town Built to Last

Substantiality seems to be the keynote of the whole enterprise. All the houses are brick, or brick and stucco. So are the stores, the school, the amusement hall, the bank, post office and hospital and other buildings....

Rents are so much lower than for similar ccommodations elsewhere within reach that, as the village will not hold of all the employees, there is a constant waiting list. Thus it becomes possible to make a certain selection of tenants, with regard both to permanence of employment and congeniality. Whenever a house becomes vacant the manager confers with the mill superintendents with regard to several of the applicants for it. That man who has the best mill record, and is most likely to remain a fixture in the plant, obtains a definite preference....

Houses for Employees Only

No one can rent a house in the village unless he is an employee of the Roebling company. On the other hand, no employee is required to live in the village. There is a group of houses and stores near the railroad station, which is not on the company's property and not under its control. Here live some of the employees, partly from choice, partly from inability to find a vacancy within the village. Here also live others catering to both employees and non-employees. And this outside community has raised several serious problems in control both of radicalism and liquor....

Consisting largely of foreigners, mainly Hungarians and Roumanians, the village has many children. To care for these a 16-room school near the southwest corner of the property was built by the Township on land donated by the company. As the school is overcrowded with its present 1,100 pupils, an addition of nine to 12 rooms is to be erected....

There are four churches, easily accessible outside the village line. One of these maintains a parochial school, with more than 100 children in attendance....

Where the People Buy

To accommodate local trade a department store is maintained in the central square, where a complete line of goods is carried. One half of the store is devoted to dry goods and notions, with kitchen utensils and furniture upstairs, while the other side comprises large grocery and butcher and bakery departments. The bakery, in an adjoining building, keeps nine people busy....

But no one has to buy at the "company store." In addition to the city stores at some distance there are the stores near the station, which get a good deal of the village trade. And many hucksters come in, particularly neighboring farmers and market gardeners with provisions. So long as these people behave themselves they are encouraged, for it is felt wise by the management to avoid all appearance of constraint.

And this idea pervades the whole theory of the control: let each man live where and how he wishes; let him buy where he wishes; let him do with his time as he wishes.

Having to deal so largely with a foreign element, this method has been found essential. It avoids the raising of that suspicion with which the average newcomer appears to regard our American way of doing things. It prevents him from feeling that the company is "keeping tabs" on him, both in the mill and out. And it gives him that liberty of action and choice which are essentially his if he is to become a worthwhile citizen.

This does not mean the necessary control is not exercised. In several cases it has become imperative to get rid of radicals who had come in and were stirring up trouble. Residents of the village are not permitted to harbor such elements and when they have done so, they had to leave the village, taking the radicals along. This is one of a number of ways in which complete control of the physical entity of the village enables the management to free it from trouble.

Providing for Activities Outside the Mill

Participation in sports is encouraged, particularly for the young men, as a means of "letting off steam" and avoiding the effects of their having too much time on their hands. Baseball teams from the different mill departments and a village football team have been developed and intense rivalry with similar teams from adjoining plants and towns has come into being. The tennis courts, maintained by the village, are in active demand....

There is an amusement hall with moving picture outfit that seats 800 on the main floor and another 100 in the balcony. The stage is adapted for plays and entertainments, and there are dressing rooms on each side. Dances and socials are held here....appropriately enough the curtain contains a picture of the Brooklyn Bridge, upon the building of which the first fame of the Roeblings was founded. Back of the balcony is a large room devoted to a circulating library, with 4,300 well selected volumes covering a wide variety of books – not only fiction but history, science, poetry, biography, religion, etc....

In the post office building is a well-equipped hospital, a new x-ray machine being the most recent piece of apparatus. Two two-bed wards, operating room, dressing room, bath, etc., with a nurse constantly in attendance, and two doctors, each having an office in the hospital, form a compact unit. The men are encouraged to make use of this facility, even for slight injuries, as a means of avoiding infection. Their families are also accommodated here for such treatment as they may require....

Caring for Workers' Savings

Formerly the "stocking bank" or its equivalent, translated into many languages and many quaint customs, were much in evidence. And it took a long time to gain enough of the confidence of the foreign element to induce them to make use of a more secure way of taking care of their savings. But now the First National Bank....has nearly 2000 accounts....

Studying the Alien Psychology

In former times it was difficult to make the foreign inhabitants understand the need for keeping their yards clean; in particular, they would dump garbage and piles. To overcome this a contest was started, with substantial money prizes, for the best looking backyards. This resulted in transforming the erstwhile dumps into luxuriant gardens, and the idea "stuck."

This is merely one instance of the psychology used and tact exercised in dealing with the alien element. Their characteristics have been studied and their wishes are respected in every way which is not detrimental to the village. They are fond of being photographed, particularly with grandiose backgrounds. Hence the photographic gallery is run by one of them who understands their idiosyncrasies and their language....

Much influence on the older people is exercised through the children. Alert, keen, mischievous, they make it needful to keep many things locked up. But what they learn in school, at the "movie," in the library, is much of it faithfully transmitted – translated, of course, into the foreign tongue – and its effect is seen. This cannot be measured in anyway, but the secondhand influence thus exerted has taught the management the importance of keeping "on the right side" of the youngsters....

Every effort is made to keep the streets and lawns attractive. The two streets crossing at the central square are parked down the center and are 120 ft. wide; the other streets are 80 ft. Trees have been planted, as well as shrubs in the park spaces, and the grass is cut by the man in charge of streets and park. He has a small experimental plot where he can raise shrubs and other plants for eventual transplanting into the park or elsewhere.

Does it pay?

Not in dollars and cents. As a matter of fact, the running expenses almost exactly balance the income – in many years creating a deficit which the company has had to underwrite. And this makes no provision for either depreciation or amortization. Hence the enterprise is operated at what it is, in last analysis, a distinct loss - measured in money.

But it most assuredly does pay in the larger sense. It pays in attracting men of the better kind. It pays in promoting permanence of employment, and hence avoiding costly labor turnover. It pays in promoting health of employees, and thus reducing absences and errors and accidents.

And Mr. Raymond H. Thompson, who has been with the project since its inception, and who lived that first winter in a little shack on the property, believes that really the company has made a long step forward, not only in solving a bothersome labor problem, but also the twin problem of the assimilation into our body politic the foreign element which forms so large a share of what we have become accustomed to call "common labor."

Trees, Hedges, Shrubs, Vines and Flowers Abound. A contest transformed back yards into bowers of blossoms

Blocks of Ten Houses In a Row (Above and at Right)

All the Streets Are Wide—Some More So Than Others

These Houses Are of the Double or Semi - Detached Type, Each Side Having Six to Nine Rooms and Bath (Above, At Right and Below). Note the parked streets

Figure 5.60: "Industrial Village on Sound Basis," *The Iron Age*, **January 3, 1924, page 11. PPL**

Open Spaces Give Ample Elbow Room. There is not the slightest suggestion of crowding. And there is room for considerable expansion

The Riverside Park

A Superintendent's House

"The Inn"

The Amusement Hall, Where Moving Pictures Are Shown and Dances and Socials Take Place. On the second floor, the library occupies the front

Main Entrance to the Kinkora Works. Showing the End of the Parked Main Street. At left are the principal store buildings, with the water tower at junction of Main Street and Fifth Avenue

Figure 5.61: "Industrial Village on Sound Basis," *The Iron Age*, **January 3, 1924, page 13. PPL**

Figure 5.62: Flat Shop No. 3, Trenton, 1926. BC
A "daylight factory" with huge windows and sawtooth skylights, the 1924 flat wire shop on South Clinton Avenue represented "the last word in factory construction."

The new rod mill enabled the Company to replace the 1886 Rolling Mill (see Fig. 4.23) on South Clinton Avenue in Trenton with Flat Shop No. 3 (Fig. 5.62) to roll flat wire for a variety of customers and uses. As Washington noted: "The Flat business has expanded - our reputation in that line stands high, though the profits are correspondingly low. If the fashions were to change and women wore steel corsets again, our fortune would be made – we excel in that line and profits are good."[144]

In November, 1925, the Company began publishing *Blue Center* for employees to bring "our organization into closer understanding and harmony" (Fig. 5.63). As the Editor noted, "We are a large family, scattered from the Atlantic to the Pacific – some eight thousand of us – each sincerely interested in the great human organization bearing the name of the John A. Roebling's Son Company, and in what is being done by our fellow-employees around us and across the continent." The first of many features on employees noted:

Figure 5:63: *Blue Center*, November, 1925.
In response to an article in the first issue on John A. Roebling's original rope walk in Trenton, Washington wrote:
Trudging out the long rope walk in cold and snow was killing work for these poor fellows. Most of the workers were German in those days. What a change between Then & Now.[149]

Ernest C. Ermeling, holds the record for the greatest length of service among the active employees, having been employed in the rope department for fifty-two years....Mr. Ermeling's interest dates back of 1873, as his father, Barnhart Ermerling, served the Company as steam engineer for forty-five years. He had been a school chum of John A. Roebling years before in Germany...Mr. Ermeling recalls many interesting incidents when he was a boy and when the Roebling plant had only a few hundred employees. One concerns the Sunday mornings in the old apple orchard, where Charles G. and Ferdinand W., then boys, indulged in the manly art of self-defense.[145]

William Anderson reported at the Annual Meeting in early 1926 that 1925 was "the maximum production year in the history of the Company, and stands fourth in the list of its most profitable years...1917, 1923, 1916, 1925." The next few years would show even more profits, proving Washington's decision to keep and modernize the Company.[146]

While Washington's health declined in early 1926, he stayed engaged in the business and continued writing about the Brooklyn Bridge, minerals, the economy, and his view of life (see box). In March he wrote to John II, "My recent attacks of indigestion have left me very weak. I can no longer rally as formerly - have not been at the mill for two weeks." As his 89th birthday approached, he wrote to a friend: "Have broken down completely – losing strength daily – cannot eat, sleep, walk, or stand – weigh 90 lbs."[147]

Washington's immediate family quietly celebrated his 89th birthday with him on May 26. A few weeks later he wrote to his daughter-in-law: "Body racks with pain – Head bowed down in sheer apathy – Bones creak when I am rolled over – Fall down when I try to stand – Please leave me alone and in peace....W.A.R." Then he continued in a postscript:[148]

A surprise: For several years - 10 - a night blooming crocus stalk has been knocked about in the greenhouse - last night it suddenly bloomed - was brought to my bedside at 10 P.M. A delicate odor filled the room - a wonderful flower - much larger than a rose – a calyx filled with snow white petals curved outward and oval pointed - this morning it is gone - to sleep the sleep of ages again.

> The human mind is incapable of comprehending the terms Infinity and Eternity. If the Universe has always existed, there was no need at any time to create it, and since matter is indestructible, it can only change its form but not cease to exist. Our puny human mind cannot get away from the idea of a personal God. To me the term God simply represents the universe. The universe is God and God is the universe and we are part of it.
> - Washington A. Roebling, December, 1925[150]

Washington remained remarkably lucid even as he grew weaker, as related by Hamilton Schuyler, a family friend:

Up to a few days before his death, officials of the Roebling Company frequently went to his house to consult him about important business matters which he settled with his customary decision. He thoroughly realized his critical condition, and shortly before his death remarked to relatives that about all of his physique which remained to serve him was his brain. He added, he was grateful for this much.[151]

On the morning of July 21, 1926, Washington slipped into a coma and died peacefully that afternoon with his wife, his son and daughter-in-law, his grandson Siegfried and his stepson at his bedside at 191 West State Street. When Governor A. Harry Moore learned of his passing, he said: "In the death of Colonel Roebling, New Jersey has lost one of, if not its most distinguished citizen." *The New York Times* noted, "The Brooklyn Bridge, which, when it was completed in 1883, was the longest suspension bridge in the world, is a monument to the engineering skill of Washington A. Roebling" (Fig. 5.64).[152]

Over 300 family members, friends and business associates gathered in the house on July 23 for a funeral service, with the Episcopal bishop of New Jersey presiding at the bottom of the staircase in the great hall, below the Tiffany window of the Brooklyn Bridge (see Fig. 4.48). On the next day, 60 family members and friends boarded a special train provided by the Pennsylvania Railroad and accompanied Washington's body to Cold Spring, New York, where, as he had stipulated, his family buried him next to the grave of his first wife, Emily.

On July 26, the Directors recognized Washington's contributions to the Company (see box) and elected Ferdinand, Jr., as President and William A. Anderson as Vice President and Treasurer and appointed Anderson as General Manager.

When his executors settled Washington's estate, they valued it at $29 million (about $357 million in 2009). He bequeathed $110,000 (about $1.35 million) to various members of his immediate family, $50,000 to Rensselaer Polytechnic Institute, $45,000 to three Trenton Hospitals, and $5,000 to be divided among household staff. He left 100 shares each of his stock in J.A.R.'s Sons to employees William Anderson, Austin Cooley and Charles Cooley, and 50 shares to Charles C. Sunderland.

In the city of Trenton Colonel Roebling was for years regarded as the leading citizens and all Trentonians are proud of his achievements and revere his memory. It is universally felt that his presence here lent distinction to the town, and that by his death it has sustained a loss which cannot be measured in words.
- Hamilton Schuyler, 1931[153]

Figure 5.64:
Washington Augustus Roebling
1837-1926 RPI

It is with profound sorrow and regret that we record the death of our President, Colonel Washington A. Roebling....In his passing away this Company has sustained an irreparable loss. It is futile for us to attempt to express adequately our sense of this loss, yet we desire to record our appreciation of his long life of service and the privilege which has been ours to have been associated with him in the direction of this Company's affairs.

To few men has it fallen the lot to take up active duties as the head of a great business after having reached the age of more than four score years. We have watched with admiration the courage with which he accepted this responsibility and the able and gallant manner in which he performed his duties.

His long connection with the Company which practically dates from the very commencement of the business in Trenton over 75 years ago; his early association with his father, John A. Roebling, the founder of the business, in carrying out to successful completion the many great enterprises in the early years of its history; his keen observation of the growth and expansion of the business during the last half-century of our country's industrial development; and his devotion to the welfare of the business to which he dedicated his accumulated wisdom and experience, placed him in a unique and invaluable position of usefulness and influence as the head of our Company.

His attainments and character have given added prestige to the Roebling name. We honor and cherish his memory.
Ferdinand W. Roebling Jr., Siegfried Roebling, Robert C. Roebling, William A. Anderson, William Gummere, Directors, John A. Roebling's Sons Co., July 26, 1926.[154]

To his wife he left 6,500 shares in addition to 9,000 he previously gave, plus one third of his residuary estate. To his son John II he left 63,000 shares, about 18 percent of the total shares, two thirds of the residuary, his papers, including his father's papers, and his mineral collection. Siegfried had inherited 191 West State from his grandmother, Emily, in 1903.

A month before he died, Washington wrote that his mineral collection "cost me $150,000 (about $1.8 million in 2009) and contains all the rare minerals in the world" (right). A few weeks later he wrote to his son: "The time has come for me to give up minerals – can no longer keep up – entirely too many new ones." John II donated the collection to the Smithsonian along with $150,000 (below). *The New York Times* noted: "It is reputed to be the finest private collection in the world and it's worth is estimated at $300,000 (about $3.6 million). Its scientific value is said by experts to be inestimable."[155]

To George Frederick Collins, President, New York Mineralogical Club,

I was both surprised and highly pleased with the announcement of my election as an honorary member of the New York Mineralogical…. Although I have been collecting for 40 years I feel that I am still a neophyte in the science and that there is more than ever for us to learn in the future. Most collections have a small beginning. My motive was chiefly to while away the tedium of a sick room when reading and writing were forbidden for some years – and well it served its purpose. As in all large collections, a time comes when specimens come so fast that they threaten to crowd one out of house and home – case after case is filled and one room after the other commandeered. The process of culling out helps but little.

To acquire at least one specimen of every known mineral proves to be an impossible task for a private individual. Only museums live forever. When I began there were only a few hundred of the principal minerals – now there are thousands, with annual accretions of new varieties in species of fifty to a hundred more. My specialty has been to collect rare minerals – and in that way I have been able to be of a little assistance to the many masters of the Science in this country.

- Washington A. Roebling, October 24, 1917

"Roebling Collection of Rare Minerals Puts Smithsonian in the Highest Rank," *Washington Star*, March 13, 1927

The mineral collection of the late Colonel Washington A. Roebling, the man who built the Brooklyn Bridge, has been given to the Smithsonian Institution by his son, John A. Roebling II. It is the finest private mineral collection in the world. But more than that, it represents the lifetime solace and relaxation of one of America's greatest figures. In fact, the collection more intimately reveals the man and embodies the personality of Col. Roebling than the professional achievements which ensure his fame.

Begun when Col. Roebling was a college student in the '50s' of the last century, the collection grew to over 16,000 carefully selected specimens. Every one of the 16,000 bears a label in the handwriting of Col. Roebling, and many bear notations which have to do with the circumstances under which the specimen was obtained, or some facts on its character and history.

The owner kept his minerals in a huge room in his Trenton residence (see Fig. 4.49). The walls were lined with cases and cabinets full of drawers, and though he maintained no catalogue, Col. Roebling was able up to the very last month to select at once the drawer in which any particular specimen was kept. In later years he converted a basement bowling alley into a similar room.

It was his habit from time to time to take out a drawer full of specimens and examine each with the delight of a connoisseur. This seemed to bring peace to a body that was often in pain…

Colonel Roebling was able to supply a considerable number of specimens to many great public collections….That he began to collect before graduating from Rensselaer Polytechnic Institute in 1857, where a course in mineralogy first awakened his interest in the subject, gave him a decided advantage over many present day private collectors….

In the collection is an opal weighing 18.6 ounces, perhaps the largest precious opal in the world….which was found in Virgin Valley, Nevada….Another unusual stone is a peridot of 310 carats, which was found on the island of St. John in the Red Sea, and was originally set in a figure of a saint in Austria…. Another rarity is a 32-carat alexandriate from Ceylon….

A 64-carat black diamond of unusually fine crystal, and believed to be one of the largest crystals of black diamonds, comes from the river diggings of South Africa. An 18-carat stone of a fine canary yellow color, was found in Arizona near Murfreesboro….Three exceptional specimens of beryls from Brazil are in the collection. Also in the collection is one of the largest pink spodumenes, found in Pala in San Diego County, California, and tourmalines from Mesa Grande, California.

A crystal of apatite from Maine is remarkable for its deep purple color, large size and perfection of the crystal form it shows. One of the specimens is of a species named after the collector, Roeblingite. It was found at Franklin Furnace, N.J. by Penfield, late mineralogist of Yale. It is the only mineral with a sulfite radical on it….

Col. Roebling was not a collector of 'showy' stones only. He had a scientific interest in minerals; he wished to acquire a complete collection of fine specimens, of the most obscure species and their varieties, as well as of those which are considered precious stones. Many of the very rare species are represented by unusually fine examples.

Accompanying the gift of the Roebling collection to the Smithsonian, John A. Roebling II added an endowment of $150,000 to ensure the maintenance of the collection in the front rank position to which Col. Roebling brought it.

Chapter 6: *Another bold leap forward*

Figure 6.1:
J.A.R.'s Sons Company
Trenton Works, N.J., 1926. BC
The Aero Service Corporation photographed the Roebling plants just a few months before Washington Roebling died in July 1926. Tracking the progress of the Industrial Revolution, the Roebling Company had grown phenomenally since John A. Roebling moved his wire rope factory to Trenton in 1849 (see Fig. 3.2).
The plant reached its greatest density in the late 1920s, with scores of buildings and multistory mills covering nearly the entire 25 acre site. The Delaware & Raritan Canal separated the Roebling Plant from the American Steel & Wire Co. (top), the successor to Peter Cooper's Trenton Iron Co.

John A. Roebling made his first wire rope in 1841 and manufactured wire rope for 28 years until his death in 1969. The second generation Roeblings operated their wire rope and wire business for a remarkable 57 years until Washington's death in 1926, when control passed completely to the third generation. The founder would have been amazed and delighted to the extent to which his sons expanded his business (Figs. 6.1-6.2).

Washington divided his 30 percent share of J.A.R.'s Sons Co. among: John II, 59, his only child, who now had 18.4 percent, making him the largest individual shareholder; his grandsons, Siegfried, 36, and Donald, 18, who each had 3.5 percent; and Cornelia Witsell Roebling, his second wife, who owned 4.5 percent. Francis S. MacIlvaine, a relative of John II's first wife, Margaret MacIlvaine Roebling, served as guardian of Donald's shares and Austin Cooley held a proxy for Cornelia's shares.

Figure 6.2:
J.A.R.'s Sons Company
Roebling Village
and Kinkora Works
Roebling, N.J., 1926. BC
The Kinkora Works (in the middle background) occupied over 200 acres in a country environment just ten miles south of Trenton. With its more than 720 houses, athletic fields and the Roebling School (bottom), the Village constituted an orderly community of about 4,000 workers and members of their families.
The Delaware River flows around Newbold Island (top) just north of the plant.

Ferdinand had equally divided his 30 percent share to his two sons. Karl had left his 15 percent in four equal portions of 3.75 percent to his widow, Blanche Estabrook Roebling, and his children, Robert, 22, Allison, 19, and Caroline, 15. Robert held the proxy for his mother's and sister's shares. Ferdinand, Jr., 48, owned 15 percent of the stock. Ferdinand, like his father John, had provided for his daughters, Margaret Roebling Perrine, 58, and Augusta Roebling White, 53, in other ways.

Charles had placed his 30 percent share in trusts for his daughters, Emily Roebling Cadwalader, 47, and Helen Roebling Tyson, 42, and their offspring, and he had appointed Herbert Noble, Emily and Helen as co-trustees. Ten third generation Roeblings or their surrogates now controlled J.A.R.'s Sons Co. Edmund, John A. Roebling's fourth son, was 72 and retained his 10 percent share, but, as Washington had arranged, Austin Cooley, a loyal executive employee, held his power of attorney.

With Washington's bequest, five loyal employees now held Roebling stock: William A. Anderson, 123 shares: Austin Cooley, 100; Charles C. Cooley, 100; Charles C. Sunderland, 50; and William Gummere, 1. While these shares amounted to only .01 percent of the stock, they enabled the five employees to serve on the Board of Directors and help run the Company.

The stockholders and representatives elected eight Directors: Ferdinand, Jr., Siegfried and Robert Roebling, long-time employees and executives William Anderson, William Gummere, and Austin Cooley (who represented Cornelia and Edmund), Francis S. MacIlvaine, (who represented Donald), and Herbert Noble (who represented Emily and Helen).

As the Company entered its third management era, Roebling family members served as only three of its eight directors, and no one represented John II, the largest individual holding. The Directors appointed Ferdinand, Jr., as President, William W. Anderson as 1st Vice President, Treasurer and General Manager, Siegfried as 2nd Vice President, Austin Cooley as Secretary and Assistant Treasurer, and his brother Charles Cooley as Assistant Secretary.

Anderson reported 1926 profits of $6.1 million (about $75.2 million in 2009), the second highest in the Company's history, and investment in the plants that year of $854,000 ($10.5 million). He noted $400,000 ($4.9 million) in savings from electrification and other upgrades, and from reorganizing some production. Anderson also reported a distribution of $198,720 ($2.4 million) to himself and 29 other managers under a Profits Participation Plan that the Directors instituted to further enlist "the cooperation, efforts and zeal of its employees in increasing the future successful operations of the business." The Company paid dividends of $4.1 million ($50 million), the second highest annual dividends recorded to date.

Figure 6.3: J.A.R.'s Sons Co. "New General Office," 1927. BC Hoggson Brothers, a prominent New York firm of Architects & Builders, designed and erected the new office at 640 South Broad Street in Trenton of "modern fire proof construction."[2]

Since the administration of the business had outgrown its headquarters, the Directors authorized $500,000 ($6.1 million) to construct a new General Office south of the existing building to "provide for the consolidation of departmental activity and normal expansion of work" (Figs. 6.3-6.4). Over the next four years the Company would undertake other big construction projects "to eliminate obsolete and inefficient buildings," including John A. Roebling's original rope shops, which Washington would have been reluctant to demolish.[1]

It should be given consideration

Washington had closely followed proposals since the 1890s to build an unprecedented suspension bridge across the Hudson River, and had met with Gustav Lindenthal in 1923 about his proposal to build a bridge at 57th Street in Manhattan. That same year, Othmar Ammann, who had previously worked for Lindenthal, proposed a bridge between Fort Washington Park at 179th Street in New York and Fort Lee in New Jersey. With a span of 3,500 feet, Amman's bridge would have twice the span of the Camden Bridge (named the Benjamin Franklin Bridge in 1956), the longest at that time.

The directors of the Port of New York Authority, which the states of New York and New Jersey established in 1921 and is now called the Port Authority of New York and New Jersey, agreed in 1925 to build Amman's proposed bridge. The directors appointed Amman as the Authority's Chief Bridge Engineer, and in December 1926, they authorized $60 million (about $737 million) of New York and New Jersey Interstate Bridge Gold Bonds yielding 4.2 percent for the construction of the Hudson River Bridge. The Authority's finance staff estimated that bridge tolls would generate about $4 million ($49 million) annually, more than enough to pay for maintenance and debt service.

Figure 6.4: J.A.R.'s Sons Co. General Office, 1928. BC
The Company modernized the old General Office (left center), which contained remnants of John Roebling's 1855 house (see Figs. 3.11 & 4.76-77), to complement the new building (right).

Amman projected that 8.5 million cars, trucks and buses would cross in the first full year of operation after the bridge opened in 1932, and that annual traffic would reach 15.5 million by 1954, exceeding the capacity of a single deck. He therefore proposed to build the bridge strong enough to support a second deck that would be added when it was needed.

Amman preferred building the bridge with eyebar chains as the suspension system, and the Port Authority's illustrations of the bridge showed eyebar chains. It seemed that the Roebling Company might be excluded from making the cables of the greatest suspension bridge ever proposed.

Worried that the Company might lose out on building the Hudson River Bridge cables, the Directors authorized Anderson to write a letter to Governor A. Harry Moore objecting to the Port Authority's consideration of eyebar chains for the cables. In his letter, Anderson expressed doubt about the uniformity and durability of eyebars and the ability to erect them over the proposed span of 3,500 ft. The longest eyebar bridge had a span of 1,114 ft., less than one third of the proposed Hudson River span, whereas the longest wire cable span, the 1,750 ft. Camden Bridge, was only half the required length. Anderson reminded Moore that only two steel companies could manufacture eyebars and that: "Neither of these is located in the State of New Jersey" (see box).

Governor Moore, who was also concerned about the autonomy of the Port Authority, responded by having the State Legislature adopt a bill that required the approval of the State House Commission over all of the Port Authority's bridge contracts. When New York Governor Alfred Smith strenuously objected to New Jersey's potential interference in Port Authority business, Moore released Anderson's letter to the press with an accompanying statement:

Millions of dollars will be expended for this bridge, and I do not see why New Jersey concerns should be excluded from bidding, thus depriving hundreds of our people of the work which this gigantic undertaking would supply.

It is true that specifications have not been adopted, but the report of the Bridge Engineer, which has been received and approved by the Port Authority, pictures a bridge of eye-bar construction....The Brooklyn Bridge, which has stood the test of time; the new Bear Mountain Bridge; and the very latest word in bridges - the Delaware River Bridge (Benjamin Franklin Bridge)*, are all of steel wire construction....*

When such objection is made by a concern of the reputation of the John A. Roebling's Sons Company, it should be given consideration.[3]

After Governor Smith threatened to sue New Jersey over the State House Commission bill, Othmar Ammann assured both governors that the Port Authority would request bids for both eyebar chain cables and for wire cables, and Moore subsequently had his bill repealed. Anderson's letter and Moore's support had succeeded in assuring that J.A.R.'s Sons Co. could bid on the Hudson River Bridge cables.

March 16, 1927

Governor A. Harry Moore,
State Capital, Trenton, New Jersey,

We wish to register our opposition to the consideration at the New York Port Authority of a bridge of the eye-bar design for the Hudson River....Galvanized High Strength Steel Bridge Wire is an important commodity of the State of New Jersey and other States. This commodity is recognized to be a high-grade and most uniform material. The practice of testing both ends of each coil of wire for its physical properties, and testing the galvanized coating for uniformity and durability, warrants the belief that this material excels any other steel commodity for uniformity and durability.

When Galvanized High Strength Steel Bridge Wire is used in the construction of Parallel Wire Suspension Bridge Cables for Long Span Suspension Bridges, it ensures the most economical construction for these cables, both as to material and erection, and further insures the maximum durability.... The maximum benefits to the people of New Jersey will be secured by constructing the Hudson River Bridge cables of Galvanized High Strength Steel Bridge Wire....

The durability of this structure is of great importance, as a bridge of this magnitude must be judged by its strength and durability 200 years hence, not in terms of 50 or 75 years, as a smaller structure would be considered.

Very truly yours,
JOHN A. ROEBLING'S SONS CO.,
W. A. Anderson, Vice President

Figure 6.5 (left): The *Spirit of St. Louis*, 1927. BC Charles Lindbergh outfitted his airplane on the first transatlantic flight with "Roebling aircord control cords" and electrical cables. Figure 6.6 (above): A 1927 J.A.R.'s Sons Co. ad equated Lindbergh and Roebling with "STRENGTH - ENDURANCE - RELIABILITY."

Guided in its flight by Roebling aircraft control cords

On May 21, 1927, after 33 hours on the first solo transatlantic flight, Charles Lindbergh landed his Spirit of St. Louis at 10:22 P.M. at Le Bourget Field outside Paris, and 100,000 waiting people rushed the airplane. The June issue of *Blue Center* noted: "Our readers will be interested to learn that the one-motor airplane, the *Spirit of St. Louis*, which was recently flown from New York to Paris by Captain Lindbergh was guided in its flight by Roebling aircraft control cords. The plane was braced with our tinned aircraft wire, and our lighting and ignition cables were also used" (Figs. 6.5-6).

That summer the Port Authority issued specifications for combined bids for the Hudson River Bridge towers and deck and the cables, which could be built of eyebar chains or wire. Charles Sunderland submitted J.A.R.'s Sons Co.'s bid for wire cables in conjunction with bids for the towers and deck by three steel companies: the American Bridge Company, a division of U.S. Steel; Bethlehem Steel; and the McClintic-Marshall Company of Steelton, Pennsylvania. Bethlehem, American Bridge, American Cable and McClintic-Marshall also submitted various combinations of bids to build the bridge with either cables or eyebars.

Port Authority officials announced on October 3 that the J.A.R.'s Sons Co. - McClintic-Marshall combined bid was the lowest at $22,474,000 (about $273 million in 2009), consisting of $12,340,000 (about $150 million) for the wire cables and $10,134,000 (about $123 million) for the towers and deck. J.A.R.'s Sons Co. underbid the second lowest bid for wire cables - by American Cable - by less than three percent. At a presentation to the Trenton Rotary Club two weeks later,

Charles Sunderland called the Hudson River Bridge "a sudden leap forward into a whole new range of magnitude (see box)."[4]

For such exacting service

Sunderland and his bridge engineering staff faced many unprecedented challenges in building the Hudson River Bridge cables, including erecting the temporary footbridges with wire ropes that would have to span more than 3,600 ft. between the towers. As the Editor of *Engineering News-Record* noted, "No ropes so long as would be required to support these walks had ever been built for such exacting service." After laying the wire for the cables, Sunderland planned on cutting the footbridge ropes into premarked lengths and using them as suspender ropes for the deck. The construction of the bridge required 36 2-15/16 in. diameter footbridge ropes that totaled 185,000 ft. or 32 miles in length, and 106,000 miles of 3/16 in. bridge wire. To produce and install these huge quantities of galvanized bridge wire and wire rope to meet the Port Authority's opening date in 1932, the Company expanded production and developed the capacity to prestretch and test the footbridge ropes to minimize sagging after installation.[5]

Meanwhile, on the other side of the country, after more than a decade of planning, California legislators in 1928 created the Golden Gate Bridge and Highway District to finance and build a 4,200 ft. span suspension bridge between San Francisco and Marin County that would surpass the Hudson River Bridge span by 20 per cent. Roebling engineers and Directors followed the development of this project closely, especially since Joseph Strauss, the Chief Engineer of the proposed Golden Gate Bridge, had served on the Port Authority's board of advisory engineers for the Hudson River Bridge.

"The Super Bridge of Today," Charles C. Sunderland, Chief Bridge Engineer, J.A.R.'s Sons Co., Trenton Rotary Club, 1927

From 1844 to 1867 John A. Roebling was proving to skeptical engineers that the accepted impossible was possible, safe and scientifically correct. He not only designed original and bold projects, he proved them possible and safe by building them. So when he designed and offered to build that wonderful structure, the Brooklyn Bridge, his position as the outstanding engineer of his day made it impossible for the skeptics to ridicule the idea. Nevertheless, the idea of building a bridge, having nearly twice the span length of the Niagara Bridge, was strikingly bold, and required courage of the highest order, in addition to the scientific knowledge and great experience at his command.

The Brooklyn Bridge, having a span of approximately 1600 ft., stands as the oldest, most beautiful and durable engineering feat of its day, a monument, not only to John A. Roebling, but also to his son, Washington A. Roebling, who carried the structure to completion after his father's death….

The bridges of our day are of the same order of magnitude as the Brooklyn Bridge. The Williamsburg Bridge, 1600 ft. span, Manhattan Bridge, 1470 ft. span, Bear Mountain Bridge, 1632 ft. span. The Philadelphia-Camden Bridge, 1750 ft. span, the longest of these bridges, shows an increase of only eleven percent in span length over the Brooklyn Bridge.

Therefore the solution of design and erection problems, as developed on the Brooklyn Bridge have applied on the latter bridges. We have simply used stronger materials as they have been developed, fabricated and erected heavier members, and increased the speed of erection as our skill improved. In our day engineering progress usually moves cautiously, step by step, but the Hudson River Bridge is a sudden leap forward into a whole new range of magnitude. Just as the Brooklyn Bridge was a bold step forward into a field of greater magnitude, so does the Hudson River Bridge make another bold leap forward.

It is only right and proper that the Roebling Company, founded by John A. Roebling, should undertake the furnishing and erecting of the cables for this super-bridge. It is a tribute to his memory which we cannot ignore. We profoundly regret that Colonel Washington A. Roebling was not spared for a few more years until he could have finished the main cables for this super-bridge, for he was keenly interested in this development up to the time of his death. His knowledge and mature judgment would have made our problems much easier. Nevertheless the history and experience of these great men, master engineers, are available, and the men they have trained to continue their work will carry it to a successful completion.

The Hudson River Bridge is distinctly a bridge of the future. One hundred years hence, bridges of this magnitude will be common practice. Unlike the Philadelphia-Camden Bridge, which will reach its maximum capacity in ten years, the Hudson River Bridge will be increasing capacity as the demand requires. The towers and main cables will be built for the full capacity. The additional roadways on the suspended structure will be built to meet the need as the demand increases. The bridge must be open within four years, in 1932. This means that a bridge having twice the span of the Philadelphia-Camden Bridge, must be erected in the same amount of time. It was considered that the Philadelphia-Camden Bridge erection represented the maximum speed possible….

If you need a comparison, place the tower of the Philadelphia-Camden Bridge on top of the Brooklyn Bridge Tower and the total height will correspond with the Hudson River Bridge Tower. Consider this tower as a skyscraper, and you will have a 54-story building above the water line.

Another feature that will make you realize the size of this bridge, stand on the roadway at the center of the main span, and you will be 250 feet above the water. The total height of the Brooklyn Bridge Tower is 273 feet, so you are only 23 feet below the top of the Brooklyn Bridge Tower when at the center of the Hudson River Bridge….

The main cables for this super bridge must support over three times the weight of the Philadelphia-Camden Bridge….and will be constructed of wires 3/16" in diameter, laid parallel. The minimum strength of each wire is 6,800 pounds. There are 26,774 wires in each main cable, therefore the ultimate strength of each main cable is 180,000,000 pounds (90,000 tons), and the four main cables have a total of 720,000,000 (360,000 tons) pounds strength. The length of main cables from anchorage to anchorage is one mile, therefore in the four main cables there is a total of 106,000 miles of wire, enough to go four times around the Earth. The total weight of the four main cables is 57,000,000 pounds, or 28,500 tons….

To give a better idea of the size and weight of the Hudson River Bridge cables, the total weight of wire in the main cables of the Brooklyn, Williamsburg, Manhattan, Philadelphia-Camden and Bear Mountain Bridges is 22,400 tons. Add to this the weight of wire in the cables of the suspension bridges now being erected at Poughkeepsie, N.Y., and at Detroit, Michigan, making a total of 27,800 tons of wire, and you will still lack 1,300 tons of wire to equal the weight of wire in the Hudson River Bridge.

Just imagine, the combined weight of wire in the main cables of the seven largest suspension bridges in the world is not sufficient to construct the cables of this super bridge.

The Roebling Company will produce this material within the time specified, without, in any way, affecting our commercial production of wire and wire rope. It is gratifying to know that there has grown up in our midst an industry capable of producing and erecting the material of this super-bridge, and further gratifying to know that, as in the past, when the workmen, mechanics and engineers of Trenton produced the material and helped to build the Brooklyn Bridge - the super-bridge of its day - so will the sons, grandsons and great grandsons of these same men perform the same distinctive service on the Hudson River Bridge - the Super-Bridge of today.

Figure 6.7: Kinkora Works Expansion, 1928. BC
To prepare for the huge quantities of wire needed for the Hudson River Bridge and other projects, Company engineers erected a new continuous Rod Mill and expanded the capacity of two of the nine open hearth furnaces in the Steel Mill (right) from 25 to 40 tons.

Figure 6.8: Physical Testing Laboratory, Trenton Works, 1987. Jet Lowe, HAER
Charles Sunderland erected the tall laboratory in 1928 to house the world's largest testing machine for testing the tensile strength of strands and wire ropes for the Hudson River Bridge and other special projects.

With production requirements for the Hudson River Bridge and the prospect of other bridge contracts, the Directors authorized major improvements at the Company's plants, including a new rod mill at the Kinkora Plant to increase wire production (Fig. 6.7). At the Upper Works in Trenton, Charles Sunderland built a Physical Testing Laboratory on the site of the old galvanizing shop that Charles Roebling had erected in the 1880s. Sunderland installed a huge testing machine in this laboratory to test sections of the footbridge ropes to the required load of 1.2 million lbs. (Figs. 6.8-9 & box). He also built models of the suspension system and a full size section of a cable (Fig. 6.10) to perfect their designs.

Figure 6.9: Physical Testing Laboratory, Trenton Plant, 1928. RC Charles Sunderland and his bridge engineering staff conducted many tests to prepare for building the Hudson River Bridge cables, including this model of a single strand of wires over a tower.

> **"See Hudson River Bridge Cables Made and Tested,"**
> *- Telegraph & Telephone Age*, **1929**
>
> *And such a test! It was made on the Rhiele Automatic Testing Machine, the largest precision testing machine of its kind in the world, capable of exerting the tremendous pull of 2,000,000 lbs. The machine itself weighs 275,000 lbs. and stands 43-feet high, power being applied by a 75-horsepower electric motor through three big screws and a four-speed transmission gearing....*
>
> *On went the power, and an engineer watching the dials announced through a megaphone the details of the strain. Up and up went the indicators on the dials! - up to 350,000 lbs., than to half a million lbs., then to 750,000 lbs., then to over 1,000,000 lbs., then past the 1,200,000 lbs. strain that every suspender rope for the new bridge must stand to pass official inspection. And all this quietly, almost noiselessly, while the assembled spectators held their breath expecting that the cable must surely snap under such a terrific pull. Then on up to 1,300,000 lbs. strain, after which separate wires on the outside of the rope began to snap, one by one!*
>
> *Soon after the polls had passed the 1,365,000 lbs. mark the cable snapped in twain with a resounding crack that could be heard a block away! Iron latticework prevented any of the pieces from flying out upon the spectators or workers. A big sigh of relief when up involuntarily from the watchers, followed by a burst of applause. It was a test for a break, and the machine won as usual, but the Roebling engineers were prepared to put the strain up to 2,000,000 pounds, until either the cable or the machine gave way. The steel rope that was tested was nearly 3 inches in diameter.*[6]

One of the most important advances

To prestretch the 3,600 ft.-long footbridge ropes for the Hudson River Bridge so that they wouldn't sag when suspended between the towers, Sunderland and his staff created an 1,850 ft. track at the Kinkora Works along the Delaware River bank, where the Company had extended its property with steel mill slag and soil. The editor of *Engineering News-Record* called the prestretcher "one of the most important advances made in the

suspension bridge field in many years" (Fig. 6.11 & box), and it enabled the construction of even longer suspension bridges.

The Roebling prestretcher also enabled the Company to produce "Roebling prestressed bridge strand," which could be bundled together to efficiently build cables of medium length suspension bridges. These built-up cables did not require a footbridge, which saved additional time and money. Sunderland used this Roebling innovation for the first time in 1929 on a 987- ft. span suspension bridge designed by Robinson and Steinman of New York to cross the Saint-Maurice River in Grand'Mere, a small town about 100 miles northeast of Montreal. David B. Steinman, the bridge's chief engineer, had grown up a few blocks from the Brooklyn Bridge and as a teenager had watched the construction of the Williamsburg Bridge. His admiration of the Brooklyn Bridge and John and Washington Roebling culminated in his authoring of *The Builders of the Bridge* about them in 1945.

Figure 6.11: Pre-Stretcher, Kinkora Works, c1929. SI On the 1,850 ft. standard-guage track, a flat car fitted with a sheave wheel enabled a wire rope to be looped or doubled back to its starting point for a total length of 3,750 ft. An hydraulic tensioning machine at the western end could apply a maximum of 600,000 lbs. of tension on an 1,875 ft. rope or 300,000 lbs. on a 3,750 ft. looped rope. The operators prestretched each of the 36 footbridge ropes for the Hudson River Bridge to 200,000 lbs., 25 percent more than the required prestretched load of 160,000 lbs.

It was a great experience

In November of 1928, J.A.R's Sons Co. officials celebrated the 50th anniversary of their subsidiary, the New Jersey Wire Cloth Company at the Kinkora Works (Figs. 6.12, 6.14-16 & boxes). The celebration was especially meaningful for the women working in the "screen shop," as the employees called the division, which had been employing women for several decades. Alice Mae Agostinelli (Fig. 6.13), who worked in the screen shop from 1943 to 1946, recalled in 2008:

When the word came out that they were hiring at the mill and hiring women, at 19 I needed a job, so I went down there to get this job in the screen shop and they hired me and said come back for two weeks of training.

The first day I walked into that screen shop and I looked at those looms, all 95 lbs. of me, and I thought, oh well, I can do that, one of them. So the foreman proceeded to tell us about the looms, and I said, 'Which one will be mine?' He said, 'All ten.' We had to run ten looms....It was hard work, it was dirty work, but it was a great experience.[8]

"Fiftieth Anniversary - The New Jersey Wire Cloth Company," *Blue Center*, 1928

The New Jersey Wire Cloth Company was established at Trenton, N.J., as a subsidiary of John A. Roebling's Sons Company, to utilize its wire in the manufacture of wire fabrics.

It at first made painted wire cloth for windows and door screens to exclude insects. Later metal coated, copper, brass and bronze cloths were added to the line for the same purpose.

About 15 years ago it introduced Jersey Copper Insect Screened Cloth, which is much stronger and more resiliant than the ordinary copper screen cloth. This has met with a large and increasing demand and has been approved by leading architects.

The Company was established at a time when the advantage of screens was beginning to be recognized and since then the industry has developed to very large proportions. Screens are now regarded as a necessity to keep flies and mosquitoes from infecting human beings.

A few years after its establishment, Wire Lath was added to its line, which has been extensively employed in building construction. In 1885 the Company introduced an improved wire lath (patented) which was made with ribs, woven in

between the wires, which served to offset the fabric, thereby permitting the plaster when applied, to pass through the meshes and form a continuous surface over the face of timbers as well as the open space between them.

The wire lath made by this Company has been installed in many large hotels, apartment buildings, office buildings, stores and warehouses throughout the United States. It has been employed as a plaster foundation in hundreds of private homes.

The Company also manufactures at the present time an innumerable variety of wire fabrics (wire cloth and wire netting) both with rectangular and hexagonal matches, some of which are used for building work, while many are used for manufacturing, mining, agricultural and many other industrial purposes.

From the beginning the Company has utilized special automatic machinery, most of which has been developed and made in its own works.

It manufactures fabrics of iron, steel, copper, bronze, brass, nickel and many metals and alloys and employs as finishes or coatings when required, zinc for galvanizing, tin and paint.

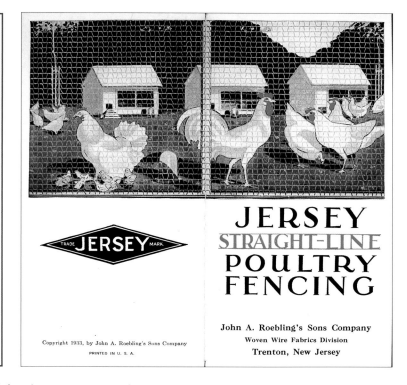

Figure 6.14 (right): "Jersey Straight-Line Pountry Fencing," 1933. RU
Besides producing industrial screening and wire lath for construction, J.A.R.'s Sons Co.'s wire cloth subsidiary
produced agricultural fencing and residential screens sold in hardware stores.

Figures 6.15-16: "Zintex" Insect Screen Cloth, 1936. RU
The Woven Wire Fabrics Division developed Zintex in 1927 by electro-galvanizing steel wire with zinc.
It later added a varnish coating to further prevent rust. Insect screen was one of the few consumer products
that J.A.R.'s Sons Co. produced and marketed directly to homeowners as a cheaper alternative to copper screens.

Figure 6.17: New Rope Shop No. 1, Trenton Works, 1929. BC
New bridge contracts impelled the Company to replace
its old rope shops and wire mills with a big rope shop
connecting the Physical Testing House (right - see Fig. 6.8)
to the 1885 and 1893 Rope Rooms (see Figs. 4.29 & 4.32)
just out of the frame on the left. The roof of the 1890-1901
Machine Shop (see Figs. 4.42-43) and the five-story 1890s
Insulated Wire building (se Fig. 4.58) are visible in the rear.

Figure 6.18: Interior View of New Rope Shop No. 1, 1930. BC
The Company's modern single-story buildings used steel trusses
with glass-lined roof monitors to maximize daylight on the
interior. Workers used 20-ton traveling cranes, far right,
to move products and machinery through the shops.

With manufacturing and investment income on track to reach all-time highs, the Directors allocated $400,000 (about $5 million in 2009) to modernize the rope shops in Trenton. The Company demolished John A. Roebling's 1850's wire mill (see Fig. 4.1, left) and his sons' 1870s wire mill (see Fig. 4.9, left center), and erected a new Rope Shop No. 1 (Figs. 6.17-8) incorporating the 1885 and 1893 Rope Rooms with the big wire rope machines (see Figs. 4.28 & 4.30-31). It replaced the 1890s Galvanizing Shop along the canal (see Fig. 4.74, right) with a wire rope warehouse (Fig. 6.19) and erected another warehouse between the 1917 Elmer Street Rope Shop and Hamilton Ave (Fig. 6.20). The Directors allocated $500,000 ($6.2 million) to build a Copper Wire Mill at the Kinkora Works.

In March, 1929, *Blue Center* reported: "Joseph Roebling takes up duties in the Trenton plant....We are glad to welcome 'Joe' into our organization family. He is the eldest son of our President, Mr. F.W. Roebling, Jr., and is beginning a study of all the products that have made the name of Roebling famous.... He is at present learning the manufacture of Flat Wire." Joseph Metcalf Roebling, 22, was the first member of the fourth generation to work for the Company and he followed the family tradition of learning the business by working in various production departments for two years.[9]

As stock prices had soared in the late 1920s, the Directors sought to increase their investment portfolio's returns, which often rivaled manufacturing profits, and in May, 1929, they engaged a financial counseling firm to review their holdings. John A. Roebling and his three sons had always invested

Figure 6.19: New Wire Rope Warehouse, Trenton Works, 1930. BC
The new warehouse for shipping large wire ropes provided a
distinctly modern appearance along the Delaware & Raritan Canal
at the South Broad Street crossing. The modernized
General Office (see Fig. 6.4) is visible on the right.

Figure 6.20: Elmer Street Rope Shop Extension, 1930. BC
The extension at the northern end of the Trenton Plant on
Hamilton Avenue at the canal crossing provided warehouse
and shipping space for smaller wire ropes and created
"an impressive finish to the north end of the Upper Works."[10]

Figure 6.21 (left):
Joseph M. Roebling,
c1942. WSR
The oldest son of
Ferndinand W. Roebling,
Jr., joined the Company
in 1929 and became
Chairman in 1946.

Figure 6.22 (right):
"Roebling Float in Historic
Pageant," 1929. BC
Om Monmouth Street
in Trenton, the float
compared the size of the
Brooklyn Bridge with the
Hudson River Bridge.

conservatively in bonds, utilities, and railroads, and in major customers like Otis Elevator. On the advice of their financial counselors that summer, the Directors sold many of their long-term holdings, including a large portion of their Otis Elevator shares, and purchased more speculative stocks.

On October 28, 1929, the City of Trenton celebrated its 250th anniversary and the Roebling Company celebrated its 60th anniversary in Trenton with a float in the city's Historic Pageant (Fig. 6.22). On that day, a two-day crash began at the New York Stock Exchange that wiped out 25 percent of its value. The reduced value of the Company's investment portfolio would hinder its ability to invest in plant upgrades for years to come, and while revenues would later surpass 1920s levels,

profits and dividends would never regain their consistent highs during that decade.[11]

The stock market crash set back the financing plans for the Golden Gate Bridge in San Francisco but some other big projects that had been financed before the crash continued to generate large orders for wire and wire rope. In the Fall of 1929, the developers of the Empire State Building, led by former New York Governor Al Smith, approved a $2.9 million ($36.6 million) contract with the Otis Elevator Company for sixty-six elevators in the world's tallest building. J.A.R.'s Sons Co., which still owned a large block of Otis shares, supplied over 120 miles of elevator ropes and over 1,550 miles of electrical wire for the building (Figs. 6.23-24).

Roebling elevator ropes and Roebling electrical cables are in use throughout the Empire State elevator setup, supplied to Otis Elevator Company through the Roebling New York Branch sales office. The total length of elevator hoist ropes, compensating ropes and governor ropes in operation in the great structure is 626,361 feet or over 120 miles. Nearly 8,000,000 feet or over 1,515 miles of rubber-covered wire and 190,000 feet or approximately 36 miles of conduit wire are utilized in the elevator installation.

Figure 6.23 (left):
Empire State Building,
Roebling Magazine,
1947. TPL
Roebling supplied all
the wire ropes for the
building's 66 elevators.

Figure 6.24 (right):
*Roebling Elevator
Wire Ropes and Cables,*
1938. RU
Citing "years of
experience and skill"
in wire drawing,"
the Company's
brochure noted:
"A large majority
of the important
buildings in every
locality are equipped
with Roebling
elevator ropes."

With its bond financing in place, the Port Authority proceeded with the construction of the Hudson River Bridge, and the Kinkora Works' railroad crew shipped a huge load of prestretched 2 15/16 in. wire ropes for the footbridges (Fig. 6.25). When Roebling bridgemen hoisted the first 3,600 ft. long footbridge rope into position to connect the New York and New Jersey towers (Fig. 6.26), the Port Authority held a ceremony marking this milestone achievement (see box).

With work on the footbridges and preparations for laying the cable wire, the Roebling Company had about 175 men working at the bridge site (Fig. 6.27), and they soon started laying the cable wires.

Figure 6.25 (above):
"Train Load of Wire Rope For New Hudson River Bridge," Kinkora Works, 1929. BC
The shipment of 32 miles of wire ropes was the "the largest ever made from any one plant at one time."

Figure 6.26 (left):
Blue Center, September, 1929.
Blue Center's resident artist deftly illustrated a Roebling bridgeman on top of the New York Tower securing the first pair of 36 footbridge ropes.

Figure 6.27 (below):
J.A.R.'s Sons Co. Blotter, 1930.
The colored photograph shows the first four of 36 wire ropes crossing the river for hoisting atop the towers to support the footbridges needed to build the bridge cables.

Four of the 52 wire rope cables which will support the temporary foot-walks on the Hudson River Bridge; crossing the river, preparatory to hoisting into position.

John A. Roebling's Sons Company Trenton, New Jersey

174

"THE BRIDGE BUILDERS," *The New York Times*, Editorial, July 10, 1929

Behind the public men who graced yesterday's occasion stood the engineers. They met to celebrate the larger political and social significance of what is after all a physical one - a cable, a rope of wire strands hoisted from the river bottom. Here were the two great towers, nearly a mile apart; somehow they must be joined. The wire rope that was raised yesterday is merely one of thirty-six that will carry the footbridges from which the main cables will be spun.

Mr. O. H. AMMANN, chief engineer of the bridge, tells us just how it is going to be done. One reads of cold drawn wire and spinning wheels and cable saddles and "squeezers," of cables made of 26,474 wires, each so strong that it would sustain the pull of ten heavy horses without breaking. They will have to be strong, those four cables, to support trains and trucks and motorcars in addition to their own not inconsiderable weight! If stretched out in one length, the wire which the Roeblings are now making for the bridge would reach halfway to the moon.

Steel made by the open hearth process is cast into ingots fourteen inches square and five feet long. They are rolled down to two inches, cut into thirty foot billets, rolled again into round rods, tempered, cold drawn through holes of successively decreasing diameter. Finally, reduced to a little less than the thickness of a lead pencil, the wire is wound on reels, thirty miles of wire to a reel. After the footbridges are in place – the

wire rope that is being slung across the Towers this week will ultimately be cut up for "suspenders" - the work of spinning begins. Spinning wheels traveling on an endless chain to and fro pull one loop of wire after another across the river to the anchorages on each side: 434 wires make a strand, sixty-one strands a cable. When all the strands are in place and have just the right sag, the squeezer comes along to give the final touch. It is capable of exerting a pressure of about a thousand pounds to the square inch. Under its gentle ministrations the cross-section changes from a hexagon of bundles of wire to a circle three feet in diameter, to all intents and purposes a single cable, only of course infinitely stronger and more manageable.

Later each cable has to be wrapped in seizing wire to hold the main wire in place after the removal of the squeezer. At intervals steel bands are placed around the cables to carry the suspenders. Then they are allowed to rest a while and stretch by their own weight before they are finally wrapped and painted against corrosion. The whole undertaking involves no untried operations. Mr. AMMANN assures us this type of steel wire cable having been used in all large cable bridges since JOHN A. ROEBLING first spun it over Brooklyn Bridge. But the engineers are now able to spin the cables faster than has ever been done before, so that this great bridge over the Hudson, 200 feet high, 8,800 feet long, joining the highway systems of two commonwealths, may be opened to traffic in 1932.

Figure 6.28: Roebling Bridgemen at the Hudson River Bridge, September, 1930. BC
The Company's crew of some 175 men building the bridge cables gathered in the Fort Lee cut through the top of the Palisades.

Hudson River Bridge Cable Construction, 1929. Figures 6.29 (left) & 6.30 (top right): SI J.A.R.'s Sons Co. mounted electic signs on the New Jersey Tower to prominently advertise its cable making. Figure 6.31 (bottom right): PANYNJ Roebling bridgemen loading bridge wire on a traveler, invented by John A. Roebling in 1845 (see Fig. 2.15), for laying it into one of the four cables.

Visible each night for miles

As the Roebling bridgemen laid the cable wires faster than expected, the Port Authority granted the Company permission to erect two huge lighted signs on both sides of the New Jersey tower advertising its cable making (Figs. 6.29-32 & box). As *Blue Center* noted: "These signs, said to be the highest in the country, are visible each night for miles in upper New York City and Bergen County, N.J."

A distinct triumph

Three other bridge projects made news in the Fall of 1929 for their innovative cables made with Roebling prestressed bridge strand, which Charles Sunderland had developed on the prestretcher at the Kinkora Works, the Grand'Mere Bridge opened in Quebec (Fig. 6.33 & box), and the Company won contracts for cables on the St. John's Bridge in Portland, Oregon, and for a bridge at Maysville, Kentucky.

"Wire and Space," *Fortune Magazine*, January, 1931

Over the bridge's gaunt steel towers as they stand, dimly enormous against the deep violet night, on either side of the silently flowing river, there blazes a sign: 'Roebling Cables.' And over the entire evolution of the suspension bridges shines the potent name of Roebling….

There were suspension bridges before those the Roeblings built, it is true….Not until steel-wire cable was devised, however, was the modern suspension bridge a possibility. Nor did it become an actuality until the Roeblings had built the Brooklyn Bridge….That their bridge still remains one of the world's great suspension bridges, that it still remains at all,

in fact, is proof enough of its significance….

When the Roeblings built their bridge, they used steel wire cables to support it – the most vital of many innovations. This wire they manufactured in Trenton, and this same wire, materially strengthened by decades of research and experience, their company still manufactures at Trenton.

Hence the glittering sign over the Hudson Bridge, and hence the contemporary significance of the name Roebling….

It is the cables after all that are the vitals of a suspension bridge, and the name of Roebling deserves its eminence on the Hudson River Bridge.

Roebling Standards

Acknowledging the Company's prominence in bridge engineering, the Directors elected Charles Sunderland to the Board and appointed him as Chief Engineer of Bridges. Sunderland organized a new Bridge Engineering Department for designing suspension bridges, tramways, and structures like antennas and transmission towers. Born in Yorkshire, England, Sunderland was revered by colleagues for his gentlemanly manner, professionalism, and devotion to J.A.R.'s Son Co. In a typical memo to foremen at the Kinkora Works, Sunderland wrote in December, 1930, about the wire for the Maysville Bridge:

We ask that you take particular pains with the surface inspection of wire before fabrication to determine defective galvanizing, for we cannot accept any finished strand that shows wire with flaked galvanizing....We are emphasizing, Quality, Workmanship and Durability of ROEBLING CABLES and we cannot afford to erect any material that does not conform to Roebling Standards.[12]

Figure 6.33: Grand'Mere Bridge, Grand'Mere, Quebec, 2010. FL J.A.R.'s Sons Co. first used its innovative prestressed bridge strand in 1929 on the cables for this 950 ft. span bridge over the Saint-Maurice River.

"Another Advance,"
Engineering News-Record, February 13, 1930

Completion of a 950 ft. span suspension bridge with rope strand cables at Grand'Mere, Quebec and, the beginning of work on a similar structure with 1,207 ft. span in Portland, Oregon, signalize a development that has long been considered an ideal by many engineers. Cables built of assembled ropes were common in the early days of suspension bridges, but their shortcomings, chiefly their large and variable stretch and the resultant difficulty of good load distribution, were so grave that it remained for the parallel wire construction of cables to bring long-span bridges into being.

The difficulty and slowness of the process of stringing cables wire by wire have always made the assembled rope construction an attractive possibility, but manufacturers were not able to make rope or strand accurate in length, free from permanent stretch. Production of strands of high modulus - up to 24,000,000 pounds per sq.in. – and pre-stretched in long lengths at high stress to give them their set, has now made possible strand construction of cables in large bridges. The ability to guarantee a twisted wire rope to within ½-in. of specified length under any tension up to 60,500 pounds, as was the case for the 1,700 ft. 1 ¼-inch diameter ropes at Grand'Mere and for the 2,700 ft. 1 ½-in. diameter ropes which make up the cables of the Portland Bridge, is a distinct triumph for the wire manufacturer.

Also, it provides another flexibility in suspension bridge construction, with several potential advantages. Field work can be simplified. The footwalks can be entirely dispensed with. Speed in construction can be augmented, since the strands can be manufactured before the towers and anchorages are completed. Strand adjustment can be freed from much of its intricacy.

The rope-strand cable is one of the important byproducts of the present activity of suspension-bridge construction. A direct result of research which the manufacturer carried out in studies of the footwalk ropes for the Fort Lee-Hudson River Bridge, it represents an important advance in the suspension bridge field.[13]

Figure 6.34: J.A.R's Sons Co. Headquarters, Trenton Works, 1987. Jet Lowe, HAER To consolidate its research, the Company built a Research Laboratory (right) in 1930 adjacent to its General Office (left), and Physical Testing House (rear). Roebling engineers erected the experimental footbridge in 1943.

With engineering and other staff increases, the Directors approved the addition of two stories on top of the General Office in Trenton, which had opened 18 months earlier. The Directors also approved the construction of a Research Laboratory next to the General Office to consolidate "this Company's large amount of original research....in a single department, provided with all the necessary equipment of the very latest type....It will be conveniently near the Physical Laboratory so that the two laboratories can be operated together with all the advantages" (Fig. 6.34 & box above).

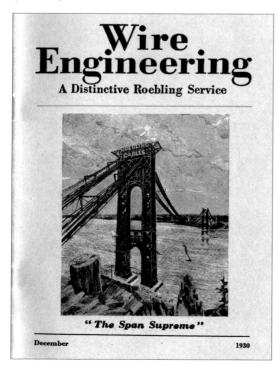

Figure 6.35: *Wire Engineering*, November, 1930. TPL

Spun at a rate never attained before

The Company's Hudson River Bridge contract specified that one pair of cables would be ready for hanging suspender ropes by December 1, 1930, and the other pair on December 1, 1931. Roebling bridge engineers and bridgemen completed all four cables by the end of October, 1930 – 13 months ahead of schedule. As Othmar Ammann, the Port Authority's Chief Bridge Engineer, later wrote: "Many refinements and improvements were introduced by the contractor, the John A. Roebling's Sons Company, which permitted the wire to be spun at a rate never attained before."[14]

This achievement, however, was overshadowed by a sharp decline in business in the latter half of 1930. To focus more on sales, the Company stopped publishing *Blue Center* that October and began publishing *Wire Engineering: A Distinctive Roebling Service*, in November as a "technical House Organ" for customers (Fig. 6.35 & below). By the end of 1930, sales had shrunk by 20 percent and operating profits by nearly 80.

On December 21, 1930, Edmund Roebling, the last of John and Johanna Roebling's children, died at age 76. John had bequeathed Edmund 10 percent of his Company in the hope that he would work alongside his brothers. As *The New York Times* noted in his obituary: "After a few years of active participation in the work of the firm Mr. Roebling was forced by ill health to retire, but he retained a financial interest. He tried in vain to improve his condition by foreign travel. Throughout his long years as an invalid he read a great deal and never lost interest in the outside world." Edmund never married and for many years Washington managed his financial affairs.[15]

The appraisers of Edmund's estate valued it at $13.8 million (about $175 million in 2009), 99 percent of it in stocks and bonds. They valued his personal effects at $90 and his 34,500 Roebling Company shares at $3.3 million ($41 million), about $95 ($1,195) per share. At this value, the 345,000 outstanding shares in the Company had a total value of $32.8 million ($412.5 million). In his will, Edmund bequeathed his net estate to his 12 nieces and nephews, each of whom received $1.1 million ($13.8 million). John A. Roebling had not left any of his wire rope business to his three daughters, Laura, Elvira, and Josephine, but thanks to Edmund's bequest, their living descendents now held shares in the Company.

1931 marked the centennial of John A. Roebling's immigration to America and the Roebling Company's completion of the cables on four suspension bridges: the St. John's Bridge over the Willamette River in Portland, Oregon, the Maumee River Bridge in Toledo, Ohio, the Maysville Bridge over the Ohio River at Maysville, Kentucky, and the Hudson River Bridge (see box and Figs. 6.36-38).

Roebling Bridge Cables of 1931

Figure 6.36 (top): St. John's Bridge, Portland, Oregon, 2005. WK J.A.R.'s Sons Co. built the 16 1/2 in. cables of prestressed bridge strand on this 1,207 ft. span bridge designed by David B. Steinman.

Figure 6.37 (center): Anthony Wayne Bridge, Toledo, Ohio, 2006. HB The Company built the 13 1/4 in. cables on this 785 ft. span bridge with traditional wire construction.

Figure 38: (bottom): Simon Kenton Bridge, Maysville, Kentucky. UCB The Company used prestressed bridge strand to build the 13 1/2 in. cables on this 1,060 ft. span bridge, and it also erected the steel towers and deck.

HAIL! THE SPAN SUPREME

THE MIGHTY GEORGE WASHINGTON . . . KING OF SUSPENSION
BRIDGES . . . SPANNING THE HUDSON RIVER BETWEEN NEW YORK
AND NEW JERSEY . . . FORMALLY OPENED SATURDAY THE TWENTY
FOURTH DAY OF OCTOBER, NINETEEN HUNDRED & THIRTY ONE

Cables By Roebling

Figure 6.39 (left): *HAIL! THE SPAN SUPREME, WIRE ENGINEERING*, Oct.-Nov., 1931. TPL

The completion of this structure was an epic-making achievement in engineering and construction. Particular emphasis is placed on this accomplishment when it is realized that during the 43 years between the opening of the Brooklyn Bridge in 1883 and the Delaware River Bridge in 1926, the increase in main-span length was only 12 per cent, whereas in the short period of time to 1931 - 5 years - the George Washington Bridge reaches 3500 feet - an increase of 100 percent.

Figure 6.40 (right): *WIRE ENGINEERING*, Vols. 1-3, 1933. TPL J.A.R.'s Sons Co. proudly hailed the 'Super Bridge' in its publications and advertisements for several years.

WIRE ENGINEERING

JOHN A. ROEBLING'S SONS COMPANY
TRENTON · · · NEW JERSEY ·

As workers completed the Hudson River Bridge eight months ahead of schedule, the directors of the Port Authority voted to name it the George Washington Memorial Bridge to commemorate the bicentennial of the birth of the nation's first president in 1732 (Figs. 6.39-40 & box). The honor was also fitting as the Super Bridge spanned between the sites of Fort Washington in New York and Fort Lee in New Jersey, where General Washington had unsuccessfully tried to prevent British troops from seizing New York in 1776.

The Port Authority directors also decided to hold off on cladding the towers in granite, as the architect of the bridge, Cass Gilbert, had originally designed them, mostly to keep the project within its budget. Like many other observers, however, *The New York Times* credited "the effect upon the bridge planners and upon the public of the naked steel structures standing there as an observed part of the landscape. The notion has gotten considerably diffused that what has already been achieved in carrying out the monumental design

---

"Two Governors Open Great Hudson Bridge As Throngs Look On," *The New York Times*, October 25, 1931

More than 5,000 guests of the Port of New York Authority, which built the new bridge, opened it eight months ahead of schedule and held costs down considerably below the original estimates, saw the picturesque ceremonies in the center of the span. Altogether, nearly 30,000 citizens of New York and New Jersey were present, according to police estimates. In addition to the 5,000 in the grandstand, 20,000 stood in the Manhattan plaza and 4,000 in the Fort Lee plaza listening to the exercises from amplifiers. Additional thousands lined Riverside Drive and the top of the Palisades.

During the exercises more than thirty Army airplanes flew in various formations over the bridge up and down the Hudson. Another airplane gave the spectators a thrill when it flew under the span. Following the formal celebrations, the bridge was open to pedestrians from six until eleven o'clock last evening.

'In dedicating this the George Washington Bridge,' said Governor Franklin D. Roosevelt of New York, '....we offer homage to the great ideals, exemplified in Washington's career and stamped indelibly upon our national thought....the works of integrity, the need for intelligence and the fact that our

interdependence....as an example of constructive cooperation between two great States, this bridge is worthy of its name....

'Today, faced with critical problems in every field, we are inclined to put our faith in mechanical panaceas, underestimating the most powerful of all machines, the human mind. These steel spans, these fine cables are a vivid reminder that skill and scientific planning must be the keynote of all great achievements. Behind this mighty structure, that seems almost superhuman in its perfection, is an inspiring background of high intelligence'....

Governor Morgan F. Larsen of New Jersey stated: 'As George Washington has been an inspiration to the people of this county and the people of the world to do the right and just things, so this bridge, the George Washington Bridge....shall also be an inspiration to the people of this nation and an example to other nations of what can be accomplished for the common good'....

Charles Francis Adams, Secretary of the Navy, said: 'George Washington would have felt a proud satisfaction that he had known that day would come when so noble a bridge, bearing his own name, was to be conceived, designed and executed by American engineers and architects.'

in steel provides an eyeful that could hardly be better by trying to make the steel towers look like stone piers" (Fig. 6.41). As another article in *The New York Times* noted (see box):[17]

> *By the time the bridge is completed, it will have required at least 1,000,000 man days of labor, besides a much greater amount devoted to producing and manufacturing materials and equipment in mines and shops and in transporting them.*
> *The cables, each a mile long, are strong enough to resist the pull of a thousand powerful locomotives at each end.*
> *The remarkably rapid and safe completion of these enormous cables, many times more difficult to spin than their longest and largest predecessors, solved practical problems that had for many years been a barrier to the construction of such long spans and demonstrated the practicability of much longer ones.*[18]

In its October-November, 1931, issue, *Wire Engineering* credited 19 Roebling innovations specifically developed for the George Washington Bridge, including the prestretcher at the Kinkora Works, for "one big achievement – speed in cable making." In comparing the George Washington Bridge to U.S. Steel's Delaware River Bridge (Benjamin Franklin Bridge), the previous record holder, the author noted that besides spanning twice the distance:

> *The suspended load of the greatest bridge of all is fifty per cent greater per linear foot…*(and) *the required strength of the cables….is three times greater. This data clearly indicates the magnitude of the engineering achievement…. The construction problem, however, was one of even greater magnitude, taxing the skill of the engineers to the maximum….*
> *The cable construction required the creation of new high standards and the application of scientific and mechanical investigations resulting in improved methods and equipment that assured greater safety, efficiency and economy than ever before approached in similar work.*[19]

Figure 6.41: George Washington Bridge, 1932.

A Dream Realized: Here the Builder of Bridge Cables
sees the Realization of his Dreams.
The Largest Suspension Bridge in the World
carried on Cables made of Wire.
He sees Wire Cables above all other features.
- Wire Engineering, October-November, 1931.

After the bridge opened, Port Authority Chief Bridge Engineer Amman wrote to Charles Sunderland to thank him and his engineering staff for "the excellent and efficient manner in which you have carried out this unusual and important work."[20]

During this time of business depression

While Roebling Directors and employees relished the completion of the great bridge, the deteriorating economy dampened any enthusiasm they had for celebrating. General Manager William Anderson reported to the Directors in April, 1931, on "the efforts of the management to reduce the overhead cost and….curtail expenses during this time of business depression." The Directors approved a ten percent pay cut for all salaried employees, and Anderson furloughed many hourly and piece-work employees and reduced the hours of those still working.[21]

Figure 6.42:
J.A.R.'s Sons Company,
Trenton Works, 1931. HM&L
In 1931 the Company ended
a multi-year modernization of
its Upper Works in Trenton.
The single story rope shops
and warehouse it built in
1928-30 behind the 5-story
General Office on South
Broad Street (left center)
contrasted sharply
with the 5-story wire mills
that Charles Roebling built
in the late 19th Century.

The Company's construction crews completed several projects in its remodeling and expansion program (Figs. 6.42-43), and Anderson postponed any others still in planning.[18] In early October, Anderson reduced wages for all hourly and piecemeal employees by 10 percent and the Directors authorized "the officers to expend not over $20,000 per month (about $257,000 in 2009), for approximately 30 weeks, for the purpose of unemployment relief to needy Roebling employees, whose services have been temporarily discontinued, and their families and for special payrolls for work to be created for such employees." Like John A. Roebling and his sons had

done during several previous downturns, the Directors were resolved to sustain their employees until business picked up.[22]

As Ken Ibach, a mason in the steel mill at the Kinkora Works, recalled in a 2007 interview:

When the Depression came and people couldn't pay their rent, Roebling allowed them to stay and gave them a chance to pay back one dollar a week or whatever....nobody was put out because they couldn't pay their rent or electric or gas. Roebling was good to their people.[23]

Figure 6.43:
J.A.R.'s Sons Company,
Kinkora Works, 1931. HM&L
The Company also completed
a major expansion
and upgrade of its
steel and wire plant
in Roebling, N.J.
The plant and
the adjacent
Roebling Village
constituted one
of the most distinctive
industrial communities
in the United States.

The spectacular job

Despite the depression, the Golden Gate Bridge and Highway District finally managed to secure the financing to build its big bridge between San Francisco and Marin County, and it requested bids in the summer of 1932. The Roebling Company's innovations on the George Washington Bridge gave Charles Sunderland and his engineering staff some advantages in developing their bid to build the cables, but the competition from U.S. Steel and other bidders was intense. After the District opened the bids in October, one year after the George Washington Bridge opened, *Time Magazine* reported:

> *The contract for the spectacular job of fabricating and erecting the cable work on the Golden Gate Bridge was awarded to John A. Roebling's Sons Co. of Trenton. N. J. The winning Roebling bid was $5,885.000 ($83.3 million). It was only $31,000 (.5 percent) below that of Columbia Steel Co. (of Portland, Oregon). This greatly vexed United States Steel Corp. which had bought Columbia in the hope of getting more Pacific Coast business.*[24]

Roebling had underbid U.S. Steel despite having to ship its wire through the Panama Canal. McClintic-Marshall, which Bethlehem Steel had acquired in February, 1931, won the contract to erect the towers and deck.

The most trying year in the Company's history

Everyone associated with J.A.R.'s Sons Co. welcomed this great news, especially because of the terrible economy. The Gross National Product (GNP) fell a record 13.4 percent in 1932 and unemployment rose to a record 23.6 percent. In the three years since the stock market crash, the GNP fell 31 percent, the value of stocks on the New York Stock exchange plunged 80 percent, more than 5,000 banks and over 100,000 businesses failed, and industrial production shrank by one half.

J.A.R.'s Sons Co. suffered its first operating loss in 1932. Sales shrank 71 percent from their 1928 high of $29 million ($357 million in 2009) to $8.4 million ($118.2 million). The Company's payroll fell 45 percent from 6,648 in 1929 to 3,618. Income from the investment portfolio shrank from $2.7 million ($33.6 million) in 1928 to $358,000 ($5 million). With the cost of operating four plants, ten regional sales offices and warehouses, and the town of Roebling, plus the cost of relief for employees, the Company recorded a loss of $2.8 million ($39.1 million). At the Annual Meeting in February, 1933, John A. Roebling II requested that "a vote of thanks be tendered to the Directors, Officers and Employees for the splendid manner in which they conducted the affairs of the Company during what has perhaps been the most trying year in the Company's history."[25]

Figure 6.44: Ferdinand W. Roebling III c1935. MRF
Ferd, as everyone called him, graduated from Princeton University in 1933 and worked in the Roebling wire mills and the Trenton rope shops for two years, and then joined the engineering staff.

At this same meeting the Directors authorized the officers to bid on "the cables, suspenders and accessories for the San Francisco – Oakland Bay Bridge." The U.S. Reconstruction Finance Corporation had recently financed this 3.6 mile-long bridge, which included a 2,300 ft. span that would be the third longest suspension bridge. When the California Toll Bridge Authority opened the bids in May, 1933, two U.S. Steel subsidiaries won the major contracts, American Bridge for the steel structure and American Steel & Wire for the cables.

Up until this time, large suspension bridge projects typically had separate contractors for cable making and for steel erection because of the expertise each required, and J.A.R.'s Sons Co. could successfully compete for cable contracts. With its subsidiaries, U.S. Steel could now underbid the cable making and still make profits on the steel erection. As Washington Roebling had predicted years earlier, the Company would continue to be challenged by this competitive disadvantage.

In June, 1933, Ferdinand Roebling III (Fig. 6.44) graduated from Princeton University and his service there in the Reserve Officers Training Corps led to a commission in the Army Reserves as a second lieutenant. He went to work that summer at the Kinkora Works, as he later said, "to find out how the wire that goes into wire rope is made." He also worked in the Trenton rope shops and then he joined the Wire Rope Engineering department. As one superintendent recalled:

> *Ferd won the men's respect by showing up for work on time every morning and by pitching right in doing whatever job he was on as well as he could do it. He didn't mind getting his hands dirty. And he never thought he knew it all, and admitted what he didn't know and when he was wrong. He hadn't been down there very long before he was "Ferd" to the boys and they were "Joe" and "Mike" to him. He would have made a swell foreman.*[26]

183

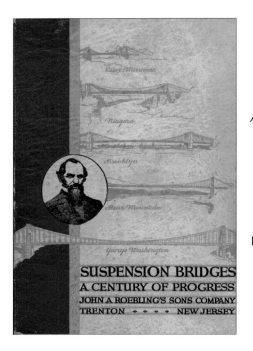

Figure 6.45: Suspension Bridges: A Century of Progress, 1933. RM J.A.R.'s Sons Co. highlighted its leadership in suspension bridges in a booklet for the Century of Progress Exposition in Chicago.

A distinctive Roebling innovation

In the summer of 1933, 1.5 million visitors to the "Century of Progress" Exposition in Chicago enjoyed views of four states from the "Sky Ride," an 1,850 ft. tramway rigged with Roebling wire rope. The Company also completed a 452 ft. span bridge over the Yaque del Norte River at Mao in the Dominican Republic in just ten weeks after the foundations were done. In a *Century of Progress* booklet (Fig. 6.45), Roebling engineers attributed the success of both of these projects to: "Prestressing, *a distinctive Roebling innovation.*"[27]

With various small engineering projects, preparations for the Golden Gate Bridge, and wire and wire rope business stimulated by President Franklin D. Roosevelt's "First New Deal" programs, sales increased 25 percent in 1933. After two years of operating losses, the Company recorded an operating profit of $211,000 (about $3.3 million in 2009). The Company's investment portfolio returned three times as much profit.

One New Deal program, the National Industrial Recovery Administration (NIRA), set minimum wages of 20 to 45 cents per hour and a maximum workweek of 35 to 45 hours for various industries, and it abolished child labor. The NIRA also set minimum product prices to stop the spiral of deflation. Roebling and other manufacturers liked the minimum prices but resented the wage and hour controls. At the Annual Meeting in February, 1934, John A. Roebling II noted that in 1933: "It was not only a question of successfully carrying on through the greatest depression of all time, but this was added to by problems occasioned by unprecedented changes in Government policies toward industry, the adjustment to which called for the most careful and painstaking efforts."[28]

The Company's sales increased in 1934 by 23 percent, but its operating profit shrank to $476 (about $7,880 in 2009). In his financial statement to stockholders, President Ferdinand Roebling, Jr., noted:

> *This decrease in profits in manufacturing is due to wage increases....adding more than $600,000 to our manufacturing payrolls, and thus reducing the better profit showing which would have otherwise been possible. Operating under the several basic codes provided by the National Recovery Act has added considerable expense and has also restricted our sales activity to some extent. It is, of course, problematical as to the ultimate benefits to be derived, but we are continuing to cooperate with the various recovery agencies.*[29]

The Company's investment portfolio earned a profit of $590,000 ($9.8 million) in 1934. The Directors spent most of their meeting time reviewing investments and approving the sale and purchase of stocks and bonds. They approved far less funds for plant upgrades than in earlier years.

You can never forget that first impression

In 1934, Charles Sunderland hired Blair Birdsall, a 27-year -old engineer, to work on the Golden Gate Bridge. Birdsall grew up in Newark and had climbed one of the footbridges on the Hudson River Bridge while completing his degree in civil engineering at Princeton University. In 1993, he recalled:

> *I was the second man in the group of two doing the cable calculations for the Golden Gate Bridge. The other fellow had gone all through the cable calculations on the George Washington Bridge....We did all the cable calculations for the main cables and all the footbridges and the suspender ropes for the Golden Gate Bridge.*
> *Then in August of '35 they sent me out to the site.... I will never forget the sensation I had walking right up to the base of that tower, which was practically finished then. To see this massive structure - you can never forget that first impression as a young man of a great structure like that.*[30]

The 746 ft. towers were 17 percent higher than the George Washington Bridge towers, the overall length of 6,450 ft. was 35 percent longer, and the 4,200 ft. main span was 20 percent longer. With less projected traffic, the Golden Gate engineers designed the bridge with only two main cables, which would have 21,500 tons of Roebling wire. As *Trenton Magazine* noted:

> *Ships have been leaving the Port of Trenton for some time past with Roebling galvanized wire for the great Golden Gate Bridge. On the docks here may be seen coils of wire of about 380 pounds each. The steamers for the Pacific Coast take on this cargo, and arriving at the Golden Gate, sail under the*

Golden Gate Bridge Construction, 1935 - Figure 6.46 (left): Roebling engineer Harold Hills photographed Roebling bridgemen on a platform between the footbridges at the center of the bridge. TPL   Figure 6.47 (right): With the footbridges in place, the bridgemen started laying the first cable wire with a "spinning wheel" based on John A. Roebling's 1845 invention (see Fig. 2.15). RM

great bridge on which the cables are now being erected, to the Roebling factory in California city, about 5 ½ miles from the bridge. Here the smaller coils are spliced to larger ones and wound on great spools or drums that weigh 7 ½ times each small coil, and the wire in one of them, if stretched out, would reach from Trenton to New Brunswick, or 30 miles....

The Roebling force of workmen on the bridge numbers 350, while 150 more are engaged in splicing and reeling of the wire in the special plant at California city....C. C. Sunderland, chief bridge engineer of the Roebling Company, is on the scene of action. With him are several engineers and other assistants from the Trenton office and plant....

The 'spinning wheel' travels back and forth along the cable being formed above the "catwalk," threading out the wire as it goes. Sometimes the wheel makes the trip in as low as 13 minutes....The marvelous thing about the construction of the Golden Gate Bridge is the speed at which the spinning is progressing (Figs. 6.46-47).[31]

The Roebling family and Company experienced some major changes in 1936. Siegfried Roebling, who had served as Second Vice President since 1927, died suddenly in January. Encouraged by her father-in-law, John A. Roebling II, Mary G. Roebling (Fig. 6.48), Siegfried's second wife, assumed her husband's position as a director of the Trenton Trust Company. A year later the bank directors elected her president, and she continued pioneering leadership positions for women in finance over nearly four decades.

With inheritances and distributions, there were now 33 family and four employee shareholders. At the Annual Meeting in February, 1936, they increased the number of Directors from eight to 13 and re-elected seven current Directors: Ferdinand Roebling, Jr., President; Robert C. Roebling, representing

himself and his mother, Blanch Roebling O'Brien; Richard M. Cadwalader, Jr., representing his mother, Emily Roebling Cadwalader; Francis MacIlvaine, a relative of John A. Roebling II's first wife; and three employees, William Anderson, General Manager, William Gummere, Kinkora Works Superintendent, and Austin C. Cooley, Secretary-Treasurer and representative of three Roebling descendents. The shareholders elected six new Directors: Donald Roebling, John A. Roebling II's youngest son; Joseph M. Roebling, Ferdinand, Jr.'s, oldest son; Charles R. Tyson, Helen Roebling Tyson's son and Charles G. Roebling's grandson; Alexander B. Hagner, husband of Caroline Roebling Hagner; T. Girard Wharton, representing Siegfried Roebling's Estate, and Charles M. Jones, Manager of Engineering.

Only five of the 13 Directors were descendents of John A. Roebling, and only four Roeblings worked for the Company: Ferdinand, Jr., and his two sons, Joseph, 29, and Ferd, 26, and Charles R. Tyson, 21, grandson of Charles Roebling. Tyson grew up outside Philadelphia and joined the Company after graduating from Princeton University that year.

Figure 6.48: Mary G. Roebling, c1938. RU When her husband Siegfried Roebling died in 1936, Mary took his place as a director of the Trenton Trust Company, and she became the first woman to run a major American bank when she was elected president in 1937. She merged the bank with the National State Bank of Elizabeth in 1972, and became chairman. She was also the first woman governor on the American Stock Exchange.

**Figure 6.49: Golden Gate Bridge, 1936. SI
Roebling engineers developed a triple spinning wheel to speed cable making, which they completed months ahead of schedule.**

The first attempt to achieve the perfect cable

Roebling bridgemen laid the last of 55,144 wires in the two Golden Gate Bridge cables on May 22, 1936. They improved upon John A. Roebling's patented traveling wheel with a three-wheel design that laid 24 wires with each pass, which enabled them to lay the wire four times faster than on the George Washington Bridge. Blair Birdsall credited Charles Sunderland for this and other improvements:

> *Sunderland succeeded a whole lot better than he expected. From 22 percent voids* (the amount of air space between cable wires) *on the George Washington Bridge cables we went down to 17 percent voids on the Golden Gate Bridge cables. That was so small, in fact, that the semi-circular cable bands that we had made for the cables were too big…. We had to remake the whole set of cable bands. But that was a great contribution he made.*[32]

Sunderland's compaction innovation enabled the cables to be more circular as they passed over the tower saddles than previous cables that widened there. As his assistant, Charles M. Jones, wrote in April, 1936: "The Golden Gate Bridge represents the first attempt to achieve the perfect cable."[33]

One week after the cable wire laying was completed, Ferdinand Roebling, Jr., (see Fig. 5.35), died at the age of 57. In 35 years with the Company, he had worked in the mills and in engineering, and had served as assistant treasurer, secretary treasurer, vice president, and since 1926, as President. He and his wife, Ruth Metcalf Roebling, had since Washington's death served as the "chief representatives of the Roebling name in Trenton," and participated in "all worthwhile movements for Trenton's civic and philanthropic betterment." They were the last Roebling couple to play this role in the capital city.[34]

**Figure 6.50: Golden Gate Bridge, 1936. RM
Roebling bridgemen compressing one of the 36 in. cables in preparation for wrapping it with wire.
The Marin Tower is in the distance.**

The Roebling Directors appointed Ferdinand W. Roebling III to the Board and appointed William Anderson as President. Anderson was the only person who was not a Roebling descendant to hold the office, although he was a cousin of Ferdinand, Jr. He was also the obvious choice for President, since he had worked at the Company since 1888, and after 46 years, knew more about its manufacturing and finances than anyone else.

It has been a very good year

The U.S. Supreme Court had declared the National Industrial Recovery Act unconstitutional in 1935, scrapping the government's minimum wages and maximum hours, and just five weeks later, President Franklin Roosevelt had signed the National Labor Relations Act, giving workers the right to organize and making it illegal for employers to interfere.

On June 7, 1936, the Congress of Industrial Organizations (CIO) formed the Steel Workers Organizing Committee (SWOC) in Pittsburgh and funded it with $500,000 (about $7.9 million in 2009). The Committee elected Phillip Murray, a Scottish immigrant who rose to power in the United Mine Workers under John L. Lewis, as Chairman. Murray started with 36 organizers and soon built the force to over 200.

SWOC"s formation was timely, as the GNP grew a record 14.1 percent in 1936 and unemployment fell to 16.9 percent. As U.S. Steel, the nation's largest steel company, informed its stockholders:

The revival in general business activity....brought about a broadening and expanding demand for all iron and steel products....and increases of substantially 47 percent in the aggregate tonnage of rolls and finished products shipped.... This more satisfactory and sustained trade volume brought about a gratifying improvement in earnings.[34]

The scrapping of the NIRA's wage and hour controls helped push steel industry production to 90 percent of capacity, and U.S. Steel increased its workforce 14 percent to 222,372, more than one quarter of steel industry jobs. Its revenues increased 47 percent to $1.1 billion (about $17 billion) and profits rose to $62 million (about $971 million), of which it distributed 81 percent to preferred shareholders.

J.A.R.'s Sons Co. occupied a small niche within the steel industry, but demand for its specialized products and services increased revenues 32 percent in 1936 to $20.5 million (about $322 million), a little less than 2 percent of U.S. Steel's revenues. The Golden Gate Bridge accounted for 18 percent of sales; Wire Rope and Strand, 34 percent; Insulated Wire, 16 percent; Steel Round Wire & Rods, 12 percent; Flat Wire and Copper Wire, 7 percent each; Woven Wire Fabrics, 5 percent; and miscellaneous sales, 1 percent.

The Roebling Payroll climbed to 5,617 employees, 70 percent higher than in 1932. Operating profits spiked 68 percent to $1.5 million (about $23.1 million). Investment portfolio profits climbed 40 percent to $789,000 (about $12.3 million), some 35 percent of total profits. The Company paid dividends of $1.8 million (about $28.4 million), about 80 percent of total profits. When John A. Roebling II heard the growth in earnings for 1936, thanks in large part to the Golden Gate Bridge, he commented: "It has been a very good year, and of course, this is due to the men who make it so."[35]

The Company's balance sheet on December 31, 1936, showed assets of $51.4 million (about $807.6 million), which worked out to about $149 per share (about $2,341). Financial assets constituted 56 percent of the total: Investments, 46 percent, and Cash & Accounts Receivable, 10 percent. Tangible assets constituted only 44 percent of the total: Real Estate & Machinery, 26 percent, and Inventories, 18 percent. The Company had no debts. In a marked contrast, U.S. Steel's tangible assets of Real Estate, Machinery and Inventories accounted for 87 percent of its total assets and Investments accounted for only 3 percent. U.S. Steel reported debt obligations totaling about 6 percent of its assets.

Labor organizers had wanted to unionize U.S. Steel since its founding in 1901, but never had the strength to do so. With the high steel industry employment, Murray and other SWOC leaders focused much of their efforts on U.S. Steel, thinking that once the industry leader agreed to collective bargaining, the smaller firms would capitulate as well.

To counter SWOC's drive, U.S. Steel and other firms formed "company unions" to represent workers. The National Labor Relations Act prohibited company domination or financing of these "independent" unions, but it had little leverage. When a SWOC team started a campaign to organize Roebling workers, Company managers and sympathetic workers incorporated the Roebling Employee Association. The workers soon termed the Association a "chocolate drop union" because it resembled a company union formed by the Hershey Corporation in Hershey, Pennsylvania, and because the managers could "sweet talk" the union with minor concessions.

SWOC organizers infiltrated U.S. Steel's company union and turned it against the company. To maintain production, U.S. Steel Chairman Moses C. Taylor signed a collective bargaining agreement with SWOC on March 2, 1937, that set a common wage rate of $5 per day (about $77 in 2009), an eight hour workday, time-and-a-half for overtime, and binding arbitration for disagreements. Armed with this milestone victory against "Big Steel," as U.S. Steel was known, Murray and his SWOC colleagues turned their attention to unionizing Bethlehem, Republic, Inland and other smaller companies, including J.A.R.'s Sons Co., collectively known as "Little Steel."

To defeat their organization drive

While San Franciscans prepared for the opening of the Golden Gate Bridge, striking employees of Republic Steel picketed the company's steel mill in South Chicago. The managers of most of the "Little Steel" companies had adopted the wage and hour provision of the SWOC-U.S. Steel contract, but they refused to recognize the union because they didn't want union officials interfering in how they operated their plants. When SWOC called a strike on May 26 against Republic Steel, Inland Steel and the Youngstown Sheet and Tube Company, Inland and Youngstown closed their plants, but Republic kept operating its South Chicago plant.

On Sunday, May 30, Memorial Day, Chicago policemen opened fire on some 1,000 strikers and their supporters, killing ten of them and wounding thirty. Another six strikers died at a Republic Steel plant in Ohio, but the deaths turned public sentiment against militant unionizing, and SWOC's "Little Steel Strike" collapsed. Exhausted and in-debt, SWOC leaders turned to the National Labor Relations Board (NLRB) for help in unionizing "Little Steel," including J.A.R.'s Sons Co.

Figure 6.51 (left): *Roebling Wire Products,* J.A.R.'s Sons Co., c1941. Company brochures proudly displayed the Golden Gate Bridge.

Figure 6.52 (right): Golden Gate Bridge San Francisco Tower & J.A.R.'s Sons Co. Cable Section, 2009. The Company built the cable section before construction started to show its size, wrapping, and a hanger for the suspender ropes.

It speaks for itself

Just three days before the Memorial Day massacre at Republic Steel, an employee of the California Golden Gate Bridge and Highway District on Thursday, May 27, 1937, sounded a fog horn at 6 AM signaling the official opening of the Golden Gate Bridge (see boxes). Eighteen thousand people rushed the toll plazas at each end of the bridge to be among the first to cross. At the dedication, Joseph B. Strauss, the engineer who designed the bridge, said in a low voice: "This bridge needs neither praise, eulogy nor encomium. It speaks for itself. We who have labored long are grateful. What Nature rent asunder long ago, man has joined today." By the end of

the day, over 100,000 people had paid the nickel toll to cross, some of them sprinting, skating and tap dancing. On the next day, 32,000 drivers paid the 50 cent toll to drive across. A year after the bridge opened, Joseph Strauss died at the age of 68.[36]

Following the Roebling tradition, J.A.R.'s Sons Co. featured the bridge prominently in marketing various products (Fig. 6.51). The Golden Gate Bridge and Highway District installed the Company's pre-construction cable section at its San Francisco overlook with a plaque of statistics. Thanks to the efforts of John Dimon and other Roebling, N.J., residents who attended the bridge's 50th Anniversary in 1987, a replacement plaque credits J.A.R.'s Sons Co. for the bridge cables (Fig. 6.52).

"Golden Gate Completed," San Francisco, May 30, 1937

A great work has been accomplished in the completion of the Golden Gate Bridge. Once more the bounds of what man can do have been pushed forward, establishing a new base for further progress. The Golden Gate Bridge stands as a symbol of the long way that bridge engineering art has advanced in three quarters of a century in overcoming the barriers of space.

Those who built the structure at San Francisco stood on the shoulders of the bridge builders who went before, and what they now have wrought will in due time become the starting point for further progress – just as the far-famed Brooklyn Bridge, despite its now puny proportions, was the work that made possible the great spans across the Hudson River, San Francisco Bay and Golden Gate.

Because the Brooklyn Bridge achievement of 53 years ago prepared for the grander accomplishments of bridge construction of current years, there is meaning in the fact that the work of the '80s is linked to the bridge just completed by a

direct line of succession of human endeavor. John A. Roebling, suspension bridge pioneer, made the Brooklyn Bridge possible; his direct successors in tradition, knowledge and spirit played a determining part in building the Golden Gate.

We see before us an instance of that continuity of effort which – be it called experience or tradition or accumulated skill – plays an unmistakable part in the progress of the arts.

More is at issue than the mere survival of shop craft, or a name, or of commercial acumen. The basic restudy of suspension bridge problems that is made evident by the emphatic advance of cable erection performance at Golden Gate tells of the survival of some of the same spirit that the elder Roebling built into his great span across the East River. It is fair to conclude that virile tradition has a value that we cannot afford to neglect – though such tradition of course can never remain virile unless re-created every day by the same kind of effort and idealism as that of its founders.[37]

The influence of the George Washington Bridge is manifest. There are the same lean towers, the same simplicity, the same willingness to let steel speak for itself as an architectural material, and, as a result, the same dignity and impressiveness....

From two graceful cables hangs a 60-foot roadway flanked by 11-foot sidewalks. There is a lesson in those cables – so delicate to the eye, so strong in reality. In each are 27,572 wires less than two-tenths of an inch in diameter. Separately the wires are but threads; banded into ropes over three feet in diameter they support thousands of tons of steel and more thousands of tons of live load in the form of vehicles and foot passengers. The strength that lies in union is nowhere more dramatically and powerfully symbolized....

A century ago Richard Henry Dana wrote of the Golden Gate: 'If ever California becomes a prosperous country, this bay will be the center of its prosperity.'

This new bridge is the very highway of the prosperity that he foresaw....A great State has fulfilled Dana's prophecy with one of the greatest engineering structures of man.

Interfered with, restrained, and coerced their employees

Since the economic nadir of 1932-33, the government's deficit spending had fueled four years of recovery. President Roosevelt and members of Congress shifted their concern to the growing deficit and they reduced spending in 1937. The recovery soon stalled and the economy fell back into a recession. J.A.R.'s Sons Co. had already started downsizing since completing the Golden Gate Bridge contract, and this new downturn worsened its prospects.

In February, 1938, the NLRB dealt another blow when it filed a suit in Federal court based on a SWOC complaint that J.A.R.'s Sons Co. "attempted to discourage membership of employees in the Steel Workers Organizing Committee, a labor organization,....caused to be formed the Roebling Employee Association, Inc.,....and have since dominated and interfered with the administration of the Association....and have interfered with, restrained, and coerced their employees in the exercise of their rights guarantees in Section 7 of the National Labor Relations Act."[38]

The trial examiner ruled in August that the Company had violated the Act's fair labor practices. The Company agreed to abide by the ruling but the Roebling Employee Association appealed the ruling, its lawyer arguing that the association was "independent and unaffiliated." SWOC's representatives countered that "the Association was formed to defeat their organization drive in the company's plants." The Third Circuit Court of Appeals in Philadelphia denied the Association's appeal later that year. To increase pressure on the Company, SWOC chartered union Locals 2110 in Roebling and 2111 in Trenton and held meetings to educate workers about the benefits of collective bargaining and to share information about the Company's efforts to resist unionization.

1938 marked the 50th anniversary of John A. Roebling II's graduation in 1988 from Rensselaer Polytechnic Institute, where his father, Washington, had graduated in 1857, and he made a gift of $60,000 (about $900,000 in 2009) to RPI that summer. The gift raised the total family's contributions to RPI within the last 15 years to $250,000 (about $3.7 million)

The Gross National Product fell in 1938 by 4.5 percent and unemployment rose to 19 percent. J.A.R.'s Sons Co.'s sales dropped by nearly one-third and it reported a loss, the second and only additional loss in its history, of $1.04 million (about $15.5 million), 170 percent below its 1930s peak of operating profits in 1936.

To help out its employees, the Company reduced payroll by only 10 percent from its 1930s peak in 1936. The Directors drew upon the profits from the Company's investment portfolio to maintain employment and reduced dividends by 76 percent from their 1930s peak in 1936.

A comprehensive study

At the Directors meeting in March, 1939, President William Anderson cited the operating losses in 1938 and in the first two months of the current year, and he advised the Directors to hire an engineering firm, Ford, Bacon & Davis, "to make a comprehensive study of our business operations and business methods and management, and to formulate recommendations for changes and improvements." Based in New York, Ford, Bacon & Davis consulted on construction, valuations and management. The Directors engaged the firm to make "a survey of the organization, personnel policies of the Company and of its selling and accounting methods and practices, for the purpose of presenting views concerning their effectiveness and of making recommendations."[39]

That same month in Europe, German Chancellor Adolph Hitler demanded that Poland return Danzig and the "Polish Corridor," (which the Allies had carved out of Germany with the Treaty of Versailles in 1918), the Polish Government refused, England and France pledged to defend Polish independence, and Francisco Franco overthrew the republican government in Madrid, ending the Spanish Civil War. As European countries prepared for another war, the American economy expanded and orders grew for all types of steel products.

Where the gravy is flowing thickest

With the increase in steel production, SWOC officials pushed Roebling workers to demand higher wages and they distributed leaflets describing the Company's exploitation of its workers and its use of "fly cops," "hatchet men," "grindstones," "ace snoopers" and "stooges" to spy on them (see box). A "Jekyll and Hyde" in the Trenton plant named William, the organizers noted, "was a C.I.O. member when we looked strong, and when he got a better job he joined the Company Union as a do-nothing representative. What some people will do for a mess of pottage. At this writing it is no telling where loyal William is standing but you can bet your bottom dollar that he is standing where the gravy is flowing thickest."

"Roebling Workers in Drive to Raise Wage Rates,"
Voice of 2110 & 2111,
Official Organ – SWOC Lodges 2110-2111
Roebling Plants - August 1, 1939

We want to extend our appreciation to the workers in both plants for the courteous way in which they have been receiving our leaflets. The interest shown by the workers indicates that they are alive to the conditions that exist in the plant....

In a desperate attempt to chisel on his employees further Roebling Co is now introducing women into certain operations formerly done by men at half the pay the men were getting.

For instance in Department 56 Trenton on the smaller spooling operations women now work the jobs at 35 cents per hour that men worked for 64 cents per hour plus. As a union we respect the rights of women the same as men and our policy is that they should get the same pay as men regardless of sex....

Encouraged by the militancy and picketing of the C.I.O. unions, the rank and file in the various depts. in the Roebling, N.J. plant have started a drive for wage increases to counteract wage cutting, speed up program of the company....

The Company under pressure from the C.I.O. and now the rank and file is in a tough spot and it will take more than a lot of promises from their 'stooges' to satisfy the legitimate demands of their employees.

Meanwhile all depts, both in Trenton and Roebling should start a drive for wage increases and raise the cry everywhere for raises. Get a committee together in your department, draw a petition and present to your boss. Make sure a C.I.O. man is on your committee. If you get no results then communicate with us and we will give you further instructions.

ACT NOW. RAISES FOR ALL EMPLOYEES.

When Hitler ordered the German Army into Poland on September 1, President Roosevelt accelerated defense spending and everyone involved with J.A.R.'s Sons Co. knew that business and production would soon increase dramatically.

The Company will find itself in a more difficult position

On October 1, the business analysts at Ford, Bacon & Davis submitted their report to the Directors, noting:[40]

> *We believe that measurable improvement can be made in the general profitability of the Company's operations....*
>
> *No single industry is a dominant factor in the Company's volume of business. Most of the industries purchasing products from the Company are those with businesses which fluctuate with the production of heavy capital goods....*
>
> *Between 1929 and 1937 the Company has generally decreased its participation in the available markets....The reasons for this general decline are many and varied. In wire rope the quality of competitors' products has improved whereas that of the Company's rope has remained about the same or at least it has not improved as rapidly, thereby narrowing and some times eliminating the gap which previously existed in the Company's favor....*
>
> *Within the American steel industry....the Company is not a tonnage producer, by which we mean that the large integrated steel companies can turn out tonnage products or standard products which are sold in great volume at a considerably lower cost. We believe that the Company's field is in the specialty business including special products and standard products with special characteristics....Many items in this class are sold in limited quantities to satisfy specific requirements and we believe that by more aggressive salesmanship the Company can place itself in a position to serve that important section of this market.*

The consultant noted the "more aggressive leadership" assumed by competitors, and the high expense of operating the Company's ten regional sales offices, which it had established over the decades to sell directly to customers. The consultant recommended selling products through distributors as competitors were doing. While acknowledging that "The Company's reputation for fair dealing is excellent," the consultant also noted the high average age of salesmen and the lack of an incentive plan and specialized training, and it recommended revamping sales policies, controls, and practices. The consultant found that:

> *The Company's advertising is too heavy on prestige and too light on performance....The Company should emphasize, to an even greater degree, the sale of Blue Center rope in order to create a brand preference and to overcome the effect of price cutting tactics by competitors.*

The consultant recommended more advertising about secondary products, like flat wire and welding wire (Fig. 6.53), and a review of insulated wire and woven wire products to determine whether these could be produced profitably in light of larger competitors. Regarding the Company's longstanding prominence in suspension bridges, the consultant concluded:

The Company enjoys a very fine reputation in the suspension bridge field but the obtaining of suspension bridge business will become increasingly competitive in the future because of the more complete integration of its competitors.

The Company will find itself in a more difficult position competitively on medium and large sized suspension bridge construction because, in addition to U.S. Steel Corporation with its subsidiaries – American Bridge Company and American Steel and Wire Company - the Bethlehem Steel Corporation, with its subsidiaries, McClintic-Marshall and Williamsport Wire Rope Division, will be in a position to bid on the complete fabrication and erection of the superstructures....

The Company should continue its practice of operating the bridge business as a separate division. At the expiration of three years, the operation of that division should be restudied and a decision reached at that time as to the advisability of further continuing that operation....

The Company has been and is very much of a one-man organization and there is no understudy for that one.... An extraordinarily large number of individuals (seventeen) report directly to the President....Major changes must be made in the general organization set up of the Company to the end that lines of authority and responsibility will be much more clearly defined. Each executive must know his duties and the extent of his authority, and he must be made to realize that if he does not function successfully, he will be replaced by someone who can....

Two or three competent individuals not connected with the Company's organization, but active in other lines of business, should be added to the Board of Directors.

We have given thought to the possibility and to the advisability of the Company consolidating its activities with some other large organization either through sale, merger or other means. Even though this be done ultimately, the changes outlined in this report should be made, because the company could then negotiate the longest line to much better advantage if it seemed desirable to do so.

The Ford, Bacon & Davis report confirmed the Company's declining prospects for competing profitably against the big steel firms. The impending unionization also threatened to hinder management's control of the workplace, increase labor costs and further reduce profits. While the Company's ability to remain independent looked increasingly uncertain, getting 36 family stockholders to agree on a course of action was

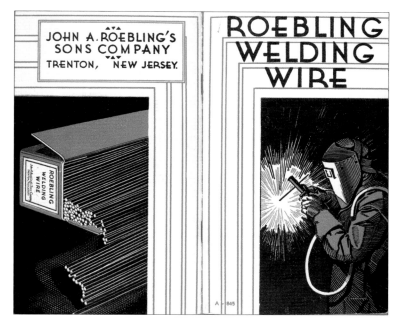

Figure 6.53: *Roebling Welding Wire* Brochure, 1938. RU J.A.R.'s Sons Co. made made a number of specialty wire products, but larger manufacturers made similar products in greater quantities and were able to sell them at lower prices.

daunting, and the three third generation family members who controlled nearly 50 percent of the stock, John A. Roebling II, Emily Roebling Cadwalader, and Helen Roebling Tyson, wanted to maintain the status quo as a family business.

President Anderson, aged 69, who had celebrated his 50th anniversary with the Company in 1938, owned only a token number of shares, so he also had little incentive for making changes. Roebling presidents remained in office until they died, but to assist Anderson the Directors hired Charles G. Williams in December, 1939, as Executive Vice President and General Manager, and they made him a Director as well. Williams had been vice-president of the American Chain & Cable Company of Detroit, and he soon brought in other executives to manage sales, exports, and the regional offices, and they started selling Roebling products through distributors, as Ford, Bacon & Davis had recommended (Fig. 6.54).

Figure 6.54: *JAR Roebling Authorized Distributor,* c1940. RM On the advice of its consultant, J.A.R.'s Sons Co. started selling its products through distributors, like its competitors did, instead of relying solely on its regional offices.

By April, 1940, defense orders and prospects dominated the Directors' attention. Anderson presented Income and Expense prospects for "the manufacture and sale of 3,000,000 French 75 millimeter shells." After discussing the proposal, the Directors unanimously authorized "a new corporation to be formed for the purpose of engaging in the business of manufacturing and selling munitions of war and other metal products, to be known as 'The Roebling Steel Products Corporation,' and to subscribe for 51 percent of the capital stock…not to exceed the sum of $25,500" (about $394,000 in 2009).[41]

A vital and inspiring contribution

In the Fall, the U.S. Navy announced the order of 200 "amphibian tanks," also known as "Roebling Alligators," from Donald Roebling (see box), the youngest son of John A. Roebling II. After a hurricane devastated the Lake Okeechobee area near John II's Red Hill Estate in Lake Placid, Florida, he encouraged Donald to develop an amphibious vehicle that could reach remote areas of the wetlands. Donald built a prototype boat-vehicle with wide treads to traverse the wetlands in 1935 (Fig. 6.55), and he gradually improved upon it through several models.

U.S. Navy Rear Admiral Edward Kalbfus read about Donald's "amphibian tractor" in *Life* magazine in 1938, and shared the article with the Commandant of the Marine Corps, Major General Thomas Holcomb, who ordered the vehicle's evaluation for use in the Pacific. Donald donated his design to the war effort and the Navy ultimately established Amphibian Tractor Battalions. The "Roebling Alligators" provided crucial landing capabilities at Guadalcanal and many other battles in the Pacific and in Europe. In 1947, the Navy awarded Donald a Medal for Merit for "a vital and inspiring contribution to the defense of his country" (Fig. 6.56).[42]

Do the work or go home

Thanks to the wartime economy, J.A.R.'s Sons Co.'s annual revenues jumped in 1940 to $22.4 million (about $348 million in 2009), 62 percent higher than in 1938 and 270 percent higher than in 1932. By early 1941, the need for steel workers had reinvigorated SWOC's campaign to unionize the "Little Steel" companies, and it's leaders decided to focus on Bethlehem Steel, which by then had over $1.3 billion (about $20 billion) in defense contracts, 47 percent more than it's defense contracts during all of the First World War.

In January, 1,500 SWOC supporters at Bethlehem's Lackawanna Steel plant next to Buffalo, New York, laid down their tools and staged a one-day "spontaneous demonstration" to protest the company's refusal to recognize SWOC. A month later Lackawanna workers walked off their jobs demanding SWOC recognition and a 25 percent increase in pay, and police clashed with picketers blocking the gates to prevent employees who wanted to work from entering.

"Navy Orders 200 Mechanical 'Alligators' Made by Donald Roebling for Land or Sea,"
- The New York Times, November 26, 1940

The novel feature of the 'alligators' is that they depend on the same equipment for traction on land or water and consequently are able to slash and crash through swamp and mud. Traction is supplied from caterpillar treads equipped with extremely wide cleats, which act as fins or paddles in mud and water but are close enough to provide fairly smooth transit on land.

Mr. Donald Roebling built his first "alligator" in 1935. Compared with the later model, it was somewhat crude but effective. The later model weighs 8,000 pounds and is twenty feet long and eight feet wide.

It travels twenty-five miles an hour on land eight and a half in the water, and looks like a machine from Mars.

In tests the vehicle was driven from land into water and back again as easily as its animal prototype. Mr. Roebling then tried it in mushy swampland, where a land vehicle would bog down and a boat could not run. The alligator wallowed along without hesitating. Logs, seaweed, grass, slime – none had any effect. Trees up to eight inches in diameter were battered down.

Figure 6.55 (above): The first 'Roebling Alligator' developed by Donald Roebling in 1935 to help rescue efforts in Florida wetlands.

Figure 6.56 (left): In 1947, Donald Roebling, the youngest son of John A. Roebling II, received a Presidential Medal of Merit for donating the design of his 'Alligator' to the U.S. Navy in World War II. RR

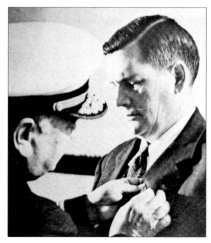

In early March, SWOC organizers in Bethlehem, Pa., called a strike at the Bethlehem Steel plant and claimed that 80 percent of the 18,000 workers there walked out. Governor Arthur James sent in 250 state troopers to protect scabs from angry picketers. "Policemen can't make steel," a SWOC leaflet noted, "The overwhelming majority of Bethlehem Steel workers and citizens are behind the strike. They believe in democracy and the rights of common people against industrial dictatorship."[43]

In Trenton, SWOC's Subregional Director, Michael Harris, demanded that J.A.R.'s Sons Co. bargain solely with SWOC, but Company officials resisted because the Roebling Employee Association had an appeal pending at the U.S. Circuit Court in Philadelphia on the National Labor Relations Board's (NLRB) order to disband. After Harris petitioned the NLRB on "the question of employees choosing a union as bargaining agent," and set a strike date of March 29, Company officials agreed to cooperate, and Harris rescinded the strike deadline.[44]

SWOC's national leaders appealed to President Roosevelt for help, and after he met with them and subsequently with representatives of Bethlehem, U.S. Steel, Republic, and other 'Little Steel' companies, the companies agreed on Monday, April 14, to a ten-cent-an-hour wage increase and to negotiate with SWOC towards a collective bargaining agreement.

On the following day, April 15, J.A.R.'s Sons Co. announced a ten cent an hour wage increase, bringing the rate for common labor to 72 ½ cents an hour. On Wednesday, April 16, the Company announced "a vacation of one week with pay for all employees with three years of service and two weeks with pay for those employed for 15 years."[45]

On that same day, the Trenton rope shop superintendent increased the production schedule in the strand department, where he had installed new machines "for a greater and more rapid production of aircraft strand, urgently required in aircraft factories throughout the country at this time." When the men running the machines objected, their foreman told them to "do the work or go home." Harris called this response a "lockout," and led some 3,000 workers out of the Trenton and Roebling plants, claiming that "the trouble started when employees were told to operate six machines instead of four…. The production speed up nullified the wage increase."[46]

On the next day, April 17, nearly all of the workers in the Company's Trenton plants and 75 percent in Roebling stayed out, but SWOC leaders permitted the "furnace men to stay on until the steel had been drained off." Two days later, Company officials announced that "the plant at Roebling was in operation and a substantial number of employees were at work there, many of them having returned to work today. The Company has contracts for wire strand and cable and other defense materials costing several million dollars and therefore considered itself obligated to keep the plants open to employees who want to work." SWOC organizers handed out 500 baseball bats to strikers picketing the gates to keep workers from entering the plants (see box).[47]

On April 21 at the Trenton Works, as *The Trenton Evening Times* reported, "a considerable number of employees reported at the gates apparently with the intention of going to work, but only a few dared to cross the picket lines." At the Kinkora Works, Company officials estimated that two-thirds of the workers had returned, many of them believing that SWOC had brought in communist agitators from Trenton and elsewhere. Some women passed lunches through the plant fence for their husbands, while others formed a back-to-work line against their striking husbands who were picketing. The police arrested three picketers for shouting at workers leaving the plant and for swinging "baseball bats supporting placards in a menacing manner at workers entering the plant at Roebling on the day shift at the plant gates." The conflict continued into the night:[48]

Carrying an American flag and marching to fife and drum rhythm, five hundred workers shoved aside pickets at the plant gates at midnight. The marchers, many of whom had worked 12 hour shifts, turned about and entered the plant again to work. A thousand men and women cheered the strikebreaking workers, while Sheriff F. George Furth directed police in maintaining order.[49]

"Roebling Girl Worker Stripped In Attempt to Pass Picket Line; Police Patrol Strike-Bound Area," *The Philadelphia Inquirer*, April 22, 1941

Striking women workers at the John A. Roebling's Sons Company Buckthorn Plant stripped a girl worker near the plant late yesterday afternoon as CIO pickets armed with baseball bat placards succeeded in keeping the day shift from returning to their jobs. Confirming the stripping action, Morris Malmignatti, CIO organizer, said last night that the woman was 'stripped of all but her shoes and stockings' by a 'reception committee' of women members of the Steel Workers Organizing Committee, after she had ignored the union picket line and returned to her job at the Buckthorn works.

Although 700 employees reported to the firm's gate here yesterday morning with the announced intention of returning to work, less than a dozen, the majority of them girl workers, chose to cross the picket line. More than 35 policemen patrolled this strikebound area throughout the day and pickets were instructed by the police to use their baseball bats only as placard standards…. Commenting on the use of baseball bats by the pickets, Malmignati said: 'These pickets have a legal right to carry placard standards and anyway, we intend to organize a baseball team when the strike is over.'

Kinkora Works Strike April, 1941. RM

Figure 6.57 (left): Picketers at Main Gate.

Figure 6.58 (middle left): Strikers sprayed by police.

Figure 6.59 (middle right): Anxious family members.

Figure 6.60: (bottom left): Injured striker.

Figure 6.61 (bottom right): SWOC Leader Michael Harris.

A test of the picketing law

SWOC organizers held a meeting in Roebling that evening at Hungarian Hall, as *The Trenton Evening Times* reported:

The crowd overflowed the auditorium, and loudspeakers were set up outside. Afterward, the strikers marched to the plant in what was termed a 'test of the picketing law.' A union spokesman said the company threatened the marchers with fire hoses but the firm denied this.[50]

Tensions boiled over the next day, April 22, when 500 workers emerged from the Kinkora Plant at the end of the day shift and marched into a picket line of 200 strikers brandishing baseball bats in front of nearly 1,000 onlookers (Figs. 6.57-61). As strikers and workers swung fists and bats, 35 town and county police sprayed them with water from fire hoses. About a dozen people were injured, and the sheriff arrested several, including SWOC Subregional Director Harris. The violence left bitter feelings among both the strikers and workers.

That same day, the NLRB directed the Company to "disestablish the employee association and stop dealing with it as the exclusive bargaining agent for workers at it's plants." Five days later, judges at the U.S. Circuit Court in Philadelphia unanimously upheld the NLRB's finding to disband the "company dominated" Roebling Employee Association. The judges rebuked SWOC for distributing circulars stating that "the President wants you to join the union," implying that President Roosevelt supported SWOC's organizing efforts. The judges also rebuked the Company, noting that: "While the company has a right to counteract this move, W.A. Anderson, Roebling President, went beyond the limits to the law in letters to employees urging them, in effect, not to join the union."[51]

The National Mediation Defense Board called Company and SWOC representatives to Washington and on March 29 announced an agreement to end the 13 day strike: "In view of America's need for maximum defense production and in order to promote cooperation in the Roebling Plant for this purpose." The agreement specified that: "The company and SWOC are to cooperate promptly for fair, orderly and harmonious conduct and for intelligent and efficient production in the Roebling plants, which are the producers of material immediately necessary and vital to the defense of the nation." The agreement also called for an employee election for union representation by secret ballot within 30 days. Three weeks later, on May 20, *The New York Times* reported:[52]

> Voting approximately two to one in favor of union affiliation, employees of the John A. Roebling's Sons Company selected the Steel Workers Organizing Committee (C.I.O.) as their collective bargaining agency in tonight's National Labor Relations Board election held in Trenton and at Roebling, New Jersey. With 4,472 workers balloting out of a total of 5,004 eligibles at both Roebling plants, 2,912 votes were cast for the C.I.O. in comparison to 1,477 opposed to union affiliation.[53]

Three months later, on August 24, Roebling workers ratified a contract, as *The New York Times* reported:

> Michael Harris said the contract provided for payment of the wage scale prevalent in the steel industry, with time and a half pay for Sunday work. The contract included also a five-day workweek and a vacation clause. Provision was also made for arbitration of grievances, abolition of a unit system, and establishment of a five-day suspension period before an employee may be dismissed.[54]

Most of the workers welcomed the changes that the contract brought to the mills and shops as long overdue (see box).

Now You're Set For Life - John Smith
J.A.R.'s Sons Co. Oral Histories, Trenton, N.J., 1993

I started working at Roebling's in 1939. It was very difficult getting work then. I put my application in, went to people who worked there and tried to use them. Finally, I was accepted. When I went home, I told my mother. She said: 'Now you're set for life.' She believed it at that time. I believed it, because nobody quit Roebling's. You either died or you were fired. Nobody walked out and quit because they were dissatisfied there....

They had a lot of aircraft orders, for warplanes. So, in 1940, I started on the third floor in Department 75 F – the aircraft cord department. The foreman who took me there said: 'You're going to have a lot of noise. You better use cotton in your ears.' When they opened that door it was as if 1,000 machine guns were going off. Couldn't hear, just noise, noise. The noise just overwhelmed you. He gave me some cotton. I put it in my ears, and they broke me in on the machine. One day I forgot to put the cotton in. When I went home at four o'clock, I couldn't hear until about eight o'clock. It really frightened me. I thought I lost my hearing, but it came back. You could stand ten feet from a person and scream at the top of your lungs, and he wouldn't hear you. He wouldn't hear anything.

The mills were going seven days a week, 24 hours a day and they didn't stop. I don't even think they stopped on the Fourth of July; they just kept right on going.

Before the union there was a lot of favoritism. Roeblings' was a family-oriented place. Most of the employees were related: uncles, cousins, brothers-in-law. And the foreman had a lot of power. He was the one who assigned you a machine when you went in. He had maybe 65 to 70 machines, and he'd say, 'You go here, you go there.' Most of the time he kept you on the same machine. But, if you had a machine that was very profitable, that was a good moneymaking machine at piecework rates, he would normally assign one of his family to it. I mean, he would assign his brother-in-law to it, because he was helping out his sister's family. They were making good money on that machine.

The foreman had the power to fire you. He could say, 'You're fired. Clean your locker out and go!' And that was it. There was no recourse. You were done. After the union came in, that was no longer so. We had shop stewards who were on your side. They just couldn't do that anymore. Everybody had to get a fair shake, and a lot of seniority came into play, as far as the machines went.

And of course, the shifts. Everybody had to work three shifts. Before, the old-timers had the dayshift locked up. You never went on the day shift, never. These guys were working the day shift for 40 years and you're not going to crack that. The union came in, that was gone. So these were some of the changes the union made. It was good for the workers. We were guaranteed two weeks vacation. We were guaranteed a raise in salary. Safety conditions were improved. The foreman being God was taken away. The foreman no longer had the power to fire you, if you looked at him cross-eyed.

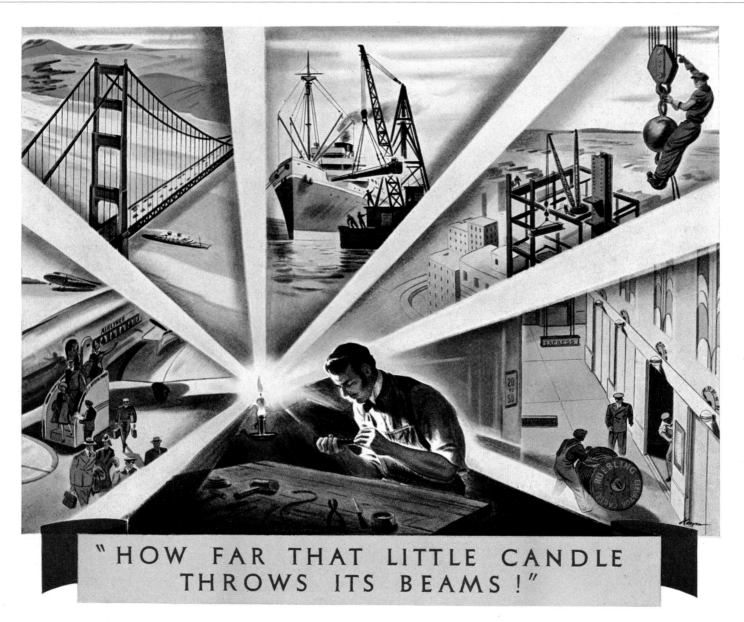

"HOW FAR THAT LITTLE CANDLE THROWS ITS BEAMS!"

Over a hundred years ago a young engineer by the name of John A. Roebling conceived the thought of making rope of strong steel wires twisted together, to replace costly, short-lived hemp hawsers used for hauling Pennsylvania Canal portage cars over the 2300 foot barrier of the Alleghanies.

Today, canal boats are all but forgotten — but Roebling wire rope plays a vital role throughout commerce and industry. It is used in the marine field for rigging and hoisting purposes. Thousands of building elevators depend on its safety. It has endless uses ranging from control cables for giant air transports and fighting planes to crane ropes used in skyscraper erection.

Roebling main cables and suspender ropes are found on

104 years ago the idea of twisting wire into rope, stronger, more useful, than ever made before, took root in John A. Roebling's mind.

mighty suspension bridges from coast to coast — from the George Washington, spanning the Hudson River between New York and New Jersey, to the Golden Gate Bridge in San Francisco.

Today, Roebling serves industry with an organization of over 6,000 employees and 217 acres of manufacturing facilities.

Roebling Products · WIRE ROPE AND STRAND · WIRE ROPE SLINGS AND FITTINGS · SUSPENSION BRIDGES AND CABLES · AERIAL WIRE ROPE SYSTEMS · ELECTRICAL WIRES AND CABLES · HIGH AND LOW CARBON COLD ROLLED STRIP · ROUND AND SHAPED WIRE · WIRE CLOTH AND NETTING · STEEL AND COPPER RODS HIGH AND LOW CARBON ACID AND BASIC OPEN-HEARTH STEELS

JOHN A. ROEBLING'S SONS COMPANY
TRENTON · NEW JERSEY

1841 ☆ ROEBLING BRIDGES A CENTURY WITH WIRE ☆ 1941

After all the turmoil of the strike, the negotiations and finally the acceptance of collective bargaining after decades of resisting it, the Roebling stockholders and Directors could finally turn their attention to celebrating the Company's Centennial. In the Company's marketing efforts, Robert T. Bowman, the Director of Public Relations, traced its roots to the first wire rope that John A. Roebling made by hand with his neighbor-farmers in Saxonburg, Pennsylvania, in 1841.

Bowman commissioned a Pathescope film, *Bridging a Century*, with scenes of building the George Washington and Golden Gate Bridge cables to illustrate J.A.R.'s Sons Co.'s history of innovation in suspension bridges and cables. He developed centennial advertisements with a "Roebling 100th Anniversary" Golden Gate Bridge logo (Fig. 6.62). To emphasize the Company's diverse products, he created a stylish series of catalogs targeting specific industries (Fig. 6.63), telling customers: "The high quality of Roebling Wire Rope and Wire Products is nowhere left to chance."

In September, Company officials invited 150 editors and publishers of business and news publications for a tour of the Trenton and Roebling plants and a centennial dinner at the Nassau Inn in Princeton. *The Iron Age, Time Magazine, The New York Times* and the local press all featured glowing stories of the Company's heritage (see box). Readers also learned that J.A.R.'s Sons Co. employed 6,200 people and currently devoted 75 percent of its efforts to defense orders, including specialty products like harbor defense nets, degaussing cable

> ### "The Roebling Centenary,"
> ### - *The New York Times*, September 19, 1941
> *In 1841 a young civil engineer of Prussian origin established at Saxonburg, Pennsylvania, a wire rope factory which was destined to develop into one of America's great industries. Moving his plant later to Trenton, New Jersey....and in designing and pushing forward the erection of the Brooklyn Bridge performed what still remains one of the great engineering feats of the 19th century....The story of John A. Roebling and his cables is the story of an American epoch, and today's centenary exercises fittingly recall one of the most romantic chapters in American industrial pioneering.*

for demagnetizing ship hulls to resist mines, wiring for battleships and cantonments, signal wire, anchor cables for captive balloons, and instrument parts. Defense contracts helped boost Roebling sales in 1941 by 61 percent, and despite the new union wage levels, operating profits spiked more than 700 percent to the level of the highly profitable 1920s.

In early 1942, the Directors addressed "the tremendously increased demands by the U.S. Government's War and Navy Departments and allocations under the Lend-Lease program for Fine Wire Strand, Cord and Fittings, namely: Aircraft Cord (Fig. 6.64), Tractor Tread Cord, Assault Wire Strand, Field Wire Strand and Aircraft Fittings." They allocated $572,000 (about $8.4 million in 2009) "to meet these demands by extending our productive facilities with modern equipment, thus placing us in a more favorable competitive position as well as furthering the Nation's war effort." By mid-1942, the Company's payroll had reached 7,353, including about 600 women.[55]

Figure 6.62 (opposite): J.A.R.'s Sons Co. Centennial Ad, *Fortune*, 1941. One of four in a series on Roebling heritage and products from "coast-to-coast."

New catalogs for specific markets:

Figure 6.63 (left): *Roebling Marine Products*, c1941. *Roebling controls every step of manufacture - from the production of raw materials to the final testing.*

Figure 6.64: *Roebling Aircraft Products*, 1941. *Roebling Aircraft Cord and Strand will meet all the requirements of various Army and Navy specifications for these materials.*

In January, 1942, the U.S. Navy awarded J.A.R.'s Sons Co. an "E" pennant for ordnance production. The Navy traditionally awarded this "coveted emblem of excellence," to vessels and crews for distinguished service, but President Roosevelt authorized the Navy to award it to industries that have gone "all out for national defense." As a leaflet distributed at the award ceremony at the War Memorial in Trenton noted: "The John A. Roebling's Sons Co. and its crew - the men and women of that company - were deemed worthy of the highest service award the Navy can make. To these men and women the Navy has said, 'WELL DONE ROEBLING!'"[56]

That may, SWOC officials reorganized the union as the United Steel Workers of America, and SWOC Chairman Phillip Murray became president. A month later, 165 workers in the "melt shop," or steel mill, at the Kinkora Works staged a midnight "sit down strike" to protest inefficient management and to demand the higher pay prevailing at other steel plants. The union wanted the Company to bring in an outside expert to help operate the open hearths more efficiently, and to use the resulting savings to increase wages by 25 percent.

A National War Labor Board official investigating the dispute reported: "Parties hopelessly deadlocked. Trenton plant may go down in sympathy with Roebling plant and more employees may go out at Roebling, thus shutting down entire plant." While the official found that: "The strike is definitely a violation of the contract," the Company agreed to a small pay increase but dismissed the need for an outside expert.[57]

In August, 29 shippers and tractor drivers at the Kinkora Works quit working, demanding more pay and resolution of several grievances. As materials piled up, foremen had to halt work in several departments, including the wire rope department at the Trenton Works. A few weeks later, melt shop workers at Kinkora refused to charge a furnace and demanded more pay. The heads of the United Steel Workers locals in Trenton and Roebling, Francis McIntyre and John Kelley, cooperated with plant officials to end both of these stoppages.

By late 1942, about 16 percent of the Company's employees had joined the armed forces, including 56 pairs of brothers and one father and son. To highlight the Company's war efforts and cooperation with the union, its Industrial Relations staff began publishing the *Roebling War Worker* in November, and President Anderson announced in it the formation of Labor-Management War Production Drive Committees at the Trenton and Roebling plants, to "call upon Roebling employees in both plants for a still greater effort for victory." Anderson also announced that the Navy Board of Production Awards had awarded the Company its new Army-Navy "E" (Fig. 6.65).

Figure 6.65: *Roebling War Worker,* November 20, 1942. RM The newsletter helped build support for the war effort, and the first issue celebrated an award for production excellence for "the splendid work to help the Army and Navy do their big job."

It has to be perfect

When the Labor-Management Committees launched an "all out United States War Bond drive for 100 percent enrollment of Roebling company employees in the war bond payroll deduction plan," the cooperation for war production and financing represented quite a turnaround from the earlier acrimony. In a joint statement on the Army-Navy "E" award, McIntyre and Kelley declared in the *Roebling War Worker*:

> *We want to congratulate the men and women of the Roebling plants for the splendid production record which they had to make in order to obtain this high honor from the United States government. But we are all Americans. And Americans are never satisfied with just a good record. It has to be perfect. Everyone in these plants has been working hard and well, but there are still ways in which our Victory job can be improved.*
>
> *It is to investigate these possible ways of improving the job we are doing, to make suggestions and to prove to Uncle Sam and the world that American free labor can out produce and outfight Axis slave labor, that the Labor-Management War Production Drive Committee has been formed.*
>
> *All of us should be deeply grateful to have received the Army-Navy tribute today and it marks a great day in company history. But the greatest award and reward that any of us can hope for is the surrender of our enemies. Let's do our part for complete victory by constantly improving our production for victory and by cooperating to the fullest with the Labor-Management Committee in its war production drive.*[58]

Figure 6.66: Peace River Bridge, c1943. RU Roebling engineers and bridgemen completed this 903 ft. span bridge – a key link in the Alaska-Canada Highway – in just 18 weeks in 1943 to support the defense of Alaska. A landslide in 1957 shifted the foundations of the towers and collapsed parts of the deck, but the Roebling cables held firm.

War production boosted sales 40 percent in 1942 to $52.5 million, (about $768 million in 2009). Operating profits spiked 80 percent to $7.6 million (about $111 million), the highest profits of the Second World War years. The Directors raised dividends 50 percent to $1.5 million (about $22.5 million), or $4.46 (about $65) per share. Following government efforts to control windfall profits, the Directors suggested "a basis for reducing profits to eliminate any excessive amount."[59]

Union officials wanted to share in the extra profits and asked the War Labor Board for a wage increase of 5.5 cents per hour retroactive to February, 1942. To protest the Board's inaction, about 1,000 workers struck for six hours at the Trenton Plant in January, 1943. In February, Admiral C. C. Block informed William Anderson that because of "the excessive number of man-hours lost to production through work stoppages during the last four months of 1942," the Navy had withdrawn the Army-Navy "E" it had conferred the previous summer. Admiral Bloch admonished the Company and its employees "to realize the urgency of our armed services' need for war material of all kinds and unite to work your hardest and best, not only to regain your award but to serve our country in its most desperate hour." In March, the War Labor Board granted the union's request for the retroactive pay increase.[60]

Four and a half months from foundation to traffic

To help defend Alaska, President Roosevelt authorized the Army Corps of Engineers in 1942 to build a 1,422 mi. highway between the Canadian railhead at Dawson Creek in British Columbia and the American railhead at Delta Junction near Fairbanks. In early 1943, the Public Roads Administration contracted with J.A.R.'s Sons Co. to build a 930 ft. span suspension bridge for the highway across the Peace River at Taylor, about 40 miles northwest of Dawson Creek.

Roebling engineers and bridgemen set up "Camp Roebling" and worked two shifts a day in temperatures that sometimes dipped to 55 degrees below zero in order to complete the foundations and towers before the spring thaw. They then made the cables in just six weeks with Roebling prestressed bridge strand, and by August, U.S. Army trucks began hauling vital supplies 24 hours a day over the bridge to Fairbanks. A Roebling engineer called the Peace River crossing "the Bridge Division's greatest single contribution to World War II – Four and a half months from foundation to traffic" (Fig. 6.66 & box).

**"Peace River Bridge -
Here in the wilderness a great bridge,"**
- Engineering News Record, September 23, 1943

There's a lot of river. Two thousand feet wide, running 8 miles an hour. And here in the wilderness a great bridge. They trucked it here – 100 freight car loads of material and equipment. It was in the winter and spring of 1943. Bitter cold, snowing, blowing....

There wasn't much here when the men arrived. Roebling carpenters built weather-tight shacks for the men. Roebling men cut wood for Roebling cooks who kept their stoves heated red. Disease struck, and at one time 80 men were down. From Trenton, medicine was packed, and flown in by plane.

The river was frozen 54 inches thick – 4 ½ feet of ice. So they used the ice, built their construction tower on it, because it was the fastest way. But they gambled, for they knew the ice would thaw. The breakup would come in March. They raised one bridge tower, then skidded their 100-ton construction tower across the ice to raise the other one. Just like a sled. They had to hurry. But they won.

After the breakup, the bridge towers stood safely pointing to the sky. They needed motorboats, but there were none. They built them. The 'John A. Roebling' and the 'Washington Roebling,' nicknamed for America's bridge building pioneers, helped the Army ferry as they worked to build the bridge. This bridge was so vital that as soon as the cables were spun across, they carried a gasoline pipe line over on them. Trucks shuttled to one end of it, and from the other end towards the Alaska-based bombers and fighters - and Tokyo....

'Surpassing their 100-year record as bridge builders, Roebling has done a magnificent job at Peace River,' says Commissioner Thomas H. McDonald of the U.S. Public Roads Administration, 'Construction is complete....7 ½ months after the contract signing....18 weeks after the setting of the first piece of steel....cutting in half the best previous construction time.'

Figure 6.67: Roebling Physical Laboratory, c1943. TPL Chief Bridge Engineer Charles C. Sunderland (right) and Assistant Chief Engineer Blair Birdsall (left), developed a "Roebling bridge of tomorrow" with "revolutionary principles" using diagonal cables for stiffening instead of steel trusses.

Figure 6.68: General Office Footbridge, c1943. WSR Sunderland and Birdsall's lightwieght cable-stiffened bridge represented a "radical departure from accepted practices," and they erected the first real version as a footbridge between the Company's General Office and and its Physical Laboratory on South Broad Street in Trenton.

This bridge stretches a scant 53 feet between the Roebling main office building and Roebling's modern laboratory. But it is the 'stiffest' bridge for its weight ever built.
- Trenton Sunday Times Advertizer, May 20, 1945.

Our thinking turned to wire

Building the Peace River Bridge quickly in a remote location was the kind of challenge that inspired Charles Sunderland. As Blair Birdsall recalled in a 1993 interview: "Sunderland was a really great engineer with a tremendous amount of ingenuity and he always came up with fresh ideas of how to do something." In considering how to build lightweight suspension bridges in remote locations, as Blair later wrote, "our thinking turned to wire as a possible means of providing stiffness. Our investigation involved experimental structures which were sometimes purely academic, and in other cases also functional. First came studies on paper, then preliminary laboratory models (fig. 6.67), then a small office footbridge."[61]

Their cable-truss concept, also known as cable stiffening, continued the tradition of Roebling innovations in suspension bridges. In place of the standard vertical suspender ropes, their design used crossed diagonal ropes attached to the main cables to support and stiffen the deck at the same time. To test the concept over a period of time, Sunderland and Birdsall built a 53 ft. long cable-truss footbridge between the General Office and the Physical Laboratory on South Broad Street in Trenton in 1943 (Fig. 6.68), and this experimental bridge remains in place today as a testament to their ingenuity.

Sunderland was also a visionary in developing Roebling products for prestressed concrete. A San Francisco inventor had patented a concrete prestressing method in 1886 and the French engineer Eugene Freyssinet started building prestressed

concrete bridges in France in the early 20th century. Freyssinet and a few other European engineers used prestressed parallel wires to place concrete in compression and thereby strengthen it to resist tension at the bottom of a beam or slab when a load is placed on it. As Birdsall recalled:

In the early 1940s, when prestressed concrete hadn't come into this country at all except in circular structures, like tanks, Sunderland began hearing about using prestressed concrete for things like bridges and buildings.

An engineer from Europe came in about once a week and had long talks with him and after that Sunderland was able to convince our management to let him spend real money on research and development in prestressed concrete.

At one point he said to me, 'Blair, you wait and see. You know the precast concrete products made in little shops all over the country, cut concrete blocks and square stones? You are going to see shops like that go up for making prestressed concrete, this is going to catch on'....He was ahead of his time, he could see what was coming. He was a great man.[62]

Sunderland and Birdsall tested various types of wires and strands for putting concrete under compression, and they installed some prototype prestressed concrete deck slabs for testing on their cable-truss office bridge at the Trenton Works.

USS John A. Roebling

Under the Navy's program to build Liberty Ships for transporting cargo, any group that raised $2 million in war bonds could propose a name for a ship. Thanks to J.A.R.'s Sons Co.'s War Bond Drives, the Navy announced in October, 1943, that its 286th 10,500-ton Liberty Ship under construction at the California Shipbuilding Corporation's shipyard in Wilmington, California, would be named the *USS John A. Roebling*. The 440 ft. ship was one of more than 2,700 Liberty Ships built during the war in 18 American shipyards.

With the Peace River Bridge and other defense contracts, the Company's sales grew by 9 percent in 1943 to the highest level of the Second World War, but because of the excessive profits negotiations with the government, operating profits fell nearly 29 percent. Although the Company's 1943 sales, in inflation adjusted numbers, almost doubled 1928 sales, the previous peak, 1943 operating profits were only 25 percent higher than those in 1928. Union wage scales and government price controls were now limiting the Company's profitability.

At the end of 1943, the Company held investments totaling $17 million (about $224 million in 2009), the largest holding being U.S. Government Bonds, Notes and Obligations, 45 percent of the total, and Otis Elevator stock, 17 percent. The total portfolio returned about 2.8 percent in income, and although the investments were almost equally divided between stocks and bonds, the stocks returned an average of 5 percent and the bonds an average of only 1 percent. The Directors were clearly investing patriotically, as their U.S. Government holdings returned far less than their stock holdings.

We do not think it a minor issue

By 1944, the "universal manpower shortage" had led the officers to make "every effort to recruit and carefully select employees willing and able to take their part in the Company's war production program. Women have been trained to perform men's jobs where ever possible. Jobs and machines have been restudied and revised to make work easier, safer and more efficient." While the Company saw the tight labor market as an opportunity to increase efficiency, it also paid some of the female employees less than the men they had replaced for the same work.[63]

When a War Labor Board arbitrator rejected a petition by the union in early 1944 for equal pay and seniority recognition for nineteen women in the aircraft cord department at the Trenton Works, all 2,700 workers at the plant walked out. B.F. McClancy, the Company's industrial relations manager, told a reporter: "Certainly, a minor difference between this company and such a small number of employees cannot justify a work stoppage involving 2,700 employees. Only the nation's enemies can profit from this walkout." Michael Harris, the United Steel Workers leader in Trenton, cited "the unwillingness of the company to give jobs back to discharged serviceman" as a contributing factor to the walkout. The War Labor Board ordered the striking employees to return to work while the Company and union settled the dispute.[64]

Another grievance involving a handful of workers shut down all the Company's plants that summer, after the foreman in the tempering shop at the Kinkora Works reassigned nine workers to lower-paying jobs. Over the next several days the nine men staged a slow-down that created a bottleneck in other departments, and when the foreman dismissed them, most of the other 3,000 workers in the plant walked out. A company spokesman termed the reassignments as a "minor dispute," but Charles Kovacs, president of Local 2111, told a reporter: "We do not think it a minor issue when the take-home pay of the men fired yesterday was reduced $24 to $30 a week."[65]

Three days later, 1,700 workers at the Trenton Works walked out in support of the nine fired men. The chairman of the War Labor Board sent Kovacs a telegram two days later stating that "your Government expects you to terminate this strike at once," but Kovacs ignored it for three days until the Board ordered the Company to rescind its dismissal of the nine men pending a hearing with union officials about the reassignments.[66]

A straight shooter

To meet its war production drive, the Directors had approved a "continuance in employment" in 1943 for 14 administrative employees and more than 100 production employees over the Company's mandatory retirement age of 65. Company President William Anderson, 74, topped the 1943 continuance list (see Fig. 6.65). After serving nearly 56 years with the Company, Anderson died at his home in Princeton in September, 1944.

A Trenton native and a cousin of Ferdinand Roebling, Jr., Anderson started as a time keeper in the wire mills in 1888 at the age of 18 and worked his way up to Superintendent of Wire Drawing. The Directors elected him to the Board in 1922, appointed him General Manager in 1923 and First Vice President and Treasurer in 1927, and elected him as President in 1936 to succeed Ferdinand Roebling, Jr. Upon his death, an employee quoted in the *War Worker* commented: "Affectionately referred to in the mills as 'Big Bill,' Mr. Anderson was a big man with a big heart who always had time to hear both sides of any story. His door was always open to any and all employees….Possessed of a remarkable memory, he was a stern but understanding man, a straight shooter."[67]

Figure 6.69:
Charles Roebling Tyson,
Roebling War Worker,
1943. RM
The grandson of
Charles Roebling,
Charlie Tyson graduated
from Princeton University
in 1936, joined the
Company as a Director
and employee that year,
and learned the business
working in the mills.
The Directors elected him
Secretary-Treasurer in 1941
and President in 1944
at the age of 29.

Fully aware of its obligation to the nation

With Lt. Joe Roebling, serving in the Army overseas, and Lt. Col. Ferd Roebling serving with the Army Corps of Engineers, the Directors elected Charles Roebling Tyson (Fig. 6.69) as President at the age of 29. Charlie, as everyone called him, proposed a new position of Company Chairman, and nominated Joe for the position, and the Directors approved.

In their Fifth War Bond Drive, the Company and the union set a goal of 90 percent employee participation to raise $250,000 to pay for two Army Air Force bombers. In less than three weeks, employees bought $517,000 (about $6.4 million in 2009) in bonds, enough to pay for four bombers. The Sixth War Loan Drive in November, 1944, set a goal of $500,000 and instead sold $640,000 (about $7.9 million) in four weeks

to pay for four tanks, three troop carriers, an amphibious truck and a jeep. The Seventh War Bond Drive in April, 1945, raised $609,000 (about $7.6 million) to pay for a B-29 Super-Fortress. As Charlie noted in the Annual Report for 1944:

During 1944 your company continued to devote substantially all of its productive and engineering facilities to aid in the prosecution of the war. On every battlefront around the globe, on the high seas, in the mines, oil fields and forests, in factories and munitions plants, the use of our products in such large quantities is ample evidence that a modern war cannot be fought without the use of wire and wire products (Fig. 6.70). Your company is fully aware of its obligation to the nation.

Profound tribute is paid to the 3,064 employees who left our Plants and Offices to enter the fight for our Country and particularly to the sixty-nine young men who made the supreme sacrifice. The number of veterans returning to work during the last few months has been indeed gratifying.

The reemployment of these experienced men and women has been a most helpful factor in improving our operations. We anticipate with pleasure the return in the near future of many of those still serving with the military forces.[68]

An inspiration to all

When the war ended on August 14, thousands celebrated on the streets in Trenton and Roebling. Among the many veterans returning to their Roebling jobs, Sgt. Kenneth E. Ibach stood out for his "heroic achievement" in combat (Fig. 6.71). As a private in the 10th Mountain Division in Careglio, Italy, Ibach risked his life capturing enemy soldiers in April, 1944. As the Division's commanding general noted in

Figure 6.70:
Roebling Aircraft Products ad,
Aero Digest, 1943.

Smoke in the Sky Spells Teamwork.
Smoke signals....mushroom up
mile-high, signaling the
end of ammunition dumps
and fuel tanks....
every one subtracting
days from the war....
We at Roebling are proud
of our part in that teamwork.
Proud that in the big job ahead
and in the peace that follows,
Roebling aircraft products
will carry their part of the load.

**Figure 6.71
Kenneth E. Ibach
Roebling War Worker,
1944. RM
Born in Trenton
and raised in Roebling,
Ken started at the Kinkora
Works in 1939
at the age of 20.
He earned a Bronze Star as
a "battlefield hero" during
the war and then returned
to the Kinkora Works,
where he worked
until it closed in 1974.**

Ibach's Bronze Star citation, "His conspicuous heroism was an inspiration to all who witnessed this brave deed, and has earned Private Ibach the highest commendation and praise." Ibach's wife Eloise worked for the Company in Standards Engineering during the war. He returned to the Kinkora Works Wire Mills, used the G.I. Bill to learn the masonry trade, and became a steel mill mason and then a foreman rebuilding furnaces, and worked until the plant closed in 1974.[69]

The War Department cancelled contracts worth $10 million (about $122 million) with the Company when the war ended, and its revenues in the last four months of 1945 fell by 35 percent. The Company's peacetime transition included layoffs so returning veterans could resume their jobs (see box).

"THE CHALLENGE of the days ahead!," *Trenton Sunday Times-Advertiser,* May 20, 1945

How one of America's great industrial concerns now devoted almost entirely to war work, plans to meet the challenge and responsibilities of peace....JOBS! It's America's number one postwar problem, and Roebling is doing something about it. Back of all the sweeping postwar plans and projects you read about is one major objective: jobs. Jobs for returning servicemen. Jobs for war workers. Jobs for all of us, so that we may enjoy the fruits of peace time production....better homes, new cars, a greater opportunity for ourselves and our children....When our fighting men come home to pick up the pursuits of peace, Roebling will be ready....

At Roebling the spirit of the pioneer still runs deep and strong, and it bodes well for the energy, courage and foresight with which postwar problems will be tackled...Roebling products will help rebuild the war-torn world. Wire in its endless thousands of forms is an essential servant of mankind, whether at war or in peace.

Product development that is ongoing will be one of the most vital forces in postwar prosperity. We are improving the quality of many wire products, designing types and forms to meet increasing and changing demands. The wire world of tomorrow is being born in the research laboratory today, and will be ready to make its contribution towards solving the problems of peace....

We acknowledge a great debt to the men of Roebling who have gone to war. Their sacrifice has been great....We intend to express our appreciation in a practical way....by setting up a system that ensures each servicemen returning to the best possible job for which he is fitted. To do this and to assure profitable employment through the years for all our employees who have been faithful to their wartime tasks means vision and planning on the part of every department. Roebling teamwork. With it we hope to do our share toward winning the peace....making better jobs for the men who have saved America for us, and a better world in which to live.

Union and management face the same problems and share the same opportunities for the future. In recent years union and management have worked as a team to gain the same great objective – win the war. This willingness to pitch in and do the job resulted in a tremendous upsurge of production.

The problems of peace that labor and management will face continued to be of mutual concern, and are closely linked with the happiness and well-being of all of us. The men at Roebling machines, and the leaders in their labor unions are keenly aware of this responsibility. They look forward to taking a place beside Roebling executives in an effort to make a smooth transition from war to peace, to do their part to assure jobs, loyal workers, and a bright future for America.

For every Roebling employee, good health, good working conditions, a chance for advancement, that is always our goal.

Getting the veteran back on the right job will be our major objective. We plan to consider each man's individual capacity and requirements, and place him where he can do the best work for himself and for the company.

Our plans continue for the improvement of facilities to ensure the best of health and working conditions for all Roebling employees. Only contented workers are good workers, and the welfare of our employees will always receive first consideration.

Production is the key to a stronger America in war or peace. History will record that it was the vast productive capacity of America that turned the tide of the war against enemy hordes. The cost was of secondary importance to getting the job done....

Roebling had kept pace with technological developments....and there will be ample opportunity and work for men with foresight who will help us achieve the important goals we have set.

Roebling products will spring from mighty machines to supply a postwar world. But even the most efficient machines need the guiding hand of skilled workers.

The Roebling bridge of tomorrow will incorporate new principles. War has accelerated development in bridge design as well as in other fields. New principles have been devised and tested, and will be incorporated in Roebling postwar bridges. Wire and wire rope will play an even greater role in the bridge of tomorrow, with the great savings in weight and result in economy. Thus in a tangible way Roebling will help to bridge the gap between demobilization and normal peacetime living.

With the war over, the *Roebling War Worker* editor offered a $100 Victory Bond for the best new name for the Company's newsletter, and George Acock of the Electrical Engineering Department won it for proposing *The Roebling Record*.

Phillip Murray and other United Steel Workers officials now believed that it was time for their members to benefit from wartime sacrifices, and in September they called for a 25 cent per hour wage increase. Contending that government price ceilings limited wage increases, Charlie Tyson proposed an alternative Income Security Plan with 26 weeks of pay for full time employees with five years of service who were laid off and who had exhausted their 26 weeks of State unemployment compensation. Tyson earlier told his fellow Directors that the Company's employment record over the past 16 years indicated that the Plan would generate little if any cost.

The United Steel Workers rejected this and other proposals by steel companies and called a general strike on January 21, 1946. With Roebling and most other steel plants shut down, negotiations dragged until the Federal Office of Price Administration assured steel company executives that it would raise price ceilings five to eight percent. Company and union representatives signed an agreement ending the strike on March 2. The contract provided an 18.5 cent per hour increase for common labor and included a union pledge "to cooperate with the company in an all-out effort to eliminate waste and to increase productivity….and to cooperate in securing a fair day's work from every member of the union."[70]

Ferd Roebling returned in early 1946 after five years in the U.S. Army with the rank of Lieutenant Colonel in the Officers Reserve Corps. At the Annual Meeting, the Directors appointed him Vice President of Engineering. Ferd was the fifth Roebling to head engineering, and three 4th generation Roeblings were now running the Company.

In some ways this 4th generation resembled the 2nd, though with some switched roles. While Ferdinand, Sr., had managed the business, his grandson, Ferd, now oversaw engineering. Where Charles, an engineer, had managed production, his grandson, Charlie, now ran the business side. Washington and Joe both helped run the Company without operating responsibilities. With personal and financial stakes in the Company's history and future, the three young Roeblings would now oversee a golden postwar era of the family business that the changing times would make all too brief (Fig. 6.72).

To enhance post-war production, the Directors instituted a Building and Equipment Program "to reduce manufacturing costs, improve quality and expand capacities in those profitable

Figure 6.72: *Maintaining a family tradition of active company management.* **4th Generation Roeblings, 1952. RMg left to right Joseph M. Roebling Chairman, Ferdinand W. Roebling III Vice President - Engineering, Charles Roebling Tyson President**

lines were future growth is indicated." The $6 million (about $71 million in 2009) program, the Company's largest plant investment since the late 1920s, represented about 50 percent of the book value of its land, buildings and equipment. The program included major upgrades in the Wire Rope, Cold Rolled Products, and Electrical Wire divisions, in Maintenance and Power, and in the copper and steel mills.[71]

For the growing auto industry, the Company developed new wire products for seat springs, valve springs and tires, the latter to replace cotton cording. To prepare for the anticipated growth of the ski industry, the engineering department developed a triple line of ski lifts. To serve the growing suburban population, the Company introduced the *Roebling Lawn Mower – the Lawn Mower of the Future* (Fig. 6.73).

Figure 6.73 *The New Roebling Rotary Power Mower, 1946. RU*

Built on an entirely new principle... to save time and work, and give you a more healthier, beautiful lawn.

The Roebling mower leaves an even, beautiful green carpet behind it.

While Charles, Ferdinand and Washington had originally sought a four percent return on their investment in Roebling village, the Company had operated it over four decades largely as an amenity for its Kinkora workers (Fig. 6.74). The housing had given the Roeblings some leverage over their employee tenants, since they could dismiss and evict them on a week's notice, but the union contract now prevented quick dismissals.

In September, 1946, Treasurer Archibald Brown, who had started with the Company in 1902, reported to the Directors that it had spent $3.3 million (about $39.3 million) to build the village, but that its depreciated book value was now $760,000 (about $9.1 million). Over the past 28 years the Company had lost $1.3 million (about $16.1 million) operating the village, an average of $47,000 annually (about $562,000). Real estate brokers estimated the value of the village as a whole at $2 million (about $23 million), but selling the 752 houses and 15 commercial buildings individually would bring more.

The Directors decided to sell the buildings individually and to donate the streets and park to Florence Township due to "the operating losses, the inability to secure Office of Price Administration approval for rent increases, the risks in operating the Village and in furnishing utilities and services, such as police and fire protection, gas and electricity, street maintenance, etc.; and the Company's proposed program of capital expenditures, the cost of which could in part be defrayed by the proceeds from the sale of the Village properties."[72]

At a meeting with union officials, Archibald Brown said that the Directors had decided to sell the village several years ago and had received a "very attractive offer" from a mid-western firm. They decided, however, to sell the houses individually to "see to it that not too much hardship was placed on the tenants." Brown assured the group that "no one on pension would be put out on the streets if they were unable to meet the price asked for and all disabled persons would be shown special considerations....The company would also work out a suitable solution for those people who were to encounter hardships in meeting the down payment."[73]

The Directors engaged the Clarke Real Estate Company to appraise the homes and commercial buildings and prepare them for sale starting on January 1, 1947. Tenants had first preference, followed by Roebling employees with the highest seniority, and then war veterans, who also qualified for Federal Housing Agency mortgages and could purchase their parents' home. A *New York Herald Tribune* reporter noted some complaints about the house prices, but also that: "Many employees say they are digging into old-age nest eggs to purchase homes they cannot bear to leave."[74]

Figure 6.74: Roebling, New Jersey, Main Street, 1947. RM

By March, Charlie Tyson reported that it was "gratifying to know of the large percentage of Village residents who have indicated their willingness to purchase the houses they now occupy" (see box). The Company sold nearly all the properties in 1947 and netted $2.7 million (about $30 million in 2009), and it also donated its garage at Hornberger and Second Avenues to Florence Township for use as an ambulance house.

Many families that had saved money were able to buy houses on "better streets" than their own because of their seniority and in many cases their war service as well, and the ethnic character of some of the streets started to change.[75]

"Residents Agree to Buy Jersey Village Built for Employees of John A. Roebling," - *The New York Times*, **February 1, 1947**

A majority of the occupants of the 752 company houses in this village of 3,000 met today's deadline with offers to purchase the homes they or their parents have lived in for 40 years as employees of John A. Roebling's Sons Co., wire manufacturers....

Archibald W. Brown, treasurer of the Roebling company, said the majority of the townspeople are paying cash for their homes, while others are financing the purchase through the Federal Housing Authority or their banks....

The residents have been paying the company from $18 to $30 a month rent for the single and double brick buildings, ranging in size from four to nine rooms. They were sold to their occupants at prices ranging from $3,000 to $6,500 (about $33-71,000), while three mansions were sold to company officials at $16,000 (about $177,000)....

Florence Township is absorbing the entire Roebling community, the four miles of streets and the sewerage and street systems, having been deeded free to the Township by the Company on Jan. 1.

We depend on each other.

In his first "Report to Employees" in March, 1947, Charlie Tyson reported 1946 revenues of $33 million (about $369 million in 2009), a 45 percent decline from their peak in 1943, and operating income of $99,000 (about $1 million), a meager .3 percent of sales and a 99 percent drop from the wartime peak in 1942. The Company had increased the average wage of its 6,500 employees by 112% since 1936, while the cost of living had increased by only 54%. As Charlie Tyson noted:

> *It is our purpose to keep the men and women of the Roebling Company more fully informed as to developments and conditions within our organization. It is our belief that you will want to know more about our mutual problems....*
>
> *Job security and stability depend primarily on whether the company is in a healthy condition or an unhealthy condition, whether it makes money or loses money. All of us like to play on a winning team....*
>
> *It can be seen from the distribution of our sales dollar that it is not management, not the owners, not the workers, but the combined effort of all which makes the business go.*
>
> *The heart of our organization is the men and women whose knowledge, skill, ability and cooperative efforts make the difference between success and failure....*
>
> *Roebling is a good place to work. We take pride that we are an important part of it. For us to continue to have that pride, Roebling must continue to be a good place in which to work and continue to be an organization worthy of that pride.*
>
> *To these ends our efforts will be devoted. It is not a one-man job. Each of us must do his share. We depend on each other.*

Charlie reported to the Directors that the 1946 strike cost $1 million (about $12 million) in operating profits. The Company's 1946 union contract expired on April 30, and while the union had reached agreements with U.S. Steel and several other companies for about one third of its 850,000 members, no agreement had been reached after seven weeks of negotiations with the remaining companies, including Roebling. The steel workers walked out on May 1, and as Charlie later noted:

> *The precise reason for the strike still remains obscure. No economic issues were involved as we had offered the same wage increases and other liberalizations as those generally agreed upon by the basic steel industry and the United Steel Workers. The strike completely paralyzed production for three weeks. It was orderly in that there were no mass picket lines, no violence and no attempt to interfere with office employees entering or leaving the company's premises.*[76]

Company and union representatives settled the strike with an average 12.5-cents-per-hour pay increase plus additional benefits. Charlie estimated that this strike cost $500,000, (about $5.5 million) in operating profit and that the new contract would cost an additional $2 million (about $22 million) annually. He cautiously also noted that:

> *Unfortunately, some employees have been imbued by their union leadership with the philosophy that they should fall into the path of those who expect to obtain better living for less effort and less enterprise. Certainly the results of the workers adopting this philosophy in the European nations should provide the correct solution to this condition.*

Like most other business owners and leaders, the Roeblings were alarmed about the spread of Communism and socialism in Europe, and they worked to reinforce American values of freedom and initiative in their communities. As the Roebling Company noted in *Trenton Magazine* (see box):

> *Today, we enjoy comforts and pleasures that were undreamed of a hundred years ago - that are unknown to the people of other countries even today.*
>
> *Our future looks even brighter if our desire for a more abundant life is strong enough to impel us to create it as our fathers have created what we are enjoying....if we continue to improve the output of our minds and our hands....*
>
> *Our kind of well-being is the product of creative, not covetous minds. It is made with tools, not with weapons. It will flourish only so long as we place no limits on individual achievement, so long as we use our heads instead of our fists.*

"What Do YOU See In the Future?"
- *Trenton Magazine*, June 1947

Life seems more complicated today.

Just about now the world appears to be in pretty much of a mess. Some of us are lost completely in the wilderness of theories and 'isms' that surround us and have given up trying to find our own way....All the theories and isms can not alter the fact that life depends upon our ability to earn a living.... or that our American Way has produced the greatest nation on earth, enjoying the world's highest standards of living.

All the theorists and neoists cannot change these fundamentals: Business is the exchange of money for goods and services. Our earning power depends upon our ability to supply these goods or services.

But our earning power also depends upon our neighbors. We can prosper only as our community prospers - as our country prospers – and as the company with which we are connected prospers....Too many people fail to realize that these simple fundamentals are the basis of all sound business - that they are the key to every man's welfare. Let those of us cling to these fundamentals who want our children to inherit a country that continues to offer freedom and equal opportunity for all. - John A. Roebling's Sons Company.

Figure 6.75 (above): J.A.R.'s Sons Co. General Office, 1947. TPL Employees at 640 South Broad Street, Trenton, admiring the new *Roebling Magazine*. At left is Peter Rossi, Public Relations head.

Figure 6.76 (below left): *Roebling Magazine,* **1948. TPL** General Store salesgirl Mary Arnold Montalto helps newlewed employees Harold & Jean Miller select paint for their new home in Roebling.

The great American 'melting pot' in action

In October, 1947, the Company began publishing *Roebling* - a monthly magazine of "stories and pictorial reviews of products and the Roebling line the world around" (Figs. 6.75-76). *Roebling Magazine* celebrated the American way of life with articles like "Roebling, New Jersey, An American Community," which noted that the 3,500 residents had access to a General Store, food market, drugstore, dentist,

physicians, barbershop, a bank, a motion picture theatre with "the latest in Hollywood offerings," parent-teacher and civic associations, social clubs, lodges, an American Legion Post, and six churches - Methodist, Roman Catholic, two Greek Catholic, Greek Orthodox, and Hungarian Reformed. *Roebling* also celebrated the local diversity:

> *Working together in close community cooperation are people not too far removed from more than one half dozen European countries. With its commendable civic consciousness, a sense of community responsibility, and it's highly developed group loyalty, the town of Roebling is an outstanding example of the great American 'melting pot' in action (Fig. 6.77).*[77]

Charlie Tyson cited the Roebling, N.J., article as "timely and appropriate in light of today's unsettled conditions, setting out as it does the vital importance of the community as the basic unit in our American system....Healthy communities almost of a certainty make for progressive counties, States, and when viewed cumulatively, progressive, democratic nations." In the following issue, Tyson wrote:

> *Roebling management firmly believes in the American system of free enterprise, a system under which labor and management working together in harmony, provide a winning combination against which the blast of foreign 'isms' of all shades and descriptions prove fruitless.*[78]

The International Council of Industrial Editors gave *Roebling Magazine* its Highest Award rating among 3,000 industrial publications in 1948, including a perfect score in "accomplishment of purpose."[79]

Figure 6.77: *Roebling Magazine,* **1948. TPL** To promote understanding and tolerance of the many different backgrounds of Company employees, *Roebling* featured articles on ethnic cooking and other family traditions.

Figure 6.78: "Blue Center," *Roebling Magazine*, **1947. TPL Bridge Engineer Normal Sollenberger, right, and other employees used the Company airplane to attend the opening of the 423 ft. span Hal W. Adams Bridge, which the Company erected in 1947 with Prestressed Roebling Bridge Strand.**

Roebling Magazine also featured articles on "Blue Center," the Company's five-passenger Beechcraft airplane that enabled "top management to make important sales contacts and attend vital conferences with a minimum of delay (Fig. 6.78):"[84]

> *With the purchase of this ultramodern, five passenger Beechcraft, Roebling joins the ranks of those progressive, wide-awake firms throughout the nation who are utilizing air power to further improve and strengthen their sales effort and customer relationships.*[80]

Being Squeezed

Revenues rebounded 45 percent in 1947, but profits were only two percent of sales, less than a third the average American manufacturing profits. In his 1947 Annual Report to stockholders, Charlie cited the May strike and the resulting wage and benefit increases as "adversely affecting" profits, but the biggest problem was the Company's inability to raise prices to reflect its increased materials costs:

> *Since the elimination of government price controls, the cost of pig iron and scrap has increased 65%, whereas the average price of wire and wire rope, our principal product groups consuming these materials, has advanced but 19%.*[81]

The Company's head of sales also noted "the narrow spread between cost and selling prices caused by our position in the steel industry. The large integrated steel firms profit from the sale of materials to us while restricting price increases of fabricated materials they sell in competition."[82]

In his 1947 Report to Employees, Charlie cautioned:

> *The year found us being squeezed between increased costs of materials we purchase and prices we receive for selling our products. In our Company both material costs and selling prices are mainly determined by our larger competitors.*
>
> *This is a serious problem and one which we must continue to face, for the security of us all is at stake. The Company must continue to make money if our jobs are to be secure.*[83]

The meager profits prompted Charlie to examine long-term capital needs, as he told the Directors, in early 1948:

> *For the first time in the Company's history a long-range capital program had been projected....in two surveys, one by the Freyn Engineering Company, of Chicago, covering our Open Hearth, Blooming Mill and attendant facilities and one by our Production Division concerning all other plant and equipment needs. The Freyn survey offered several alternate plans at costs ranging from $2-$10 million (about $19-96 million in 2009) to put our steelmaking facilities on a basis competitive with larger integrated steel companies.*
>
> *Since the cost requirements of such a program are out of proportion to the resources of the Company, relating as they did to but one Division of the Company, it appeared to the management advisable that we should - First, maintain our steelmaking facilities as now constituted, effecting such minimum improvements as would yield a quick return; and, Second, continue efforts to purchase rerolling billets whenever market conditions permit.*
>
> *The Production Division has compiled a list of replacements and improvements in all other manufacturing facilities that should be undertaken within the next several years and would cost approximately $10 million. On average such expenditures would provide a return of at least 10% per annum through cost reduction, assuming an average level of operations of two shifts per day, five days per week, forty weeks per year. This program should be spread over six or seven years in order that it be financed within the bounds of our financial resources without resort to borrowing.*[84]

Charlie continued the Roebling aversion to borrowing and the Company's reliance on its investment portfolio for capital funds when needed. At the end of 1947, the portfolio had a value of $15 million (about $145 million), only 50 percent more than just the Production Division's required "replacements and improvements," and certainly not enough to modernize steel production. In the early 20th Century, Charles, Ferdinand, and Washington had sufficient funds to build their own steel mill and the adjacent village and they didn't have to consult with anyone else. Now, the Company would have to borrow money to fully modernize, and 35 family stockholders had a say in any decision to do so.

Figure 6.79 (left):
Roebling Magazine,
1949. TPL
By the 1949 season,
J.A.R.'s Sons Co. had
installed Roebling T-Bar lifts
and chair lifts at ski resorts
in the Pocono Mountains in
Pennsylvania, in New York,
Massachusetts, Vermont, New
Hampshire and Quebec.

Figure 6.80 (right):
Roebling Magazine,
1947. TPL
Roebling Assistant Chief
Engineer Blair Birdsall
walking on a J.A.R.'s Sons Co.
natural gas pipeline bridge
over the Colorado River
in Colorado.

Widespread use

By 1947, the Roebling Bridge Division was capitalizing on its heritage and innovations to secure a variety of projects in the expanding postwar economy. As a Company brochure noted:

During the early days of his career John A. Roebling introduced the novelty of the aerial tramway....a wire rope stretched between two towers from which a suspended carriage transported across a stream the materials he needed to construct a bridge. This method of haulage rapidly came into widespread use, especially where waterways, marshes or rugged terrain made the conveyance of materials a slow, difficult and expensive operation.[85]

The Division built a 10 mile tramway over the continental divide at an elevation of 15,500 ft. in Peru to deliver 50 tons of copper ore per hour. It also outfitted "Skyhook" tramways built by the Pointer-Willamette Company in Portland, Oregon, for hauling logs in Oregon, sugar cane in Hawaii, and pipeline equipment in Saudi Arabia for the Arabian American Oil Company. To serve the growing ski industry, the Division licensed some technology from Switzerland and developed a line of Roebling Ski Lifts (Fig. 6.79). It also built several unique pipeline bridges for gas companies in several states to meet the demand for gas in the expanding postwar economy, including one over the Colorado River in Colorado (see Fig. 6.80).

The Division also secured three important bridge contracts in 1948. Charles Sunderland, Blair Birdsall and Norman Sollenberger, who joined the Division in 1945 (see Fig. 6.78), got their first chance to build a public cable-stiffened bridge, an innovation which Sunderland and Birdsall had developed during the war (see Figs. 6.67-68), when state officials decided to replace an 1856 covered bridge over the Delaware River between Raven Rock, New Jersey, and Lumberville, Pennsylvania. The Roebling engineers designed and erected a five-span cable-stiffened bridge, with the longest span at 156 ft., and built it on top of the 1856 stone piers (Fig. 6.81).

Figure 6.81: Lumberville Bridge, *Roebling Magazine,* **1950. TPL**
Roebling bridge engineers combined their cable stiffening and prestressed concrete innovations in this 688 ft. long footbridge, which remains a popular crossing on the Delaware River today.

A thoroughly absorbing subject

Figure 6.82: San Marcos Bridge, El Salvador, c1952. RM Roebling engineers completed their largest cable-stiffened bridge with 5-spans in 1952. Guerillas destroyed it in 1981.

The bridge was a product of the unique engineering, fabrication, and construction expertise of the J.A.R.'s Sons Co. Bridge Division. No other design firm in the world was able to design and construct such a bridge, much less advance the concept.[89]

Roebling bridge engineers underbid their competitors by 20 percent with a cable-stiffened design for a bridge near San Marcos in El Salvador (Fig. 6.82). They encountered many challenges building the innovative bridge at its remote site, and Blair Birdsall later noted in *Civil Engineering*, "for all who have been connected with it, either in design or construction, the structure is a thoroughly absorbing subject, with countless facets of general and professional interest." He called the bridge "a memorial to Charles Sunderland's vision and genius."[86]

The engineers won a $3 million contract (about $30 million in 2009) with the Washington State Toll Bridge Authority for the cables of the new Tacoma Narrows Bridge to replace the "Galloping Gertie" suspension bridge that had dramatically collapsed just four months after it opened in 1940. Like its predecessor, the new 2,800 ft. span bridge was the third longest suspension bridge when it opened (Fig. 6.83).

Figure 6.83: Tacoma Narrows Bridge, c1952. WSR Roebling bridgemen built the 20 in. cables for the 2,800 ft. span bridge that replaced the infamous "Galloping Gertie" bridge that collapsed in 1940. The new bridge soon became known as "Sturdy Gertie."

A steel industry wage increase of nine percent in 1948 raised the cost of pig iron for the Company, but it couldn't raise prices because its competitors didn't. An economic downturn began in the fall, but the Company's revenues that year reached "an all-time high, excluding the abnormal war years, of $49.9 million" (about $482 million). Operating profits, however, were only $879,000 (about $8.4 million), just 1.6 percent of sales, which, as Charlie Tyson told the Directors, "is certainly not satisfactory when related to the high volume of business." The Directors decreased dividends for the first time in 10 years, by 22 percent. In his Report to Employees, Charlie cautioned:[87]

> *The financial results of 1948 are certainly not good. The Company operated at a loss from January through August, partly because of the continued squeeze between our cost of materials purchased and the selling price of our products. Over these two basic business factors your Company has little control. We do however have control over our manufacturing operations. Here the more efficient use of manpower and machines results in lower, competitive costs.*
>
> *Profits are essential to pay for use of plant, equipment, tools and materials, and the owner is entitled to a fair return on his investment. Out of retained profits must come the money to pay for new plant and equipment. Without profits our business becomes stagnant; our prosperity, our hopes for a better living, and even our security are placed in jeopardy.*
>
> *The conditions here at Roebling are serious. There was ample evidence observed by you in 1948 that the company invested large sums of money in improved plant and equipment. This investment is far greater than the profits realized in 1948, but this alone is not enough to assure a healthy and secure institution. The sure strength of a company is in the keeping of those men and women whose daily efforts spell our greater production. If we falter, our Company falters.*
>
> *The average Roebling employee has been with the Company nearly 17 years. This means that by and large we are mature people, who intend to continue as Roebling employees. If this be true, let us be honest with ourselves and our Company. It is only through hard work and intelligent cooperation that we can hope to find the road to good living and security. Let each of us carry his allotted share of the load.*[88]

As sales declined in early 1949, the Directors authorized Charlie to borrow up to $1.5 million (about $13.4 million) to cover operating expenses without tapping their investments.

Figure 6.84 (left): Rio Paz Bridge, Guatemala-El Salvador Border, 1949. RR Roebling engineers built the 210 ft. span with their innovative prestressed bridge strand and prestressed concrete. Figure 6.85 (right): Construction of Walnut Lane Bridge, Philadelphia, 1949. RM With its 160 ft. span concrete girders made with Roebling "stress relieved wires," this groundbreaking bridge over the Schuylkill River "inspired the creation of the precast/prestressed concrete industry." The ASCE designated the bridge an "Outstanding Civil Engineering Achievement" in 1977.[93]

An American invention

Roebling bridge engineers marked a new "epoch in the construction of highway bridges" in 1949 with the opening of "the first all-prefabricated, all prestressed bridge" in a remote location on the border between Guatemala and El Salvador (Fig. 6.84). They used Roebling prestressed bridge strand for the cables, and made concrete walkway and deck slabs on-site using other innovative prestressed strand. At a presentation on "the Roebling method of pre-stressed concrete" to the American Society of Civil Engineers (ASCE), Blair Birdsall noted another innovative project (Fig. 6.85):[90]

> *The Walnut Lane Memorial Bridge in Philadelphia, now under construction, will be equipped with prestressed concrete girders which use a wire of special properties developed by the Company after years of extensive research and development.*

He called these special "stress-relieved wires....an American invention....(and) an improvement over European prestressing steels." The Company soon started advertising "Roebling Prestressed Concrete Wire and Strand" (Fig. 6.86).[91]

Figure 6.86: *Today it's Roebling* **ad, 1950. After years of testing, J.A.R.'s Sons Co. proudly marketed** *Americanized Prestressed Concrete - an exclusive Roebling development.*

"Prestressed Concrete," *Roebling Magazine,* **1950**

Out of the laboratory era and into practical, everyday application, the Roebling principle of prestressed concrete has definitely come of age....Roebling engineers sought to develop more suitable and simplified methods and found a reliable material in galvanized bridge wire....

Analyzing the results of the several applications in which the Roebling design and construction principle has been used to date, Company engineers confidently predict a bright future for this new type of prestressing system.

Meanwhile, constant research and development operations involving the prestressing of concrete continue to move forward in the Roebling laboratories and additional, practical uses, for the new products are being uncovered daily.[92]

The Company's principal trouble spots

Despite the progress in prestressed concrete products, the Bridge Division lost money in 1949 because of wage and price increases and delays from severe weather and an earthquake on the Tacoma Narrows Bridge. The Company's revenues fell nine percent in 1949 and it reported an operating loss of $580,000 (about $5 million in 2009), but thanks to investment portfolio profits, it posted a profit of $55,000 (about $491,000).

The Company lost money on wire rope, its signature product, because of competitors' prices, but as Charlie Tyson told the stockholders, "The Company's principal trouble spots were the Electrical Wire and Woven Wire Fabrics Divisions" (Fig. 6.87), which the Ford, Bacon & Davis report had predicted ten years earlier. Fourteen other companies made insulated electrical wire at an average 4.6 percent profit, and "several principal competitors own their own copper ore mines," which enabled them to produce their electrical wire at lower cost. Charlie reorganized the latter division and discontinued unprofitable products, including the Roebling Lawn Mower, which after three years had lost $639,000 (about $5.7 million).[94]

Charlie had increased sales through distributors, as Ford Bacon & Davis had recommended, and now had 246 wire rope agents and 252 electrical wire distributors around the country, but the consultants' assessment of the various Roebling product lines remained true. Wire, wire rope, woven wire fabrics and electrical wire profits all continued to be squeezed by larger competitors with lower production costs. The Cold Rolled Products Division that produced specialty flatwire remained the only consistently profitable line.

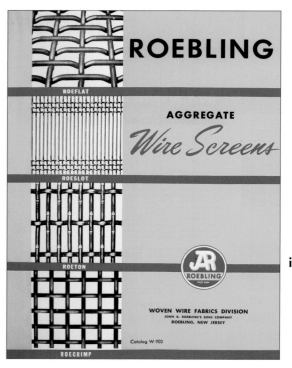

Figure 6.87: *Roebling Aggregate Wire Screen,* c1948. RU Started by Ferdinand Roebling in the 1870s to use up excess wire, the Woven Wire Fabrics Division produced a variety of products from insect to industrial screens, but its profits were limited by larger competitors with lower costs.

As business picked in early 1950, Charlie raised prices to boost profits about $1 million (about $9 million), and hired a management consultant to help improve operations. When wire mill workers staged a two-day strike, he sued the union for damages and leased one of the mills to the Standard Steel Spring Co. of Coraopolis, Pa., for making auto springs.

Shoulder to shoulder as a strong confident team

The start of the Korean War on June 25 spiked the demand for steel products, and in August 1,400 workers walked out of the Trenton rope shops to protest "the installation of two new machines...that would require attendance of only one man for both." While the union had not authorized the strike, it halted wire rope production for nearly four weeks.[95]

President Truman in September set up wage and price controls and signed the Defense Production Act authorizing the requisition of factories for national defense. When China entered the war in October, people began hoarding food and other basics, and steel producers had trouble filling orders. The Company added 600 employees in 1950, revenues climbed 20 percent to $54 million (about $492 million), and profits rebounded to $2 million (about $24.7 million), 4.6 percent of revenues. During the "unpleasant" downturn of 1949, Charlie had asked for "the cooperation and help of all of our employees." Now he told them in the 1950 Employees Report:

> Today we can say that a goodly majority of us did meet that challenge in splendid fashion. During the course of our last year important changes were affected....to strengthen our production and marketing efforts and to improve our overall efficiency as a business organization....
>
> During 1950, products manufactured by Roebling Co. employees in the mills at Trenton and Roebling were sold to customers located in every part of the United States. The Company's Export Division promoted the sale of Roebling products in world markets. Wire rope was sent to the coal fields, the logging camps and the mining centers. Cold rolled products serviced the automotive industry. New bridges by Roebling were built in Central and South America. Electrical wires and cables and screen cloth were purchased for use in scores of diversified trades and industries....
>
> This is a picture of industrial progress from which we can all quite rightly derive satisfaction. Your Company today is in a healthy condition. We are in good shape.
>
> One of the dangers facing us now is complacency. Though we met last year's challenge, today's fast-moving events make it imperative that all of us resolve to maintain a high degree of conscientious effort if we are to continue to move forward along the road of industrial prosperity....I personally know that all of us will face future months resolutely, standing shoulder to shoulder as a strong, confident team.[96]

Roebling Magazine. TPL **Figure 6.88 (left): "Strikeout Queen" Kathy "Tink" Dougherty of the Championship Roebling Girls Softball Team at a 1950 game. Figure 6.89 (center): The Company's Roebling Baseball Team defeated its Trenton Team in 1951. Figure 6.90 (right): Football in Roebling, N.J., enjoys a long tradition of winning and avid community support that continues today.**

You don't lose, you win

In the post World War II prosperity, employees increased their participation in Company-sponsored sports, and the communities around the factories embraced them, particularly in Roebling (Figs. 6.88-90). As Roebling resident and former railroad engineer Lonnie Brown recalled in a 2008 interview:

> *Our big thing was football, and 'nobody's gonna beat us' - that was the attitude we had. We went out on a football field and we were sure we were going to win and we really played hard and we kind of had a tradition - 'you don't lose, you win.'*[97]

A considerable amount of obsolete equipment

The Company increased its dividends in 1950 to $1.1 million (about $10 million), which was about 72 percent of the typical dividends it paid during World War II and less than one third of the high dividends of the 1920s. Since 1945, the Company had distributed about 66 percent of its net profits in dividends, as compared to the 40 percent distributed by the large steel companies. From 1946 to 1950, the Company had invested $13.4 million (about $121 million) in capital improvements, "to restore obsolete equipment, to reduce costs, and to improve quality." The Company took a total depreciation in plant and equipment during that period of $5.7 million (about $51.5 million), leaving a net capital investment of $7.7 million (about $69.6 million). As Joe Roebling told the Directors,

> *It is expected that this considerable excess of capital expenditures over depreciation will continue for some time.*

> *We still have a considerable amount of obsolete equipment; one of the outstanding examples is the Blooming Mill, the replacement of which - at a cost of some $6 or $7 million - we will be confronted with in the not too distant future....*

> *The Company does not expect to maintain the current rate of profits. It is almost certain that we will not be able to increase prices to the extent that our material, and particularly our labor costs, will increase, and our margin of profit is also decreasing because of regulations and the increased requirements of less profitable defense orders.*[98]

The Company's financing of the 1946-1950 improvements drained its investment portfolio from $17 million (about $153.6 million) to $7.4 million (about $42.5 million). Charlie Tyson investigated raising capital through a Roebling stock offering, but the investment bankers he consulted valued the stock at only $55 per share (about $497), including the investment portfolio, and he abandoned the idea. The Directors allocated $617,000 (about $5.5 million) in 1951 for additional improvements to be financed from investments and profits.[99]

The Bridge Division contracted with Bethlehem Steel in 1951 to supply footbridge equipment and prestressed bridge strands and for the 1,600 ft. span Chesapeake Bay Bridge in Maryland for $800,000 (about $7.1 million). Bethlehem was using specialty products and equipment pioneered by Roebling and making the big profits because it won the contract to build the entire bridge. As Ford, Bacon & Davis had predicted in 1939, J.A.R.'s Sons Co. could no longer compete against the big steel companies on cable contracts, and this diminished it's prospects for remaining an independent producer.

Besides the Company's problems, several third-generation Roeblings, including John A. Roebling II, 84, the largest stockholder with 18.4 percent of the shares, faced the prospect of having their estates tied up for years in disputes with the Internal Revenue Service over the value of their stock.

At a special Directors meeting in May, 1951, at the Stacy-Trent Hotel in Trenton, Chairman Joe Roebling requested authority to establish a subcommittee "to explore the possibilities of a merger with a fully integrated steel company," which he said "will offer substantial benefits to the stockholders of this Company." The Directors authorized Joe, Charlie Tyson and T.G. Wharton confidentially "to direct and review negotiations with a fully integrated steel company looking toward a merger or other combination of business with such a company on a basis calculated to accomplish the following results for the stockholders of this Corporation:"[100]

1) A larger dividend return on the stockholders' investment than they are currently receiving in this Corporation,
2) Substituting for their present stock holdings, through a tax-free exchange of stock, marketable securities which could be readily disposed of by individual stockholders in accordance with their own estate requirements and wishes to diversify their investments and which would be subject to ready evaluation for transfer and estate tax purposes.

The Roebling family had seriously considered selling their Company at least three times before. Ferdinand had opposed a sale to the American Steel & Wire Co. in 1898, the three Roebling brothers had turned down an offer in 1912, and Washington had turned down another in 1922. The majority of the stockholders now agreed that selling was their best option, and the Directors engaged McKinsey & Co. of New York to help negotiate with potential buyers.

Thanks to the Korean War and a construction boom, Company revenues grew 23 percent in 1951 to a record $66.7 million (about $595 million in 2009). The war and recent plant upgrades helped push operating profits up 112 percent to $5.9 million (about $52.4 million), and the Directors increased dividends by 54 percent and refunded the investment portfolio to $15 million (about $133.7 million).

A critical shortage in structural steel accelerated the acceptance of prestressed concrete in buildings and bridges, as it reduced the amount of steel required by 60-80 percent. The Bridge Division developed prefabricated strands at the Kinkora Works for imbedding in concrete at construction sites, and by the end of 1951, the Company had produced wire, strand and fittings for eight bridges, two stadiums and two

Cuban Prestressed Concrete Bridge Nears Completion

Figure 6.91: 246-ft. span Las Canas Bridge, Cuba, 1952. RR
The increasing acceptance of prestressed concrete was gratifying for Charles C. Sunderland, who had initiated the Company's research and production of prestressed products. The Cuban Government used the Roebling specialty products in four bridges.

buildings, and had orders for five more bridges (Fig. 6.91), a seven-story garage, and a dome. As the editor of *The Roebling Record* noted: "With the expanding program of Prestressed Concrete construction throughout the country, Roebling anticipates increased production of prestressing materials."[101]

The interest in prestressed concrete was gratifying for Charles C. Sunderland (Fig. 6.92), who had developed the Company's prestressed products during World War II, as he celebrated his 50th anniversary with the Company in December, 1951. Born in Yorkshire, England, Sunderland had started as a draftsman in the Roebling Bridge and Tramway Department in New York in 1901. He became Assistant Engineer under Charles Roebling in Trenton in 1905, and then the Chief Engineer of the Bridge and Tramway and the Wire Rope Departments in 1910. The Directors elected him to the Board in 1929, when he established the Bridge Division.

At a banquet in Trenton in his honor, he told his friends and colleagues: "Looking back over the 50 years I have spent with the Roebling Company doesn't seem that long as the years have been full and happy ones for me." In his engineering work for the Company over five decades, Sunderland distinguished himself in the tradition of the great Roebling engineers. He resigned in May, 1952, and died in July.[102]

In February, 1952, John A. Roebling II died at his home in Bernardsville. The only child of Washington and Emily Warren Roebling, John had graduated in 1888 from Rensselaer Polytechnic Institute in Troy, New York, where his father graduated in 1857. The Directors appointed Judge Clarence Case of Somerville, John II's executor, to the Board to represent his estate's share of Company stock.[103]

Charles C. Sunderland

*The career of Charles C. Sunderland was one of outstanding
and notable performance in the field of suspension bridges,
aerial tramways and prestressed concrete. Recognized as one
of the world's foremost bridge engineers, his work in these
fields made possible such achievements as the world's longest
suspension bridge, the Golden Gate Bridge, the adoption of
the mono cable Tramway, and the expanding use of prestressed
concrete in the construction of bridges and buildings....
His work in expanding the economic use of suspension
bridges through the prestressing of ropes and cables,
the adoption of parallel strand cables, and the development
of the cable stiffening principle, has made possible
the erection of major suspension bridges with
a resultant reduction in costs and increase in quality....
In prestressed concrete, his research has led toward new
applications for Roebling products, placing the company
in its present position as one of the leaders.*

- The Roebling Record, August 8, 1952

"After long and careful consideration," Charlie Tyson announced that March that the Directors had decided to "discontinue all operations of the Woven Wire Fabrics Division" at the Kinkora Works. Tyson revealed that the Division had "not been profitable for a great many years:"

*Because the foreseeable future not only fails to promise
any improvement, but instead promises a continued drain on
the Company's resources, it was reluctantly concluded that it
is in the Company's best interests to cease this operation.*

*During the past several years, the Company had exerted
a tremendous effort and gone to great expense to make the
operation of this Division a competitive enterprise....*

*It was impossible despite the fact that our geographical
location in relation to the market is favorable, our supply
of raw material has been adequate, our volume of sales has
been good, and the equipment used for a producing the
finished product has been made competitive....*

*Despite the effort and expense of the Company, we did
not become competitive in the fields of manpower costs
and manpower productivity. These two vitally important
factors have fallen far short of the improvement necessary to
continue operations.*[104]

Ferdinand and Charles had started producing woven wire fabrics 74 years earlier as a way to sell additional wire, and this business had never made much money, but the Directors were no longer willing to carry it now that they were trying to sell the Company. Tyson ultimately sold the Woven Wire Fabrics Division machinery for $500,000 (about $4.1 million in 2009).

Seizure of the Company's properties

After months of meetings and hearings with the national Wage Stabilization Board, negotiators from the steel industry and the United Steel Workers failed to reach an agreement on a new contract, and USW President Phillip Murray set a strike deadline of 12:01 AM on April 9. President Truman believed that a strike would harm the war effort, and he announced at 10:30 PM on April 8 that the government was seizing the nation's steel mills under the authority of the Defense Production Act in order to maintain production. Murray called off the strike and several steel companies filed suit the next day to overturn the seizure.

Charlie Tyson informed the Directors that he had "received a telegram from the Secretary of Commerce, Mr. Charles W. Sawyer, notifying him of the seizure and appointing him Operating Manager for the United States. Joe Roebling added that "it cannot be predicted at this time what the outcome of the controversy may be or to what extent it may affect the interests of the stockholders."[105]

Less than a week later on April 29, U.S. District Court Judge David Pine issued a restraining order against the seizure of the steel mills, stating that the President had no constitutional authority to do so, and Phillip Murray ordered his union members out on strike the next day. The President won a stay of the restraining order on May 1, and the case headed to the Supreme Court. Murray called off the strike on May 2 at President Truman's request, pending the court's ruling.

> ## Roebling Anual Report to Employees for 1951
> *We wonder sometimes how many of us fully realize the tremendous economic and cultural impact which Roebling has on the life of the community.... In Florence Township, we are the largest taxpayer, carrying 53% of the tax burden.... We do feel that an important relationship exists between our Company and the communities in which our mills and offices are located. We think that our position as a successful business enterprise does have far-reaching effects on the economic well-being of these communities and the people who live in them. - Charles R. Tyson, June 19, 1952*

Figure 6.93: *Roebling, Spring, 1952, Annual Report to Employees for 1951*. TPL 2 in. & 4 in. sq. billets passing through the 18 in. Blooming Mill.

benefits, just one cent below the Wage Stabilization Board's recommendation three months earlier. The companies won a price increase of $5.60 per ton, just $1.10 above what they were offered in April. Murray won his "union shop" demand requiring workers to join the union. Fourteen weeks later, Murray died of a heart attack at age 66. The 58 day strike cost the country $4 billion (about $33 billion in 2009) in lost production. Charlie calculated that the wage and price settlements cost the Company $600,000 (about $5 million).

If such a transaction were consummated

At a Directors' meeting on May 22, 1952, Charlie Tyson reviewed negotiations with the Colorado Fuel & Iron Corp. (CF&I), of Pueblo, Colorado, which had "evidenced interest in acquiring the fixed assets and inventory of this Company.... and the advantages to the Roebling Stockholders if such a transaction were consummated." The Directors authorized Charlie to proceed "toward a sale....on terms and conditions in the best interests of the stockholders, 1) to place them in a more liquid position, and 2) to enable those who may wish to do so to realize a part or all of the value of their investment in this Company." The Directors also instructed him to "give due consideration to obtaining adequate assurance that the policies heretofore followed by this Company in the conduct of its operations and treatment of its personnel shall not be repudiated or discarded." In his *Spring 1952 Report to Employees*, Charlie discussed the Company's impact on it's communities (Fig. 6.93 & box).[106]

On June 2, the Supreme Court denied President Truman's authority to seize the nation's steel mills, and he returned the control of the mills to their owners. Phillip Murray ordered his United Steel Workers out on strike, halting all production at the Company's Trenton and Roebling plants. The strike dragged on for eight weeks until President Truman called Murray and U.S. Steel President Benjamin Fairless into his office to tell them that the strike had crippled production of war materials. After threatening to seize the steel mills again on more solid legal grounds, he sent Murray and Fairless to the White House Cabinet Room, where they agreed that afternoon to a 22 cent an hour increase in wages and

In the best interests of the Company

The union contract was one of CF&I's prerequisites to a sale in order to justify the purchase price. On August 21, 1952, Charlie signed a memorandum to sell the Company's fixed assets for $25 million (about $207 million), with the stockholders retaining the investment portfolio as J.A.R.'s Sons Company's only asset. On November 28, the Directors agreed to accept $15 million (about $124 million) in cash from CF&I and $10 million (about $82.7 million) in 200,000 shares of CF&I stock valued at $50 per share. When they reviewed the sales agreement on December 5, the price had dropped to $23 million (about $190 million), but they passed a resolution:[107]

The Board of Directors, deeming it expedient and in the best interests of the Company, approves the sale and transfer by the Company of all of its fixed assets, including plants and equipment, and its inventories of materials, supplies and work in progress, its good will and certain other of its assets to Colorado Steel Corp. (a CF&I subsidiary in Delaware).[108]

The Directors also agreed "to change the name of this Company to 'The Roebling Securities Corporation' and to amend the First Article of the Certificate of Incorporation of this Company, by striking out the words 'JOHN A. ROEBLING'S SONS COMPANY' and substituting in lieu thereof the words 'THE ROEBLING SECURITIES CORPORATION.' On December 8, the owners of 94 percent of the shares approved the sale, and Joe Roebling estimated the assets of the Roebling Securities Corporation at $48.7 million (about $403 million) in cash, securities, and accounts receivable, which amounted to $143 per share (about $1,168).

John A. Roebling's Sons Company

December 8, 1952

Dear Fellow Employees,

Tomorrow you will read in the papers that a contract has been made for the sale of all the manufacturing business, plants and inventories of the John A. Roebling's Sons Co. to a wholly owned subsidiary of the Colorado Fuel & Iron Corp. The contract is subject to various conditions but we expect the sale to take place on December 31, 1952. There is nothing to be alarmed about, so don't let it bother you. As a matter of fact I truly believe that the transaction will benefit all of us. We'll become members of a large diversified and aggressive steel family - the ninth largest steel producer in America. I will continue to direct the Company's operations. No change in personnel, plants or products that would not have otherwise occurred is anticipated....

Those of you who are members of the several bargaining units will continue to operate under the prersent contracts.

This change of ownership follows the natural course of events in industrial history. The vast majority of corporations, including the Colorado Fuel and Iron Corp., are owned by thousands of people. Their stocks are on the open market and can be bought and sold by the owners as they choose. Many of the larger steel companies today grew out of a number of smaller companies that were 'family-owned' or 'closely held' such as we. The disadvantage of closely held stock by relatively few people is that it cannot be easily disposed of. It has no ready market and is, therefore, not a liquid asset. With the extremely high inheritance taxes of today any estate with a large proportion of non-liquid stock presents a most difficult tax problem. This is one reason and a big one why this action will be taken.

The transfer of Roebling ownership was inevitable at some time and we believe that the best solution for all concerned has been reached. The present owners of the John A. Roebling's Sons Company wish to express to you their appreciation of your loyal service to their organization. I earnestly request and urge your continued cooperation and support of our new ownership.

Sincerely Yours, Charles R. Tyson, President

Charlie Tyson distributed a letter that day to all the employees informing them of the sale, and reassuring them, "There is nothing to be alarmed about, so don't let it bother you" (see box & Fig. 6.94). In another letter to employees published a few weeks later in *Roebling Magazine*, he wrote:

As an important operating unit of one of the nation's largest steel producers, we will be called upon to continue to give our best efforts toward maintaining a most creditable record. From now on, the success of the Colorado Fuel and Iron Corporation operations will be our success, and vice versa. We become a part of a larger industrial team, doing a bigger job. The need for turning in our usual high level performance will be most desirous and necessary.[109]

Figure 6.94: *The Roebling Record*, **December 26, 1952. RR The newsletter carried the sale news on the day after Christmas.**

A table name throughout the country

The Directors kept the sale a secret, as Blair Birdsall recalled: "Not a word had peeped out about it before, even the Vice President in charge of sales knew nothing about it." Charlie had asked Birdsall to prepare a report on the Bridge Division, and he dedicated it to his mentor, Charles Sunderland:[110]

To the memory of the late C. C. Sunderland, whose name will always remain at the side of those of John A. Roebling and Washington A. Roebling in the Roebling tradition.

As a trainer of men, as an inspiration and a source of confidence to his employees and all who came in contact with him directly or indirectly, as a loyal and able employee with his sights always fixed on the long view of what was best for the Company, and as an inventive creator with inspired vision; he will never be surpassed. His spirit will live on as an inspiration to those who carry on his work and reap the benefits of the great heritage he has left them.

In his forecast of future bridge prospects, Blair wrote,

The Bridge Division has a better than reasonable expectancy of being able to carry itself and a part of the Company overhead charged to it, year by year, and of being able to produce an average net profit of the order of magnitude of $120,000 (about $992,000) a year over a period of several years into the foreseeable future. Only Management can decide whether this, coupled with the fact that it is the operations of the Bridge Division that make 'Roebling' a table name throughout the country, is sufficient.

To generate more profits, Birdsall recommended that the Bridge Division concentrate on "selling wire for bridge cables with a minimum of additional services or labor….at the same time maintaining our ability to handle an erection contract, striving to take an erection contract from time to time to keep our tools sharp and our name before the public." For tramways, he recommended concentrating on selling wire rope to independent tramways manufacturers while "getting at least as many Roebling tramway jobs as we do now (very few), resulting in more profitable business and continuance of our reputation as acknowledged experts in this field." He also recommended "expanding our sales contacts to keep more fully informed on the mushrooming market for Prestressed Concrete materials."

Birdsall identified eight big suspension bridge projects in various planning stages, including the Narrows Bridge in New York (Verrazano Narrows Bridge), the South Philadelphia Bridge (Walt Whitman Bridge), and the Mackinac Straits Bridge in Michigan, but it was clear from his report that the future of the Roebling Bridge Division lay primarily in selling wire and wire rope for bridges, tramways and prestressed concrete, rather than actually erecting bridge cables and tramways and engineering prestressed concrete.

Despite the long strike that year, the increase in demand from the Korean War and the growing economy pushed the Company's revenues in 1952 to $67.4 million (about $557.2 million in 2009). Operating profits also climbed to $7.8 million (about $64.1 million), rivaling the highest recorded profits in the Company's history during the late 1920s. The Roebling family stockholders sold the Company's fixed assets at the end of one of its very best years.

The ownership and operation of the Company through four generations constituted a remarkable legacy for the Roeblings. A recent study showed that only 15 percent of family businesses survive under family control past the second generation. In the high profit years before income taxes and unions, a small number of Roebling family stockholders could comfortably retain earnings to expand or update the Company.

By the time the fourth generation sold the plants and inventory, 39 family members held stock, only three worked at the Company and most of the rest preferred steady income to erratic manufacturing profits and risky investments to keep up with the competition of the big steel companies. The lower profit margins from the competition left the Company with inadequate capital to fund the needed improvements, and the family's traditional aversion to borrowing precluded outside financing. The close family ownership and control that had served the Roeblings well through four generations had finally become unsustainable.

"Industrial Milestone Marked in Roebling's Sale of Firm"
- *The Trentonian*, December 9, 1952

The Roebling family's grip on holdings of the John A. Roebling's Sons Co., which was relaxed after a century of industrial history, will represent to many Trentonians one of the last vestiges of another era. Family operation of vast industrial enterprises was once an accepted mode of American life. Today, it is exemplified by only a handful of stubborn holdouts such as the DuPonts and Fords. That the Roebling family held control of the firm for more than one hundred years, defying the encroachment of mass ownership, consolidation and depression, not only points up a great consideration for tradition, but a family tenacity which has been handed down from the company's founder, John A. Roebling.

After selling the plants, inventory and name, Charlie Tyson and Joe Roebling ran the Roebling Securities Company, gradually selling the investments and distributing the proceeds to the stockholders. They closed the Company in 1960, when they sold the 200,000 shares of CF&I stock taken as partial payment in the 1952 sale, and distributed the remaining shares of Otis Elevator stock, which was too profitable to sell. According to Charlie, the stockholders ultimately received about $168 (about $1,242) per share for their Roebling stock, more than three times the $55 (about $497) per share offered by investment bankers a decade earlier.

For Trenton, the Roebling sale signaled the end of its era of civic capitalism, where manufacturers lived near their plants and participated prominently in civic, social, cultural and philanthropic activities. The trend towards national consolidation of manufacturing into large conglomerates had started more than five decades earlier, and the Roeblings had held on long after other local factory owners had sold out. In reporting the sale of the Roebling plants in Trenton and in Roebling to CF&I, the *Trenton Sunday Times Advertiser* noted that they had now become part of an "industrial empire" that stretched from coast to coast.[111]

When the Roeblings sold their business, it had reached across the U.S. and into foreign markets with major engineering and bridge projects, provided innovations in technology, supplied an expanding world market for wire rope products, contributed to the national efforts in four wars, brought fame and fortune to an exceptionally talented family of engineers and businessmen, employed tens of thousands of native-born and immigrant Americans, and provided the foundations for vital industrial communities in both Trenton and Roebling.

Chapter 7: *Roebling will continue to be Roebling*

We are particularly enthusiastic about the addition of Roebling, which has established an excellent reputation through the years as a producer of high quality products. Our inspection of the plants shows the buildings have been well maintained and many recent improvements have been made to the machinery and equipment, which is well arranged for high speed and efficient operation. Most important to us also is the research knowledge and steelmaking qualifications that have been demonstrated by the Roebling personnel. Alwin F. Franz, President, CF&I[1]

Colorado Fuel and Iron Corporation (CF&I) acquired the Roebling manufacturing business, plants and inventory through its Delaware-based subsidiary, the Colorado Steel Corporation, which it reorganized and renamed the John A. Roebling's Sons Corporation on December 31, 1952. It took less than a week for the national corporation's reach to become apparent in the Roebling operations. While the Roeblings had always avoided borrowing money, the Roebling Corporation announced on January 6 that Allen & Company, an investment banking firm in New York, had sold $15 million in bonds to insurance companies and 200,000 shares of CF&I stock to finance the Roebling purchase.

CF&I was the ninth-largest steel producer in the country, with 1952 revenues of $195 million (about $1. 6 billion in 2009), almost three times the size of Roebling's revenues of $67.4 million (about $557 million). CF&I operated plants in Pueblo, Buffalo, and Claymount in Delaware, and seven specialty steel plants in California, Pennsylvania and Massachusetts, including the Worcester wire rope plants of the former Wickwire Spencer Steel Corporation, which CF&I had acquired in 1949. The net value of CF&I's plants and inventory in 1952 was $86.9 million (about $718.5 million), about 3.7 times the $23 million (about $190 million) it paid for the Roebling business, plants and inventory.

CF&I's corporate culture was quite a contrast to the Roebling family business. John A. Roebling was a civil engineer who started a business to manufacture wire rope, and three generations of his descendents had run the family company as engineers and businessmen. Financiers had established CF&I and a succession of financiers had always controlled it.

CF&I traced it roots to the Colorado Coal and Iron Company, founded in Pueblo in 1881 by Civil War General William J. Palmer and other owners of the Denver and Rio Grande Railroad to make rails for their line and for others in the West. They built their steel plant in Pueblo because it was a transportation center and because the Arkansas River there

Figure 7.1: Colorado Fuel and Iron Company Office, c1905. BHS John C. Osgood, a mining entrepreneur, founded the Colorado Fuel Company in 1883, and he merged it with the Colorado Coal and Iron Company to form CF&I in 1892. He built the CF&I office in the Mission Style in Pueblo, Colorado.

could provide the large amounts of water needed to make steel. Colorado Coal and Iron was the first fully integrated steel company west of St. Louis, with coal and iron mines, coke-ovens, and a Bessemer steel plant for making steel rails and fittings, bars, plates, wire, and nails.

In 1883, John Cleveland Osgood and some fellow investors founded the Colorado Fuel Company to supply coal to the Burlington (Iowa) and Missouri Railroad, a subsidiary of the Chicago, Burlington and Quincy Railroad. Osgood was born in Brooklyn in 1851 and left school at the age of 14 to work as an office boy in a Providence, Rhode Island cotton mill. He moved to Burlington at the age of 19 and became a bank cashier.

At the age of 26, he acquired control of the Whitebreast Coal and Mining Company, which supplied coal to the Burlington and Missouri Railroad. At the request of the railroad's directors, Osgood went to Colorado in 1882 to assess its coal resources, and he started buying coal lands there with some of his railroad associates. After establishing Colorado Fuel, he expanded it by buying more coal reserves, mines, and coke-oven plants.

An economic downturn in 1890-91 weakened Colorado Coal and Iron's finances and Osgood negotiated its merger with Colorado Fuel in 1892 to form the Colorado Fuel and Iron Company, which came to be known as CF&I. Over the next ten years, Osgood built CF&I into one of Colorado's largest businesses. He expanded the Pueblo steel plant and erected a big office building there (Fig. 7.1).

Like George Pullman in Chicago, and later the Roebling brothers, Osgood built a model company town to benefit his workers and to discourage them from joining unions. Starting in 1901, Osgood spent $5 million (about $146 million in 2009) building the town of Redstone, about 285 miles west of Denver, with over 100 cottages in a Swiss Chalet style with indoor plumbing for the "appreciative….Italians, Huns and Austrians" who worked in his coking plant in Carbondale, 16 miles to the north. He built a 40 room Redstone Inn for single men, plus a bathhouse, a clubhouse with a library and a theatre, a school, and a 42 room Tudor mansion called the Redstone Castle. With its beautiful setting above the Crystal River, Redstone soon became known as "the Ruby of the Rockies." Osgood also built model facilities for other employees, including a company hospital in Pueblo in the Mission Style.[2]

In 1901, John W. Gates, the financier who had assembled the American Steel and Wire Corp. and had tried to buy J.A.R.'s Sons Co. from the Roebling brothers in 1898, purchased a large block of CF&I stock with some other investors. Gates committed CF&I to make major improvements with the goal of taking over when Osgood failed to raise the required capital. Osgood turned to George Jay Gould, who controlled the Denver and Rio Grande Railroad, for a $3 million loan (about $83 million) in April, 1903. Gould was the son of Jay Gould, the railroad tycoon, and he got John D. Rockefeller, the oil tycoon, to finance half the loan. By July, Gould and Rockefeller had taken over CF&I and Osgood soon departed.

Osgood had developed CF&I for major growth in the expanding western economy. Its mines and quarries produced iron ore, limestone and dolomite for its own use and for sale. Its Minnequa Steel Plant (Fig. 7.2), which the Pueblo plant was now called, was the only rail plant west of the Mississippi. Its Colorado Supply Co. sold its finished products, and its Colorado and Wyoming Railroad transported its raw materials to its plants and its products to customers. Its Colorado and Wyoming Telegraph Company operated much of the region's telegraph and telephone service. With access to eastern capital, CF&I grew into a dominating economic and political force that employed some ten percent of Colorado's workforce by 1906.

Under Rockefeller's remote and conservative management, CF&I spent less than Osgood had on its company towns and it resisted safety improvements in its mines, which had high injury rates. To frustrate union organizing, CF&I hired immigrants from Eastern Europe and Mexico and mixed them in the mines so they couldn't communicate with each other. In 1913, the United Mine Workers of America (UMWA) targeted CF&I for its harsh tactics and demanded union recognition, pay increases, and adherence to safety laws. When the UMWA

Figure 7.2: CF&I's Minnequa Steel Plant, Pueblo, Colorado. Founded in 1881 to make rails for western railroads, CF&I expanded the plant to 565-acres, the largest integrated steel mill in the west, with over 8,500 workers who produced rails and fastenings, structural and plate steel, wire fencing and barbed wire. Today, a Russian steel firm owns the plant and employs about 1,000 workers making rods, bars and seamless pipes.

called a strike that September, CF&I evicted the strikers and they moved to tent camps. The Colorado governor sent the National Guardsmen to check the ensuing violence, but had to recall most of them after the funds ran out. CF&I hired militias to harass the camps, and fighting broke out on April 20, 1914, in Ludlow, 75 miles south of Pueblo, that left 20 people dead, including 11 children. The "Ludlow Massacre" incited a 10 day uprising that left another 30 people dead.

The Colorado Coalfield War, as the conflict came to be known, greatly tarnished the Rockefeller reputation, and John D. Rockefeller, Jr., brought in William L. M. King, a labor relations expert and former Canadian labor minister, to help. King developed an Industrial Representation Plan (IRP) to enable employee-elected representatives to negotiate grievances, working conditions and wages. In October, 1915, Rockefeller and King toured CF&I's mills, mines, stores, and camps, where employees invited them into their homes to see how they lived. Rockefeller responded that the four pillars of industry – stockholders, directors, officers and employees – all needed to cooperate to ensure a company's success.

CF&I directors and employees approved the IRP on January 1, 1916, and established four labor-management committees to implement it: Cooperation and Conciliation, Safety and Accidents, Sanitation, Health and Housing, and Recreation and Education. After three years, Rockefeller declared the IRP a success, but dissatisfied workers wanted an independent union and many went out on strike in 1919, 1921-22 and in 1927-28. When the National Industrial Recovery Act of 1933 gave workers the right to organize, CF&I officials signed an

Figure 7.3: "New Roebling Corporation Officers,"
Roebling Record, **Feb 6, 1953. RR**
**CF&I Chairman Charles Allen, Jr., and President Alwin Franz
assumed the same positions at the John A. Roebling's Sons
Corp., Charles R. Tyson became Executive Vice President and
Ferdinand W. Roebling III Vice President for Engineering.**

agreement with the United Mine Workers for its coal mining employees but beefed up their IRPs to resist unionizing efforts in their iron mines and steel plant. J.A.R.'s Sons Co. coincidently created the Roebling Employee Association in 1937 to resist the Steel Workers Organizing Committee (SWOC).

During the Second World War CF&I became even more dominant as the largest heavy industry in the Rocky Mountains, but it remained a regional producer. In 1944, Charles Allen, Jr., acquired control of CF&I through his investment banking firm, Allen & Company, which he had founded in 1922. Allen was born in 1903, left school at the age of 15 to become a runner at the New York Stock Exchange, and four years later, at the age of 19, he founded Allen & Company, which remains in existence today. A voracious reader and brilliant financier, Allen was known as the "shy Midas of Wall Street," and he set out to expand CF&I through acquisitions into a national steel company for the expected postwar boom.[3]

In 1945, CF&I acquired Wickwire Spencer Steel Corp. of Worcester, Massachusetts, the second largest steel and wire company after J.A.R. Son's Co. Wickwire Spencer produced rods and other steel products at its steel plant in Buffalo, established by Thomas and Chester Wickwire in 1906, the same year Charles Roebling started production at the Kinkora Works, and it produced wire, wire rope, screening, netting, fencing, and hardware at its wire works in Worcester. Alwin F. Franz had been the general superintendent of the Buffalo plant, and Allen put him in charge of CF&I's steel plant in Pueblo. Franz had started as an open hearth pitman at the Otis Steel Corp. and had worked his way up through first helper, melter and other jobs to become the general superintendent of the

---

Alan Wood Iron and Steel Co. in Philadelphia, and then the general superintendent of CF&I's Buffalo plant. Allen made Franz a director of CF&I in 1948 and its President in 1952.

Allen became Chairman of the John A. Roebling's Sons Corporation, and Franz became President. Charlie Tyson continued running the plants as Executive Vice President, and Ferd Roebling continued overseeing engineering as a Vice President (Fig. 7.3). In a letter to his 4,800 new "Fellow Employees," Franz pledged: "Roebling will continue to be Roebling in every sense of the word!" (see box).

Figure 7.4:
J.A.R.'s Sons Co.
Trenton Plant, c1952. RM
In this aerial of the plant around the time of its sale to CF&I, the former route of the Delaware & Raritan Canal, which was filled in the 1930s, is visible as a diagonal green strip in the lower left quadrant (see Fig. 4.62).
The multi-story, late 19th Century wire mills (see Figs. 4.70) are in the middle above the 5-story General Office (see Figs. 6.3-4).
The Chambersburg section of Trenton extends around the north, east and south sides of the plant.

In preparation for the sale to CF&I, J.A.R.'s Sons Company President Charlie Tyson commissioned a series of photographs of the Trenton and Roebling plants, including key manufacturing processes (Figs. 7.4-9). In an article entitled "CF&I Building for Tomorrow" in the Spring, 1953 *Roebling Magazine*, the new John A. Roeblings' Sons Corporation President described CF&I's future under Allen's leadership as simply, "New products, new customers and new markets:"

The keynote to our program has been Diversification…. I want to emphasize that the ability to produce diversified products is most important in a highly competitive industry like the steel industry. We have been fortunate in being able to implement our diversification program by taking advantage of opportunities that developed in the form of new company acquisitions, which gave us additional new capacity and a wider range of products and customer contacts.

Our diversification program has essentially been twofold: geographical and product. CF&I products are now used by a number of the basic industries of this country. Our confidence in building CF&I for greater service is based on our belief that our customers represent almost every important segment of American industry - mining, agricultural, oil and gas, railroad, construction, manufacturing, lumbering, electrical, and others. These obviously serve both civilian and defense needs.

Figure 7.5: Reeling wire rope from the 80-Ton Rope Machine (see Figs. 4.30-31) at the Trenton Works, c1952. RM

Figure 7.6: Cutting Wire Rope to length in the Wire Rope Warehouse (see Fig. 6.19) at the Trenton Works, c1952. RM

**Figure 7.7:
J.A.R.'s Sons Co.
Kinkora Works, Roebling,
N.J. c1952. RM
(see Figs. 5.3-4)
The nearly 1,000-ft. long
Steel Mill is along the
bottom with the nine
chimneys, one for each of
the open hearth furnaces.
The three Wire Mills are
the large buildings with
sawtooth skylights at
center and right.
Beyond Newbold Island
in the Delaware River
is U.S. Steel's
Fairless Works,
in Fairless Hills, Pa.,
which opened in 1952.**

To illustrate the success of CF&I's strategy, Franz noted that its revenues sales had more than tripled from an average of $55 million (about $657 million in 2009) in the years 1943-1946 to $195 million (about $1.6 billion) in 1952. In the same period, J.A.R.'s Sons Co. revenues had increased by less than half. After Franz described CF&I's "Building for Tomorrow" strategy in the spring issue, he discontinued *Roebling Magazine.*

In acquiring Roebling, CF&I not only expanded its wire and wire rope capacity, but it also added important new product lines, including cold rolled products, electrical wire, prestressed strand, and bridge wire. It acquired the enormous skill and experience of employees ranging from the steelmakers in the steel mill and the wire drawers in the wire mills to the engineers in the Bridge Division, and it acquired the Roebling brand built up by four generations of Roebling over 11 decades.

With its California Wire Cloth and American Wire Fabrics Divisions, CF&I didn't need any additional woven wire capacity, which no doubt contributed to Charlie Tyson's decision to close the Woven Wire Fabrics Division in 1952 prior to the sale to CF&I. By April, 1953, the Roebling Corporation announced plans to demolish most of the Woven Wire Fabrics buildings, which dated to 1912, when Charles Roebling moved the N.J. Wire Cloth Company to the Kinkora Works.

Figure 7.8: Tapping the furnace to pour molton steel into a ladle in the Steel Mill at the Kinkora Works (see Fig. 5.8). RM

Figure 7.9: Collecting wire coils in the Wire Mill at the Kinkora Works (see Figs. 5.10-11), c1952. RM

**Figure 7.10:
"There's only
ONE reason!"
Fortune,
May 1953.
The Roebling
Corporation's
engagment
of renowned
artist
Normal
Rockwell
illustrated
its national
approach to
marketing.**

The Roebling Corporation's sales staff began marketing it as "A subsidiary of the Colorado Fuel and Iron Corporation," with both JAR and CF&I logos, and it drew upon the parent corporation's broader sales experience with a new series of advertisements, including a few selling Roebling wire rope with illustrations by Normal Rockwell (Fig. 7.10).

The self sacrificing devotion of a Woman

On May 24, 1953, the 70th anniversary of the opening of the Brooklyn Bridge and 50 years after the death of Emily Warren Roebling, the City of New York held a ceremony on the Brooklyn tower to unveil a plaque erected by the Brooklyn Engineers Club to recognize her, as David Steinman noted in his speech, "as one of the Builders of the Bridge" (Figs. 7.11-12).

As *The Roebling Record* noted on May 22:

Through her unselfish efforts and courage, Emily Warren Roebling made possible completion of the bridge linking Manhattan and Brooklyn. When her husband, chief engineer on the project, was rendered incapacitated following successive attacks of 'the bends' after going down in the bridge caissons, Mrs. Roebling became his 'eyes' and 'ears,' serving as liaison between him and the construction personnel. Her efforts brought to realization the dreams of John A. Roebling and his son, Colonel Washington A. Roebling. Inscribed on the plaque are the words, "Back of Every Great Work We Can Find the Self-sacrificing Devotion of a Woman."

The growing interest in prestressed concrete

In October, 1953, the CF&I directors elected Charlie Tyson as a director and he launched a Roebling Construction Materials Division to serve "the growing interest in prestressed concrete and the increasing part that the corporation is playing in the development of products concerned with its use" (Figs. 7.13-14). The Roebling Corporation soon won several contracts totaling $1.2 million (about $8.5 million) that demonstrated the growing acceptance of prestressed concrete.[4]

The Port Authority of New York bought three million feet of Roebling prestressed strand for its new 700 ft. long Pier C in Hoboken. The Garden State Parkway Authority approved the use of 500,000 ft. of 3/8-in. prestressed strand for 218 girders ranging from 40 ft. to 61 ft. in length for eight overpass bridges between Atlantic City and Ocean City. Other projects using Roebling prestressed strand included the 24 mile Lake Pontchartrain Bridge in New Orleans, two bridge sections

**Figure 7.11 (above) : Brooklyn Borough President John Cashmore, left, congratulating Paul Roebling on the plaque for his great grandmother, Emily Warren Roebling, 1953. RR
Figure 7.12 (right): Plaque for Emily Warren Roebling, 2008.**
*Whose faith and courage helped her stricken husband
Col. Washington A. Roebling C.E.
complete the construction of this bridge.*

CONSTRUCTION MATERIALS DIVISION JOHN A. ROEBLING'S SONS CORPORATION
SUBSIDIARY OF THE COLORADO FUEL AND IRON CORPORATION TRENTON 2 · NEW JERSEY

Figure 7.13 (above): *Roebling Tensioning Materials, 1957.* WSR
The Roebling Construction Materials Division brochure shows a pre-stressed concrete beam being hoisted into place on a highway bridge.

Prestressed concrete combines the strength of steel with the durability of concrete to improve on the characteristics of both materials.... Roebling pioneered prestressed techniques in America and is constantly making availble new developments.

Figure 7.14 (right): "Flexible Concrete!" 1956 ad for Roebling "stress relieved steel wire and strand," showing a a 183 ton test on a prestressed beam.

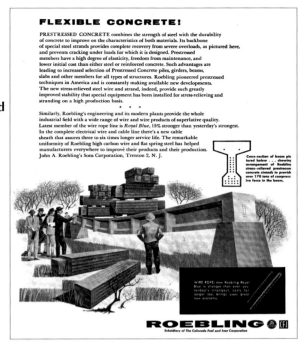

totaling 2.6 miles for the Hampton Roads Bridge and Tunnel in Norfolk, Virginia, and the 1,700 ft. Greater Egg Harbor Bridge in Egg Harbor, New Jersey.[5]

Charles Sunderland and Blair Birdsall had spent several years researching and developing Roebling's prestressed wire and strand, and under CF&I's marketing prowess, the Roebling Corporation was now capitalizing on their efforts with these and other innovative construction projects.

With the end of the Korean War, demand for steel products declined 21 percent in 1954, but CF&I's diversification strategy

helped it weather the downturn. As the economy rebounded in 1955 with a 7.6 percent growth rate, the highest of the decade, CF&I was well positioned to meet the demand.

In February, 1955, New York City's Commissioner of Public Works announced a $2.2 million (about $17.6 million) contract with the Roebling Corporation to replace the cable bands and bridge suspenders that J.A.R's Sons Co. had installed on the Manhattan Bridge in 1908 (Figs. 7.15-16). The Commissioner cited heavy traffic as the cause for the slippage of some of the original bands and had made the decision to install new suspender ropes as well.

Manhattan Bridge 1955. Figure 7.15 (left): Roebling bridgemen replacing the suspender ropes installed by their predecessors five decades earlier. WSR **Figure 7.16:** Roebling Bridge Division staff, from left - Pat Galotti, Harold Hills, Resident Engineer, Leroy Patterson, Jack Nixon, Blair Birdsall, Chief Bridge Engineer, and Ted Yanushevski, 1955. RM

THE ROEBLING Record

Published every two weeks by
JOHN A. ROEBLING'S SONS CORPORATION
Subsidiary of The Colorado Fuel and Iron Corporation
TRENTON 2, NEW JERSEY

OUR DEMOCRACY

THE MORE ABUNDANT LIFE

HERE IN AMERICA, A LUXURY SELDOM REMAINS A LUXURY FOR LONG. NOT TOO MANY YEARS AGO, THERE WEREN'T MANY AUTOMOBILES FOR THE AVERAGE INCOME FAMILIES — AND THEN ABRUPTLY THERE WERE AUTOS FOR ALMOST EVERYONE. WHAT OUTSIDERS STILL REGARD AS LUXURY ITEMS WE CONSIDER ESSENTIALS:

RADIOS — TELEVISION SETS — TELEPHONES
ELECTRIC STOVES — CAMERAS — VACUUM CLEANERS
HOMES

—HUBERT MATHIEU—

IN A SINGLE LIFETIME, INGENUITY AND INDUSTRIAL SKILL, BACKED BY THE SAVINGS OF THE PEOPLE, HAVE GIVEN US ALL THIS. WE HOLD IT CASUALLY, RARELY WONDERING — AN ABUNDANCE THAT GIVES OPPORTUNITY, TOO, FOR THE DEVELOPMENT OF CULTURAL AND SPIRITUAL VALUES.

In the early-1950s, high employment, savings and birth rates, and low inflation created an unprecedented period of prosperity and contentment, raising the standard of living for most working Americans, and particularly for those with union jobs. Industrial companies like the Roebling Corp. stressed the "abundant" benefits and opportunities provided by American capitalism (Figs. 7.17-20).

Figure 7.17 (left): *The Roebling Record*, May 12, 1954, celebrated "The More Abundant Life" enjoyed by employees & their families.
Figure 7.18 (top): The Roebling Corporation-sponsored "Roebling Steel Workers" Baseball Team, 1955. TPL
Figure 7.19 (center): The Roebling Volunteer Fire Co. #3 bought the 1914 Roebling Auditorium for the community, 1954. RR
Figure 7.20 (above): Roebling employees' children at the United Steel Workers 1955 outing. RR

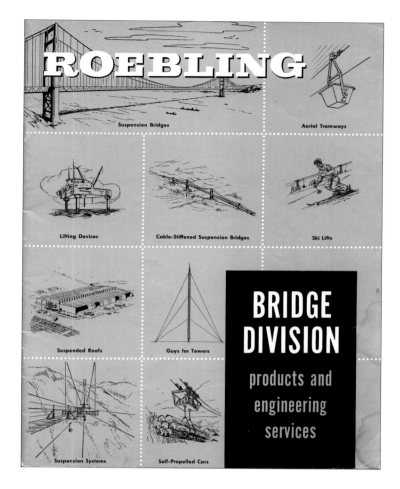

Figure 7.21 (right): *Roebling Bridge Division
Products and Engineering Services, 1957.* WSR
In promoting the Bridge Division's specialized services,
the Roebling Corporation's new brochure noted:

*Let Roebling help with your problem. Allow us to search
for possible solutions. You'll find that Roebling is particularly
well equipped to handle complicated engineering problems.
We've been doing just that since 1841.*

On the 150th anniversary of the founder's birth, *The New York Times* acknowledged John A. Roebling's genius in designing the "universally known symbol of the spirit of New York" (see box).

In the absence of contracts for any big bridges, Blair Birdsall marketed the Bridge Division's reputation for other engineered uses of wire rope (Fig. 7.21). He saw opportunities for using Roebling prestressed ropes and strands to meet "the rising demand for long span unobstructed spaces within buildings," and he built a working model in the Physical Testing house to demonstrate their potential for suspended roofs.[5]

Under pressure from CF&I executives to reduce expenses, Charlie Tyson finally had to deal with the obsolete multi-story buildings that his grandfather, Charles Roebling, had erected at the Trenton Works. He tore down the 1890s Insulated Wire Division Rubber Mill on Hudson Street (see Fig. 4.58) and the 1880s Elmer Street Wire Mill (see Fig. 4.26), and he removed three floors from the 1899 Clinton Avenue Wire Mill (see Figs. 4.70-71 & 7.22-23). In their day, each of these buildings had been prominent symbols of J.A.R.'s Sons Co.'s dominating presence in Trenton.

Figure 7.22: Elmer Street, Trenton, c1954. TPL
In dealing with obsolete buildings, the Roebling Corporation
kept part of the 1899 Clinton Avenue Wire Mill, left, but
demolished the 1880s Elmer Street Wire Mill, center.

Figure 7.23: Clinton Avenue Wire Mill, Trenton, 1956. RR
The Roebling Corporation removed the top three floors
from the wire mill, "long a Chambersburg landmark,"
and converted the two bottom floors to storage.

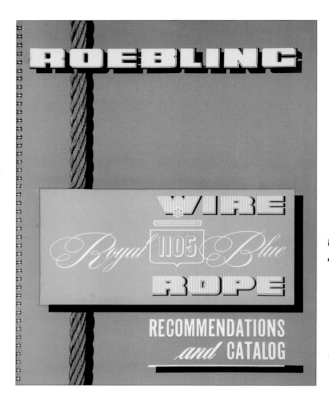

Figure 7.24 (left): *Roebling Royal Blue Wire Rope Catalog, 1956. RM* The Company promised its new "1105" steel wire rope provided "15 percent greater strength" over comparable ropes

Figure 7.25 (right): "Here is Perfection" ad, 1956. RM *Roebling makes the finest high carbon wire available to industry today. Manufacturers who try Roebling wire once, become Roebling customers from then on. You pay for the best when you buy high carbon wire. Make sure you get it. Always specify Roebling.*

Unequalled resistance

Starting in the 1920s, J.A.R.'s Sons Co. had marketed its best wire rope as *Blue Center*, made with "superior grade Improved Plow Steel" produced in the Kinkora Works Steel Mill. In the mid-1950s, Roebling metallurgists developed "Roebling Type 1105 Wire, the finest high carbon rope wire ever produced," and the Corporation used it in a new line of "Roebling Royal Blue Wire Rope" with "15 percent greater strength than any standard wire rope of the same size and construction." The Corporation marketed "Royal Blue" as offering "unequalled resistance to impact, crushing, abrasion and fatigue," and especially valuable "in drilling, mining, construction, earth-moving and logging" (Fig. 7.24). It also marketed the high strength wire as "Perfection" in other products (Fig. 7.25).[6]

American steel is in trouble

With the economy growing, the Eisenhower administration reduced the Federal budget to hold down inflation, but by 1957 the decrease in government spending helped push the economy into recession and unemployment to 7.7 percent. American steel production declined from 93 percent of capacity in 1955 to 60 percent in 1958. An increased use of cheaper imported steel contributed to this decline.

The economy recovered in 1959 and steel manufacturers reported high profits just as the industry's three-year contract with the United Steel Workers of America was set to expire. Steel company executives offered a moderate wage increase in

exchange for work rule concessions, but union leaders wanted a substantial wage increase because of the high industry profits.

In his 23 years at Roebling, Charlie Tyson had experienced many tough labor conflicts and didn't need to face another one. He resigned his position as Executive Vice President in the summer of 1959 but remained a CF&I director. He was also a director of Philadelphia's Penn Mutual Life Insurance Company, where he became Executive Vice president and eventually President.

On July 15, 500,000 steel workers went out on strike at most of the nations' steel mills including CF&I's. The strike dragged on into the fall, threatening production at automobile and other plants that relied on steel. Concerned about national security, President Eisenhower ordered the strikers back to work under the 1947 Taft-Hartley Act, which enabled injunctions against strikes if they "imperiled the national health or safety." The United Steel Workers sued to have the act declared unconstitutional, but the Supreme Court denied the suit on November 7, forcing the strikers back to work after being out for 116 days.

Steel industry and union officials agreed to a modest wage increase and some work rule concessions on January 15, 1960. With more than 85 percent of steel production shut down during the long strike, customers had significantly increased their purchases of foreign steel. Rod imports rose over 75 percent in 1959, and imports of wire rope rose 65 percent. Some historians believe that the 1959 strike accelerated the decline of the American steel industry by stimulating imports of foreign steel, but other factors like overcapacity and the substitution of other materials for steel also contributed.

From 1955 to 1960, worldwide steel production increased 28 percent while American steel production dropped 16 percent. In adjusting to the loss of business, American steel executives needed to further reduce costs and increase efficiency. In a sobering message in September, 1961, Alwin Franz, President of both CF&I and the Roebling Corporation, told his employees that "American Steel is in trouble" (see box). CF&I had spent nearly $130 million (about $945 million in 2009) between 1953 and 1960 to upgrade production, but now announced another round of upgrades:

'Operation Progress' at CF&I plants means a planned program of technological advance designed to modernize the art of steelmaking....This is a major step in the modernization program CF&I has undertaken during the past few years to bolster our competitive position with both domestic and foreign steel producers.

Franz also faced the reality that some product lines weren't worth modernizing. Charles Roebling had started the Insulated Wire Division in the 1880s when "the whole manufacturing world was going mad about electricity," as Washington Roebling had recalled, and although J.A.R.'s Sons Co. had sold a lot of electrical wire, he also claimed that the division was never very profitable. Since 1953, the Roebling Corporation had invested substantial sums to upgrade and expand the Division at the Buckthorn Plant "to produce new items for new customers and new and expanding markets."[7]

The Corporation's contract with the steel workers union, however, made its electrical wire production costs higher than those of manufacturers that operated under less expensive contracts with less powerful unions or with no unions at all. By 1961, Franz acknowledged that the competition made it unlikely that the Division would earn a sufficient profit, and he shut it down, eliminating 250 jobs. He sold the machinery to the Reynolds Metals Company of Chester, Pennsylvania, and sold the Buckthorn Plant with its 14 buildings to a Philadelphia real estate firm for an industrial park.

"An Important Message for all CF&I Employees: Cold Facts About the American Steel Industry," Alwin Franz, *CF&I BLAST*, September 18, 1961

American steel is in trouble. Low-priced imports from foreign countries are choking markets for certain types of American steel in this country. American exports are falling off as an ever-increasing number of modernized foreign steel producers woo and win existing and new world markets. American costs are spiraling upwards at a dizzying pace....

I pointed out this critical situation in an earlier article entitled "Imports are Exporting Your Job".... Foreign competition is playing particular havoc with the sales and profits of America's "little steel" companies, like CF&I. Companies manufacturing CF&I-type products are particularly hard hit by the imbalance between imports and exports....

Any way you look at it, we are at a definite disadvantage. We are not meeting foreign competition now, and prospects for the future are equally dim - unless constructive, cooperative action by government, labor and management is taken immediately....

Our troubles with foreign steel producers are only beginning ....The United States is still the world's leading steel producer. Since 1951, however, we have been losing our front running position. More of our foreign and domestic markets have been seized by steel from abroad - steel from Western Europe, Eastern Europe, Japan and elsewhere....

Since 1950, steal ingot production in the rest of the world has increased rapidly - much more so than in the United States. The result is that the U.S. share of total world steel ingot production has declined by nearly half, from forty-six percent to twenty six percent....Decreased American steel production means decreasing profits....In reviewing the reports of nineteen

integrated steel companies, we find that seven did not earn their regular dividend, some have not paid a common stock dividend for some time, several returned a small and inadequate profit, and five of the companies showed an actual loss....

Profit is the one great motivating force in our American free enterprise system. Profit and the expectation of profit distinguish our mode of production and our way of life from those who threaten our very existence. It is the tonic and energizer of the American economic life stream. Profit gives our national security its industrial muscle to resist aggression....

Only under the profit system has man attained those ends by which we set so much store: independence, ownership of property, savings, a rational planning of one's own life, and that greatest boon of all, the freedom of choice and the courage to make it....To meet rising costs, steel profits must be increased.

Only if the American Steel Industry realizes increased profits can it (a) Attract and hold shareholders and pay them their full share for the use of invested funds, (b) Build employment and job security, (c) Reduce industry's long-term debt, (d) Expand and modernize American plants to compete with foreign steel....

Modernizing is a costly necessity. We are hamstrung by inefficiency. Many American steel plants - especially the smaller ones - are antiquated and outdated. One of the major reasons foreign steel producers can compete so well price wise is that they have modern, efficient machinery and modern, streamlined plants - thanks to capital from the United States. We must modernize in order to cut costs and increase productivity and efficiency - so that we can survive.

Figure 7.26 (left): Cable Construction, Vincent Thomas Bridge, Los Angeles, California, *CF&I BLAST*, April, 1963. RM
A Roebling bridgeman on a footbridge checks the traveling wheel, based on John A. Roebling's 1846 patent (see Fig. 2.15),
laying one of the 8,000 bridge wires for each of the two 13-1/2-in. cables. Fifty Roebling bridgemen laid
6,000 miles of the bridge wire, produced at the Kinkora Works and shipped through the Panama Canal, in ten weeks.
Figure 7.27 (right): Vincent Thomas Bridge, 2009. WK The 1,500 ft. span bridge crosses Los Angeles Harbor to Terminal Island.

A job of a lifetime

Franz also recognized that competition severely limited the profitability of the Roebling Bridge Division, which had been the most prominent Roebling business since the 1920s. The Division's last big suspension bridge project had been building the cables for the new 2,800 ft. span Tacoma Narrows Bridge in Washington in 1951.

U.S. Steel's American Bridge and American Steel & Wire subsidiaries jointly won the contracts for the other big suspension bridges of the 1950s: the 2,150 ft. span Delaware Memorial Bridge between New Jersey and Delaware in 1951, the 2,000 ft. span Walt Whitman Bridge between Camden and Philadelphia in 1957, the 3,800 ft. span Mackinac Bridge in Michigan in 1957, and the 1,800 ft. span Throggs Neck Bridge in New York, completed in 1961.

American Steel & Wire had built a pre-stretcher track at its plant across the canal from the Roebling plant in Trenton, so Charles Sunderland's pre-stretcher track at the Kinkora Works, which he had built in 1928 for the George Washington Bridge cables, no longer provided a competitive advantage for Roebling on big bridge contracts.

The Roebling Corporation's Bridge Division finally won a contract in 1961 to build the cables for a medium-size suspension bridge over the Main Channel at Los Angeles Harbor from San Pedro to Terminal Island. With a 1,500 ft. span, the Vincent Thomas Bridge is just 95 five feet shorter than the Brooklyn Bridge, but it was the first big suspension bridge in southern California (Figs 7.26-27).

Leroy Patterson (see Fig. 7.16) of the Bridge Division spent a year in Los Angeles working on the Vincent Thomas Bridge. Born in Florence Township, which includes the village of Roebling, Leroy got a job right out of high school in the Roebling Physical Testing House at the Trenton Plant in 1945, thanks to his brother, who was working in the Construction Materials Division selling prestressed concrete strand. Leroy soon became a draftsman in the Bridge Division, and recalled working on the Vincent Thomas Bridge in a 2007 interview:

There was never a dull moment, really....if you weren't on the towers, you were out on the catwalk where they were spinning and putting the wires in place, or you were in mid-span....and to be out there all day on the bridge and looking down and watching a boat headed for Hawaii with all the people on the deck waving to us. It was a job of a lifetime for me – it was the best job I ever had.[8]

While this project was underway, Blair Birdsall, the head of the Bridge Division, submitted a bid for the cables of the Verrazano Narrows Bridge across the Hudson River between Staten Island and Brooklyn. With a span of 4,260 ft., it would surpass the record Golden Gate Bridge span by 60 ft. to become the world's longest suspension bridge. Ferd Roebling, who as Vice President for Engineering oversaw the Bridge Division, was very disappointed as were other Roebling employees when U.S. Steel won the contract to build the cables, but there was some consolation. The bridge's four 36 in. cables required 41,000 tons of bridge wire, enough to stretch 143,000 miles, but since American Steel & Wire couldn't supply all of it in time, it subcontracted with the Roebling Corporation to make about 25 percent of the bridge wire, some 10,000 tons.

It was dirty, rotten, hot work and I loved it

While Roebling steel men produced the high carbon steel for the Verrazano Narrows Bridge wire at the Roebling Plant, it was all-too obvious that Charles Roebling's nine open hearth furnaces were obsolete. Charles had installed the first four in 1906 and the other five by 1918 (see Figs. 5.6-8). These 30 and 50-ton open hearth furnaces sprayed heated air mixed with fuel oil in flaming jets at close to 3,000 degrees over scrap steel and other ingredients spread out on the hearths to create a "melt" of molten steel. The steel making process took ten hours from one tap - pouring out the molten steel - to the next, and the open hearth furnaces had to be shut down every 12 or 13 weeks so hot-mill masons could reline their interiors with new refractory bricks to protect the furnace walls.

Ken Ibach (see Fig. 6.71) relined those furnaces numerous times. Ken grew up in Roebling with his father working at the Roebling Plant, and got a job in the rod mill at the age of 20. As a sergeant in the U.S. Army infantry during the war, Ken received a Bronze Star for "heroic achievement in action near Careglio, Italy," and after the war he returned to the plant and became an apprentice mason. He started out working with the yard masons on buildings and finished his apprenticeship as a hot mill mason in the steel mill, where he later became a foreman. As he recalled in a 2007 interview:[9]

When I first became a foreman in the steel mill, I was in charge of tearing out the furnaces....We would tear them out and move to the next furnace and a repair crew would come in and do their work....When the bricks in the open hearths burnt out, they had to be torn down to where you can get to a solid place to start and rebuild them....

Those furnaces were generally up around 3000° and if you shut them down even for four hours, they're still a few thousand degrees yet - pretty darn hot....We'd take burlap bags and soak them in water and cover ourselves with these bags and you'd go in and work as long as you could, then come out and get cooled off and the next group would go in....

Sometimes a break in the roof would fall in and we'd go in and crawl on that roof and replace those bricks without shutting those furnaces down....They were some mean jobs. I used to come home sometimes with blisters on my face....

We had masks, but you couldn't wear them inside, you could wear them if you're working outside, like reaching in. We used to have big spoons and sometimes we'd stand on the outside and pick up bricks with these spoons and stick them in, then you could wear a mask, but if you went inside you couldn't wear one because it'd fog all up and you couldn't see what you were doing....We used to do different things to try and overcome some of the heat, but I loved it, loved the work just the same....I enjoyed my work - it was dirty, rotten, hot work and I loved it, I really did.

Charles' open hearth furnaces had produced millions of tons of steel over nearly six decades for "unthinkable" feet of wire and wire rope, but the Roebling Corporation could no longer operate the furnaces competitively. Leonard Rose, who was now President of CF&I, faced similar problems with CF&I's other steel and wire plants, including its Buffalo Plant, which had opened a year after the Kinkora Works in 1907 as the Wickwire Steel Plant, and its Palmer Plant in Palmer, Massachusetts. Newer foreign plants, primarily in Japan, produced wire and wire rope at significantly lower costs than CF&I could produce them at its three old plants.

When CF&I's efforts to make the Buffalo Plant competitive fell short, Rose decided to consolidate wire and wire rope production at the Palmer Plant and at the Kinkora Works. In announcing the decision in June, 1963, Rose stated:

Wire and wire products have been harder hit by foreign competition than most other types of steel.

The Buffalo Plant has been severely squeezed between foreign competition, which has made adequate prices impossible, and rising labor and material costs over which we have little or no control.

As a result, despite extensive programs of cost reduction and plant improvement, operating losses at Buffalo have increased year after year....

By concentrating our Eastern manufacturing at the Roebling and Palmer plants we expect to lower costs, improve customer service, and strengthen our competitive position....

The planned installation of new electric steelmaking furnaces at our Roebling plant will more than offset the reduction in steel ingot producing capacity occasioned by the closing of the Buffalo plant.[10]

Fourteen hundred employees lost their jobs at the Buffalo plant when CF&I shut it down, and Rose later said: "Closing our Buffalo steel plant was one of the most difficult steps our management has ever had to take." The plant personnel director set up an employment center to help the employees find new jobs and thanked the United Steel Workers local staff for their help in this effort, but it was all a chilling indicator of the vulnerability of older steel plants.[11]

CF&I industrial relations executives concluded a new labor contract with United Steel Workers negotiators in 1963 without any interruptions of operations, thanks to "the high degree of labor statesmanship" exhibited by both sides. Steel industry executives had sufficient profits to agree to a wage increase and higher insurance, vacation and pension benefits, while the union executives realized that the increasing competition of foreign steel warranted a compromise that would help preserve jobs.

Figure 7.28: Electric Furnace, Roebling Steel Mill, c1965. RM
A "melt shop" worker checking molten steel in the furnace.

Figure 7.29: Roebling Steel Mill, c1965. RM
Workers pouring molten steel from a ladle into ingot molds.

If we are to meet the keen competition facing this plant

The decision by CF&I executives to invest $4.5 million (about $31.7 million in 2009) to upgrade the old Kinkora Works gave both Roebling plants a new lease on life. In announcing the investment, Rose stated that:

> *Installation of the electric furnaces and other improvements should result in a very substantial reduction in costs, which is absolutely necessary if we are to meet the keen competition facing this plant at the present time and for the foreseeable future. Coming on the heels of the recent consolidation of CF&I's operations in the Eastern Division, these furnaces represent another important phase in our corporate-wide modernization program.*[12]

Workers started shutting down several of the open hearth furnaces that December to prepare for the installation of the three electric arc furnaces to replace them. A French scientist named Paul Heroult invented the electric arc steel furnace in 1900 and the first one was installed in the U.S. in 1907. Electric arc furnaces were generally used for special alloy steels until improvements after the Second World War made them practical for large-scale production. In an electric arc furnace, scrap steel and other ingredients are placed in a hardened steel vessel, a cover is placed on top, and large electrodes are inserted through the cover. When the current is turned on, an electric arc between the electrodes and the scrap generates the nearly 3,000 degree temperatures needed to melt the scrap steel along with some iron ore, limestone and other ingredients, depending on the type of steel required.

CF&I contracted with American Bridge to build the three electric arc furnaces, which had the same capacity of producing about 240,000 tons of steel annually as the nine old open hearth furnaces. Producing a "heat," also known as a "melt" or "tap," of steel took just four hours in the electric furnaces, compared with 11 hours in the open hearths. The electric furnaces required many fewer men to operate than the open hearths, and they took up a lot less space, allowing for improved scrap handling in the rest of the huge steel mill building. J.G. Blythe, the superintendent of the "melt shop," as the steel mill was now called, told a reporter that the electric arc furnaces saved time, space, and money: "It was a matter of cutting costs. It was either putting in the electric furnaces or going out of business. It was that simple."[13]

In addition to dealing with antiquated mills, CF&I executives soon found themselves facing another problem that threatened their Roebling operations. By the spring of 1964, officials at the New Jersey Department of Health had become seriously concerned about pollution in the lower Delaware River, from which several municipalities drew drinking water. Department of Health investigators prepared a Status Report in May, 1964, stating that at CF&I's Roebling Plant, "15 million gallons per day (MGD) were being discharged into the Delaware River; 1 MGD used for acid solutions and rinsing. These effluents did not undergo neutralization and were low in pH, high levels of iron and other heavy metals, suspended solids and oil." The Kinkora Works had been discharging toxic waste into the Delaware River for nearly six decades. The Department of Health officials recommended that CF&I install a wastewater treatment facility.[14]

With no big bridge projects to work on, Blair Birdsall and his Bridge Division staff spent their time engineering wire rope and bridge strand for prestressed concrete, pipe bridges, ski lifts and suspended roofs. In a sizeable ski-lift project, the Division contracted with the State of New Hampshire to design, build and install four double-chair lifts, two each at

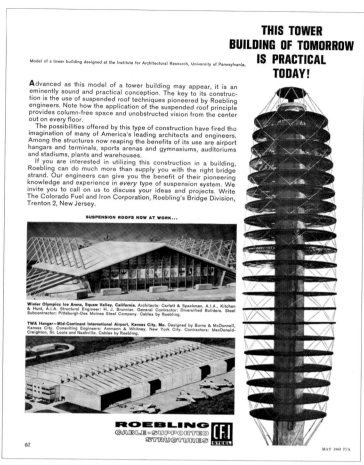

Figure 7.30: Roebling Cable-Supported Structures ad, 1963. By 1963, the Roebling Bridge Division was marketing its innovative uses of wire rope and strand for suspended roofs like the Winter Olympics Ice Arena in Squaw Valley, California, upper left, and the TWA Hanger in Kansas City, Missouri, lower left. For a conceptual Tower Building of Tomorrow designed at the University of Pennsylvania, the ad noted:

The Key to its construction is the use of suspended roof techniques pioneered by Roebling engineers.

Franconia State Park and Mt. Sunapee State Park, where one of the lifts was 6,000 ft. long. The contract included 500 chairs and 32,000 ft. of Roebling wire rope.

Blair had started testing and promoting suspended roof designs in 1956, and by the early 1960s, as a CF&I Roebling ad noted in 1963: "The possibilities offered by this type of construction have fired the imagination of many of America's leading architects and engineers" (Fig. 7.30). In the Bridge Division's most prominent suspended roof project, it contracted to supply 96 custom cables for the world's largest suspended roof, designed by the noted New York architect Philip Johnson, at the 250 ft. wide by 320 ft. long elliptical New York State Pavilion at the New York World's Fair (Fig. 7.31). The Bridge Division also furnished custom cables for suspending the New Jersey Pavilion's 21 canopies, one for each county, from 80 ft. guyed booms (Fig. 7.32).

Figure 7.31: Roebling Cable-Supported Structures, *Architectural Record*, **1964.** Phillip Johnson designed the New York Pavilion at the N.Y. World's Fair with a 55,000 sq.ft. suspended roof, the world's largest at that time. Workers assembled the roof with Roebling Wire Ropes at ground level and raised it to 100 ft. New York State designated the structure a Landmark in 2009.

Figure 7.32: New Jersey Pavillion, N.Y. World's Fair, 1964. CUH2A Phillip S. Collins designed the Pavilion with 21 canopies, one for each county, suspended with Roebling Wire Ropes.

Ever since Charles Sunderland had established the Bridge Division in 1929, he and then Blair, who became its head in 1952, had run it as an autonomous department for engineering and construction contracts. As Leroy Patterson recalled in 2007:

The Bridge Department was a separate entity really.... There were five office clerical staff, three engineers, the chief draftsman, and probably eight to ten draftsmen depending on how many jobs there were....We didn't have to report to any plant managers or anything like that....

Blair was the chief engineer of the Bridge Department and he reported to Ferd Roebling, who had an office across the hall and, of course, knew what was going on....Blair's whole soul and body was to build big bridges - that's what he did. He was one of the best, really. You couldn't want a better supervisor. He would listen to anybody and everybody in the department and wouldn't treat anybody higher than anybody else. He always joined everybody at parties, Christmastime celebrations, but by the same token he demanded that you pay attention to your work and not goof off, but nobody had a desire to. There was no one there that made you feel miserable like some shops and offices that have a guy who won't let up on employees, there was none of that at all....There wasn't anybody who was undesirable in the Bridge Department, everybody melded in and it was a great bunch....I couldn't want a better job really.

Sunderland built a sterling reputation for the Bridge Division through its innovative work on the George Washington and Golden Gate Bridge cables. When CF&I bought the Roebling plants, its executives continued to give Blair a free hand in running the department, as he recalled in a 1993 interview:

CF&I really didn't fuss with Roebling very much. They let us run our own show. We had one boss there just as we always had, selected by us, and so we went along very much as usual and we did a lot of things in the Bridge Department during that time.

At the end of 1963, CF&I began to look more closely at Roebling. Before long we saw we no longer had a single boss there, we found eight, nine department heads in our building reporting to different people in Denver, Colorado (at CF&I's main office), and you would find one department head investigating another department for the benefit of his boss.

It was just terrible, depressing attitudes and actions on the people that worked there. Right away they began trying to close down the Bridge Department because we were the only little group in the whole corporation that did any contracting at all, or any engineering other than plant engineering. So right away they started saying that we should shut down.

Well, during the spring of 1964 everybody at Roebling

above me and I were all in favor of keeping the Bridge Department going. We had a big meeting up in New York with the corporate headquarters of CF&I and we finally talked them down. The problem was, I could not promise them a profit every year. I could show them a good forecast for a five-year period, because we were up and down like that in our market, but they couldn't tolerate that. They were practically owned by insurance companies themselves and they had to insist everybody make a profit all the time. But they did let us go for a while.

Then along came the cable contract for the second Delaware Memorial Bridge. We lost that contract, but only because Bethlehem Steel, which had all the years previous used us whenever they wanted to do any cable work, decided to get into the business themselves. So they bid a price there to buy that job that was so low it was just ridiculous, nobody could even touch it. That gave the CF&I people in Denver the reason they wanted. They said, 'Okay, you lost that, and what other bridges are coming along? Let's forget it.'

Then they decided to shut down the Bridge Department, in September....I spent the rest of the year working down the order book and trying to find places for my people and then my actual employment terminated the end of 1964.... Steinman was the place that looked like it needed me the most and I could probably do more for myself up there.[15]

CF&I's vice president of sales announced in the *CF&I BLAST* in October, 1964, that, "as part of the corporation's continuing policy to strengthen its competitive position, the Roebling Bridge Department will be consolidated with other functions within the corporation. The lack of any appreciable Bridge work in the foreseeable future made the move necessary.... Although we are going out of the contracting and erection end of the bridge business, you'll still be manufacturing and selling those elements that go into bridge building such as bridge wire, strand and wire rope." As Patterson recalled in 2007:[16]

They closed the Bridge Department just for lack of work. They had a lot of expensive people there and a big corporation couldn't see forking out all that money when there were no jobs ahead of us that we could see....

CF&I made the announcement and Blair came out and said they were going to shut us off because there weren't enough jobs to support the people. Everybody understood, but it didn't make us feel any better. Everybody went their own way and got jobs....I went back into wire rope engineering - small engineering problems and drawings of new socket types they were exploring....

Blair left when the Bridge Department closed. There was no other place for him and he didn't want to stay and manufacture wire rope, that's why he went to Steinman Boynton Engineers in New York....that's where he got a job and stayed until re retired.

Figure 7.33: **Specialties of the House** ad, c1965. RM In the mid-1960s, Colorado Fuel & Iron Corp. changed its name to CF&I Steel, and operated its Roebling plants as the Roebling Wire and Cold Rolled Steel Products Division

With strong growth in the housing and automobile markets, the introduction of main-frame computers, the Vietnam War, and low unemployment, the U.S. economy in the 1960s recorded the nation's longest period of uninterrupted expansion. In 1965, the U.S. steel industry employed 600,000 people who produced a record 131 million tons of steel, but steel company executives faced a number of problems that clouded the industry's future prospects.[18]

With 85 companies making steel in the U.S., 26 producing more than 500,000 tons annually, and a total of 275 different companies manufacturing steel products, there was a lot of excess capacity that would be idled by an economic downturn. The high cost of wages and benefits in the U.S. contributed to record imports of cheaper foreign steel, and lighter and less expensive plastic and aluminum materials continued to displace steel in finished products. Companies with older plants also had higher costs than the 21 companies that made steel in more efficient postwar plants.

The industry needed significant investment in research and development and productivity improvements, but the cyclical nature of the steel business provided inconsistent profits to fund these adequately. Rising concerns about air and water pollution forced steel executives to install expensive dust collectors and other pollution control equipment that contributed little to productivity. There was also a growing shortage of metallurgists with advanced degrees.

CF&I's investment in the electric furnaces at the Roebling Plant updated steel making there and a new gas-scrubber reduced toxic emissions, but the electric furnaces also generated additional ground pollution. J.A.R.'s Sons Co. workers had transported cold slag from the open hearth furnaces to the western end of its property along the Delaware River and dumped it there for decades. With the electric furnaces, workers used a 50 ton LaTourneau forklift to carry molten slag to the dumping area and dumped it while it was still hot, which left the resulting waste more congealed after it cooled. CF&I executives cited the more efficient molten slag dumping as a benefit of their cost control program at the Roebling Plant.[19]

CF&I President Rudolph Smith assured the company's employees at the beginning of 1966 that strong profits "have strengthened the ability of CF&I to undertake major programs for plant modernization and improvement, which are essential to the future of the corporation….With the improvements of the financial structure and the various programs underway in all areas of the Corporation, I am confident that we are building for the future well-being of the Corporation."[20]

Steinman Boynton was the successor to Robinson & Steinman, the engineering firm of David B. Steinman, the prominent engineer and author of *Builders of the Bridge*, his 1942 book on John and Washington Roebling and the Brooklyn Bridge. In 1984, Birdsall became a partner in Steinman Boynton Gronquist & Birdsall, and the Manhattan Borough President proclaimed May 24 as Blair Birdsall Day, giving him the honorific title of "Mr. Bridges." When he died at the age of 90 in 1997, Blair was consulting on the design of the Great Belt (Storebaelt) Bridge in Denmark. With a span of 5,328 feet, it was 1,128 feet longer than the Golden Gate Bridge, on which Blair had worked when he started at Roebling in 1934.[17]

When it closed the Bridge Division in 1964, CF&I employed 12,000 people, operated 42 sales offices, and made over 1,200 products at its manufacturing plants in Colorado, California, Massachusetts, and New Jersey. CF&I managers consolidated the Trenton and Roebling Plants with their Palmer, Massachusetts, plant in a new "Eastern Division" headquartered at 630 South Broad Street in Trenton, the old Roebling General Office, and they started referring to them as the "Trenton Plants" or "New Jersey Plants." They started marketing prestressed wire and strand produced at the Trenton and Roebling plants as "suspension systems," and various wire products as "CF&I-Roebling" (Fig. 7.33). Maintaining the Roebling brand seemed less and less important to CF&I executives in New York and Denver, and they eventually used it only for wire rope and slings made in Trenton. To modernize the Colorado Fuel and Iron Corporation's image, the directors changed its name to CF&I Steel Corporation.

World's first 5-inch wire rope made by CF&I

CF&I Steel's new preforming head turns out the world's first 5-inch diameter wire rope as Mary Jane Bodnar, Trenton Wire Rope Sales, watches. First user of the new wire rope will be the Bucyrus-Erie Company on a giant dragline they are building for the Ohio Power Company's coal mining operation.

Trenton produced wire rope to be used on world's largest mobile land machine

TRENTON, New Jersey— Marking its 120th year in the rope making business, CF&I Steel Corporation's Trenton Plant has come up with another first for the Corporation — the world's first 5-inch diameter wire rope.

First customer for the new wire rope is the Bucyrus-Erie Company of Milwaukee, who is building the world's largest mobile land machine — a 220-cubic yard dragline — to be used by the Ohio Power Company's huge coal surface-mining and land reclamation operation in Southern Ohio. Bucyrus-Erie officials, other prospective customers and members of the press previewed the 5-inch rope at ceremonies in Trenton earlier this month.

The dragline will have four hoist ropes made of CF&I-Roebling Royal Blue 5-inch wire rope to lift a total of 550 tons, including the dragline bucket and 325 tons of earth and rock. Nearly one mile of the wire rope will be used.

Weighing 27-million pounds—more than 150 Boeing "727" jetliners — the $20-million dragline will have a reach of 310 feet. It could be positioned between two football fields, reach over one goal post with its 220-cubic yard bucket and dig 325 tons of material, hoist it 18 stories high and dump it beyond the goal post of the second football field in less than one minute. It can do this continuously day after day with shutdown periods only for crew changes and maintenance.

A marketing breakthrough for CF&I Steel, the 5-inch wire rope typifies the

company's accelerated program of product improvement and development through engineering and research.

To help implement this aggressive program, future plans call for a modern laboratory for basic and applied research that will enable CF&I to develop new products and improve existing lines. Areas for new or improved products that are being investigated include aluminum coated wire, improved grinding media, plastic coated wire, improved prestressed strand, a broader range of wide flange beams, hardened rails, and different types of cutting edges.

CF&I 5-INCH WIRE ROPE

Figure 7.34: *CF&I BLAST*, **February, 1968. RM**
In 1968, engineers at the Trenton Works modified Charles Roebling's 1893 80-Ton Wire Rope Machine to produce a 5 in. wire rope for a giant excavator at a strip mine near Zanesville, Ohio.
In the photo at left, Mary Jane Bodnar, of CF&I's Trenton Wire Rope Sales office, stands next to the huge closing head that the engineers created to lay 6 strands around a core strand to form the 5 in. wire rope.
As the *BLAST* noted in an earlier issue about a 2.1 million lb. tensioning test of the rope at Lehigh University's Fritz Laboratory in Bethlehem, Pa.,

The largest wire rope in the world, manufactured at CF&I Steel Corporation's Trenton Plant, passed its breaking test by almost breaking down the powerful machine that inflicted its punishment.[22]

Got a tough wire rope problem?

In February, 1968, CF&I announced that it was making the world's largest wire rope at its Trenton plant (Figs. 7.34-35) for the 320 ft. draglines on a giant Bucyrus-Erie excavator called "Big Muskie," the world's largest mobile land machine. Charlie Brenner, who was born on Hewitt Street in Trenton, had studied engineering at Rutgers University and had worked for J.A.R.'s Sons Co. since 1946, oversaw the production of this unprecedented wire rope. By the mid-1960s he had become the plant engineer in the wire rope division, which included the 80-Ton Wire Rope Machine that Charles Roebling had built in 1893 to make 30,000 ft. long wire ropes for cable cars. As Brenner explained in a 1993 interview:

Bucyrus-Erie, the equipment manufacturing company, and American Electric Power wanted to build the biggest strip mining shovel in the world out in the Midwest. They wanted to build a shovel that could take the overburden off a coal mine out there, to take 75 feet of earth off the top of coal. They wanted to pick up 300 tons of earth in one scoop and they needed 5 in. wire rope for the shovel.

At that point in time, we could make a 4 in. diameter rope and nobody else could make it. They asked us if we could make 5 in. rope and we decided we could with the 80-Ton Wire Rope Machine. We made alterations to the

machine and produced the 5 in. wire rope for them. It weighs 46 pounds a foot. We made 1,300 ft. lengths which were then cut into two pieces and shipped on ten ft. reels out to their site where the shovel was built.[21]

Figure 7.35: "From CF&I-Roebling, of course" brochure, 1968.

CF&I-Roebling Royal Blue, the extra rugged wire rope. CF&I controls every step in the manufacturing of Royal Blue from steel making up... roll our own rods, draw our own CF&I-Roebling developed Type 1105 rope wire, the world's toughest wire.

The Bucyrus-Erie excavator required nearly one mile of the 5 in. rope to drag and lift a 550 ton load of earth and rock in a 220 cu. yd. bucket and lift it 18 stories high. As CF&I noted in its press release: "Got a tough wire rope problem? Take it to the leader. CF&I-Roebling." CF&I rope shop workers continued making the 5 in. wire ropes until the Trenton Plant closed in 1973. U.S. Steel's American Steel & Wire subsidiary across the D&R Canal right-of-way subsequently leased the 80-Ton Wire Rope Machine and continued making 5 in. wire ropes on it for several years.

Cease polluting the river

In the four years since New Jersey Department of Health officials had recommended that CF&I treat the Roebling Plant's wastewater before discharging it into the Delaware River, CF&I had not complied. In May, 1968, frustrated officials "ordered CF&I to cease polluting the river, requiring the plant to construct a wastewater treatment facility." CF&I executives incorporated the treatment facility into a five-year, $115 million (about $741 million in 2009) "Blueprint for Progress" program of capital improvements, which they approved in November 1968. As the *CF&I BLAST* noted:[23]

> *'Blueprint for Progress' is designed to increase earnings capability, primarily through modernized equipment and improved operations. The program contemplates strengthening the corporation's competitive position through greater flexibility in manufacturing processes and quality of products - enabling it take maximum advantage of unique geographical and marketing positions.*
>
> *The Blueprint program is a major part of a long-range plan reaching into many corporate areas in addition to manufacturing. Because its immediate aim is more efficient and economical operations, it is expected to quickly enhance the ability to earn more….in a more reliable and predictable manner.*[24]

CF&I is here to stay

The program included $23 million (about $148 million in 2009) for upgrading the Trenton and Roebling plants. While CF&I officials noted that the investment "should strongly reinforce our corporate structure and indicate our resolve to remain competitive in the New Jersey area," the program also included some cutbacks in Trenton:

> *The wire rope manufacturing operations at Trenton are in the process of being rearranged and consolidated to eliminate multilevel operations in diverse locations. Increased efficiency and substantial costs savings are expected to result from the centralization of facilities.*
>
> *The cold rolled steel facilities will be transferred from Trenton to Roebling providing a concentration of both steel and wire manufacturing at one location. This move will facilitate the capability of the Roebling Plant to successfully compete with the mini steel plants being built or projected for the eastern part of the United States.*
>
> *An additional benefit to accrue as a result of these moves will be the release of more than half of the presently occupied buildings at Trenton for sale, lease or other utilization.*

As the *CF&I BLAST* noted: "Reduction in operating space will exceed fifty percent and provide maximum operating efficiency at reduced cost." The reductions vacated the Trenton Plant's north and east blocks, and consolidated the remaining production into the 1930s rope shops on the central block.[25]

In December, 1968, CF&I announced that it planned to vacate its Eastern Division Office at 640 South Broad Street in Trenton. With rumors spreading that after closing two-thirds of its Trenton Plant and its office there, CF&I was going to leave Trenton altogether, a "top company official" went to see the editor of the *Trenton Evening Times* to clear up this "false impression" and told him: "Nothing could be further from the truth, CF&I is here to stay."[26]

At the Roebling Plant, CF&I installed "an 18 in. Cold Rolling Mill to meet customer requirements of quality and close tolerances." The "Blueprint for Progress" also included environmental controls at CF&I's plants:

> *Air and water quality equipment to be incorporated at manufacturing facilities has been allocated approximately $11 million (about $70.1 million). Programs for the Palmer (Mass.) and Roebling Plants are concerned with abatement of river pollution, while the maintenance of both air and water quality standards will be of prime concern at Pueblo.*[27]

Environmental concerns rose to national prominence in January, 1969, when an underwater pipe burst on a Union Oil Company platform off the coast of Santa Barbara, California, and discharged 100,000 barrels of oil that fouled hundreds of square miles of ocean and some 35 miles of the coast. Public outrage over such an egregious example of industrial pollution led to the passage of the National Environmental Protection Act that President Richard Nixon had originally opposed but signed, creating the U.S. Environmental Protection Agency (EPA) with an unprecedented mandate:

> *To declare national policy which will encourage productive and enjoyable harmony between man and his environment; to promote efforts which will prevent or eliminate damage to the environment and biosphere and stimulate the health and welfare of man; to enrich the understanding of the ecological systems and natural resources important to the nation.*[28]

Charles Allen, who was now 66 years old, had approved the "Blueprint for Progress," but he had controlled CF&I for 25 years, and, like the Rockefeller heirs back in 1944, he had lost interest in the corporation's future. While domestic steel production increased in the 1960s, the U.S. portion of world steel production had fallen by more than half from 47 percent in 1950 to 22 percent in 1969. For Allen, increasing labor and environmental costs, foreign competition and the obsolescence of its plants suggested limited growth potential for CF&I. Allen was a genteel investment banker and he wasn't interested in wringing out more profits by closing facilities and slashing costs, especially when it meant laying off long-time employees. But Allen knew someone who had no such reservations.

Allen had assisted Thomas Mellon Evans (Fig. 7.36) in his failed takeover attempt of the Westinghouse Air Brake Company a year earlier, and he suggested that Evans take a look at CF&I. Evans was Chairman of the Crane Corporation, a family-run Chicago manufacturer of plumbing fixtures when Evans took it over in 1958. One of his earliest moves was to lay off 700 people at Crane's main plant, which prompted angry union members to picket Crane's annual stockholder meeting in 1960 with signs reading: "Money-Mad Evans Has No Hart." By this time Evans already had a reputation as "the leading practitioner of a strange new form of corporate ruthlessness, one that squeezed 'fat' out of profitable corporations in the relentless pursuit of greater profit."[29]

Figure 7.36: Thomas Mellon Evans, c1960. Born in Pittsburgh, the financier took took control of the Crane Corporation in 1958, and devised Crane's takeover of CF&I in 1968. After Evans closed several companies and laid off many workers in the 1960s, New Jersey Congressman Frank Thompson, Jr., called him "the corporate embodiment of Jaws, the great white shark." [33]

Evans built Crane into a profitable conglomerate of companies with a tight management overseeing diverse products, including industrial valves and pumps and equipment for plumbing, heating, water treatment, and aerospace projects. In 1968, *The Wall Street Journal* described Evans as "something of a legend for his tough methods of operating the company once he wins control. He demands prompt profit performance from both assets and men: if he doesn't get it, he sells the assets or fires the men." With 1968 sales of $410 million (about $2.6 billion in 2009), Crane was a little less than twice the size of CF&I, which had sales of $210 million in 1967 (about $1.4 billion).[30]

Evans had grown up in Pittsburgh as a "stranger in paradise." His mother was a distant cousin of Andrew Mellon, the famous banker, industrialist, philanthropist, art collector, Secretary of the Treasury, and Ambassador to Great Britain. That connection and his father's presidency of a small bank earned the family "a comfortable and secure spot on the lower slopes of the Iron City's formidable industrial aristocracy."[31]

His father died suddenly when he was three and his mother died when he was 11, having set aside the insurance money from her husband's death to pay for the education of Thomas and his sister. As they were raised by relatives and as Evans attended Yale, like his father had, he was always on the fringe of the wealth and culture of the Mellons and other elite Pittsburgh families. A biographer speculated that Mellon's early loss of his parents hardened his heart, and his longing to live like the Mellons drove his hunger for wealth – a potent combination for a ruthless capitalist.

When Allen suggested that Evans take a look at CF&I, Evans already knew a fair amount about the steel industry. The foundation of his wealth was the H.K. Porter Company of Pittsburgh, which had been a manufacturer of steam locomotives when Evans took it over in 1939. In the three decades since then, Evans had built it into a conglomerate of some 30 companies, including a steel division manufacturing specialty products.

Evans' son, Robert Sheldon Evans, known as Shel, joined Crane in 1968 at the age of 24 after obtaining an MBA from Columbia University and did the financial analysis on CF&I. After reviewing this analysis and touring CF&I's Pueblo steel plant, Thomas Evans said: "It's an excellent fully integrated mill and it services a booming part of the country - Texas, Oklahoma and the Southwest. It would cost $700 million (about $4.5 billion) to build a mill like that today. And CF&I owns 360,000 acres of undeveloped land out there, which isn't a bad thing to have in a time of inflation." With its common shares trading for about two-thirds of their book value, CF&I was "exactly the kind of situation Evans loved."[32]

Crane had earned $5 million (about $32 million) in Evans' failed attempt to takeover the Westinghouse Air Brake Company and he used it to quietly buy CF&I stock. By early spring, 1969, Evans had accumulated 380,000 shares and he made his move on CF&I. On March 29, he announced an exchange offer in which CF&I shareholders could exchange their stock for Crane Corporation bonds with a 15 year maturity. One half of the bonds could be converted to Crane stock. As a veteran CF&I executive later recalled, "the steel company was shaken."[34]

At the CF&I board meeting in May, Evans listened to a "Blueprint for Progress" update and then asked to speak:

> *Although he was not a director, he was a major stockholder, he said, and he felt he ought to review any proposal to spend such a substantial amount of the company's money. 'A chill came over the whole group,' said Al Pocius (chief of CF&I public relations). 'Everything froze at that point.' The managers soon filed out of the boardroom, leaving the shaken directors to continue their meeting with their aggressive guest.*
>
> *Evans had done his homework. He earmarked units that could be put on his famous cost-cutting diet, but he also was willing to put money in to modernize and support profitable operations. He could not understand the American steel industry's fixation on the quantity of tonnage produced, rather than the profits generated by that production.*
>
> *Imports were a problem, certainly. 'The auto companies have cheaper import competition,' he reasoned. 'But they make money on the cars they sell.' The only way American steel makers could prosper would be if they could make money on every ton of steel they sold.[35]*

In June, Crane announced that it had acquired 80 percent of CF&I's outstanding stock. CF&I President Frederick A. Fielder stated that:

> *The association of our two companies greatly enhances the future business prospects for both of us. Crane's broad range of manufacturing facilities both here and abroad and CF&I's wide range of steelmaking operations fit together perfectly for a future of increased income for debenture and shareholders and job security for employees.*
>
> *Mr. Thomas M. Evans, Chairman of Crane, has expressed that one of the major reasons Crane became interested in CF&I was the high regard they have for the accomplishments and abilities of the CF&I management team and the steelmaking capabilities of our employees.*
>
> *Crane also has no plans for making any changes in the officers or management of CF&I and intends to continue existing pension and other employee benefit programs in accordance with their terms.[36]*

Evans' actions quickly belied his words. He moved CF&I's headquarters from Denver to Pueblo so its managers could maintain better control over its flagship steel plant there, and longtime employees soon found themselves at risk of losing much of what they had loyally worked for:

> *Evans' brisk, sometimes rude manner severely jolted the Colorado management. In a letter submitted as a congressional exhibit five years later, Al Pocius described Evans' reign at CF&I in extraordinarily harsh terms: 'He instituted a management housecleaning, zeroing in particularly on those who had a long service but were still a couple of years or so from qualifying for pensions. Some people were fired summarily....one associate committed suicide; another attempted to do so.'[37]*

Obsolete for our purposes

Governor William T. Cahill signed legislation creating the New Jersey Department of Environmental Protection (N.J. DEP) on April 22, 1970, the nation's first "Earth Day." The new department, the third in the country, consolidated previous environmental programs into a "unified major agency to administer aggressive environmental protection and conservation efforts."[38]

By spring, 1970, Crane Corporation had sold the J.A.R.'s Sons Co. General Office buildings at 640 South Broad Street at the Trenton Plant to Mercer County for its administrative offices. Crane sold the 12 buildings at the plant that CF&I's 1968 "Blueprint for Progress" had targeted for vacating to the Newark Parafine Paper Company, also known as Norpac. The sale included the Plant's entire north block (Block 3), with the Elmer and Clark Street Rope Shops, the Boiler House, Engine House and Carpenter Shop, plus the Clinton Avenue Wire Mill and the Machine Shop on the central block (Block 1).

Charles Roebling had erected these buildings between 1890 and 1918. A spokesman for the Crane Corporation told a reporter that "the buildings are considered obsolete for our purposes but are excellent for light manufacturing and warehousing." Norpak labeled its new property the Trenton Industrial Center and stored huge rolls of paper in some of the buildings, and it leased others for light manufacturing and warehousing that created several hundred jobs.

Thomas Evans came to Trenton and Roebling in 1971 to see the CF&I plants there for himself. CF&I continued scaling back wire rope production at the Trenton plant because the lower cost of imported wire rope made the operation uncompetitive. Evans was more optimistic about steel and wire production at the Roebling Plant and continued to invest in improvements there.

In 1972, CF&I completed its $3.5 million (about $18.6 million in 2009) wastewater treatment facility at the Roebling Plant, eight years after the N.J. Department of Health had called for its construction. The facility included "a raw waste pumping station, an acid neutralization system, flocculation tanks, settling tanks, an oil collection and reclamation system, sludge lagoons, and a control building and laboratory." CF&I invested another $1.2 million (about $6.4 million) in air pollution control equipment and ordered a new Morgan "No-Twist" Rod Mill to replace the 1928 Rod Mill, giving everyone hope there that the plant would keep operating for many more years. In April, 1973, CF&I shut down the Trenton plant because of "continuing losses" (see box).[39]

That October, when the Syrian and Egyptian armies attacked Israel and started the Yom Kippur War, the United States resupplied Israel with military equipment, and the Organization of Petroleum Exporting Companies (OPEC) retaliated with a 70 percent increase in its oil price, a reduction in output, and an embargo against selling to the United States. As the embargo took effect, Americans lined up at gasoline stations to get some of the limited supply available. Within a few months the price of oil nearly tripled, triggering a spike in inflation. With the increased cost of fuel oil for heating rods, CF&I shut down one of the rod mills at the Roebling Plant, idling 50 workers. U.S. Steel's Fairless Works across the Delaware River in Bucks County laid off 200 workers.

While steel demand and prices were gradually increasing, the price of scrap steel on the east coast spiraled because of European demand, making it impossible for plants like Roebling that made steel from scrap to produce steel profitably. Another unanticipated expense arose when the contractor installing the new rod mill at Roebling had trouble reaching solid ground for the footings, and demanded $1.5 million (about $6 million) more for the installation. In addition, CF&I's contract with the United Steel Workers at Roebling was up for renewal in August, and a new contract would undoubtedly raise wage and pension costs as the union wanted to protect its members from inflation. Faced with current losses and limited prospects for future profits, Evans gave up on the Roebling Plant and CF&I issued a press release:

Roebling, N.J., April 2, 1974 - CF&I Steel Corporation announced today that its Roebling, New Jersey, plant had stopped entering orders for delivery after June 30. J.R. Nelson, General Manager, stated that the Company had been unable to stem continuing losses arising principally from the increased costs of scrap:

'Those steel companies which have their own supply of iron ore are in position to hold down their raw material

---

"An Industrial Giant Dies Quietly in City,"
- *Trenton Sunday Times Advertizer*, April 30, 1973

A company which for more than a century was Trenton's largest, a worldwide leader in its industry, died quietly during the past week. At the end it was a wasted shadow of its once vibrant self. Only a relative handful of people were directly affected by its passing. But it is mourned by many who remember what it was like in its vigorous prime....

Eighty-five people were employed on the last day in a small section of the huge South Trenton manufacturing complex where many thousands once worked, producing billions of miles of wire every year.

Thus ended a long chapter in the city's industrial history which began in 1848. John Augustus Roebling, an immigrant from Germany, built his first small rope mill here. The tiny company went on to become the largest specialty wire manufacturer in the United States. No manufacturer in the world made more different types of wire rope then did the John A. Roebling's Sons Company....So important a factor was it in the city's economy that the saying was frequently heard: 'As Roebling's goes, so goes Trenton.'....

Many former officials and employees look back fondly on the close relationship between management and workers during the Roebling regime. 'It was a family relationship, a loyalty second to none,' commented one....

Why did CF&I close up shop here? Continuing losses is the only explanation given by the company.

---

costs, but the Roebling Plant is entirely dependent upon scrap which has now reached a price of $118 per ton, compared with $40 per ton approximately a year ago. This scrap situation on the East Coast is particularly bad with a substantial amount of scrap being exported. Increased labor and energy costs have also contributed to these losses.'

Mr. Nelson acknowledged that the Company had discussed the sale of the plant with a number of potential purchasers, but has thus far been unable to work out any firm commitment. 'We are continuing to study the situation,' Mr. Nelson said, 'but unless some unforeseen change develops, it may be necessary to consider termination of operations at the Roebling Plant.'

"Roebling...An Ideal is Shaken"
- J.J. Sciortino, April 25, 1974

The fate of the Roebling plant today, is in question. It's employees, many of whom have spent their entire lives there, ponder the eventual outcome of the plant, as well as their pensions, and even perhaps their pride. From the beginning, the Roebling family gave their employees hope for survival. In witness, strength and a deep sense of pride - a Roebling spirit - the community is determined to hold on.[40]

Figure 7.37 (above):
"Employees, town, share alike in fate of CF&I,"
Burlington County Times, May 12, 1974. LB
Man walks past near empty scrap yards at CF&I in Roebling.

Figure 7.38 (right): "The Week Roebling Closed,"
Trenton Times, June 30, 1974. LB
*One day last week, an angry woman here called
a Florence Township official and exploded:
'I could fill that old Mr. Evans full of lead,' she said.*

SILENT STEEL MILL — There is a sense of uneasiness in the village of Roebling after the closing of the CF&I steel plant at the top of this aerial photo. The view is north from Hornberger Avenue, with United Steelworkers Local 2110 headquarters at the bottom right.

The Week Roebling Closed: Fear Mingles With Anger

It's the only thing I know

CF&I employed 1,323 people at the Roebling Plant and about 40 percent of them had worked there for more than 30 years. Harry Danley, president of United Steel Workers Local 2111, told a reporter that the workers "were shook up" over the news (Figs. 7.37-78). One worker asked, "How can they close the plant down with such a big domestic and worldwide need for steel?" Andy Kotch, 59, a 40 year man, said: "What in the heck am I going to do? I've been driving a tractor at this place since I was 18." Ray Arnold, 56, said: "I've been pulling wire for 38 years. It's the only thing I know." An estimated 400 workers risked losing their pensions if the plant shutdown.[41]

CF&I paid $418,000 (about $2 million) in real estate taxes to Florence Township, 25 percent of the total taxes, and about one-half of Roebling residents depended on the plant for a livelihood. Florence Township Mayor Kenneth Wilkie suggested to New Jersey's representatives that Congress enact a tariff on the export of scrap steel, but the inaction in Washington frustrated him and many others, and he wished Congress would "get back on the job," as he vehemently told a reporter: "No one's minding the store. There are vital pieces of legislation which should be passed, but Congress is so wrapped up in Watergate that nothing gets done."[42]

He better not come round here

Harry Danley said that many men at the plant believed that "the current owner is a realtor who works a plant until it collapses and then sells it." As chairman of both the H.K. Porter Company and the Crane Corporation, Evans had already shutdown four plants in Trenton in six years, putting 1,300 people out of work at Porter's Thermoid Rubber and Riverside-Alloy Metal divisions, Crane's Trenton pottery and CF&I's Trenton plant.[43]

When one steelworker at the Roebling Plant said, "Somebody ought to put a contract out on that guy," another replied, "I don't know about that, but he better not come around here."

Evans claimed that he had tried to sell the Roebling Plant for 18 months before he directed Nelson, the general manager, to stop taking orders for steel. Bethlehem Steel executives showed some serious interest in acquiring the plant, but with Washington officials preoccupied by Watergate, they gave up on getting the necessary waiver from federal anti-trust regulations that prohibited too much control of production facilities by any one company. The Bethlehem executives were also put off by CF&I's huge pension obligations to the plant's current and retired employees.

We tried everything we could

At the beginning of June, Evans told a *Philadelphia Bulletin* reporter: "I'll bet it's been shown to 50 people, but we can't find a buyer. Nobody will touch it with a ten foot pole.... Bethlehem has lost interest. Everybody's lost interest. Nobody wants it" (Fig. 7.39). Evans termed the $15 million (about $73 million in 2009) selling price "a rare bargain. You couldn't build it now for $75 million (about $364 million)." He cited two reasons why the Roebling Plant was unprofitable:

> *One, the plant is dependent on scrap metal and the price of scrap has risen in one year from $40 a ton to $118. And two, wages. This is a mini plant but we have to pay big steel wages. We can't make a go of it. We've been slow facing up to the situation. Going along for years not making any money. Improving the plant but not getting anything back. We tried everything we could and finally gave up.*[44]

The *Bulletin* reporter noted that: "Evans is viewed as a wheeler dealer who milks companies of their assets, selling them or closing them, with never a care for the economic impact on workers." Regarding the effect of the closing on the town, Evans commented: "I guess it won't help it any."

Figure 7.39: "For Immediate Sale," 1974. Equipment categories included Steel Making, Rolling Mills, Heating, Wire Mill, Wire Drawing Machines, Galvanizing & Plating, Stranders, Welded Fabric, Cold Rolling, and Service Locomotives.

A few days later the president of the Kurt Orban Steel Company of Wayne, New Jersey, announced that he had negotiated an "agreement in principal" with Evans to buy the plant. Orban Steel had four wire mills but the owners wanted to make their own steel. Members of the United Steel Workers Local 2111 voted to extend their contract for three years with a 12 percent wage increase so Orban could calculate its labor costs during that period.

International United Steel Workers officials demanded that CF&I guarantee the contract's shutdown benefits for three years, a liability that could reach $20 million (about $97 million). At the agreement signing meeting in New York on June 25, Evans refused to accept the union's demand and the deal died. The next day Nelson announced that CF&I would shut the plant in four days.

How much I'm leaving behind

George Sampson, who was a foreman in the Tempering Shop with nearly 20 years of service, recalled the shutdown:

> *It was a surprise....this came pretty sudden. I had enough time just to pack up my things, and you drove out in your car and that was the end of the story....End of shift, goodbye.*
> *Just before they closed they did a lot of renovation in there, they constructed a new flat shop with all ultramodern equipment and did a lot of refurbishing in the Tempering Shop where I was....It seemed like a shame to spend all this money, then it's gone. It was strange.*
> *I remember driving out the last day. I felt very bad, very sad about it, and when I drove out the gate, I thought, 'How much I'm leaving behind, this history of mine that got me there, and I'm leaving it there on the other side of the fence.*[45]

Bill Lovelett, a plant engineer at Roebling who had graduated from Rensselaer Polytechnic Institute, where Washington and Charles Roebling had also studied engineering, recalled:

> *There were no tears....Every person did a heck of a job cleaning up. The place was cleaner than your living room. All the material that could be shipped, was shipped....*
> *A lot of people had already been furloughed because they started at the beginning of the production line and worked all the way down until the last piece came out at the end....*
> *A lot of people I think they had the feeling that somebody would buy the place and it would come alive again. They put out a wide circulation of brochures advertising the place for sale and after the closing we had an endless parade of buyers who wanted to buy everything from a pencil sharpener, right up to the whole thing. Some of my staff stayed on and we conducted guided tours, one after the other, for quite some time.*[46]

Crane Corporation executives started selling the plant equipment to various buyers, expecting to net $20-25 million (about $97-121 million) if they sold everything separately. Bethlehem Steel purchased wire drawing and stranding equipment and Cooper Industries of Houston, Texas, bought the cold rolled department for its Lufkin Rule subsidiary, a long-time Roebling customer for the flat wire it used to manufacture its measuring tapes.

Evans also negotiated with firms interested in buying the rest of the equipment and the site, including three that showed serious interest: the New York Wire Company, a division of the Canadian steel company Ivaco Incorporated; Southwire, an electrical wire manufacturer in Carrollton, Georgia; and the Federal Steel and Wire Corporation, a family-owned company in Cleveland headed by Robert Alpert, its 25-year-old president.

While Evans negotiated with Alpert, the president of the Crane Corporation summoned Bill Lovelett to its New York headquarters to ask him whether it was worth keeping the 1928 Rod Mill out of the deal, which Evans wanted to do. As Lovelett recalled:

> Dante Fabriani, the president of Crane Corporation said, 'Well you know more about the rod mill than I do, so let's go tell Evans.' We went down to Mr. Evans' office and the secretary said, 'Mr. Evans is talking on the phone and has sixteen calls waiting.' Fabriani, said, 'I'm exercising my prerogative,' and that permitted him to move on top— so we went in.
>
> I was introduced to Evans and Fabriani said real quick, 'Yesterday you took out the rod mill, the locomotive and three railroad cars. Mr. Lovelett said he would not keep the rod mill.'
>
> Evans asked me, 'Why would you not keep the rod mill?'
>
> I told him, 'It's from 1929, antiquated, technologically behind, and it's not up to today's standards of quality.'
>
> He immediately turned to Fabriani and quoted off some financial jargon which I didn't follow and told him, 'Put the rod mill back in, put the engine back in and put the cars back in.'
>
> Then he said to me, 'Could you unequivocally without any reservation say that nobody would ever buy the rod mill?'
>
> I said, 'No, I can't say that, but I would not tell anybody to buy the rod mill.'
>
> Then he said this statement that left me aghast, 'What do you do in a rod mill?'
>
> So I said, 'You take square steel bars, heat them red hot and roll them down into rods the size of a pencil.' He said, 'That's good enough, thank you,' and picked up the phone.
>
> I dare say that Evans was beyond 60. He sat behind a desk but he was impressive. I never saw him again.[47]

Figure 7.40: "Old Roebling Plant fires for new life," *Trenton Evening Times*, **November 20, 1974. LB Roebling Steel & Wire Corporation President Robert Albert, his father, Ferdinand Alpert, and Mary G. Roebling (see Fig. 6.48), President of National State Bank, watched the first melt of steel at the Roebling Plant in five months.**

It's a beautiful sight

Alpert originally paid $4.5 million (about $21.6 million) in cash for the remaining equipment with plans to ship it to Michigan. On October 19, however, he announced that the Alpert Brothers Leasing Company, another family business in Troy, Michigan, had purchased the Roebling Plant for $3.5 million (about $17 million), $1 million in cash and the rest with a mortgage, and had formed the Roebling Steel and Wire Corp. to operate it. He estimated that Roebling Steel and Wire would employ about 1,000 workers, utilize about half of the plant's two million sq. ft. of buildings and lease the other half.

Alpert told a reporter: "Our organization is a privately held family operation with substantial know-how in the metalworking industry. The family operates numerous plants throughout the country producing ferrous and non ferrous metal and has been in the business three generations." Florence Township Mayor Kenneth Wilkie said: "The prayers of many people have been answered. It will cease the worries of many who have been affected by the plant closing. We hope this company will stay as long as the original Roebling Company."[48]

Four weeks later, Roebling Steel and Wire fired up one of the three steel mill furnaces and a crowd of 200 cheered as workers poured 40 tons of molten steel from the furnace into a ladle with a deafening roar (Fig. 7.40). Sam Balcom, of Trenton, a 17 year man, told a reporter: "It's a beautiful sight. I worked here a long time and I can tell you I've seen a lot of changes at this plant but the feeling here today is unbeatable."[49]

We're going to plant flowers out here

On the day that Alpert made his first melt of steel, Mayor Wilkie said: "We've seen some dark days in Roebling for the past few months. We are very much appreciative that the plant is going to open again and we hope to make a lot of steel....Thank God for people like the Alpert family."

When Alpert walked out of the steel mill that day, he said: "We're going to clean this plant. I'm going to get everything painted. I want this to be a place where people enjoy coming to work. And in the spring, we're going to plant flowers out here."[50]

With the change in ownership, N.J. DEP officials met with Alpert that November to "discuss various aspects of the operations at the site (Fig. 7.41), including the absence of liners under the sludge lagoons, groundwater contamination, oil unloading, landfill, transmission and storage."[51]

Before reopening the plant, Alpert had signed an agreement with the Miscellaneous and Industrial Workers Union of America, an independent union, to represent Roebling Steel employees. By December, Roebling Steel and Wire had 135 employees making steel and rolling billets, but start up, repairs and environmental costs exceeded Alpert's estimates and sales were lower than expected. He asked the union to forgo overtime pay, but its officers declined, saying that it was against state law. Roebling Steel soon owed Florence Township $242,000 in back taxes (about $1.2 million in 2009).

CF&I reported its best year ever in 1974, with revenues increasing 28 percent to $439 million (about $2.1 billion) and earnings increasing to $35 million (about $170 million). As President Clay Crawford proudly noted in the CF&I *BLAST*:

CF&I's record-braking performance reflected the increased profitability and efficiency of the company's improved and modernized facilities that came online during the past six years as part of CF&I's capital expenditure program, the continued high worldwide demand for most of CF&I product lines, and price adjustments that were made during the year after government controls were lifted in May 1974.

The outstanding dedication and efforts of all employees played a large part in the company's success during 1974.[52]

Figure 7.41: The Roebling Steel and Wire Corporation's Plant in Roebling, N.J., *The Trenton Times,* **Feb. 20, 1976. LB   After 70 years of operation, much of the old J.A.R's Sons Company's Kinkora Works was obsolete and contaminated with industrial waste.**

Epilogue: *The people here are ambitious and industrious*

We weren't going to fold up and go away

The Roeblings and their employees over many decades created one of the great legacies of America's industrial age – several of the word's greatest suspension bridges and many other noteworthy bridges, a treasure trove of archival materials in several locations, some outstanding examples of American industrial architecture, one of America's best company towns, and remarkable stories of vision, heroism, ingenuity, innovation, quality, immigration, community, perseverance, and hard work. Like many historic industrial legacies, it also includes contaminated sites that had to be cleaned up.

The Roebling works in Trenton had operated continuously for 124 years when CF&I closed it in 1973 and the Kinkora Works in Roebling for 68 years when CF&I closed it in 1974. Obsolescence, high operating costs, environmental regulations, the international oil crisis, and a stock market decline all contributed to the closings, which are part of the overall waning of America's industrial age. As manufacturing jobs move elsewhere or disappear altogether, former workers and their families and entire communities have had to find new livelihoods and investment. In many cases, communities, states, and the Federal government were also left to deal with obsolete sites and decades of industrial wastes.

Figure E.1: "Iron Willed Roebling Keeps Going - without steel," ***The Trenton Times*, October 25, 1975. LB By the time the plant closed, the town of Roebling had become a suburban community.**

As CF&I shut down in Trenton, Mercer County acquired the Roebling office buildings and private investors purchased the old mills and shops for warehousing and some light manufacturing, which helped fill some of the void left by the closing. The redevelopment of many of these buildings and sites has brought new investment and jobs that have preserved much of their historic character and have helped create a new image for the City, though others remain to be redeveloped.

At the old Kinkora Works in Roebling, a series of businesses attempted to revitalize steel and wire production but struggled with financing and pollution issues. Roebling Steel and Wire Corp. produced steel ingots and billets for five months but missed a $100,000 (about $485,000 in 2009) mortgage payment in April, 1975, and was forced to declare bankruptcy. The Alperts told the judge that they had invested $2.2 million (about $10.7 million) in start up and operating costs. They halted production but leased some of the site for storage and recycling. The second shut down in less that a year made some people wonder about the future of the town, as Mayor Kenneth Wilkie told a *Trenton Times* reporter in October, 1975:[1]

> When the plant closed we had some Philadelphia newsmen come to ask what was going to happen to the town, but I couldn't get them to understand that we weren't going to fold up and go away. The people here are ambitious and industrious....There is a strong family life.
> The people own their homes, no one is going to leave.

As the *Times* reporter noted:

> There has been no mass evacuation from Roebling. A walk down the quiet streets will show that the homes for sale are far outnumbered by the homes that are being repaired and expanded. Why doesn't the mammoth plant dominate the social and economic life of the town as it once did?
> The 1947 sale of the homes is the answer. Before that all the buildings and homes were owned by the Roebling Co. and in order to live in Roebling you had to work in the plant.
> The sale began a slow transformation of the town that is still continuing. Families not connected to the plant began to move into town until Roebling finally changed from company town to suburb. In the end when CF&I closed the plant in 1974 only 150 of the 1400 who lost their jobs lived in Roebling....
> Roebling today is a quaint combination of pensioners, established families who have lived in the town for years and young couples who have found the town with its compact brick homes an economical way to begin their families.
> The three groups are held together by strong family ties and a fierce civic pride.

245

I felt there was so much history here

The American Bicentennial in 1976 raised awareness of the nation's colonial heritage but also of other aspects of our history as well. When CF&I closed the Roebling Plant in 1974, Louis Borbi (Fig. E.2), a sixth grade teacher and Roebling native whose father and other family members worked at the plant, started collecting oral histories and documents about the town and the plant. As Lou recalled in a 2008 interview:

> *I wanted to gather the information because no one was doing it....I felt there was so much history here in town, and no one was collecting it....*
>
> *I used to go to the local bars in town....and the old timers would be there and I'd buy them drinks....They enjoyed talking about Roebling and I enjoyed gathering their stories.*[2]

Thanks to Lou and others interested in the local history, Roebling Village was listed on the State and National Registers of Historic Places and the Roebling Plant was recognized as eligible for the State Register in 1977.

Public awareness of industrial pollution increased markedly in 1978 when President Jimmy Carter declared a "Federal health emergency" at Niagara Falls' Love Canal, where the Hooker Chemical Co. had dumped and covered 21,000 tons of waste between 1942 and 1952. Houses and a school were later built there and by the mid-1970s, residents were exhibiting multiple health problems. EPA officials estimated that there were more than 5,000 hazardous waste sites in the country.

Back to life

In May, 1979, four executives of small steel firms formed the John A. Roebling Steel Corp., "JARSCO," and

purchased the Roebling Plant for $9.5 million (about $31.4 million in 2009). The price included $2 million for equipment, as they noted: "The steel making equipment consists of modern electric arc furnaces and a billet mill. It is in our intention to operate this modern equipment to produce high quality steel billets for the forging industry." The partners planned to lease out about 60 percent of the buildings. They financed JARSCO with $3 million (about $10 million) and a Marine Midland Bank loan for $17 million (about $56 million) that was guaranteed by the N.J. Economic Development Authority and the U.S. Economic Development Administration. In the permitting process, N.J. DEP officials cited JARSCO for health and safety violations for hazardous wastes on the site.[3]

The Bordentown Register News reported that fall: "Doubters were silenced and area businessmen were encouraged when the 75-year-old steel plant in Roebling came back to life after five dormant years." Jack Nelson, who ran the plant for CF&I and was now running it again, said: "I think this time the people are really enthusiastic, really committed to making it work. It's a tremendous group." The 90 workers, mostly "old timers," produced ingots and billets for farm and construction equipment, railroad cars and automobiles. As JARSCO started shipping steel billets in January, 1980 (see box), N.J. DEP

"After a four-year layoff steel furnace heats up,"
- Burlington County Times, **January 27, 1980**

Each night, 47 tons of mangled auto bodies and other scrap metal are loaded by a heavy magnet and giant buckets into an electric arc furnace, 15 feet in diameter. Then three electrodes, resembling stacks atop the furnace, begin to pump and glow as they create a giant short-circuit that melts the scrap.

After about three hours of heating, the steel is ready to be poured. The heavy furnace thunders and groans as it is tilted forward. Through a spout, a stream of brilliant white and yellow liquid steel spills into the ladle sitting in a 22 foot pit below. For four minutes, sparks splash in all directions as a sound like exploding fireworks pierces the air. Thick, orange and black smoke billows. Steam hisses and spits.

With enormous cranes, the ladle, containing 43 tons (four tons less than the scrap) of molten steel is lifted and hauled across the shop to be tapped. Through a hole in the bottom of the ladle, the steel trickles into 30 ingot molds, 15-square inches in size. At this time, a sample is taken to make certain the chemical composition is correct. 'It is the same as making a cake,' said Lou Boldizar, superintendent of the melt shop, 'You have to follow a recipe exactly.'

---

officials named the Roebling Plant as "one of 38 hazardous waste sites most urgently needing cleanup in New Jersey." "Potential pollution problems" included slag piles, 40,000 tires, baghouse dust, and abandoned oil and chemical storage tanks. The U.S. economy slipped into recession that month from the doubling of oil prices during the 1979 energy crisis.[4]

Roebling residents got together in 1980 to mark the 75th anniversary of the village (see box), as Lou Borbi recalled:

A couple of parents of students in my room....they were interested and they said: 'Let's start an historical society.' We contacted John Dimon (see Fig. E.2), he was very interested and he drew up the charter....He grew up here and he was very encouraging to the historical society. He was a motivator, he did a lot, gathered a lot of information. We signed it and we had the historical society that we always wanted.... to preserve the memory of people growing up here. We didn't want that to be lost. People were very excited, and one of the first activities we had was the 75th anniversary of Roebling.

JARSCO increased employment to about 145 workers but had to scale back as the inflation rate climbed to 13.5 percent. When *The Trenton Times* reported in November, "JARSCO survives first year," Jack Nelson stated, "Practically overnight... when the interest rates hit 20 percent, the bottom fell out of the market....We couldn't have gone into business during a worse time. I think considering that, we've done reasonably well."[5]

Amid public outrage over industrial wastes at Love Canal and many other sites, New Jersey Congressman Jim Florio sponsored the Comprehensive Environmental Response, Compensation and Liability Act (CERCLA) that created the "Superfund" program within the U.S. EPA in December, 1980, to clean up polluted sites. JARSCO continued producing steel billets at the Roebling Plant until November, 1981, when it shut down following citations from N.J. DEP and EPA for hazardous waste violations.

In January 1982, JARSCO sold wire equipment and leased a wire mill to a startup called the Roebling Wire Company, which bought rods to make wire. That summer, N.J. DEP officials directed JARSCO to install groundwater monitoring wells and EPA officials issued a Complaint and Compliance Order "to stop storing hazardous waste without a permit, to remove spilled dust and contaminated soil, and to address contaminant migration." EPA officials proposed the plant as a Superfund site in December, 1982, JARSCO abandoned it on January 1, 1983, and the U.S. EDA foreclosed on its loan a week later. EPA officials designated "Roebling Steel" as a Superfund site in September, 1983. The Roebling Wire Company and other tenants stayed on the site until 1985, when EPA began a remediation study to identify the cleanup requirements.[6]

"A Time to Remember," by John Dimon
- *Diamond Jubilee News & Views*, September, 1980

As we celebrate the 75th anniversary of the founding of our village, we should take stock and reflect on the part each person, association and time have played in making this possible.

Roebling's growth and progress have been the result of contributions first by the Roebling family; then by our ancestors who preceded us individually and collectively as part of churches, societies and organizations; finally be members of the present generation who are still willing to give time and effort to preserve and perpetuate the fair name of the community that has meant so much to us.

Roebling is a beautiful community, and it has withstood the pressures of changing and fickle time, mores and philosophy. 75 years is a long time but it went by quickly as is attested by Wesley Renshaw who was here on day one and who still remembers vividly the construction of the mill and the village.

One Hundred Years – Two Hundred Years – Three hundred years will be upon us, too. Let us safeguard the history of the community and its people. Pictures, articles of the era and other artifacts should be sought out and carefully preserved.

Oral recall should be perpetuated on tape, transcribed and placed in safekeeping. Roebling: We love you and cherish you and stand proud to be a townie.

The Centennial of the Brooklyn Bridge in 1983 generated a lot of interest in the tragic and heroic story of its construction, which David McCullough chronicled in his popular book, *The Great Bridge*. Ken Burns' PBS film, *Brooklyn Bridge*, also focused attention on the bridge's remarkable iconography. 120 members of the Roebling family celebrated the Centennial with a gathering at the foot of the bridge in May, 1983, organized by Paul Roebling, Washington's great grandson, and Connie Moore, Ferdinand's great granddaughter (Fig. E.3).

Figure E.3: Roebling Family Members celebrating the Brooklyn Bridge Centennial in May, 1983. RM

Figure E.4: The former J.A.R.'s Sons Company's Trenton Works in the City's Chambersburg section, 1987.

Revitalization with historical and cultural significance

In December, 1984, the author completed a study of the Roebling Company's 25 acre Trenton Plant and proposed "The Roebling Works," a mixed-use redevelopment of 20 of its buildings, "to serve the surrounding community as a local center providing additional or currently non-existent facilities, and to serve the larger Trenton region as a focus of economic revitalization with historical and cultural significance."[7]

In 1979, a proposal to demolish a third of the historic site for a strip mall generated opposition from residents concerned about preserving the site's history, and led in 1980 to the State Historic Preservation Office declaring the site as eligible for the N.J. Register of Historic places. Anthony Anastasio, a native of Chambersburg and the East Ward Councilman of Trenton, wanted to see the buildings preserved and he organized a number of local residents, business owners, and professionals to form along with the author the non-profit Trenton Roebling Community Development Corporation (TRCDC) in 1985 to plan and oversee the redevelopment of the site (Fig. E.4), and the author became TRCDC's executive director.

Among the many people who contributed to TRCDC's success, Nancy G. Beer of Princeton University's Program for N.J. Affairs at the Woodrow Wilson School championed the local and regional benefits of a Roebling redevelopment and the crucial role of government in urban revitalization. As she wrote in 1987: "Government can and should take steps to overcome the biases in government programs and tax policies that favor growth in the suburbs." With City, Mercer County, State and foundation grants and private donations, TRCDC organized the documentation of the Trenton Roebling Plant and the adjacent American Steel & Wire Co. plant by the Historic American Engineering Record (HAER), a program of the National Park Service (Fig. E.5 & multiple HAER photos).[8]

Cellars full of artifacts and memorabilia

In the town of Roebling that year, John Dimon compiled a list of 151 living Roebling employees, aged 60 to 96, who helped make the Golden Gate Bridge wire at the Kinkora Works or helped build the bridge cables, and he organized a contingent of residents and workers to attend the Bridge's 50th anniversary in San Francisco in May, 1987. Appalled at

248

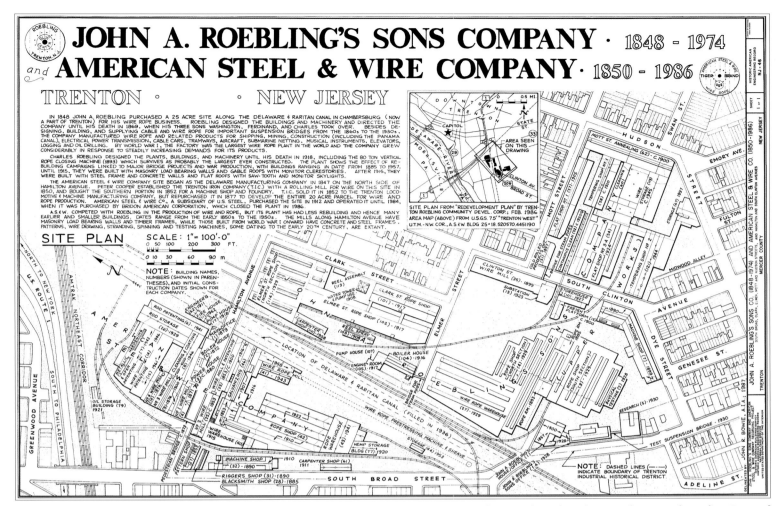

Figure E.5: J.A.R.'s Sons Co. and the American Steel & Wire Co., Trenton, 1987. John Bowie, Historic American Engineering Record.

the lack of credit given to J.A.R.'s Sons Co. and its workers for building the cables, John distributed information on their role to set the record straight (see box).

With the renewed pride in Roebling accomplishments and history from the Golden Gate Bridge celebration, John, Lou Borbi and other members of the Roebling Historical Society and the Friends of Roebling launched *The Roebling Record* newsletter that July to collect and share Roebling stories. In an article in the March, 1988, edition titled, "Museum Needed Now To House Artifacts," John wrote, "No one will deny that our community is in an enviable position when it comes to history....How do we preserve all this? Where do we store and display it? We have cellars full of artifacts and memorabilia that need sunshine, attention and affection" (Fig. E.6).

> *The record should be clear that Roebling with its hundreds of proud, faithful and accomplished workers was the prime contractor and builder of the Golden Gate Bridge Suspension Systems.*
> – John Dimon, Friends of the Golden Gate Bridge, Roebling, New Jersey, May 9, 1987

Figure E.6: *The Roebling Record,* March, 1988.

The Roebling Historical Society named its newsletter after the J.A.R.'s Sons Co. newsletter, and called for a museum to collect Roebling history.

Figure E.7: The Trenton Roebling Community Development Corporation Newsletter, Spring, 1988. TRCDC's plan to preserve the historical significance of the J.A.R.'s Sons Co.'s Trenton Plant while adapting it for modern uses won City approval in 1989.

The Roebling Project is an exciting urban redevelopment project that enjoys the support of community groups, local and State officials and the private sector.

I am well aware of the success of similar projects such as the old mills in Lowell, Massachusetts, and the buildings surrounding the fish markets at South Street Seaport....

I applaud your efforts in developing a well-thought-out and creative reuse plan for a very important neighborhood project in Trenton.[9]

With support from the Geraldine R. Dodge Foundation and planning by Michael Schaffer Productions of Cambridge, Massachusetts, TRCDC in 1988 proposed rehabilitating the Roebling Machine Shop for "The Invention Factory" - an interactive learning center "to stimulate creative thinking, foster problem solving skills, and explore 100 years of N.J.'s industrial heritage." In 1989, TRCDC collaborated with Richard Brackin and the Greater Trenton Section of the American Society of Mechanical Engineers (ASME) in securing the Society's designation of Charles Roebling's 1893 80-Ton Wire Rope Machine as its 93rd National Mechanical Engineering Landmark (Fig. E.8-9 & see box & Figs. 4.30-31).[10]

A well-thought-out and creative reuse plan

With the HAER documentation of the Trenton Roebling Plant and additional analysis of its adaptive reuse potential, the author drafted the "Roebling Area Redevelopment Plan" in 1988 for TRCDC and the City (Fig. E.7). "To maintain the historic significance of the site," the Plan included Design Guidelines for the rehabilitation of the buildings and site based in part on guidelines for Lowell National Historical Park in Lowell, Massachusetts. In response to TRCDC's request for State support for the redevelopment plan, Governor Thomas H. Kean wrote to TRCDC Board Members:

> *This machine is a symbol of America's 19th Century industrial leadership. The Roeblings embodied American dreams of industry. Their work manifested itself in monuments to American progress. Their bridges, to which they gave so much of their lives, are awe inspiring.*
> *The cable cars, telegraphs, elevators and other machines that have changed our lives and haved shaped the 20th Century were made feasible with Roebling wire.*
>
> - Nancy Fitzroy, ASME Past President, October 31, 1989

Figure E.8: TRCDC and DKM properties hosted the American Society of Mechanical Engineers' 1989 ceremony designating Charles Roebling's 80-Ton Wire Rope Machine as ASME's 93rd National Mechanical Engineering Landmark. It remains in place today in a corner of the Roebling Market.

Figure E.9: American Society of Mechanical Engineers' Designation Brochure, 1989. ASME designated the Machine a Landmark "not only for its individual engineering merit but also as a symbol of the achievements of the Roebling family and their company."

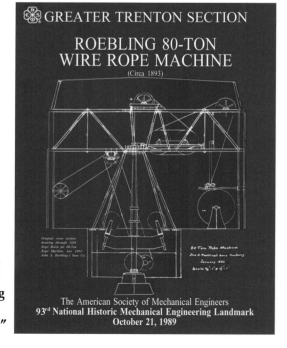

GREATER TRENTON SECTION

ROEBLING 80-TON WIRE ROPE MACHINE
(Circa 1893)

The American Society of Mechanical Engineers
93rd National Historic Mechanical Engineering Landmark
October 21, 1989

Figure E.10: Governor Jim Florio in front of the former Roebling Physical Testing House announcing the N.J. Housing Mortgage Finance Agency's purchase of office space to anchor the redevelopment of Trenton's Roebling Plant.

The century-long success of the Roebling Company is a testimony to New Jersey's ingenuity and hard work. In the redevelopment of this historic treasure is proof that we still possess those qualities in abundance. This is what the public and private sectors can accomplish when they work together toward a common goal. We're not abandoning our cities. Some have walked away from the cities. Not here in New Jersey. Not here in the 1990s.
- New Jersey Governor Jim Florio

THE TIMES, WEDNESDAY, OCTOBER 23, 1991

State approval brings life to Roebling plan

By CHRIS W. BIDDLE
Staff Writer

TRENTON — At the turn of the century, the John A. Roebling Wire Rope Co. was the industrial hub of this city, turning out miles of steel cable for the nation's great suspension bridges.

By next fall, if all goes as planned, the once-great factory will become the retail hub of Chambersburg with a large 24-hour Foodtown supermarket and a Thrift Drug store as its anchor stores.

The transformation — from factory to shopping center — will be carried out by DKM Properties Corp. of Lawrence, the developer that owns the site.

Although it had been talked about for more than a decade, the redevelopment project finally was made possible with the state's decision to purchase a large chunk of space to make a new home for the New

• see ROEBLING, A10

Gov. Jim Florio speaks at yesterday's kick-off ceremony for the Roebling complex, as an array of city and state dignitaries stand behind him.

Staff photo by Frank Jacobs III

Ron Berman, who grew up in Trenton and was the President of DKM Properties Corporation, the owner of about half of the Trenton Roebling Plant, endorsed TRCDC's mixed-use plan for the complex and worked with TRCDC, City, County and State officials to develop a proposal for the initial phase of redevelopment to include offices, stores and apartments in rehabilitated Roebling buildings. Trenton City Council adopted TRCDC's Roebling Redevelopment Plan with some modifications in 1989.

In July, 1991, DKM unveiled a $24 million plan (about $44 million in 2009) to rehabilitate 66,000 sq.ft. of former Roebling buildings for office space, 90,000 sq.ft. for a Roebling Market that would include Trenton's first full size supermarket in many years, plus 25,000 sq.ft. of flexible space. In support of the project, Alan Mallach, Director of Trenton's Department of Housing and Development, told a reporter: "We want this thing to happen right. This is the single most important development project in the city for the next five to ten years."[11]

The N.J. Casino Reinvestment Development Authority awarded the project a $1.6 million (about $2.9 million) loan for the supermarket in 1991, and that October, Governor Jim Florio announced that the N.J. Housing Mortgage Finance Agency would move from its suburban location and purchase the office space to anchor the Roebling Redevelopment (Fig. E.10).

Veronica Brady, Artistic Director of Trenton's Passage Theatre Company, commissioned playwright Jim McGrath in 1991 to write a play about working for Roebling and living in Chambersburg. Passage produced the play in 1992 in an 1897 wire shop to wide acclaim (Fig. E.11-12 & See Fig. 4.59).

Jim McGrath, once a student at Princeton Theological Seminary and now a full-time writer in Los Angeles, spoke about the development of his play: 'I knew I had my focus when I began to understand what work meant to these people. The power and nobility of their work in that factory was the richest vein of all for me.' The playwright's insights are revealed in such lines as those spoken by Anthony, a member of the play's Carrera family, recalling the day when the Roebling factories ceased production. 'Then after they sold the place, the noise stopped for good,' Anthony recalls, 'My Aunt Isabel couldn't sleep at night. The silence kept her awake.'
- The New York Times, May 17, 1992

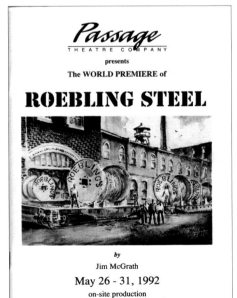

Passage
THEATRE COMPANY
presents
The WORLD PREMIERE of

ROEBLING STEEL

by
Jim McGrath
May 26 - 31, 1992
on-site production
John A. Roebling's Sons Company Factory
676 South Clinton Avenue
Trenton, NJ

Figure E.11 (left): Passage Theatre Company's *Roebling Steel* Playbill, May, 1992. Trenton artist Tom Malloy painted the cover image based on a 1927 photograph (see Fig. 4.32). The eight performances sold out a week ahead and won praise from attendees and the press.

Figure E.12 (right): *Roebling Steel* review, *The New York Times*, May 17, 1992.

THE NEW YORK TIMES, SUNDAY, MAY 17, 1992

At Trenton Factory, the Spirit of the Past Lives Again on Stage

By SALLY FRIEDMAN

'God looked like Roebling Steel.'

Members of the Passage Theater Company rehearsing script for "Roebling Steel," at the former cable and wire factory in Trenton.

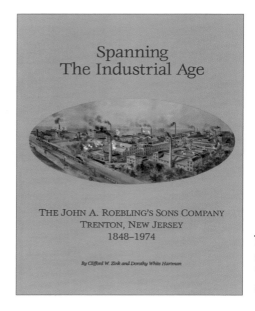

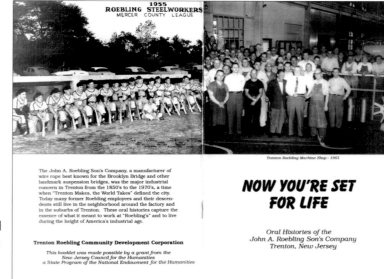

Figure E.13 (left): *Spanning the Industrial Age,* 1992. TRCDC published the history of the John A. Roebling's Sons Company to document its local and national contributions.

Figure E.14 (right): *Now You're Set For Life,* 1993. TRCDC also published oral histories excerpts from former Roebling employees in Trenton.

In 1992, TRCDC published *Spanning the Industrial Age: The John A Roebling's Sons Company, Trenton, New Jersey, 1848-1974*, by the author and Dorothy White Hartman, with support from the N.J. Historical Commission (Fig. E.13). The following year TRCDC recorded oral histories of former Roebling employees and produced *Now You're Set for Life*, a documentary film and accompanying booklet, with support from the N.J. Council for the Humanities (Fig. E.14). With another Council grant in 1994, TRCDC's created the "Roebling Online History Archive" to provide Internet access to primary documents illustrating Roebling history.[12]

We are creating hope and opportunity

Governor Christine Todd Whitman supported the Roebling Redevelopment when she took office in 1994, and presided over the grand opening of the project's first phase in June, 1996 (Fig. E.15). "Rather than making Roebling cables," Governor

Whitman told the audience of over 500 people: "We are creating hope and opportunity." As provided in the Redevelopment Plan's Design Guidelines, DKM's rehabilitation preserved the historical significance of the buildings' exteriors.

The rehabilitation of the 1928 Physical Testing House for the N.J. Housing Mortgage Finance Agency's headquarters preserved its 3 story interior (Figs. E.16-17 & see Figs. 6.8-9). In adapting the 1930 Rope Shop for the Roebling Market, DKM Properties preserved the shop's traveling craneway (Figs. E.18-19 & see Fig. 6.18) and the Roebling 80-Ton Rope Machine (Fig. E.20). Penrose Properties rehabilitated Charles Roebling's 1899 Clinton Avenue Wire Mill for Pellettieri Homes' senior apartments (Fig. E.21 & see Figs. 4.71 & 7.23).

TRCDC secured two State grants in 1995 and 1996 to begin rehabilitating the Roebling Machine Shop at the Trenton Plant: a $1 million grant (about $1.5 million in 2009) administered by the N.J. Department of Transportation from the Federal Intermodal Surface Transportation Enhancement Act, known as ISTEA, and a $1.25 million grant (about $1.8 million) from the N.J. Historic Trust.

Figure E.15: *The Trenton Times*, June 11, 1996. Governor Christine Todd Whitman presides over the opening of the first phase of the Roebling Redevelopment in Trenton.

> **"Dream finally a reality,"** *Trenton Times*, June 11, 1996
> *Here, where a family-owned manufacturing business employed thousands of workers at its peak and transformed the city of Trenton, we inaugurate a new era of job creation, of entrepreneurship, of transformation. Rather than making Roebling cables we are creating hope and opportunity. We are building bridges. Bridges that join the public, private and not-for-profit sectors. Bridges that link residents with the businesses that will serve and employ them. Bridges that span the great history of this complex and connect a glorious past to a dynamic future.*
> – Governor Christine Todd Whitman.

Figure E.16: N.J. Housing Mortgage Finance Agency, 1996. CCH Trenton architects Clarke Caton Hintz adapted the 1928 Roebling Physical Testing House for HMFA's headquarters.

Figure E.17: N.J. Housing Mortgage Finance Agency, 2010. Princeton architects Farewell Mills & Gatsch adapted the interior of the 1928 Physical Testing House for HMFA.

Figure E.18: Roebling Market, Trenton, 2006
Architects Clarke Caton Hintz preserved a steel frame, left, as a gateway to the Roebling Market, right, and the Millyard, flanked at the top by the Machine Shop and HMFA offices.

Figure E.19: Roebling Market, 2001.
Following the Roebling Redevelopment Plan's Design Guidelines, architects Clark Caton Hintz preserved the 1930 Rope Shop's traveling craneway as a key industrial feature.

Figure E.20: Roebling 1893 80-Ton Wire Rope Machine, 1995. Located within a corner of the Roebling Market, Charles Roebling's 1893 Wire Rope Machine awaits rehabilitation and interpretation as a National Mechanical Engineering Landmark (see Figs. 4.30-31 & E.8-9).

Figure E.21: Pellettieri Homes, c2001. CCH
The Roebling Company removed the three top stories of the 1899 Clinton Street Wire Mill in the 1950s (see Figs. 4.70-71 & 7.22-23). Architects Clark Caton Hintz added one story in adapting the building in 1997 for the Pellettieri Homes senior apartments.

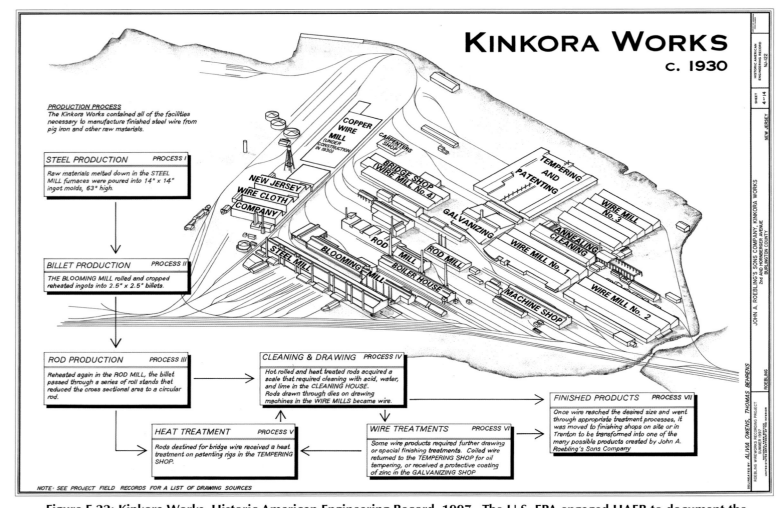

Figure E.22: Kinkora Works, Historic American Engineering Record, 1997. The U.S. EPA engaged HAER to document the J.A.R.'s Sons Company plant in Roebling prior to its cleanup. Drawing No. 4 of 14 illustrates the Production Process, noting:
The Kinkora Works contained all of the facilities necessary to manufacture finished steel wire from pig iron and other raw materials.

The diligence to continue his works

By 1996, EPA had completed the first two stages in the multi-year cleanup of the Roebling Plant in Roebling, removing tons of contaminants and contaminated soils, and identifying remedial actions for slag areas and for long-term monitoring to ensure the effectiveness of the various remedies. EPA's Remedial Investigation & Feasibility Study for the site indicated that most of the historic buildings and structures would have to be demolished because they were too contaminated and/or deteriorated to preserve, or were otherwise unusable.

To comply with the National Historic Preservation Act of 1966, EPA officials identified two ways to mitigate the adverse effect that the demolitions would have on the site's historic significance. In the first of these, they arranged for HAER to document the site's historic buildings and identify the processes that took place in them (Fig. E.22). As with all HAER documentation, the photographs and drawings of the Kinkora Works are preserved in the Library of Congress.[13]

EPA's second mitigation focused on a local benefit. As part of EPA's community relations efforts, Tamara Rossi, the Remedial Project Manager for the site, kept the members of the Roebling Historical Society and other residents informed on the scope and progress of the cleanup. Mary Montalto, a Roebling native and a Society member, had suggested at a meeting that the Kinkora Works' Main Gate Building would make a good museum of the site's and the town's history. Donna McElrea, a lifelong Roebling resident whose father worked in the Copper Mill, and who became president of the Society in 1996, asked Tamara if the Society could get the Main Gate for a museum, and in a follow-up letter, she wrote:

We are a proud people with strong roots and we love our town....

The Main Gate Building will serve as an excellent museum for the many items and artifacts that the Roebling Historical Society has been collecting over the years....

John A. Roebling instilled in us a strong community pride and the diligence to continue his works.[14]

Figure E.23 (left): Roebling Historical Society members toured the Kinkora Works to identify industrial objects for the proposed Roebling Museum, c1999. PV Figure E.24 (right): Society President Donna Mc Elrea and Diane Schlagel in the Steel Mill. DM

Abuzz with excitement

EPA officials approved more remedial work in 1996, and began demolishing unstable structures. Florence Township officials foreclosed on the property because of delinquent taxes, and agreed with EPA to preserve the Main Gate Building as a museum, and Roebling Historical Society members began tagging objects to save (Figs. E.23-24). Roebling and Florence residents and officials celebrated the 100th anniversary of the Village in 2005 with multiple activities (Figs. E.25-26).

EPA began rehabilitating the Main Gate and seven acres for the Museum in 2005, and Donna McElrea soon reported in *The Roebling Record*: "The village of Roebling is abuzz with excitement" (Fig. E.27). To raise the funds necessary to create and sustain the museum, the Society created the Roebling Museum, Inc., with six Roebling family members on the board, in 2007.[15]

Figure E.25 (right): Roebling Village and Florence Township residents and officials celebrated the village's Centennial in 2005 with signs at the village entrances and with multiple events and activities.

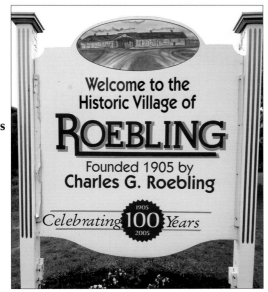

Figure E.26 (left): Roebling Family at Roebling Centennial, 1905. Front row, Martha Moore, Mary Roebling Foster, Audrey Roebling; second row, Connie Moore, Allison Gibbons, Eudora Roebling, Bill Roebling; rear, Rip Roebling. GL Figure E.27 (right): Main Gate Rehabilitation, 2007. EPA's Jeff Josephson and Tamara Rossi, Remedial Project Manager, 3rd & 4th from left, hosted Roebling Museum Tustees, from left, Emma Cartier, Linda McDonald, Mark Magyar, George & Kathy Lengel, and Paul Varga, and the author.

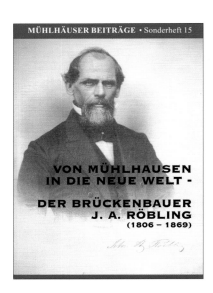

Figure E.28 (left): "From Mühlhausen to the New World - The Bridgebuilder J.A. Roebling" Exhibition, Mühlhausen Museum, Mühlhausen, Germany.

Figure E.29 (right): "From Mühlhausen to the New World - The Bridgebuilder J.A. Roebling" book cover, 2006.

Several exhibitions and events in 2006 celebrated the bicentennial of John A. Roebling's birth in Mühlhausen, Germany. The Mühlhausen Museum mounted an exhibition incorporating new research by Dr. Nele Guntheroth, Foundartion of the City Museum of Berlin, and Andreas Kahlow, University of Applied Science, Potsdam, on John's education and work experience in Germany, noted in Chapter 1 (Fig. E. 28). The Museum also published a compendium in German of this research and other scholar's research on John, including work by Don Sayenga, a former general manager of Bethlehem Steel's wire rope division and the historian for the Wire Association International (Figs. E.29-30).

Rutgers University's Special Collections and University Archives mounted an exhibition from its Roebling Collection. As Curator Fernanda Perrone noted in the exhibit catalog (Fig. E.31): "The bridges and aqueducts he built bear witness to his genius as an engineer, while his farsighted decision to manufacture wire rope on his farm in Saxonburg, Pa., laid the foundations of an industrial empire." Ellarslie, the Trenton City, Museum mounted an exhibition (Fig. E.32) on

Figure E.30: Wire Rope Historian, Don Sayenga, left, with Dr. Nele Guntheroth, Foundation of the City Museum of Berlin, and Dr. Andreas Kahlow, University of Applied Science, Potsdam, at the Roebling Chapter of the Society for Industrial Archaeology's 2006 Symposium at Drew University in Madison, N.J. DS

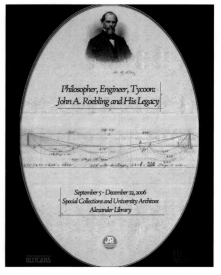

Figure E.31 (left): *Philosopher, Engineer, Tycoon: John A. Roebling and His Legacy*. RU Catalog of Rutgers University's John A. Roebling Bicentennial Exhibition, 2006.

Figure E.32 (right): "John A. Roebling: His Life And Legacy" Exhibition, Ellarslie, the Trenton City Museum, 2006. EM

Figure E.33: John A. Roebling Statue Unveiling, Mühlhausen, Germany, 2007. KR   Kriss Roebling, left, a descendant of Washington A. Roebling, attended the unveiling, which was hosted by Chief Mayor Hans-Dieter Doerbaum, right.

Figure E.34: Roebling Chapter SIA Tour of Roebling, N.J., 2007. From left, Robert Vogel, former Curator of Civil Engineering at the Smithsonian, Martha Moore and her daughter Allison, Kriss and Meg Roebling with August Roebling. Robert has authored many works on John A. Roebling (see Bibliography).

John's "Industry, Ingenuity and Trenton History." As Museum Director Brian O. Hill noted, John "moved to Trenton to put his industrial dreams to work," and when he died, "the entire city of Trenton felt the integral nature of Roebling's participation in its industry, history, economy and social development."[16]

The American Society of Civil Engineers, which designated the Brooklyn Bridge as a National Historic Engineering Landmark in 1972, hosted a bicentennial symposium on John A. Roebling in 2006. In 2007, the City of Mühlhausen dedicated a John A. Roebling statue in its Lower Market Square (Fig. E.33), and the Roebling Chapter of the Society for Industrial Archaeology, named for Roebling at its founding in 1987, hosted a tour of Roebling, N.J. (Fig. E.34). The Town of Saxonburg has preserved its Roebling history (see Fig. 2.1) in the Saxonburg Museum and in several original buildings (Figs. E.35-7).

Figure E.35: Roebling Room, Saxonburg Museum, 2010. Built in 1991, the Museum highlights Saxonburg's founding by John A. Roebling, his brother, Karl, and other settlers in 1831.

Figure E.36: Main Street, Saxonburg, Pennsylvania, 2008. SS The town John A. Roebling and his brother Karl founded in 1831 today has about 1,400 residents. His house is on the right.

Figure E.37: John A. Roebling House, Saxonburg, Pa. 2010 John and Karl built the house c1832 (see Fig. 2.6), and today it is the office of the Saxonburg Memorial Presbyterian Church.

Figure E.38: Roebling Museum Oral History Project, 2008. Museum Board Member and Roebling descendant Martha Moore, center, interviewing former Roebling employee Charles Detterer, left, as Scott Neilson, center, and Dick Blofsom, right, of Telequest, Inc., record, with assistance from Carl Reeverts.

In preparation for the opening of the Roebling Museum, Executive Director Mark Magyar initiated the Roebling Oral History Project in 2007 to record the recollections of former Kinkora Works employees and local residents (Fig. E.38), and Board Members introduced the Museum to the community at local events (Fig. E.39). Board members, staff and consultants worked with EPA staff to salvage historic industrial objects for display in the Museum Millyard (Fig. E.40).

To help visitors understand the Kinkora Works, which has now been almost completely demolished, the Museum has drawn upon the rich interpretations of local artists like photographer Barbara Gilmer, who exhibited her photographs of the abandoned Kinkora Works in the Main Gate, and painters Don Jones and Lou Borbi (Figs. E.41-42).

Figure E.39: Roebling Museum Board Members, Roebling Park, 2008. Don Cammus (left), Kathie & Georgle Lengel, Don Jones, Dennis O'Hara, Florence Township Council, Peg Manser and Linda McDonald, Museum President and Roebling descendant.

Figure E.40: Roebling Museum Millyard Tour, 2008. From left, Bobbie Dease, EPA, George Lengel, Steve Cannon, Jeff Josephson and Tami Rossi, EPA, Gary McGowan, CPR Conservation, and Pat Millen, Museum Executive Director

Figure E.41: Kinkora Works at Main Gate, c1955. DJ Don Jones, a Roebling native and Museum Board Member, painted this view in 2008 from the Main Gate archway at the end of a shift.

Figure E.42: Kinkora Works Steel Mill, c1950. LB Lou Borbi, a Roebling native and former Roebling School teacher, painted this view in 2000 of workers tending the open hearth furnaces.

Figure E.43: Roebling Museum Open House, June, 2009. Museum supporters and townspeople at the eastern entrance to the Main Gate observing an Honor Guard from Fort Dix rasing the U.S. flag on the 1918 Kinkora Works flagpole.

Figure E.44: Roebling Museum Open House, June 2009. From left, Florence Township Mayor William Berry, Museum Vice President George Lengel, Roebling descendant and Museum President Martha Moore, and Don Cammus.

When EPA completed the Main Gate rehabilitation in 2009, the Museum introduced supporters and local residents to the facility at an open house (Figs. E.43-44).

The Friends of Roebling and the Roebling Garden Club in 2009 unveiled a statue of Charles G. Roebling, created by Hopewell, New Jersey, sculptor Morris Doktor and mounted in the Roebling village circle (Fig. 4.45).

Museum Board Member and Roebling descendant Karl Darby organized a Mercer Automobile Company Centennial Reunion at the Museum in 2009 that attracted some 1,800 people (Figs. E.46-47). Mercer owners from Maine to California, and Illinois to Arkansas brought 23 Mercers to the Reunion, the largest assemblage of Mercers since the demise of the company in the 1920s, and they drove through Roebling and Florence Township in a Centennial parade.

Figure E.45: Charles Roebling Statue Unveiling, 2009. GL From left, Mary Roebling Foster and her daughters Laurie and Sara, Mary Roebling and her father Bill Roebling.

Figure E.46 (left): Mercer Automobile Company Centennial Reunion, Roebling Museum, 2009, with 23 Mercers lined up in the Museum Millyard east of the Main Gate.   Figure E.47 (right): Museum Board Member, Roebling descendant and Reunion organizer Karl Darby driving his 1921 Mercer Touring Car with family members in front of the Main Gate in the Reunion parade.

Figure E.48: N.J. League of Municipalities Headquarters, 2007. CCH The League's rehabilitation of the Ferdinand Roebling House on West State Street in Trenton included an addition, right, all designed by Trenton Architects Clark Caton Hintz.

Figure E.49: Mercer County Administrative Office, Trenton, 2010. The County purchased the Roebling General Offices, left & center, after CF&I Steel vacated them in 1970, and it recently acquired the former Research Laboratory, far right.

The Roebling legacy remains prominent in Trenton thanks to additional public, private and non-profit investments. The N.J. League of Municipalities rehabilitated the Ferdinand Roebling House on West State Street for its offices in 2007 (Fig. E.48 & see Figs. 4.51-52). Mercer County has preserved the Roebling General Office and Research Lab on South Broad Street as its administrative offices (Fig. E.49 & see Figs. 4.76-77, 6.3-4, & 6.34). Proservices Corporation adapted a 1919 Roebling building for its offices in 2007 (Fig. E.50).

The N.J. Schools Construction Corporation has planned the reuse of Roebling buildings for a Roebling School (Figs E.51-52), and the city-owned Roebling Machine Shop has become a premier event space (Figs. E.53-56 & see Figs. 4.42-43). Nexus Properties adapted the Roebling Buckthorn Plant starting in the 1990s (Fig. E.57). Mercer County has designated HHG Development Associates for more redevelopment (Fig. E.58).

Figure E.50: Trenton Creates Technology Building, 2010. Proservices Corp. rehabilitated the 1919 Roebling Employment Office on South Clinton Avenue in 2007 for its headquarters.

Figure E.51: Proposed Roebling School, Trenton, 2004. CCH Architects Clarke Caton Hintz designed the rehabilitation of the 1924 Roebling Flat Shop for a K-8 school for the New Jersey Schools Construction Corporation.

Figure E.52: 1924 Roebling Flat Shop, Trenton, 2010. With the Roebling School proposed for the site on hold, the future of the 1924 Flat Shop (see Fig. 5.61) across from the Roebling Market on South Clinton Avenue remains uncertain.

Figure E.53: Art All Night at Roebling Machine Shop, Trenton, 2010. FJP The 1890-1901 Machine Shop and the adjacent Roebling Millyard provide spectacular indoor and outsdoor spaces for events like Trenton Artworks' annual Art All Night.

Figure E.54: Art All Night, Roebling Millyard, Trenton, 2008. Mercer County converted the J.A.R.'s Sons Co. millyard into an urban County Park adjacent to the Machine Shop, N.J. HMFA Headquarters and the Roebling Market.

Figure E.55: Art All Night, Roebling Machine Shop, Trenton, 2008. The 1890 section of the Machine Shop is the oldest complete building erected by the John A. Roebling's Sons Co.

Figure E.56: Art All Night, Roebling Machine Shop, Trenton, 2008. The Machine Shop, 1901 section above, represents the apex of industrial architecture built by the Roeblings.

Figure E.57: Roebling Metro Complex, Trenton, 1995. NP Nexus Properties of Lawrenceville, N.J., adapted the former Roebling Buckthorn Plant (see Fig. 5.42) for offices and a warehouse.

Figure E.58: Roebling Block 3, Trenton, 2010. In early 2011, Mercer County designated HHG Development Associates to rehabilitate five buildings for housing, offices, stores and studios.

Figure E.59: Roebling Village Inn, Roebling, N.J., 2008.
The Burlington County Community Action Program converted
the former Roebling Inn to 14 senior apartments in 2000.

Figure E.60: Riverside Avenue, Roebling, N.J., 2008.
The former Kinkora Works managers' houses are
highly prized by their current owners.

While the Roebling buildings in Trenton are monuments to the industrial era, the well-maintained buildings and tree-lined streets in Roebling village testify to the ideals of the age, when factory owners and workers shared common interests in work, community, and prosperity (Figs. E.59-63). Fred Kent, founding president of the Project for Public Spaces, said in 2000: "If you were to rate all the New Urbanist communities on a scale of 1 to 10, Roebling would be a nine. It has connected housing, separate family homes, narrow streets, commercial areas....It seems so perfect you can't believe it's real, but it is."[17]

In 2010, the Roebling Museum opened its exhibits (Fig. E.64), and celebrated Florence Township's renovation of the Roebling Auditorium (Fig. E.65) by hosting Mark Violi's play about the Roeblings and the Brooklyn Bridge (Figs. E.66-67).

Further afield, portions of the Roebling legacy are extant in the Archbold Biological Station in Florida (Fig. E.68), the Skidaway Institute of Oceanography in Georgia (Fig. E.69), and Highland Hammock State Park in Florida.

Figure E.61: Roebling, N.J., 2009. U.S. EPA
Roebling Village thrives as the EPA completes
the remediation of the former Kinkora Works (top) for
redevelopment, and its slag area (left) for a riverfront park.

Figure E.62: Fourth Avenue, Roebling, N.J., 2008.
Many Roebling residents continue to live in houses their
families bought from J.A.R.'s Sons Company in 1947.

Figure E.63: Third Avenue, Roebling, N.J., 2008.
Roebling natives and former employees like George Lengel,
with white hat, retain vivid memories of their "family streets."

Figure E.64: Roebling Museum, Roebling Family Gallery, 2010.
Museum Executive Director Pat Millen and intern Leah
Southerland review the Roebling Family and Brooklyn Bridge
exhibits designed by Steve Tucker and opened in 2010.

Figure E.65: 1914 Roebling Auditorium, Roebling N.J., 2010.
Florence Township rehabilitated the Auditorium as
a community center in 2010, and it opened with
an inaugural production of Mark Violi's *Roebling* play.

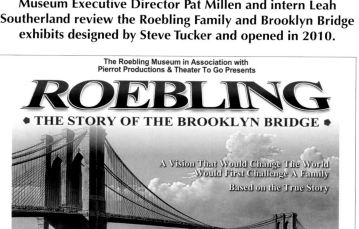

Figure E.66 (left): *Roebling - The Story of the Brooklyn Bridge*, 2010. TTG The Roebling Museum hosted Theatre To Go's production
of Mark Violi's play of the Roebling family's struggle to build the Brookyn Bridge. Figure E.67 (right): *Roebling - The Story of the
Brooklyn Bridge* in the Roebling Auditorium, 2010. TTG From left to right, Emily Warren Roebling (Sarah McIlhenny), Washington
Roebling (Derek Capre), Mary Martin (Jennifer Huckleberry), Charles Martin (Mark Ott), and E.F. Farrington (Lee Benson).

Figure E.68: Archbold Biological Station, 2010. ABS
John A. Roebling II's donation in 1941 of his 1,050-acre
Red Hill Estate near lake Placid, Florida, enabled ecological
explorer Richard Archbold to establish the Station.

Figure E.69: Skidaway Institute of Oceanography, 2010. SKIO
Robert and Dorothy Roebling's donation of their 1,062-acre
Modena Plantation enabled the State of Georgia to establish
its world reknowned marine research institute in 1867.

Figure E.70 (left): John A. Roebling Bridge, 2008. Cincinnati and Covington citizens erected a statue of the bridge engineer holding a triangular ruler (see Figs. 3.39-40). Figure E.71 (right): "Vision and Ingenuity" Mural, Covington, Ky., 2008. Robert Dafford's painting depicts John A. Roebling and Amos Shinkle, President of the Covington and Cincinnati Bridge Co., at the opening in 1867.

The utimate monuments of the Roebling legacy are the landmark bridges built by the Roeblings and the pioneering cables built by the John A. Roebling's Sons Company. In recognition of the significance of the John A. Roebling Bridge (Fig. E.70 & see Figs. 3.39-40) to Cincinnati, Ohio, and Covington, Kentucky, the Northern Kentucky Legacy, a group of community-minded young professionals, launched its Roebling Murals project along the Ohio Riverfront in Covington, and one of the first murals by artist Robert Dafford illustrates the bridge as it opened in 1867 (Fig. E.71).

The National Park Service acquired John A. Roebling's Delaware Aqueduct in 1980, and preserved its original cables and nearly all of its other ironwork in restoring it for vehicles and pedestrians, and it is now known simply as Roebling Bridge (Fig. E.72 & see Figs. 2.21-24).

The Brooklyn Bridge is the crowning achievement of John A. Roebling (E.73) and Washington A. Roebling as bridge engineers, and the symbol of New York. In 2008, the City celebrated its 125th anniversary with a bridge birthday party in Empire Fulton Ferry Park, where more than 10,000 people enjoyed music, a lightshow, and fireworks (Figs. E.74-75).

Several smaller bridges represent the continuing engineering ingenuity of the J.A.R.'s Sons Co. Bridge Division, like the St. John's Bridge (Fig. E.76) in Portland, Ore., and the Lumberville Bridge (Fig. E.77) over the Delaware River at Lumberville, Pa.

The great bridges of the 1930s are J.A.R.'s Sons Co.'s crowning achievements. New York celebrated the 75th anniversary of the George Washington Bridge in 2006, and San Francisco will celebrate the Golden Gate Bridge's 75th in 2012 (E.78-79).

Figure E.72: Delaware Aqueduct, c2005. NPS Restored in 1986 and operated as a vehicular and pedestrian bridge by the National Park Service, John A. Roebling's 1848 aqueduct is the oldest suspension bridge in America.

Figure E.73: John A. Roebling Statue, Trenton, 2008. In the 1908 statue erected by his sons in Trenton's Cadawalader Park, the bridge engineer surveys the horizon while holding plans of the Brooklyn Bridge.

Figure E.74 (left): Brooklyn Bridge 125th Anniversary Program, 2008. The Brooklyn Bridge has become the universal symbol of New York City. Figure E.75 (right): Brooklyn Bridge 125th Anniversary Celebration, Empire Fulton Ferry Park, 2008.

Figure E.76: St. John's Bridge, Portland, Oregon, 2006. WK J.A.R.'s Sons Co.'s innovative prestessed bridge strand increased the efficiency of building cables for small to medium size bridges like the St. John's Bridge, which it built in 1931.

Figure E.77: Lumberville Bridge, Lumberville, Pennsylvania, 2010. J.A.R.'s Sons Co.'s wartime innovations of cable-stiffening and prestressed concrete considerably reduced the amount of steel needed in this 1947 pedestrian bridge.

Figure E.78: George Washington Bridge, 1997. Dave Frieder J.A.R.'s Sons Co. pioneered the great 36-in. cables that support 14 lanes on two decks on the world's busiest suspension bridge.

Figure E.79: Golden Gate Bridge, San Francisco, 2009. J.A.R.'s Sons Company built its 36-in. cables in record time in 1937, and the bridge has become the symbol of San Francisco.

Notes for Chapter 1: *John August Röbling*
Pages 2-18

1 Roebling, Washington A., "Biography of J.A. Roebling," Rutgers University, Special Collections and University Archives. See also an edited and illustrated version of the biography: Donald Sayenga, Editor, *Washington Roebling's Father: A Memoir of John A. Roebling*, New York: American Society of Civil Engineers, 2009.

2 Schuyler, Hamilton, *The Roeblings: A Century of Engineers. Bridge Builders and Industrialists*, Princeton, N.J.: Princeton University Press, 1931, 6-8; Roebling, "Biography," 4. Roeblingen am See is a small town about 75 miles east of Mühlhausen in Sachsen-Anhalt, but the Roebling family connection to it is unknown.

3 Roebling, "Biography," 4.

4 Roebling, "Biography," 2.

5 Roebling, "Biography," 2-3.

6 Guentheroth, Nele. "The Young Roebling, Biographical Notes," in *John A. Roebling: A Bicentennial Celebration of His Birth, 1806-2006*, edited by Theodore Green, New York: American Society of Civil Engineers, 2006, 5; Steinman, David B., *The Builders of the Bridge*, New York: Harcourt Brace & Company, 1945, 5.

7 Roebling, "Biography," 3; Guentheroth, 6-7.

8 Guentheroth, 6.

9 Roebling, "Biography," 3-4. Washington also noted, "The History of the town of Eschwege in Hessen, not far from Mühlhausen, was illustrated by lithographs from his drawings and the frontispiece of the history of Mühlhausen is also from his pencil."

10 Johann took the government surveyor's exam in Erfurt on May 26th, which was coincidently the day of the year on which Washington was born thirteen years later.

11 Röbling, Johann A., Mühlhausen, March 24, 1823, to Friedrich Carl Röbling.

12 Roebling, "Biography," 3.

13 Pfammatter, Ulrich, *The Making of the Modern Architect and Engineer*, Boston: Birkhäuser, 2000, 222-3; Guentheroth, 8.

14 Guentheroth, 8-9.

15 Roebling, "Biography," 7-8.

16 Roebling, "Biography," 8.

17 Roebling, "Biography," 8.

18 Steinman, 12.

19 Roebling, "Biography," 9.

20 Guentheroth, 8. Washington characterized his father as Hegel's "favorite pupil," but this seems highly unlikely as the evidence suggests he may have attended Hegel's lectures for only one term.

21 Roebling, "Biography," 6.

22 Hegel, Georg Wilhelm Friedrich, *The Philosophy of History*, John Sibree, Translator, New York: Wiley Book Co., 1900.

23 http://www.marxists.org/reference/archive/hegel/

24 Of the university education of his time, Washington wrote: "I do not consider the lecture system a success. Good text books are better and are of use later on in life. The notes are always taken in haste and written in a cramped hand so that later you cannot read your own handwriting. So much time is taken up in writing that the mind gets tired and cannot properly understand the subject. That was my father's testimony, and I second it. One cause of it was the want of proper textbooks at the time. To this one may add the vanity and ambition of the various professors to write their own textbooks, and ignore previous works. Their lectures were the matter of their future books. A few subjects can perhaps be better taught by lectures and made more entertaining, such as physics, popular sciences and philosophy, but the professional subjects which you intend to follow in life are better in books." Roebling, "Biography," 5-6.

25 Roebling, "Biography," 9; Guentheroth, 11.

26 Mende, Michael, "Early 19th Century Suspension Bridges on the Upper Ruhr: Johann August Röbling's 1828 Freienohl Project and the 1839 Bridge by A. Bruns at Laer Manner," http://www.ticcihcongress2006.net/paper/Paper%207/Mende%207.pdf

27 Guentheroth, 11.

28 Andreas Kahlow, "Johann August Röbling (1806-1869): Early Projects in Context," in *John A. Roebling: A Bicentennial Celebration of His Birth, 1806-2006*, edited by Theodore Green, New York: American Society of Civil Engineers, 2006, 5.

29 Guentheroth, 11.

30 Guentheroth, 12.

31 Roebling, "Biography," 5.

32 "The Personal Diary, J.A. Röbling," 1981 Translation of unpublished manuscript, Smithsonian Institution, 13.

33 Röbling, "Personal Diary," 15.

34 Röbling, "Personal Diary," 16-19.

35 Röbling, "Personal Diary," 20-21.

36 Röbling, "Personal Diary," 20.

37 Röbling, "Personal Diary," 22.

38 Röbling, "Personal Diary," 35.

39 Röbling, "Personal Diary," 50, 64.

40 Roebling, "Biography," 10.

41 Roebling, "Biography," 11.

42 Guentheroth, 13.

43 Etzler, Johann Adolphus, *The Paradise Within Reach of All Men, Without Labour by Powers of Nature and Machinery,* London: John Brooks, 1836, 1, 3, 4, 121-2, 211-2.

44 Etzler, v & 5.

45 Schuyler, 27.

46 Roebling, "Biography," 11.

47 Johann August Röbling, "Diary of our Sea-Voyage from Bremen to Philadelphia on the Transport August Eduard in the Year 1831," Manuscript Translation in Special Collections, Rutgers University, 1-2. Originally published in Eschwege, Germany, 1832; published at the diary's centennial by the John A. Roebling's Sons Company as *Dairy of My Journey from Mühlhausen in Thuringia via Bremen to the United States and North America in the year 1831*, Trenton: Roebling Press, 1931.

48 Röbling, "Sea-Voyage," 8, 12.

49 Roebling, "Biography," 12.

50 Röbling, "Sea-Voyage," 14-15.

51 Röbling, "Sea-Voyage," 38, 42.

52 Röbling, "Sea-Voyage," 47, 68-9.

53 Röbling, "Sea-Voyage," 78-79.

54 Röbling, "Sea-Voyage," 83-4.

Notes for Chapter 2: *The Village of Saxonburg*
Pages 19-44

1 Röbling, "Sea-Voyage," 84-104.

2 Roebling, "Biography," 14-16.

3 Röbling, Johann, Pittsburgh, to Mr. F. Baehr in Mühlhausen, November 2, 1831, Karel J. R. Arndt and Patrick R. Brostowin, "Pragmatists and Profits: George Rapp and J. A. Roebling versus J. A. Etzler and Count Leon," *The Western Pennsylvania Historical Magazine*, Vol. 52, No. 1, January 1969, 8-13. After he immigrated to the United States, Baehr changed the spelling of his name to Baer.

4 Roebling, "Biography," 19-20.

5 Röbling to Baer, November 2, 1831, 21-22, 25-27.

6 Röbling, Johann, Röbling's Farm in Butler County, Pennsylvania, to Mr. F. Baer in Mühlhausen, December 13, 1831, "Opportunities for Immigrants," *Western Pennsylvania Historical Magazine*, June 1935, 75, 84, 88-89.

7 Röbling, Johann, Röbling's Farm in Butler County, Pennsylvania, to Mr. F. Baer in Mühlhausen, January 14, 1832, "Opportunities for Immigrants," *Western Pennsylvania Historical Magazine*, June, 1935, 92-103.

8 Roebling, "Biography," 21, 27-28, 32, 33-34.

9 Roebling, "Biography," 36-38.

10 Roebling, "Biography," 41-3, 51.

11 John A. Roebling, to E.H. Gill, Sandy and Beaver Co., New Lisbon, Ohio, from Saxonburg, B. Co. Pa., June 28th, 1837.

12 Roebling, "Biography," 40-42.

13 Roebling, "Biography," 59.

14 Roebling, "Biography," 54-59.

15 John A. Roebling, Harrisburg, to Charles Ellet, Philadelphia, January 28th 1840

16 Charles Ellet Jr., Philadelphia, to John. A. Roebling, Harrisburg, Feb. 8th 1840.

17 Roebling, "Biography, 60.

18 Roebling, "Biography, 61.

19 Roebling, "Biography," 81; Washington wrote "1839" in his memoir, but archival sources indicate that John made his first rope in 1841.

20 Thomas P. Jones, Washington, D.C., to John A. Roebling, March 24th, 1841; Charles Ellet, Philadelphia, to John A. Roebling, March 27th, '41.

21 Roebling, "Biography," 81.

22 Roebling, "Biography," 81-86.

23 Roebling, "Biography," 61, 80.

24 Roebling, "Biography," 87-88.

25 L. Chamberlain, L., 84 Walnut St., Phila. Aug. 5th, 1842, to John A. Roebling.

26 John A. Roebling, August 13th, 1842, to L. Chamberlain.

27 C.L. Schlatter, Harrisburg, to John A. Roebling, May 8th, 1843; C.L. Schlatter, Chicago, to John A. Roebling, November. 24th, 1843: C. L. Schlatter, Chicago, to John A. Roebling, February 20th, 1844.

28 D.K. Minor, New York, to John A Roebling, Esqr., December 29, '43.

29 Roebling, "Biography," 89-91.

30 John A. Roebling, Saxonburg, Butler Co. Pa. March 30, 1844, to "Beloved father and brother Christel," Mühlhausen.

31 R. Townsend, Pittsburgh, to John A Roebling, May 28, 1844.

32 Roebling, "Biography," 92-93.

33 Mahan, Dennis Hart, *An elementary course of civil engineering, for the use of cadets of the United States' Military Academy*, New York: John Wiley, 1861, (first published c1846), 275.

34 Roebling, "Biography," 94-96.

35 Roebling, "Biography," 98.

36 Roebling, "Biography," 100.

37 Mahan, 274-5.

38 Roebling, "Biography," 99-100.

39 Roebling, "Biography," 109-110.

40 Roebling, John A., "The Wire Suspension Bridge Over the Monongahela River at Pittsburgh," *The American Railroad Journal*, Vol. 19, April 4, 1846, 216, also June 13, 1846, 376.

41 Steinman, 97.

42 Roebling, "Biography," 115.

43 Roebling, "Biography," 116-117.

44 Roebling, "Biography," 111-114.

45 Schuyler, 119-121.

46 Schuyler, 121-122.

47 Nevins, Allan, *Abram S. Hewitt, With Some Account of Peter Cooper*, New York: Harper & Brothers, 1937, 106-107.

48 Roebling, "Biography," 135-6.

49 *Trenton State Gazette*, August 21, 1848.

Notes for Chapter 3: *First class facilities* Pages 45-74

1 Roebling, "Biography," 136; Washington's 11,000 population figure for Trenton in 1848 includes some of the adjacent towns. The 1850 Federal Census reported a population of 6,400 for Trenton itself.

2 Roebling, "Biography," 137.

3 Roebling, "Biography, 138.

4 Roebling, "Biography," 143-145.

5 John A. Roebling, High Falls, Ulster County, N.Y., August 20, 1849, to Charles Swan, Trenton. While John was away from Trenton on bridge projects, he wrote frequently to Swan with instructions about money, the factory and his family. Their surviving correspondence totals several hundred letters.

6 Roebling, "Biography," 138-9; *Trenton State Gazette*, November 13, 1850.

7 Roebling, "Biography," 147-149.

8 Roebling, "Biography," 139, 142.

9 Roebling, "Biography," 174; Steinman, 165.

10 Roebling, "Biography," 164-165.

11 Roebling, "Biography," 156.

12 Roebling, "Biography," 152.

13 Roebling, "Biography," 172.

14 Roebling, "Biography," 177.

15 John A. Roebling, January 27, 1854, to Samuel Backus.

16 Roebling, "Biography," 174-175.

17 John A. Roebling, Susp. Br., June 8th, 1854, to Charles Swan, Trenton.

18 Roebling, "Biography," 155-157.

19 John A. Roebling, Suspension Bridge, N.Y., March, 1855, to Charles Swan, Trenton.

20 John A. Roebling, *Report of John A. Roebling, Civil Engineer, to the Directors, the Niagara Falls International & Suspension Bridge Companies*, Buffalo: Steam Press of Jewett, Thomas & Co., 1852.

21 Clemens, Samuel, *Sketches New and Old*, Hartford, Conn.: American Publishing Company, 1875.

22 Roebling's vision of mile-long suspension bridge spans was reached and surpassed in 1998 with the completion of the Storebaelt Bridge in Denmark, spanning 5,328 feet, and the Akashi-Kaikyo Bridge in Japan spanning 6,529 feet. In 2007, the Xihoumen Bridge opened in China with a span of 5,414 feet.

23 "John A. Roebling, The Funeral Services in Trenton," *The Brooklyn Eagle*, July 24, 1869.

24 Washington also noted that: "Much work was done on the Kentucky Bridge; four stone towers were built, the anchorages were put in, some of the cable wire had arrived, carpenter shops were built for cable making, lumber contracted for the superstructure, and another 18 months would have completed the work. The span was much longer than the Niagara, some 1250 feet, and the cables were much larger, but there was no highway bridge connected with it." The bridge was never completed but John's stone towers became local curiosities until they were torn down in 1929; Roebling, "Biography," 182.

25 John A. Roebling, Susp. Br., Aug. 31, 1854, to Charles Swan, Trenton.

26 John A. Roebling, Susp. Br., Sep. 6, 1854, to Charles Swan, Trenton.

27 John A. Roebling, Susp. Br., May 2, 1855, to Charles Swan, Trenton.

28. John A. Roebling, Susp. Br., Mar. 14, 1854, to Charles Swan, Trenton. Roebling monitored the heating system's performance after living in the house, and noted on a drawing for modifying the system's "Evaporating Pan" humidifier: "It is evident from the Cracking of the Woodwork and furniture that there is not moisture enough evaporated. Double the Capacity of present pan will answer."

29 John A. Roebling, Notebook c1854-1855, RPI; Donald Sayenga letter, 12/20/06. Don has studied and written extensively about the development of wire rope and the machinery used to make it.

30 John A. Roebling, Susp. Br., April 3rd, 1854, to Charles Swan, Trenton.

31 Roebling, "Biography," 198.

32 Griggs, Francis E., Jr., "John A. Roebling and His East River Bridge Proposals, 1847 - 1869," in *John A. Roebling: A Bicentennial Celebration of His Birth, 1806 - 2006*, Theodore Green, editor, New York: American Society of Civil Engineers, 2006, 169.

33 John A. Roebling, "Bridge Over the East River Between New York and Brooklyn," *New York Herald Tribune*, March 27, 1857.

34 John A. Roebling, Monongahela House, Pittsburgh, October 11, 1857, to Charles Swan, Trenton.

35 John A. Roebling, Monongahela House, Pittsburgh, July 30, 1857, to Charles Swan, Trenton.

36 Roebling, "Biography," 196-8.

37. Schuyler, 98; Roebling, "Biography," 142.

38 Roebling, "Biography," 200-1.

39 John A. Roebling, Monongahela House, Pittsburgh, July 31, 1858, to Charles Swan, Trenton.

40 John A. Roebling, Monongahela House, Pittsburgh, July 2, 1858, to Charles Swan, Trenton.

41 Roebling, "Biography," 201.

42 Ferdinand W. Roebling, Washington, D.C., Oct. 13, 1858, to Washington Roebling, Pittsburgh.

43 John A. Roebling, Pittsburgh, June 11 and 21, 1860, to Charles Swan, Trenton.

44 Ferdinand W. Roebling, Trenton, May 7th, 1860, to John A. Roebling, Pittsburgh.

45 Roebling, "Biography," 202-3, 207-9.

46 Roebling, "Biography," 172.

47 John A. Roebling, Pittsburgh, June 21, 1860, to Charles Swan, Trenton.

48 John A. Roebling, Pittsburgh, Febr. 18, 1860, to Charles Swan, Trenton.

49 Roebling, "Biography," 212-3.

50 Charles Roebling, Stapleton, S.I., Sep. 6, 1862, to John A. Roebling.

51 Roebling, "Biography," 220-1.

52 Steinman, 253.

53 Roebling, "Biography," 225-6.

54 Roebling, "Biography," 236.

55 Roebling, "Biography," 237-9.

56 Brigadier General G. K. Warren, Headquarters Engineers, Army of the Potomac, July 16, 1863, to General Williams.

57 Roebling, "Biography," 235.

58 Washington A. Roebling: Trenton, August 2, 1864, to Emily Warren.

59 Washington A. Roebling: Trenton, October 18, 1864, to Emily Warren; Headquarters 5th Army Corps, October, 23, 1864, to Emily Warren.

60 John A. Roebling, Office Covington & Cincinnati Bridge Company, Covington, Ky., Nov. 17, 1864, to Washington Roebling.

61 Schuyler, 99.

62 Excerpts of Washington's writings about his Civil War experience, published as a booklet: *Wash Roebling's War*, Newark, Delaware: The Curtis Paper Company, 1961.

63 John A. Roebling, Cin., April 17, 1865, to Charles Swan.

64 John A. Roebling, Cin., May 16, 1865, to Charles Swan.

65 Washington A. Roebling, Cincinnati, March 16, 1865, to Emily W. Roebling; McCullough, David, *The Great Bridge*, New York: Simon & Shuster, 1972, 70.

66 Roebling, "Biography," 239, 242-245.

67 Roebling, "Biography," 245-52.

68 Washington A. Roebling, Cincinnati, February 9, 1867, to John A. Roebling.

69 John A. Roebling, *Report of John A. Roebling Civil Engineer to the Covington and Cincinnati Bridge Company, Trenton, N.J., April 1st, 1867*, 22-27.

70 Roebling, Report…Cincinnati Bridge, 85-86.

71 Roebling, "Biography," 254.

72 John A. Roebling, *Report of John A. Roebling, Civil Engineer to the President and Directors of the New York Bridge Company on the Proposed East River Bridge*, Brooklyn: Daily Eagle Print, September 1, 1867, 43-48.

73 Roebling, *Report…Proposed East River Bridge*, 48.

74 Charles G. Roebling, Troy, New York, September 10, 1867 to John A. Roebling.

75 Emily W. Roebling, Mühlhausen, January 6, 1868, to John A. Roebling.

76 Roebling, *Report…Proposed East River Bridge*, 18-19.

77 Roebling, "Biography," 256; Hildenbrand shared much in common with John. He was born in Germany in 1845, in

Karlsruhe in the Duchy of Baden, he studied engineering at the Polytechnic School of Karlsruhe and he was a highly skilled draftsman. Also like John, he served his obligatory post-school service working on roads in Westphalia, plus he also worked in Prussia, where John came from. Hildenbrand immigrated to New York in 1867 and John soon hired him as an assistant engineer.

[78] Roebling, "Biography," 256, 270.

[79] *The New York Times*, April 16, 1868; William Kingsley, New York, April 16, 1868, to John A. Roebling.

[80] Roebling, "Biography," 255.

[81] Roebling, "Biography," 272.

[82] A gale blew down the Falls View Suspension Bridge in 1889, just 20 years after it was completed.

[83] Roebling, "Biography," 277-80.

[84] "John A. Roebling, The Funeral Services in Trenton," *The Brooklyn Eagle*, July 24, 1869.

[85] Roebling, "Biography," 266-8.

[86] John. A Roebling, *Long and Short Span Railway Bridges*, New York: D. Van Nostrand, 1869, 1-2.

Notes for Chapter 4: *John A. Roebling's Sons* Pages 75-110

[1] "Last Will and Testament of John A. Roebling," June 5, 1868. RU

[2] John A. Roebling's Sons Agreement with Charles Swan, August 2, 1869, was drawn up within weeks of Roebling's death and before his estate was inventoried. Charles Swan's property is noted on Evert and Stewart, *Combination Atlas Map of Mercer County*, Philadelphia, 1875.

[3] Washington A. Roebling, Trenton, January 23, 1916, to General James F. Rusling.

[4] Schuyler, 324.

[5] Schuyler, 149.

[6] Schuyler, 333.

[7] Schuyler, 333.

[8] Schuyler, 335-6.

[9] Roebling, Washington, A., "In Memoriam to Charles Roebling," 1918, 24.

[10] McCullough, 343.

[11] Edmund Roebling worked for the firm for a few years, but then quit, moved to New York and lived off his dividends and investments. He is listed as Edward in a typed version of his father's will but this may have been an error.

[12] "The Bridge: Some Interesting Facts about the Enterprise," *The Brooklyn Daily Eagle*, August 11, 1876, 4.

[13] McCullough, 522.

[14] Steinman, 415; McCullough, 536; Steinman, 426.

[15] Hewitt, Abram S., *Address on the Opening of the New York and Brooklyn Bridge*, May 24, 1883, N.Y.: J. Polhemus, 1883, 56-58.

[16] Sara Wermiel has researched and written about the Roebling Company's fire proof construction: Wermiel, Sara E., "John A. Roebling's Sons Company and Early Concrete Floors in New York City, 1890s-1910," in *John A. Roebling: A Bicentennial Celebration of His Birth, 1806 - 2006*, Theodore Green, editor, New York: American Society of Civil Engineers, 2006.

[17] Schuyler, 334-335; J.A.R.'s Sons Co., Annual Report, 1877.

[18] Schuyler, 341-342.

[19] Washington A. Roebling, Chicago "World Fair", September 22, 1893 to John A. Roebling II.

[20] Schuyler, 334-34.

[21] Schuyler, 347-348.

[22] Washington A. Roebling, Niagara Falls, New York, May 30, 1888, to John A. Roebling II.

[23] Sayenga, letter, 2/14/90.

[24] Mumford, John Kimberly, *Outspinning The Spider: The Story of Wire and Wire Rope*, New York: Robert L. Stillson Co., 1921; 102.

[25] Schuyler, 346.

[26] Schuyler, 352.

[27] Schuyler, 346.

[28] John Cichoki Interview, Oral Histories of the John A. Roebling's Sons Company, Trenton, New Jersey, Trenton Roebling Community Development Corporation, 1993.

[29] George E. Harney also designed the Plumbush Inn in 1865 in Cold Spring; the Moffat Library in 1887 in Washingtonville, New York; and in New York City, the Brooks Brothers Store at 670 Broadway, opened in 1874, and the New York Mercantile Library on Astor Place, completed in 1890 and now the Astor Place Hotel. Harney published *Barns Outbuildings and Fences* in 1870, and he contributed articles and designs to other publications, including *American Architect and Building News*. The Ballantine Mansion has been the home of the Newark Museum since 1937 and was designated a National Historic Landmark in 1985.

[30] Schuyler, 260.

[31] Schuyler, 260.

[32] "Widow and Son Get Roebling's Estate," *The New York Times*, August 3, 1926.

[33] Washington A. Roebling, Trenton, January 3, 1914, to John A. Roebling II.

[34] Schuyler, 264-5.

[35] Washington A. Roebling, Trenton, April 2, 1893, to John A. Roebling II.

[36] Ibid.

[37] Ibid.

[38] Ibid.

[39] Schuyler, 343-5.

[40] Schuyler, 346.

[41] "John A. Roebling's Sons Company, Cast Steel, Iron, Copper, Plough Steel Wires and Wire Rope," *Daily State Gazette*, Trenton, July 31, 1897.

[42] "Wire Trust Meeting Called," *The New York Times*, Pittsburgh, February 24, 1898.

[43] Ibid.

[44] "The Wire and Nail Trust," *The New York Times*, March 5, 1898.

[45] "Wire Trust Completed," *The New York Times*, March 29, 1898.

[46] Washington A. Roebling, Waldorf Astoria, N.Y., February 15, 1899, to R.V. Lindaberry, Esq.

[47] Schuyler, 352.

[48] "Girls Invoke Law Against Roeblings," *Sunday Times Advertiser*, May 21, 1899;

[49] "Good Times Cause Labor Troubles," *Sunday Times Advertiser*, May 28, 1899.

[50] "Crocker's Son a Stockholder," *The New York Times*, Jan. 10, 1899.

[51] Schuyler, 252-253.

[52] Wermiel, 146.

[53] *The Roebling System of Fire Proof Construction*, Roebling

Construction Company, c1905.

54 Schuyler, 349-352.

55 Schuyler, 346-347

56 Ruth Egan Interview, Oral Histories of the John A. Roebling's Sons Company, 1993.

57 "Roebling Plant Still Reaching Out," *Sunday Times Advertiser*, May 20, 1900.

58 John A. Roebling II, Asheville, North Carolina, July 19, 1905, to Washington A. Roebling.

59 "Roebling Plant Still Reaching Out."

60 Washington A. Roebling, Trenton, July 5, 1903, to John A. Roebling II.

61 Washington A. Roebling, Trenton, July 18, 1904, to John A. Roebling II.

62 Roebling Letters, Vol. II, 645.

Notes for Chapter 5: *We are building as well as we know how*
Pages 111-162

1 Schuyler, 359-60.

2 Washington A. Roebling, Trenton, January 12, 1894, to John A. Roebling II.

3 Schuyler, 360-362.

4 Schuyler, 361, 366.

5 Schuyler, 361.

6 Schuyler, 365, 366.

7 Schuyler, 362-364.

8 Joseph Sabol, Roebling Museum Oral History Interview, 2008.

9 Schuyler, 362-363.

10 Schuyler, 364.

11 Schuyler, 366.

12 Alfred Krupp, Address to His Employees (February 11, 1877). http://germanhistorydocs.ghi-dc.org/pdf/eng/211_Krupp%20 Address%20to%20Employees_29.pdf

13 Buder, Stanley, *Pullman: An experiment in Industrial Order and Community Planning, 1880-1930*, New York: Oxford University Press, 1967, 40-41.

14 Buder, 42.

15 Buder, 43-44.

16 Buder, 69.

17 Buder, 71.

18 Washington A. Roebling, Chicago, September 22, 1893, to John A. Roebling II.

19 Moore, Martha, "Our Town: Company Paternalism and Community Participation in Roebling," Yale University, 1982, 5-6.

20 Buder, 142, 200

21 Buder, 161, 206.

22 "Kinkora: America's Latest 'Model City' Not Built Upon Ideals," *The New York Herald*, April 22, 1906.

23 "The Roebling Enterprise at Kinkora," *The Iron Age*, Vol. 76, November 30, 1905, 1457.

24 "Kinkora: America's Latest 'Model City' Not Built Upon Ideals."

25. Moore, 21.

26 Schuyler, 371.

27 "The Industrial Village at Roebling," *The Iron Age*," Vol. 82, August 6, 1908, 362.

28 "The Industrial Village," 362.

29 Roebling Company Lease with Harry Tonne, June 1, 1918.

30. In a discussion with longtime employees, the only eviction they could recall was an alcoholic who became a nuisance. Roebling, N.J. Meeting, February 24, 1990; N.J. Network, *Steelmakers*, 1974.

31 "The Industrial Village," 363.

32 "Kinkora: America's Latest 'Model City' Not Built Upon Ideals."

33 "The Industrial Village," 362-363.

34 "The Industrial Village," 364.

35 "The Biggest Rope," John A. Roebling's Sons Company Advertisement, unidentified magazine, c1915.

36 *The Wire Rope at Panama*, Trenton, N.J.: John A. Roebling's Sons Company, c1915.

37 Washington A. Roebling, Trenton, April 19, 1907, to John A. Roebling.

38 Washington A. Roebling, Trenton, September 1, 1908, to John A. Roebling.

39 Schuyler, 348-349.

40. "Roebling Plant Suffers $300,000 Loss By Fire," *Trenton Evening Times*, Feb. 5, 1908.

41 Washington A. Roebling, Trenton, March 19, 1908, to John A. Roebling II.

42 Washington A. Roebling, Trenton, January 23, 1916, to James F. Rusling.

43 "Pretty Girls Keep Men Home," *The New York Times*, December 21, 1908.

44 Washington A. Roebling, Trenton, July 18, 1904, to John A. Roebling II.

45 Washington A. Roebling, Trenton, October 15, 1908, to John A. Roebling II.

46 "Roebling and his Noted Car at Vanderbilt Races," *Trenton Evening Times*, October 24, 1908.

47 *Roebling-Planche Cars*, Trenton, N.J,: Walter Automobile Company, 1909.

48 "The Mercer Automobile Company – A Chronological History." Exhibition script for "The Car of Caliber," the New Jersey State Museum, Trenton, 1978.

49 Washington A. Roebling, Trenton, July 9, 1909, to John A. Roebling II.

50 Washington A. Roebling, Trenton, September 15, 1910, to John A. Roebling II.

51 Paul Varga Oral History Interview, July 6, 2007, Roebling Museum.

52. For a discussion of ethnic churches, see C.W. Zink & Co., "South Ward Survey, Trenton, N.J.", 1989.

53 "Fear Trouble at Roebling's, 6000 Workers Out in Trenton - Union Leaders Block Peace Terms," *The New York Times*, April 11, 1910.

54 Cumbler, John T., *A Social History of Economic Decline: Business, Politics and Work in Trenton*, New Brunswick: Rutgers University Press, 1989, 60.

55 Washington A. Roebling, Trenton, May 31, 1910, to John A. Roebling II.

56 Schuyler, 294.

57 Washington A. Roebling, Trenton, June 18, 1914, to John A. Roebling II.

58 "The Mercer Automobile Company – A Chronological History." By 1910, Etienne Planche had left the Mercer Automobile Company to join Louis Chevrolet in Detroit in building the first Chevrolet automobile.

59 Washington A. Roebling, Trenton, January 9, 1912, to John A. Roebling II.

60 Washington A. Roebling, Hotel Brighton, Atlantic City, May 15, 1912.

61 "Roebling Said Goodbye to Friends and Then Perished With Blackwell, His Companion," *Trenton Evening Times*, April 19, 1912.

62 "Roebling Said Goodbye;" Schuyler, 314.

63 "Fiftieth Anniversary – The New Jersey Wire Cloth Company," *Blue Center*, Vol. IV, No. 1, November 1928.

64 "Town Overtaxes Charity; Roebling Families Grow Too Fast for Purse of Its Benefactors," *The New York Times*, January 21, 1914.

65 Washington A. Roebling, Spring Lake, February 19, to John A. Roebling II.

66 Schuyler, 353.

67 Washington A. Roebling, Trenton, March 10, 1913, to John A. Roebling II.

68 Washington A. Roebling, Trenton, August 14, 1913, to John A. Roebling II; "Profitable Philanthropy," *Town Development*, Volume II, 1914, 72.

69 Schuyler, 365.

70 Washington A. Roebling, Trenton, November 3, 1914, to John A. Roebling II.

71 Starr, Dennis. "The Nature and Uses of Political and Social Power in Trenton, N.J., 1890-1917," PhD. Dissertation, Rutgers University, 1979. 298.

72 Washington A. Roebling, Trenton, November 13, 1914, to John A. Roebling II.

73 Washington A. Roebling, Trenton, January 13, 1915, to John A. Roebling II.

74 Schuyler, 354-5.

75 Washington A. Roebling, Trenton, April 15, 1915, to John A. Roebling II.

76 Washington A. Roebling, Trenton, May 20, 1915, to John A. Roebling II.

77 Moore, 40.

78 Moore, 40.

79 Washington A. Roebling, Trenton, September 29 & October 16, 1915, to John A. Roebling II.

80 Schuyler, 355-6; Washington A. Roebling, Trenton, November 11, 1915, to John A. Roebling II.

81 Schuyler, 356-357.

82 Washington A. Roebling, Trenton, December 15, 1915, to John A. Roebling II.

83 Washington A. Roebling, Trenton, January 23, 1916, to James F. Rusling.

84 Washington A. Roebling, Trenton, December 29, 1915, to John A. Roebling II.

85 Washington A. Roebling, Trenton, January 14, 1916, to John A. Roebling II.

86 Washington A. Roebling, Trenton, February 11, 1916, to John A. Roebling II.

87 "Plan to Unionize Roebling Workers," February 21, 1915. Trentoniana newspaper clipping.

88 Washington A. Roebling, Trenton, May 8, 1916, to John A. Roebling II.

89 Washington A. Roebling, Trenton, July 15, 1916, to John A. Roebling II.

90 The Belpre-Parkersberg Bridge was replaced with a new bridge in 1980.

91 Washington A. Roebling, Trenton, March 2, 1917, to John A. Roebling II.

92 Schuyler, 357.

93 Washington A. Roebling, Trenton, March 6, 1917, to John A. Roebling II.

94 Washington A. Roebling, Trenton, March 22, 1917, to John A. Roebling II.

95 Washington A. Roebling, Trenton, March 22, 1917, to John A. Roebling II.

96 Schuyler, 396-396.

97 Washington A. Roebling, Trenton, May 17, 1917, to John A. Roebling II.

98 Washington A. Roebling, Trenton, May 24, 1917, to John A. Roebling II.

99 Washington A. Roebling, Trenton, June 15, 1917, to John A. Roebling II.

100 Washington A. Roebling, Trenton, November 14, 1917, to John A. Roebling II.

101 *Wire Roping the German Submarine: The Barrage that Stopped the U-Boat*, Trenton, N.J.: John A. Roebling's Sons Company, 1920, 9.

102 Washington A. Roebling, Trenton, May 31, 1918, to John A. Roebling II.

103 "Striking Ropemakers Discharged," *The New York Times*, May 5, 1918.

104 Washington A. Roebling, Trenton, September 1, 1918, to John A. Roebling II.

105 Washington A. Roebling, Trenton, October 5, 1918, to John A. Roebling II.

106 Schuyler, 324-328.

107 Schuyler, 394.

108 Washington A. Roebling, Trenton, November 20, 1918, to John A. Roebling II.

109 Washington A. Roebling, Trenton, December 24, 1918, to John A. Roebling II.

110 Washington A. Roebling, Trenton, March 5 and July 28, 1919, to John A. Roebling II.

111 Washington A. Roebling, Trenton, August 2 & September 3, 1920, to John A. Roebling II; September 20, 1920, to Rita Roebling.

112 Washington A. Roebling, "History of the connection of Noble and Scammell with the J. A. Roebling's Sons Co., Trenton New Jersey," Handwritten manuscript, November, 1921, 1. Of Scott Scammell, Washington wrote: "Scammell favorably impressed me at first….The Scammell family – 4 or 5 boys and girls – settled in Chambersburg near our mill. As a young man Scott Scammell worked there as a heater – making 2 dollars a day. An ambitious mother made him take to the law." 1, 3.

113 Washington A. Roebling, Trenton, March 30, 1921, to John A. Roebling II.

114 Washington A. Roebling, Trenton, April 21, 1921, to John A. Roebling II.

115 Schuyler, 386.

116 J.A.R.'s Sons Company, Annual Meeting, January 9, 1922.

117 Washington A. Roebling, "Noble and Scammell," 3.

118 Washington A. Roebling, "Noble and Scammell," 3.

119 Washington A. Roebling, "Noble and Scammell," 9.

120 Washington A. Roebling, "Noble and Scammell," 6-7.

121 Washington A. Roebling, "Noble and Scammell," 17.

122 In devising his strategy to oust Nobel and Scammell, Washington solicited the advice of Clarence Edward Case, a State Senator from Somerset County. Case had done legal work for John II since 1914, and served the Roeblings over five decades. In his work as the executor of John II's estate in the 1950's, Case organized the voluminous Roebling family papers that Washington had collected, and apportioned them to Rensselaer Polytechnic Institute and Rutgers University for long-term preservation. As Case recalled in 1955: "My employment, which was in the capacity of an old-time family advisor, brought me into intimate ties with John and with his wife, his sons and his aging father. It formed, in its character, duration and ramifications, the most interesting and satisfying experience of my life at the bar." Clarence E. Case, editor, "Roebling Letters," June 30, 1955, unpublished, b-c; Washington A. Roebling, Trenton, December 23, 1921, to John A. Roebling II.

123 Washington A. Roebling, "Noble and Scammell," 21; Washington A. Roebling, Trenton, October 15, 1921 to John A. Roebling II.

124 Washington A. Roebling, Trenton, May 17, 1921, to John A. Roebling II.

125. Cumbler, 107.

126 Washington A. Roebling, Trenton, March 8, 1922, to John A. Roebling II.

127 Washington A. Roebling, Trenton, March 8 and March 23, 1922, to John A. Roebling II; John A. Roebling II, Bernardsville, N.J., March 18, 1922, to Washington A. Roebling.

128 Washington A. Roebling, Trenton, June 6, 1922, to John A. Roebling II.

129 George W. Pepper, Philadelphia, June 21, 1922, to Washington A. Roebling.

130 Washington A. Roebling, Trenton, June 6, 1922, to John A. Roebling II.

131 Washington A. Roebling, Trenton, June 2, 1922, to John A. Roebling II.

132 Washington A. Roebling, Trenton, June 2, 1922, to John A. Roebling II.

133 Washington A. Roebling, Trenton, June 10, 1922, to Rita.

134 Washington A. Roebling Trenton, August 26, 1922, to George W. Pepper.

135 J.A.R.'s Sons Co., Board of Directors Meetings, August 21 & November 28, 1922.

136 Washington A. Roebling, Trenton, N.J., March 8, 1922, to John A. Roebling II; For a detailed description of electrical modernization at the Trenton and Roebling works, see: "Improving Flexibility and Cost of Power," The Iron Age, Vol. 113, April 17, 1924, 1141-1143.

137 Schuyler 378-80.

138 Washington A. Roebling, Trenton, April 17, 1923, to Rita and to John A. Roebling II.

139 Washington A. Roebling, Trenton, July 19, & August 4, 1923, to John A. Roebling II.

140 Washington A. Roebling, Trenton, September 23, 1923, to Clarence Case; July 3, 1924, to John A. Roebling II.

141 "New Rod Mill for Wire and Cable Plant," The Iron Age, Vol. 112, No. 23, December 6, 1923, 1507.

142 "New Rod Mill for Wire and Cable Plant," 1507.

143 Moore, 28.

144 Washington A. Roebling, Trenton, July 24, 1925, to John A. Roebling II.

145 Blue Center, Vol. 1, No.1, November, 1925, frontispiece.

146 John A. Roebling's Sons Company, Board of Directors Meeting, January 26, 1926.

147 Washington A. Roebling, Trenton, March 3, 1926, to John A. Roebling II; May 13, 1926, to My Dear Gage.

148 Washington A. Roebling, May 14, 1926, to Margaret S. M. Roebling (Mrs. John A. Roebling II).

149 Washington A. Roebling, Trenton, November 7, 1925, To the Editor of the Blue Center.

150 Washington A. Roebling, Trenton, December 5, 1925, to John A. Roebling II.

151 Schuyler, 276.

152 "Governor and Mayor Join Priest in Honoring Dead," Trenton Gazette, July 22, 1926; "Roebling Dies: Built Brooklyn Bridge," The New York Times, July 21, 1926.

153 Schuyler, 277.

154 J.A.R.'s Sons Co., Board of Directors, Special Meeting, July 26, 1926.

155 Washington A. Roebling, Trenton New Jersey, June 6, 1926, to John A. Roebling II; "Roebling Minerals Go to Smithsonian," The New York Times, January 23, 1927; "Rare Stones Collections Go To Smithsonian," The New York Times, February 6, 1927.

**Notes for Chapter 6: *Another bold leap forward*
Pages 163-218**

1 Blue Center, August, 1927, 1.

2 For information on Hoggson Brothers, see Alfred Willis, "Design-build and Building Efficiency in the early Twentieth, Century United States," Construction History Society Newsletter, No. 65, February 2003, 7

3 "For Release Saturday Afternoon, March 26th" (1927), Papers of Governor Arthur Harry Moore (1879-1952), 1st Term, New Jersey State Archives, 130P.

4 "Open Bids for Span over Hudson River," The New York Times, October 4, 1927.

5 Sunderland, C.C., "Manufacturing High-Modulus Footbridge Ropes for Fort Lee Hudson River Bridge," Engineering News-Record, May 1, 1930, 714.

6 "John A. Roebling's Sons Co. Vast Wire Plant Thrown Open to the New York Electrical Society: See Hudson River Bridge Cables Made and Tested," Telegraph and Telephone Age, May 16, 1929, 220-2.

7 Sunderland, 714.

8 Alice Mae Agostinelli Interview, July 12, 2008, Roebling Museum.

9 Blue Center, March 1929, 8.

10 Blue Center, October, 1929, 2.

11 Zink, Clifford W., and Hartman, Dorothy White, Spanning the Industrial Age: History of the John A. Roebling's Sons Company, 1848-1974, Trenton, N.J.: Trenton Roebling Community Development Corporation, 1992, 188-9.

12 C.C. Sunderland, "John A. Roebling's Sons Co. Bridge Department Memo, Subject: Galvanized Strand Cables for Maysville, Ky., Bridge, December 30, 1930." Roebling Museum.

13 "Another Advance," Engineering News-Record, V. 104, February

13, 1930, 270.

[14] "Wire and Space," *Fortune Magazine*, January, 1931, 85.

[15] "Edmund Roebling Dies; Long An Invalid," *The New York Times*, December 22, 1930.

[16] "The Bridges of '31," *Wire Engineering*, Vol. 1, No. 11, February-March, 1932.

[17] "The Span That Symbolizes the Steel Age," *The New York Times*, September 6, 1931.

[18] "How the Bridge Was Built," *The New York Times*, October 18, 1931.

[19] "The George Washington Bridge," *Wire Engineering*, October – November 1931, 3-7.

[20] Gasparini, Dario A., "Charles C. Sunderland and the Diffusion of Prestressing Technologies in the Americas," *Proceedings of the Third international Congress on Construction History*, Cottbus, 2009, 656.

[21] J.A.R.'s Sons Co., Board of Directors, April 7, 1931.

[22] J.A.R.'s Sons Co., Board of Directors, October 6, 1931.

[23] Ken Ibach Interview, July 7, 2007, Roebling Museum.

[24] "Big Job to Roebling," *Time Magazine*, November 21, 1932.

[25] J.A.R.'s Sons Company, Board of Directors, February 7, 1933.

[26] "Ferdinand W. Roebling III," *Roebling Reel*, May-June 1942.

[27] *Suspension Bridges: A Century of Progress*, Trenton: J.A.R.'s Sons Company, c1936, 126.

[28] J.A.R.'s Sons Co., Board of Directors, February 6, 1934.

[29] J.A.R.'s Sons Co., Consolidated Income for the Year ended December 31, 1934, February 5, 1935.

[30] Blair Birdsall Interview, Oral Histories of the John A. Roebling's Sons Company, November 18, 1993.

[31] *The Golden Gate Bridge*, Friends of the Golden Gate Bridge, Roebling, N.J., May 9, 1987.

[32] Birdsall Interview.

[33] "Largest and Longest Bridge Cables Spun at New Record Rate," *Engineering News-Record*, April 30, 1936.

[34] Schuyler, 392.

[35] J.A.R.'s Sons Co., Board of Directors Minutes, February 2, 1937.

[36] http://www.fhwa.dot.gov/infrastructure/2bridges.cfm

[37] "More Kudos for JAR," *The Golden Gate Bridge,* Friends of the Golden Gate Bridge, Roebling, N.J., May 9, 1987.

[38] J.A.R.'s Sons Company, Annual Report, 1938; "NLRB Upheld on Roebling," *The New York Times*, November 21, 1939.

[39] J.A.R.'s Sons Company, Board of Directors, March 21, 1939

[40] Ford, Bacon & Davis, Report to John A. Roebling's Sons Company, October 30, 1939, 19, 9.

[41] J.A.R.'s Sons Company, Board of Directors, April 5, 1940.

[42] www.globalsecurity.org/military/library/report/1987/RRW.htm; "Award Roebling Medal," *The Roebling Record*, March 21, 1947.

[43] "250 Police Watch," *The New York Times*, March 27, 1941.

[44] "Strike at Roebling Plant," *The New York Times,* April 17, 1941.

[45] "Strike Grows, Two Roebling Plants Are Hit," *Trenton Evening Times*, April 18, 1941.

[46] "Roebling Walkout Halts Defense Work," *The New York Times*, April 18, 1941; "Strike Grows;" "Roebling Walkout."

[47] "Strike Grows;" Roebling Strike Goes On," *The New York Times*, April 20, 1941.

[48] "Pickets Carry Baseball Bats At Roebling's," *Trenton Evening Times*, April 22, 1941.

[49] "Pickets Carry."

[50] "Workers Back at Roebling's," *Trenton Evening Times*, April 23, 1941.

[51] "Roebling Union Loses," *The New York Times*, April 29, 1941; "Defense Factor in Pact," *Trenton Evening Times*, April 29, 1941.

[52] National Defense Mediation Board Case No. 18, John A. Roebling's Sons Company and the Steel Workers Organizing Committee – CIO, April 29, 1941.

[53] "C.I.O. Wins Roebling Vote," *The New York Times*, August 25, 1941.

[54] "Roebling Pact with C.I.O.," *The New York Times*, May 21, 1941.

[55] J.A.R.'s Sons Co., Board of Directors Minutes, March 26, 1942.

[56] For information on the Navy "E" Award, see www.history.navy.mil/library/online/e_award.htm#circ

[57] "Memo for the Record," National War Labor Board, June 10, 1942.

[58] "Army-Navy "E" To Roebling," *Roebling War Worker*, Vol. 1, No. 1, November 20, 1942, 1, 7.

[59] J.A.R.'s Sons Company, Board of Directors Minutes, November 27, 1942.

[60] "Roebling "E" Withdrawn," *The New York Times*, February 18, 1943.

[61] Birdsall Interview; Birdsall, Blair, "San Marcos Bridge: A prophetic design in an out-of-the-way place," *Civil Engineering*, September, 1954, 40-41.

[62] Birdsall Interview.

[63] J.A.R.'s Sons Co., Annual Report to Stockholders, March 7, 1947.

[64] "Labor Row Closes Big Trenton Plant," *The New York Times*, January 21, 1944; "Union Assails Roebling," *The New York Times*, January 22, 1944.

[65] "3,000 At War Plant Continue Walkout," *The New York Times*, July 30, 1944.

[66] "Roebling Strikers Ignore WLB," *The New York Times*, August 3, 1944.

[67] "William A. Anderson Dies; Served Company 56 Years," *Roebling War Worker*, September 18, 1944.

[68] J.A.R.'s Sons Co., Annual Report to Stockholders, March 12, 1946.

[69] "Sgt. Ibach is Cited as Battlefield Hero," *Roebling War Worker*, 1945, 8.

[70] J.A.R.'s Sons Co., Annual Report to Stockholders, March 12, 1946.

[71] J.A.R.'s Sons Co., Annual Report to Stockholders, March 12, 1946.

[72] J.A.R.'s Sons Co., Board of Directors, October 24, 1942.

[73] "Report on Meeting Between Union and Roebling Officials on Housing Problem, 1946."

[74] "Roebling, N.J., Put up for Sale by Wire Plant," *New York Herald Tribune*, June 17, 1947.

[75] J.A.R.'s Sons Co., Annual Report to Stockholders, March 17, 1947, 6.

[76] J.A.R.'s Sons Co., Annual Report to Stockholders, March 11, 1948, 8.

[77] "Roebling, New Jersey – An American Community," *Roebling Magazine*, January 1948, 9-18.

[78] "President's Message," *Roebling Magazine*, February 1948, 23.

[79] "We Win An Award," *Roebling Magazine*, June-July 1948, 12.

[80] "Roebling Buys Airplane To Promote Sales Program," *The Roebling Record*, August 21, 1946.

[81] J.A.R.'s Sons Co., Annual Report to Stockholders, March 11, 1948, 3.

[82] J.A.R.'s Sons Co., Board of Directors, April 22, 1948.

[83] J.A.R.'s Sons Co., Report to Employees, 1947.

[84] J.A.R.'s Sons Co., Board of Directors, February 26, 1948.

[85] *Aerial Wire Rope System*s, J.A.R.'s Sons Co., 1949, 2.

[86] Birdsall, Blair, "San Marcos Bridge," 40-41.

[87] J.A.R.'s Sons Co., Annual Report 1948 to the Stockholders, March 2, 1949, 3.

[88] "Report to Employees 1948," *Roebling Magazine*, Apr-May, 1948, 7.

[89] Gasparini, "Charles C. Sunderland," 657.

[90] "Roebling Span Crosses Rio Paz Between Guatemala and El Salvador," *The Roebling Record*, March 16, 1950, 4.

[91] "Birdsall Gives Chicago Address," *The Roebling Record*, February 16, 1950, volume 4, number 13, 1; Nasser, George D., "The Legacy of the Walnut Lane Memorial Bridge," www.structuremag.org/article.aspx?articleID=775.

[92] "Prestressed Concrete," *Roebling Magazine*, October-November-December, 1950, 6-9.

[93] Nasser, "Walnut Lane Memorial Bridge."

[94] J.A.R.'s Sons Co., Annual Report 1949 to the Stockholders, March 6, 1950, 4: Annual Report 1948, March 2, 1949, 4.

[95] "Roebling Assails Strike," *The New York Times*, August 31st, 1950.

[96] J.A.R.'s Sons Co., Employees Annual Report 1950, Apr. 26, 1951, 2.

[97] Lonnie Brown, Oral History Interview, July 12, 2008, Roebling Museum.

[98] J.A.R.'s Sons Co., Board of Directors, November 29, 1951.

[99] Charles Roebling Tyson explained the stockholders' rationale for selling in a meeting with the author in January, 1990, and in a subsequent letter dated February 1, 1990.

[100] J.A.R.'s Sons Co., Board of Directors, May 7, 1951.

[101] "Supply Cable Assemblies for Twelve Structures, Other Orders Expected," *The Roebling Record*, November 5, 1951.

[102] "Charles C. Sunderland, Chief Bridge Engineer, Honored by Associates," *The Roebling Record*, December 19, 1951.

[103] Judge Clarence Case organized Roebling family papers for donation to Rutgers University & Rensselaer Polytechnic Institute.

[104] "Company to Discontinue Operations at Woven Wire Fabrics Division Plant," *The Roebling Record*, March 12, 1952.

[105] J.A.R.'s Sons Co., Board of Directors, April 24, 1952.

[106] J.A.R.'s Sons Co., Board of Directors, May 22, 1952.

[107] J.A.R.'s Sons Co., Board of Directors, August 28, 1952.

[108] J.A.R.'s Sons Co., Board of Directors, November 28, 1952.

[109] Charles R. Tyson, December 19, 1952, *Roebling Magazine*, Christmas, 1952, Vol. 6, No. 2, 4.

[110] Birdsall Interview, 16; Birdsall, Blair, "The Bridge Division of the John A. Roebling's Sons Company," December 18, 1952.

[111] *Trenton Sunday Times Advertizer*, Jan. 11, 1953.

Notes for Chapter 7: *Roebling will continue to be Roebling*
Pages 219-244

[1] "CF&I - Building for Tomorrow," *Blue Center*, Spring 1953, 10.

[2] "The Newest Figure in Finance: Remarkable Career of J.C. Osgood," *The New York Times*, September 7, 1902.

[3] "Charles Allen, Jr., 91, Founder of Investment Company, Is Dead," *The New York Times*, July 17, 1994.

[4] "Form Construction Materials Unit," *The Roebling Record*, October 8, 1950 3, 1; "Employ JAR Prestressing Elements for Building of Giant Hoboken Pier, *The Roebling Record*, October 30, 1953, 1.

[5] "Suspenarch Tests Successful; New Concept in Roof Supporting Design," *The Roebling Record*, August, 1957, 1 & 3.

[6] "Roebling Markets Royal Blue Wire Rope Offering Greater Service Life," *The Roebling Record*, March 2, 1955, 1.

[7] "See Sales Rise Resulting from EWD Expansion," *The Roebling Record*, June, 1954, Vol. 7, No. 15, 1.

[8] Leroy Patterson Interview, July 7, 2007, Roebling Museum.

[9] "Sgt. Ibach Is Cited As Battlefield Hero," *Roebling War Worker*, 1945, 8.

[10] "CF&I will close the Buffalo Plant," *CF&I NEWS*, June 24, 1963, 1.

[11] "President L.C. Rose sees bright CF&I Outlook," *CF&I NEWS*, November 25, 1963, 1.

[12] "First Roebling electric arc furnace expected to operate in early 1964," *CF&I NEWS*, July 22, 1963, 1.

[13] "Open Hearths Closed," *Sunday Times Advertiser*, Sep. 26, 1965.

[14] "Final Draft Work Plan, Remedial Investigation/Feasibility Study, Roebling Steel Site, Florence Township, New Jersey," Ebasco Services Incorporated for the U.S. Environmental Protection Agency, March, 1989, 9.

[15] Birdsall Interview.

[16] "CF&I's Bridge Department to be consolidated with other functions within the corporation," *CF&I BLAST*, October 26, 1964.

[17] "Blair Birdsall, Master of Civil Engineering," *The New York Times*, July 4, 1997.

[18] By comparison, the American steel industry in 2007 employed 97,000 workers to produce 98 million tons of steel.

[19] "New slag handling method at Roebling helps CF&I's cost control program," *CF&I BLAST*, November 8, 1965, 1.

[20] "CF&I President confident of Corporation's future," *CF&I BLAST*, May 23, 1966, 1.

[21] Charles Brenner Interview, Oral Histories of the John A. Roebling's Sons Company, 1993.

[22] "World's first 5 inch wire rope made by CF&I," *CF&I BLAST*, February, 1968, 1.

[23] "Final Draft Work Plan," 9.

[24] "Blueprint for Progress," *CF&I BLAST*, May, 1969, 6.

[25] "Annual Report to CF&I Employees 1968," *CF&I BLAST*, May 1969, 3.

[26] "An Industrial Giant Dies Quietly in City," *Sunday Times Advertiser*, May 6, 1973.

[27] "Annual Report to CF&I Employees 1968," *CF&I BLAST*, May 1969, 3.

[28] http://en.wikipedia.org/wiki/National_Environmental_Policy_Act

[29] Henriques, Diana, *The White Sharks of Wall Street: Thomas Mellon Evans and the Original Corporate Raiders*, New York: Scribner, 2000, 233, 14.

[30] Henriques, 14.

[31] Henriques, 22.

[32] Henriques, 266.

[33] "Thomas Evans, a Takeover Expert, Dies," *The New York Times*, July 18, 1997.

[34] Henriques, 266.

[35] Henriques, 267-8.

[36] "Crane Co. now controlling shareholder of CF&I," *CF&I BLAST*, July, 1969, 1.

[37] Henriques, 268.

[38] www.nj.gov/dep/about.html

[39] "Final Draft Work Plan," 9.

[40] "Roebling, An Ideal Is Shaken," Newspaper Clipping, Apr. 25, 1974.

[41] "CF&I Suspends Orders, Workers Hope for a Buyer," Newspaper Clipping, April 4, 1974; "1325 Steel Workers Fearing for Their

Jobs," Newspaper Clipping, April 21, 1974.

[42] "Employees, town share alike in fate of CF&I," *Burlington County Times*, May 12, 1974, 1-2.

[43] "The Terrible Tycoon With an Axe of Gold," *The Trentonian*, April 13, 1974.

[44] "1400 Will Go If There Is No Buyer. Interested?," *The Philadelphia Bulletin*, June 2, 1974, 40.

[45] George Sampson Interview, July 6, 2007. Roebling Museum.

[46] Bill Lovelett Oral History Interview, July 8, 2007. Roebling Museum.

[47] Lovelett Interview.

[48] "Cleveland firm purchases CF&I plant," *Burlington County Times*, October 19, 1974, 1; "They've heard this sale story before," *The Trenton Times*, October 19, 1974.

[49] "Mighty Furnaces Pour Steel Again at Roebling," Newspaper Clipping, November 19, 1974.

[50] "Jolly Old St. Nicholas Slid down Roebling Chimneys Early This Year," Newspaper Clipping, November 19, 1974.

[51] "Final Draft Work Plan," 10.

[52] "CF&I posts record sales, earnings for 1974," *CF&I BLAST*, 1975/1, 1.

Notes for the Epilogue:
The people here are ambitious and industrious
Pages 245-265

[1] "Iron-willed Roebling Keeps Going Without Steel," *Sunday Times Advertiser*, October 26, 1975, B1.

[2] Lou Borbi Oral History Interview, Nov. 13, 2009, Roebling Museum.

[3] "Roebling plans to open 2,000 jobs," *Burlington County Times*, May 15, 1979, 1.

[4] "Final Draft Work Plan," 10.

[5] "JARSCO survives first year," *Trenton Times*, Nov. 2, 1980, C1.

[6] "Final Draft Work Plan," 11.

[7] Zink, Clifford W., "The Roebling Works: New life for one of Trenton's most significant cultural resources," Historic Preservation Program, Columbia University School of Architecture and Urban Planning, December, 1984. The author completed the study under the guidance of Dr. Sigurd Grava, Professor of Urban Planning, and with gracious assistance from Ken Russo, Principal Planner, Trenton Department of Housing and Economic Development. Yun Sheng Huang of the Princeton University School of Architecture and Gordon Loader of the Columbia Historic Preservation program also provided significant assistance.

[8] In addition to Trenton Councilman Anthony Anastasio, many other trustees and staff members contributed to TRCDC's success over more than 12 years: Laura Pedrick Allen, Janine Bauer, Nancy Beer, Frank Bilancio, Elizabeth Bonney Brian, Jane Chiurco, Fia Coscia, Ed Cortesini, Roberta DeAngelis, Debbie DiLeo, Lionel Ellis, John Evans, Donna Geis, Anton Geurds, Hartford Gongaware, Seth Grossman, Richard Grove, Larry Gustin, Dr. John Hamada, Lydia Hill, Richard Hueber, Myrna Kushner, Yuki Moore Laurenti, Christine Lewandoski, Eunice Levie, Eunice Lewis, Ida B. Malloy, Michael McKeever, Molly Merlino, Dan Millen, William Morales, Ralph Muldrow, Dr. Michael Newman, Angelo Nicolai, Joe Nuva, Russell Paoline, Dan Popkin, Dr. Greg Pressman, Vincent Pucciatti, Robert Rahl, Cornell Rudov, Kathy Russo, Rev. James Sauchelli, Ruth Scott, Dino Spadaccini, Herbert Spiegel, Pamela Switlik, Bill Watson, Stephen Wills, Judy Winkler, Kevin Wolfe and Uli Zimmer. Councilmen Anthony Carabelli, John Cipriano, Frank Cirillo, Anthony Conti, John Ungrady and Joe Yuhas contributed significantly to TRCDC's success. Mayor Arthur Holland, Mayor Douglas Palmer, and Mercer County Executive Bob Prunetti all provided crucial support for the redevelopment. Mercer County Freeholders Calvin Iszard and Linda Lengyel, and State Senators Dick LaRossa and Peter Inverso also provided considerable support for TRCDC's efforts. Within Trenton City Hall, Planning Directors Tom Ogren and Alan Mallach provided key planning support for the redevelopment. Ron Berman, President of DKM Properties Corporation, and Richard Bilotti, Publisher of the *Trenton Times*, also provided key support for TRCDC's redevelopment efforts. Associate State Treasurer Richard Wright also provided crucial support. Ed Banta, Anne Bucher, Ho San Chang, Joe Dean, Allison Eckis, Anne Egberts, Alexis Faust, Marie Frank, Scott Hagedorn, Peter Krumins, Dr. Stanley Krystek, Dean Matthews, Alexa McPherson, Bart Overley, Lyle Rawlings, Carol Rogers, Dr. Matt Trau, Mark Wilson and Barbara Wisneski provided volunteer support for TRCDC's educational programs, and Mark contributed key artwork as well; Beer, Nancy G., and Zink, Clifford W., "Capital Comeback: Trenton's Roebling Revival," *New Jersey Reporter*, Feb., 1988.

[9] Governor Thomas H. Kean to Members of the Trenton Roebling Community Development Corporation, February 28, 1989.

[10] The Invention Factory concept was formulated for TRCDC by Sherry Wagner, Michael Schaffer and Sarah Peskin with support form the Geraldine R. Dodge Foundation, New Jersey Bell, Griffith Electric, Suburban Chemical Corporation, Princeton Capital Corporation, DKM Properties, the City of Trenton, Mercer County, and the Mercer County Improvement Authority.

[11] "DKM Properties offers plan for Roebling Project," *The Trenton Times*, July 12, 1991, A13.

[12] Nancy Beer and Judy Winkler assisted with the *Now You're Set For Life* documentary film, which was taped and edited by Andy Fredericks at Telequest in Princeton Junction, N.J. Dennis Starr and the author conducted the interviews. Judy Winkler and the author edited the *Now You're Set For Life* booklet with assistance from Nancy Beer and Dennis Starr. Hartford Gongaware created the "Roebling Online History Archive" with assistance from Judy Winkler. The Archive remained available on the Internet until the closing of the Museum of Contemporary Science, the successor to the Invention Factory, in 2010.

[13] As part of EPA's Remedial Investigation and Feasibility Study for cleaning up the Kinkora Works and complying with the National Historic Preservation Act of 1966, the author surveyed the historic architecture of the site: Zink, C.W., "Architectural Historical Stage 1A Survey: John A. Roebling's Sons Company, Kinkora Works, Roebling, New Jersey," June 1, 1990.

[14] Donna McElrea to Tamara Rossi, EPA Remedial Project Manager, August 19, 1996.

[15] "The Village of Roebling is Abuzz…," *The Roebling Record*, Fall-Winter, 2006, 10.

[16] "John A. Roebling: His Life & Legacy," Ellarslie Museum, Trenton, Press Release, 2006.

[17] pps.org/pdf/an%20urbanist%20says.pdf., 3.

ROEBLING BIBLIOGRAPHY

Manuscript, Document, and Artifact Collections

Ellarslie Museum, Trenton, N.J.

Ferdinand W. Roebling III Archive, Roebling Museum, Roebling, N.J.

Historic American Engineering Survey, Upper Works, Trenton, N.J., 1987; Kinkora Works, Roebling, N.J., 1997.

Roebling Collection, Institute Archives and Special Collections, Folsom Library, Rensselaer Polytechnic Institute, Troy, N.Y.

Roebling Collection, Special Collections and University Archive, Alexander Library, Rutgers University, New Brunswick, N.J.

Roebling Historical Society, Roebling N.J.

Sanborn Map Company, Princeton University, Firestone Library, Princeton, N.J., and New Jersey State Library, Trenton, N.J.

Smithsonian Institution Archives, Washington, D.C.

Trentoniana Collection, Trenton Public Library, Trenton, N.J.

Books, Edited Collections, Booklets and Pamphlets

Billington, David P., *The Tower and the Bridge: The New Art of Civil Engineering*, Princeton, N.J.: Princeton University Press, 1983.

Buder, Stanley, *Pullman: An experiment in Industrial Order and Community Planning, 1880-1930*, New York: Oxford University Press, 1967.

Calvert, Monte, *The Mechanical Engineer in America, 1830-1910*, Baltimore: Johns Hopkins Press, 1967.

Clemens, Samuel, *Sketches New and Old,* Hartford, Conn.: American Publishing Company, 1875.

Cumbler, John, *A Social History of Economic Decline*, New Brunswick: Rutgers University Press, 1989.

Doig, Jonathan, *Empire on the Hudson*, New York: Columbia University Press, 2001.

Etzler, Johann Adolphus, *The Paradise Within Reach of All Men, Without Labour by Powers of Nature and Machinery*, London: John Brooks, 1836.

Goldinger, Ralph, *Historic Saxonburg and Its Neighbors*, Apollo, Pa.: Closson Press, 1990.

The Great Suspension Bridge at Cincinnati, Ohio: Centennial Year, 1966, Cincinnati, Ohio: Committee for the Celebration of the Centennial of the Great Suspension Bridge between Covington, Kentucky, and Cincinnati, Ohio, October, 15, 1966.

Griggs, Francis E., Jr., "John A. Roebling and His East River Bridge Proposals, 1847-1869," in *John A. Roebling: A Bicentennial Celebration of His Birth, at 1806-2006*, Theodore Green, editor, New York: American Society of Civil Engineers, 2006.

Guentheroth, Nele, "The Young Roebling, Biographical Notes," in *John A. Roebling: A Bicentennial Celebration of His Birth, 1806-2006*, edited by Theodore Green, New York: American Society of Civil Engineers, 2006

Güntheroth, Nele and Andreas Kahlow, editors, *Von Mühlhausen in Die Neue Welt – Der Brückenbauer, J.A. Röbling (1806 – 1869)*, Mühlhäuser Beiträge, Sonderheft 15, Mühlhausen, Thuringia, 2006.

Harrod, Kathryn, *Master Bridge Builders: The Story of the Roeblings*, New York: J. Messner, 1958.

Hegel, Georg Wilhelm Friedrich, *The Philosophy of History*, John Sibree, Translator, New York: Wiley Book Co., 1900.

Henriques, Diana, *The White Sharks of Wall Street: Thomas Mellon Evans and the Original Corporate Raiders*, New York: Scribner, 2000.

Kahlow, Andreas, "Johann August Röbling (1806-1869): Early Projects in Context," in *John A. Roebling: A Bicentennial Celebration of His Birth, 1806-2006*, edited by Theodore Green, New York: American Society of Civil Engineers, 2006.

Latimer, Margaret, Brooke Hindle and Marvin Kranzberg, *Bridge to the Future: A Celebration of the Brooklyn Bridge*, New York: Annals of the New York Academy of Science, Vol. 424, 1984.

Mahan, Dennis Hart, *An elementary course of civil engineering, for the use of cadets of the United States' Military Academy,"* New York: John Wiley, 1861, 1st Edition c1846.

McCartney, Clarence, *Where the Rivers Meet: Striking Personalities in the History of Western Pennsylvania*, Pittsburgh: Gibson Press, 1946.

McCullough, David, *The Great Bridge*, N.Y.: Simon & Shuster, 1972.

Miers, Earl Schenck, editor, *Washington Roebling's War*, Newark, Delaware: The Curtis Paper Company, 1961.

Menton, Rose M., Daniel C. Roth, Michelle V. Scott, Joseph Varga, Joseph B. Varga, Loretta M. Varga, and Paul Varga, *Images of America: Roebling*, Charleston, S.C.: Arcadia Publishing, 2001.

Menton, Rose M., Daniel C. Roth, Michelle V. Scott, Joseph Varga, Joseph B. Varga, Loretta M. Varga, and Paul Varga, *Images of America: Roebling Revisited*, Charleston, S.C.: Arcadia Publishing, 2007.

Mumford, John Kimberly, *Outspinning The Spider: The Story of Wire and Wire Rope*, New York: Robert L. Stillson Co., 1921.

Nevins, Allan, *Abram S. Hewitt, With Some Account of Peter Cooper*, New York: Harper & Brothers, 1935.

Pfammatter, Ulrich, *The Making of the Modern Architect and Engineer*, Boston: Birkhäuser, 2000.

Roebling, John A., *Long and Short Span Railway Bridges*, New York: D. Van Nostrand, 1869.

Sayenga, Donald, *Ellet & Roebling*, York, Pa.: The American Canal and Transportation Center, 1983.

Sayenga Donald, "The Remarkable Kinkora Prestretcher," in *John A. Roebling: A Bicentennial Celebration of His Birth, 1806-2006*, edited by Theodore Green, N.Y.: American Society of Civil Engineers, 2006.

Sayenga, Donald, *Washington Roebling's Father: A Memoir of John A. Roebling*, New York: American Society of Civil Engineers, 2009.

Scamehorn, H. Lee, *Mill & Mine: The CF&I in the Twentieth Century*, Lincoln, Nebraska: University of Nebraska, 1992.

Schuyler, Hamilton, *The Roeblings: A Century of Engineers. Bridge Builders and Industrialists*, Princeton, N.J.: Princeton University Press, 1931.

Steinman, David, *Builders of the Bridge*, New York: Harcourt, Brace & Company, 1945.

Stern, Joseph S., Jr., *100, The Great Suspension Bridge at Cincinnati, Ohio, Centennial Year, Nineteen Hundred and Sixty-Six,* Cincinnati, Ohio and Covington, Kentucky: Committee for the Celebration of the Centennial of the Great Suspension Bridge, 1966.

Stewart, Elizabeth C., editor, *Guide to the Roebling Collections at Rensselaer Polytechnic Institute and Rutgers University*, Troy, N.Y.: Rensselaer Polytechnic Institute, 1983.

Tolzman, Don Heinrich, *John A. Roebling and His Suspension Bridge on the Ohio River*, Milford, Ohio: Little Miami Publishing Co., 2007.

Trachtenberg, Alan, *Brooklyn Bridge: Fact and Symbol*, Chicago: University of Chicago Press, 1965.

Vogel, Robert M., *Building Brooklyn Bridge: The Design and Construction*, Smithsonian Institution: Washington, D.C., 1983.

Vogel, Robert M., "Designing Brooklyn Bridge," *Bridge to the Future: A Centennial Celebration of the Brooklyn Bridge,* Annals of the New York Academy of Sciences, Vol. 424, May, 1984.

Vogel, Robert M., *Roebling's Delaware & Hudson Aqueducts*, Washington, D.C.: Smithsonian Institution, 1971.

Weigold, Marilyn E., *Silent Builder: Emily Warren Roebling and the Brooklyn Bridge*, Port Washington, N.Y.: Assoc. Faculty Press, 1984.

Winkler, Judy L. and Clifford W. Zink, editors, *Now You're Set for Life: Oral Histories of the John A. Roebling's Sons Company, Trenton, New Jersey.* Trenton, N.J.: Trenton Roebling Community Development Corporation, 1994.

Zink, Clifford W. Zink, editor, "Roebling Oral Histories," Roebling Museum, Roebling, N.J., July 2007 and July 2008.

Zink, Clifford W., and Hartman, Dorothy White, *Spanning the Industrial Age: History of the John A. Roebling's Sons Company, 1848-1974*, Trenton, N.J.: Trenton Roebling Community Development Corporation, 1992.

Zink, Clifford W., *Mercer Magic: The Mercer Automobile Company, Founded 1909*, Roebling, N.J., Roebling Museum, 2009.

Zink, Clifford W., "Roebling 80-Ton Wire Rope Machine, 93rd National Mechanical Engineering Landmark," American Society of Mechanical Engineers, October 21, 1989.

Newspapers, Magazines, Technical Journals, Reports, Internet and Other Media

"1325 Steel Workers Fearing for Their Jobs," Newspaper Clipping, April 21, 1974.

"1400 Will Go If There Is No Buyer. Interested?," *The Philadelphia Bulletin*, June 2, 1974.

"250 Police Watch," *The New York Times*, March 27, 1941.

"3,000 At War Plant Continue Walkout," *The New York Times*, July 30, 1944.

"An Industrial Giant Dies Quietly in City," *Sunday Times Advertiser*, May 6, 1973.

"Annual Report to CF&I Employees 1968," *CF&I BLAST*, May 1969.

"Another Advance," *Engineering News-Record*, Vol. 104, February 11, 1930, 270.

"Army-Navy 'E' to Roebling!," *Roebling War Worker*, Nov. 20, 1942.

"Award Roebling Medal," *The Roebling Record*, March 21, 1947.

Beer, Nancy G., and Zink, Clifford W., "Capital Comeback: Trenton's Roebling Revival." *New Jersey Reporter*. February, 1988.

"Blair Birdsall, Master of Civil Engineering," *The New York Times*, July 4, 1997.

Blofsom, Richard, and Scott Neilson, *Steelmakers*, Film, N.J. Network, 1974.

"Blueprint for Progress," *CF&I BLAST*, May, 1969.

Birdsall, Blair, "San Marcos Bridge: A prophetic design in an out-of-the-way place," *Civil Engineering*, September, 1954.

"The Bridges of '31," *Wire Engineering*, Vol. 1, No. 11, Feb.-Mar. 1932.

"The Bridge: Some Interesting Facts about the Enterprise," *Brooklyn Daily Eagle*, August 11, 1876.

Burns, Ken, *Brooklyn Bridge*, PBS Documentary Film, 1983.

"Ceremonies in Two States Mark Opening of the George Washington Bridge," *The New York Times*, October 25, 1931.

"CF&I - Building for Tomorrow," *Blue Center*, Spring 1953.

"CF&I President confident of Corporation's future," *CF&I BLAST*, May 23, 1966.

"CF&I's Bridge Department to be consolidated with other functions within the corporation," *CF&I BLAST*, October 26, 1964.

"CF&I posts record sales, earnings for 1974," *CF&I BLAST*, 1975/1.

"CF&I Suspends Orders, Workers Hope for a Buyer," Newspaper Clipping, April 4, 1974.

"CF&I will close the Buffalo Plant," *CF&I NEWS*, June 24, 1963.

"C.G. Roebling is Called by Death at 69," *Trenton Evening Times*, October 6, 1918.

"Charles Allen, Jr., 91, Founder of Investment Company, Is Dead," *The New York Times*, July 17, 1994.

"Charles C. Sunderland, Chief Engineer, Honored By Associates," *The Roebling Record*, December 19, 1951.

"C.I.O. Wins Roebling Vote," *The New York Times*, August 25, 1941.

"Cleveland firm purchases CF&I plant," *Burlington County Times*, October 19, 1974.

"Company to Discontinue Operations at Woven Wire Fabrics Division Plant," *The Roebling Record*, March 12, 1952.

"Crane Co. now controlling shareholder of CF&I," *CF&I BLAST*, July, 1969.

"Crocker's Son a Stockholder," *The New York Times*, Jan. 10, 1899.

Cummings, Dr. Hubertus M., "Roebling and the Public Works of Pennsylvania," *Proceedings of the Canal History and Technology Symposium,* Vol. Ill, March 31, 1984, Easton Pennsylvania: The Center for Canal History and Technology, 1984.

"Defense Factor in Pact," *Trenton Evening Times*, April 29, 1941.

"DKM Properties offers plan for Roebling Project," *The Trenton Times*, July 12, 1991.

"Edmund Roebling Dies; Long An Invalid," *The New York Times*, December 22, 1930.

"Employees, town share alike in fate of CF&I," *Burlington County Times*, May 12, 1974.

"Employ JAR Prestressing Elements for Building of Giant Hoboken Pier, *Roebling Record*, October 30, 1953.

"Fear Trouble at Roebling's, 6000 Workers Out in Trenton - Union Leaders Block Peace Terms," *The New York Times*, April 11, 1910.

"Final Draft Work Plan, Remedial Investigation/Feasibility Study, Roebling Steel Site, Florence Township, New Jersey," Ebasco Services Inc. for U.S. Environmental Protection Agency, 1989.

Gasparini, Dario A., "Charles C. Sunderland and the Diffusion of Prestressing Technologies in the Americas," *Proceedings of the Third international Congress on Construction History*, Cottbus, 2009.

"The George Washington Bridge," *Wire Engineering*, Oct.–Nov., 1931.

"Girls Invoke Law Against Roeblings," *Sunday Times Advertiser*, May 21, 1899;

globalsecurity.org/military/library/report/1987/RRW.htm

"The Golden Gate Bridge," *Friends of the Golden Gate Bridge*, Roebling, N.J., May 9, 1987.

"Good Times Cause Labor Troubles," *Sunday Times Advertiser*, May 28, 1899.

"Governor and Mayor Join Priest in Honoring Dead," *Trenton Gazette*, July 22, 1926.

Hegel, Georg Wilhelm Friedrich: http://www.marxists.org/reference/archive/hegel/

"How the Bridge Was Built," *The New York Times*, October 18, 1931

"Improving Flexibility and Cost of Power," *The Iron Age*, 113, April 17, 1924.

"The Industrial Village at Roebling, N.J.," *The Iron Age*. Vol. 82, August 6, 1908.

"Industrial Village on Sound Basis," *The Iron Age*, Vol. 113, January 3, 1924.

"Iron-willed Roebling Keeps Going Without Steel," *Sunday Times Advertiser*, October 26, 1975.

"JARSCO survives first year," *The Trenton Times*, November 2, 1980.

John A. Roebling, "Bridge Over the East River Between New York and Brooklyn," *New York Herald* Tribune, March 27, 1857.

"John A. Roebling, The Funeral Services in Trenton," *Brooklyn Eagle*, July 24, 1869.

"John A. Roebling's Sons Company 100th Anniversary Supplement," *Trenton Evening Times,* September 9, 1941.

"John A. Roebling's Sons Company, Cast Steel, Iron, Copper, Plough Steel Wires and Wire Rope," *Daily State Gazette*, Trenton, July 31, 1897.

"John A. Roebling's Sons Company's Vast Wire Plant Thrown Open to the New York Electrical Society: See Hudson River Bridge Cables Made and Tested", *Telegraph and Telephone Age*, May 16, 1929.

"Jolly Old St. Nicholas Slid down Roebling Chimneys Early This Year," Newspaper Clipping, November 19, 1974.

Karel J. R. Arndt and Patrick R. Brostowin, "Pragmatists and Profits: George Rapp and J. A. Roebling versus J. A. Etzler and Count Leon," *The Western Pennsylvania Historical Magazine*, Vol. 52, No. 1, January 1969.

"Keeping Young on the Job at 84 years: Col. Roebling, Factory Head, Tells How," *New York Evening World,* June 8, 1921.

"Kinkora: America's Latest Model City Not Built Upon Ideals," *New York Herald*, April 22, 1906.

Alfred Krupp, Address to His Employees (February 11, 1877). http://germanhistorydocs.ghi-dc.org/pdf/eng/211_Krupp%20 Address%20to%20Employees_29.pdf

"Labor Row Closes Big Trenton Plant," *The New York Times*, January 21, 1944.

"Largest and Longest Bridge Cables Spun at New Record Rate," *Engineering News-Record*, April 30, 1936.

Mende, Michael, "Early 19th Century Suspension Bridges on the Upper Ruhr: Johann August Röbling's 1828 Freienohl Project and the 1839 Bridge by A. Bruns at Laer Manner;" http://www.ticcihcongress2006.net/paper/Paper%207/Mende%207.pdf

"Memo for the Record," National War Labor Board, June 10, 1942.

"Mighty Furnaces Pour Steel Again at Roebling," Newspaper Clipping, November 19, 1974.

Morris, John G. "A Century Old, the Wonderful Brooklyn Bridge," *National Geographic*, Vol. 163, No. 5 (May 1983), 565-579.

Moses, Kingsley, "Profitable Philanthropy of the Vision of John A. Roebling: Its Inception, Its Fulfillment, and Its Ultimate Success as a Producer of Wealth and Happiness to Laborer and Capitalist", *Town Development*. Vol. II, 1914.

Nasser, George D., "The Legacy of the Walnut Lane Memorial Bridge," structuremag.org/article.aspx?articleID=775.

"The Newest Figure in Finance: Remarkable Career of J. C. Osgood," *The New York Times*, September 7, 1902.

"New Magazine to Appear Next Month," *The Roebling Record*, August 15, 1947.

"New Power Lawn Mower by Roebling," *Roebling Record*, June 5, 1946.

"New Roebling Mower Wins Acclaim," *The Roebling Record*, July 1, 1946.

"The New Roebling Works," *The Iron Age*, Vol. 78, April 26, 1906.

"New Rod Mill for Wire and Cable Plant," *The Iron Age*, Vol. 112, No. 23, December 6, 1923.

"New slag handling method at Roebling helps CF&I's cost control program," *CF&I BLAST*, November 8, 1965.

Now You're Set For Life, Documentary Film Edited by Andy Fredericks, Telequest, Trenton Roebling Community Development Corporation, 1993.

"The Old Standpipe," *The Roebling Record*, November, 1948.

"Open Bids for Span over Hudson River," *The New York Times*, October 4, 1927.

"Open Hearths Closed," *Sunday Times Advertiser*, Sep. 26, 1965.

"Pickets Carry Baseball Bats At Roebling's," *Trenton Evening Times*, April 22, 1941.

"Plan to Unionize Roebling Workers," February 21, 1915. Trentoniana newspaper clipping.

"President L.C. Rose sees bright CF&I Outlook," *CF&I NEWS*, November 25, 1963.

"Prestressed Concrete," *Roebling*, October-November-December, 1950.

"Pretty Girls Keep Men Home," *The New York Times*, Dec. 21, 1908.

"Report on Meeting Between Union and Roebling Officials on Housing Problem, 1946."

"Residents Agree to Buy Jersey Village Built for Employees of John A. Roebling," *The New York Times*, February 1, 1947.

"Roebling and his Noted Car at Vanderbilt Races," *Trenton Evening Times*, October 24, 1908.

"Roebling, An Ideal Is Shaken," Newspaper Clipping, Apr. 25, 1974.

"Roebling Assails Strike," *The New York Times*, August 31, 1950.

"Roebling Buys Airplane To Promote Sales Program," *The Roebling Record*, August 21, 1946.

"Roebling Dies: Built Brooklyn Bridge," *The New York Times*, July 21, 1926.

"The Roebling Enterprise at Kinkora," *The Iron Age*, Vol. 76, November 30, 1905, 1457.

"Roebling "E" Withdrawn," *The New York Times*, February 18, 1943.

"Roebling Girl Worker Stripped In Attempt to Pass Picket Line; Police Patrol Strike-Bound Area," *Philadelphia Inquirer*, April 22, 1941.

Roebling, John A., *Report of John A. Roebling Civil Engineer to the Covington and Cincinnati Bridge Company*, Trenton, N.J., April 1st, 1867.

Roebling, John A., *Report of John A. Roebling, Civil Engineer, to the Directors of the Niagara Falls International and Suspension Bridge Companies*, Buffalo: Steam Press of Jewett, Thomas & Co., 1852.

Roebling, John A., *Report of John A. Roebling, Civil Engineer to the President and Directors of the New York Bridge Company on the Proposed East River Bridge*, Brooklyn: Daily Eagle Print, Sep. 1, 1867.

Roebling, John A., "The Wire Suspension Aqueduct Over the Allegheny River at Pittsburgh," *Journal of the Franklin Institute*. Third Series, X, 1845, 306-09.

Roebling, John A., "The Wire Suspension Bridge Over the Monongahela River at Pittsburgh," *The American Railroad Journal*, Vol. 19, April 4, 1846, and June 13, 1846.

Röbling, Johann, Pittsburgh, to Mr. F. Baehr in Mühlhausen, November 2, 1831, in Karel J. R. Arndt and Patrick R. Brostowin, "Pragmatists and Profits: George Rapp and J. A. Roebling versus J. A. Etzler and Count Leon," *The Western Pennsylvania Historical Magazine*, Vol. 52 No. 1, January 1969.

"Roebling Man Sees Nazi Horrors," *Roebling War Worker*, May 15, 1945.

"Roebling Minerals of Untold Scientific Value," *Baltimore Sun*, August 21, 1927.

"Roebling, N.J., Put up for Sale by Wire Plant," *New York Herald Tribune*, June 17, 1947.

"Roebling Pact with C.I.O.," *The New York Times*, May 21, 1941.

Roebling-Planche Cars, Trenton, N.J,: Walter Automobile Company, 1909.

"Roebling plans to open 2,000 jobs," *Burlington County Times*, May 15, 1979.

"Roebling Plant Still Reaching Out," *Trenton Sunday Times Advertiser*. May 20, 1900

"Roebling Plant Suffers $300,000 Loss By Fire," *Trenton Evening Times*, February, 5, 1908.

The Roebling Record, Roebling Historical Society, Roebling, N.J. 1987 to present.

"Roebling Said Goodbye to Friends and Then Perished With Blackwell, His Companion," *Trenton Evening Times*, April 19, 1912.

"'Roebling Steel' captured people's hearts," *The Trenton Times*, June 3, 1992.

"Roebling Strikers Ignore WLB," *The New York Times*, Aug. 3, 1944.

"Roebling Strike Goes On," *The New York Times*, April 20, 1941.

"Roebling Union Loses," *The New York Times*, April 29, 1941,

"Roebling Strike Settled," *The New York Times*, April 30, 1941.

Roebling Stories, Documentary Film Written and Directed by Clifford W. Zink, Roebling Museum, Roebling, N.J., 2009.

"Roebling Walkout Halts Defense Work," *The New York Times*, April 18, 1941.

"Roebling Workers in Drive to Raise Wage Rates," *VOICE of 2110 & 2111*, Official Organ 2110 & 2111, SWOC Lodges 2110-2111, Roebling Plants, August 1, 1939, Vol. 1, No. 3.

Sayenga, Donald, "Six Biographic Sketches of John A. Roebling, Parts 1-6, *Wire Rope News and Sling Technology*, February-December, 2006.

"See Sales Rise Resulting from EWD Expansion," *The Roebling Record*, Vol. 7, No. 15, June, 1954.

"Sgt. Ibach Is Cited As Battlefield Hero," *Roebling War Worker*, 1945.

"The Span That Symbolizes the Steel Age," *The New York Times*, September 6, 1931.

"Strike at Roebling Plant," *The New York Times*, April 17, 1941.

"Strike Grows, Two Roebling Plants Are Hit," *Trenton Evening Times*, April 18, 1941.

"Striking Ropemakers Discharged," *The New York Times*, May 5, 1918.

"Stockholders Approve Company Sale to Colorado Fuel & Iron," *The Roebling Record*, December 26, 1952.

Sunderland, C.C., "Manufacturing High-Modulus Footbridge Ropes for Fort Lee Hudson River Bridge," *Engineering News-Record*, May 1, 1930, 714-8.

Sunday Times Advertiser, May 21, 1899; Jan. 11, 1953.

"Supply Cable Assemblies for Twelve Structures, Other Orders Expected," *The Roebling Record*, November 5, 1951.

Tarr, Joel A. and Steven J. Fenves, "The Greatest Bridge Never Built," *Invention & Technology*, Fall, 1989, Vol. 5, No. 2.

"The Terrible Tycoon With an Axe of Gold," *The Trentonian*, April 13, 1974.

"They've heard this sale story before," *Trenton Times*, October 19, 1974.

"Thomas Evans, a Takeover Expert, Dies," *The New York Times*, July 18, 1997.

Time Magazine. May 25, 1987.

"Town Overtaxes Charity; Roebling Families Grow Too Fast for Purse of Its Benefactors," *The New York Times*, January 21, 1914.

The Trenton Roebling Redevelopment News, Trenton Roebling Community Development Corporation, Trenton, N.J. 1988-1993.

Trenton State Gazette, August 21, 1848.

Trenton State Gazette, November 13, 1840.

"Union Assails Roebling," *The New York Times*, January 22, 1944.

Walbert, Kate, "The Roebling Resurrection," *Rutgers Magazine*, Summer, 1993.

Wermiel, Sara E., "John A. Roebling's Sons Company and Early Concrete Floors in New York City," in *John A. Roebling: A Bicentennial Celebration of His Birth 1806-2006*, Theodore Green, editor, New York: American Society of Civil Engineers, 2006, 146.

"Widow and Son Get Roebling's Estate," *The New York Times*, August 3, 1926.

"Wilhelm Hildenbrand," *Engineering News*, February 27, 1908.

"The Wire and Nail Trust," *The New York Times*, March 5, 1898.

"Wire and Space," *Fortune Magazine*, January, 1931, 83-88.

"Wire Trust Completed," *The New York Times*, March 29, 1898.

"The Wire Suspension Bridge Over the Monongahela River at Pittsburgh," *The American Railroad Journal*, 19, Apr. 4 & Jun. 6, 1846.

"Wire Trust Meeting Called," *The New York Times*, Pittsburgh, February 24, 1898.

"Workers Return to Roebling Job," *Trenton Evening Times*, Apr. 23, 1941.

"World's first 5 inch wire rope made by CF&I," *CF&I BLAST*, February, 1968.

John A. Roebling's Sons Company Publications, Trade Catalogs and Documents

Birdsall, Blair, "The Bridge Division of the John A. Roebling's Sons Company," December 18, 1952.

Blue Center, 1925-1930.

Brown, J.C., "In Memoriam - John A. Roebling," Trenton, N.J.: Sunday Sermon, August 8th, 1896.

CF&I BLAST, CF&I NEWS

Ford, Bacon & Davis, Incorporated, Engineers, New York, "Report, Business and Sales Operations, John A. Roebling's Sons Company, Trenton, N.J., October 30, 1939, Volume 1."

Hildenbrand, Wilhelm, *The underground haulage of coal by wire ropes: including the system of wire rope tramways as a means of transportation for mining products*, Trenton, N.J.: 1884.

J.A.R.'s Sons Company, Minutes of the Board of Directors.

John A. Roebling's Sons Company, Reports to Employees.

Manufacture of Patent Wire Rope, Trenton, Trade Catalogue, c1855.

Price List of Wire Rope and Wire Rope Fastenings: Iron, Copper, Brass and Steel Wire; Galvanized Telegraph Wire and Hard Copper Telephone Wire, with descriptive notes on Cableways, Tramways, Suspension Bridges, Transmission of Power by Wire Rope, Inclined Planes, Wire Rope Haulages, Trenton, N.J., 1903.

Roebling Magazine. 1946-1953.

Roebling Handbook, 1947.

The Roebling Record, 1945-1958.

The Roebling Reel, c1940-c1943.

The Roebling System of Fire Proof Construction, Roebling Construction Company, Trenton, N.J., 1905.

The Roebling Story, c1950.

Roebling War Worker, 1941-1945.

Roebling Wire Rope, periodical, 1916 and possibly additional years.

Roebling Wire Rope and Wire, 1923, 1931.

Skinner, Frank W., *Roebling cable for the Hudson River Bridge*, Trenton, N.J., c1932.

Suspension Bridges: A Century of Progress, Trenton: John A. Roebling's Sons Co. c1936.

Wire Engineering, 1930-1933.

The Wire Rope at Panama, Trenton, N.J., c1915.

Wire Roping the German Submarine: The Barrage that Stopped the U-Boat, Trenton, N.J., 1920.

Roebling Family Documents

Roebling, John A., *Diary of My Journey from Mülhausen in Thuringia via Bremen to the United States and North America in the year 1831*, Trenton, N.J.: Roebling Press, 1931.

Röbling, Johann August, "Diary of our Sea-Voyage from Bremen to Philadelphia on the Transport August Eduard in the Year 1831."

Röbling, Johann August, "The Personal Diary, J.A. Röbling," 1981 Translation of unpublished manuscript, Smithsonian Institution.

Roebling, Washington A., "Biography of J.A. Roebling," Roebling Collection, Rutgers University.

Roebling, Washington A., "History of the connection of Noble and Scammell with the J. A. Roebling's Sons Co., Trenton New Jersey," Handwritten manuscript, November, 1921. RU

Roebling, Washington, A., "In Memoriam to Charles Roebling", 1918, Roebling Collection, Rutgers University.

Dissertations, Theses, Papers

Bartus, Mary Raimonde, Sister, "John Augustus Roebling, Inventor and Bridge Builder," Master's Thesis, Fordham University, 1957.

Beer, Donald A.E., "Engines of Prosperity: America's Investment History 1800-1978." 1988.

Czepiel, Robert, "Roebling Steel, CF&I and the Shutdown of 1974," Student Paper, 1990.

Moore, Martha, "Our Town: Company Paternalism and Community Participation in Roebling," Senior Paper, Yale University, 1982.

Starr, Dennis. "The Nature and Uses of Political and Social Power in Trenton, N.J., 1890-1917," PhD. Dissertation, Rutgers University, 1979.

Zink, Clifford W. "The Roebling Works: New Life for One of Trenton's Most Significant Cultural Resources," Columbia University, Graduate School of Architecture, Planning and Preservation, December, 1984.

Surveys and Reports

Hunter Research Associates, "Report on Excavations at the N.J. State House, 1988-1989."

Zink, C.W., "Architectural Historical Stage 1A Survey: John A. Roebling's Sons Company, Kinkora Works, Roebling, N.J," 1990.

Zink, Clifford W. "Draft Redevelopment Plan for the John A. Roebling's Company and the American Steel and Wire Company Historic Industrial Sites," Trenton Roebling Community Development Corporation, Trenton, N.J., January, 1987.

Zink, Clifford W. "Roebling Machine Shop Historic Structure Report," Trenton Roebling Community Development Corporation, Trenton, N.J. 1993.

Zink, Clifford W. "Roebling Steel RI/FS: Architectural Historical Stage 1A Survey, John A. Roebling's Sons Company, Kinkora Works, Roebling, New Jersey," Ebasco Services Incorporated, REM III Program, U.S. Environmental Protection Agency, June 1, 1990.

Zink, Clifford W. "The Roebling Works: Redevelopment of the Historical John A. Roebling's Sons Industrial Complex, in Trenton, N.J." Trenton Roebling Community Development Corporation, Trenton, N.J. 1986.

Zink, Clifford W. "The Trenton Roebling Project: Redevelopment Plan for the John A. Roebling's Sons Company and American Steel & Wire Company Historic Industrial Sites," Trenton Roebling Community Development Corp., Trenton, N.J. August 1989.

ROEBLING SUSPENSION BRIDGES AND CABLES

Bridges designed and built by John A. Roebling

1844	Allegheny Aqueduct*	Pittsburgh, Pennsylvania	7 spans, longest 162 ft.	7 in. Cables
1846	Smithfield Street Bridge*	Pittsburgh, Pennsylvania	8 spans, longest 188 ft.	4 ½ in.
1848	Lackawaxen Aqueduct*	Lackawaxen, Pennsylvania	2 spans, 114 ft. each ft.	7 in.
1848	Delaware Aqueduct	Lackawaxen, Pennsylvania	4 spans, longest 141 ft.	8 ½ in.
1850	High Falls Aqueduct*	High Falls, New York	145 ft. span	8 ½ in.
1850	Neversink Suspension Aqueduct*	Cuddlebackville, New York	170 ft. span	9 ½ In.
1855	Niagara Falls Suspension Bridge*	Niagara Falls, New York	821 ft. span	10 ½ in. (4)
1859	Allegheny Suspension Bridge*	Pittsburgh, Pennsylvania	4 spans, longest 344 ft.	7 ¼ & 4 ¼ in.
1867	Cincinnati-Covington Bridge	Cincinnati, Ohio	1,056 ft. span	12 ½ in.

* Demolished

Designed by John A. Roebling and built by Washington A. Roebling

1883	Brooklyn Bridge	Brooklyn-Manhattan	1,596 ft.	15 ½ in. (4)

Cables constructed by the John A. Roebling's Sons Company

1903	Williamsburg Bridge	New York, New York	1,600 ft.	18 ¾ in. (4)
1904	Riegelsville Bridge	Riegelsville, Pennsylvania	3 spans, longest 200 ft.	2 7/8 in.
1909	Manhattan Bridge	New York, New York	1,470 ft.	20 ¾ in. (4)
1916	Parkersburg Bridge*	Parkersburg, West Virginia	775 ft.	8 ¼ in.
1922	Rondout Creek Bridge	Kingston, New York	705 ft.	9 in.
1924	Bear Mountain Bridge	Stony Point, New York.	1,632 ft.	18 in.
1929	McPhaul Bridge (Dome)	Yuma, Arizona	802 ft.	5 ½ in.
1929	Grand'Mere Bridge**	Grand Mere, Quebec	949 ft.	6 5/8 in.
1931	St. John's Bridge**	Portland, Oregon	1,207 ft.	16 ½ in.
1931	Anthony Wayne Bridge	Toledo, Ohio	785 ft.	13 ¼ in.
1931	Simon Kenton Memorial Bridge**	Maysville, Kentucky	1,060 ft.	13 ½ in.
1931	George Washington Bridge	New York-New Jersey	3,500 ft.	36 in. (4)
1933	San Rafael Bridge**	Mao, Dominican Republic	452 ft.	9-1 3/8 in.
1934	Rio Hiquamo Bridge**	San Pedro, Dominican Rep.	3 spans, longest 554 ft.	
1937	Golden Gate Bridge	San Francisco, California	4,200 ft.	36 ½ in.
1943	Peace River Bridge* ** ***	Taylor, Alaska	930 ft.	24-1 7/8 in.
1943	Roebling General Office Bridge**	Trenton, New Jersey	53 ft.	
1947	Lumberville Bridge** ***	Lumberville, New Jersey	5 spans, longest 156 ft.	
1947	Hal W. Adams Bridge**	Mayo, Florida	423 ft.	
1950	Rio Paz Bridge** ***	Las Chinama, El Salvador	210 ft.	
1952	San Marcos Bridge* ** ***	San Salvador, El Salvador	5 spans, longest 669 ft.	24-1 ½ in.
1950	Tacoma Narrows Bridge	Tacoma, Washington	2,800 ft.	20 in.
1963	Vincent Thomas Bridge	San Pedro, California	1,500 ft.	13 ½ in.

* Demolished
** Cables made with Roebling prestressed bridge strands.
*** Entire bridge contract.
Note: J.A.R.'s Sons Co. also supplied wire and/or prestressed bridge strands for cables built by other companies on bridges such as: the Chesapeake Bay Bridge, Deer Isle Bridge, Delaware Memorial Bridge, Verrazano Narrows Bridge, and Bronx-Whitestone Bridge.

ROEBLING FAMILY TREE
Through Four Generations

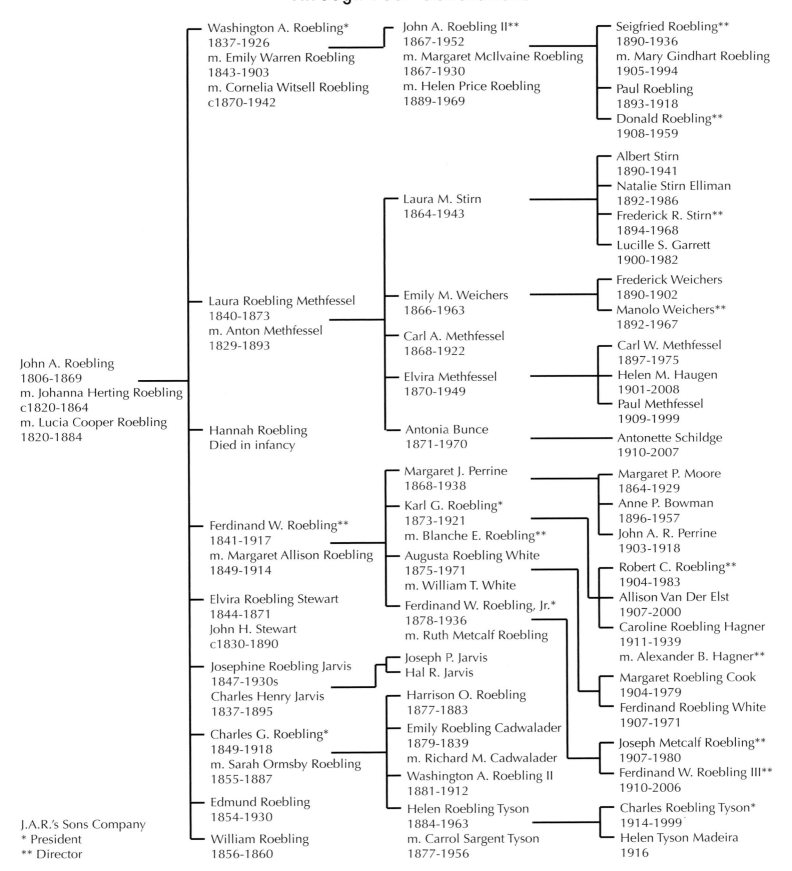

John A. Roebling
1806-1869
m. Johanna Herting Roebling
c1820-1864
m. Lucia Cooper Roebling
1820-1884

Washington A. Roebling*
1837-1926
m. Emily Warren Roebling
1843-1903
m. Cornelia Witsell Roebling
c1870-1942

John A. Roebling II**
1867-1952
m. Margaret McIlvaine Roebling
1867-1930
m. Helen Price Roebling
1889-1969

Seigfried Roebling**
1890-1936
m. Mary Gindhart Roebling
1905-1994

Paul Roebling
1893-1918

Donald Roebling**
1908-1959

Laura Roebling Methfessel
1840-1873
m. Anton Methfessel
1829-1893

Laura M. Stirn
1864-1943

Albert Stirn
1890-1941

Natalie Stirn Elliman
1892-1986

Frederick R. Stirn**
1894-1968

Lucille S. Garrett
1900-1982

Emily M. Weichers
1866-1963

Frederick Weichers
1890-1902

Manolo Weichers**
1892-1967

Carl A. Methfessel
1868-1922

Elvira Methfessel
1870-1949

Carl W. Methfessel
1897-1975

Helen M. Haugen
1901-2008

Paul Methfessel
1909-1999

Antonia Bunce
1871-1970

Antonette Schildge
1910-2007

Hannah Roebling
Died in infancy

Ferdinand W. Roebling**
1841-1917
m. Margaret Allison Roebling
1849-1914

Margaret J. Perrine
1868-1938

Margaret P. Moore
1864-1929

Anne P. Bowman
1896-1957

John A. R. Perrine
1903-1918

Karl G. Roebling*
1873-1921
m. Blanche E. Roebling**

Augusta Roebling White
1875-1971
m. William T. White

Robert C. Roebling**
1904-1983

Allison Van Der Elst
1907-2000

Caroline Roebling Hagner
1911-1939
m. Alexander B. Hagner**

Ferdinand W. Roebling, Jr.*
1878-1936
m. Ruth Metcalf Roebling

Elvira Roebling Stewart
1844-1871
John H. Stewart
c1830-1890

Josephine Roebling Jarvis
1847-1930s
Charles Henry Jarvis
1837-1895

Joseph P. Jarvis
Hal R. Jarvis

Margaret Roebling Cook
1904-1979

Ferdinand Roebling White
1907-1971

Charles G. Roebling*
1849-1918
m. Sarah Ormsby Roebling
1855-1887

Harrison O. Roebling
1877-1883

Emily Roebling Cadwalader
1879-1839
m. Richard M. Cadwalader

Washington A. Roebling II
1881-1912

Joseph Metcalf Roebling**
1907-1980

Ferdinand W. Roebling III**
1910-2006

Edmund Roebling
1854-1930

Helen Roebling Tyson
1884-1963
m. Carrol Sargent Tyson
1877-1956

Charles Roebling Tyson*
1914-1999

Helen Tyson Madeira
1916

William Roebling
1856-1860

J.A.R.'s Sons Company
* President
** Director

283

INDEX

"THE WORK MEN DO LIVES . . . AFTER THEM . . ."

It is a far cry from America's first wire rope making machine, built by John A. Roebling a hundred years ago, to present day modern Roebling wire rope making equipment. It is a far cry, too, from the few original applications of Roebling wire rope to today's almost endless uses.

Now there is hardly an industry in which Roebling wire ropes or cables are not employed. They are used for hundreds of defense purposes. They help mine coal and ore—harvest timber—build, rig, and load ships—drill oil wells—erect buildings and operate their elevators—suspend giant bridges—and, on the cranes and hoists of thousands of fac-

Illustrated above: Hand-operated wire-twisting machine invented by John A. Roebling. Used in Roebling's pioneer wire rope factory at Saxonburg, Pa. in 1841 — a hundred years ago.

tories, they help lift the burdens of industry from the backs of men. Included in the Roebling line today are not only wire ropes and cables for every conceivable use, but the many other diversified wire products listed, which range from electric wires and cables to strip steel.

Roebling Products · WIRE ROPE AND STRAND · WIRE ROPE SLINGS AND FITTINGS · SUSPENSION BRIDGES AND CABLES · AERIAL WIRE ROPE SYSTEMS · ELECTRICAL WIRES AND CABLES · HIGH AND LOW CARBON COLD ROLLED STRIP · ROUND AND SHAPED WIRE · WIRE CLOTH AND NETTING · STEEL AND COPPER RODS HIGH AND LOW CARBON ACID AND BASIC OPEN-HEARTH STEELS

JOHN A. ROEBLING'S SONS COMPANY
TRENTON · NEW JERSEY

1841 ☆ ROEBLING BRIDGES A CENTURY WITH WIRE ☆ 1941